A Modern History
From The Time Of Luther
To The Fall Of Napoleon

by

John Lord

Double 9
BOOKS

A Modern History From The Time Of Luther To The Fall Of Napoleon

by John Lord

ISBN: 978-93-59327-84-6

Published by

DOUBLE 9 BOOKS

2/13-B, Ansari Road
Daryaganj, New Delhi – 110002
info@double9books.com
www.double9books.com
Tel. 011-40042856

ABOUT THE AUTHOR

John Lord (September 10, 1810 – December 15, 1894) was a professor and historian from the United States. He graduated from Dartmouth College in 1833 and then entered the Andover Theological Seminary, where in his second year he produced a series of lectures on the Dark Ages, which he presented the following fall during a trip through northern New York. He joined the American Peace Society after graduating from Andover. He was summoned to a Congregational Church in New Marlborough, Massachusetts, and subsequently to one in Stockbridge, Massachusetts, despite not being ordained. In 1840, he resigned from his pastoral duties to become a public lecturer and devote more attention to literary pursuits. In 1843-46, he lectured about the Middle Ages in England, and upon his return to the United States, he lectured for many years in the major towns and cities, giving almost 6,000 lectures in total. He obtained his LL.D. from the City University of New York in 1864. He taught history at Dartmouth College from 1866 to 1876.

CONTENTS

PREFACE 9

CHAPTER I
STATE OF EUROPEAN SOCIETY IN THE
FIFTEENTH AND SIXTEENTH CENTURIES............................... 10

CHAPTER II
MARTIN LUTHER AND HIS ASSOCIATES................................. 18

CHAPTER III
THE EMPEROR CHARLES V... 35

CHAPTER IV
HENRY VIII... 48

CHAPTER V
EDWARD VI. AND MARY.. 61

CHAPTER VI
ELIZABETH 69

CHAPTER VII
FRANCIS II., CHARLES IX., HENRY III.,
AND HENRY IV 80

CHAPTER VIII
PHILIP II. AND THE AUSTRIAN
PRINCES OF SPAIN 89

CHAPTER IX
THE JESUITS, AND THE PAPAL POWER
IN THE SEVENTEENTH CENTURY... 94

CHAPTER X
THIRTY YEARS WAR.. 104

CHAPTER XI

ADMINISTRATIONS OF CARDINALS
RICHELIEU AND MAZARIN 114

CHAPTER XII

THE REIGNS OF JAMES I. AND CHARLES I 125

CHAPTER XIII

PROTECTORATE OF OLIVER CROMWELL 166

CHAPTER XIV

THE REIGN OF CHARLES II 176

CHAPTER XV

REIGN OF JAMES II 192

CHAPTER XVI

LOUIS XIV 212

CHAPTER XVII

WILLIAM AND MARY 228

CHAPTER XVIII

PETER THE GREAT, AND RUSSIA 245

CHAPTER XIX

GEORGE I., AND THE ADMINISTRATION
OF SIR ROBERT WALPOLE 262

CHAPTER XX

THE COLONIZATION OF AMERICA AND
THE EAST INDIES 280

CHAPTER XXI

THE REIGN OF GEORGE II 308

CHAPTER XXII

LOUIS XV 324

CHAPTER XXIII

FREDERIC THE GREAT 342

CHAPTER XXIV

MARIA THERESA AND CATHARINE II 352

CHAPTER XXV

CALAMITIES OF POLAND 362

CHAPTER XXVI
THE DECLINE OF THE OTTOMAN EMPIRE.............................. 368

CHAPTER XXVII
REIGN OF GEORGE III. TO THE
ADMINISTRATION OF WILLIAM PITT... 374

CHAPTER XXVIII
THE AMERICAN REVOLUTION.. 388

CHAPTER XXIX
ADMINISTRATION OF WILLIAM PITT.................................... 404

CHAPTER XXX
THE FRENCH REVOLUTION 423

CHAPTER XXXI
NAPOLEON BONAPARTE.. 445

CHAPTER XXXII
EUROPE ON THE FALL OF NAPOLEON.................................... 472

APPENDIX.. 477

PREFACE

In preparing this History, I make no claim to original and profound investigations; but the arrangement, the style, and the sentiments, are my own. I have simply attempted to condense the great and varied subjects which are presented, so as to furnish a connected narrative of what is most vital in the history of the last three hundred years, avoiding both minute details and elaborate disquisitions. It has been my aim to write a book, which should be neither a chronological table nor a philosophical treatise, but a work adapted to the wants of young people in the various stages of education, and which, it is hoped, will also prove interesting to those of maturer age; who have not the leisure to read extensive works, and yet who wish to understand the connection of great events since the Protestant Reformation. Those characters, institutions, reforms, and agitations, which have had the greatest influence in advancing society, only have been described, and these not to the extent which will satisfy the learned or the curious. Dates and names, battles and sieges, have not been disregarded; but more attention has been given to those ideas and to those men by whose influence and agency great changes have taken place. In a work so limited, and yet so varied, marginal references to original authorities have not been deemed necessary; but a list of standard and accessible authors is furnished, at the close of each chapter, which the young student, seeking more minute information, can easily consult. A continuation of this History to the present time might seem desirable; but it would be difficult to condense the complicated events of the last thirty years into less than another volume. Instead of an unsatisfactory compend, especially of subjects concerning which there are great differences of opinion, and considerable warmth of feeling, useful tables of important events are furnished in the Appendix. I have only to add, that if I have succeeded in remedying, in some measure, the defects of those dry compendiums, which are used for want of living histories; if I have combined what is instructive with what is entertaining; and especially if I shall impress the common mind, even to a feeble degree, with those great moral truths which history ought to teach, I shall feel that my agreeable labor is not without its reward.

J. L.

Boston, *October, 1849.*

CHAPTER I
STATE OF EUROPEAN SOCIETY IN THE FIFTEENTH AND SIXTEENTH CENTURIES

The period at which this History commences,—the beginning of the sixteenth century,—when compared with the ages which had preceded it, since the fall of the Roman empire, was one of unprecedented brilliancy and activity. It was a period very fruitful in great men and great events, and, though stormy and turbulent, was favorable to experiments and reforms. The nations of Europe seem to have been suddenly aroused from a state of torpor and rest, and to have put forth new energies in every department of life. The material and the political, the moral and the social condition of society was subject to powerful agitations, and passed through important changes.

Great *discoveries and inventions* had been made. The use of movable types, first ascribed to a German, of Mentz, by the name of Gutenberg, in 1441, and to Peter Schœffer, in 1444, changed the whole system of book-making, and vastly increased the circulation of the Scriptures, the Greek and Latin classics, and all other valuable works, which, by the industry of the monkish copyist, had been preserved from the ravages of time and barbarism. Gunpowder, whose explosive power had been perceived by Roger Bacon as early as 1280, though it was not used on the field of battle until 1346, had completely changed the art of war and had greatly contributed to undermine the feudal system. The polarity of the magnet, also discovered in the middle ages, and not practically applied to the mariner's compass until 1403, had led to the greatest event of the fifteenth century—the discovery of America by Christopher Columbus, in 1492. The impulse given to commerce by this and other discoveries of unknown continents and oceans, by the Portuguese, the Spaniards, the Dutch, the English, and the French, cannot be here enlarged on. America revealed to the astonished European her riches in gold and silver; and Indian spices, and silks, and drugs, were imported, through new channels, into all the countries inhabited by the Teutonic races. Mercantile wealth, with all its refinements, acquired new importance in the eyes of the nations. The world opened towards the east and the west. The horizon of knowledge extended. Popular delusions were dispelled. Liberality of mind was acquired. The material prosperity of the western nations was increased. Tastes became more refined, and social intercourse more cheerful.

Revival of the Arts.

Art, in all its departments, was every where revived at this epoch. Houses became more comfortable, and churches more splendid. The utensils of husbandry and of cookery were improved. Linen and woollen manufactures supplanted the coarser fabrics of the dark ages. Music became more elaborate, and the present system of notation was adopted. The genius of the sculptor again gave life and beauty to a marble block, and painting was carried to greater perfection than by the ancient Greeks and Romans. Florence, Venice, Milan, and Rome became seats of various schools of this beautiful art, of which Michael Angelo, Correggio, the Carracci, and Raphael were the most celebrated masters, all of whom were distinguished for peculiar excellences, never since surpassed, or even equalled. The Flemish artists were scarcely behind the Italian; and Rubens, of Antwerp, may well rank with Correggio and Titian. To Raphael, however, the world has, as yet, furnished no parallel.

Influence of Feudalism.

The political and social structure of society changed. The crusades, long before, had given a shock to the political importance of the feudal aristocracy, and reviving commerce and art had shaken the system to its foundations. The Flemish weavers had arisen, and a mercantile class had clamored for new privileges. In the struggle of classes, and in the misfortunes of nobles, monarchs had perceived the advantages they might gain, and fortunate circumstances enabled them to raise absolute thrones, and restore a central power, always so necessary to the cause of civilization. Feudalism had answered many useful ends in the dark ages. It had secured a reciprocity of duties between a lord and his vassal; it had restored loyalty, truth, and fidelity among semi-barbarians; it had favored the cultivation of the soil; it had raised up a hardy rural population; it had promoted chivalry, and had introduced into Europe the modern gentleman; it had ennobled friendship, and spread the graces of urbanity and gentleness among rough and turbulent warriors. But it had, also, like all human institutions, become corrupt, and failed to answer the ends for which it was instituted. It had become an oppressive social despotism; it had widened the distinction between the noble and ignoble classes; it had produced selfishness and arrogance among the nobles, and a mean and cringing sycophancy among the people; it had perpetuated privileges, among the aristocracy, exceedingly unjust, and ruinous to the general welfare of society. It therefore fell before the advancing spirit of the age, and monarchies and republics were erected on its ruins.

The people, as well as monarchs, had learned the secret of their power. They learned that, by combining their power, they could successfully resist their enemies. The principle of association was learned. Combinations of masses took place. Free cities were multiplied. A population of artificers, and small merchants, and free farmers arose. They discussed their privileges, and asserted their independence. Political liberty was born, and its invaluable blessings were conceived, if they were not realized.

Effects of Scholasticism.

And the intellectual state of Europe received an impulse as marked and beneficent as the physical and social. The scholastic philosophy, with its dry and technical logic, its abstruse formulas, and its subtle refinements, ceased to satisfy the wants of the human mind, now craving light and absolute knowledge in all departments of science and philosophy. Like feudalism, it had once been useful; but like that institution, it had also become corrupted, and an object of sarcasm and mockery. It had trained the European mind for the discoveries of the sixteenth century; it had raised up an inquisitive spirit, and had led to profound reflections on the existence of God, on his attributes and will, on the nature of the soul, on the faculties of the mind and on the practical duties of life. But this philosophy became pedantic and cold; covered, as with a funereal shade, the higher pursuits of life; and diverted attention from what was practical and useful. That earnest spirit, which raised up Luther and Bacon, demanded, of the great masters of thought, something which the people could understand, and something which would do them good.

In poetry, the insipid and immoral songs of the Provençal bards gave place to the immortal productions of the great creators of the European languages. Dante led the way in Italy, and gave to the world the "Divine Comedy"—a masterpiece of human genius, which raised him to the rank of Homer and Virgil. Petrarch followed in his steps, and, if not as profound or original as Dante, yet is unequalled as an "enthusiastic songster of ideal love." He also gave a great impulse to civilization by his labors in collecting and collating manuscripts. Boccaccio also lent his aid in the revival of literature, and wrote a series of witty, though objectionable stories, from which the English Chaucer borrowed the notion of his "Canterbury Tales." Chaucer is the father of English poetry, and kindled a love of literature among his isolated countrymen; and was one of the few men who, in the evening of his days, looked upon the world without austerity, and expressed himself with all the vivacity of youthful feeling.

Ecclesiastical Corruptions.

Such were some of the leading events and circumstances which gave a new life to European society, and created a desire for better days. All of these causes of improvement acted and reacted on each other in various ways, and prepared the way to new and great developments of action and passion. These new energies were, however, unfortunately checked by a combination of evils which had arisen in the dark ages, and which required to be subverted before any great progress could be reasonably expected. These evils were most remarkable in the church itself and almost extinguished the light which Christ and his apostles had kindled. The church looked with an evil eye on many of the greatest improvements and agitations of the age, and attempted to suppress the spirit of insurrection which had arisen against the abuses and follies of past ages. Great ideas were ridiculed, and daring spirits were crushed. There were many good men in the church who saw and who lamented prevailing corruptions, but their voice was overwhelmed by the clamors of interested partisans, or silenced by the authority of the popes. The character of the popes themselves was not what was expected of the heads of the visible church, or what was frequently exhibited in those ignorant and superstitious times, when the papacy fulfilled, in the opinion of many enlightened Protestants, a benevolent mission. None had the disinterestedness of Gregory I., or the talents of Gregory VII. There had been a time when the great central spiritual monarchy of Rome had been exercised for the peace and tranquillity of Europe, when it was uniformly opposed to slavery and war, and when it was a mild and paternal government, which protected innocence and weakness, while it punished injustice and crime. The time was, when popes had been elevated for their piety and learning, and when they lived as saints and died as martyrs. But that time had passed. The Roman church did not keep up with the spirit or the wants of the age, and moreover did not reform itself from vices which had been overlooked in ages of ignorance and superstition. In the fifteenth century, many great abuses scandalized a body of men who should have been the lights of the world; and the sacred pontiffs themselves set examples of unusual depravity. Julius II. marched at the head of armies. Alexander VI. secured his election by bribery, and reigned by extortion. He poisoned his own cardinals, and bestowed on his son Cæsar Borgia—an incarnated demon—the highest dignities and rewards. It was common for the popes to sell the highest offices in the church for money, to place boys on episcopal thrones, to absolve the most heinous and scandalous crimes for gold, to encourage the massacre of heretics, and to disgrace themselves by infamous vices. And a general laxity of morals existed among all orders of the clergy. They were ignorant, debauched, and ambitious. The monks were exceedingly numerous; had ceased to be men of prayer and contemplation, as in the days of Benedict and Bernard; and might be seen frequenting places of demoralizing excitement, devoted to pleasure, and enriched by inglorious gains.

But the evils which the church encouraged were more dangerous than the vices of its members. These evils were inherent in the papal system, and were hard to be subverted. There were corruptions of doctrine, and corruptions in the government and customs of the church.

Papal Infallibility.

There generally prevailed, throughout Christendom, the belief in papal infallibility, which notion subverted the doctrines of the Bible, and placed its truths, at least, on a level with the authority of the schoolmen. It favored the various usurpations of the popes, and strengthened the bonds of spiritual despotism.

The popes also claimed a control over secular princes, as well as the supremacy of the church. Hildebrand was content with riveting the chains of universal spiritual authority, the evil and absurdity of which cannot well be exaggerated; but his more ambitious successors sought to reduce the kings of the earth to perfect vassalage, and, when in danger of having their monstrous usurpations torn from them, were ready to fill the world with discord and war.

But the worldly popes of the fifteenth century also aspired to be temporal princes. They established the most elegant court in Europe; they supported large armies; they sought to restore the splendor of imperial Rome; they became ambitious of founding great families; they enriched their nephews and relations at the sacrifice of the best interests of their church; they affected great state and dignity; they built gorgeous palaces; they ornamented their capital with pictures and statues.

The territories of Rome were, however, small. The lawful revenues of the popes were insufficient to gratify their extravagance and pomp. But money, nevertheless, they must have. In order to raise it, they resorted to extortion and corruption. They imposed taxes on Christendom, direct and indirect. These were felt as an intolerable burden; but such was the superstition of the times, that they were successfully raised. But even these were insufficient to gratify papal avarice and rapacity. They then resorted, in their necessities, to the meanest acts, imposed on the simplicity of their subjects, and finally adopted the most infamous custom which ever disgraced the world.

The Sale of Indulgences.

They pardoned sins for money—granted sales of indulgences for crime. A regular scale for absolution was graded. A proclamation was made every fifty, and finally every twenty-five years, of a year of jubilee, when plenary remission of all sin was promised to those who should make a pilgrimage to Rome. And so great was the influx of strangers, and consequently of wealth, to Rome, that, on one occasion, it was collected into piles by rakes. It is computed that two hundred thousand deluded persons visited the city in a single month. But the vast sums they brought to Rome, and the still greater sums which were obtained by the sale of indulgences, and by various taxations, were all squandered in ornamenting the city, and in supporting a luxurious court, profligate cardinals, and superfluous ministers of a corrupted religion. Then was erected the splendid church of St. Peter, more after the style of Grecian temples, than after the model of the Gothic cathedrals of York and Cologne. Glorious was that monument of reviving art; wonderful was its lofty dome; but the vast sums required to build it opened the eyes of Christendom to the extravagance and presumption of the popes; and this splendid trophy of their glory also became the emblem of their broken power. Their palaces and temples made an imposing show, but detracted from their real strength, which consisted in the affections of their spiritual subjects. Their outward grandeur, like the mechanical agencies which kings employ, was but a poor substitute for the invisible power of love,—in all ages, and among all people, "that cheap defence" which supports thrones and kingdoms.

The Corruptions of the Church.

Another great evil was, the prevalence of an idolatrous spirit. In the churches and chapels, and even in private families, were innumerable images of saints, pictures of the Virgin, relics, crucifixes, &c., designed at first to kindle a spirit of devotion among the rude and uneducated, but gradually becoming objects of real adoration. Intercessions were supposed to be made by the Virgin Mary, and by favorite saints, more efficacious with Deity than the penitence and prayers of the erring and sinful themselves. The influence of this veneration for martyrs and saints was degrading to the mind, and became a very lucrative source of profit to the priests, who peddled the bones and relics of saints as they did indulgences, and who invented innumerable lies to attest the genuineness and antiquity of the objects they sold, all of which were parts of the great system of fraud and avarice which the church permitted.

Again; the public worship of God was in a language the people could not understand, but rendered impressive by the gorgeous dresses of the priests, and the magnificence of the altar, and the images and vessels of silver and gold, reflecting their splendor, by the light of wax candles, on the sombre pillars, roofs, and windows of the Gothic church, and the effect heightened by exciting music, and other appeals to the taste or imagination, rather than to the reason and the heart. The sermons of the clergy were frivolous, and ill adapted to the spiritual wants of the people. "Men went to the Vatican," says the learned and philosophical Ranke, "not to pray, but to contemplate the Belvidere Apollo. They disgraced the most solemn festivals by open profanations. The clergy, in their services, sought the means of exciting laughter. One would mock the cuckoo, and another recite indecent stories about St. Peter." Luther, when he visited Italy, was extremely shocked at the infidel spirit which prevailed among the clergy, who were hostile to the circulation of the Scriptures, and who encouraged persecutions and inquisitions. This was the age when the dreadful tribunal of the Inquisition flourished, although its chief enormities were perpetrated in Spain and Portugal. It never had an existence in England, and but little influence in France and Germany. But if the Church did not resort, in all countries, to that dread tribunal which subjected youth, beauty, and innocence to the inquisitorial vengeance of narrow-minded Dominican monks, still she was hostile to free inquiry, and to all efforts made to emancipate the reason of men.

The spirit of religious persecution, which inflamed the Roman Church to punish all dissenters from the doctrine and abuses she promulgated, can never be questioned. The Waldenses and Albigenses had suffered, in darker times, almost incredible hardships and miseries—had been almost annihilated by the dreadful crusade which was carried on against them, so that two hundred thousand had perished for supposed heresy. But reference is not now made to this wholesale massacre, but to those instances of individual persecution which showed the extreme jealousy and hatred of Rome of all new opinions. John Huss and Jerome of Prague were publicly burned for attempting to reform the church, and even Savonarola, who did not deny the authority of the popes, was condemned to the flames for denouncing the vices of his age, rather than the evils of the church.

Necessity for Reform.

These multiplied evils, which checked the spirit of improvement, called loudly for reform. Councils were assembled for the purpose; but councils supported, rather than diminished, the evils of which even princes complained. The reform was not destined to come from dignitaries in the church or state; not from bishops, nor philosophers, nor kings, but from an obscure teacher of divinity in a German university, whom the genius of a reviving and awakened age had summoned into the field of revolutionary warfare. It was reserved for Martin Luther to commence the first successful rebellion against the despotism of Rome, and to give the greatest impulse to freedom of thought, and a general spirit of reform, which ten centuries had seen.

The most prominent event in modern times is unquestionably the Protestant Reformation, and it was by far the most momentous in its results. It gave rise, directly or indirectly, to the great wars of the sixteenth and seventeenth centuries, as well as to those rival sects which agitated the theological world. It is connected with the enterprises of great monarchs, with the struggle of the Huguenots and Puritans, with the diffusion of knowledge, and with the progress of civil and religious liberty in Europe. An event, therefore, of such interest and magnitude, may well be adopted as a starting point in modern history, and will, accordingly, be the first subject of especial notice. History is ever most impressive and philosophical when great changes and revolutions are traced to the agency of great spiritual ideas. Moreover, modern history is so complicated, that it is difficult to unravel it except by tracing the agency of great causes, rather than by detailing the fortunes of kings and nobles.

CHAPTER II
MARTIN LUTHER AND HIS ASSOCIATES

The Early Life of Luther.

Martin Luther was born the 10th of November, 1483, at Eisleben, in Saxony. His father was a miner, of Mansfield, and his ancestors were peasants, who lived near the summit of the Thuringian Forest. His early years were spent at Mansfield, in extreme poverty, and he earned his bread by singing hymns before the houses of the village. At the age of fifteen, he went to Eisenach, to a high school, and at eighteen entered the university of Erfurt, where he made considerable progress in the sciences then usually taught, which, however, were confined chiefly to the scholastic philosophy. He did not know either Greek or Hebrew, but read the Bible in Latin. In 1505, he took his degree of bachelor of arts, and, shortly after, his religious struggles commenced. He had witnessed a fearful tempest, which alarmed him, while on a visit at his father's house, and he was also much depressed by the death of an intimate friend. In that age, the serious and the melancholy generally sought monastic retreats, and Luther, thirsty after divine knowledge, and anxious to save his soul, resolved to forsake the world, and become a monk. He entered an Augustinian monastery at Erfurt, soon after obtaining his first degree. But the duties and studies of monastic life did not give his troubled soul the repose he sought. He submitted to all the irksome labors which the monks imposed; he studied the fathers and the schoolmen; he practised the most painful austerities, and fastings, and self-lacerations: still he was troubled with religious fears. His brethren encouraged his good works, but his perplexities and doubts remained. In this state of mind, he was found by Staupitz, vicar-general of the order, who was visiting Erfurt, in his tour of inspection, with a view to correct the bad morals of the monasteries. He sympathized with Luther in his religious feelings, treated him with great kindness, and recommended the reading of the Scriptures, and also the works of St. Augustine whose theological views he himself had embraced. Although St. Augustine was a great oracle in the Roman church, still, his doctrines pertaining to personal salvation differed in spirit from those which were encouraged by the Roman Catholic divines generally, who attached less importance to justification by faith than did the venerated bishop of Hyppo. In that age of abuses, great importance was attached, by the church, to austerities, penance, and absolutions for money. But Luther, deeply imbued with the spirit of Augustine, at length found light, and repose, and joy, in the doctrine of justification by faith alone. This became more and more the idea of his life, especially at this time. The firmness of his convictions on this point became extraordinary, and his spiritual gladness now equalled his former depression and anxiety. He was soon to find a sphere for the development of his views.

Luther was consecrated as a priest in 1507, and in 1508 he was invited by Frederic, Elector of Saxony, to become a professor in the new university which he had established at Wittemberg. He was now twenty-five years of age, and the fact, that he should have been selected, at that early age, to teach dialectics, is a strong argument in favor of his attainments and genius.

He now began to apply himself to the study of the Greek and Hebrew, and delivered lectures on biblical theology; and his novel method, and great enthusiasm, attracted a crowd of students. But his sermons were more striking even than his lectures, and he was invited, by the council of Wittemberg, to be the preacher for the city. His eloquence, his learning, and his zeal, now attracted considerable attention, and the elector himself visited Wittemberg to hear him preach.

In 1512, he was sent on an embassy to Rome, and, while in Italy, obtained useful knowledge of the actual state of the hierarchy, and of morals and religion. Julius II., a warlike pontiff, sat on the throne of St. Peter; and the "Eternal City" was the scene of folly, dissipation, and clerical extortion. Luther returned to Germany completely disgusted with every thing he had seen—the levity and frivolity of the clergy, and the ignorance and vices of the people. He was too earnest in his religious views and feelings to take much interest in the works of art, or the pleasures, which occupied the attention of the Italians; and the impression of the general iniquity and corruption of Rome never passed away, and probably gave a new direction to his thoughts.

Luther's Early Religious Struggles.

On his return, in 1512, he was made doctor of divinity, then a great distinction, and renewed his lectures in the university with great ardor. He gave a new impulse to the studies, and a new form to the opinions of both professors and students. Lupinus and Carlstadt, his colleagues, were converts to his views. All within his sphere were controlled by his commanding genius, and extraordinary force of character. He commenced war upon the schoolmen, and was peculiarly hostile to Thomas Aquinas, whom he accused of Pelagianism. He also attacked Aristotle, the great idol of the schools, and overwhelmed scholasticism with sarcasm and mockery.

Such was the state of things when the preachers of indulgences, whom Leo X. had encouraged, in order to raise money for St. Peter's Church, arrived in the country round the Elbe. They had already spread over Germany, Switzerland, and France. Their luxury and extravagance were only equalled by their presumption and insolence. All sorts of crime were pardoned by these people for money. Among the most remarkable of these religious swindlers and peddlers was Tetzel. He was a friar of the Dominicans, apostolical commissioner, inquisitor, and bachelor of theology. He united profligate morals with great pretensions to sanctity; was somewhat eloquent, so far as a sonorous voice was concerned, and was very bold and haughty, as vulgar men, raised to eminence and power, are apt to be. But his peculiarity consisted in the audacity of his pretensions, and his readiness in inventing stories to please the people, ever captivated by rhetoric and anecdote. "Indulgences," said he, "are the most precious and sublime of God's gifts." "I would not exchange my privileges for those of St. Peter in heaven; for I have saved more souls, with my indulgences, than he, with his sermons." "There is no sin so great that the indulgence cannot remit it: even repentance is not necessary: indulgences save not the living alone,—they save the dead." "The very moment that the money clinks against the bottom of this chest, the soul escapes from purgatory, and flies to heaven." "And do you know why our Lord distributes so rich a grace? The dilapidated Church of St. Peter and St. Paul is to be restored, which contains the bodies of those holy apostles, and which are now trodden, dishonored, and polluted."

The Ninety-Five Propositions.

Tetzel found but few sufficiently enlightened to resist him, and he obtained great sums from the credulous people. This abomination excited Luther's intensest detestation; and he accordingly wrote ninety-five propositions, and nailed them, in 1517, to the gates of the church, in which he denounced the traffic in indulgences, and traced the doctrine of absolution to the usurped power of the pope. He denied the value of his absolution, and maintained that the divine favor would only be granted on the condition of repentance and faith.

In these celebrated propositions, he struck at the root of scholastic absurdities, and also of papal pretensions. The spirit which they breathed was bold, intrepid, and magnanimous. They electrified Germany, and gave a shock to the whole papal edifice. They had both a religious and a political bearing; religious, in reference to the grounds of justification, and political, in opening men's eyes to the unjust and ruinous extortions of Rome.

Among those who perceived with great clearness the political tendency of these propositions, and rejoiced in it, was the elector of Saxony himself, the most powerful prince of the empire, who had long been vexed, in view of the vast sums which had been drained from his subjects. He also lamented the corruptions of the church, and probably sympathized with the theological opinions of Luther. He accordingly protected the bold professor, although he did not openly encourage him, or form an alliance with him. He let things take their course. Well did Frederic deserve the epithet of *Wise*.

Erasmus — Melancthon.

There was another great man who rejoiced in the appearance of Luther's theses; and this was Erasmus, the greatest scholar of his age, the autocrat of letters, and, at that time, living in Basle. He was born in Rotterdam, in 1467, of poor parents, but early attracted notice for his attainments, and early emancipated himself from the trammels of scholasticism, which he hated and despised as cordially as Luther himself. He also attacked, with elegant sarcasm the absurdities of his age, both in literature and morals. He denounced the sins and follies of the monks, and spoke of the necessity of reform. But his distinguishing excellence was his literary talent and taste. He was a great Greek scholar, and published a critical edition of the Testament, which he accompanied with a Latin translation. In this, he rendered great service to the reformers, especially to Luther. His fascinating style and extensive erudition gave him great literary fame. But he was timid, conservative, and vain; and sought to be popular, except among the monks, whom he uniformly ridiculed. One doctor hated him so cordially, that he had his picture hung up in his study, that he might spit in his face as often as he pleased. So far as Luther opposed monkery and despotism, his sympathies were with him. But he did not desire a radical reformation, as Luther did, and always shunned danger and obloquy. He dreaded an insurrection among the people, and any thing which looked either revolutionary or fanatical. Luther, therefore, much as he was gratified by his favor at first, soon learned to distrust him; and finally these two great men were unfriendly to each other.

Melancthon was too prominent an actor in the great drama about to be performed, to be omitted in this sketch of great men who were on the side of reform. He was born in 1497, and was, therefore, fourteen years younger than Luther. He was educated under the auspices of the celebrated Greek scholar Reuchlin, who was also a relative. At twelve, he was sent to the university of Heidelberg; at fourteen, was made bachelor of arts; and at seventeen, doctor of philosophy. He began to lecture publicly at the age of seventeen; and, for his extraordinary attainments, was invited to Wittemberg, as professor of ancient languages, at the age of twenty-one. He arrived there in 1518, and immediately fell under the influence of Luther, who, however, acknowledged his classical attainments. He was considered a prodigy; was remarkably young looking, and so boyish, that the grave professors conceived but little hope of him at first. But, when he delivered his inaugural oration in Latin, all were astonished; and their prejudices were removed. Luther himself was enthusiastic in his praises, and a friendship commenced between them, which was never weakened by a quarrel. The mildness and gentleness of Philip Melancthon strongly contrasted with the boldness, energy, and tumultuous passions of Luther. The former was the more learned and elegant; the latter was the superior genius—a genius for commanding men, and guiding great enterprises.

Melancthon — Leo X.

But there was another great personage, who now viewed the movement of Luther with any thing but indifference; and this wasLeo X., the reigning pope when the theses were published. He belonged to the illustrious family of the Medici, and was chosen cardinal at the age of thirteen. He was the most elegant and accomplished of all the popes, patronized art and literature, and ornamented his capital with palaces, churches, and statues. But with his sympathy for intellectual excellence, he was prodigal, luxurious, and worldly. Indeed, his spirit was almost infidel. He was more ambitious for temporal than spiritual power; and, when he commenced his reign, the papal possessions were more extensive and flourishing, than at any previous period. His leading error was, his recklessness in the imposition of taxes, even on the clergy themselves, by which he lost their confidence and regard. With a very fine mind, he was, nevertheless, quite unfitted for his station and his times.

Thus far, he had allowed the outcry which Luther had raised against indulgences to take its course, and even disregarded the theses, which he supposed originated in a monkish squabble. But the Emperor Maximilian was alarmed, and wrote to the pope an account of Luther's differences with Tetzel. Frederic of Saxony had also written to his holiness, to palliate the conduct of Luther.

When such powerful princes became interested, Leo was startled. He summoned Luther to Rome, to be tried by Prierias. Luther, not daring to refuse, and not willing to obey, wrote to his friend Spalatin to use his influence with the elector to have his cause tried in Germany; and the pope, willing to please Frederic, appointed De Vio, his legate, to investigate the matter. Luther accordingly set out for Augsburg, in obedience to the summons of De Vio, although dissuaded by many of his friends. He had several interviews with the legate, by whom he was treated with courtesy and urbanity, and by whom he was dissuaded from his present courses. But all the persuasion and argument of the cardinal legate were without effect on the mind of Luther, whose convictions were not to be put aside by either kindness or craft. De Vio had hoped that he could induce Luther to retract; but, when he found him fixed in his resolutions, he changed his tone, and resorted to threats. Luther then made up his mind to leave Augsburg; and, appealing to the decision of the sovereign pontiff, whose authority he had not yet openly defied, he fled from the city, and returned to Wittemberg, being countenanced by the elector, to whom he also addressed letters. His life was safe so long as Frederic protected him.

The Leipsic Disputation.

The next event in the progress of Luther was the Leipsic disputation, June, 1519. The pope seemed willing to make one more effort to convince Luther, before he proceeded to more violent courses. There was then at his court a noble Saxon, Charles Miltitz, whose talents and insinuating address secured him the high office of chamberlain to the pope. He accordingly was sent into his native country, with the dignity of legate, to remove the difficulties which De Vio had attempted. He tried persuasion and flattery, and treated the reformer with great civility. But Luther still persisted in refusing to retract, and the matter was referred to the elector archbishop of Trèves.

While the controversy was pending, Dr. Eck, of the university of Ingolstadt, a man of great scholastic ingenuity and attainment, and proud of the prizes of eight universities, challenged the professors of Wittemberg to a public controversy on Grace and Free Will. He regarded a disputation with the eye of a practised fencer, and sought the means of extending his fame over North Germany. Leipsic was the appointed arena, and thither resorted the noble and the learned of Saxony. Eck was among the first who arrived, and, soon after, came Carlstadt, Luther, and Melancthon.

Principles of the Leipsic Disputation.

The place for the combat was a hall in the royal palace of Duke George, cousin to the elector Frederic, which was arranged and ornamented with great care, and which was honored by the presence of the duke, and of the chief divines and nobles of Northern Germany. Carlstadt opened the debate, which did not excite much interest until Luther's turn came, the antagonist whom Eck was most desirous to meet, and whose rising fame he hoped to crush by a brilliant victory. Ranke thus describes Luther's person at this time. "He was of the middle size, and so thin as to be mere skin and bone. He possessed neither the thundering voice, nor the ready memory, nor the skill and dexterity, of his distinguished antagonist. But he stood in the prime of manhood and in the fulness of his strength. His voice was melodious and clear; he was perfectly versed in the Bible, and its aptest sentences presented themselves unbidden to his mind; above all, he inspired an irresistible conviction that he sought the truth. He was always cheerful at home, and a joyous, jocose companion at table; he even, on this grave occasion, ascended the platform with a nosegay in his hand; but, when there, he displayed the intrepid and self-forgetting earnestness arising from the depth of a conviction, until now, unfathomed, even by himself. He drew forth new thoughts, and placed them in the fire of the battle, with a determination that knew no fear and no personal regard. His features bore the traces of the storms that had passed over his soul, and of the courage with which he was prepared to encounter those which yet awaited him. His whole aspect evinced profound thought, joyousness of temper, and confidence in the future. The battle immediately commenced on the question of the authority of the papacy, which, at once intelligible and important, riveted universal attention." Eck, with great erudition and masterly logic, supported the claim of the pope, from the decrees of councils, the opinions of scholastics, and even from those celebrated words of Christ to Peter—"Thou art Peter, and on this rock will I build my church," &c. Luther took higher and bolder ground, denied the infallibility of councils, and appealed to Scripture as the ultimate authority. Eck had probably the advantage over his antagonist, so far as dialectics were concerned, being a more able disputant; but Luther set at defiance mere scholastic logic, and appealed to an authority which dialectics could not reach. The victory was claimed by both parties; but the result was, that Luther no longer acknowledged the authority of the Roman church, and acknowledged none but the Scriptures.

The Rights of Private Judgment.

The Leipsic disputation was the grand intellectual contest of the Reformation, and developed its great idea—the only great principle, around which all sects and parties among the Protestants rally. This is the idea, that *the Scriptures are the only ultimate grounds of authority in religion, and that, moreover, every man has a right to interpret them for himself.* The rights of private judgment—that religion is a matter between the individual soul and God, and that every man is answerable to his own conscience alone how he interprets Scripture—these constitute the great Protestant platform. Different sects have different views respecting justification, but all profess to trace them to the Scriptures. Luther's views were similar to those of St. Augustine—that "man could be justified by faith alone," which was *his* great theological doctrine—a doctrine adopted by many who never left the communion of the Church of Rome, before and since his day, and a doctrine which characterized the early reformers, Zwingle, Calvin, Knox,

Cranmer, and the Puritans generally. It is as absurd to say that Luther's animating principle in religion was not this doctrine, as it is unphilosophical to make the reformation consist merely in its recognition. After Luther's convictions were settled on this point, and he had generally and openly declared them, the main contest of his life was against the papacy, which he viewed as the predicted Antichrist—the "scarlet mother of abominations." It is not the object of the writer of this History to defend or oppose Luther's views, or argue any cause whatever, but simply to place facts in their true light, which is, to state them candidly.

Although the Leipsic controversy brought out the great principle of the Reformation, Luther's views, both respecting the true doctrines and polity of the church, were not, on all points, yet developed, and were only gradually unfolded, as he gained knowledge and light. It was no trifling matter, even to deny the supremacy of the Roman church in matters of faith. He was thus placed in the position of Huss and Jerome, and other reformers, who had been destroyed, with scarcely an exception. He thus was brought in direct conflict with the pope, with the great dignitaries of the church, with the universities, and with the whole scholastic literature. He had to expect the violent opposition and vengeance of the pope, of the monks, of the great ecclesiastical dignitaries, of the most distinguished scholars, and of those secular princes who were friendly to Rome. He had none to protect him but a prince of the empire, powerful, indeed, and wise, but old and wavering. There were but few to uphold and defend him—the satirical Erasmus, who was called a second Lucian, the feeble Staupitz, the fanatical Carlstadt, and the inexperienced Melancthon. The worldly-minded, the learned, the powerful, and the conservative classes were his natural enemies. But he had reason and Scripture on his side, and he appealed to their great and final verdict. He had singular faith in the power of truth, and the gracious protection of God Almighty. Reposing on the greatness of his cause, and the providence of the omnipotent Protector, he was ready to defy all the arts, and theories, and malice of man. His weapon was truth. For truth he fought, and for truth he was ready to die. The sophistries of the schools he despised; they had distorted and mystified the truth. And he knew them well, for he had been trained in the severest dialectics of his time, and, though he despised them, he knew how to use them. The simple word of God, directed to the reason and conscience of men, seemed alone worthy of his regard.

Luther's Elements of Greatness

But, beside Scripture and unperverted reason, he had another element of power. He was master of the sympathies and passions of the people. His father was a toiling miner. His grandfather was a peasant. He had been trained to penury; he had associated with the poor; he was a man of the people; he was their natural friend. He saw and lamented their burdens, and rose up for their deliverance. .And the people distinguished their true friend, from their false friends. They saw the sincerity, earnestness, and labors of the new apostle of liberty, and believed in him, and made an idol of him. They would protect him, and honor him, and obey him, and believe what he taught them, for he was their friend, whom God had raised up to take off their burdens, and point a way to heaven, without the intercession of priests, or indulgences, or penance. Their friend was to expose the corruptions of the clergy, and to give battle to the great arch enemy who built St. Peter's Church from their hard-earned pittances. A spirit from heaven enlightened those to whom Luther preached, and they rallied around his standard, and swore never to separate, until the great enemies of the poor and the oppressed were rendered powerless. And their sympathies were needed, and best services, too; for the great man of the age—the incarnated spirit of liberty—was in danger.

Excommunication of Luther.

The pope, hitherto mild, persuasive, and undecided, now arose in the majesty of his mighty name, and, as the successor of St. Peter, hurled those weapons which had been thunderbolts in the hands of the Gregories and the Innocents. From his papal throne, and with all the solemnity of God's appointed vicegerent, he denounced the daring monk of Wittemberg, and sentenced him to the wrath of God, and to the penalty of eternal fire. Luther was excommunicated by a papal bull, and his writings were condemned as heretical and damnable.

This was a dreadful sentence. Few had ever resisted it successfully, even monarchs themselves. Excommunication was still a fearful weapon, and used only in desperate circumstances. It was used only as the last resort; for frequency would destroy its power. In the middle ages, this weapon was omnipotent; and the middle ages had but just passed away. No one could stand before that awful anathema which consigned him to the wrath of incensed and implacable Deity. Much as some professed to despise the sentence, still, when inflicted, it could not be borne, especially if accompanied with an interdict. Children were left unburied. The churches were closed. The rites of religion were suspended. A funereal shade was spread over society. The fears of hell haunted every imagination. No reason was strong enough to resist the sentence. No arm was sufficiently powerful to remove the curse. It hung over a guilty land. It doomed the unhappy offender, who was cursed, wherever he went, and in whatever work he was engaged.

But Luther was strong enough to resist it, and to despise it. He saw it was an imposition, which only barbarous and ignorant ages had permitted. Moreover, he perceived that there was now no alternative but victory or death; that, in the great contest in which he was engaged, retreat was infamy. Nor did he wish to retreat. He was fighting for oppressed humanity, and death even, in such a cause, was glory. He understood fully the nature and the consequence of the struggle. He perceived the greatness of the odds against him, in a worldly point of view. No man but a Luther would have been equal to it; no man, before him, ever had successfully rebelled against the pope. It is only in view of this circumstance, that his intrepidity can be appreciated.

What did the Saxon monk do, when the papal bull was published? He assembled the professors and students of the university, declared his solemn protest against the pope as Antichrist, and marched in procession to the gates of the Castle of Wittemberg, and there made a bonfire, and cast into it the bull which condemned him, the canon law, and some writings of the schoolmen, and then reëntered the city, breathing defiance against the whole power of the pope, glowing in the consciousness that the battle had commenced, to last as long as life, and perfectly secure that the victory would finally be on the side of truth. This was in 1520, on the 10th of December.

The attention of the whole nation was necessarily drawn to this open resistance; and the sympathy of the free thinking, the earnest, and the religious, was expressed for him. Never was popular interest more absorbing, in respect to his opinions, his fortunes, and his fate. The spirit of innovation became contagious, and pervaded the German mind. It demanded the serious attention of the emperor himself.

The Diet of Worms.

A great Diet of the empire was convened at Worms, and thither Luther was summoned by the temporal power. He had a safe-conduct, which even so powerful a prince as Charles V. durst not violate. In April, 1521, the reformer appeared before the collected dignitaries of the German empire, both spiritual and temporal, and was called upon to recant his opinions as heretical in the eyes of the church, and dangerous to the peace of the empire. Before the most august assembly in the world, without a trace of embarrassment, he made his defence, and refused to recant. "Unless," said he, "my errors can be demonstrated by texts from Scripture, I will not and cannot recant; for it is not safe for a man to go against his conscience. Here I am. I can do no otherwise. God help me! Amen."

This declaration satisfied his friends, though it did not satisfy the members of the diet. Luther was permitted to retire. He had gained the confidence of the nation. From that time, he was its idol, and the acknowledged leader of the greatest insurrection of human intelligence which modern times have seen. The great principles of the reformation were declared. The great hero of the Reformation had planted his cause upon a rock. And yet his labors had but just commenced. Henceforth, his life was toil and vexation. New difficulties continually arose. New questions had to be continually settled. Luther, by his letters, was every where. He commenced the translation of the Scriptures; he wrote endless controversial tracts; his correspondence was unparalleled; his efforts as a preacher were prodigious. But he was equal to it all; was wonderfully adapted to his age and circumstances.

Imprisonment at Wartburg.

About this time commenced his voluntary imprisonment at Wartburg, among the Thuringian forests: he being probably conducted thither by the orders of the elector of Saxony. Here he was out of sight, but not out of mind; and his retirement, under the disguise of a knight, gave him leisure for literary labor. In the old Castle of Wartburg, a great part of the Scriptures was translated into that beautiful and simple version, which is still the standard of the German language.

Carlstadt.

While Luther was translating the Scriptures, in his retreat, Wittemberg was the scene of new commotions, pregnant with great results. There were many of the more zealous converts to the reformed doctrines, headed by Carlstadt, dean of the faculty of theology, who were not content with the progress which had been made, and who desired more sweeping and radical changes. Such a party ever exists in all reforms; for there are some persons who are always inclined to ultra and extravagant courses. Carlstadt was a type of such men. He was learned, sincere, and amiable, but did not know where to stop; and the experiment was now to be tried, whether it was possible to introduce a necessary reform, without annihilating also all the results of the labors of preceding generations. Carlstadt's mind was not well balanced, and to him the reformation was only a half measure, and a useless movement, unless all the external observances of religion and the whole economy of the church were destroyed. He abolished, or desired to abolish, all priestly garments, all fasts and holydays, all pictures in the churches, and all emblematical ceremonies of every kind. He insisted upon closing all places of public amusement, the abolition of all religious communities, and the division of their possessions among the poor. He maintained that there was no need of learning, or of academic studies, and even went into the houses of the peasantry to seek explanation of difficult passages of Scripture.

For such innovations, the age was certainly not prepared, even had they been founded on reason; and the conservative mind of Luther was shocked at extravagances which served to disgust the whole Christian world, and jeopardize the cause in which he had embarked. So, against the entreaties of the elector, and in spite of the ban of the empire, he returned to Wittemberg, a small city, it was true, but a place to which had congregated the flower of the German youth. He resolved to oppose the movements of Carlstadt, even though opposition should destroy his influence. Especially did he declare against all violent measures to which the ultra reformers were inclined, knowing full well, that, if his cause were sullied with violence or fanaticism, all Christendom would unite to suppress it. His sermons are, at this time, (1522,) pervaded with a profound and conservative spirit, and also a spirit of conciliation and love, calculated to calm passions, and carry conviction to excited minds. His moderate counsels prevailed, the tumults were hushed, and order was restored. Carlstadt was silenced for a time; but a mind like his could not rest, especially on points where he had truth on his side. One of these was, in reference to the presence of Christ's body in the Eucharist, which Carlstadt totally denied. He taught "that the Lord's supper was purely symbolic, and was simply a pledge to believers of their redemption." But Luther saw, in every attempt to exhibit the symbolical import of the supper, only the danger of weakening the authority of Scripture, which was his stronghold, and became exceedingly tenacious on that point; carried his views to the extreme of literal interpretation, and never could emancipate himself from the doctrines of Rome respecting the eucharist. Carlstadt, finding himself persecuted at Wittemberg left the city, and, as soon as he was released from the presence of Luther, began to revive his former zeal against images also, and was the promoter of great disturbances. He at last sought refuge in Strasburg, and sacrificed fame, and friends, and bread to his honest convictions.

Thomas Münzer.

But, nevertheless, the views of Carlstadt found advocates, and his extravagances were copied with still greater zeal. Many pretended to special divine illumination—the great central principle of all fanaticism. Among these was Thomas Münzer, of Zwickau, mystical, ignorant, and conceited, but sincere and simple hearted. "Luther," said he, "has liberated men's consciences from the papal yoke, but has not led them in spirit towards God." Considering himself as called upon by a special revelation to bring men into greater spiritual liberty, he went about inflaming the popular mind, and raising discontents, and even inciting to a revolt. Religion now became mingled with politics, and social and political evils were violently resisted, under the garb of religion. An insurrection at last arose in the districts of the Black Forest, (1524,) near the sources of the Danube, and spread from Suabia to the Rhine provinces, until it became exceedingly formidable. Then commenced what is called the "peasants' war," which was only ended by the slaughter of fifty thousand people. As the causes of this war, after all, were chiefly political, the details belong to our chapter on political history. For this insurrection of the peasantry, however, Luther expressed great detestation; although he availed himself of it to lecture the princes of Germany on their duties as civil rulers.

The peasant war was scarcely ended, when Luther married Catharine Bora; and, as she was a nun, and he was a monk, the marriage gave universal scandal. But this marriage, which proved happy, was the signal of new reforms. Luther now emancipated himself from his monastic fetters, and lifted up his voice against the whole monastic system. Eight years had elapsed since he preached against indulgences. During these eight years, reform had been gradual, and had now advanced to the extreme limit it ever reached during the life of the reformer.

But, in another quarter, it sprang up with new force, and was carried to an extent not favored in Germany. It was in Switzerland that the greatest approximation was made to the forms, if not to the spirit, of primitive Christianity.

Ulric Zwingle.

The great hero of this Swiss movement was Ulric Zwingle, the most interesting of all the reformers. He was born in 1484, and educated amid the mountains of his picturesque country, and, like Erasmus, Reuchlin, Luther, and Melancthon, had no aristocratic claims, except to the nobility of nature. But, though poor, he was well educated, and was a master of the scholastic philosophy and of all the learning of his age. Like Luther, he was passionately fond of music, and played the lute, the harp, the violin, the flute and the dulcimer. There was no more joyous spirit in all Switzerland than his. Every one loved his society, and honored his attainments, and admired his genius. Like Luther and Erasmus, he was disgusted with scholasticism, and regretted the time he had devoted to its study. He was ordained in 1506, by the bishop of Constance, and was settled in Zurich in 1518. At first, his life did not differ from that which the clergy generally led, being one of dissipation and pleasure. But he was studious, and became well acquainted with the fathers, and with the original Greek. Only gradually did light dawn upon him, and this in consequence of his study of the Scriptures, not in consequence of Luther's preaching. He had no tempests to withstand, such as shook the soul of the Saxon monk. Nor had he ever devoted himself with the same ardor to the established church. Nor was he so much interested on doctrinal points of faith. But he saw with equal clearness the corruptions of the church, and preached with equal zeal against indulgences and the usurpations of the popes. The reformation of morals was the great aim of his life. His preaching was practical and simple, and his doctrine was, that "religion consisted in trust in God, loving God, and innocence of life." Moreover, he took a deep interest in the political relations of his country, and was an enthusiast in liberty as well as in religion. To him the town of Zurich was indebted for its emancipation from the episcopal government of Constance, and also for a reformation in all the externals of the church. He inspired the citizens with that positive spirit of Protestantism, which afterwards characterized Calvin and the Puritans. He was too radical a reformer to suit Luther, although he sympathized with most of his theological opinions.

Controversy between Luther and Zwingle.

On one point, however, they differed; and this difference led to an acrimonious contest, quite disgraceful to Luther, and the greatest blot on his character, inasmuch as it developed, to an extraordinary degree, both obstinacy and dogmatism, and showed that he could not bear contradiction or opposition. The quarrel arose from a difference of views respecting the Lord's supper, Luther maintaining not exactly the Roman Catholic doctrine of transubstantiation, but something approximating to it—even the omnipresence of Christ's body in the sacred elements. He relinquished the doctrine of the continually repeated miracle, but substituted a universal miracle, wrought once for all. In his tenacity to the opinions of the schoolmen on this point, we see his conservative spirit; for he did not deny tradition, unless it was expressly contradicted by Scripture. He would have maintained the whole structure of the Latin church, had it not been disfigured by modern additions, plainly at variance with the Scriptures; and so profoundly was he attached to the traditions of the church, and to the whole church establishment, that he only emancipated himself by violent inward storms. But Zwingle had not this lively conception of the universal church, and was more radical in his sympathies. He took Carlstadt's view of the supper, that it was merely symbolic. Still he shrunk from a rupture with Luther, which, however, was unavoidable, considering Luther's views of the subject and his cast of mind. Luther rejected all offers of conciliation, and, as he considered it essential to salvation to believe in the real presence of Christ in the sacrament, he refused to acknowledge Zwingle as a brother.

Zwingle, nevertheless, continued his reforms, and sought to restore, what he conceived to be, the earliest forms in which Christianity had manifested itself. He designed to restore a worship purely spiritual. He rejected all rites and ceremonies, not expressly enjoined in the Bible. Luther insisted in retaining all that was not expressly forbidden. And this was the main point of distinction between them and their adherents.

But Zwingle contemplated political, as well as religious, changes, and, as early as 1527, two years before his conference with Luther at Marburg, had projected a league of all the reformers against the political authorities which opposed their progress. He combated the abuses of the state, as well as of the church. This opposition created great enemies against him among the cantons, with their different governments and alliances. He also secured enthusiastic friends, and, in all the cantons, there was a strong democratic party opposed to the existing oligarchies, which party, in Berne and Basle, St. Gall, Zurich, Appenzell, Schaffhausen, and Glarus, obtained the ascendency. This led to tumults and violence, and finally to civil war between the different cantons, those which adhered to the old faith being assisted by Austria. Lucerne, Uri Schwytz, Zug, Unterwalden took the lead against the reformed cantons, the foremost of which was Zurich, where Zwingle lived. Zurich was attacked. Zwingle, from impulses of patriotism and courage, issued forth from his house, and joined the standard of his countrymen, not as a chaplain, but as an armed warrior. This was his mistake. "They who take the sword shall perish with the sword." The intrepid and enlightened reformer was slain in 1531, and, with his death, expired the hopes of his party. The restoration of the Roman Catholic religion immediately commenced in Switzerland.

Luther, more wise than Zwingle, inasmuch as he abstained from politics, continued his labors in Germany. And they were immense. The burdens of his country rested on his shoulders. He was the dictator of the reformed party, and his word was received as law. Moreover, the party continually increased, and, from the support it received from some of the most powerful of the German princes, it became formidable, even in a political point of view. Nearly one half of Germany embraced the reformed faith.

Diet of Augsburg.

The illustrious Charles V. had now, for some time, been emperor, and, in the prosecution of his conquests, found it necessary to secure the support of united Germany, especially since Germany was now invaded by the Turks. In order to secure this support, he found it necessary to make concessions in religion to his Protestant subjects. At the diet of Augsburg, (1530,) where there was the most brilliant assemblage of princes which had been for a long time seen in Germany, the celebrated confession of the faith of the Protestants was read. It was written by Melancthon, in both Latin and German, on the basis of the articles of Torgau, which Luther had prepared. The style was Melancthon's; the matter was Luther's. It was comprised in twenty-eight articles, of which twenty-one pertained to the faith of the Protestants—the name they assumed at the second diet of Spires, in 1529—and the remaining seven recounted the errors and abuses of Rome. It was subscribed by the Elector of Saxony, the Marquis of Brandenburg, the Duke of Lunenburg, the Landgrave of Hesse, the Prince of Anhalt, and the deputies of the imperial cities Nuremberg and Reutlingen. But the Catholics had the ascendency in the diet, and the "Confession of Augsburg" was condemned. But the emperor did not venture on any decisive measures for the extirpation of the "heresy." He threatened and published edicts, but his menaces had but little force. Nevertheless, the Protestant princes assembled, first at Smalcalde, and afterwards at Frankfort, for an alliance of mutual defence,—the first effective union of free princes and states against their oppressors in modern Europe,—and laid the foundation of liberty of conscience. Hostilities, however, did not commence, since the emperor was desirous of uniting Germany against the Turks; and he therefore recalled his edicts of Worms and Augsburg against the Protestants, and made important concessions, and promised them undisturbed enjoyment of their religion. This was a great triumph to the Protestants, and as great a shock to the Papal power.

League of Smalcalde.

The Confession of Augsburg and the League of Smalcalde form an important era of Protestantism, since, by these, the reformed faith received its definite form, and was moreover guaranteed. The work for which Luther had been raised up was now, in the main, accomplished. His great message had been delivered and heard.

Death and Character of Luther.

After the confirmation of his cause, his life was perplexed and anxious. He had not anticipated those civil commotions which he now saw, sooner or later, were inevitable. With the increase of his party was the decline of spirituality. Political considerations, also, with many, were more prominent than moral. Religion and politics were mingled together, not soon to be separated in the progress of reform. Moreover, the reformers differed upon many points among themselves. There was a lamentable want of harmony between the Germans and the Swiss. Luther had quarrelled with early every prominent person with whom he had been associated, except Melancthon, who yielded to him implicit obedience. But, above all, the Anabaptist disorders, which he detested, and which distracted the whole bishopric of Münster, oppressed and mortified him. Worn out with cares, labors, and vexations, which ever have disturbed the peace and alloyed the happiness of great heroes, and from which no greatness is exempt, he died at Eisleben, in 1545, while on a visit to his native place in older to reconcile dissensions between the counts of Mansfeldt.

Luther's name is still reverenced in Germany, and, throughout all Protestant countries, he is regarded as the greatest man connected with the history of the church since the apostolic age. Others have been greater geniuses, others more learned, others more devout, and others more amiable and interesting; but none ever evinced greater intrepidity, or combined greater qualities of mind and heart. He had his faults: he was irritable, dogmatic, and abusive in his controversial writings. He had no toleration for those who differed from him—the fault of the age. But he was genial, joyous, friendly, and disinterested. His labors were gigantic; his sincerity unimpeached; his piety enlightened; his zeal unquenchable. Circumstances and the new ideas of his age, favored him, but he made himself master of those circumstances and ideas, and, what is more, worked out ideas of his own, which were in harmony with Christianity. The Reformation would have happened had there been no Luther, though at a less favorable time; but, of all the men of his age that the Reformation could least spare, Martin Luther stands preëminent. As the greatest of reformers, his name will be ever honored.

References.—The attention of the student is directed only to the most prominent and valuable works which treat of Luther and the Protestant reformation. All the works are too numerous, even to be decimated. Allusion is made to those merely which are accessible and useful. Among them may be mentioned, as most important, Ranke's History of the Reformation; D'Aubigné's History of the Reformation; Michelet's Life of Luther; Audin's Life of Luther, a Catholic work, written with great spirit, but not much liberality; Stebbing's History of the Reformation; a Life of Luther, by Rev. Dr. Sears, a new work, written with great correctness and ability; Guizot's Lectures on Civilization; Plank's Essay on the Consequences of the Reformation.

CHAPTER III
THE EMPEROR CHARLES V

When Luther appeared upon the stage, the great monarchies of Europe had just arisen upon the ruins of those Feudal states which survived the wreck of Charlemagne's empire.

Charles V.

The Emperor of Germany, of all the monarchs of Europe, had the greatest claim to the antiquity and dignity of his throne. As hereditary sovereign of Austria, Styria, Carinthia, and the Tyrol, he had absolute authority in his feudal provinces; while, as an elected emperor, he had an indirect influence over Saxony, the Palatinate, the three archbishoprics of Trèves, Mentz, and Cologne, and some Burgundian territories.

Spain and France in the Fifteenth Century.

But the most powerful monarchy, at this time, was probably that of France; and its capital was the finest city in Europe, and the resort of the learned and elegant from all parts of Christendom. All strangers extolled the splendor of the court, the wealth of the nobles, and the fame of the university. The power of the monarch was nearly absolute, and a considerable standing army, even then, was ready to obey his commands.

Spain, at the beginning of the sixteenth century, was ruled by Ferdinand and Isabella, who, by their marriage, had united the crowns of Castile and Arragon. The conquest of Granada and the discovery of America had added greatly to the political importance of Spain, and laid the foundation of its future greatness under Philip II.

England, from its insular position, had not so much influence in European politics as the other powers to which allusion has been made, but it was, nevertheless, a flourishing and united kingdom. Henry VII., the founder of the house of Tudor, sat on the throne, and was successful in suppressing the power of the feudal nobility, and in increasing the royal authority. Kings, in the fifteenth century, were the best protectors of the people, and aided them in their struggles against their feudal oppressors. England, however, had made but little advance in commerce or manufactures, and the people were still rude and ignorant. The clergy, as in other countries, were the most intelligent and wealthy portion of the population, and, consequently, the most influential, although disgraced by many vices.

Italy then, as now, was divided into many independent states, and distracted by civil and religious dissensions. The duchy of Milan was ruled by Ludovico Moro, son of the celebrated Francis Sforza. Naples, called a kingdom, had just been conquered by the French. Florence was under the sway of the Medici. Venice, whose commercial importance had begun to decline, was controlled by an oligarchy of nobles. The chair of St. Peter was filled by pope Alexander VI., a pontiff who has obtained an infamous immortality by the vices of debauchery, cruelty, and treachery. The papacy was probably in its most corrupt state, and those who had the control of its immense patronage, disregarded the loud call for reformation which was raised in every corner of Christendom. The popes were intent upon securing temporal as well as spiritual power, and levied oppressive taxes on both their spiritual and temporal subjects.

The great northern kingdoms of Europe, which are now so considerable,—Russia, Denmark, Sweden, and Norway,—did not, at the beginning of the sixteenth century, attract much attention. They were plunged in barbarism and despotism, and the light of science or religion rarely penetrated into the interior. The monarchs were sensual and cruel, the nobles profligate and rapacious, the clergy ignorant and corrupt, and the people degraded, and yet insensible to their degradation, with no aspirations for freedom and no appreciation of the benefits of civilization. Such heroes as Peter and Gustavus Adolphus had not yet appeared. Nor were these northern nations destined to be immediately benefited by the impulse which the reformation gave, with the exception of Sweden, then the most powerful of these kingdoms.

The Greek empire became extinct when Constantinople was taken by the Turks, in 1453. On its ruins, the Ottoman power was raised. At the close of the fifteenth century, the Turkish arms were very powerful, and Europe again trembled before the Moslems. Greece and the whole of Western Asia were obedient to the sultan. But his power did not reach its culminating point until a century afterwards.

Such were the various states of Europe when the Reformation broke out. Maximilian was emperor of Germany, and Charles V. had just inherited, from his father, Philip the Fair, who had married a daughter of Ferdinand and Isabella, the kingdom of Spain, in addition to the dominion of the Netherlands.

By the death of Maximilian, in 1519, the youthful sovereign of Spain and the Netherlands came into possession of the Austrian dominions; and the electors, shortly after, chose him emperor of Germany.

He was born at Ghent, A. D. 1500, and was educated with great care. He early displayed his love of government, and, at fifteen, was present at the deliberations of the cabinet. But he had no taste for learning, and gave but few marks of that genius which he afterwards evinced. He was much attached to his Flemish subjects, and, during the first year of his reign, gave great offence to the grandees of Spain and the nobles of Germany by his marked partiality for those men who had been his early companions.

It is difficult to trace, in the career of Charles V., any powerful motives of conduct, separate from the desire of aggrandizement. The interests of the church, with which he was identified, and the true welfare of his subjects, were, at different times, sacrificed to his ambition. Had there been no powerful monarchs on the other thrones of Europe, his dreams of power might possibly have been realized. But at this period there happened to be a constellation of princes.

Wars between Charles and

The greatest of these, and the chief rival through life of Charles, was Francis I. of France. He had even anticipated an election to the imperial crown, which would have made him more powerful than even Charles himself. The electors feared both, and chose Frederic of Saxony; but he declined the dangerous post. Charles, as Archduke of Austria, had such great and obvious claims, that they could not be disregarded. He was therefore the fortunate candidate. But his election was a great disappointment to Francis, and he could not conceal his mortification. Francis.Peace could not long subsist between two envious and ambitious princes. Francis was nearly of the same age as Charles, had inherited nearly despotic power, was free from financial embarrassments, and ruled over an united and loyal people. He was therefore no contemptible match for Charles. In addition, he strengthened himself by alliances with the Swiss and Venetians. Charles sought the favor of the pope and Henry VIII. of England. The real causes of war were mutual jealousies, and passion for military glory. The assigned causes were, that Charles did not respect the claims of Francis as king of Naples; and, on the other hand, that Francis had seized the duchy of Milan, which was a fief of the empire, and also retained the duchy of Burgundy, the patrimonial inheritance of the emperor.

The political history of Europe, for nearly half a century, is a record of the wars between these powerful princes, of their mutual disasters, disappointments, and successes. Other contests were involved in these, and there were also some which arose from causes independent of mutual jealousy, such as the revolt of the Spanish grandees, of the peasants in Germany, and of the invasion of the empire by the Turks. During the reign of Charles, was also the division of the princes of Germany, on grounds of religion—the foundation of the contest which, after the death of Charles, convulsed Germany for thirty years. But the Thirty Years' War was a religious war—was one of the political consequences of the Reformation. The wars between Charles and Francis were purely wars of military ambition. Charles had greater territories and larger armies; but Francis had more money, and more absolute control over his forces. Charles's power was checked in Spain by the free spirit of the Cortes, and in Germany by the independence of the princes, and by the embarrassing questions which arose out of the Reformation.

It would be tedious to read the various wars between Charles and his rival. Each of them gained, at different times, great successes, and each experienced, in turn, the most humiliating reverses. Francis was even taken prisoner at the battle of Pavia, in 1525, and confined in a fortress at Madrid, until he promised to the victors the complete dismemberment of France— an extorted promise he never meant to keep. No sooner had he recovered his liberty, than he violated all his oaths, and Europe was again the scene of fresh hostilities. The passion of revenge was now added to that of ambition, and, as the pope had favored the cause of Francis, the generals of Charles invaded Italy. Rome was taken and sacked by the constable Bourbon, a French noble whom Francis had slighted, and cruelties and outrages were perpetrated by the imperial forces which never disgraced Alaric or Attila.

Charles affected to be filled with grief in view of the victories of his generals, and pretended that they acted without his orders. He employed every artifice to deceive indignant Christendom, and appointed prayers and processions throughout Spain for the recovery of the pope's liberty, which one stroke of his pen could have secured. Thus it was, that the most Catholic and bigoted prince in Europe seized the pope's person, and sacked his city, at the very time when Luther was prosecuting his reform. And this fact shows how much more powerfully the emperor was influenced by political, than by religious considerations. It also shows the providence of God in permitting the only men, who could have arrested the reformation, to spend their strength in battling each other, rather than the heresy which they deplored. Had Charles been less powerful and ambitious, he probably would have contented himself in punishing heretics, and in uniting with his natural ally, the pope, in suppressing every insurrection which had for its object the rights of conscience and the enjoyment of popular liberty.

The war was continued for two years longer between Francis and Charles, with great acrimony, but with various success, both parties being, at one time, strengthened by alliances, and then again weakened by desertions. At last, both parties were exhausted, and were willing to accede to terms which they had previously rejected with disdain. Francis was the most weakened and disheartened, but Charles was the most perplexed. The troubles growing out of the Reformation demanded his attention, and the Turks, at this period a powerful nation, were about invading Austria. The Spaniards murmured at the unusual length of the war, and money was with difficulty obtained.

Hence the peace of Cambray, August 5, 1529; which was very advantageous to Charles, in consequence of the impulsive character of Francis, and his impatience to recover his children, whom he had surrendered to Charles in order to recover his liberty. He agreed to pay two millions of crowns for the ransom of his sons, and renounce his pretensions in the Low Countries and Italy. He, moreover, lost reputation, and the confidence of Europe, by the abandonment of his allies. Charles remained the arbiter of Italy, and was attentive to the interests of all who adhered to him. With less *chivalry* than his rival, he had infinitely more *honor*. Cold, sagacious, selfish, and ambitious, he was, however, just, and kept his word. He combined qualities we often see in selfish men—a sort of legal and technical regard to the letter of the law, with the constant violation of its spirit. A Shylock might not enter a false charge upon his books, while he would adhere to a most extortionate bargain.

Charles, after the treaty of Cambray was signed, visited Italy with all the pomp of a conqueror. At Genoa, he honored Doria with many marks of distinction, and bestowed upon the republic new privileges. He settled all his difficulties with Milan, Venice, and Florence, and reëstablished the authority of the Medici. He was then crowned by the pope, whom he had trampled on, as King of Lombardy and Emperor of the Romans, and hastened into Germany, which imperatively required his presence, both on account of dissensions among the princes, which the reformation caused, and the invasion of Austria by three hundred thousand Turks. He resolved to recover the old prerogatives of the emperor of Germany, and crush those opinions which were undermining his authority, as well as the power of Rome, with which his own was identified.

Diet of Spires.

A Diet of the empire was accordingly summoned at Spires, in order to take into consideration the state of religion, the main cause of all the disturbances in Germany. It met on the 15th of March, 1529, and the greatest address was required to prevent a civil war. All that Charles could obtain from the assembled princes was, the promise to prevent any further innovations. A decree to that effect was passed, against which, however, the followers of Luther protested, the most powerful of whom were the Elector of Saxony, the Marquis of Brandenburg, the Landgrave of Hesse, the Duke of Lunenburg, the Prince of Anhalt, and the deputies of fourteen imperial cities. This protest gave to them the name of *Protestants*—a name ever since retained. Soon after, the diet assembled at Augsburg, when the articles of faith among the Protestants were read,—known as the Confession of Augsburg,—which, however, the emperor opposed. In consequence of his decree, the Protestant princes entered into a league at Smalcalde, (December 22, 1530,) to support one another, and defend their religion. Circumstances continually occurred to convince Charles, that the extirpation of heresy by the sword was impossible in Germany, and moreover, he saw it was for his interest—to which his eye was peculiarly open—to unite all the German provinces in a vigorous confederation. Accordingly after many difficulties, and with great reluctance, terms of pacification were agreed upon at Nuremburg, (1531,) and ratified in the diet at Ratisbon, shortly after, by which it was agreed that no person should be molested in his religion, and that the Protestants, on their part, should assist the emperor in resisting the invasion of the Turks. The Germans, with their customary good faith, furnished all the assistance they promised, and one of the best armies ever raised in Germany, amounting to ninety thousand foot, and thirty thousand horse, took the field, commanded by the emperor in person. But the campaign ended without any memorable event, both parties having erred from excessive caution.

Hostilities between Charles and Francis.

Francis soon availed himself of the difficulties and dangers of his rival, formed an alliance with the Turks, put forth his old claims, courted the favor of the German Protestants, and renewed hostilities. He marched towards Italy, and took possession of the dominions of the duke of Savoy, whom the emperor, at this juncture, was unable to assist, on account of his African expedition against the pirate Barbarossa. This noted corsair had built up a great power in Tunis and Algiers, and committed shameful ravages on all Christian nations. Charles landed in Africa with thirty thousand men, took the fortress of Goletta, defeated the pirate's army, captured his capital, and restored the exiled Moorish king to his throne. In the midst of these victories Francis invaded Savoy. Charles was terribly indignant, and loaded his rival with such violent invectives that Francis challenged him to single combat. The challenge was accepted, but the duel was never fought. Charles, in his turn, invaded France, with a large army, for that age—forty thousand foot and ten thousand horse; but the expedition was unfortunate. Francis acted on the defensive with admirable skill, and was fortunate in his general Montmorency, who seemed possessed with the spirit of a Fabius. The emperor, at last, was compelled to return ingloriously, having lost half of his army without having gained a single important advantage. The joy of Francis, however, was embittered by the death of the dauphin, attributed by some to the infamous Catharine de Medicis, wife of the Duke of Orleans, in order to secure the crown to her husband. War did not end with the retreat of Charles, but was continued, with great personal animosity, until mutual exhaustion led to a truce for ten years, concluded at Nice, in 1538. Both parties had exerted their utmost strength, and neither had obtained any signal advantage. Notwithstanding their open and secret enmity, they had an interview shortly after the truce, in which both vied with each other in expressions of esteem and friendship, and in the exhibition of chivalrous courtesies — a miserable mockery, as shown by the violation of the terms of the truce, and the renewal of hostilities in 1541.

African Wars.

These were, doubtless, facilitated by Charles's unfortunate expedition against Algiers in 1541, by which he gained nothing but disgrace. His army was wasted by famine and disease, and a tempest destroyed his fleet. All the complicated miseries which war produces were endured by his unfortunate troops, but a small portion of whom ever returned. Francis, taking advantage of these misfortunes, made immense military preparations, formed a league with the Sultan Solyman, and brought five armies into the field. He assumed the offensive, and invaded the Netherlands, but obtained no laurels. Charles formed a league with Henry VIII., and the war raged, with various success, without either party obtaining any signal advantage, for three years, when a peace was concluded at Crespy, in 1544. Charles, being in the heart of France with an invading army, had the apparent advantage but the difficulty of retreating out of France in case of disaster, and the troubles in Germany, forced him to suspend his military operations. The pope, also, was offended because he had conceded so much to the Protestants, and the Turks pressed him on the side of Hungary. Moreover, he was afflicted with the gout, which indisposed him for complicated enterprises. In view of these things, he made peace with Francis, formed a strong alliance with the pope, and resolved to extirpate the Protestant religion, which was the cause of so many insurrections in Germany.

Council of Trent.

In the mean time, the pope resolved to assemble the famous Council of Trent, the legality of which the Protestants denied. It met in December,

1545, and was the last general council which the popes ever assembled. It met with a view of healing the dissensions of the church, and confirming the authority of the pope. The princes of Europe hoped that important reforms would have been made; but nothing of consequence was done, and the attention of the divines was directed to dogmas rather than morals. The great number of Italian bishops enabled the pope to have every thing his own way, in spite of the remonstrance of the German, Spanish, and French prelates, and the ambassadors of the different monarchs, who also had seats in the council. The decrees of this council, respecting articles of faith, are considered as a final authority by the Roman church. It denounced the reform of Luther, and confirmed the various ecclesiastical usurpations which had rendered the reformation necessary. It lasted twenty-two years, at different intervals, during the pontificate of five popes. The Jesuits, just rising into notice, had considerable influence in the council, in consequence of the learning and ability of their representatives, and especially of Laynez, the general of the order. The Dominicans and Franciscans manifested their accustomed animosities and rivalries, and questions were continually proposed and agitated, which divided the assembly. The French bishops, headed by the Cardinal of Lorraine, were opposed to the high pretensions of the Italians, especially of Cardinal Morone, the papal legate; but, by artifice and management, the more strenuous adherents of the pope attained their ends.

About the time the council assembled, died three distinguished persons — Henry VIII. of England, Francis I., and Luther. Charles V. was freed from his great rival, and from the only private person in his dominions he had reason to fear. He now, in good earnest, turned his attention to the internal state of his empire, and resolved to crush the Reformation, and, by force, if it were necessary. He commenced by endeavoring to amuse and deceive the Protestants, and evinced that profound dissimulation, which was one of his characteristics. He formed a strict alliance with the pope, made a truce with Solyman, and won over to his side Maurice and other German princes. His military preparations and his intrigues alarmed the Protestants, and they prepared themselves for resistance. Religious zeal seconded their military ardor. One of the largest armies, which had been raised in Europe for a century, took the field, and Charles, shut up in Ratisbon, was in no condition to fight. Unfortunately for the Protestants, they negotiated instead of acting. The emperor was in their power, but he was one of those few persons who remained haughty and inflexible in the midst of calamities. He pronounced the ban of the empire against the Protestant princes, who were no match for a man who had spent his life in the field: they acted without concert, and committed many errors. Their forces decreased, while those of the emperor increased by large additions from Italy and Flanders. Instead of decisive action, the Protestants dallied and procrastinated, unwilling to make peace, and unwilling to face their sovereign. Their army melted away, and nothing of importance was effected.

Treachery of Maurice.

Maurice, cousin to the Elector of Saxony, with a baseness to which history scarcely affords a parallel, deserted his allies, and joined the emperor, purely from ambitious motives, and invaded the territories of his kinsman with twelve thousand men. The confederates made overtures of peace, which being rejected, they separated, and most of them submitted to the emperor. He treated them with haughtiness and rigor, imposed on them most humiliating terms, forced them to renounce the league of Smalcalde, to give up their military stores, to admit garrisons into their cities, and to pay large contributions in money.

The Elector of Saxony and the Landgrave of Hesse, however held out; and such was the condition of the emperor, that he could not immediately attack them. But the death of Francis gave him leisure to invade Saxony, and the elector was defeated at the battle of Muhlhausen, (1547,) and taken prisoner. The captive prince approached the victor without sullenness or pride. "The fortune of war," said he, "has made me your prisoner, most gracious emperor, and I hope to be treated − −" Here Charles interrupted him−"And am I, at last, acknowledged to be emperor? Charles of Ghent was the only title you lately allowed me. You shall be treated as you deserve." At these words he turned his back upon him with a haughty air.

The unfortunate prince was closely guarded by Spanish soldiers, and brought to a trial before a court martial, at which presided the infamous Duke of Alva, afterwards celebrated for his cruelties in Holland. He was convicted of treason and rebellion, and sentenced to death−a sentence which no court martial had a right to inflict on the first prince of the empire. He was treated with ignominious harshness, which he bore with great magnanimity, but finally made a treaty with the emperor, by which, for the preservation of his life, he relinquished his kingdom to Maurice.

Captivity of the Landgrave of Hesse.

The landgrave was not strong enough to resist the power of Charles, after all his enemies were subdued, and he made his submission, though Charles extorted the most rigorous conditions, he being required to surrender his person, abandon the league of Smalcalde, implore pardon on his knees, demolish his fortifications, and pay an enormous fine. In short, it was an unconditional submission. Beside infinite mortifications, he was detained a prisoner, which, on Charles's part, was but injury added to insult−an act of fraud and injustice which inspired the prince, and the Protestants, generally, with unbounded indignation. The Elector of Brandenburg and Maurice in vain solicited for his liberty, and showed the infamy to which he would be exposed if he detained the landgrave a prisoner. But the emperor listened to their remonstrances with the most provoking coolness, and showed very plainly that he was resolved to crush all rebellion, suppress Protestantism, and raise up an absolute throne in Germany, to the subversion of its ancient constitution.

To all appearances, his triumph was complete. His great rival was dead; his enemies were subdued and humiliated; Luther's voice was hushed; and immense contributions filled the imperial treasury. He now began to realize the dreams of his life. He was unquestionably, at that time, the most absolute and powerful prince Europe has ever seen since Charlemagne, with the exception of Napoleon.

But what an impressive moral does the history of human greatness convey! The hour of triumph is often but the harbinger of defeat and shame. "Pride goeth before destruction." Charles V., with all his policy and experience, overreached himself. The failure of his ambitious projects and the restoration of Protestantism, were brought about by instruments the least anticipated.

Heroism of Maurice..

Misfortunes of Charles.

The cause of Protestantism and the liberties of Germany were endangered by the treachery of Maurice, who received, as his reward, the great electorate of Saxony. He had climbed to the summit of glory and power. Who would suppose that this traitor prince would desert the emperor, who had so splendidly rewarded his services, and return to the rescue of those princes whom he had so basely betrayed? But who can thread the labyrinth of an intriguing and selfish heart? Who can calculate the movements of an unprincipled and restless politician? Maurice, at length, awoke to the perception of the real condition of his country. He saw its liberties being overturned by the most ambitious man whom ten centuries had produced. He saw the cause, which his convictions told him was the true one, in danger of being wrecked. He was, moreover, wounded by the pride, coldness, and undisguised selfishness of the emperor. He was indignant that the landgrave, his father-in-law, should be retained a prisoner, against all the laws of honor and of justice. He resolved to come to the rescue of his country. He formed his plans with the greatest coolness, and exercised a power of dissimulation that has no parallel in history. But his address was even greater than his hypocrisy. He gained the confidence of the Protestants, without losing that of the emperor. He even obtained the command of an army which Charles sent to reduce the rebellious city of Magdeburg, and, while he was besieging the city, he was negotiating with the generals who defended it for a general union against the emperor. Magdeburg surrendered in 1551. Its chieftains were secretly assured that the terms of capitulation should not be observed. His next point was, to keep the army together until his schemes were ripened, and then to arrest the emperor, whose thoughts now centred on the council of Trent. So he proposed sending Protestant divines to the council, but delayed their departure by endless negotiations about the terms of a safe conduct. He, moreover, formed a secret treaty with Henry II., the successor of Francis, whose animosity against Charles was as intense as was that of his father. When his preparations were completed, he joined his army in Thuringia, and took the field against the emperor, who had no suspicion of his designs, and who blindly trusted to him, deeming it impossible that a man, whom he had so honored and rewarded, could turn against him. March 18, 1552, Maurice published his manifesto, justifying his conduct; and his reasons were, to secure the Protestant religion, to maintain the constitution of the empire, and deliver the Landgrave of Hesse from bondage. He was powerfully supported by the French king, and, with a rapidly increasing army, marched towards Innspruck, where the emperor was quartered. The emperor was thunderstruck when he heard the tidings of his desertion, and was in no condition to resist him. He endeavored to gain time by negotiations, but these were without effect. Maurice, at the head of a large army, advanced rapidly into Upper Germany. Castles and cities surrendered as he advanced, and so rapid was his progress, that he came near taking the emperor captive. Charles was obliged to fly, in the middle of the night, and to travel on a litter by torchlight, amid the passes of the Alps. He scarcely left Innspruck before Maurice entered it—but too late to gain the prize he sought. The emperor rallied his armies, and a vigorous war was carried on between the contending parties, to the advantage of the Protestants. The emperor, after a while, was obliged to make peace with them, for his Spanish subjects were disgusted with the war, his funds were exhausted, his forces dispersed, and his territories threatened by the French. On the 2d of August, 1552, was concluded the peace of Passau, which secured the return of the landgrave to his dominions, the freedom of religion to the Protestants, and the preservation of the German constitution. The sanguine hopes of the emperor were dispelled, and all his ambitious schemes defeated, and he left to meditate, in the intervals of the pains which he suffered from the gout, on the instability of all greatness, and the vanity of human life. Maurice was now extolled as extravagantly as he had been before denounced, and his treachery justified, even by grave divines. But what is most singular in the whole affair, was, that the French king, while persecuting Protestants at home, should protect them abroad. But this conduct may confirm, in a signal manner, the great truth of history, that God regulates the caprice of human passions, and makes them subservient to the accomplishment of his own purposes.

Treaty of Passau.

The labors and perplexities of Charles V. were not diminished by the treaty of Passau. He continued his hostilities against the French and against the Turks. He was obliged to raise the siege of Metz, which was gallantly defended by the Duke of Guise. To his calamities in France, were added others in Italy. Sienna revolted against his government, and Naples was threatened by the Turks. The imperialists were unsuccessful in Italy and in Hungary, and the Archduke Ferdinand was obliged to abandon Transylvania. But war was carried on in the Low Countries with considerable vigor.

Charles, whose only passion was the aggrandizement of his house, now projected a marriage of his son, Philip, with Mary, queen of England. The queen, dazzled by the prospect of marrying the heir of the greatest monarch in Europe, and eager to secure his powerful aid to reëstablish Catholicism in England, listened to his proposal, although it was disliked by the nation. In spite of the remonstrance of the house of commons, the marriage treaty was concluded, and the marriage celebrated, (1554.)

Character of Charles V.

Soon after, Charles formed the extraordinary resolution of resigning his dominions to his son, and of retiring to a quiet retreat. Diocletian is the only instance of a prince, capable of holding the reins of government, who had adopted a similar course. All Europe was astonished at the resolution of Charles, and all historians of the period have moralized on the event. But it ceases to be mysterious, when we remember that Charles was no nearer the accomplishment of the ends which animated his existence, than he was thirty years before; that he was disgusted and wearied with the world; that he suffered severely from the gout, which, at times, incapacitated him for the government of his extensive dominions. It was never his habit to intrust others with duties and labors which he could perform himself, and he felt that his empire needed a more powerful protector than his infirmities permitted him to be. He was grown prematurely old, he felt his declining health; longed for repose, and sought religious consolation. Of all his vast possessions, he only reserved an annual pension of one hundred thousand crowns; resigning Spain and the Low Countries into the hands of Philip, and the empire of Germany to his brother Ferdinand, who had already been elected as King of the Romans. He then set out for his retreat in Spain, which was the monastery of St. Justus, near Placentia, situated in a lovely vale, surrounded with lofty trees, watered by a small brook, and rendered attractive by the fertility of the soil, and the delightful temperature of the climate. Here he spent his last days in agricultural improvements and religious exercises, apparently regardless of that noisy world which he had deserted forever, and indifferent to those political storms which his restless ambition had raised. Here his grandeur and his worldly hopes were buried in preparing himself for the future world. He lived with great simplicity, for two years after his retreat, and died (1558,) from the effects of the gout, which, added to his great labors, had shattered his constitution. He was not what the world would call a great genius, like Napoleon; but he was a man of great sagacity, untiring industry, and respectable attainments. He was cautious, cold, and selfish; had but little faith in human virtue, and was a slave, in his latter days, to superstition. He was neither affable nor courteous, but was sincere in his attachments, and munificent in rewarding his generals and friends. He was not envious nor cruel, but inordinately ambitious, and intent on aggrandizing his family. This was his characteristic defect, and this, in a man so prominent and so favored by circumstances, was enough to keep Europe in a turmoil for nearly half a century.

References.—Robertson's History of Charles V. Ranke's History of the Reformation. Kohlrausch's History of Germany. Russell's Modern Europe. The above-mentioned authors are easily accessible, and are all that are necessary for the student. Robertson's History is a classic, and an immortal work.

CHAPTER IV
HENRY VIII

The history of Europe in the sixteenth century is peculiarly the history of the wars of kings, and of their efforts to establish themselves and their families on absolute thrones. The monotonous, and almost exclusive, record of royal pleasures and pursuits shows in how little consideration the people were held. They struggled, and toiled, and murmured as they do now. They probably had the same joys and sorrows as in our times. But, in these times, they have considerable influence on the government, the religion, the literature, and the social life of nations. In the sixteenth century, this influence was not so apparent; but power of all kinds seemed to emanate from kings and nobles; at least from wealthy and cultivated classes. When this is the case, when kings give a law to society, history is not unphilosophical which recognizes chiefly their enterprises and ideas.

Rise of Absolute Monarchy.

The rise of absolute monarchy on the ruins of feudal states is one of the chief features of the fifteenth and sixteenth centuries. There was every where a strong tendency to centralization. Provinces, before independent, were controlled by a central government. Standing armies took the place of feudal armies. Kings took away from nobles the right to coin money, administer justice, and impose taxes. The power of the crown became supreme and unlimited.

But some monarchs were more independent than others, in proportion as the power of nobles was suppressed, or, as the cities sided with the central government, or, as provinces were connected and bound together. The power of Charles V. was somewhat limited, in Spain, by the free spirit of the Cortes, and, in Germany, by the independence of the princes of the empire. But, in France and England, the king was more absolute, although he did not rule over so great extent of territory as did the emperor of Germany; and this is one reason why Francis I. proved so strong an antagonist to his more powerful rival.

The history of France, during the reign of this monarch, is also the history of Charles V., since they were both engaged in the same wars; which wars have already been alluded to. Both of these monarchs failed in the objects of their existence. If Charles did not realize his dream of universal empire, neither did Francis leave his kingdom, at his death, in a more prosperous state than he found it.

Francis I. was succeeded by his son Henry II., a warlike prince, but destitute of prudence, and under the control of women. His policy, however, was substantially that of his father, and he continued hostilities against the emperor of Germany, till his resignation. He was a bitter persecutor of the Protestants, and the seeds of subsequent civil wars were sown by his zeal. He was removed from his throne prematurely, being killed at a tournament, in 1559, soon after the death of Charles V. Tournaments ceased with his death.

Henry VIII.

The reign of Henry VIII., the other great contemporary of Charles V., merits a larger notice, not only because his reign was the commencement of a new era in England, but, also, because the affairs, which engaged his attention, are not much connected with continental history.

He ascended the throne in the year 1509, in his eighteenth year, without opposition, and amid the universal joy of the nation; for his manners were easy and frank, his disposition was cheerful, and his person was handsome. He had made respectable literary attainments, and he gave promise of considerable abilities. He was married, soon after his accession, to Catharine, daughter of the King of Spain, and the first years of his reign were happy, both to himself and to his subjects. He had a well-filled treasury, which his father had amassed with great care, a devoted people and an obedient parliament. All circumstances seemed to conspire to strengthen his power, and to make him the arbiter of Europe.

But this state did not last long. The young king was resolved to make war on France, but was diverted from his aim by troubles in Scotland, growing out of his own rapacity—a trait which ever peculiarly distinguished him. These troubles resulted in a war with the Scots, who were defeated at the memorable battle of Flodden Field, which Sir Walter Scott, in his Marmion, has immortalized. The Scotch commanders, Lenox and Argyle, both perished, as well as the valiant King James himself. There is scarcely an illustrious Scotch family who had not an ancestor slain on that fatal day, September 9, 1513. But the victory was dearly bought, and Surrey, the English general, afterwards Duke of Norfolk, was unable to pursue his advantages.

Rise of Cardinal Wolsey.

About this time, the celebrated Cardinal Wolsey began to act a conspicuous part in English affairs. His father was a butcher of Ipswich; but was able to give his son a good education. He studied at Oxford, was soon distinguished for his attainments, and became tutor to the sons of the Marquis of Dorset. The marquis gave him the rich living of Limington; but the young parson, with his restless ambition, and love of excitement and pleasure, was soon wearied of a country life. He left his parish to become domestic chaplain to the treasurer of Calais. This post introduced him to Fox, bishop of Winchester, who shared with the Earl of Surrey the highest favors of royalty. The minister and diplomatist, finding in the young man learning, tact, vivacity, and talent for business, introduced him to the king, hoping that he would prove an agreeable companion for Henry, and a useful tool for himself. But those who are able to manage other people's business, generally are able to manage their own. The tool of Fox looked after his own interest chiefly. He supplanted his master in the loyal favor, and soon acquired more favor and influence at court than any of the ministers or favorites. Though twenty years older than Henry, he adapted himself to all his tastes, flattered his vanity and passions, and became his bosom friend. He gossiped with him about Thomas Aquinas, the Indies, and affairs of gallantry. He was a great refiner of sensual pleasures, had a passion for magnificence and display, and a real genius for court entertainments. He could eat and drink with the gayest courtiers, sing merry songs, and join in the dance. He was blunt and frank in his manners; but these only concealed craft and cunning. "It is art to conceal art," and Wolsey was a master of all the tricks of dissimulation. He rose rapidly after he had once gained the heart of the king. He became successively dean of York, papal legate, cardinal, bishop of Lincoln, archbishop of York, and lord chancellor. He also obtained the administration and the temporalities of the rich abbey of St. Albans, and of the bishoprics of Bath and Wells, Durham and Winchester. By these gifts, his revenues almost equalled those of the crown; and he squandered them in a style of unparalleled extravagance. He dressed in purple and gold, supported a train of eight hundred persons, and built Hampton Court. He was the channel through which the royal favors flowed. But he made a good chancellor, dispensed justice, repressed the power of the nobles, encouraged and rewarded literary men, and endowed colleges. He was the most magnificent and the most powerful subject that England has ever seen. Even nobles were proud to join his train of dependants. There was nothing sordid or vulgar, however, in all his ostentation. Henry took pleasure in his pomp, for it was a reflection of the greatness of his own majesty.

Magnificence of Henry VIII.

The first years of the reign of Henry VIII., after the battle of Flodden Field, were spent in pleasure, and in great public displays of magnificence, which charmed the people, and made him a popular idol. Among these, the interview of the king with Francis I. is the most noted, on the 4th of June, 1520; the most gorgeous pageant of the sixteenth century, designed by Wolsey, who had a genius for such things. The monarchs met in a beautiful valley, where jousts and tournaments were held, and where was exhibited all the magnificence which the united resources of France and England could command. The interview was sought by Francis to win, through Wolsey, the favor of the king, and to counterbalance the advantages which it was supposed Charles V. had gained on a previous visit to the king at Dover.

The getting up of the "Field of the Cloth of Gold" created some murmurs among the English nobility, many of whom were injured by the expensive tastes of Wolsey. Among these was the Duke of Buckingham, hereditary high constable of England, and connected with the royal house of the Plantagenets. Henry, from motives of jealousy, both on account of his birth and fortune, had long singled him out as his victim. He was, also, obnoxious to Wolsey, since he would not flatter his pride, and he had, moreover, insulted him. It is very easy for a king to find a pretence for committing a crime; and Buckingham was arrested, tried, and executed, for making traitorous prophecies. His real crime was in being more powerful than it suited the policy of the king. With the death of Stafford, Duke of Buckingham, in 1521, commenced the bloody cruelty of Henry VIII.

Soon after the death of Buckingham, the king made himself notorious for his theological writings against Luther, whose doctrines he detested. He ever had a taste for theological disputation, and a love of the schoolmen. His tracts against Luther, very respectable for talent and learning, though disgraced by coarse and vulgar vituperation, secured for him the favor of the pope, who bestowed upon him the title of "Defender of the Faith;" and a strong alliance existed between them until the divorce of Queen Catharine.

The difficulties and delays, attending this act of cruelty and injustice, constitute no small part of the domestic history of England during the reign of Henry VIII. Any event, which furnishes subjects of universal gossip and discussion, is ever worthy of historical notice, inasmuch as it shows prevailing opinions and tastes.

Queen Catharine, daughter of Ferdinand, King of Spain, was eight years older than her husband, whom she married in the first year of his reign. She had been previously married to his brother Arthur, who died of the plague in 1502. For several years after her marriage with Henry VIII., her domestic happiness was a subject of remark; and the emperor, Charles V., congratulated her on her brilliant fortune. She was beautiful, sincere, accomplished, religious, and disinterested, and every way calculated to secure, as she had won, the king's affections.

Anne Boleyn.

But among her maids of honor there was one peculiarly accomplished and fascinating, to whom the king transferred his affections with unwonted vehemence. This was Anne Boleyn, daughter of Sir Thomas Boleyn, who, from his great wealth, married Elizabeth Howard, daughter of the first duke of Norfolk. This noble alliance brought Sir Thomas Boleyn into close connection with royalty, and led to the appointment of his daughter to the high post which she held at the court of Queen Catharine. It is probable that the king suppressed his passion for some time; and it would have been longer concealed, even from its object, had not his jealousy been excited by her attachment to Percy, son of the Earl of Northumberland. The king at last made known his passion; but the daughter of the Howards was too proud, or too politic, or too high principled, to listen to his overtures. It was only *as queen of England*, that she would return the passion of her royal lover. Moreover, she resolved to be revenged on the all-powerful cardinal, for assisting in her separation from Percy, whom she loved with romantic attachment. The king waited four years, but Anne remained inflexibly virtuous. He then meditated the divorce from Catharine, as the only way to accomplish the object which now seemed to animate his existence. He confided the matter to his favorite minister; but Wolsey was thunderstruck at the disclosure, and remained with him four hours on his knees, to dissuade him from a step which he justly regarded as madness. Here Wolsey appears as an honest man and a true friend; but royal infatuation knows neither wisdom, justice, nor humanity. Wolsey, as a man of the world, here made a blunder, and departed from the policy he had hitherto pursued— that of flattering the humors of his absolute master. Wolsey, however, recommended the king to consult the divines; for Henry pretended that, after nearly twenty years of married life, he had conscientious scruples about the lawfulness of his marriage. The learned English doctors were afraid to pronounce their opinions, and suggested a reference to the fathers. But the king was not content with their authority; he appealed to the pope, and to the decisions of half of the universities of Europe. It seems very singular that a sovereign so unprincipled, unscrupulous, and passionate, and yet so absolute and powerful as was Henry, should have wasted his time and money in seeking countenance to an act on which he was fully determined, and which countenance he never could reasonably hope to secure. But his character was made up of contradictions. His caprice, violence, and want of good faith, were strangely blended with superstition and reverence for the authority of the church. His temper urged him to the most rigorous measure of injustice; and his injustice produced no shame, although he was restrained somewhat by the opinions of the very men whom he did not hesitate to murder.

Queen Catharine.

Queen Catharine, besides being a virtuous and excellent woman, was powerfully allied, and was a zealous Catholic. Her repudiation, therefore, could not take place without offending the very persons whose favor the king was most anxious to conciliate especially the Emperor Charles, her nephew, and the pope, and all the high dignitaries and adherents of the church. Even Wolsey could not in honor favor the divorce, although it was his policy to do so. In consequence of his intrigues, and the scandal and offence so outrageous an act as the divorce of Catharine must necessarily produce throughout the civilized world, Henry long delayed to bring the matter to a crisis, being afraid of a war with Charles V., and of the anathemas of the pope. Moreover, he hoped to gain him over, for the pope had sent Cardinal Campeggio to London, to hold, with his legate Wolsey, a court to hear the case. But it was the farthest from his intention to grant the divorce, for the pope was more afraid of Charles V. than he was of Henry VIII.

Disgrace and Death of Wolsey.

The court settled nothing, and the king's wrath now turned towards Wolsey, whom he suspected of secretly thwarting his measures. The accomplished courtier, so long accustomed to the smiles and favors of royalty, could not bear his disgrace with dignity. The proudest man in England became, all at once, the meanest. He wept, he cringed, he lost his spirits; he surrendered his palace, his treasures, his honors, and his offices, into the hands of him who gave them to him, without a single expostulation: wrote most abject letters to "his most gracious, most merciful, and most pious sovereign lord;" and died of a broken heart on his way to a prison and the scaffold. "Had I but served my God as diligently as I have served the king, he would not have given me over in my gray hairs"—these were the words of the dying cardinal; his sad confessions on experiencing the vanity of human life. But the vindictive prince suffered no word of sorrow or regret to escape him, when he heard of the death of his prime minister, and his intimate friend for twenty years.

More — Cranmer — Cromwell.

Shortly after the disgrace of Wolsey, which happened nearly a year before his death, (1529,) three remarkable men began to figure in English politics and history. These were Sir Thomas More, Thomas Cranmer, and Thomas Cromwell. More was the most accomplished, most learned, and most enlightened of the three. He was a Catholic, but very exemplary in his life, and charitable in his views. In moral elevation of character, and beautiful serenity of soul, the annals of the great men of his country furnish no superior. His extensive erudition and moral integrity alone secured him the official station which Wolsey held as lord chancellor. He was always the intimate friend of the king, and his conversation, so enlivened by wit, and so rich and varied in matter, caused his society to be universally sought. He discharged his duties with singular conscientiousness and ability; and no one ever had cause to complain that justice was not rendered him.

Cranmer's elevation was owing to a fortunate circumstance, notwithstanding his exalted merit. He happened to say, while tutor to a gentleman of the name of Cressy, in the hearing of Dr. Gardiner, then secretary to Henry, that the proper way to settle the difficulty about the divorce was, to appeal to learned men, who would settle the matter on the sole authority of the Bible, without reference to the pope. This remark was reported to the king, and Cranmer was sent to reside with the father of Anne Boleyn, and was employed in writing a treatise to support his opinion. His ability led to further honors, until, on the death of Warham, archbishop of Canterbury, he was appointed to the vacant see, the first office in dignity and importance in the kingdom, and from which no king, however absolute, could eject him, except by the loss of life. We shall see that, in all matters of religion, Cranmer was the ruling spirit in England until the accession of Mary.

Cromwell's origin was even more obscure than that of Wolsey's; but he received his education at one of the universities. We first hear of him as a clerk in an English factory at Antwerp, then as a soldier in the army of the Constable Bourbon when it sacked Rome, then as a clerk in a mercantile house in Venice, and then again as a lawyer in England, where he attracted the attention of Wolsey, who made him his solicitor, and employed him in the dissolution of monasteries. He then became a member of the house of commons, where his address and business talents were conspicuous. He was well received at court, and confirmed in the stewardship of the monasteries, after the disgrace of his master. His office brought him often into personal conference with the king; and, at one of these, he recommended him to deny the authority of the pope altogether, and declare himself supreme head of the church. The boldness of this advice was congenial to the temper of the king, worried by the opposition of Rome to his intended divorce, and Cromwell became a member of the privy council. His fortune was thus made by his seasonable advice. All who opposed the king were sure to fall, and all who favored him were sure to rise, as must ever be the case in an absolute monarchy, where the king is the centre and the fountain of all honor and dignity.

With such ministers as Cranmer and Cromwell, the measures of Henry were now prompt and bold. Queen Catharine was soon disposed of; she was divorced and disgraced, and Anne Boleyn was elevated to her throne, (1533.) The anathemas of the pope and the outcry of all Europe followed. Sir Thomas More resigned the seals, and retired to poverty and solitude. But he was not permitted to enjoy his retirement long. Refusing to take the oath of supremacy to Henry, as head of the church as well as of the state, he was executed, with other illustrious Catholics. The execution of More was the most cruel and uncalled-for act of the whole reign, and entailed on its author the execrations of all the learned and virtuous men in Europe, most of whom appreciated the transcendent excellences of the murdered chancellor, the author of the Utopia, and the Boethius of his age.

Quarrel with the Pope.

The fulminations of the pope only excited Henry to more decided opposition. The parliament, controlled by Cromwell, acknowledged him as the supreme head of the Church of England, and the separation from Rome was final and irrevocable. The tenths were annexed to the crown, and the bishops took a new oath of supremacy.

The independence of the Church of England, effected in 1535, was followed by important consequences, and was the first step to the reformation, afterwards perfected by Edward VI. But as the first acts of the reformation were prompted by political considerations, the reformers in England, during the reign of Henry VIII., should be considered chiefly in a political point of view. The separation from Rome, during the reign of this prince, was not followed by the abolition of the Roman Catholic worship, nor any of the rites and ceremonies of that church. Nor was religious toleration secured. Every thing was subservient to the royal conscience, and a secular, instead of an ecclesiastical pope, still reigned in England.

Abolition of Monasteries.

Henry soon found that his new position, as head of the English Church, imposed new duties and cares: he therefore established a separate department for the conduct of ecclesiastical affairs, over which he placed the unscrupulous, but energetic Cromwell—a fit minister to such a monarch. A layman, who hated the clergy, and who looked solely to the pecuniary interests of his master, was thus placed over the highest prelates of the church. But Cromwell, in consulting the pecuniary interests of the king, also had an eye to the political interests of the kingdom. He was a sagacious and practical man of the world, and was disgusted with the vices of the clergy, and especially with the custom of sending money to Rome, in the shape of annates and taxes. This evil he remedied, which tended greatly to enrich the country, for the popes at this time were peculiarly extortionate. He then turned his attention to the reform of the whole monastic institution, but with an eye also to its entire destruction. Cromwell hated the monks. They were lazy, ignorant, and debauched. They were a great burden on the people, and were as insolent and proud as they were idle and profligate. The country swarmed with them. The roads, taverns, and the houses of the credulous were infested with them. Cranmer, who sympathized with the German reformers, hated them on religious grounds, and readily coöperated with Cromwell; while the king, whose extortion and rapacity knew no bounds, listened, with glistening eye, to the suggestions of his two favorite ministers. The nation was suddenly astounded with the intelligence that parliament had passed a bill, giving to the king and his heirs all the monastic establishments in the kingdom, which did not exceed two hundred pounds a year. Three hundred and eighty thus fell at a blow, whereby the king was enriched by thirty-two thousand pounds a year, and one hundred thousand pounds ready money—an immense sum in that age. By this spoliation, perhaps called for, but exceedingly unjust and harsh, and in violation of all the rights of property, thousands were reduced to beggary and misery, while there was scarcely an eminent man in the kingdom who did not come in for a share of the plunder. Vast grants of lands were bestowed by the king on his favorites and courtiers, in order to appease the nation; and thus the foundations of many of the great estates of the English nobility were laid. The spoliations, however, led to many serious riots and insurrections, especially in Lincolnshire. At one place there were forty thousand rebels under arms; but they were easily suppressed.

Suppression of Monasteries.

The rapacious king was not satisfied with the plunder he had secured, and, in 1539, the final suppression of all the monasteries in England was decreed. Then followed the seizure of all the church property in England connected with monasteries—shrines, relics, gold and silver vessels of immense value and rarity, lands, and churches. Canterbury, Bath, Merton, Stratford, Bury St. Edmonds, Glastonbury, and St. Albans, suffered most, and many of those beautiful monuments of Gothic architecture were levelled with the dust. Their destruction deprived the people of many physical accommodations, for they had been hospitals and caravansaries, as well as "cages of unclean birds." Neither the church nor the universities profited much from the confiscation of so much property, and only six new bishoprics were formed, and only fourteen abbeys were converted into cathedrals and collegiate churches. The king and the nobles were the only gainers by the spoil; the people obtained no advantage in that age, although they have in succeeding ages.

After renouncing the pope's supremacy, and suppressing the monasteries, where were collected the treasures of the middle ages, one would naturally suppose that the king would have gone farther, and changed the religion of his people. But Henry hated Luther and his doctrines, and did not hate the pope, or the religion of which he was the sovereign pontiff. He loved gold and new wives better than the interests of the Catholic church. Reform proceeded no farther in his reign; while, on the other hand, he caused a decree to pass both houses of his timid, complying parliament, by which the doctrines of transubstantiation, the communion of one kind, the celibacy of the clergy, masses, and auricular confession, were established; and any departure from, or denial of, these subjected the offender to the punishment of death.

Execution of Anne Boleyn.

But Henry had new domestic difficulties long before the suppression of monasteries—the great political act of Thomas Cromwell. His new wife, Anne Boleyn, was suspected of the crime of inconstancy, and at the very time when she had reached the summit of power, and the gratification of all worldly wishes. She had been very vain, and fond of display and of ornaments; but the latter years of her life were marked by her munificence, and attachment to the reform doctrines. But her power ceased almost as soon as she became queen. She could win, but she could not retain, the affections of her royal husband. His passion subsided into languor, and ended in disgust. The beauty of Anne Boleyn was soon forgotten when Jane Seymour, her maid of honor, attracted the attention of Henry. To make this lady his wife now became the object of his life, and this could only be effected by the divorce of his queen, who gave occasion for scandal by the levity and freedom of her manners. Henry believed every insinuation against her, because he wished to believe her guilty. There was but a step between the belief of guilt and the resolution to destroy her. She was committed to the Tower, impeached, brought to trial, condemned without evidence, and executed without remorse. Even Cranmer, whom she had honored and befriended, dared not defend her, although he must have believed in her innocence. He knew the temper of the master whom he served too well to risk much in her defence. She was the first woman who had been beheaded in the annals of England. Not one of the Plantagenet kings ever murdered a woman. But the age of chivalry was past, and the sentiments it encouraged found no response in the bosom of such a sensual and vindictive monarch as was Henry VIII.

The very day after the execution of that accomplished lady, for whose sake the king had squandered the treasures of his kingdom, and had kept Christendom in a ferment, he married Jane Seymour, "the fairest, discreetest, and most meritorious of all his wives," as the historians say, yet a woman who did not hesitate to steal the affections of Henry and receive his addresses, while his queen was devoted to her husband. But Anne Boleyn had done so before her, and suffered a natural retribution.

Jane Seymour lived only eighteen months after her marriage, and died two days after giving birth to a son, afterwards Edward VI. She was one of those passive women who make neither friends nor enemies. She indulged in no wit or repartee, like her brilliant but less beautiful predecessor, and she passed her regal life without uttering a sentence or a sentiment which has been deemed worthy of preservation.

Anne of Cleves — Catharine Howard.

She had been dead about a month, when the king looked round for another wife, and besought Francis I. to send the most beautiful ladies of his kingdom to Calais, that he might there inspect them, and select one according to his taste. But this Oriental notion was not indulged by the French king, who had more taste and delicacy; and Henry remained without a wife for more than two years, the princesses of Europe not being very eager to put themselves in the power of this royal Bluebeard. At last, at the suggestion of Cromwell, he was affianced to Anne, daughter of the Duke of Cleves, whose home was on the banks of the Rhine, in the city of Dusseldorf.

The king no sooner set his eyes on her than he was disappointed and disgusted, and gave vent to his feelings before Cromwell, calling her a "great Flanders mare." Nevertheless, he consummated his marriage, although his disgust constantly increased. This mistake of Cromwell was fatal to his ambitious hopes. The king vented on him all the displeasure which had been gathering in his embittered soul. Cromwell's doom was sealed. He had offended an absolute monarch. He was accused of heresy and treason,—the common accusations in that age against men devoted to destruction,—tried by a servile board of judges, condemned, and judicially murdered, in 1540. In his misfortunes, he showed no more fortitude than Wolsey. The atmosphere of a court is fatal to all moral elevation.

But, before his execution, Anne of Cleves, a virtuous and worthy woman, was divorced, and Catharine Howard, granddaughter of the victor of Flodden Field, became queen of England. The king now fancied that his domestic felicity was complete; but, soon after his marriage, it was discovered that his wife had formerly led a dissolute life, and had been unfaithful also to her royal master. When the proofs of her incontinence were presented to him, he burst into a flood of tears; but soon his natural ferocity returned, and his guilty wife expiated her crime by death on the scaffold, in 1542.

Henry's sixth and last wife was Catharine Parr, relict of Lord Latimer, a woman of great sagacity, prudence, and good sense. She favored the reformers, but had sufficient address to keep her opinions from the king, who would have executed her, had he suspected her real views. She survived her husband, who died four years after her marriage, in 1547.

The last years of any tyrant are always melancholy, and those of Henry were embittered by jealousies and domestic troubles. His finances were deranged, his treasury exhausted, and his subjects discontented. He was often at war with the Scots, and different continental powers. He added religious persecution to his other bad traits, and executed, for their opinions, some of the best people in the kingdom. His father had left him the richest sovereign of Europe, and he had seized the abbey lands, and extorted heavy sums from his oppressed people; and yet he was poor. All his wishes were apparently gratified; and yet he was the most miserable man in his dominions. He exhausted all the sources of pleasure, and nothing remained but satiety and disgust. His mind and his body were alike diseased. His inordinate gluttony made him most inconveniently corpulent, and produced ulcers and the gout. It was dangerous to approach this "corrupt mass of dying tyranny." It was impossible to please him, and the least contradiction drove him into fits of madness and frenzy.

Last Days of Henry.

In his latter days, he ordered, in a fit of jealousy, the execution of the Duke of Norfolk, the first nobleman of the kingdom, who had given offence to the Earl of Hertford, uncle to the young prince of Wales, and the founder of the greatness of the Seymours. But the tyrant died before the sentence was carried into effect, much to the joy of the good people of England, whom he had robbed and massacred. Several thousands perished by the axe of the executioner during his disgraceful reign, and some of them were the lights of the age, and the glory of their country.

Tyrannical as was Henry VIII., still he ever ruled by the laws. He did not abolish parliament, or retrench its privileges. The parliament authorized all his taxes, and gave sanction to all his violent measures. The parliament was his supple instrument; still, had the parliament resisted his will, doubtless he would have dissolved it, as did the Stuart princes. But it was not, in his reign, prepared for resistance, and the king had every thing after his own way.

Death of Henry VIII.

By nature, he was amiable, generous, and munificent. But his temper was spoiled by self-indulgence and incessant flattery. The moroseness he exhibited in his latter days was partly the effect of physical disease, brought about, indeed, by intemperance and gluttony. He was faithful to his wives, so long as he lived with them; and, while he doted on them, listened to their advice. But few of his advisers dared tell him the truth; and Cranmer himself can never be exculpated from flattering his perverted conscience. No one had the courage to tell him he was dying but one of the nobles of the court. He died, in great agony, June, 1547, in the thirty-eighth year of his reign, and the fifty-sixth of his age, and was buried, with great pomp, in St. George Chapel, Windsor Castle.

References.—The best English histories of the reign of Henry VIII. are the standard ones of Hume and Lingard. The Pictorial History, in spite of its pictures, is also excellent. Burnet should be consulted in reference to ecclesiastical matters, and Hallam, in reference to the constitution. See also the lives of Wolsey, Sir Thomas More, and Cranmer. The lives of Henry's queens have been best narrated by Agnes Strickland.

CHAPTER V
EDWARD VI. AND MARY

Henry VIII. was succeeded by his son, Edward VI., a boy of nine years of age, learned, pious, and precocious. Still he was a boy; and, as such, was a king but in name. The history of his reign is the history of the acts of his ministers.

The late king left a will, appointing sixteen persons, mostly members of his council, to be guardians of his son, and rulers of the nation during his minority. The Earl of Hertford, being uncle of the king, was unanimously named protector.

The first thing the council did was to look after themselves, that is, to give themselves titles and revenues. Hertford became Duke of Somerset; Essex, Marquis of Northampton; Lisle, Earl of Warwick; the Chancellor Wriothesley, Earl of Southampton. At the head of these nobles was Somerset. He was a Protestant, and therefore prosecuted those reforms which Cranmer had before projected. Cranmer, as member of the council, archbishop of Canterbury, and friend of Somerset, had ample scope to prosecute his measures.

The history of this reign is not important in a political point of view, and relates chiefly to the completion of the reformation, and to the squabbles and jealousies of the great lords who formed the council of regency.

War with Scotland.

The most important event, of a political character, was a war with Scotland, growing out of the attempts of the late king to unite both nations under one government. In consequence, Scotland was invaded by the Duke of Somerset, at the head of eighteen thousand men. A great battle was fought, in which ten thousand of the Scots were slain. But the protector was compelled to return to England, without following up the fruits of victory, in consequence of cabals at court. His brother, Lord Seymour, a man of reckless ambition, had married the queen dowager, and openly aspired to the government of the kingdom. He endeavored to seduce the youthful king, and he had provided arms for ten thousand men.

The protector sought to win his brother from his treasonable designs by kindness and favors; but, all his measures proving ineffectual, he was arrested, tried, and executed, for high treason.

Rebellions and Discontents.

But Somerset had a more dangerous enemy than his brother; and this was the Earl of Warwick, who obtained great popularity by his suppression of a dangerous insurrection, the greatest the country had witnessed since Jack Cade's rebellion, one hundred years before. The discontent of the people appears to have arisen from their actual suffering. Coin had depreciated, without a corresponding rise of wages, and labor was cheap, because tillage lands were converted to pasturage. The popular discontent was aggravated by the changes which the reformers introduced, and which the peasantry were the last to appreciate. The priests and ejected monks increased the discontent, until it broke out into a flame.

The protector made himself unpopular with the council by a law which he caused to be passed against enclosures; and, as he lost influence, his great rival, Warwick, gained power. Somerset, at last, was obliged to resign his protectorship; and Warwick, who had suppressed the rebellion, formed the chief of a new council of regency. He was a man of greater talents than Somerset, and equal ambition, and more fitted for stormy times.

As soon as his power was established, and the country was at peace, and he had gained friends, he began to execute those projects of ambition which he had long formed. The earldom of Northumberland having reverted to the crown, Warwick aspired to the extinct title and the estates, and procured for himself a grant of the same, with the title of duke. But there still remained a bar to his elevation; and this was the opposition of the Duke of Somerset, who, though disgraced and unpopular, was still powerful. It is unfortunate to be in the way of a great man's career, and Somerset paid the penalty of his opposition—the common fate of unsuccessful rivals in unsettled times. He was accused of treason, condemned, and executed, (1552.)

Northumberland, as the new dictator, seemed to have attained the highest elevation to which a subject could aspire. In rank, power, and property, he was second only to the royal family, but his ambition knew no bounds, and he began his intrigues to induce the young king, whose health was rapidly failing, and who was zealously attached to Protestantism, to set aside the succession of his sister Mary to the throne, really in view of the danger to which the reformers would be subjected, but under pretence of her declared illegitimacy, which would also set aside the claims of the Princess Elizabeth. Mary, Queen of Scots, was to be set aside on the ground of the will of the late king, and the succession would therefore devolve on the Lady Jane Grey, granddaughter of the Duke of Suffolk and of the French queen, whom he hoped to unite in marriage with his son. This was a deeply-laid scheme, and came near being successful, since Edward listened to it with pleasure. Northumberland then sought to gain over the judges and other persons of distinction, and succeeded by bribery and intimidation. At this juncture, the young king died, possessed of all the accomplishments which could grace a youth of sixteen, but still a tool in the hands of his ministers.

Rivalry of the Great Nobles.

Religious Reforms.

Such were the political movements of this reign—memorable for the rivalries of the great nobles. But it is chiefly distinguished for the changes which were made in the church establishment, and the introduction of the principles of the continental reformers. No changes of importance were ever made beyond what Cranmer and his associates effected. Indeed, all that an absolute monarch could do, was done, and done with prudence, sagacity, and moderation. The people quietly—except in some rural districts—acquiesced in the change. Most of the clergy took the new oath of allegiance to Edward VI., as supreme head of the church; and very few suffered from religious persecution. There is no period in English history when such important changes were made, with so little bloodshed. Cranmer always watched the temper of the nation, and did nothing without great caution. Still a great change was effected—no less than a complete change from Romanism to Protestantism. But it was not so radical a reform as the Puritans subsequently desired, since the hierarchy and a liturgy, and clerical badges and dresses, were retained. It was the fortune of Cranmer, during the six years of Edward's reign, to effect the two great objects of which the English church has ever since been proud—the removal of Roman abuses, and the establishment of the creed of Luther and Calvin; and this without sweeping away the union of church and state, which, indeed, was more intimate than before the reformation. The papal power was completely subverted. Nothing more remained to be done by Cranmer. He had compiled the Book of Common Prayer, abolished the old Latin service, the worship of images, the ceremony of the mass, and auricular confessions. He turned the altars into communion tables, set up the singing of psalms in the service, caused the communion to be administered in both kinds to the laity, added the litany to the ritual, prepared a book of homilies for the clergy, invited learned men to settle in England, and magnificently endowed schools and universities.

The Reformation is divested of much interest, since it was the work of *authority*, rather than the result of *popular convictions*. But Cranmer won immortal honor for his skilful management, and for making no more changes than he could sustain. A large part of the English nation still regard his works as perfect, and are sincerely and enthusiastically attached to the form which he gave to his church.

The hopes of his party were suddenly dispelled by the death of the amiable prince whom he controlled, 6th of July, 1553. The succession to the throne fell to the Princess Mary, or, as princesses were then called, the *Lady* Mary; nor could all the arts of Northumberland exclude her from the enjoyment of her rights. This ambitious nobleman contrived to keep the death of Edward VI. a secret two days, and secure from the Mayor and Alderman of London a promise to respect the will of the late king. In consequence, the Lady Jane Grey was proclaimed Queen of England. "So far was she from any desire of this advancement, that she began to act her part of royalty with many tears, thus plainly showing to those who had access to her, that she was forced by her relations and friends to this high, but dangerous post." She was accomplished, beautiful, and amiable, devoted to her young husband, and very fond of Plato, whom she read in the original.

Execution of Northumberland.

But Mary's friends exerted themselves, and her cause—the cause of legitimacy, rather than that of Catholicism—gained ground. Northumberland was unequal to this crisis, and he was very feebly sustained. His forces were suppressed, his schemes failed, and his hopes fled. From rebellion, to the scaffold, there is but a step; and this great nobleman suffered the fate of Somerset, his former rival. His execution confirms one of the most striking facts in the history of absolute monarchies, when the idea of legitimacy is firmly impressed on the national mind; and that is, that no subject, or confederacy of subjects, however powerful, stand much chance in resisting the claims or the will of a legitimate prince. A nod or a word, from such a king, can consign the greatest noble to hopeless impotence. And he can do this from the mighty and mysterious force of ideas alone. Neither king nor parliament can ever resist the omnipotence of popular ideas. When ideas establish despots on their thrones, they are safe. When ideas demand their dethronement, no forces can long sustain them. The age of Queen Mary was the period of the most unchecked absolutism in England. Mary was apparently a powerless woman when Lady Jane Grey was proclaimed queen by the party of Northumberland, and still she had but to signify her intentions to claim her rights, and the nation was prostrate at her feet. The

Protestant party dreaded her accession; but loyalty was a stronger principle than even Protestantism, and she was soon firmly established in the absolute throne of Henry VIII.

Then almost immediately followed a total change in the administration, which affected both the political and religious state of the country. Those who had languished in confinement, on account of their religion, obtained their liberty, and were elevated to power. Gardiner, Bonner, and other Catholic bishops, were restored to their sees, while Cranmer, Ridley, Latimer, Hooper Coverdale, and other eminent Protestants, were imprisoned. All the statutes of Edward VI. pertaining to religion were repealed, and the queen sent assurances to the pope of her allegiance to his see. Cardinal Pole, descended from the royal family of England, and a man of great probity, moderation, and worth, was sent as legate of the pope. Gardiner, Bishop of Winchester, was made lord chancellor, and became the prime minister. He and his associates recommended violent councils; and a reign, unparalleled in England for religious persecution, commenced.

Marriage of the Queen.

Soon after the queen's accession, she married Philip, son of the Emperor Charles, and heir of the Spanish monarchy. This marriage, brought about by the intrigues of the emperor, and favored by the Catholic party, was quite acceptable to Mary, whose issue would inherit the thrones of Spain and England. But ambitious matches are seldom happy, especially when the wife is much older than the husband, as was the fact in this instance. Mary, however, was attached to Philip, although he treated her with great indifference.

This Spanish match, the most brilliant of that age, failed, however, to satisfy the English, who had no notion of becoming the subjects of the King of Spain. In consequence of this disaffection, a rebellion broke out, in which Sir Thomas Wyatt was the most conspicuous, and in which the Duke of Suffolk, and even the Lady Jane and her husband, were implicated, though unjustly. The rebellion was easily suppressed, and the leaders sent to the Tower. Then followed one of the most melancholy executions of this reign— that of the Lady Jane Grey, who had been reprieved three months before. The queen urged the plea of self-defence, and the safety of the realm—the same that Queen Elizabeth, in after times, made in reference to the Queen of the Scots. Her unfortunate fate excited great popular compassion, and she suffered with a martyr's constancy, and also her husband—two illustrious victims, sacrificed in consequence of the ambition of their relatives, and the jealousy of the queen. The Duke of Suffolk, the father of Lady Jane, was also executed, and deserved his fate, according to the ideas of his age. The Princess Elizabeth expected also to be sacrificed, both because she was a Protestant and the next heiress to the throne. But she carefully avoided giving any offence, and managed with such consummate prudence, that she was preserved for the future glory and welfare of the realm.

Religious Persecution.

The year 1555 opened gloomily for the Protestants. The prisons were all crowded with the victims of religious persecution, and bigoted inquisitors had only to prepare their fagots and stakes. Over a thousand ministers were ejected from their livings, and such as escaped further persecution fled to the continent. No fewer than two hundred and eighty-eight persons, among whom were five bishops, twenty-one clergymen, fifty-five women, and four children, were burned for religious opinions, besides many thousands who suffered various other forms of persecution. The constancy of Ridley, Latimer, and Hooper has immortalized their names on the list of illustrious martyrs: but the greatest of all the victims was Cranmer, Archbishop of Canterbury. The most artful and insinuating promises were held out to him, to induce him to retract. Life and dignities were promised him, if he would consent to betray his cause. In an evil hour, he yielded to the temptation, and consented to sell his soul. Timid, heartbroken, and old, the love of life and the fear of death were stronger than the voice of conscience and his duty to his God. But, when he found he was mocked, he came to himself, and suffered patiently and heroically. His death was glorious, as his life was useful; and the sincerity of his repentance redeemed his memory from shame. Cranmer may be considered as the great author of the English Reformation, and one of the most worthy and enlightened men of his age; but he was timid, politic, and time-serving. The Reformation produced no perfect characters in any country. Some great defect blemished the lives of all the illustrious men who have justly earned imperishable glory. But the character of such men as Cranmer, and Ridley, and Latimer, present an interesting contrast to those of Gardiner and Bonner. The former did show, however, some lenity in the latter years of this reign of Mary; but the latter, the Bishop of London, gloated to the last in the blood which he caused to be shed. He even whipped the Protestant prisoners with his own hands, and once pulled out the beard of an heretical weaver, and held his finger in the flame of a candle, till the veins shrunk and burnt, that he might realize what the pain of burning was. So blind and cruel is religious intolerance.

But Providence ordered that the religious persecution, which is attributed to Mary, but which, in strict justice, should be ascribed to her counsellors and ministers, should prepare the way for a popular and a spiritual movement in the subsequent reign. The fires of Smithfield, and the cruelties of the pillory and the prison, opened the eyes of the nation to the spirit of the old religion, and also caused the flight of many distinguished men to Frankfort and Geneva, where they learned the principles of both religious and civil liberty. "The blood of martyrs proved the seed of the church"—a sublime truth, revealed to Cranmer and Ridley amid the fires which consumed their venerable bodies; and not to them merely, but to all who witnessed their serenity, and heard their shouts of triumph when this mortal passed to immortality. Heretics increased with the progress of persecution, and firm conviction took the place of a blind confession of dogmas. "It was not," says Milman, "until Christ was lain in his rock-hewn sepulchre, that the history of Christianity commenced." We might add, it was not until the fires of Smithfield were lighted, that great spiritual ideas took hold of the popular mind, and the intense religious earnestness appeared which has so often characterized the English nation. The progress which man makes is generally seen through disaster, suffering, and sorrow. This is one of the fundamental truths which history teaches.

Character of Mary.

The last years of the reign of Mary were miserable to herself, and disastrous to the nation. Her royal husband did not return her warm affections, and left England forever. She embarked in a ruinous war with France, and gained nothing but disgrace. Her health failed, and her disposition became gloomy. She continued, to the last, most intolerant in her religious opinions, and thought more of restoring Romanism, than of promoting the interests of her kingdom. Her heart was bruised and broken, and her life was a succession of sorrows. It is fashionable to call this unfortunate queen the "bloody Mary," and not allow her a single virtue; but she was affectionate, sincere, high-minded, and shrunk from the dissimulation and intrigue which characterized "the virgin queen"—the name given to her masculine but energetic successor. Mary was capable of the warmest friendship; was attentive and considerate to her servants, charitable to the poor, and sympathetic with the unfortunate, when not blinded by her religious prejudices. She had many accomplishments, and a very severe taste, and was not addicted to oaths, as was Queen Elizabeth and her royal father. She was, however, a bigoted Catholic; and how could partisan historians see or acknowledge her merits?

Accession of Elizabeth.

But her reign was disastrous, and the nation hailed with enthusiasm the accession of Elizabeth, on the 17th of November, 1558. With her reign commences a new epoch, even in the history of Europe. Who does not talk of the Elizabethan era, when Protestantism was established in England, when illustrious poets and philosophers adorned the literature of the country, when commerce and arts received a great impulse, when the colonies in North America were settled, and when a constellation of great statesmen raised England to a pitch of glory not before attained?

References.—See Hume's, and Lingard's, and other standard Histories of England; Miss Strickland's Lives of the Queens of England; Burnet's History of the Reformation; Life of Cranmer; Fox's Book of Martyrs. These works contain all the easily-accessible information respecting the reigns of Edward and Mary, which is important.

CHAPTER VI
ELIZABETH

Elizabeth, daughter of Henry VIII., by Anne Boleyn, was in her twenty-sixth year when she ascended the throne. She was crowned the 15th of June, 1559, and soon assembled her parliament and selected her ministers. After establishing her own legitimacy, she set about settling the affairs of the church, but only restored the Protestant religion as Cranmer had left it. Indeed, she ever retained a fondness for ceremonial, and abhorred a reform spirit among the people. She insisted on her supremacy, as head of the church, and on conformity with her royal conscience. But she was not severe on the Catholics, and even the gluttonous and vindictive Bonner was permitted to end his days in peace.

Mary, Queen of Scots.

As soon as the Protestant religion was established, the queen turned her attention towards Scotland, from which much trouble was expected.

Scotland was then governed by Mary, daughter of James V., and had succeeded her father while a mere infant, eight days after her birth, (1542.) In 1558, she married the dauphin, afterwards King of France, by which marriage she was Queen of France as well as of Scotland.

John Knox.

According to every canonical law of the Roman church, the claim of Mary Stuart to the English throne was preferable to that of her cousin Elizabeth. Her uncles, the Guises, represented that Anne Boleyn's marriage had never been lawful, and that Elizabeth was therefore illegitimate. In an evil hour, she and her husband quartered the arms of England with their own, and assumed the titles of King and Queen of Scotland and England. And Elizabeth's indignation was further excited by the insult which the pope had inflicted, in declaring her birth illegitimate. She, therefore, resolved to gratify, at once, both her ambition and her vengeance, encouraged by her ministers, who wished to advance the Protestant interest in the kingdom. Accordingly, Elizabeth, with consummate art, undermined the authority of Mary in Scotland, now distracted by religious as well as civil commotions. Mary was a Catholic, and had a perfect abhorrence and disgust of the opinions and customs of the reformers, especially of John Knox, whose influence in Scotland was almost druidical. The Catholics resolved to punish with fire and sword, while the Protestants were equally intent on defending themselves with the sword. And it so happened that some of the most powerful of the nobility were arrayed on the side of Protestantism. But the Scotch reformers were animated with a zeal unknown to Cranmer and his associates. The leaders had been trained at Geneva, under the guidance of Calvin, and had imbibed his opinions, and were, therefore, resolved to carry the work of reform after the model of the Genevan church. Accordingly, those pictures, and statues, and ornaments, and painted glass, and cathedrals, which Cranmer spared, were furiously destroyed by the Scotch reformers, who considered them as parts of an idolatrous worship. The antipathy to bishops and clerical vestments was equally strong, and a sweeping reform was carried on under the dictatorship of Knox. Elizabeth had no more sympathy with this bold, but uncouth, reformer and his movements, than had Mary herself, and never could forgive him for his book, written at Geneva, aimed against female government, called the "First Blast of a Trumpet against the monstrous Regiment of Women." But Knox cared not for either the English or the Scottish queens, and zealously and fearlessly prosecuted his work, and gained over to his side the moral strength of the kingdom. Of course, a Catholic queen resolved to suppress his doctrines; but nearly the whole Scottish nobility rallied around his standard, marching with the Bible in one hand, and the sword in the other. The queen brought in troops from France to support her insulted and tottering government, which only increased the zeal of the Protestant party, headed by the Earls of Argyle, Arran, Morton, and Glencairn, and James Stuart, Prior of St. Andrews, who styled themselves "Lords of the Congregation." A civil war now raged in Scotland, between the queen regent, who wished to suppress the national independence, and extinguish the Protestant religion, and the Protestants, who comprised a great part of the nation, and who were resolved on the utter extirpation of Romanism and the limitation of the regal power. The Lords of the Congregation implored the aid of England, which Elizabeth was ready to grant, both from political and religious motives. The Protestant cause was in the ascendant, when the queen regent died, in 1560. The same year died Francis II., of France; and Mary, now a widow, resolved to return to her own kingdom. She landed at Leith, August, 1561, and was received with the grandest demonstration of joy. For a time, affairs were tolerably tranquil, Mary having intrusted the great Protestant nobles with power. She was greatly annoyed, however, by Knox, who did not treat her with the respect due to a queen, and who called her Jezebel; but the reformer escaped punishment on account of his great power.

Marriage of Mary — Darnley.

In 1565, Mary married her cousin, Lord Darnley, son of the Earl of Lennox,—a match exceedingly distasteful to Elizabeth, who was ever jealous of Mary, especially in matrimonial matters, since the Scottish queen had not renounced her pretensions to the throne of her grandfather, Henry VII. The character of Elizabeth now appears in its worst light; and meanness and jealousy took the place of that magnanimity which her admirers have ascribed to her. She fomented disturbances in Scotland, and incited the queen's natural brother, the Prior of St. Andrews, now Earl of Murray, to rebellion, with the expectation of obtaining the government of the country. He formed a conspiracy to seize the persons of Mary and her husband. The plot was discovered, and Murray fled to England; but it was still unremittingly pursued, till at length it was accomplished.

Darnley, the consort of Mary, was a man of low tastes, profligate habits, and shallow understanding. Such a man could not long retain the affections of the most accomplished woman of her age, accustomed to flattery, and bent on pursuing her own pleasure, at any cost. Disgust and coldness therefore took place. Darnley, enraged at this increasing coldness, was taught to believe that he was supplanted in the queen's affections by an Italian favorite, the musician Rizzio, whom Mary had made her secretary. He therefore signed a bond, with certain lords, for the murder of the Italian, who seems to have been a man of no character. One evening, as the queen was at supper, in her private apartment, with the countess of Argyle and Rizzio, the Earl of Morton, with one hundred and sixty men, took possession of the palace of Holyrood, while Darnley himself showed the way to a band of ruffians to the royal presence. Rizzio was barbarously murdered in the presence of the queen, who endeavored to protect him.

Darnley, in thus perpetrating this shocking murder, was but the tool of some of the great lords, who wished to make him hateful to the queen, and to the nation, and thus prepare the way for his own execution. And they succeeded. A plot was contrived for the murder of Darnley, of which Murray was probably the author. Shortly after, the house, in which he slept, was blown up by gunpowder, in the middle of the night.

Bothwell — Civil War in Scotland.

The public voice imputed to the Earl of Bothwell, a great favorite of the queen, the murder of Darnley. Nor did the queen herself escape suspicion. "But no inquiry or research," says Scott, "has ever been able to bring us either to that clear opinion upon the guilt of Mary which is expressed by many authors, or guide us to that triumphant conclusion in favor of her innocence of all accession, direct or tacit, to the death of her husband, which others have maintained with the same obstinacy." But whatever doubt exists as to the queen's guilt, there is none respecting her ministers—Maitland, Huntley, Morton, and Argyle. Still they offered a reward of two thousand pounds for the discovery of the murderers. The public voice accused Bothwell as the principal: and yet the ministers associated with him, and the queen, entirely exculpated him. He was brought to a trial, on the formal accusation of the Earl of Lennox, in the city of Edinburgh, which he was permitted to obtain possession of. In a place guarded by his own followers, it was not safe for any witnesses to appear against him, and he was therefore acquitted, though the whole nation believed him guilty.

Mary was rash enough to marry, shortly after, the man whom public opinion pronounced to be the murderer of her husband; and Murray, her brother, was so ambitious and treacherous, as to favor the marriage, with the hope that the unpopularity of the act would lead to the destruction of the queen, and place him at the helm of state. No sooner was Mary married to Bothwell, than Murray and other lords threw off the mask, pretended to be terribly indignant, took up arms against the queen, with the view of making her prisoner, and with the pretence of delivering her from her husband. Bothwell escaped to Norway, and the queen surrendered herself, at Carberry Hill, to the insurgent army, the chiefs of which instantly assumed the reins of government, and confined the queen in the castle of Lochleven, and treated her with excessive harshness. Shortly after, (1567,) she resigned her crown to her infant son, and Murray, the prime mover of so many disturbances, became regent of the kingdom. Murray was a zealous Protestant, and had the support of Knox in all his measures, and the countenance of the English ministry. Abating his intrigue and ambition, he was a most estimable man, and deserved the affections of the nation, which he retained until his death. M'Crie, in his Life of Knox, represents him as a model of Christian virtue and integrity, and every way worthy of the place he held in the affections of his party.

Captivity of Queen Mary.

The unfortunate queen suffered great unkindness in her lonely confinement, and Knox, with the more zealous of his party, clamored for her death, as an adulteress and a murderer. She succeeded in escaping from her prison, raised an army, marched against the regent, was defeated at the battle of Langside, fled to England, and became, May, 1568, the prisoner-guest of her envious rival. Elizabeth obtained the object of her desires. But the captivity of Mary, confined in Tutbury Castle, against all the laws of hospitality and justice, gave rise to incessant disturbances, both in England and Scotland, until her execution, in 1587. And these form no inconsiderable part of the history of England for seventeen years. Scotland was the scene of anarchy, growing out of the contentions and jealousies of rival chieftains, who stooped to every crime that appeared to facilitate their objects. In 1570, the regent Murray was assassinated. He was succeeded by his enemy, the Earl of Lennox, who, in his turn, was shot by an assassin. The Earl of Mar succeeded him, but lived only a year. Morton became regent, the reward of his many crimes but retribution at last overtook him, being executed when James assumed the sovereignty.

Execution of Mary.

Meanwhile, the unfortunate Mary pined in hopeless captivity. It was natural for her to seek release, and also for her friends to help her. Among her friends was the Duke of Norfolk, the first nobleman in England, and a zealous Catholic. He aspired to her hand; but Elizabeth chose to consider his courtship as a treasonable act, and Norfolk was arrested. On being afterwards released, he plotted for the liberation of Mary, and his intrigues brought him to the block. The unfortunate captive, wearied and impatient, naturally sought the assistance of foreign powers. She had her agents in Rome, France, Spain, and the Low Countries. The Catholics in England espoused her cause, and a conspiracy was formed to deliver her, assassinate Elizabeth, and restore the Catholic religion. From the fact that Mary was privy to that part of it which concerned her own deliverance, she was brought to trial as a criminal, found guilty by a court incompetent to sit on her case, and executed without remorse, 8th February, 1587.

Few persons have excited more commiseration than this unfortunate queen, both on account of her exalted rank, and her splendid intellectual accomplishments. Whatever obloquy she merited for her acts as queen of Scotland, no one can blame her for meditating escape from the power of her zealous but more fortunate rival; and her execution is the greatest blot in the character of the queen of England, at this time in the zenith of her glory.

Next to the troubles with Scotland growing out of the interference of Elizabeth, the great political events of the reign were the long and protracted war with Spain, and the Irish rebellion. Both of these events were important.

Spain was at this time governed by Philip II., son of the emperor Charles, one of the most bigoted Catholics of the age, and allied with Catharine de Medicis of France for the entire suppression of Protestantism. She incited her son Charles IX. to the massacre of St. Bartholomew, and Philip established the inquisition in Flanders. This measure provoked an insurrection, to suppress which the Duke of Alva, one of the most celebrated of the generals of Charles V., was sent into the Netherlands with a large army, and almost unlimited powers. The cruelties of Alva were unparalleled. In six years, eighteen thousand persons perished by the hands of the executioner, and

Alva counted on the entire suppression of Protestantism by the mere force of armies. He could count the physical resources of the people, but he could not estimate the degree of their resistance when animated by the spirit of liberty or religion. Providence, too, takes care of those who strive to take care of themselves. A great leader appeared among the suffering Hollanders, almost driven to despair—the celebrated William of Nassau, Prince of Orange. He appeared as the champion of the oppressed and insulted people; they rallied around his standard, fought with desperate bravery, opened the dikes upon their cultivated fields, expelled their invaders, and laid the foundation of their liberties. But they could not have withstood the gigantic power of the Spanish monarchy, then in the fulness of its strength, and the most powerful in Europe, had it not been for aid rendered by Elizabeth. She compassionated their sufferings, and had respect for their cause. She entered into an alliance, defensive and offensive, and the Netherlands became the great theatre of war, even after they had thrown off the Spanish yoke. Although the United Provinces in the end obtained their liberty, they suffered incredible hardships, and lost some of the finest of their cities, Antwerp among the rest, long the rival of Amsterdam, and the scene of Rubens's labors.

Military Preparations of Philip II.

The assistance which Elizabeth rendered to the Hollanders, of course, provoked the resentment of Philip II., and this was increased by the legalized piracies of Sir Francis Drake, in the West Indies, and on the coasts of South America. This commander, in time of peace, insisted on a right to visit those ports which the Spaniards had closed, which, by the law of nations, is piracy. Philip, according to all political maxims, was forced to declare war with England, and he made immense preparations to subdue it. But the preparations of Elizabeth to resist the powerful monarch were also great, and Drake performed brilliant exploits on the sea, among other things, destroying one hundred ships in the Bay of Cadiz, and taking immense spoil. The preparations of the Spanish monarch were made on such a gigantic scale, that Elizabeth summoned a great council of war to meet the emergency, at which the all-accomplished Sir Walter Raleigh took a leading part. His advice was to meet the Spaniards on the sea. Although the royal navy consisted, at this time, of only thirty-six sail, such vigorous measures were prosecuted, that one hundred and ninety-one ships were collected, manned by seventeen thousand four hundred seamen. The merchants of London granted thirty ships and ten thousand men, and all England was aroused to meet the expected danger. Never was patriotism more signally evinced, never were more decisive proofs given of the popularity of a sovereign. Indeed, Elizabeth was always popular with the nation; and with all her ceremony, and state, and rudeness to the commons, and with all their apparent servility, she never violated the laws, or irritated the people by oppressive exactions. Many acts of the Tudor princes seem to indicate the reign of despotism in England, but this despotism was never grievous, and had all the benignity of a paternal government. Capricious and arbitrary as Elizabeth was, in regard to some unfortunate individuals who provoked her hatred or her jealousy, still she ever sedulously guarded the interests of the nation, and listened to the counsel of patriotic and able ministers. When England was threatened with a Spanish invasion, there was not a corner of the land which did not rise to protect a beloved sovereign; nor was there a single spot, where a landing might be effected, around which an army of twenty thousand could not be rallied in forty-eight hours.

Spanish Armada.

But Philip, nevertheless, expected the complete conquest of England; and, as his "Invincible Armada" of one hundred and thirty ships, left the mouth of the Tagus, commanded by Medina Sidonia, and manned by the noblest troops of Spain, he fancied his hour of triumph was at hand. But his hopes proved dreams, like most of the ambitious designs of men. The armada met with nothing but misfortunes, both from battle and from storms. Only fifty ships returned to Spain. An immense booty was divided among the English sailors, and Elizabeth sent, in her turn, a large fleet to Spain, the following year, (1589,) under the command of Drake, which, after burning a few towns, returned ingloriously to England, with a loss of ten thousand men. The war was continued with various success till 1598, when a peace was negotiated. The same year, died Philip II., and Lord Burleigh, who, for forty years, directed the councils of Elizabeth, and to whose voice she ever listened, even when opposed by such favorites as Leicester and Essex. Burleigh was not a great genius, but was a man admirably adapted to his station and his times,—was cool, sagacious, politic, and pacific, skilful in the details of business competent to advise, but not aspiring to command. He was splendidly rewarded for his services, and left behind him three hundred distinct landed estates.

Meanwhile the attention of the queen was directed to the affairs of Ireland, which had been conquered by Henry II. in the year 1170, but over which only an imperfect sovereignty had been exercised. The Irish princes and nobles, divided among themselves, paid the exterior marks of obedience, but kept the country in a constant state of insurrection.

Irish Rebellion.

The impolitic and romantic projects of the English princes for subduing France, prevented a due attention to Ireland, ever miserably governed.

Elizabeth was the first of the English sovereigns to perceive the political importance of this island, and the necessity for the establishment of law and order. Besides furnishing governors of great capacity, she founded the university of Dublin, and attempted to civilize the half-barbarous people. Unfortunately, she also sought to make them Protestants, against their will, which laid the foundation of many subsequent troubles, not yet removed. A spirit of discontent pervaded the country, and the people were ready for rebellion. Hugh O'Neale, the head of a powerful clan, and who had been raised to the dignity of Earl of Tyrone, yet attached to the barbarous license in which he had been early trained, fomented the popular discontents, and excited a dangerous rebellion. Hostilities, of the most sanguinary character, commenced. The queen sent over her favorite, the Earl of Essex, with an army of twenty thousand men, to crush the rebellion. He was a brave commander, but was totally unacquainted with the country and the people he was expected to subdue, and was, consequently, unsuccessful. But his successor, Lord Mountjoy, succeeded in restoring the queen's authority, though at the cost of four millions and a half, an immense sum in that age, while poor Ireland was devastated with fire and sword, and suffered every aggravation of accumulated calamities.

The Earl of Essex.

Meanwhile, Essex, who had returned to England against the queen's orders, was treated with coldness, deprived of his employments, and sentenced to be confined. This was more than the haughty favorite could bear, accustomed as he had been to royal favor. At first, he acquiesced in his punishment, with every mark of penitence, and Elizabeth was beginning to relax in her severity for she never intended to ruin him; but he soon gave vent to his violent temper, indulged in great liberties of speech, and threw off all appearance of duty and respect. He even engaged in treasonable designs, encouraged Roman Catholics at his house, and corresponded with James VI. of Scotland about his succession. His proceedings were discovered, and he was summoned before the privy council. Instead of obedience, he armed himself and his followers, and, in conjunction with some discontented nobles, and about three hundred gentlemen, attempted to excite an insurrection in London, where he was very popular with the citizens. He was captured and committed to the Tower, with the Earl of Southampton. These rash but brave noblemen were tried by their peers, and condemned as guilty of high treason. In this trial, the celebrated Bacon appeared against his old patron, and likened him to the Duke of Guise. The great lawyer Coke, who was attorney-general, compared him to Catiline.

Essex disdained to sue the queen for a pardon, and was privately beheaded in the Tower. He merited his fate, if the offence of which he was guilty deserved such a punishment. It is impossible not to be interested in the fate of a man so brave, high-spirited, and generous, the idol of the people, and the victor in so many enterprises. Some historians maintain that Elizabeth relented, and would have saved her favorite, had he only implored her clemency; but this statement is denied by others; nor have we any evidence to believe that Essex, caught with arms against the sovereign who had honored him, could have averted his fate.

Elizabeth may have wept for the death of the nobleman she had loved. It is certain that, after his death, she never regained her spirits, and that a deep melancholy was visible in her countenance. All her actions showed a deeply-settled inward grief, and that she longed for death, having tasted the unsubstantial nature of human greatness. She survived the execution of Essex two years, but lived long enough to see the neglect into which she was every day falling, and to feel that, in spite of all her glory and power, she was not exempted from drinking the cup of bitterness.

Character of Elizabeth.

Whatever unamiable qualities she evinced as a woman, in spite of her vanity, and jealousy, and imperious temper, her reign was one of the most glorious in the annals of her country. The policy of Burleigh was the policy of Sir Robert Walpole—that of peace, and a desire to increase the resources of the kingdom. Her taxes were never oppressive, and were raised without murmur; the people were loyal and contented; the Protestant religion was established on a firm foundation; and a constellation of great men shed around her throne the bright rays of immortal genius.

The most unhappy peculiarity of her reign was the persecution of the Non-conformists, which, if not sanguinary, was irritating and severe. For some time after the accession of Elizabeth, the Puritans were permitted to indulge in their peculiarities, without being excluded from the established church; but when Elizabeth felt herself secure, then they were obliged to conform, or suffered imprisonment, fines, and other punishments. The original difficulty was their repugnance to the surplice, and to some few forms of worship, which gradually extended to an opposition to the order of bishops; to the temporal dignities of the church; to the various titles of the hierarchy; to the jurisdiction of the spiritual courts; to the promiscuous access of all persons to the communion table; to the liturgy; to the observance of holydays; to the cathedral worship; to the use of organs; to the presentation of living by patrons; and finally, to some of the doctrines of the established church. The separation of the Puritans from the Episcopal church, took place in 1566; and, from that time to the death of Elizabeth, they enjoyed no peace, although they sought redress in the most respectful manner, and raised no opposition to the royal authority. Thousands were ejected from their livings, and otherwise punished, for not conforming to the royal conscience. But persecution and penal laws fanned a fanatical spirit, which, in the reign of Charles, burst out into a destructive flame, and spread devastation and ruin through all parts of the kingdom.

If the queen and her ministers did not understand the principles of religious toleration, they pursued a much more enlightened policy in regard to all financial and political subjects, than during any former reign. The commercial importance of England received a new impulse. The reign of Henry VIII. was a reign of spoliation. The king was enriched beyond all former precedent, but his riches did not keep pace with his spendthrift habits. The value of the abbey lands which Henry seized amounted, a century after his death, to six million pounds. The lands of the abbey of St. Alban's alone rented for two hundred thousand pounds. The king debased the coin, confiscated chapels and colleges, as well as monasteries, and raised money by embargoes, monopolies, and compulsory loans.

Improvements Made in the Reign of Elizabeth.

But Elizabeth, instead of contracting debts, paid off the old ones, restored the coin to its purity, and was content with an annual revenue of five hundred thousand pounds, even at a time when the rebellion in Ireland cost her four hundred thousand pounds. Her frugality equalled the rapacity of her father, and she was extravagant only in dress, and on great occasions of public rejoicings. But her economy was a small matter compared with the wise laws which were passed respecting the trade of the country, by which commercial industry began to characterize the people. Improvements in navigation followed, and also maritime discoveries and colonial settlements. Sir Francis Drake circumnavigated the globe, and the East India Company was formed. Under the auspices of Sir Walter Raleigh, Virginia was discovered and colonized. Unfortunately, also, the African slave trade commenced—a traffic which has been productive of more human misery, and led to more disastrous political evils, than can be traced to any other event in the history of modern times.

During this reign, the houses of the people became more comfortable; chimneys began to be used; pewter dishes took the place of wooden trenchers, and wheat was substituted for rye and barley; linen and woollen cloth was manufactured; salads, cabbages, gooseberries, apricots, pippins, currants, cherries, plums, carnations, and the damask rose were cultivated, for the first time. But the great glory of this reign was the revival of literature and science. Raleigh, "the soldier, the sailor, the scholar, the philosopher, the poet, the orator, the historian, the courtier," then, adorned the court, and the prince of poets, the immortal Shakspeare, then wrote those plays, which, for moral wisdom and knowledge of the human soul, appear to us almost to be dictated by the voice of inspiration. The prince of philosophers too, the great miner and sapper of the false systems of the middle ages, Francis Bacon, then commenced his career, and Spenser dedicated to Elizabeth his "Fairy Queen," one of the most truly poetical compositions that genius ever produced. The age produced also great divines; but these did not occupy so prominent a place in the nation's eye as during the succeeding reigns.

Reflections.

While the virgin queen was exercising so benign an influence on the English nation, great events, though not disconnected with English politics, were taking place on the continent. The most remarkable of these was the persecution of the Huguenots. The rise and fortunes of this sect, during the reigns of Henry II., Francis II., Charles IX., Henry III., and Henry IV., now demand our attention. If a newspaper had, in that age, been conducted upon the principles it now is, the sufferings of the Huguenots would always be noticed. It is our province to describe just what a modern newspaper would have alluded to, had it been printed three hundred years ago. It would not have been filled with genealogies of kings, but with descriptions of great popular movements. And this is history.

References.—For the history of this reign, see Hume,
Lingard, and Hallam; Miss Strickland's Queens of England;
Life of Mary, Queen of Scots; M'Crie's Life of Knox;
Robertson's History of Scotland; Macaulay's Essay on
Nares's Life of Burleigh; Life of Sir Walter Raleigh; Neale's
History of the Puritans. Kenilworth may also be profitably
read.

CHAPTER VII
FRANCIS II., CHARLES IX.,
HENRY III., AND HENRY IV

The history of France, from the death of Francis I. to the accession of Henry IV. is virtually the history of religious contentions and persecutions, and of those civil wars which grew out of them. The Huguenotic contest, then, is a great historical subject, and will be presented in connection with the history of France, until the death of Henry IV., the greatest of the French monarchs, and long the illustrious head of the Protestant party.

The reform doctrines first began to spread in France during the reign of Francis I. As early as 1523, he became a persecutor, and burned many at the stake, among whom the descendants of the Waldenses were the most numerous. In 1540, sentence was pronounced against them by the parliament of Aix. Their doctrines were the same in substance as those of the Swiss reformers.

While this persecution was raging, John Calvin fled from France to Ferrara, from which city he proceeded to Geneva. This was in the year 1536, when his theological career commenced by the publication of his Institutes, which were dedicated to Francis I., one of the most masterly theological works ever written, although compended from the writings of Augustine. The Institutes of Calvin, the great text-book of the Swiss and French reformers, were distasteful to the French king, and he gave fresh order for the persecution of the Protestants. Notwithstanding the hostility of Francis, the new doctrines spread, and were embraced by some of the most distinguished of the French nobility. The violence of persecution was not much arrested during the reign of Henry II., and, through the influence of the Cardinal of Lorraine, the inquisition was established in the kingdom.

Catharine de Medicis.

The wife of Henry II. was the celebrated Catharine de Medicis; and she was bitterly opposed to the reform doctrines, and incited her husband to the most cruel atrocities. Francis II. continued the persecution, and his mother, Catharine, became virtually the ruler of the nation.

The power of the queen mother was much increased when Francis II. died, and when his brother, Charles IX., a boy of nine years of age, succeeded to the French crown. She exercised her power by the most unsparing religious persecution recorded in the history of modern Europe. There had been some hope that Protestantism would be established in France; but it did not succeed, owing to the violence of the persecution. It made, however, a desperate struggle before it was overcome.

At the head of the Catholic party were the queen regent, the Cardinal of Lorraine, the Duke of Guise, his brother, and the Constable Montmorency. They had the support of the priesthood, of the Spaniards, and a great majority of the nation.

The Protestants were headed by the King of Navarre, father of Henry IV., the Prince of Condé, his brother, and Admiral Coligny; and they had the sympathy of the university, the parliaments, and the Protestants of Germany and England.

Civil War in France.

Between these parties a struggle lasted for forty years, with various success. Persecution provoked resistance, but resistance did not lead to liberty. Civil war in France did not secure the object sought. Still the Protestants had hope, and, as they could always assemble a large army, they maintained their ground. Their conduct was not marked by the religious earnestness which characterized the Puritans, or by the same strength of religious principle. Moreover, political motives were mingled with religious. The contest was a struggle for the ascendency of rival chiefs, as well as for the establishment of reformed doctrines. The Bourbons hated the Guises, and the Guises resolved to destroy the Bourbons. In the course of their rivalry and warfare, the Duke of Guise was assassinated, and the King of Navarre, as well as the Prince of Condé, were killed.

Charles IX. was fourteen years of age when the young king of Navarre,— at that time sixteen years of age,—and his cousin, the Prince of Condé, became the acknowledged heads of the Protestant party. Their education was learned in the camp and the field of battle.

Charles IX., under the influence of his hateful mother, finding that civil war only destroyed the resources of the country, without weakening the Protestants, made peace, but formed a plan for their extermination by treachery. In order to cover his designs he gave his sister, Margaret de Valois, in marriage to the King of Navarre, first prince of the blood, then nineteen years of age. Admiral Coligny was invited to Paris, and treated with distinguished courtesy.

Massacre of St. Bartholomew.

It was during the festivities which succeeded the marriage of the King of Navarre that Coligny was murdered, and the signal for the horrid slaughter of St. Bartholomew was given. At midnight, August 23, 1572, the great bell at the Hotel de Ville began to toll; torches were placed in the windows, chains were drawn across the streets, and armed bodies collected around the hotels. The doors of the houses were broken open, and neither age, condition, nor sex was spared, of such as were not distinguished by a white cross in the hat. The massacre at Paris was followed by one equally brutal in the provinces. Seventy thousand people were slain in cold blood. The King of Navarre and the Prince of Condé only escaped in consequence of their relationship with the king, and by renouncing the Protestant religion.

Most of the European courts expressed their detestation of this foulest crime in the history of religious bigotry; but the pope went in grand procession to his cathedral, and ordered a *Te Deum* to be sung in commemoration of an event which steeped his cause in infamy to the end of time.

The Protestants, though nearly exterminated, again rallied, and the King of Navarre and his cousin the Prince of Condé escaped, renounced the religion which had been forced on them by fear of death, and prosecuted a bloody civil war, with the firm resolution of never abandoning it until religious liberty was guarantied.

Meanwhile, Charles IX. died, as it was supposed, by poison. His last hours were wretched, and his remorse for the massacre of St. Bartholomew filled his soul with agony. He beheld spectres, and dreamed horrid dreams; his imagination constantly saw heaps of livid bodies, and his ears were assailed with imaginary groans. He became melancholy and ferocious, while his kingdom became the prey of factions and insurrections. But he was a timid and irresolute king, and was but the tool of his infamous mother, the grand patroness of assassins, against whom, on his death bed, he cautioned the king of Navarre.

Henry III. — Henry IV.

He was succeeded by his brother, the King of Poland, under the title of Henry III. The persecutions of the Huguenots were renewed, and the old scenes of treachery, assassination, and war were acted over again. The cause of religion was lost sight of in the labyrinth of contentions, jealousies, and plots. Intrigues and factions were endless. Nearly all the leaders, on both sides, perished by the sword or the dagger. The Prince of Condé, the Duke of Guise, and his brother, the Cardinal of Lorraine, were assassinated.

Shortly after, died the chief mover of all the troubles, Catharine de Medicis, a woman of talents and persuasive eloquence, but of most unprincipled ambition, perfidious, cruel, and dissolute. She encouraged the licentiousness of the court, and even the worst vices of her sons, that she might make them subservient to her designs. All her passions were subordinate to her calculations of policy, and every womanly virtue was suppressed by the desire of wielding a government which she usurped.

Henry III. soon followed her to the grave, being, in turn, assassinated by a religious fanatic. His death (1589) secured the throne to the king of Navarre, who took the title of Henry IV.

Henry IV., the first of the Bourbon line, was descended from Robert, the sixth son of St. Louis, who had married the daughter and heiress of John of Burgundy and Agnes of Bourbon. He was thirty-six years of age when he became king, and had passed through great experiences and many sorrows. Thus far he had contended for Protestant opinions, and was the acknowledged leader of the Protestant party in France. But a life of contention and bloodshed, and the new career opened to him as king of France, cooled his religious ardor, and he did not hesitate to accept the condition which the French nobles imposed, before they would take the oaths of allegiance. This was, that he should abjure Protestantism. "My kingdom," said he, "is well worth a mass." It will be ever laid to his reproach, by the Protestants, that he renounced his religion for worldly elevation. Nor is it easy to exculpate him on the highest principles of moral integrity. But there were many palliations for his conduct, which it is not now easy to appreciate. It is well known that the illustrious Sully, his prime minister, and, through life, a zealous Protestant, approved of his course. It was certainly clear that, without becoming a Catholic, he never could peaceably enjoy his crown, and France would be rent, for another generation, by those civil wars which none lamented more than Henry himself. Besides, four fifths of the population were Catholics, and the Protestants could not reasonably expect to gain the ascendency. All they could expect was religious toleration, and this Henry was willing to grant. It should also be considered that the king, though he professed the reform doctrines, was never what may be called a religious man, being devoted to pleasure, and to schemes of ambition. It is true he understood and consulted the interests of his kingdom, and strove to make his subjects happy. Herein consists his excellence. As a magnanimous, liberal-minded, and enterprising man, he surpassed all the French kings. But it is ridiculous to call him a religious man, or even strongly fixed in his religious opinions. "Do you," said the king to a great Protestant divine, "believe that a man may be saved by the Catholic religion?" "Undoubtedly," replied the clergyman, "if his life and heart be holy." "Then," said the king, "prudence dictates that I embrace the Catholic religion, and not yours; for, in that case, according to both Catholics and Protestants, I may be saved; but, if I embrace your religion, I shall not be saved, according to the Catholics."

But the king's conversion to Catholicism did not immediately result in the tranquillity of the distracted country. The Catholics would not believe in his sincerity, and many battles had to be fought before he was in peaceable enjoyment of his throne. But there is nothing so hateful as civil war, especially to the inhabitants of great cities; and Paris, at last, and the chief places in the kingdom, acknowledged his sway. The king of Spain, the great Catholic prelates, and the pope, finally perceived how hopeless was the struggle against a man of great military experience, with a devoted army and an enthusiastic capital on his side.

The peace of Verviens, in 1598, left the king without foreign or domestic enemies. From that period to his death, his life was devoted to the welfare of his country.

Edict of Nantes.

His first act was the celebrated Edict of Nantes, by which the Huguenots had quiet and undisturbed residence, the free exercise of their religion, and public worship, except in the court, the army, and within five leagues of Paris. They were eligible to all offices, civil and military; and all public prosecutions, on account of religion, were dropped. This edict also promulgated a general amnesty for political offences, and restored property and titles, as before the war; but the Protestants were prohibited from printing controversial books, and were compelled to pay tithes to the established clergy.

Henry IV., considering the obstacles with which he had to contend, was the greatest general of the age; but it is his efforts in civilization which entitle him to his epithet of *Great*.

Improvements during the Reign of Henry IV.

The first thing which demanded his attention, as a civil ruler, was the settlement of the finances—ever the leading cause of troubles with the French government. These were intrusted to the care of Rosny, afterward Duke of Sully, the most able and upright of all French financiers—a man of remarkable probity and elevation of sentiment. He ever continued to be the minister and the confidant of the king, and maintained his position without subserviency or flattery, almost the only man on the records of history who could tell, with impunity, wholesome truths to an absolute monarch. So wise were his financial arrangements, that a debt of three hundred million of livres was paid off in eight years. In five years, the taxes were reduced one half, the crown lands redeemed, the arsenals stored, the fortifications rebuilt, churches erected, canals dug, and improvements made in every part of the kingdom. On the death of the king, he had in his treasury nearly fifty millions of livres. Under the direction of this able minister, the laws were enforced, robbery and vagrancy were nearly stopped, and agriculture received a great impulse. But economy was the order of the day. The king himself set an illustrious example, and even dressed in gray cloth, with a doublet of taffeta, without embroidery, dispensed with all superfluity at his table, and dismissed all useless servants.

The management and economy of the king enabled him to make great improvements, besides settling the deranged finances of the kingdom. He built innumerable churches, bridges, convents, hospitals, fortresses, and ships. Some of the finest palaces which adorn Paris were erected by him. He was also the patron of learning, the benefits of which he appreciated. He himself was well acquainted with the writings of the ancients. He was particularly fond of the society of the learned, with whom he conversed with freedom and affability. He increased the libraries, opened public schools, and invited distinguished foreigners to Paris, and rewarded them with stipends. Lipsius, Scaliger, and De Thou, were the ornaments of his court.

And his tender regard to the happiness and welfare of his subjects was as marked as his generous appreciation of literature and science. It was his ambition to be the father of his people; and his memorable saying, "Yes, I will so manage matters that the poorest peasant in my kingdom may eat meat each day in the week, and, moreover, be enabled to put a fowl in the pot on a Sunday," has alone embalmed his memory in the affections of the French nation, who, of all their monarchs, are most partial to Henry IV.

Peace Scheme of Henry IV.

But this excellent king was also a philanthropist, and cherished the most enlightened views as to those subjects on which rests the happiness of nations. Though a warrior, the preservation of a lasting peace was the great idea of his life. He was even visionary in his projects to do good; for he imagined it was possible to convince monarchs that they ought to prefer purity, peace, and benevolence, to ambition and war. Hence, he proposed to establish a Congress of Nations, chosen from the various states of Europe, to whom all international difficulties should be referred, with power to settle them—a very desirable object, the most so conceivable; for war is the greatest of all national calamities and crimes. The scheme of the enlightened Henry, however, did not attract much attention; and, even had it been encouraged, would have been set aside in the next generation. What would such men as Frederic the Great, or Marlborough, or Louis XIV., or Napoleon have cared for such an object? But Henry, in his scheme, also had in view the regulation of such forces as the European monarchs should sustain, and this arose from his desire to preserve the "Balance of Power"—the great object of European politicians in these latter times.

Death of Henry IV.

But Henry was not permitted, by Providence, to prosecute his benevolent designs. He was assassinated by a man whom he had never injured—by the most unscrupulous of all misguided men—a religious bigot. The Jesuit Ravaillac, in a mood, as it is to be hoped, bordering on madness, perpetrated the foul deed. But Henry only suffered the fate of nearly all the distinguished actors in those civil and religious contentions which desolated France for forty years. He died in 1610, at the age of fifty-seven, having reigned twenty-one years, nine of which were spent in uninterrupted warfare.

By his death the kingdom was thrown into deep and undissembled mourning. Many fell speechless in the streets when the intelligence of his assassination was known; others died from excess of grief. All felt that they had lost more than a father, and nothing was anticipated but storms and commotions.

He left no children by his wife, Margaret de Valois, who proved inconstant, and from whom he was separated. By his second wife, Mary de Medicis, he had three children, the oldest of whom was a child when he ascended the throne, by the title of Louis XIII. His daughter, Henrietta, married Charles I. of England.

Though great advances were made in France during this reign, it was still far from that state of civilization which it attained a century afterwards. It contained about fifteen million of inhabitants, and Paris about one hundred and fifty thousand. The nobles were numerous and powerful, and engrossed the wealth of the nation. The people were not exactly slaves, but were reduced to great dependence, were uneducated, degraded, and enjoyed but few political or social privileges. They were oppressed by the government, by the nobles, and by the clergy.

The highest official dignitary was the constable, the second the keeper of the seals, the third the chamberlain, then the six or eight marshals, then the secretary of state, then gentlemen of the household, and military commanders. The king was nearly absolute. The parliament was a judicial tribunal, which did not enact laws, but which registered the edicts of the king.

Commerce and manufactures were extremely limited, and far from flourishing; and the arts were in an infant state. Architecture, the only art in which half-civilized nations have excelled, was the most advanced, and was displayed in the churches and royal palaces. Paris was crowded with uncomfortable houses, and the narrow streets were favorable to tumult as well as pestilence. Tapestry was the most common and the most expensive of the arts, and the hangings, in a single room, often reached a sum which would be equal, in these times, to one hundred thousand dollars. The floors of the palaces were spread with Turkey carpets. Chairs were used only in kings' palaces, and carriages were but just introduced, and were clumsy and awkward. Mules were chiefly used in travelling, the horses being reserved for war. Dress, especially of females, was gorgeous and extravagant; false hair, masks, trailed petticoats, and cork heels ten inches high, were some of the peculiarities. The French then, as now, were fond of the pleasures of the table, and the hour for dinner was eleven o'clock. Morals were extremely low, and gaming was a universal passion, in which Henry IV. himself extravagantly indulged. The advice of Catharine de Medicis to her son Charles IX. showed her knowledge of the French character, even as it exists now: "Twice a week give public assemblies, for the specific secret of the French government is, to keep the people always cheerful; for they are so restless you must occupy them, during peace, either with business or amusement, or else they will involve you in trouble."

France at the Death of Henry IV.

Such was France, at the death of Henry IV., 1610, one of the largest and most powerful of the European kingdoms, though far from the greatness it was destined afterwards to attain.

A more powerful monarchy, at this period, was Spain. As this kingdom was then in the zenith of its power and glory, we will take a brief survey of it during the reign of Philip II., the successor of Charles V., a person to whom we have often referred. With his reign are closely connected the struggles of the Hollanders to secure their civil and religious independence. The Low Countries were provinces of Spain, and therefore to be considered in connection with Spanish history.

> References.—For a knowledge of France during the reign of Henry IV., see James's History of Henry IV.; James's Life of Condé; History of the Huguenots. Rankin's and Crowe's Histories of France are the best in English, but far inferior to Sismondi's, Millot's, and Lacretelle's. Sully's Memoirs throw considerable light on this period, and Dumas's Margaret de Valois may be read with profit.

CHAPTER VIII
PHILIP II. AND THE AUSTRIAN PRINCES OF SPAIN

Bigotry of Philip II.

Spain cannot be said to have been a powerful state until the reign of Ferdinand and Isabella; when the crowns of Castile and Arragon were united, and when the discoveries of Columbus added a new world to their extensive territories. Nor, during the reign of Ferdinand and Isabella, was the power of the crown as absolute as during the sway of the Austrian princes. The nobles were animated by a bold and free spirit, and the clergy dared to resist the encroachments of royalty, and even the usurpations of Rome. Charles V. succeeded in suppressing the power of the nobles, and all insurrections of the people, and laid the foundation for the power of his gloomy son, Philip II. With Philip commenced the grandeur of the Spanish monarchy. By him, also, were sown the seeds of its subsequent decay. Under him, the inquisition was disgraced by ten thousand enormities, Holland was overrun by the Duke of Alva, and America conquered by Cortes and Pizarro. It was he who built the gorgeous palaces of Spain, and who, with his Invincible Armada, meditated the conquest of England. The wealth of the Indies flowed into the royal treasury, and also enriched all orders and classes. Silver and gold became as plenty at Madrid as in old times at Jerusalem under the reign of Solomon. But Philip was a different prince from Solomon. His talents and attainments were respectable, but he had a jealous and selfish disposition, and exerted all the energies of his mind, and all the resources of his kingdom, to crush the Protestant religion and the liberties of Europe.

Among the first acts of his reign was the effort to extinguish Protestantism in the Netherlands, an assemblage of seigniories, under various titles, subject to his authority. The opinions of Luther and Calvin made great progress in this country, and Philip, in order to repress them, created new bishops, and established the Inquisition. The people protested, and these protests were considered as rebellious.

Revolt of the Netherlands.

At the head of the nobility was William, the Prince of Orange, on whom Philip had conferred the government of Holland, Zealand, Friesland, and Utrecht, provinces of the Netherlands. He was a haughty but resolute and courageous character, and had adopted the opinions of Calvin, for which he lost the confidence of Philip. In the prospect of destruction, he embraced the resolution of delivering his country from the yoke of a merciless and bigoted master. Having reduced the most important garrisons of Holland and Zealand, he was proclaimed stadtholder, and openly threw off his allegiance to Spain. Hostilities, of course, commenced. Alva, the general of Philip, took the old city of Haerlem, and put fifteen hundred to the sword, among whom were all the magistrates, and all the Protestant clergy.

Don John, Archduke of Austria, and the brother of Philip, succeeded the Duke of Alva, during whose administration the seven United Provinces formed themselves into a confederation, and chose the Prince of Orange to be the general of their armies, admiral of their fleets, and chief magistrate, by the title of *stadtholder*. But William was soon after assassinated by a wretch who had been bribed by the exasperated Philip, and Maurice, his son, received his title, dignities, and power. His military talents, as the antagonist of the Duke of Parma, lieutenant to Philip, in the Netherlands, secured him a high place in the estimation of warriors. To protect this prince and the infant republic of Holland, Queen Elizabeth sent four thousand men under the Earl of Leicester, her favorite; and, with this assistance, the Hollanders maintained their ground against the most powerful monarch in Europe, as has been already mentioned in the chapter on Elizabeth.

After the loss of the Netherlands, the next great event of his reign was the acquisition of Portugal, to which he laid claim on the death of Don Henry, in 1581. There were several other claimants, but Philip, with an army of twenty thousand, was stronger than any of the others. He gained a decisive victory over Don Antonio, uncle to the last monarch, and was crowned at Lisbon without opposition.

Revolt of the Moriscoes.

The revolt of the Moriscoes occupies a prominent place in the annals of this reign. They were Christianized Moors, but, at heart, Mohammedans. A decree had been published that their children should frequent the Christian church, that the Arabic should no longer be used in writing, that both men and women should wear the Spanish costume, that they no longer should receive Mohammedan names, or marry without permission. The Moriscoes contended that no particular dress involved religious opinions, that the women used the veil according to their notions of modesty, that the use of their own language was no sin, and that baths were used, not from religious motives, but for the sake of cleanliness. These expostulations were, however, without effect. Nothing could move the bigoted king. So revolt followed cruelty and oppression. Great excesses were committed by both parties, and most horrible barbarities were exhibited. The atrocious nature of civil war is ever the same, and presents nearly the same undeviating picture of misery and crime. But in this war there was something fiendish. A clergyman was roasted over a brazier, and the women, wearied with his protracted death, despatched him with their needles and knives. The rebels ridiculed the sacrifice of the mass by slaughtering a pig on the high altar of a church. These insults were retaliated with that cruelty which Spanish bigotry and malice know so well how to inflict. Thousands of defenceless women and children were murdered in violation of the most solemn treaties. The whole Moorish population was finally exterminated, and Granada, with its beautiful mountains and fertile valleys, was made a desert. No less than six hundred thousand were driven to Africa—an act of great impolicy, since the Moriscoes were the most ingenious and industrious part of the population; and their exile contributed to undermine that national prosperity in which, at that day, every Spaniard gloried. But destruction ever succeeds pride: infatuation and blindness are the attendants of despotism.

The destruction of the Spanish Armada, and the losses which the Spaniards suffered from Sir Francis Drake and Admiral Hawkins, have already been mentioned. But the pride of Philip was mortified, rather than that his power was diminished. His ambition received a check, and he found it impossible to conquer England. His finances, too, became deranged; still he remained the absolute master of the richest kingdom in the world.

Causes of Decline of the Spanish Monarchy.

The decline of the Spanish monarchy dates from his death which took place in his magnificent palace of the Escurial, in 1598. Under his son Philip III., decline became very marked, and future ruin could be predicted.

The principal cause of the decline of prosperity was the great increase of the clergy, and the extent of their wealth. In the Spanish dominions, which included Spain, Naples, Milan, Parma, Sicily, Sardinia, the Netherlands, Portugal, and the Indies, there were fifty-four archbishops, six hundred and eighty-four bishops, seven thousand hospitals, one hundred thousand abbeys and nunneries, six hundred thousand monks, and three hundred and ten thousand secular priests—a priest to every ten families. Almost every village had a monastery. The diocese of Seville had fourteen thousand priests, nearly the present number of all the clergy of the establishment in England. The cathedral of Seville gave support and occupation to one hundred priests.

And this numerous clergy usurped the power and dignities of the state. They also encouraged that frightful inquisition, the very name of which conjures up the most horrid images of death and torture. This institution, committed to the care of Dominican monks, was instituted to put down heresy; that is, every thing in poetry, philosophy, or religion, which was distasteful to the despots of the human mind. The inquisitors had power to apprehend people even suspected of heresy, and, on the testimony of two witnesses, could condemn them to torture, imprisonment, and death. Resistance was vain; complaint was ruin. Arrests took place suddenly and secretly. Nor had the prisoner a knowledge of his accusers, or of the crimes of which he was accused. The most delicate maidens, as well as men of hoary hairs and known integrity, were subjected to every outrage that human nature could bear, or satanic ingenuity inflict. Should the jailer take compassion, and bestow a few crumbs of bread or drops of water, he would be punished as the greatest of traitors. Even nobles were not exempted from the supervision of this court, which was established in every village and town in Portugal and Spain, and which, in the single city of Toledo, condemned, in one year, seventeen thousand people. This institution was tolerated by the king, since he knew very well that there ever exists an intimate union between absolutism in religion and absolutism in government.

The Increase of Gold and Silver.

Decline of the Spanish Monarchy.

Besides the spiritual despotism which the clergy of Spain exercised over a deluded people, but a people naturally of fine elements of character, the sudden increase of gold and silver led to luxury, idleness, and degeneracy. Money being abundant, in consequence of the gold and silver mines of America, the people neglected the cultivation of those things which money could procure. Then followed a great rise in the prices of all kinds of provision and clothing. Houses, lands, and manufactures also soon rose in value. Hence money was delusive, since, with ten times the increase of specie, there was a corresponding decrease in those necessaries of life which gold and silver would purchase. Silver and gold are only the medium of trade, not the basis of wealth. The real prosperity of a country depends upon the amount of productive industry. If diamonds were as numerous as crystals, they would be worth no more than crystals. The sudden influx of the precious metals into Spain doubtless gave a temporary wealth to the kingdom; but when habits of industry were lost, and the culture of the soil was neglected, the gold and silver of the Spaniards were exchanged for the productive industry of other nations. The Dutch and the English, whose manufactures and commerce were in a healthy state, became enriched at their expense. With the loss of substantial wealth, that is, industry and economy, the Spaniards lost elevation of sentiment, became cold and proud, followed frivolous pleasures and amusements, and acquired habits which were ruinous. Plays, pantomimes, and bull-fights now amused the lazy and pleasure-seeking nation, while the profligacy of the court had no parallel in Europe, with the exception of that of France. The country became exhausted by war. The finances were deranged, and province after province rebelled. Every where were military reverses, and a decrease of population. Taxes, in the mean while, increased, and a burdened people lamented in vain their misfortune and decline. The reign of Philip IV. was the most disastrous in the annals of the country. The Catalan insurrection, the loss of Jamaica, the Low Countries, and Portugal, were the results of his misrule and imbecility. So rapidly did Spain degenerate, that, upon the close of the Austrian dynasty, with all the natural advantages of the country, the best harbors and sea-coast in Europe, the richest soil, and the finest climate, and with the possession of the Indies also, the people were the poorest, the most ignorant, and the most helpless in Europe. The death of Charles II., a miserable, afflicted, superstitious, priest-ridden monarch, left Spain without a king, and the vacant throne became the prize of any monarch in Europe who could raise and send across the Pyrenees the largest army. It fell into the power of Louis XIV., and the Bourbon princes have ever since in vain attempted the restoration of the broken monarchy to its former glory. But, alas, Spain has, since the spoliation of the Mexicans and Peruvians, only a melancholy history—a history of crime, bigotry, anarchy, and poverty. The Spaniards committed awful crimes in their lust for gold and silver. "They had their request," but God, in his retributive justice, "sent leanness into their souls."

> For the history of Spain during the Austrian princes, see
> a history in Lardner's Encyclopedia; Watson's Life of
> Philip II.; James's Foreign Statesmen; Schiller's Revolt
> of the Netherlands; Russell's Modern Europe; Prescott's
> Conquest of Mexico and Peru.

CHAPTER IX
THE JESUITS, AND THE PAPAL POWER
IN THE SEVENTEENTH CENTURY

The Roman Power in the Seventeenth Century.

During the period we have just been considering, the most marked peculiarity was, the struggle between Protestantism and Romanism. It is true that objects of personal ambition also occupied the minds of princes, and many great events occurred, which were not connected with the struggles for religious liberty and light. But the great feature of the age was the insurrection of human intelligence. There was a spirit of innovation, which nothing could suppress, and this was directed, in the main, to matters of religion. The conflict was not between church and state, but between two great factions in each. "No man asked whether another belonged to the same country as himself, but whether he belonged to the same sect." Luther, Calvin, Zwingle, Knox, Cranmer, and Bacon were the great pioneers in this march of innovation. They wished to explode the ideas of the middle ages, in philosophy and in religion. They made war upon the Roman Catholic Church, as the great supporter and defender of old ideas. They renounced her authority. She summoned her friends and vassals, rallied all her forces, and, with desperate energy, resolved to put down the spirit of reform. The struggles of the Protestants in England, Germany, France, and the Netherlands, alike manifested the same spirit, were produced by the same causes, and brought forth the same results. The insurrection was not suppressed.

Rise of the Jesuits.

The hostile movements of Rome, for a while, were carried on by armies, massacres, assassinations, and inquisitions. The duke of Alva's cruelties in the Netherlands, St. Bartholomew's massacre in France, inquisitorial tortures in Spain, and Smithfield burnings in England, illustrate this assertion. But more subtle and artful agents were required, especially since violence had failed. Men of simple lives, of undoubted piety, of earnest zeal, and singular disinterestedness to their cause, arose, and did what the sword and the stake could not do,—revived Catholicism, and caused a reaction to Protestantism itself. These men were Jesuits, the most faithful, intrepid, and successful soldiers that ever enlisted under the banners of Rome. The rise and fortunes of this order of monks form one of the most important and interesting chapters in the history of the human race. Their victories, and the spirit which achieved them, are well worth our notice. In considering them, it must be borne in mind, that the Jesuits have exhibited traits so dissimilar and contradictory, that it is difficult to form a just judgment. While they were achieving their victories, they appeared in a totally different light from what distinguished them when they reposed on their laurels. In short, the *earlier* and the *latter* Jesuits were entirely different in their moral and social aspects, although they had the same external organization. The principles of their system were always the same. The men who defended them, at first, were marked by great virtues, but afterwards were deformed by equally as great vices. It was in the early days of Jesuitism that the events we have recorded took place. Hence our notice, at present, will be confined to the Jesuits when they were worthy of respect, and, in some things, even of admiration. Their courage, fidelity, zeal, learning, and intrepidity for half a century, have not been exaggerated.

The founder of the order was Ignatius Loyola, a Spanish gentleman of noble birth, who first appeared as a soldier at the siege of Pampeluna, where he was wounded, about the time that Luther was writing his theses, and disputing about indulgences. He amused himself, on his sick bed, by reading the lives of the saints. His enthusiastic mind was affected, and he resolved to pass from worldly to spiritual knighthood. He became a saint, after the notions of the age; that is, he fasted, wore sackcloth, lived on roots and herbs, practised austerities, retired to lonely places, and spent his time in contemplation and prayer. The people were attracted by his sanctity, and followed him in crowds. His heart burned to convert heretics; and, to prepare himself for his mission, he went to the universities, and devoted himself to study. There he made some distinguished converts, all of whom afterwards became famous. In his narrow cell, at Paris, he induced Francis Xavier, Faber, Laynez Bobadilla, and Rodriguez to embrace his views, and to form themselves into an association, for the conversion of the world. On the summit of Montmartre, these six young men, on one star-lit night, took the usual monastic vows of *poverty, chastity,* and *obedience,* and solemnly devoted themselves to their new mission.

They then went to Rome, to induce the pope to constitute them a new missionary order. But they were ridiculed as fanatics. Moreover, for several centuries, there had been great opposition in Rome against the institution of new monastic orders. It was thought that there were orders enough; that the old should be reformed, not new ones created. Even St. Dominic and St.

Francis had great difficulty in getting their orders instituted. But Loyola and his companions made extraordinary offers. They professed their willingness to go wherever the pope should send them, among Turks, heathens, or heretics, instantly, without condition, or reward.

Rapid Spread of the Jesuit Order.

How could the pope refuse to license them? His empire was in danger; Luther was in the midst of his victories; the power of ideas and truth was shaking to its centre the pontifical throne; all the old orders had become degenerate and inefficient, and the pope did not know where to look for efficient support. The venerable Benedictines were revelling in the wealth of their splendid abbeys, while the Dominicans and the Franciscans had become itinerant vagabonds, peddling relics and indulgences, and forgetful of those stern duties and virtues which originally characterized them. All the monks were inexhaustible subjects of sarcasm and mockery. They even made scholasticism ridiculous, and the papal dogmas contemptible. Erasmus laughed at them, and Luther mocked them. They were sensual, lazy, ignorant, and corrupt. The pope did not want such soldiers. But the followers of Loyola were full of ardor, talent, and zeal; willing to do any thing for a sinking cause; able to do any thing, so far as human will can avail. And they did not disappoint the pope. Great additions were made. They increased with marvellous rapidity. The zealous, devout, and energetic, throughout all ranks in the Catholic church, joined them. They spread into all lands. They became the confessors of kings, the teachers of youth, the most popular preachers, the most successful missionaries. In sixteen years after the scene of Montmartre, Loyola had established his society in the affections and confidence of Catholic Europe, against the voice of universities, the fears of monarchs, and the jealousy of the other monastic orders. In sixteen years, from the condition of a ridiculed fanatic, whose voice, however, would have been disregarded a century earlier or later, he became one of the most powerful dignitaries of the church, influencing the councils of the Vatican, moving the minds of kings, controlling the souls of a numerous fraternity, and making his power felt, even in the courts of Japan and China. Before he died, his spiritual sons had planted their missionary stations amid Peruvian mines, amid the marts of the African slave trade, in the islands of the Indian Ocean, and in the cities of Japan and China. Nay, his followers had secured the most important chairs in the universities of Europe, and had become confessors to the most powerful monarchs, teachers in the best schools of Christendom, and preachers in its principal pulpits. They had become an organization, instinct with life, endued with energy and will, and forming a body which could outwatch Argus with his hundred eyes, and outwork Briareus with his hundred arms. It had forty thousand eyes open upon every cabinet and private family in Europe, and forty thousand arms extended over the necks of both sovereigns and people. It had become a mighty power in the world, inseparably connected with the education and the religion of the age, the prime mover of all political affairs, the grand prop of absolute monarchies, the last hope of the papal hierarchy.

Rapid Spread of the Jesuits.

The sudden growth and enormous resources of the "Society of Jesus" impress us with feelings of amazement and awe. We almost attribute them to the agency of mysterious powers, and forget the operations of natural causes. The history of society shows that no body of men ever obtained a wide-spread ascendency, except by the exercise of remarkable qualities of mind and heart. And this is the reason why the Jesuits prospered. When Catholic Europe saw young men, born to fortune and honors, voluntarily surrendering their rank and goods, devoting themselves to religious duties, spending their days in hospitals and schools, wandering, as missionaries, into the most unknown and dangerous parts of the world, exciting the young to study, making great attainments in all departments of literature and science, and shedding a light, wherever they went, by their genius and disinterestedness, it was natural that they would be received as preachers, teachers, and confessors. That they were characterized, during the first fifty years, by such excellencies, has never been denied. The Jesuit missionary called forth the praises of Baxter, and the panegyric of Leibnitz. He went forth, without fear, to encounter the most dreaded dangers. Martyrdom was nothing to him, for he knew that the altar, which might stream with his blood, would, in after times, be a cherished monument of his fame, and an impressive emblem of the power of his religion. Francis Xavier, one of the first converts of Loyola, a Spaniard of rank, traversed a tract of more than twice the circumference of the globe, preaching, disputing, and baptizing, until seventy thousand converts attested the fruits of his mission. In perils, fastings, and fatigues, was the life of this remarkable man passed, to convert the heathen world; and his labors have never been equalled, as a missionary, except by the apostle Paul. But China and Japan were not the only scenes of the enterprises of Jesuit missionaries. As early as 1634, they penetrated into Canada, and, shortly after to the sources of the Mississippi and the prairies of Illinois. "My companion," said the fearless Marquette, "is an envoy of France, to discover new countries; but I am an ambassador of God, to enlighten them with the gospel." But of all the missions of the Jesuits, those in Paraguay were the most successful. They there gathered together, in *reductions*, or villages, three hundred thousand Indians, and these were bound together by a common interest, were controlled by a paternal authority, taught useful arts, and trained to enjoy the blessings of civilization. On the distant banks of the La Plata, while the Spanish colonists were hunting the Mexicans and Peruvians with bloodhounds, or the English slave traders were consigning to eternal bondage the unhappy Africans, the Jesuits were realizing the ideal paradise of More—a Utopia, where no murders or robberies were committed, and where the blessed flowers of peace and harmony bloomed in a garden of almost primeval loveliness.

Extraordinary Virtues of the Older Jesuits.

In that age, the Jesuit excelled in any work to which he devoted his attention. He was not only an intrepid missionary, but a most successful teacher. Into the work of education he entered heart and soul. He taught gratuitously, without any crabbed harshness, and with a view to gain the heart. He entered into the feelings of his pupils, and taught them to subdue their tempers, and avoid quarrels and oaths. He excited them to enthusiasm, perceived their merits, and rewarded the successful with presents and favors. Hence the schools of the Jesuits were the best in Europe, and were highly praised even by the Protestants. The Jesuits were even more popular as preachers than they were as teachers; and they were equally prized as confessors. They were so successful and so respected, that they soon obtained an ascendency in Europe. Veneration secured wealth, and their establishments gradually became magnificently endowed. But all their influence was directed to one single end—to the building up of the power of the popes, whose obedient servants they were. Can we wonder that Catholicism should revive?

The Constitution of the Jesuits.

Again, their constitution was wonderful, and admirably adapted to the ends they had in view. Their vows were indeed substantially the same as those of other monks, but there was among them a more practical spirit of obedience. All the members were controlled by a single will—all were passive, instruments in the hands of the general of the order. He appointed presidents of colleges and of religious houses; admitted, dismissed, dispensed, and punished at his pleasure. His power was irresponsible, and for life. From his will there was no appeal. There were among them many gradations in rank, but each gradation was a gradation in slavery. The Jesuit was bound to obey even his own servant, if required by a superior. Obedience was the soul of the institution, absolute, unconditional, and unreserved—even the submission of the will, to the entire abnegation of self. The Jesuit gloried in being made a puppet, a piece of machinery, like a soldier, if the loss of his intellectual independence would advance the interests of his order. The *esprit de corps* was perfectly wonderful, and this spirit was one secret of the disinterestedness of the body. "*Ad majorem Dei gloriam*," was the motto emblazoned on their standards, and written on their hearts; but this glory of God was synonymous with the ascendency of their association.

The unconditional obedience to a single will, which is the genius of Jesuitism, while it signally advanced the interests of the body, and of the pope, to whom they were devoted, still led to the most detestable and resistless spiritual despotism ever exercised by man. The Jesuit, especially when obscure and humble, was a tool, rather than an intriguer. He was bound hand and foot by the orders of his superiors, and they alone were responsible for his actions.

Degeneracy of the Jesuits.

We can easily see how the extraordinary virtues and attainments of the early Jesuits, and the wonderful mechanism of their system, would promote the growth of the order and the interests of Rome, before the suspicions of good people would be aroused. It was a long time after their piety had passed to fraud, their simplicity to cunning, their poverty to wealth, their humility to pride, and their indifference to the world to cabals, intrigues, and crimes, before the change was felt. And, moreover, it was more than a century before the fruits of the system were fully reaped. With all the excellences of their schools and missions, dangerous notions and customs were taught in them, which gradually destroyed their efficacy. A bad system often works well for a while, but always carries the seeds of decay and ruin. It was so with the institution of Loyola, in spite of the enthusiasm and sincerity of the early members, and the masterly wisdom displayed by the founders. In after times, evils were perceived, which had, at first, escaped the eye. It was seen that the system of education, though specious, and, in many respects, excellent, was calculated to narrow the mind, while it filled it with knowledge. Young men, in their colleges, were taught blindly to follow a rigid mechanical code; they were closely watched; all books were taken from them of a liberal tendency; mutilated editions of such as could not be denied only were allowed; truths of great importance were concealed or glossed over; exploded errors were revived, and studies recommended which had no reference to the discussion of abstract questions on government or religion. And the boys were made spies on each other, their spirits were broken, and their tastes perverted. The Jesuits sought to guard the avenues to thought, not to open them, were jealous of all independence of mind, and never sought to go beyond their age, or base any movement on ideal standards.

Evils in the Jesuit System.

Again, as preachers, though popular and eloquent, they devoted their talents to convert men to the *Roman church* rather than to *God*. They were bigoted sectarians; strove to make men Catholics rather than Christians. As missionaries, they were content with a mere nominal conversion. They gave men the crucifix, but not the Bible, and even permitted their converts to retain many of their ancient superstitions and prejudices. And thus they usurped the authority of native rulers, and sought to impose on China and Japan their despotic yoke. They greatly enriched themselves in consequence of the credulity of the natives, whom they flattered, and wielded an unlawful power. And this is one reason why they were expelled, and why they made no permanent conquests among the millions they converted in Japan. They wished not only to subjugate the European, but the Asiatic mind. Europe did not present a field sufficiently extensive for their cupidity and ambition.

Finally, as confessors, they were peculiarly indulgent to those who sought absolution, provided their submission was complete. Then it was seen what an easy thing it was to bear the yoke of Christ. The offender was told that sin consisted in wilfulness, and wilfulness in the perfect knowledge of the nature of sin, according to which doctrine blindness and passion were sufficient exculpations. They invented the doctrine of mental reservation, on which Pascal was so severe. Perjury was allowable, if the perjured were inwardly determined not to swear. A man might fight a duel, if in danger of being stigmatized as a coward; he might betray his friend, if he could thus benefit his party. The Jesuits invented a system of casuistry which confused all established ideas of moral obligation. They tolerated, and some of them justified, crimes, if the same could be made subservient to the apparent interests of the church. Their principle was to do evil that good might come. Above all, they conformed to the inclinations of the great, especially to those of absolute princes, on whom they imposed no painful penance, or austere devotion. Their sympathies always were with absolutism, in all its forms and they were the chosen and trusted agents of the despots of mankind, until even the eyes of Europe were open to their vast ambition, which sought to erect an independent empire within the limits of despotism itself. But the corruptions of the Jesuits, their system of casuistry, their lax morality, their disgraceful intrigues, their unprincipled rapacity, do not belong to the age we have now been considering. These fruits of a bad system had not then been matured; and the infancy of the society was as beautiful as its latter days were disgraceful and fearful. In a future chapter, we shall glance at the decline and fall of this celebrated institution—the best adapted to its proposed ends of any system ever devised by the craft and wisdom of man.

The great patrons of the Jesuits—the popes and their empire in the sixteenth century, after the death of Luther—demand some notice. The Catholic church, in this century, was remarkable for the reformation it attempted within its own body, and for the zeal, and ability, and virtue, which marked the character of many of the popes themselves. Had it not been for this counter reformation, Protestantism would have obtained a great ascendency in Europe. But the Protestants were divided among themselves, while the Catholics were united, and animated with singular zeal. They put forth their utmost energies to reconquer what they had lost. They did not succeed in this, but they secured the ascendency, on the whole, of the Catholic cause in Europe. For this ascendency the popes are indebted to the Jesuits.

The Popes in the Seventeenth Century.

Nepotism of the Popes.

At the close of the sixteenth century, the popes possessed a well-situated, rich, and beautiful province. All writers celebrated its fertility. Scarcely a foot of land remained uncultivated. Corn was exported, and the ports were filled with ships. The people were courageous, and had great talents for business. The middle classes were peaceful and contented, but the nobles, who held in their hands the municipal authority, were turbulent, rapacious, and indifferent to intellectual culture. The popes were generally virtuous characters, and munificent patrons of genius. Gregory XIII. kept a list of men in every country who were likely to acquit themselves as bishops, and exhibited the greatest caution in appointing them. Sixtus V., whose father was an humble gardener, encouraged agriculture and manufactures, husbanded the resources of the state, and filled Rome with statues. He raised the obelisk in front of St. Peter's, and completed the dome of the Cathedral. Clement VIII. celebrated the mass himself, and scrupulously devoted himself to religious duties. He was careless of the pleasures which formerly characterized the popes, and admitted every day twelve poor persons to dine with him. Paul V. had equal talents and greater authority, but was bigoted and cold. Gregory XIV. had all the severity of an ancient monk. The only religious peculiarity of the popes, at the latter end of the sixteenth century, which we unhesitatingly condemn, was, their religious intolerance. But they saw that their empire would pass away, unless they used vigorous and desperate measures to retain it. During this period, the great victories of the Jesuits, the establishment of their colleges, and the splendid endowments of their churches took place. Gregory XV. built, at his own cost, the celebrated church of St. Ignatius, at Rome, and instituted the Propaganda, a missionary institution, under the control of the Jesuits.

Rome in the Seventeenth Century.

The popes, whether good or bad, did not relinquish their nepotism in this century, in consequence of which great families arose with every pope, and supplanted the old aristocracy. The Barberini family, in one pontificate, amassed one hundred and five millions of scudi—as great a fortune as that left by Mazarin. But they, enriched under Urban VII., had to flee from Rome under Innocent X. Jealousy and contention divided and distracted all the noble families, who vied with each other in titles and pomp, ceremony and pride. The ladies of the Savelli family never quitted their palace walls, except in closely veiled carriages. The Visconti decorated their walls with the portraits of the popes of their line. The Gaetana dwelt with pride on the memory of Boniface VIII. The Colonna and Orsini boasted that for centuries no peace had been concluded in Christendom, in which they had not been expressly included. But these old families had become gradually impoverished, and yielded, in wealth and power, though not in pride and dignity, to the Cesarini, Borghesi, Aldobrandini, Ludovisi, Giustiniani, Chigi, and the Barberini. All these families, from which popes had sprung, had splendid palaces, villas, pictures, libraries, and statues; and they contributed to make Rome the centre of attraction for the elegant and the literary throughout Europe. It was still the moral and social centre of Christendom. It was a place to which all strangers resorted, and from which all intrigues sprung. It was the scene of pleasure, gayety, and grandeur. And the splendid fabric, which was erected in the "ages of faith," in spite of all the calamities and ravages of time, remained still beautiful and attractive. Since the first secession, in the sixteenth century, Rome has lost none of her adherents, and those, who remained faithful, have become the more enthusiastic in their idolatry.

References.—Ranke's History of the Popes. Father Bouhour's Life of Ignatius Loyola. A Life of Xavier, by the same author. Stephens's Essay on Loyola. Charlevoix's History of Paraguay. Pascal's Provincial Letters. Macaulay's

Review of Ranke's History of the Popes. Bancroft's chapter, in the History of the United States, on the colonization of Canada. "Secreta Monita." Histoire des Jésuites. "Spiritual Exercises." Dr. Williams's Essay. History of Jesuit Missions. The works on the Jesuits are very numerous; but those which are most accessible are of a violent partisan character. Eugene Sue, in his "Wandering Jew," has given false, but strong, impressions. Infidel writers have generally been the most bitter, with the exception of English and Scotch authors, in the seventeenth century. The great work of Ranke is the most impartial with which the author is acquainted. Ranke's histories should never be neglected, of which admirable translations have been made.

CHAPTER X
THIRTY YEARS WAR

Political Troubles after the Death of Luther.

The contests which arose from the discussion of religious ideas did not close with the sixteenth century. They were, on the other hand, continued with still greater acrimony. Protestantism had been suppressed in France, but not in Holland or Germany. In England, the struggle was to continue, not between the Catholics and Protestants, but between different parties among the Protestants themselves. In Germany, a long and devastating war of thirty years was to be carried on before even religious liberty could be guaranteed.

This struggle is the most prominent event of the seventeenth century before the English Revolution, and was attended with the most important religious and political consequences. The event itself was one of the chief political consequences of the Reformation. Indeed, all the events of this period either originated in, or became mixed up with, questions of religion.

From the very first agitation of the reform doctrines, the house of Austria devoted against their adherents the whole of its immense political power. Charles V. resolved to suppress Protestantism, and would have perhaps succeeded, had it not been for the various wars which distracted his attention, and for the decided stand which the Protestant princes of Germany took respecting Luther and his doctrines. As early as 1530, was formed the league of Smalcalde, headed by the elector of Saxony, the most powerful of the German princes, next to the archduke of Austria. The princes who formed this league, resolved to secure to their subjects the free exercise of their religion, in spite of all opposition from the Catholic powers. But hostilities did not commence until after Luther had breathed his last. The Catholics gained a great victory at the battle of Mühlberg, when the Elector of Saxony was taken prisoner. With the treaty of Smalcalde, the freedom of Germany seemed prostrate forever, and the power of Austria reached its meridian. But the cause of liberty revived under Maurice of Saxony, once its formidable enemy. All the fruits of victory were lost again in the congress of Passau, and the diet of Augsburg, when an equitable peace seemed guaranteed to the Protestants.

Diet of Augsburg.

The diet of Augsburg, 1555, the year of the resignation of Charles V., divided Germany into two great political and religious parties, and recognized the independence of each. The Protestants were no longer looked upon as rebels, but as men who had a right to worship God as they pleased. Still, in reality, all that the Lutherans gained was toleration, not equality. The concessions of the Catholics were made to necessity, not to justice. Hence, the treaty of Augsburg proved only a truce, not a lasting peace. The boundaries of both parties were marked out by the sword, and by the sword only were they to be preserved.

For a while, however, peace was preserved, and might have continued longer, had it not been for the dissensions of Protestants among themselves, caused by the followers of Calvin and Luther. The Lutherans would not include the Calvinists in their communion, and the Calvinists would not accede to the Lutheran church. During these dissensions, the Jesuits sowed tares, and the Protestants lost the chance of establishing their perfect equality with the Catholics.

Notwithstanding all the bitterness and jealousy which existed between sects and parties, still the peace of Germany, in a political sense, was preserved during the reign of Ferdinand, the founder of the German branch of the house of Austria, and who succeeded his brother Charles V. On his death, in 1564, his son Maximilian II., was chosen emperor, and during his reign, and until his death, in 1576, Germany enjoyed tranquillity. His successor was his son Rodolph, a weak prince, and incapable of uniting the various territories which were hereditary in his family—Austria, Hungary, Transylvania, Bohemia, Moravia, and Styria. There were troubles in each of these provinces, and one after another revolted, until Rodolph was left with but the empty title of emperor. But these provinces acknowledged the sway of his brother Matthias, who had delivered them from the Turks, and had granted the Protestants liberty of conscience. The emperor was weak enough to confirm his brother in his usurpation. In 1612, he died, and Matthias mounted the imperial throne.

Commencement of the Thirty Years War.

It was during the reign of this prince, that the Thirty Years' War commenced. In proportion as the reformed religion gained ground in Hungary and Bohemia,—two provinces very difficult to rule,—the Protestant princes of the empire became desirous of securing and extending their privileges. Their demands were refused, and they entered into a new confederacy, called the *Evangelical Union*. This association was opposed by another, called the *Catholic League*. The former was supported by Holland, England, and Henry IV., of France. The humiliation of Austria was the great object of Henry in supporting the Protestant princes of Germany, and he assembled an army of forty thousand men, which he designed to head himself. But, just as his preparations were completed, he was assassinated, and his death and the dissensions in the Austrian family prevented the war breaking out with the fury which afterwards characterized it.

The Emperor Matthias died in 1618, and was succeeded by his cousin Ferdinand, Duke of Styria, who was an inveterate enemy to the Protestant cause. His first care was to suppress the insurrection of the Protestants, which, just before his accession had broken out in Bohemia, under the celebrated Count Mansfeldt. The Bohemians renounced allegiance to Ferdinand II., and chose Frederic V., elector palatine, for their king. Frederic unwisely accepted the crown, which confirmed the quarrel between Ferdinand and the Bohemians. Frederic was seconded by all the Protestant princes, except the Elector of Saxony, by two thousand four hundred English volunteers, and by eight thousand troops from the United Provinces. But Ferdinand, assisted by the king of Spain and all the Catholic princes, was more than a match for Frederic, who wasted his time and strength in vain displays of sovereignty. Maximilian, Duke of Bavaria, commanded the forces of the Catholics, who, with twenty-five thousand troops from the Low Countries, invaded Bohemia. The Bohemian forces did not amount to thirty thousand, but they intrenched themselves near Prague, where they were attacked (1620) and routed, with immense slaughter. The battle of Prague decided the fate of Bohemia, put Frederic in possession of all his dominions, and invested him with an authority equal to what any of his predecessors had enjoyed. All his wishes were gratified, and, had he been wise, he might have maintained his ascendency in Germany. But he was blinded by his success, and, from a rebellion in Bohemia, the war extended through Germany, and afterwards throughout Europe.

The Emperor Frederic.

The emperor had regained his dominions by the victorious arms of Maximilian, Duke of Bavaria. To compensate him, without detriment to himself, he resolved to bestow upon him the dominions of the Count Palatine of the Rhine, who had injudiciously accepted the crown of Bohemia. Frederic must be totally ruined. He was put under the ban of the empire, and his territories were devastated by the Spanish general Spinola, with an army of twenty-five thousand men.

Apparently there was no hope for Frederic, or the Protestant cause. The only Protestant princes capable of arresting the Austrian encroachments were the Electors of Saxony and Brandenburg. But the former, John George, preferred the aggrandizement of his house to the emancipation of his country, and tamely witnessed the victories of the emperor, without raising an arm for the relief of the Protestants, of whom he was the acknowledged head. George William of Brandenburg was still more shamefully fettered by the fear of Austria, and of losing his dominions; and he, too, cautiously avoided committing himself to either party.

But while these two great princes ingloriously abandoned Frederic to his fate, a single soldier of fortune, whose only treasure was his sword, Ernest Count Mansfield, dared, in the Bohemian town of Pilsen, to defy the whole power of Austria. Undismayed by the reverses of the elector palatine, he succeeded in enlisting an army of twenty thousand men. With such an army, the cause of Frederic was not irretrievably lost. New prospects began to open, and his misfortunes raised up unexpected friends. James of England opened his treasures, and Christian of Denmark offered his powerful support. Mansfeldt was also joined by the Margrave of Baden. The courage of the count palatine revived, and he labored assiduously to arouse his Protestant brethren. Meanwhile, the generals of the emperor were on the alert, and the rising hopes of Frederic were dissipated by the victories of Tilly. The count palatine was again driven from his hereditary dominions, and sought refuge in Holland.

Count Wallenstein.

But, though the emperor was successful, his finances were exhausted, and he was disagreeably dependent on Bavaria. Under his circumstances, nothing was more welcome than the proposal of Wallenstein, an experienced officer, and the richest nobleman in Bohemia.

Character of Wallenstein.

He offered, at his own expense, and that of his friends, to raise, clothe, and maintain an army for the emperor, if he were allowed to augment it to fifty thousand men. His project was ridiculed as visionary; but the offer was too valuable to be rejected. In a few months, he had collected an army of thirty thousand. His reputation, the prospect of promotion, and the hope of plunder, attracted adventurers from all parts of Germany. Knowing that so large a body could not be held together without great resources, and having none of his own, he marched his troops into the most fertile territories, which had not yet suffered from the war, where they subsisted by contributions and plunder, as obnoxious to their friends as they were to their enemies. Nothing shows the weakness of the imperial power, with all its apparent strength, and the barbarous notions and customs of the country, more than this grant to Wallenstein. And, with all his heroism and success, he cannot now be viewed in any other light than as a licensed robber. He was virtually at the head of a troop of banditti, who fought for the sake of plunder, and who would join any side which would present the greatest hopes of gain. The genius of Schiller, both in his dramas and histories, has immortalized the name of this unprincipled hero, and has excited a strange interest in his person, his family, and his fortunes. He is represented as "born to command. His acute eye distinguished at a glance, from among the multitude, such as were competent, and he assigned to each his proper place. His praise, from being rarely bestowed, animated and brought into full operation every faculty; while his steady, reserved, and earnest demeanor secured obedience and discipline. His very appearance excited awe and reverence; his figure was proud, lofty, and warlike, while his bright, piercing eye expressed profundity of thought, combined with gravity and mystery. His favorite study was that of the stars, and his most intimate friend was an Italian astrologer. He had a fondness for pomp and extravagance. He maintained sixty pages; his ante-chamber was guarded by fifty life-guards, and his table never consisted of less than one hundred covers. Six barons and as many knights were in constant attendance on his person. He never smiled, and the coldness of his temperament was proof against sensual seductions. Ever occupied with grand schemes, he despised those amusements in which so many waste their lives. Terror was the talisman with which he worked: extreme in his punishments as in his rewards, he knew how to keep alive the zeal of his followers, while no general of ancient or modern times could boast of being obeyed with equal alacrity. Submission to his will was more prized by him than bravery, and he kept up the obedience of his troops by capricious orders. He was a man of large stature, thin, of a sallow complexion, with short, red hair, and small, sparkling eyes. A gloomy and forbidding seriousness sat upon his brow, and his munificent presents alone retained the trembling crowd of his dependants."

Such was this enterprising nobleman, to whom the emperor Ferdinand committed so great authority. And the success of Wallenstein apparently justified the course of the emperor. The greater his extortions, and the greater his rewards, the greater was the concourse to his standard. Such is human nature. It is said that, in seven years, Wallenstein exacted not less than sixty millions of dollars from one half of Germany—an incredible sum, when the expenditure of the government of England, at this time, was less than two million pounds a year. His armies flourished, while the states through which they passed were ruined. What cared he for the curses of the people, or the complaints of princes, so long as his army adored him? It was his object to humble all the princes of the empire, and make himself so necessary to the emperor that he would gradually sink to become his tool. He already was created Duke of Friedland, and generalissimo of the imperial armies. Nor had his victorious career met with any severe check, but uninterrupted success seemed to promise the realization of his vast ambition. Germany lay bleeding at his feet, helpless and indignant.

But the greatness and the insolence of Wallenstein raised up enemies against him in all parts of the empire. Fear and jealousy increased the opposition, even in the ranks of the Catholics. His dismissal was demanded by the whole college of electors, and even by Spain. Maximilian, Duke of Bavaria, felt himself eclipsed by the successful general, and was at the head of the cabals against him.

The emperor felt, at this crisis, as Ganganelli did when compelled to disband the Jesuits, that he was parting with the man to whom he owed all his supremacy. Long was he undecided whether or not he would make the sacrifice. But all Germany was clamorous, and the disgrace of Wallenstein was ordained.

Would the ambitious chieftain, at the head of one hundred thousand devoted soldiers, regard the commands of the emperor? He made up his mind to obey, looking to the future for revenge, and feeling that he could afford to wait for it. Seni had read in the stars that glorious prospects still awaited him. Wallenstein retired to his estates in Bohemia, but maintained the pomp and splendor of a prince of the empire.

Gustavus Adolphus.

Scarcely had he retired from the command of the army before his services were again demanded. One hero produces another. A Wellington is ever found to oppose a Napoleon. Providence raised up a friend to Germany, in its distress, in the person of Gustavus Adolphus, King of Sweden. It was not for personal aggrandizement that he lent his powerful arm to the Protestant princes, who, thus far, had vainly struggled against Maximilian, Tilly, and Wallenstein. Zeal for Protestantism, added to strong provocations, induced him to land in Germany with fifteen thousand men—a small body to oppose the victorious troops of the emperor, but they were brave and highly disciplined, and devoted to their royal master. He himself was indisputably the greatest general of the age, and had the full confidence of the Protestant princes, who were ready to rally the moment he obtained any signal advantage. Henceforth, Gustavus Adolphus was the hero of the war. He was more than a hero; he was a Christian, regardful of the morals of his soldiers, and devoted to the interests of spiritual religion. He was frugal, yet generous, serene in the greatest danger; and magnanimous beyond all precedent in the history of kings. On the 20th of May, 1630, taking his daughter Christiana in his arms, then only four years of age, he presented her to the states as their future sovereign, and made his farewell address. "Not lightly, not wantonly," said he, "am I about to involve myself and you in this new and dangerous war. God is my witness that I do not fight to gratify my own ambition; but the emperor has wronged me, has supported my enemies, persecuted my friends, trampled my religion in the dust, and even stretched forth his revengeful arm against my crown. The oppressed states of Germany call loudly for aid, which, by God's help, we will give them.

"I am fully sensible of the dangers to which my life will be exposed. I have never yet shrunk from them, nor is it likely that I shall always escape them. Hitherto, Providence has protected me; but I shall at last fall in defence of my country and my faith. I commend you to the protection of Heaven. Be just, conscientious, and upright, and we shall meet again in eternity. For the prosperity of all my subjects, I offer my warmest prayer to Heaven; and bid you all a sincere—it may be an eternal—farewell."

He had scarcely landed in Germany before his victorious career began. France concluded a treaty with him, and he advanced against Tilly, who now headed the imperial armies.

Loss of Magdeburg.

The tardiness of the Electors of Saxony and Brandenburg in rendering assistance caused the loss of Magdeburg, the most important fortress of the Protestants. It was taken by assault, even while Gustavus was advancing to its relief. No pen can paint, and no imagination can conceive, the horrors which were perpetrated by the imperial soldiers in the sack of that unfortunate place. Neither childhood nor helpless age—neither youth, beauty, sex, nor rank could disarm the fury of the conquerors. No situation or retreat was sacred. In a single church fifty-three women were beheaded. The Croats amused themselves with throwing children into the flames. Pappenheim's Walloons stabbed infants at the breast. The city was reduced to ashes, and thirty thousand of the inhabitants were slain.

But the loss of this important city was soon compensated by the battle of Leipsic, 1630, which the King of Sweden gained over the imperial forces, and in which the Elector of Saxony at last rendered valuable aid. The rout of Tilly, hitherto victorious, was complete, and he himself escaped only by chance. Saxony was freed from the enemy, while Bohemia, Moravia, Austria, and Hungary, were stripped of their defenders. Ferdinand was no longer secure in his capital; the freedom of Germany was secured. Gustavus was every where hailed as a deliverer, and admiration for his genius was only equalled by the admiration of his virtues. He rapidly regained all that the Protestants had lost, and the fruits of twelve years of war were snatched away from the emperor. Tilly was soon after killed, and all things indicated the complete triumph of the Protestants.

It was now the turn of Ferdinand to tremble. The only person who could save him was dismissed and disgraced. Tilly was dead. Munich and Prague were in the hands of the Protestants, while the king of Sweden traversed Germany as a conqueror, law giver, and judge. No fortress was inaccessible; no river checked his victorious career. The Swedish standards were planted in Bavaria, Bohemia, the Palatinate, Saxony, and along the banks of the Rhine. Meanwhile the Turks were preparing to attack Hungary, and a dangerous insurrection threatened his own capital. None came to his assistance in the hour of peril. On all sides, he was surrounded by hostile armies, while his own forces were dispirited and treacherous.

Wallenstein Reinstated in Power.

From such a hopeless state he was rescued by the man whom he had injured, but not until he had himself to beg his assistance. Wallenstein was in retirement, and secretly rejoiced in the victories of the Swedish king, knowing full well that the emperor would soon be compelled to summon him again to command his armies. Now he could dictate his terms. Now he could humiliate his sovereign, and at the same time obtain all the power his ambition craved. He declined entering his service unless he had the unlimited command of all the armies of Austria and Spain. No commission in the army was to be granted by the emperor, without his own approval. He demanded the ordinary pay, and an imperial hereditary estate. In short, he demanded sovereign authority; and with such humiliating terms the emperor, in his necessities, was obliged to comply.

Death of Gustavus Adolphus.

No sooner did he raise his standard, than it was resorted to by the unprincipled, the rapacious, and the needy from all parts of the empire. But Wallenstein now resolved to pursue, exclusively, his own selfish interests, and directed all his aims to independent sovereignty. When his forces were united with those of Maximilian, he found himself at the head of sixty thousand men. Then really commenced the severity of the contest, for Wallenstein was now stronger than Gustavus. Nevertheless, the heroic Swede offered to give his rival battle at Nuremburg, which was declined. He then attacked his camp, but was repulsed with loss. At last, the two generals met on the plains of Lutzen, in Saxony, 1632. During the whole course of the war, two such generals had not been pitted against each other, nor had so much been staked on the chance of a battle. Victory declared for the troops of Gustavus, but the heroic leader himself was killed, in the fulness of his glory. It was his fortune to die with an untarnished fame. "By an untimely death," says Schiller, "his protecting genius rescued him from the inevitable fate of man—that of forgetting moderation in the intoxication of success, and justice in the plenitude of power. It may be doubted whether, had he lived longer, he would still have deserved the tears which Germany shed over his grave, or maintained his title to the admiration with which posterity regards him,—as the first and only just conqueror that the world has produced. But it was no longer the benefactor of Germany who fell at Lutzen; the beneficent part of his career Gustavus Adolphus had already terminated; and now the greatest service which he could render to the liberties of Germany was—to die. The all-engrossing power of an individual was at an end; the equivocal assistance of an over-powerful protector gave place to a more noble self-exertion on the part of the estates; and those who formerly were the mere instruments of his aggrandizement, now began to work for themselves. The ambition of the Swedish monarch aspired, unquestionably, to establish a power within Germany inconsistent with the liberties of the estates. His aim was the imperial crown; and this dignity, supported by his power, would be liable to more abuse than had ever been feared from the house of Austria. His sudden disappearance secured the liberties of Germany, and saved his own reputation, while it probably spared him the mortification of seeing his own allies in arms against him, and all the fruits of his victories torn from him by a disadvantageous peace."

Assassination of Wallenstein.

After the battle of Lutzen we almost lose sight of Wallenstein, and no victories were commensurate with his reputation and abilities. He continued inactive in Bohemia, while all Europe was awaiting the exploits which should efface the remembrance of his defeat. He exhausted the imperial provinces by enormous contributions, and his whole conduct seems singular and treacherous. His enemies at the imperial court now renewed their intrigues, and his conduct was reviewed with the most malicious criticism. But he possessed too great power to be openly assailed by the emperor, and measures were concerted to remove him by treachery. Wallenstein obtained notice of the designs against him, and now, too late, resolved on an open revolt. But he was betrayed, and his own generals, on whom he counted, deserted him, so soon as the emperor dared to deprive him of his command. But he was only removed by assassination, and just at the moment when he deemed himself secure against the whole power of the emperor. No man, however great, can stand before an authority which is universally deemed legitimate, however reduced and weakened that authority may be. In times of anarchy and revolution, there is confusion in men's minds respecting the persons in whom legitimate authority should be lodged, and this is the only reason why rebellion is ever successful.

Treaty of Westphalia.

The death of Wallenstein, in 1634, did not terminate the war. It raged eleven years longer, with various success, and involved the other European powers. France was then governed by Cardinal Richelieu, who, notwithstanding his Catholicism, lent assistance to the Protestants, with a view of reducing the power of Austria. Indeed, the war had destroyed the sentiments which produced it, and political motives became stronger than religious. Oxenstiern and Richelieu became the master spirits of the contest, and, in the recesses of their cabinets, regulated the campaigns of their generals. Battles were lost and won on both sides, and innumerable intrigues were plotted by interested statesmen. After all parties had exhausted their resources, and Germany was deluged with the blood of Spaniards, Hollanders, Frenchmen, Swedes, besides that of her own sons, the peace of Westphalia was concluded, (1648,)—the most important treaty in the history of Europe. All the princes and states of the empire were reëstablished in the lands, rights, and prerogatives which they enjoyed before the troubles in Bohemia, in 1619. The religious liberties of the Lutherans and Calvinists were guaranteed, and it was stipulated that the Imperial Chamber should consist of twenty-four Protestant members and twenty-six Catholic, and that the emperor should receive six Protestants into the Aulic Council, the highest judicial tribunal in the empire. This peace is the foundation of the whole system of modern European politics, of all modern treaties, of that which is called the freedom of Germany, and of a sort of balance of power among all the countries of Western Europe. Dearly was it purchased, by the perfect exhaustion of national energies, and the demoralizing sentiments which one of the longest and bloodiest wars in human history inevitably introduced.

References.—Schiller's History of the Thirty Years' War. Russell's Modern Europe. Coleridge's Translation of Wallenstein. Kohlrausch's History of Germany. See also a history of Germany in Dr. Lardner's Cyclopedia. History of Sweden. Plank on the Political Consequences of the Reformation. The History of Schiller, however is a classic, and is exceedingly interesting and beautiful.

CHAPTER XI
ADMINISTRATIONS OF CARDINALS RICHELIEU AND MAZARIN

While Germany was rent with civil commotions, and the power of the emperors was limited by the stand taken against it by the Protestant princes, France was ruled with an iron hand, and a foundation was laid for the despotism of Louis XIV. The energetic genius of Cardinal Richelieu, during the whole period of the thirty years' war, affected the councils of all the different courts of Europe. He was indisputably the greatest statesman of his age and nation. To him France is chiefly indebted for the ascendency she enjoyed in the seventeenth century. Had Henry IV. lived to the age of Louis XIV., France would probably have been permanently greater, although the power of the king might not have been so absolute.

Regency of Mary de Medicis.

When Henry IV. died, he left his kingdom to his son Louis XIII., a child nine years of age. The first thing to be done was the appointment of a regent. The Parliament of Paris, in whom this right seems to have been vested, nominated the queen mother, Mary de Medicis, and the young king, in a bed of justice,—the greatest of the royal prerogatives,—confirmed his mother in the regency. Her regency was any thing but favorable to the interests of the kingdom. The policy of the late king was disregarded, and a new course of measures was adopted. Sully, through whose counsels the reign of Henry IV. had been so beneficent, was dismissed. The queen regent had no sympathy with his views. Neither the corrupt court nor the powerful aristocracy cared any thing for the interests of the people, for the improvement of agriculture, commerce, and manufactures, for the regulation of the finances, or for increasing the productive industry of the country, on which its material prosperity ever depends. The greedy courtiers obtained from a lavish queen the treasures which the wise care of Henry had amassed, and which he thoughtlessly bestowed in order to secure their fidelity. The foreign policy also was changed, and a strong alliance was made with the pope, with Spain, and with the Jesuits.

On the retirement of the able and incorruptible Sully, favorites of no talent or worth arose to power. Concini, an Italian, controlled the queen regent, and through him all her favors flowed. He was succeeded by Luynes, a mere falconer, who made himself agreeable to the young king, and usurped the power of Concini, when the king attained his majority. He became constable of France, the highest officer in the realm, and surpassed all the old nobility in arrogance and cupidity. His mismanagement and selfishness led to an insurrection of some of the great nobles among whom were Condé and D'Épernon.

Rise of Cardinal de Richelieu.

While the kingdom was thus convulsed with civil war, and in every way mismanaged, Richelieu, Bishop of Luçon, appeared upon the stage. He was a man of high birth, was made doctor of the Sorbonne at the age of twenty-two, and, before he was twenty-five, a bishop. During the ascendency of Mancini, he attracted the attention of the queen, and was selected as secretary of state. Soon after the death of Luynes, he obtained a cardinal's hat, and a seat in the council. The moment he spoke, his genius predominated, and the monarch, with all his pride, bowed to the ascendency of intellect, and yielded, with a good grace, to a man whom it was impolitic to resist.

From that moment, in 1622, the reins of empire were in the hands of a master, and the king himself, were it not for the splendor of his court, would have disappeared from the eye, both of statesmen and historians. The reign of anarchy, for a quarter of a century, at least, was over, and the way was prepared for the aggrandizement of the French monarchy. When Richelieu came into power, universal disorder prevailed. The finances were deranged, the Huguenots were troublesome, and the nobles were rebellious. Such was the internal state of France,—weakened, distracted, and anarchical. She had lost her position among the great powers, and Austria threatened to overturn the political relations of all the states of Europe. Austria, in the early part of the seventeenth century, was, unquestionably, the leading power in Christendom, and her ascendency boded no good to the liberties which men were beginning to assert.

Suppression of the Huguenots.

Three great objects animated the genius of Richelieu, and in the attainment of these he was successful. These were, the suppression of the Huguenots, as a powerful party, the humiliation of the great barons, and the reduction of the power of Austria. For these objects he perseveringly contended for twenty years; and his struggles and intrigues to secure these ends constitute the history of France during the reign of Louis XIII. And they affected not only France, but the whole continent. His policy was to preserve peace with England and Spain,—the hereditary enemies of France,—with Sweden, and with the Protestants of Germany, even while he suppressed their religion within his own realm. It was the true policy of England to prevent the ruin of the Huguenots in France, as before she had aided the Protestants in Holland. But, unfortunately, England was then ruled by James and Charles, and they were controlled by profligate ministers, who were the tools of the crafty cardinal. A feeble assistance was rendered by James, but it availed nothing.

In order to annihilate the political power of the Huguenots,—for Richelieu cared more for this than for their religious opinions,—it was necessary that he should possess himself of the city of La Rochelle, on the Bay of Biscay, a strong fortress, which had resisted, during the reign of Charles IX., the whole power of the Catholics, and which continued to be the stronghold of the Huguenots. Here they could always retire and be safe, in times of danger. It was strongly fortified by sea, as well as by land; and only a vigorous blockade could exclude provisions and military stores from the people. But England was mistress of the ocean, and supplies from her would always relieve the besieged.

After ineffectual but vigorous attempts to take the city by land, Richelieu determined to shut up its harbor, first by stakes, and then by a boom. Both of these measures failed. But the military genius of the cardinal was equal to his talents as a statesman. He remembered what Alexander did at the siege of Tyre. So, with a volume of Quintus Curtius in his hand, he projected and finished a mole, half a mile in length, across a gulf, into which the tide flowed. In some places, it was eight hundred and forty feet below the surface of the water, and sixty feet in breadth. At first, the besieged laughed at an attempt so gigantic and difficult. But the work steadily progressed, and the city was finally cut off from communication with the sea. The besieged, wasted by famine, surrendered; the fortifications were destroyed, the town lost its independence, and the power of the Huguenots was broken forever. But no vengeance was taken on the heroic citizens, and they were even permitted to enjoy their religion. Fifteen thousand, however, perished at this memorable siege.

The next object of Richelieu was the humiliation of Austria. But the detail of his military operations would be complicated and tedious, since no grand and decisive battles were fought by his generals, and no able commanders appeared. Turenne and Condé belonged to the next age. The military operations consisted in frontier skirmishes, idle sieges, and fitful expeditions, in which, however, the cardinal had the advantage, and by which he gained, since he could better afford to pay for them. War is always ruinously expensive, and that party generally is successful which can the longer furnish resources. It is a proof that religious bigotry did not mainly influence him, since he supported the Protestant party. All motives of a religious kind were absorbed in his prevailing passion to aggrandize the French monarchy. Had it not been for the intrigues and forces of Richelieu, the peace of Westphalia might not have been secured, and Austria might again have overturned the "Balance of Power."

The Depression of the Great Nobles.

The third great aim of the minister, and the one which he most systematically pursued to the close of his life, was the depression of the nobles, whose power was dangerously exercised. They had almost feudal privileges, were enormously wealthy, numerous, corrupt, and dissolute. His efforts to suppress their power raised up numerous conspiracies.

Among the earliest was one supported by the queen mother and Gaston, Duke of Orleans, brother to the king, and presumptive heir to the throne. Connected with this conspiracy were the Dukes of Bourbon and Vendome, the Prince de Chalais, and several others of the highest rank. It was intended to assassinate the cardinal and seize the reins of government. But he got timely notice of the plot, informed the king, and guarded himself. The conspirators were too formidable to be punished in a body; so he dissembled and resolved to cut them off in detail. He moreover threatened the king with resignation, and frightened him by predicting a civil war. In consequence, the king gave orders to arrest his brothers, the Dukes of Bourbon and Vendome, while the Prince of Chalais was executed. The Duke of Orleans, on the confession of Chalais, fled from the kingdom. The queen mother was arrested, Bassompierre was imprisoned in the Bastile, and the Duke of Guise sent on a pilgrimage to Rome. The powerful D'Épernon sued for pardon.

Still Richelieu was not satisfied. He resolved to humble the parliament, because it had opposed an ordinance of the king declaring the partisans of the Duke of Orleans guilty of treason. It had rightly argued that such a condemnation could not be issued without a trial. "But," said the artful minister to the weak-minded king, "to refuse to verify a declaration which you yourself announced to the members of parliament, is to doubt your authority." An extraordinary council was convened, and the parliament, which was simply a court of judges, was summoned to the royal presence. They went in solemn procession, carrying with them the record which showed their refusal to register the edict. The king received them with stately pomp. They were required to kneel in his presence, and their decree was taken from the record and torn in pieces before their eyes, and the leading members were suspended and banished.

The Court of Aids, by whom the money edicts were registered, also showed opposition. The members left the court when the next edict was to be registered. But they were suspended, until they humbly came to terms.

"All the malcontents, the queen, the prince, the nobles, the parliament, and the Court of Aids hoped for the support of the people, and all were disappointed." And this is the reason why they failed and Richelieu triumphed. There never have been, among the French, disinterestedness and union in the cause of liberty, which never can be gained without perseverance and self-sacrifice.

The next usurpation of Richelieu was the erection of a new tribunal for trying state criminals, in which no record of its proceedings should be preserved, and the members of which should be selected by himself. This court was worse than that of the Star Chamber.

Richelieu showed a still more culpable disregard of the forms of justice in the trial of Marshal Marrillac, charged with crimes in the conduct of the army. He was brought before a commission, and not before his peers, condemned, and executed.

In view of this judicial murder, the nobles, generally, were filled with indignation and alarm. They now saw that the minister aimed at the complete humiliation of their order, and therefore made another effort to resist the cardinal. At the head of this conspiracy was the Duke of Montmorency, admiral and constable of France, one of the most powerful nobles in the kingdom. He was governor of Provence, and deeply resented the insult offered to his rank in the condemnation of Marrillac. He moreover felt indignant that the king's brother should be driven into exile by the hostility of a priest. He therefore joined his forces with those of the Duke of Orleans, was defeated, tried, and executed for rebellion, against the entreaty and intercession of the most powerful families.

Power of Richelieu.

The cardinal minister was now triumphant over all his enemies. He had destroyed the political power of the Huguenots, extended the boundary of France, and decimated the nobles. He now turned his attention to the internal administration of the kingdom. He created a national navy, protected commerce and industry, rewarded genius, and formed the French Academy. He attained a greater pitch of greatness than any subject ever before or since enjoyed in his country, greater even than was possessed by Wolsey. Wolsey, powerful as he was, lived, like a Turkish vizier, in constant fear of his capricious master. But Richelieu controlled the king himself. Louis XIII. feared him, and felt that he could not reign without him. He did not love the cardinal, and was often tempted to dismiss him, but could never summon sufficient resolution. Richelieu was more powerful than the queen mother, the brothers of the king, the royal mistresses, or even all united, since he obtained an ascendency over all, doomed the queen mother to languish in exile at Cologne, and compelled the duke of Orleans to succumb to him. He was chief of three of the principal monastic orders, and possessed enormous wealth. He erected a palace as grand as Hampton Court, and appeared in public with great pomp and ceremony.

Character of Richelieu.

But an end came to his greatness. In 1642, a mortal malady wasted him away; he summoned to his death bed his royal master; recommended Mazarin as his successor; and died like a man who knew no remorse, in the fifty-eighth year of his age, and the eighteenth of his reign as minister. He was eloquent, but his words served only to disguise his sentiments; he was direct and frank in his speech, and yet a perfect master of the art of dissimulation; he could not be imposed upon, and yet was passionately fond of flattery, which he liked in such large doses that it seemed hyperbolical; he was not learned, yet appreciated learning in others, and magnificently rewarded it; he was fond of pleasure, and easily fascinated by women, and yet was cold, politic, implacable, and cruel. But he was a great statesman, and aimed to suppress anarchy and preserve law. In view of his labors to preserve order, we may almost excuse his severity. "Placed," says Montrésor, as quoted by Miss Pardoe, "at an equal distance between Louis IX., whose aim was to abolish feudality, and the national convention, whose attempt was to crush aristocracy, he appeared, like them, to have received a mission of blood from heaven." The high nobility, repulsed under Louis XI. and Francis I., almost entirely succumbed under Richelieu, preparing, by its overthrow, the calm, unitarian, and despotic reign of Louis XIV., who looked around him in vain for a great noble, and found only courtiers. The great rebellion, which, for nearly two centuries, agitated France, almost entirely disappeared under the ministry of the cardinal. The Guises, who had touched with their hand the sceptre of Henry III., the Condés, who had placed their foot on the steps of the throne of Henry IV., and Gaston, who had tried upon his brow the crown of Louis XIII.,—all returned, at the voice of the minister, if not into nothingness, at least into impotency. All who struggled against the iron will, enclosed in that feeble body, were broken like glass. And all the struggle which Richelieu sustained, he did not sustain for his own sake, but for that of France. All the enemies, against whom he contended, were not his enemies merely, but those of the kingdom. If he clung tenaciously by the side of a king, whom he compelled to live a melancholy, unhappy, and isolated life, whom he deprived successively of his friends, of his mistresses, and of his family, as a tree is stripped of its leaves, of its branches, and of its bark, it was because friends, mistresses, and family exhausted the sap of the expiring royalty, which had need of all its egotism to prevent it from perishing. For it was not intestinal struggles merely,—there was also foreign war, which had connected itself fatally with them. All those great nobles whom he decimated, all those princes of the blood whom he exiled, were inviting foreigners to France; and these foreigners, answering eagerly to the summons, were entering the country on three different sides,—the English by Guienne, the Spaniards by Roussillon, and the Austrians by Artois.

Effects of Richelieu's Policy.

"He repulsed the English by driving them to the Isle of Ré, and by besieging La Rochelle; the Spaniards, by creating beside them the new kingdom of Portugal; and the imperialists, by detaching Bavaria from its alliance, by suspending their treaty with Denmark, and by sowing dissensions in the Catholic league. His measures were cruel, but not uncalled for. Chalais fell, but he had conspired with Lorraine and Spain; Montmorency fell, but he had entered France with arms in his hand; Cinq-Mars fell, but he had invited foreigners into the kingdom. Bred a simple priest, he became not only a great statesman, but a great general. And when La Rochelle fell before those measures to which Schomberg and Bassompierre were compelled to bow, he said to the king, 'Sire, I am no prophet, but I assure your majesty that if you will condescend to act as I advise, you will pacificate Italy in the month of May, subjugate Languedoc in the month of July, and be on your return in the month of August.' And each of these prophecies he accomplished in its time and place, and in such wise that, from that moment, Louis XIII. vowed to follow forever the counsels of a man by which he had so well profited. Finally, he died, as Montesquieu asserts, after having made the monarch enact the secondary character in the monarchy, but the first in Europe; after having abased the king, but after having made his reign illustrious; and after having mowed down rebellion so close to the soil, that the descendants of those who had composed the league could only form the Fronde, as, after the reign of Napoleon, the successors of the La Vendée of '93 could only execute the Vendée of '32."

Louis XIII. did not long survive this greatest of ministers. Naturally weak, he was still weaker by disease. He was reduced to skin and bone. In this state, he called a council, nominated his queen, Anne of Austria, regent, during the minority of his son Louis XIV., then four years of age, and shortly after died, in 1643.

Richelieu's Policy.

Mazarin, the new minister, followed out the policy of Richelieu. The war with Austria and Spain was continued, which was closed, on the

Spanish side, by the victory of Rocroi, in 1643, obtained by the Prince of Condé, and in which battle twenty-three thousand Frenchmen completely routed twenty-six thousand Spaniards, killing eight thousand, and taking six thousand prisoners—one of the bloodiest battles ever fought. The great Condé here obtained those laurels which subsequent disgrace could never take away. The war on the side of Germany was closed, in 1648, by the peace of Westphalia. Turenne first appeared in the latter campaign of this long war, but gained no signal victory.

Cardinal Mazarin, a subtle and intriguing Italian, while he pursued the policy of Richelieu, had not his genius or success. He was soon involved in domestic troubles. The aristocracy rebelled. Had they been united, they would have succeeded; but their rivalries, jealousies, and squabbles divided their strength and distracted their councils. Their cause was lost, and Mazarin triumphed, more from their divisions than from his own strength.

He first had to oppose a clique of young nobles, full of arrogance and self-conceit, but scions of the greatest families. They hoped to recover the ancient ascendency of their houses. The chief of these were the Dukes of Beaufort, Épernon, and Guise. They made use, as their tool, of Madame Chevreuse, the confidential friend of the queen regent. And she demanded of the minister that posts of honor and power should be given to her friends, which would secure that independence which Richelieu had spent his life in restraining. Mazarin tried to amuse her, but, she being inexorable, he was obliged to break with her, and a conspiracy was the result, which, however, was easily suppressed.

Cardinal de Retz.

But a more formidable enemy appeared in the person of De Retz, coadjutor archbishop of Paris, and afterwards cardinal, a man of boundless intrigue, unconquerable ambition, and restless discontent. To detail his plots and intrigues, would be to describe a labyrinth. He succeeded, however, in keeping the country in perpetual turmoil, now inflaming the minds of the people, then exciting insurrections among the nobles, and then, again, encouraging the parliaments in resistance. He never appeared as an actor, but every movement was directed by his genius. He did not escape suspicion, but committed no overt acts by which he could be punished. He and the celebrated Duchess de Longueville, a woman who had as great a talent for intrigue as himself, were the life and soul of the Fronde—a civil war which ended only in the reëstablishment of the monarchy on a firmer foundation. As the Fronde had been commenced by a troop of urchins, who, at the same time, amused themselves with slings, the wits of the court called the insurgents *frondeurs*, or slingers, insinuating that their force was trifling, and their aim mischief.

Prince of Condé.

Nevertheless, the Frondeurs kept France in a state of anarchy for six years, and they were headed by some of the most powerful nobles, and even supported by the Parliament of Paris. The people, too, were on the side of the rebels, since they were ground down by taxation, and hoped to gain a relief from their troubles. But the rebels took the side of the oppressed only for their private advantage, and the parliament itself lacked the perseverance and intrepidity necessary to secure its liberty. The civil war of the Fronde, though headed by discontented nobles, and animated by the intrigues of a turbulent ecclesiastic, was really the contest between the parliament and the arbitrary power of the government. And the insurrection would have been fearful and successful, had the people been firm or the nobles faithful to the cause they defended. But the English Revolution, then in progress, and in which a king had been executed, shocked the lovers of constitutional liberty in France, and reacted then, even as the French Revolution afterwards reacted on the English mind. Moreover, the excesses which the people perpetrated at Paris, alarmed the parliament and the nobles who were allied with it, while it urged on the ministers to desperate courses. The prince of Condé, whose victories had given him an immortality, dallied with both parties, as his interests served. Allied with the court, he could overpower the insurgents; but allied with the insurgents, he could control the court. Sometimes he sided with the minister and sometimes with the insurgents, but in neither case unless he exercised a power and enjoyed a remuneration dangerous in any government. Both parties were jealous of him, both feared him, both hated him, both insulted him, and both courted him. At one time, he headed the royal troops to attack Paris, which was generally in the hands of the people and of parliament; and then, at another, he fought like a tiger to defend himself in Paris against the royal troops. He had no sympathy with either the parliament or the people, while he fought for them; and he venerated the throne, while he rebelled against it. His name was Louis de Bourbon, and he was a prince of the blood. He contended against the crown only to wrest from it the ancient power of the great nobles; and to gain this object, he thought to make the parliament and the Parisian mob his tools. The parliament, sincerely devoted to liberty, thought to make the nobles its tools, and only leagued with them to secure their services. The crafty Mazarin quietly beheld these dissensions, and was sure of ultimate success, even though at one time banished to Cologne. And, like a reed, he was ever ready to bend to difficulties he could not control. But he stooped to conquer. He at last got the Prince of Condé, his brother the Prince of Conti, and the

Duke of Longueville, in his power. When the Duke of Orleans heard of it, he said, "He has taken a good haul in the net; he has taken a lion, a fox, and a monkey." But the princes escaped from the net, and, leagued with Turenne, Bouillon, La Rochefoucault, and other great nobles reached Paris, and were received with acclamations of joy by the misguided people. Then, again, they obtained the ascendant. But the ascendency was no sooner gained than the victors quarrelled with themselves, and with the parliament, for whose cause they professed to contend. It was in their power, when united, to have deprived the queen regent of her authority, and to have established constitutional liberty in France. But they would not unite. There was no spirit of disinterestedness, nor of patriotism, nor public virtue, without which liberty is impossible, even though there were forces enough to batter down Mount Atlas. Condé, the victor, suffered himself to be again bribed by the court. He would not persevere in his alliance with either nobles or the parliament. He did not unite with the nobles because he felt that he was a prince. He did not continue with the parliament, because he had no sympathy with freedom. The cause of the nobles was lost for want of mutual confidence; that of the parliament for lack of the spirit of perseverance. The parliament, at length, grew weary of war and of popular commotions, and submitted to the court. All parties hated and distrusted each other, more than they did the iron despotism of Mazarin. The power of insurgent nobles declined. De Retz, the arch intriguer, was driven from Paris. The Duchess de Longueville sought refuge in the vale of Port Royal; and, in the Jansenist doctrines, sought that happiness which earthly grandeur could not secure. Condé quitted Paris to join the Spanish armies. The rest of the rebellious nobles made humble submission. The people found they had nothing to gain from any dominant party, and resigned themselves to another long period of political and social slavery. The magistrates abandoned, in despair and disgust, their high claims to political rights, while the young king, on his bed of justice, decreed that parliament should no more presume to discuss or meddle with state affairs. The submissive parliament registered, without a murmur, the edict which gave a finishing stroke to its liberties. The Fronde war was a complete failure, because all parties usurped powers which did not belong to them, and were jealous of the rights of each other. The nobles wished to control the king, and the magistracy put itself forward to represent the commons, when the states general alone was the ancient and true representative of the nation, and the body to which it should have appealed. The Fronde rebellion was a failure, because it did not consult constitutional forms, because it formed unnatural alliances, and because it did not throw itself upon the force of immortal principles, but sought to support itself by mere physical strength rather than by moral power, which alone is the secret and the glory of all great internal changes.

Power of Mazarin.

The return of Cardinal Mazarin to power, as the minister of Louis XIV., was the era of his grandeur. His first care was to restore the public finances; his second was to secure his personal aggrandizement. He obtained all the power which Richelieu had enjoyed, and reproved the king, and such a king as Louis XIV., as he would a schoolboy. He enriched and elevated his relatives, married them into the first families of France; and amassed a fortune of two hundred millions of livres, the largest perhaps that any subject has secured in modern times. He even aspired to the popedom; but this greatest of all human dignities, he was not permitted to obtain. A fatal malady seized him, and the physicians told him he had not two months to live. Some days after, he was seen in his dressing-gown, among his pictures, of which he was extravagantly fond, and exclaimed, "Must I quit all these? Look at that Correggio, this Venus of Titian, this incomparable deluge of Carracci. Farewell, dear pictures, that I have loved so dearly, and that have cost me so much."

Death of Mazarin.

The minister lingered awhile, and amused his last hours with cards. He expired in 1661; and no minister after him was intrusted with such great power. He died unlamented, even by his sovereign, whose throne he had preserved, and whose fortune he had repaired. He had great talents of conversation, was witty, artful, and polite. He completed the work which Richelieu began; and, at his death, his master was the most absolute monarch that ever reigned in France.

References.—Louis XIV. et son Siècle. Miss Pardoe's History of Louis XIV. Voltaire's and James's Lives of Louis XIV. Memoirs of Cardinal Richelieu. Memoirs of Mazarin. Mémoires de Mademoiselle de Montpensier. Mémoires du Duc de Saint Simon. Life of Cardinal de Retz, in which the Fronde war is well traced. Memoir of the Duchess de Longueville. Lacretelle's History of France. Rankin's History of France. Sismondi's History of France. Crowe's History, in Lardner's Cyclopedia. Rowring's History of the Huguenots. Lord Mahon's Life of the Prince of Condé. The above works are the most accessible to the American student.

CHAPTER XII
THE REIGNS OF JAMES I. AND CHARLES I

While the Protestants in Germany were struggling for religious liberty, and the Parliaments of France for political privileges, there was a contest going on in England for the attainment of the same great ends. With the accession of James I. a new era commences in English history, marked by the growing importance of the House of Commons, and their struggles for civil and religious liberty. The Commons had not been entirely silent during the long reign of Elizabeth, but members of them occasionally dared to assert those rights of which Englishmen are proud. The queen was particularly sensitive to any thing which pertained to her prerogative, and generally sent to the Tower any man who boldly expressed his opinion on subjects which she deemed that she and her ministers alone had the right to discuss. These forbidden subjects were those which pertained to the management of religion, to her particular courts, and to her succession to the crown. She never made an attack on what she conceived to be the constitution, but only zealously defended what she considered as her own rights. And she was ever sufficiently wise to yield a point to the commons, after she had asserted her power, so that concession, on her part, had all the appearance of bestowing a favor. She never pushed matters to extremity, but gave way in good time. And in this policy she showed great wisdom; so that, in spite of all her crimes and caprices, she ever retained the affections of the English people.

Accession of James I.

The son of her rival Mary Stuart, Queen of Scots, ascended the throne, (1603,) under the title of *James I.*, and was the first of the Stuart kings. He had been king of Scotland under the title of *James VI.*, and had there many difficulties to contend with, chiefly in consequence of the turbulence of the nobles, and the bigotry of the reformers. He was eager to take possession of his English inheritance, but was so poor that he could not begin his journey until Cecil sent him the money. He was crowned, with great ceremony, in Westminster Abbey, on the 25th of June.

The first acts of his reign were unpopular; and it was subsequently disgraced by a continual succession of political blunders. To detail these, or to mention all the acts of this king, or the events of his inglorious reign would fill a volume larger than this History. Moreover, from this period, modern history becomes very complicated and voluminous, and all that can be attempted in this work is, an allusion to the principal events.

The Genius of the Reign of James.

The genius of this reign is the contest between *royal prerogative and popular freedom*. The proceedings in parliament were characterized by a spirit of boldness and resistance never before manifested, while the speeches and acts of the king were marked by an obstinate and stupid pertinacity to those privileges which absolute kings extorted from their subjects in former ages of despotism and darkness. The boldness of the Commons and the bigotry of the king led to incessant disagreement and discontent; and, finally, under Charles I., to open rupture, revolution, and strife.

The progress of this insurrection and contest furnishes one of the most important and instructive chapters in the history of society and the young student cannot make himself too familiar with details, of which our limits forbid a description.

The great Puritan contest here begins, destined not to be closed until after two revolutions, and nearly a century of anxiety, suffering, and strife. Providence raised up, during the whole of the Stuart dynasty, great patriots and statesmen, who had an eye to perceive the true interests and rights of the people, and a heart and a hand to defend them. No period and no nation have ever been more fertile in great men than England was from the accession of James I. to the abdication of James II., a period of eighty-five years. Shakspeare, Raleigh, Coke, Bacon, Cecil, Selden, Pym, Wentworth, Hollis, Leighton, Taylor, Baxter, Howe, Cromwell, Hampden, Blake, Vane, Milton, Clarendon, Burnet, Shaftesbury, are some of the luminaries which have shed a light down to our own times, and will continue to shine through all future ages. They were not all contemporaneous, but they all took part, more or less, on one side or the other, in the great contest of the seventeenth century. Whether statesmen, warriors, poets, or divines, they alike made their age an epoch, and their little island the moral centre of the world.

But we must first allude to some of the events of the reign of James I., before the struggle between prerogative and liberty attracted the attention of Europe.

Conspiracy of Sir Walter Raleigh.

One of the first was the conspiracy against the king, in which Lord Cobham and Sir Walter Raleigh were engaged. We lament that so great a favorite with all readers as Sir Walter Raleigh, so universal a genius, a man so learned, accomplished, and brave, should have even been suspected of a treasonable project, and without the excuse of some traitors, that they wished to deliver their country from tyranny. But there is no perfection in man. Sir Walter was restless and ambitious, and had an eye mainly to his own advantage. His wit, gallantry, and chivalry were doubtless very pleasing qualities in a courtier, but are not the best qualities of a patriot. He was disappointed because he could not keep pace with Cecil in the favor of his sovereign, and because the king took away the monopolies he had enjoyed. Hence, in conjunction with other disappointed politicians, he was accused of an attempt to seize the king's person, to change the ministry, and to place the Lady Arabella Stuart on the throne. Against Raleigh appeared no less a person than the great Coke, who prosecuted him with such vehemence that Raleigh was found guilty, and condemned to death. But the proofs of his guilt are not so clear as the evidence of his ambition; and much must be attributed to party animosity. Though condemned, he was not executed; but lived to write many more books, and make many more voyages, to the great delight both of the cultivated and the adventurous. That there was a plot to seize the king is clear, and the conspirators were detected and executed. Raleigh was suspected of this, and perhaps was privy to it; but the proofs of his crime were not apparent, except to the judges, and to the attorney-general, Coke, who compared the different plots to Samson's foxes, joined in the tails, though their heads were separated.

Gunpowder Plot.

Persecution of the Catholics.

The most memorable event at this time in the domestic history of the kingdom was the Gunpowder Plot, planned by Catesby and other disappointed and desperate Catholics for the murder of the king, and the destruction of both houses of parliament. Knowing the sympathies of James for their religion, the Catholics had expected toleration, at least. But when persecution continued against them, some reckless and unprincipled men united in a design to blow up the parliament. Percy, a relation of the Earl of Northumberland, was concerned in the plot, and many of the other conspirators were men of good families and fortunes, but were implacable bigots. They hired a cellar, under the parliament house, which had been used for coals; and there they deposited thirty-one barrels of gunpowder, waiting several months for a favorable time to perpetrate one of the most horrid crimes ever projected. It was resolved that Guy Fawkes, one of the number, should set fire to the train. They were all ready, and the 5th of November,

1605, was at hand, the day to which parliament was prorogued; but Percy was anxious to save *his* kinsman from the impending ruin, Sir Everard Digby wished to warn some of *his* friends, and Tresham was resolved to give *his* brother-in-law, Lord Mounteagle, a caution. It seems that this peer received a letter so peculiar, that he carried it to Cecil, who showed it to the king, and the king detected or suspected a plot. The result was, that the cellar was explored by the lord chamberlain, and Guy Fawkes himself was found, with all the materials for striking a light, near the vault in which the coal and the gunpowder were deposited. He was seized, interrogated, tortured, and imprisoned; but the wretch would not reveal the names of his associates, although he gloried in the crime he was about to commit, and alleged, as his excuse, that violent diseases required desperate remedies, the maxim of the Jesuits. But most of the conspirators revealed their guilt by flight. They might have escaped, had they fled from the kingdom; but they hastened only into the country to collect their friends, and head an insurrection, which, of course, was easily suppressed. The leaders in this plot were captured and executed, and richly deserved their fate, although it was clear that they were infatuated. But in all crime there is infatuation. It was suspected that the Jesuits were at the bottom of the conspiracy; and the whole Catholic population suffered reproach from the blindness and folly of a few bigots, from whom no sect or party ever yet has been free. But there is no evidence that any of the Catholic clergy were even privy to the intended crime, which was known only to the absolute plotters. Some Jesuits were indeed suspected, arrested, tortured, and executed; but no evidence of guilt was brought against them sufficient to convict them. But their acquittal was impossible in such a state of national alarm and horror. Nothing ever made a more lasting and profound impression on the English mind than this intended crime; and it strengthened the prejudices against the Catholics even more than the persecutions under Queen Mary. Had the crime been consummated, it would only have proved a blunder. It would have shocked and irritated the nation beyond all self-control; and it is probable that the whole Catholic population would have been assassinated, or hunted out, as victims for the scaffold, in every corner of England. It proved, however, a great misfortune, and the severest blow Catholicism ever received in England. Thus God overrules all human wickedness. There was one person who suffered, in consequence of the excited suspicions of the nation, whose fate we cannot but compassionate; and this person was the Earl of Northumberland, who was sentenced to pay a fine of thirty thousand pounds, to be deprived of all his offices, and to be imprisoned in the Tower for life, and simply because he was the head of the Catholic party, and a promoter of toleration. Indeed, penal statutes against the Catholics were fearfully multiplied. No Catholic was permitted to appear at court, or live in

London, or within ten miles of it, or remove, on any occasion, more than five miles from his home, without especial license. No Catholic recusant was permitted to practise surgery, physic, or law; to act as judge, clerk, or officer of any court or corporation; or perform the office of administrator, executor, or guardian. Every Catholic who refused to have his child baptized by a Protestant, was obliged to pay, for each omission, one hundred pounds. Every person keeping a Catholic servant, was compelled to pay ten pounds a month to government. Moreover, every recusant was outlawed; his house might be broken open; his books and furniture destroyed; and his horses and arms taken from him. Such was the severe treatment with which the Catholics, even those who were good citizens, were treated by our fathers in England; and this persecution was defended by some of the greatest jurists, divines, and statesmen which England has produced. And yet some maintain that there has been no progress in society, except in material civilization!

One of the peculiarities of the reign of James was, the ascendency which favorites obtained over him, so often the mark of a weak and vacillating mind. Henry VIII. and Elizabeth had their favorites; but they were ministers of the royal will. Moreover, they, like Wolsey, Cromwell, Burleigh, and Essex, were great men, and worthy of the trust reposed in them. But James, with all his kingcraft and statecraft, with all his ostentation and boasts of knowledge and of sagacity, reposed his confidence in such a man as Villiers, Duke of Buckingham. It is true he also had great men to serve him; Cecil was his secretary, Bacon was his chancellor, and Coke was his chief justice. But Carr and Villiers rose above them all in dignity and honor, and were the companions and confidential agents of their royal master.

Robert Carr, Earl of Somerset.

Greatness and Fall of Somerset.

Robert Carr was a Scottish gentleman, poor and cunning, who had early been taught that personal beauty, gay dress, and lively manners, would make his fortune at court. He first attracted the attention of the king at a tilting match, at which he was the esquire to Lord Dingwall. In presenting his lord's shield to the king, his horse fell and threw him at James's feet. His leg was broken, but his fortune was made. James, struck with his beauty and youth, and moved by the accident, sent his own surgeon to him, visited him himself, and even taught him Latin, seeing that the scholastic part of his education had been neglected. Indeed, James would have made a much better schoolmaster than king; and his pedantry and conceit were beyond all bounds, so that Bacon styled him, either in irony or sycophancy, "the Solomon of the age." Carr now became the pet of the learned monarch. He was knighted, rich presents were bestowed on him, all bowed down to him as they would have done to a royal mistress; and Cecil and Suffolk vied with each other in their attempts to secure the favor of his friends. He gradually eclipsed every great noble at court, was created Viscount Rochester, received the Order of the Garter, and, when Cecil, then Earl of Salisbury, died, received the post of the Earl of Suffolk as lord chamberlain, he taking Cecil's place as treasurer. Rochester, in effect, became prime minister, as Cecil had been. He was then created Earl of Somerset, in order that he might marry the Countess of Essex, the most beautiful and fascinating woman at the English court. She was daughter of the Earl of Suffolk, and granddaughter of the old Duke of Norfolk, executed in 1572, and, consequently, belonged to the first family in the realm. She was married to Essex at the age of thirteen, but treated him with contempt and coldness, being already enamored of the handsome favorite. That she might marry Carr she obtained a divorce from her husband on the most frivolous grounds, and through the favor of the king, who would do any thing for the man he delighted to honor. She succeeded in obtaining her end, and caused the ruin of all who opposed her wishes. But she proved a beautiful demon, a fascinating fury, as might be expected from such an unprincipled woman, although ennobled by "the blood of all the Howards." Her reign lasted, however, only during the ascendency of her husband. For a time, "glorious days were succeeded by as glorious nights, when masks and dancings had a continual motion, and when banquetings rapt up the spirit of the sacred king, and kept it from descending to earthly things." But whatever royal favor stamps, royal favor, like fashion, leaves. Carr was supplanted by Villiers, and his doom was sealed. For the murder of his old friend Sir Thomas Overbury, who died in the Tower, as it was then supposed by poison, he and his countess were tried, found guilty, and disgraced. But he was not executed, and, after a few years' imprisonment, retired to the country, with his lady, to reproach and hate each other. Their only child, the Lady Anna Carr, a woman of great honor and virtue, married the first duke of Bedford, and was the mother of Lord Russell who died on the scaffold, a martyr to liberty, in the reign of Charles II. The origin of the noble families of England is curious. Some few are descended from successful Norman chieftains, who came over with William the Conqueror, and whose merit was in their sword. Others are the descendants of those who, as courtiers, statesmen, or warriors, obtained great position, power, and wealth, during former reigns. Many owe their greatness to the fact that they are the offspring of the illegitimate children of kings, or the descendants of the ignoble minions of kings. Some few are enrolled in the peerage on account of their great wealth; and a still smaller number for the eminent services they have rendered their country like Wellington, Brougham, or Ellenborough. A vast majority can boast only the merit or the successful baseness of their ancestors. But all of them are interlinked by marriages, and therefore share together the glory or the shame of their progenitors, so far as glory and shame can be transmitted from father to son, independently of all individual virtue or vice.

Duke of Buckingham.

Lord Bacon.

Carr was succeeded in the royal favor by Villiers, and he, more fortunate, ever retained the ascendency over the mind and heart of James, as well as of his son Charles I. George Villiers owed his fortune, not to his birth or talents, but to his fine clothes, his Parisian manners, smooth face, tall figure, and bland smiles. He became cup-bearer, then knight, then gentleman of the privy council, then earl, then marquis, and finally duke of Buckingham, lord high admiral, warden of the Cinque Ports, high steward of Westminster, constable of Windsor Castle, and chief justice in eyre of the parks and forests. "The doting and gloating king" had taught Somerset Latin; he attempted to teach Buckingham divinity, and called him ever by the name of "Steenie." And never was there such a mixture of finery, effeminacy, insolence, and sycophancy in any royal minion before or since. Beau Brummell never equalled him in dress, Wolsey in magnificence, Mazarin in peculation, Walpole in corruption, Jeffries in insolence, or Norfolk in pride. He was the constant companion of the king, to whose vices he pandered, and through him the royal favor flowed. But no rewards, or favors, or greatness satisfied him; not so much because he was ambitious, as because, like a spoiled child, he did not appreciate the magnitude of the gifts which were bestowed on him. Nor did he ever know his place; but made love to the queen of France herself, when he was sent on an embassy. He trampled on the constitution, subverted the laws, ground down the people by taxes, and taught the king to disregard the affections of his subjects, and to view them as his slaves. But such a triumph of iniquity could not be endured; and Buckingham was finally assassinated, after he had gained an elevation higher than any English subject ever before attained, except Wolsey, and without the exercise of any qualities which entitled him to a higher position than a master of ceremonies at a fashionable ball. It is easy to conceive that such a minion should arrive at power under such a monarch as James; but how can we understand that such a man as Lord Bacon, the chancellor, the philosopher, the statesman, the man of learning, genius, and wisdom, should have bowed down to the dust, in vile subserviency, to this infamous favorite of the king. Surely, what lessons of the frailty of human nature does the reign of James teach us! The most melancholy instance of all the singular cases of human inconsistency, at this time, is the conduct of the great Bacon himself, who reached the zenith of his power during this reign. It is not the receiving of a bribe, while exercising the highest judicial authority in the land, on which alone his shame rests, but his insolent conduct to his inferiors, his acquiescence in wrong, his base and unmanly sycophancy, his ingratitude to his friends and patrons, his intense selfishness and unscrupulous ambition while climbing to power, and, above all, his willingness to be the tool of a despot who trampled on the rights and liberties which God had given him to guard; and this in an age of light, of awakened intelligence, when even his crabbed rival Coke was seeking to explode the abuses of the Dark Ages. But "the difference between the soaring angel and the creeping snake, was but a type of the difference between Bacon the philosopher and Bacon the attorney-general, Bacon seeking for truth and Bacon seeking for the Seals." As the author of the Novum Organum, as the pioneer of modern science, as the calm and patient investigator of nature's laws, as the miner and sapper of the old false systems of philosophy which enslaved the human mind, as the writer for future generations, he has received, as he has deserved, all the glory which admiring and grateful millions can bestow, of his own nation, and of all nations. No name in British annals is more illustrious than his, and none which is shaded with more lasting shame. Pope alone would have given him an immortality as the "wisest, brightest, meanest of mankind." The only defence for the political baseness of Bacon—and this is insufficient—is, that all were base around him. The years when he was in power are among the darkest and most disgraceful in English history.

Trial and Execution of Raleigh.

Allusion has been made to the reign of favorites; but this was but a small part of the evils of the times. Every thing abroad and at home was mismanaged. Patents of monopolies were multiplied; the most grievous exactions were made; indefensible executions were ordered; the laws were perverted; justice was sold; and an ignominious war was closed by a still more ignominious peace. The execution of Raleigh was a disgrace to the king, the court, and the nation, because the manner of it was so cowardly and cruel. He had been convicted, in the early part of the reign, of treason, and committed to the Tower. There he languished twelve years, amusing himself by writing a universal history, and in seeking the elixir of life; for, in the mysteries of chemistry, and in the mazes of historical lore, as in the intrigues of courts, and dangers of camps, he was equally at home.

He was released from his prison in order to take command of an adventurous expedition to Guiana in quest of gold. In a former voyage he had visited the banks of the Oronoco in quest of the city of Manoa, where precious stones and gold existed in exhaustless treasures. That El Dorado he could not find; but now, in prison, he proposed to Secretary Winwood an expedition to secure what he had before sought in vain. The king wavered a while between his cupidity and fear; for, while he longed for gold, as the traveller does for water on the desert of Sahara, he was afraid of giving offence to the Spanish ambassador. But his cupidity was the stronger feeling, and Raleigh was sent with fourteen ships to the coasts of South America. The expedition was in every respect unfortunate to Raleigh and to the king. The gallant commander lost his private fortune and a promising son, 'the Spaniards attacked his armament, his troops mutinied and deserted, and he returned to England, with a sullied fame, to meet a disappointed sovereign and implacable enemies. In such times, failure is tantamount to crime, and Raleigh was tried for offences he never committed. The most glaring injustice, harshness, and sophistry were resorted to, even by Bacon; but still Raleigh triumphantly defended himself. But no innocence or eloquence could save him; and he was executed on the sentence which had been pronounced against him for treason fifteen years before. To such meanness and cowardice did his enemies resort to rid the world of a universal genius, whose crime—if crime he ever committed—had long been consigned to oblivion.

Encroachments of James.

But we cannot longer dwell on the lives of eminent individuals during the reign of James. However interesting may be the details of their fortunes, their history dwindles into insignificance when compared with the great public injuries which an infatuated monarch inflicted. Not cruel in his temper, not stained by personal crimes, quite learned in Greek and Latin, but weak and ignorant of his duties as a king, he was inclined to trespass on the rights of his subjects. As has been already remarked, the genius of his reign was the contest between prerogative and liberty. The Commons did not acquiesce in his measures, or yield to his wishes, as they did during the reign of Elizabeth. He had a notion that the duty of a king was to command, and that of the subject was to obey, in all things; that kings ruled by divine right, and were raised by the Almighty above all law. But such notions were not approved by a parliament which swarmed with Puritans, and who were not careful to conceal their views from the king. They insisted on their privileges as tenaciously as the king insisted on his prerogative, and often came into collision with him. And they instituted an inquiry into monopolies, and attacked the monstrous abuses of purveyance, and the incidents of feudal tenure, by which, among other things, the king became guardian to wards, and received the profits of their estates during their minority. These feudal claims, by which the king, in part, received his revenue, were every year becoming less valuable to the crown, and more offensive to the people. The king, at length, was willing to compound, and make a bargain with the Commons, by which he was to receive two hundred thousand pounds a year, instead of the privileges of wardship, and other feudal rights. But his necessities required additional grants, which the Commons were unwilling to bestow; and the king then resorted to the sale of monopolies and even peerages, sent the more turbulent of the Commons to prison, and frequently dissolved parliament. He was resolved to tax the people if supplies were not granted him, while the Commons maintained that no taxation could be allowed without their consent. Moreover, the Commons refused to grant such supplies as the king fancied he needed, unless certain grievances were redressed, among which was the High Commission Court, an arbitrary tribunal, which fined and imprisoned without appeal. But James, though pressed for money, stood firm to his notions of prerogative, and supplied his most urgent necessities by illegal means. People were dragged to the Star Chamber, on all kinds of accusations, that they might be sentenced to pay enormous fines; new privileges and monopolies were invented, and new dignities created. Baronets, who are hereditary knights, were instituted, and baronetcies were sold for one thousand pounds each.

Quarrel between James and Parliament.

But the monopolies which the king granted, in order to raise money, did not inflame the Commons so much as the projected marriage between the prince of Wales and the infanta of Spain. James flattered himself that this Spanish match, to arrange which he had sent Buckingham to the court of Madrid, would procure the restitution of the Palatinate to the elector, who had been driven from his throne. But the Commons thought differently. They, as well as the people generally, were indignant in view of the inactivity of the government in not sending aid to the distressed Protestants of Germany; and the loss of the Palatinate was regarded as a national calamity. They saw no good which would accrue from an alliance with the enemies and persecutors of these Protestants; but, on the other hand, much evil. As the constitutional guardians, therefore, of the public welfare and liberty, they framed a remonstrance to the king, representing the overgrown power of Austria as dangerous to the liberties of Europe, and entreated his majesty to take up arms against Spain, which was allied with Austria, and by whose wealth Austrian armies were supported.

James was inflamed with indignation at this remonstrance, which militated against all his maxims of government; and he forthwith wrote a letter to the speaker of the House of Commons, commanding him to admonish the members "not to presume to meddle with matters of state which were beyond their capacity, and especially not to touch on his son's marriage." The Commons, not dismayed, and conscious of strength, sent up a new remonstrance in which they affirmed that they *were* entitled to interpose with their counsel in all matters of state, and that entire freedom of speech was their ancient and undoubted right, transmitted from their ancestors. The king, in reply, told the Commons, that "their remonstrance was more like a denunciation of war, than an address of dutiful subjects, and that their pretension to inquire into state affairs was a plenipotence to which none of their ancestors, even during the weakest reigns, had ever dared to aspire." He farther insinuated that their privileges were derived from royal favor. On this, the Commons framed another protest,—that the liberties, franchises, privileges, and jurisdictions of parliament are the ancient and undoubted birthright of Englishmen, and that every member has the right of freedom of speech. This protest they entered upon their journals, upon which James lost all temper, ordered the clerk to bring him the journals, erased the protestation with his own hand, in presence of the judges and the council, and then dissolved the parliament.

Nothing else of note occurred in this reign, except the prosecution of the Spanish match, which was so odious to the nation that Buckingham, to preserve his popularity, broke off the negotiations, and by a system of treachery and duplicity as hateful as were his original efforts to promote the match. War with Spain was the result of the insult offered to the infanta and the court. An alliance was now made with France, and Prince Charles married Henrietta Maria, daughter of Henry IV. The Commons then granted abundant supplies for war, to recover the Palatinate; and liberty of conscience was granted by the monarch, on the demands of Richelieu, to the Catholics—so long and, perseveringly oppressed.

Death of James I.

Shortly after, (March 27, 1625,) King James died at Theobalds, his favorite palace, from a disease produced by anxiety, gluttony, and sweet wines, after a reign in England of twenty-two years; and his son, Charles I., before the breath was out of his body, was proclaimed king in his stead.

The course pursued by James I. was adopted by his son; and, as their reigns were memorable for the same struggle, we shall consider them together until revolution gave the victory to the advocates of freedom.

Charles I. was twenty-five years of age when he began his reign. In a moral and social point of view he was a more respectable man than his father, but had the same absurd notions of the royal prerogative, the same contempt of the people, the same dislike of constitutional liberty, and the same resolution of maintaining the absolute power of the crown, at any cost. He was moreover, perplexed by the same embarrassments, was involved in debt, had great necessities, and was dependent on the House of Commons for aid to prosecute his wars and support the dignity of the crown. But he did not consider the changing circumstances and spirit of the age, and the hostile and turbulent nature of his people. He increased, rather than diminished, the odious monopolies which irritated the nation during the reign of his father; he clung to all the old feudal privileges; he retained the detestable and frivolous Buckingham as his chief minister; and, when Buckingham was assassinated, he chose others even more tyrannical and unscrupulous; he insisted on taxing the people without their consent, threw contempt on parliament, and drove the nation to rebellion. In all his political acts he was infatuated, after making every allowance for the imperfections of human nature. A wiser man would have seen the rising storm, and might possibly have averted it. But Charles never dreamed of it, until it burst in all its fury on his devoted head, and consigned him to the martyr's grave. We pity his fate, but lament still more his blindness. And so great was this blindness, that it almost seems as if Providence had marked him out to be a victim on the altar of human progress.

With the reign of Charles commences unquestionably the most exciting period of English history, and a period to which historians have given more attention than to any other great historical era, the French Revolution alone excepted. The attempt to describe the leading events in this exciting age and reign would be, in this connection, absurd; and yet some notice of them cannot be avoided.

The Struggle of Classes.

For more than ten centuries, great struggles have been going on in society between the dominant orders and sects. The victories gained by the oppressed millions, over their different masters, constitute what is called the Progress of Society. Defenders of the people have occasionally arisen from orders to which they did not belong. When, then, any great order defended the cause of the people against the tyranny and selfishness of another order, then the people have advanced a step in civil and social freedom.

When Feudalism weighed fearfully upon the people, "the clergy sought, on their behalf, a little reason, justice, and humanity, and the poor man had no other asylum than the churches, no other protectors than the priests; and, as the priests offered food to the moral nature of man, they acquired a great ascendency, and the preponderance passed from the nobles to the clergy." By the aid of the church, royalty also rose above feudalism, and aided the popular cause.

The church, having gained the ascendency, sought then to enslave the kings of the earth. But royalty, borrowing help from humiliated nobles and from the people, became the dominant power in Europe.

Rise of Popular Power.

In these struggles between nobles and the clergy, and between the clergy and kings, the people had acquired political importance. They had obtained a knowledge of their rights and of their strength; and they were determined to maintain them. They liked not the tyranny of either nobles, priests, or kings; but they bent all their energies to suppress the power of the latter, since the two former had been already humiliated.

The struggle of the people against royalty is preëminently the genius of the English Revolution. It is to be doubted whether any king could have resisted the storm of popular fury which hurled Charles from his throne. But no king could have managed worse than he, no king could be more unfortunately and unpropitiously placed; and his own imprudence and folly hastened the catastrophe.

The House of Commons, which had acquired great strength, spirit, and popularity during the reign of James, fully perceived the difficulties and necessities of Charles, but made no adequate or generous effort to relieve him from them. Some of the more turbulent rejoiced in them. They knew that kings, like other men, were selfish, and that it was not natural for people to part with their privileges and power without a struggle, even though this power was injurious to the interests of society. In the Middle Ages, barons, bishops, and popes had fought desperately in the struggle of classes; and it was only from their necessities that either kings or people had obtained what they demanded. King Charles, no more than Pope Boniface VIII., would surrender, as a boon to man, without compulsion, his supposed omnipotence.

Quarrel between the King and the Commons.

The king ascended his throne burdened by the debts of his father, and by an expensive war, which the Commons incited, but would not pay for. They granted him, to meet his difficulties and maintain his honor, the paltry sum of one hundred and forty thousand pounds, and the duties of tonnage and poundage, not for life, as was customary, but for a year. Nothing could be more provoking to a young king. Of course, the money was soon spent, and the king wanted more, and had a right to expect more. But, if the Commons granted what the king required, he would be made independent of them, and he would rule tyrannically, as the kings of England did before him. So they resolved not to grant necessary supplies to carry on the government, unless the king would part with the prerogatives of an absolute prince, and those old feudal privileges which were an abomination in the eyes of the people. Charles was not the man to make such a bargain. Few kings, in his age, would have seen its necessity. But necessity there was. Civil war was inevitable, without a compromise, provided both parties were resolved on maintaining their ground. But Charles fancied that the Commons could be browbeaten and intimidated into submission; and, moreover, in case he was brought into collision with his subjects, he fancied that he was stronger than they, and could put down the spirit of resistance. In both of these suppositions he was wrong. The Commons were firm, and were stronger than he was, because they had the sympathy of the people. They believed conscientiously, especially the Puritans, that he was wrong; that God gave him no divine right to enslave them, and that they were entitled, by the eternal principles of justice, and by the spirit of the constitution, to civil and religious liberty, in the highest sense of that term. They believed that their rights were inalienable and absolute; that, among them, they could not be taxed without their own consent; and that their constitutional guardians, the Commons, should be unrestricted in debate. These notions of the people were *ideas*. On ideas all governments rest. No throne could stand a day unless the people felt they owed it their allegiance. When the main support of the throne of Charles was withdrawn, the support of popular ideas, and this support given to the House of Commons, at issue with the sovereign, what could he do? What could Louis XVI. do one hundred and fifty years afterwards? What could Louis Philippe do in our times? A king, without the loyalty of the people, is a phantom, a mockery, and a delusion, unless he have physical force to sustain him; and even then armies will rebel, if they feel they are not bound to obey, and if it is not for their interest to obey.

Now Charles had neither *loyalty* nor *force* to hold him on his throne. The agitations of an age of unprecedented boldness in speculations destroyed the former; the House of Commons would not grant supplies to secure the latter. And they would not grant supplies, because they loved themselves and the cause of the people better than they loved their king. In short, it was only by his concessions that they would supply his necessities. He would not make the concessions, and the contest soon ended in an appeal to arms.

The Counsellors of Charles.

But Charles was not without friends, and some of his advisers were men of sagacity and talent. It is true they did not fully appreciate the weakness of the king, or the strength of his enemies; but they saw his distress, and tried to remove it. They, very naturally in such an age, recommended violent courses—to grant new monopolies, to extort fines, to exercise all his feudal privileges, to pawn the crown jewels, even, in order to raise money; for money, at all events, he must have. They advised him to arrest turbulent and incendiary members of the Commons, to prorogue and dissolve parliaments, to raise forced loans, to impose new duties, to shut up ports, to levy fresh taxes, and to raise armies friendly to his cause. In short, they recommended unconstitutional measures—measures which both they and the king knew to be unconstitutional, but which they justified on the ground of necessity. And the king, in his perplexity, did what his ministers advised. But every person who was sent to the Tower, every new tax, every sentence of the Star Chamber, every seizure of property, every arbitrary command, every violation of the liberties of the people, raised up new enemies to the king, and inflamed the people with new discontents.

Death of Buckingham — Petition of Right.

At first the Commons felt that they could obtain what they wanted—a redress of grievances, if the king's favorite adviser and minister were removed. Besides, they all hated Buckingham—peers, commons, and people,—and all sought his downfall. He had no friends among the people, as Essex had in the time of Elizabeth. His extravagance, pomp, and insolence disgusted all orders; and his reign seemed to be an insult to the nation. Even the people regarded him as an upstart, setting himself above the old nobility, and enriching himself by royal domains, worth two hundred eighty-four thousand three hundred and ninety-five pounds. So the Commons violently attacked his administration, and impeached him. But he was shielded by the king, and even appointed to command an expedition to relieve La Rochelle, then besieged by Richelieu. But he was stabbed by a religious fanatic, by the name of Felton, as he was about to embark at Portsmouth. His body was removed to London, and he was buried with great state in Westminster Abbey, much lamented by the king, who lost his early friend, one of the worst ministers, but not the worst man, which that age despised, (1628.)

Meanwhile the indignant Commons persevered with their work. They passed what is called the "Petition of Right," —a string of resolutions which asserted that no freeman ought to be detained in prison, without being brought to trial, and that no taxes could be lawfully levied, without consent of the Commons—the two great pillars of the English constitution, yet truths involved in political difficulty, especially in cases of rebellion. The personal liberty of the subject is a great point indeed; and the act of *habeas corpus*, passed in later times, is a great step in popular freedom; but, if never to be suspended, no government could guard against conspiracy in revolutionary times.

The Petition of Right, however, obtained the king's assent, though unwillingly, grudgingly, and insincerely given; and the Commons, gratified for once, voted to the king supplies.

But Charles had no notion of keeping his word, and soon resorted to unconstitutional measures, as before. But he felt the need of able counsellors. His "dear Steenie" was dead, and he knew not in whom to repose confidence.

Earl of Strafford.

The demon of despotism raised up an agent in the person of Thomas Wentworth, a man of wealth, talents, energy, and indomitable courage; a man who had, in the early part of his career, defended the cause of liberty; who had even suffered imprisonment sooner than contribute to an unlawful loan, and in whom the hopes of the liberal party were placed. But he was bribed. His patriotism was not equal to his ambition. Seduced by a peerage, and by the love of power, he went over to the side of the king, and defended his arbitrary rule as zealously as he had before advocated the cause of constitutional liberty. He was created Viscount Wentworth, and afterwards earl of Strafford—the most prominent man of the royalist party, and the greatest traitor to the cause of liberty which England had ever known. His picture, as painted by Vandyke, and hung up in the princely hall of his descendant, Earl Fitzwilliam, is a faithful portrait of what history represents him—a cold, dark, repulsive, unscrupulous tyrant, with an eye capable of reading the secrets of the soul, a brow lowering with care and thought, and a lip compressed with determination, and twisted into contempt of mankind. If Wentworth did not love his countrymen, he loved to rule over them: and he gained his end, and continued the prime minister of absolutism until an insulted nation rose in their might, and placed his head upon the block.

Under the rule of this minister, whom every one feared, the Puritans every where fled, preferring the deserts of America, with freedom, to the fair lands of England, with liberty trodden under foot. The reigns of both James and Charles are memorable for the resistance and despair of this intrepid and religious sect, in which were enrolled some of the finest minds and most intelligent patriots of the country. Pym, Cromwell, Hazelrig, and even Hampden, are said to have actually embarked; but Providence detained them in England, they having a mission of blood to perform there. In another chapter, the Puritans, their struggles, and principles, will be more fully presented; and we therefore, in this connection, abstain from further notice. It may, however, be remarked, that they were the most inflexible enemies of the king, and were determined to give him and his minister no rest until all their ends were gained. They hated Archbishop Laud even more intensely than they hated Wentworth; and Laud, if possible, was a greater foe to religious and civil liberty. Strafford and Laud are generally coupled together in the description of the abuses of arbitrary power. The churchman, however, was honest and sincere, only his views were narrow and his temper irritable. His vices were those of the bigot—such as disgraced St. Dominic or Torquemada, but faults which he deemed excellencies. He was an enthusiast in high churchism and toryism; and his zeal in defence of royal prerogative and the divine rights of bishops has won for him the panegyrics of his friends, as well as the curses of his enemies. For Strafford, too, there is admiration, but only for his talents, his courage, his strength—the qualities which one might see in Milton's Satan, or in Carlyle's picture gallery of heroes.

John Hampden.

While the king and his minister were raising forced loans and contributions, sending members of the House of Commons to the Tower, fining, imprisoning, and mutilating the Puritans, a new imposition called out the energies of a great patriot and a great man, John Hampden—a fit antagonist of the haughty Wentworth. This new exaction was a tax called *ship money.*

It was devised by Chief Justice Finch and Attorney-General Noy, two subordinate, but unscrupulous tools of despotism, and designed to extort money from the inland counties, as well as from the cities, for furnishing ships—a demand that Elizabeth did not make, in all her power, even when threatened by the Spanish Armada. Clarendon even admits that this tax was not for the support of the navy, "but for a spring and magazine which should have no bottom, and for an everlasting supply on all occasions." And this the nation completely understood, and resolved desperately to resist.

Hampden, though a wealthy man, refused to pay the share assessed on him, which was only twenty shillings, deeming it an illegal tax. He was proceeded against by the crown lawyers. Hampden appealed to a decision of the judges in regard to the legality of the tax, and the king permitted the question to be settled by the laws. The trial lasted thirteen days, but ended in the condemnation of Hampden, who had shown great moderation, as well as courage, and had won the favor of the people. It was shortly after this that Hampden, as some historians assert, resolved to leave England with his cousin Oliver Cromwell. But the king prevented the ships, in which they and other emigrants had embarked, from sailing. Hampden was reserved for new trials and new labors.

Insurrection in Scotland.

About a month after Hampden's condemnation, an insurrection broke out in Scotland, which hastened the crisis of revolution. It was produced by the attempt of Archbishop Laud to impose the English liturgy on the Scottish nation, and supplant Presbyterianism by Episcopacy. The revolutions in Scotland, from the time of Knox, had been popular; not produced by great men, but by the diffusion of great ideas. The people believed in the spiritual independence of their church, and not in the supremacy of a king. The instant, therefore, that the Episcopal worship was introduced, by authority, in the cathedral of Edinburgh, there was an insurrection, which rapidly spread through all parts of the country. An immense multitude came to Edinburgh to protest against the innovation, and crowded all the houses, streets, and halls of the city. The king ordered the petitioners home, without answering their complaints. They obeyed the injunction, but soon returned in greater numbers. An organization of resistance was made, and a provisional government appointed. All classes joined the insurgents, who, menaced, but united, at last bound themselves, by a solemn league and covenant, not to separate until their rights and liberties were secured. A vast majority of all the population of Scotland—gentlemen, clergy, citizens, and laborers, men, women, and children—assembled in the church, and swore fealty to the covenant. Force, of course, was necessary to reduce the rebels, and civil war commenced in Scotland. But war increased the necessities of the king, and he was compelled to make peace with the insurgent army.

Eleven years had now elapsed since the dissolution of the last parliament, during which the king had attempted to rule without one, and had resorted to all the expedients that the ingenuity of the crown lawyers could suggest, in order to extort money. Imposts fallen into desuetude, monopolies abandoned by Elizabeth, royal forests extended beyond the limits they had in feudal times, fines past all endurance, confiscations without end, imprisonments, tortures, and executions,—all marked these eleven years. The sum for fines alone, in this period, amounted to more than two hundred thousand pounds. The forest of Rockingham was enlarged from six to sixty miles in circuit, and the earl of Salisbury was fined twenty thousand pounds for encroaching upon it. Individuals and companies had monopolies of salt, soap, coals, iron, wine, leather, starch, feathers, tobacco, beer, distilled liquors, herrings, butter, potash, linen cloth, rags, hops, gunpowder, and divers other articles, which, of course, deranged the whole trade of the country. Prynne was fined ten thousand pounds, and had his ears cut off, and his nose slit, for writing an offensive book; and his sufferings were not greater than what divers others experienced for vindicating the cause of truth and liberty.

At last, the king's necessities compelled him to summon another parliament. He had exhausted every expedient to raise money. His army clamored for pay; and he was overburdened with debts.

Long Parliament.

On the 13th of April, 1640, the new parliament met. It knew its strength, and was determined now, more than ever, to exercise it. It immediately took the power into its own hands, and from remonstrances and petitions it proceeded to actual hostilities; from the denunciation of injustice and illegality, it proceeded to trample on the constitution itself. It is true that the members were irritated and threatened, and some of their number had been seized and imprisoned. It is true that the king continued his courses, and was resolved on enforcing his measures by violence. The struggle became one of desperation on both sides—a struggle for ascendency—and not for rights.

One of the first acts of the House of Commons was the impeachment of Strafford. He had been just summoned from Ireland, where, as lord lieutenant, he had exercised almost regal power and regal audacity; he had been summoned by his perplexed and desponding master to assist him by his counsels. Reluctantly he obeyed, foreseeing the storm. He had scarcely arrived in London when the intrepid Pym accused him of high treason. The Lords accepted the accusation, and the imperious minister was committed to the Tower.

The impeachment of Laud soon followed; but he was too sincere in his tyranny to understand why he should be committed. Nor was he feared, as Strafford was, against whom the vengeance of the parliament was especially directed. A secret committee, invested with immense powers, was commissioned to scrutinize his whole life, and his destruction was resolved upon. On the 22d of March his trial began, and lasted seventeen days, during which time, unaided, he defended himself against thirteen accusers, with consummate ability. Indeed, he had studied his charges and despised his adversaries. Under ordinary circumstances, he would have been acquitted, for there was not sufficient evidence to convict him of high treason; but an unscrupulous and infuriated body of men were thirsting for his blood, and it was proposed to convict him by bill of attainder; that is, by act of parliament, on its own paramount authority, with or without the law. The bill passed, in spite of justice, in spite of the eloquence of the attainted earl. He was condemned, and remanded to the Tower.

Had the king been strong he would have saved his minister; had he been magnanimous, he would have stood by him to the last. But he had neither the power to save him, nor the will to make adequate sacrifices. He feebly interposed, but finally yielded, and gave his consent to the execution of the main agent of all his aggressions on the constitution he had sworn to maintain. Strafford deserved his fate, although the manner of his execution was not according to law.

Rebellion of Ireland.

A few months after the execution of Strafford, an event occurred which proved exceedingly unfortunate to the royal cause; and this was the rebellion of Ireland, and the massacre of the Protestant population, caused, primarily, by the oppressive government of England, and the harsh and severe measures of the late lord lieutenant. In the course of a few weeks, the English and Scottish colonies seemed almost uprooted; one of the most frightful butcheries was committed that ever occurred. The Protestants exaggerated their loss; but it is probable that at least fifty thousand were massacred. The local government of Dublin was paralyzed. The English nation was filled with deadly and implacable hostility, not against the Irish merely, but against the Catholics every where. It was supposed that there was a general conspiracy among the Catholics to destroy the whole nation; and it was whispered that the queen herself had aided the revolted Irish. The most vigorous measures were adopted to raise money and troops for Ireland. The Commons took occasion of the general spirit of discontent and insurrection to prepare a grand remonstrance on the evils of the kingdom, which were traced to a "coalition of Papists, Arminian bishops and clergymen, and evil courtiers and counsellors." The Commons recited all the evils of the last sixteen years, and declared the necessity of taking away the root of them, which was the arbitrary power of the sovereign. The king, in reply, told the Commons that their remonstrance was unparliamentary; that he could not understand what they meant by a wicked party; that bishops were entitled to their votes in parliament; and that, as to the removal of evil counsellors, they must name whom they were. The remonstrance was printed and circulated by the Commons, which was of more effect than an army could have been.

Thus were affairs rapidly reaching a crisis, when the attempt to seize five of the most refractory and able members of parliament consummated it. The members were Hollis, Hazelrig, Pym, Hampden, and Strode; and they were accused of high treason. This movement of the king was one of the greatest blunders and one of the most unconstitutional acts he ever committed. The Commons refused to surrender their members; and then the king went down to the house, with an armed force, to seize them. But Pym and others got intelligence of the design of Charles, and had time to withdraw before he arrived. "The baffled tyrant returned to Whitehall with his company of bravoes," while the city of London sheltered Hampden and his friends. The shops were shut, the streets were filled with crowds, and the greatest excitement prevailed. The friends of Charles, who were inclined to constitutional measures, were filled with shame. It was now feared that the king would not respect his word or the constitution, and, with all his promises, was still bent on tyrannical courses. All classes, but bigoted royalists, now felt that something must be done promptly, or that their liberties would be subverted.

Then it was, and not till then, that the Commons openly defied him, while the king remained in his palace, humbled, dismayed, and bewildered, "feeling," says Clarendon, "the trouble and agony which usually attend generous minds upon their having committed errors;" or, as Macaulay says, "the despicable repentance which attends the bungling villain, who, having attempted to commit a crime, finds that he has only committed a folly."

Flight of the King from London.

In a few days, the king fled from Whitehall, which he was never destined to see again till he was led through it to the scaffold. He went into the country to raise forces to control the parliament, and the parliament made vigorous measures to put itself and the kingdom in a state of resistance. On the 23d of April, the king, with three hundred horse, advanced to Hull, and were refused admission by the governor. This was tantamount to a declaration of war. It was so considered. Thirty-two Lords, and sixty members of the Commons departed for York to join the king. The parliament decreed an army, and civil war began.

Before this can be traced we must consider the Puritans, which is necessary in order fully to appreciate the Revolution. The reign of Charles I. was now virtually ended, and that of the Parliament and Cromwell had begun.

Rise of the Puritans.

Dissensions among the Protestants themselves did not occur until the reign of Elizabeth, and were first caused by difficulties about a clerical dress, which again led to the advocacy of simpler forms of worship, stricter rules of life, more definite forms of faith, and more democratic principles of government, both ecclesiastical and civil. The first promoters of these opinions were the foreign divines who came from Geneva, at the invitation of Cranmer, of whom Peter Martyr, Martin Bucer, John à Lasco, were the most distinguished. Some Englishmen, also, who had been travelling on the continent, brought with them the doctrines of Calvin. Among these was Hooper, who, on being nominated to the bishopric of Gloucester, refused to submit to the appointed form of consecration and admission. He objected to what he called the *Aaronical* habits—the square cap, tippet, and surplice, worn by bishops. But dissent became more marked and determined when the exiles returned to England, on the accession of Elizabeth, and who were for advancing the reformation according to their own standard. The queen and her advisers, generally, were content with King Edward's liturgy; but the majority of the exiles desired the simpler services of Geneva. The new bishops, most of whom had been their companions abroad, endeavored to soften them for the present, declaring that they would use all their influence at court to secure them indulgence. The queen herself connived at non-conformity, until her government was established, but then firmly declared that she had fixed her standard, and insisted on her subjects conforming to it. The bishops, seeing this, changed their conduct, explained away their promises, and became severe towards their dissenting brethren.

The standard of the queen was the Thirty-Nine Articles. She admitted that the Scriptures were the sole rule of faith, but declared that individuals must interpret Scripture as expounded in the articles and formularies of the English church, in violation of the great principle of Protestantism, which even the Puritans themselves did not fully recognize—the right and the duty of every individual to interpret Scripture himself, whether his interpretation interfered with the Established Church or not.

Original Difficulties and Differences.

The first dissenters did not claim this right, but only urged that certain points, about which they felt scruples, should be left as matters indifferent. On all essential points, they, as well as the strictest conformists, believed in the necessity of a uniformity of public worship, and of using the sword of the magistrate in defence of their doctrines. The standard of conformity, according to the bishops, was the queen's supremacy and the laws of the land; according to the Puritans, the decrees of provincial and national synods.

At first, many of the Puritans overcame their scruples so far as to comply with the required oath and accept livings in the Establishment. But they indulged in many irregularities, which, during the first year of the reign of Elizabeth, were winked at by the authorities. "Some performed," says an old author, "divine service in the chancel, others in the body of the church; some in a seat made in the church; some in a pulpit, with their faces to the people; some keeping precisely to the order of the book; some intermix psalms in metre; some say with a surplice, and others without one. The table stands in the body of the church in some places, in others it stands in the chancel; in some places the table stands altarwise, distant from the wall a yard, in others in the middle of the chancel, north and south. Some administer the communion with surplice and cap, some with a surplice alone, others with none; some with chalice, others with a communion cup, others with a common cup; some with unleavened bread, and some with leavened; some receive kneeling, others standing, others sitting; some baptize in a font, some in a basin; some sign with the sign of the cross, other sign not; some minister with a surplice, others without; some with a square cap, others with a round cap; some with a button cap, and some with a hat, some in scholar's clothes, some in common clothes."

These differences in public worship, which, by many, were considered as indifferent matters, and by others were unduly magnified, seem to have constituted the chief peculiarity of the early Puritans. In regard to the queen's supremacy, the union of church and state, the necessity of supporting religion by law, and articles of theological belief, there was no disagreement. Most of the non-conformists were men of learning and piety, and among the ornaments of the church.

The metropolitan bishop, at this time, was Parker, a great stickler for the forms of the church, and very intolerant in all his opinions. He and others of the bishops had been appointed as commissioners to investigate the causes of dissent, and to suspend all who refused to conform to the rubric of the church. Hence arose the famous Court of the Ecclesiastical Commission, so much abused during the reigns of James and Charles.

Persecution during the Reign of Elizabeth.

Under the direction of Parker, great numbers were suspended from their livings for non-conformity, and sent to wander in a state of destitution. Among these were some of the most learned men in the church. They had no means of defence or livelihood, and resorted to the press in order to vindicate their opinions. For this they were even more harshly dealt with; an order was issued from the Star Chamber, that no person should print a book against the queen's injunctions, upon the penalty of fines and imprisonment; and authority was given to church-wardens to search all suspected places where books might be concealed. Great multitudes suffered in consequence of these tyrannical laws.

But the non-conformists were further molested. They were forbidden to assemble together to read the Scriptures and pray, but were required to attend regularly the churches of the Establishment, on penalty of heavy fines for neglect.

At length, worried, disgusted, and irritated, they resolved upon setting up the Genevan service, and upon withdrawing entirely from the Church of England. The separation, once made, (1566,) became wider and wider, and the Puritans soon after opposed the claims of bishops as a superior order of the clergy. They were opposed to the temporal dignities annexed to the episcopal office to the titles and office of archdeacons, deans, and chapters; to the jurisdiction of spiritual courts; to the promiscuous access of all persons to the communion; to the liturgy; to the prohibition, in the public service of prayer, by the clergyman himself; to the use of godfathers and godmothers; to the custom of confirmation; to the cathedral worship and organs; to pluralities and non-residency; to the observance of Lent and of the holy days; and to the appointment of ministers by the crown, bishops, or lay patrons, instead of election by the people.

The schism was now complete, and had grown out of such small differences as refusing to bow at the name of Jesus, and to use the cross in baptism.

In our times, the Puritans would have been permitted to worship God in their own way, but they were not thus allowed in the time of Elizabeth. Religious toleration was not then understood or practised; and it was the fault of the age, since the Puritans themselves, when they obtained the power, persecuted with great severity the Quakers and the Catholics. But, during the whole reign of Elizabeth, especially the life of Archbishop Parker, they were in a minority, and suffered—as minorities ever have suffered—all the miseries which unreasonable majorities could inflict.

Archbishops Grindal and Whitgift.

Archbishop Grindal, who succeeded Parker in 1575, recommended milder measures to the queen; but she had no charity for those who denied the supremacy of her royal conscience.

Grindal was succeeded, in 1583, by Dr. Whitgift, the antagonist of the learned Dr. Cartwright, and he proved a ruler of the church according to her majesty's mind. He commenced a most violent crusade against the non-conformists, and was so harsh, cruel, and unreasonable, that Cecil—Lord Burleigh—was obliged to remonstrate, being much more enlightened than the prelate. "I have read over," said he, "your twenty-four articles, and I find them so curiously penned, that I think that the Spanish Inquisition used not so many questions to entrap the priests." Nevertheless fines, imprisonment, and the gibbet continued to do their work in the vain attempt to put down opinions, till within four or five years of the queen's death when there was a cessation of persecution.

Persecution under James.

Puritans in Exile.

But the Scottish Solomon, as James was called, renewed the severity which Elizabeth found it wise to remit. Hitherto, the Puritans had been chiefly Presbyterians; but now the Independents arose, who carried their views still further, even to wildness and radicalism. They were stricter Calvinists, and inclined to republican views of civil government. Consequently, they were still more odious than were the Presbyterians to an arbitrary government. They were now persecuted for their doctrines of faith, as well as for their forms of worship. The Church of England retained the thirty-nine articles; but many of her leading clergy sympathized with the views of Arminius, and among them was the primate himself. So strictly were Arminian doctrines cherished, that no person under a dean was permitted to discourse on predestination, election, reprobation, efficacy, or universality of God's grace. And the king himself would hear no doctrines preached, except those he had condemned at the synod of Dort. But this act was aimed against the Puritans, who, of all parties, were fond of preaching on what was called "the Five Points of Calvinism." But they paid dearly for their independence. James absolutely detested them, regarded them as a sect insufferable in a well-governed commonwealth, and punished them with the greatest severity. Their theological doctrines, their notions of church government, and, above all, their spirit of democratic liberty, were odious and repulsive. Archbishop Bancroft, who succeeded Whitgift in 1604, went beyond all his predecessors in bigotry, but had not their commanding intellects. His measures were so injudicious, so vexatious, so annoying, so severe, and so cruel, that the Puritans became, if possible, still more estranged. With the popular discontents, and with the progress of persecution, their numbers increased, both in Scotland and England. With the increase of Puritanism was also a corresponding change in the Church of England, since ceremony and forms increased almost to a revival of Catholicism. And this reaction towards Rome, favored by the court, incensed still more the Puritans, and led to language unnecessarily violent and abusive on their side. Their controversial tracts were pervaded with a spirit of bitterness and treason which, in the opinion of James, fully justified the imprisonments, fines, and mutilations which his minister inflicted. The Puritans, in despair, fled to Holland, and from thence to New England, to establish, amid its barren hills and desolate forests, that worship which alone they thought would be acceptable to God. Persecution elevated them, and none can deny that they were characterized by moral virtues and a spirit of liberty which no people ever before or since exhibited. Almost their only fault was intolerance respecting the opinions and pleasures of many good people who did not join their ranks.

James's death did not remit their sufferings; but, by this time, they had so multiplied that they became a party too formidable to be crushed. The High Commission Court and the Star Chamber still filled the prisons and pillories with victims; but every sentence of these courts fanned the flame of discontent, and hastened the catastrophe which was rapidly approaching. The volcano, over whose fearful brink the royal family and the haughty hierarchy were standing, was now sending forth those frightful noises which indicated approaching convulsions.

During the years that Charles dispensed with the parliaments, when Laud was both minister and archbishop, the persecution reached its height, and also popular discontent. During this period, the greatest emigration was made to New England, and even Hampden and Cromwell contemplated joining their brethren in America. Arianism and Popery advanced with Puritanism, and all parties prepared for the approaching contest. The advocates of royal usurpation became more unreasonable, the friends of popular liberty became more violent. Those who had the power, exercised it without reflection. The history of the times is simply this—despotism striving to put Puritanism and liberty beneath its feet, and Puritanism aiming to subvert the crown.

But the greatest commotions were in Scotland, where the people were generally Presbyterians; and it was the zeal of Archbishop Laud in suppressing these, and attempting to change the religion of the land, which precipitated the ruin of Charles I.

Troubles in Scotland.

Ever since the time of Knox, Scotland had been the scene of violent religious animosities. In that country, the reformation, from the first, had been a popular movement. It was so impetuous, and decided under the guidance of the uncompromising Knox, that even before the dethronement of Mary, it was complete. In the year 1592, through the influence of Andrew Melville, the Presbyterian government was fairly established, and King James is said to have thus expressed himself: "I praise God that I was born in the time of the light of the gospel, and in such a place as to be king of the purest kirk in the world." The Church of Scotland, however, had severe struggles from the period of its institution, 1560, to the year 1584, when the papal influence was finally destroyed by the expulsion of the earl of Arran from the councils of the young king. Nor did these struggles end even there. James, perceiving that Episcopacy was much more consonant with monarchy than Presbyterianism, attempted to remodel the Scottish church on the English basis, which attempt resulted in discontent and rebellion. James, however, succeeded in reducing to contempt the general assemblies of the Presbyterian church, and in confirming Archbishop Spotswood in the chief administration of ecclesiastical affairs, which, it must be confessed, were regulated with great prudence and moderation.

When Charles came to the throne, he complained of the laxity of the Scotch primate, and sent him a set of rules by which he was to regulate his conduct. Charles also added new dignities to his see, and ordained that he, as primate, should take precedence over all the temporal lords, which irritated the proud Scotch nobility. He moreover contemplated the recovery of tithes and church lands for the benefit of the Episcopal government, and the imposition of a liturgy on the Scotch nation, a great majority of whom were Presbyterians. This was the darling scheme of Laud, who believed that there could scarcely be salvation out of his church, and which church he strove to make as much like the Catholic as possible, and yet maintain independence of the pope. But nothing was absolutely done towards changing the religion of Scotland until Charles came down to Edinburgh (1633) to be crowned, when a liturgy was prepared for the Scotch nation, subjected to the revision of Laud, but which was not submitted to or seen by, the General Assembly, or any convocation of ministers in Scotland. Nothing could be more ill timed or ill judged than this conflict with the religious prejudices of a people zealously attached to their own forms of worship. The clergy united with the aristocracy, and both with the people, in denouncing the conduct of the king and his ministers as tyrannical and unjust. The canons, especially, which Laud had prepared, were, in the eyes of the Scotch, puerile and superstitious; they could not conceive why a Protestant prelate should make so much account of the position of the font or of the communion table, turned into an altar. Indeed, his liturgy was not much other than an English translation of the Roman Missal, and excited the detestation of all classes. Yet it was resolved to introduce it into the churches, and the day was fixed for its introduction, which was Easter Sunday, 1637. But such a ferment was produced, that the experiment was put off to Sunday, 23d of July. On that day, the archbishops and bishops, lords of session, and magistrates were all present, by command, in the Church of St. Giles. But no sooner had the dean opened the service book, and begun to read out of it, than the people, who had assembled in great crowds, began to fill the church with uproar. The bishop of Edinburgh, who was to preach, stepped into the pulpit, and attempted to appease the tumultuous people. But this increased the tumult, when an old woman, seizing a stool, hurled it at the bishop's head. Sticks, stones, and dirt followed the stool, with loud cries of "Down with the priest of Baal!" "A pape, a pape!" "Antichrist!" "Pull him down!" This was the beginning of the insurrection, which spread from city to village, until all Scotland was in arms, and Episcopacy, as an established religion, was subverted. In February, 1638, the covenant was drawn up in Edinburgh, and was subscribed to by all classes, in all parts of Scotland; and, in November, the General Assembly met in Glasgow, the first that had been called for twenty years, and Presbyterianism was reëstablished in the kingdom, if not legally, yet in reality.

From the day on which the Convocation opened, until the conquest of the country by Cromwell, the Kirk reigned supreme, there being no power in the government, or in the country, able or disposed to resist or question its authority. This was the golden age of Presbyterianism, when the clergy enjoyed autocratic power —a sort of Druidical ascendency over the minds and consciences of the people, in affairs temporal as well as spiritual.

Peculiarities of Puritanism in England.

Puritanism did not pervade the English, as it did the Scotch mind, although it soon obtained an ascendency. Most of the great political chieftains who controlled the House of Commons, and who clamored for the death of Strafford and Laud, were Puritans. But they were not all Presbyterians. In England, after the flight of the king from Whitehall, the Independents attracted notice, and eventually seized the reins of government. Cromwell was an Independent.

The difference between these two sects was chiefly in their views about government, civil and ecclesiastical. Both Presbyterians and Independents were rigid Calvinists, practised a severe morality, were opposed to gay amusements, disliked organs and ceremonies, strictly observed the Sabbath, and attached great importance to the close observance of the Mosaic ritual. The Presbyterians were not behind the Episcopalians in hatred of sects and a free press. They had their model of worship, and declared it to be of divine origin. They looked upon schism as the parent of licentiousness, insisted on entire uniformity, maintained the divine right of the clergy to the management of ecclesiastical affairs, and claimed the sword of the magistrate to punish schismatics and heretics. They believed in the union of church and state, but would give the clergy the ascendency they possessed in the Middle Ages. They did not desire the entire prostration of royal authority, but only aimed to limit and curtail it.

The Independents wished a total disruption of church and state, and disliked synods almost as much as they did bishops. They believed that every congregation was a distinct church, and had a right to elect the pastor. They preferred the greatest variety of sects to the ascendency of any one, by means of the civil sword. They rejected all spiritual courts, and claimed the right of each church to reject, punish, or receive members. In politics, they wished a total overthrow of the government—monarchy, aristocracy, and prelacy; and were averse to any peace which did not secure complete toleration of opinions, and the complete subversion of the established order of things.

Conflicts among the Puritans.

Between the Presbyterians and the Independents, therefore, there could not be any lasting sympathy or alliance. They only united to crush the common foe; and, when Charles was beheaded, and Cromwell installed in power, they turned their arms against each other.

The great religious contest, after the rise of Cromwell, was not between the Puritans and the Episcopalians, but between the different sects of Puritans themselves. At first, the Independents harmonized with the Presbyterians. Their theological and ethical opinions were the same, and both cordially hated and despised the government of the Stuarts. But when the Presbyterians obtained the ascendency, the Independents were grieved and enraged to discover that religious toleration was stigmatized as the parent of all heresy and schism. While in power, the Presbyterians shackled the press, and their intolerance brought out John Milton's famous tract on the liberty of unlicensed printing—one of the most masterly arguments which the advocates of freedom have ever made. The idea that any dominant religious sect should be incorporated with the political power, was the fatal error of Presbyterianism, and raised up enemies against it, after the royal power was suppressed. Cromwell was persuaded that the cause of religious liberty would be lost unless Presbyterianism, as well as Episcopacy, was disconnected with the state; and hence one great reason of his assuming the dictatorship. And he granted a more extended toleration than had before been known in England, although it was not perfect. The Catholics and the Quakers were not partakers of the boon which he gave to his country; so hard is it for men to learn the rights of others, when they have power in their own hands.

Character of the Puritans.

The Restoration was a victory over both the Independents and the general swarm of sectaries which an age of unparalleled religious excitement had produced. It is difficult to conceive of the intensity of the passions which inflamed all parties of religious disputants. But if the Puritan contest developed fanatical zeal, it also brought out the highest qualities of mind and heart which any age has witnessed. With all the faults and weaknesses of the Puritans, there never lived a better class of men,—men of more elevated piety, more enlarged views, or greater disinterestedness, patriotism, and moral worth. They made sacrifices which our age can scarcely appreciate, and had difficulties to contend with which were unparalleled in the history of reform. They made blunders which approximated to crimes, but they made them in their inexperience and zeal to promote the cause of religion and liberty. They were conscientious men—men who acted from the fear of God, and with a view to promote the highest welfare of future generations. They launched their bark boldly upon an unknown sea, and heroically endured its dangers and sufferings, with a view of conferring immortal blessings on their children and country. More prudent men would have avoided the perils of an unknown navigation; but, by such men, a great experiment for humanity would not have been tried. It may have failed, but the world has learned immortal wisdom from the failure. But the Puritans were not mere adventurers or martyrs. They have done something of lasting benefit to mankind, and they have done this by the power of faith, and by loyalty to their consciences, perverted as they were in some respects.

The Puritans were not agreeable companions to the idle, luxurious, or frivolous; they were rigid ever, to austerity; their expressions degenerated into cant, and they were hostile to many innocent amusements. But these were peculiarities which furnished subjects of ridicule merely, and did not disgrace or degrade them. These were a small offset to their moral wisdom, their firm endurance, their elevation of sentiment, their love of liberty, and their fear of God. Such are the men whom Providence ordains to give impulse to society, and effect great and useful reforms.

We now return to consider the changes which they attempted in government. The civil war, of which Cromwell was the hero, now claims our attention.

The refusal of the governor of Hull to admit the king was virtually the declaration of war, for which both parties had vigorously prepared.

The standard of the king was first raised in Nottingham, while the head-quarters of the parliamentarians were in London. The first action of any note was the battle of Edge Hill, (October 23, 1642,) but was undecisive. Indeed, both parties hesitated to plunge into desperate war, at least until, by skirmishings and military manœuvres, they were better prepared for it.

The forces of the belligerents, at this period, were nearly equal but the parliamentarians had the ablest leaders. It was the misfortune of the king to have no man of commanding talents, as his counsellor, after the arrest of Strafford. Hyde, afterwards lord chancellor, and Earl of Clarendon, was the ablest of the royalist party. Falkland and Culpeper were also eminent men; but neither of them was the equal of Pym or Hampden.

John Hampden.

The latter was doubtless the ablest man in England at this time, and the only one who could have saved it from the evils which afterwards afflicted it. On him the hopes and affections of the nation centred. He was great in council and great in debate. He was the acknowledged leader of the House of Commons. He was eloquent, honest, unwearied, sagacious, and prudent. "Never had a man inspired a nation with greater confidence: the more moderate had faith in his wisdom; the more violent in his devoted patriotism; the more honest in his uprightness; the more intriguing in his talents." He spared neither his fortune nor his person, as soon as hostilities were inevitable. He subscribed two thousand pounds to the public cause, took a colonel's commission, and raised a regiment of infantry, so well known during the war for its green uniform, and the celebrated motto of its intrepid leader, — "*Vestigia nulla retrorsum*." He possessed the talents of a great statesman and a great general, and all the united qualities requisite for the crisis in which he appeared — "the valor and energy of Cromwell, the discernment and eloquence of Vane, the humanity and moderation of Manchester, the stern integrity of Hale, the ardent public spirit of Sydney. Others could conquer; he alone could reconcile. A heart as bold as his brought up the cuirassiers who turned the tide of battle on Marston Moor. As skilful an eye as his watched the Scottish army descending from the heights over Dunbar. But it was when, to the sullen tyranny of Laud and Charles, had succeeded the fierce conflict of sects and factions, ambitious of ascendency, and burning for revenge; it was when the vices and ignorance, which the old tyranny had generated, threatened the new freedom with destruction, that England missed that sobriety, that self-command, that perfect soundness of judgment, that perfect rectitude of intention, to which the history of revolutions furnishes no parallel, or furnishes a parallel in Washington alone."[1]

Oliver Cromwell.

This great man was removed by Providence from the scene of violence and faction at an early period of the contest. He was mortally wounded in one of those skirmishes in which the detachments of both armies had thus far engaged, and which made the campaigns of 1642-3 so undecided, so tedious, and so irritating—campaigns in which the generals of both armies reaped no laurels, and which created the necessity for a greater genius than had thus far appeared. That genius was Oliver Cromwell. At the battle of Edge Hill he was only captain of a troop of horse, and at the death of his cousin Hampden, he was only colonel. He was indeed a member of the Long Parliament, as was Hampden, and had secured the attention of the members in spite of his slovenly appearance and his incoherent, though earnest speeches. Under his rough and clownish exterior, his talents were not perceived, except by two or three penetrating intellects; but they were shortly to appear, and to be developed, not in the House of Commons, but on the field of battle. The rise of Oliver Cromwell can scarcely be dated until the death of John Hampden; nor were the eyes of the nation fixed on him, as their deliverer, until some time after. The Earl of Essex was still the commander of the forces, while the Earl of Bedford, Lord Manchester, Lord Fairfax, Skippon, Sir William Waller, Leslie, and others held high posts. Cromwell was still a subordinate; but genius breaks through all obstacles, and overleaps all boundaries. The time had not yet come for the exercise of his great military talents. The period of negotiation had not fully passed, and the king, at his head-quarters at Oxford, "that seat of pure, unspotted loyalty," still hoped to amuse the parliament, gain time, and finally overwhelm its forces. Prince Rupert—brave, ardent, reckless, unprincipled—still ravaged the country without reaping any permanent advantage. The parliament was perplexed and the people were disappointed. On the whole, the king's forces were in the ascendant, and were augmenting; while plots and insurrections were constantly revealing to the parliamentarians the dangers which threatened them. Had not an able leader, at this crisis, appeared among the insurgents, or had an able general been given to Charles, it is probable that the king would have secured his ends; for popular enthusiasm without the organization which a master spirit alone can form, soon burns itself out.

The King at Oxford.

The state of the contending parties, from the battle of Edge Hill, for nearly two years, was very singular and very complicated. The king remained at Oxford, distracted by opposing counsels, and perplexed by various difficulties. The head-quarters of his enemies, at London, were no less the seat of intrigues and party animosities. The Presbyterians were the most powerful, and were nearly as distrustful of the Independents as they were of the king, and feared a victory over the king nearly as much as they did a defeat by him, and the dissensions among the various sects and leaders were no secret in the royalist camp, and doubtless encouraged Charles in his endless intrigues and dissimulations. But he was not equal to decisive measures, and without them, in revolutionary times, any party must be ruined. While he was meditating and scheming, he heard the news of an alliance between Scotland and the parliament, in which the Presbyterian interest was in the ascendency. This was the first great blow he received since the commencement of the war, and the united forces of his enemies now resolved upon more vigorous measures.

At the opening of the campaign, the parliament had five armies— that of the Scots, of twenty-one thousand; that of Essex, ten thousand five hundred; that of Waller, five thousand one hundred; that of Manchester, fourteen thousand; and that of Fairfax, five thousand five hundred—in all, about fifty-six thousand men, of whom the committee of the two kingdoms had the entire disposal. In May, Essex and Waller invested Oxford, while Fairfax, Manchester, and the Scots met under the walls of York. Thus these two great royalist cities were attacked at once by all the forces of parliament. Charles, invested by a stronger force, and being deprived of the assistance of the princes, Rupert and Maurice, his nephews, who were absent on their marauding expeditions, escaped from Oxford, and proceeded towards Exeter. In the mean time, he ordered Prince Rupert to advance to the relief of York, which was defended by the marquis of Newcastle. The united royalist army now amounted to twenty-six thousand men, with a numerous and well appointed cavalry; and this great force obliged the armies of the parliament to raise the siege of York. Had Rupert been contented with this success, and intrenched himself in the strongest city of the north of England, he and Newcastle might have maintained their ground; but Rupert, against the advice of Newcastle, resolved on an engagement with the parliamentary generals, who had retreated to Marston Moor, on the banks of the Ouse, five miles from the city.

The next day after the relief of York was fought the famous battle of Marston Moor, (July 2, 1644,) the bloodiest in the war, which resulted in the entire discomfiture of the royalist forces, and the ruin of the royal interests at the north. York was captured in a few days. Rupert retreated to Lancashire to recruit his army, and Newcastle, disgusted with Rupert, and with the turn affairs had taken, withdrew beyond seas. The Scots soon stormed the town of Newcastle, and the whole north of England fell into the hands of the victors.

Cromwell after the Battle.

Enthusiasm of the Independents.

This great battle was decided by the ability of Cromwell, now lieutenant-general in the army of the parliament. He had distinguished himself in all subordinate stations, in the field of battle, in raising forces, and in councils of war, for which he had been promoted to serve as second under the Earl of Manchester. But his remarkable military genius was not apparent to the parliament until the battle of Marston Moor, and on him the eyes of the nation now began to be centred. He was now forty-five years of age, in the vigor of his manhood, burning with religious enthusiasm, and eager to deliver his country from the tyranny of Charles I., and of all kings. He was an Independent and a radical, opposed to the Episcopalians, to the Presbyterians, to the Scots, to all moderate men, to all moderate measures, to all jurisdiction in matters of religion, and to all authority in political affairs, which did not directly emanate from the people, who were called upon to regulate themselves by their individual reason. He was the idol of the Independent party, which now began to gain the ascendency in that stormy crisis. For three years, the Presbyterians had been in the ascendant, but had not realized the hopes or expectations of the enthusiastic advocates of freedom. By turns imperious and wavering, fanatical and moderate, they sought to curtail and humble the king, not to ruin him; to depress Episcopacy, but to establish another religion by the sword of the magistrate. Their leaders were timid, insincere, and disunited; few among them had definite views respecting the future government of the realm: and they gradually lost the confidence of the nation. But the Independents reposed fearlessly on the greatness and grandeur of their abstract principles, and pronounced, without a scruple, those potent words which kindled a popular enthusiasm—equality of rights, the just distribution of property, and the removal of all abuses. Above all, they were enthusiasts in religion, as well as in liberty, and devoutly attached to the doctrines of Calvin. They abominated all pleasures and pursuits which diverted their minds from the contemplation of God, or the reality of a future state. Cromwell himself lived in the ecstasy of religious excitement. His language was the language of the Bible, and its solemn truths were not dogmas, but convictions to his ardent mind. In the ardor of his zeal and the frenzy of his hopes, he fondly fancied that the people of England were to rise in simultaneous confederation, shake off all the old shackles of priests and kings, and be governed in all their actions, by the principles of the Bible. A sort of Jewish theocracy was to be restored on earth, and he was to be the organ of the divine will, as was Joshua of old, when he led the Israelites against the pagan inhabitants of the promised land. Up to this time, no inconsistencies disgraced him. His prayers and his exhortations were in accordance with his actions, and the most scrutinizing malignity could attribute nothing to him but sincerity and ardor in the cause which he had so warmly espoused. As magistrate, as member of parliament, as farmer, or as general, he slighted no religious duties, and was devoted to the apparent interests of England. Such a man, so fervent, enthusiastic, honest, patriotic, and able, of course was pointed out as a future leader, especially when his great military talents were observed at Marston Moor. From the memorable 2d of July he became the most marked and influential man in England. Hampden had offered up his life as a martyr, and Pym, the great lawyer and statesman, had died from exhaustion. Essex had won no victory commensurate with the public expectations, and Waller lost his army by desertions and indecisive measures. Both Essex and Manchester, with their large estates, their aristocratic connections, and their Presbyterian sympathies, were afraid of treating the king too well. The battle of Newbury, which shortly after was gained by the parliamentarians, was without decisive results, in consequence of the indecision of Manchester. The parliament and the nation looked for another leader, who would pursue his advantages, and adopt more vigorous measures. At this point, the Presbyterians would have made peace with the king, who still continued his insincere negotiations; but it was too late. The Independents had gained the ascendency, and their voice was for war—no more dallying, no more treaties, no more half measures, but uncompromising war. It was plain that either the king or the Independents must be the absolute rulers of England.

Then was passed (April 3, 1645) the famous Self-Denying Ordinance, by which all members of parliament were excluded from command in the army, an act designed to get rid of Essex and Manchester, and prepare the way for the elevation of Cromwell. Sir Thomas Fairfax was appointed to the supreme command, and Cromwell was despatched into the inland counties to raise recruits. But it was soon obvious that the army could do nothing without him, although it was remodelled and reënforced; and even Fairfax and his officers petitioned parliament that Cromwell might be appointed lieutenant-general again, and commander-in-chief of the horse; which request was granted, and Cromwell rejoined the army, of which he was its hope and idol.

Battle of Naseby.

He joined it in time to win the most decisive battle of the war, the battle of Naseby, June 14, 1645. The forces of both armies were nearly balanced, and the royalists were commanded by the king in person, assisted by his ablest generals. But the rout of the king's forces was complete, his fortunes were prostrated, and he was driven, with the remnants of his army, from one part of the kingdom to the other, while the victorious parliamentarians were filled with exultation and joy. Cromwell, however, was modest and composed, and ascribed the victory to the God of battles, whose servant, he fancied, he preëminently was.

Success of the Parliamentary Army.

The parliamentary army continued its successes. Montrose gained the battle of Alford; Bridgewater surrendered to Fairfax; Glasgow and Edinburgh surrendered to Montrose; Prince Rupert was driven from Bristol, and, as the king thought, most disgracefully, which misfortune gave new joy to the parliament, and caused new thanksgivings from Cromwell, who gained the victory. From Bristol, the army turned southward, and encountered what royalist force there was in that quarter, stormed Bridgewater, drove the royalist generals into Cornwall, took Winchester, battered down Basing House, rich in provisions, ammunition, and silver plate, and completely prostrated all the hopes of the king in the south of England. Charles fled from Oxford, secretly, to join the Scottish army.

By the 24th of June, 1646, all the garrisons of England and Wales, except those in the north, were in the hands of the parliament. In July, the parliament sent their final propositions to the king at Newcastle, which were extremely humiliating, and which he rejected. Negotiations were then entered into between the parliament and the Scots, which were long protracted, but which finally ended in an agreement, by the Scots, to surrender the king to the parliament, for the payment of their dues. They accordingly marched home with an instalment of two hundred thousand pounds, and the king was given up, not to the Independents, but to the Commissioners of parliament, in which body the Presbyterian interest predominated.

At this juncture, (January, 1647,) Cromwell, rather than the king, was in danger of losing his head. The Presbyterians, who did not wish to abolish royalty, but establish uniformity with their mode of worship, began to be extremely jealous of the Independents, who were bent on more complete toleration of opinions, and who aimed at a total overthrow of many of the old institutions of the country. So soon as the king was humbled, and in their hands, it was proposed to disband the army which had gloriously finished the war, and which was chiefly composed of the Independents, and to create a new one on a Presbyterian model. The excuse was, that the contest was ended, while, indeed, the royalists were rather dispersed and humbled, than subdued. It was voted that, in the reduced army, no one should have, except Fairfax, a higher rank than colonel, a measure aimed directly at Cromwell, now both feared and distrusted by the Presbyterians. But the army refused to be disbanded without payment of its arrears, and, moreover, marched upon London, in spite of the vote of the parliament that it should not come within twenty-five miles. Several irritating resolutions were passed by the parliament, which only had the effect of uniting the army more strongly together, in resistance against parliament, as well as against the king. The Lords and Commons then voted that the king should be brought nearer London, and new negotiations opened with him, which were prevented from being carried into effect by the seizure of the king at Holmby House, by Cornet Joyce, with a strong party of horse belonging to Whalley's regiment, probably at the instigation of Cromwell and Ireton. His majesty was now in the hands of the army, his worst enemy, and, though treated with respect and deference, was really guarded closely, and watched by the Independent generals. The same day, Cromwell left London in haste, and joined the army, knowing full well that he was in imminent danger of arrest. He was cordially received, and forthwith the army resolved not to disband until all the national grievances were redressed, thus setting itself up virtually against all the constituted authorities. Fairfax, Cromwell, Ireton, and Hammond, with other high officers, then waited on the king, and protested that they had nothing to do with the seizure of his person, and even invited him to return to Holmby House. But the king never liked the Presbyterians, and was willing to remain with the army instead, especially since he was permitted to have Episcopal chaplains, and to see whomsoever he pleased.

Seizure of the King.

The generals of the army were not content with the seizure of his majesty's person, but now caused eleven of the most obnoxious of the Presbyterian leaders of parliament to be accused, upon which they hid themselves, while the army advanced towards London. The parliament, at first, made a show of resistance, but soon abandoned its course, and now voted that the army should be treated with more respect and care. It was evident now to all persons where the seat of power rested.

In the mean time, the king was removed from Newmarket to Kingston, from Hatfield to Woburn Abbey, and thence to Windsor Castle, which was the scene of new intrigues and negotiations on his part, and on the part of parliament, and even on the part of Cromwell. This was the last chance the king had. Had he cordially sided now with either the Presbyterians or the Independents, his subsequent misfortunes might have been averted. But he hated both parties, and trifled with both, and hoped to conquer both. He was unable to see the crisis of his affairs, or to adapt himself to it. He was incapable of fair dealing with any party. His duplicity and dissimulation were fully made known to Cromwell and Ireton by a letter of the king to his wife, which they intercepted; and they made up their minds to more decided courses. The king was more closely guarded; the army marched to the immediate vicinity of London; a committee of safety was named, and parliament was intimidated into the passing of a resolution, by which the city of London and the Tower were intrusted to Fairfax and Cromwell. The Presbyterian party was forever depressed, its leading members fled to France, and the army had every thing after its own way. Parliament still was ostensibly the supreme power in the land; but it was entirely controlled by the Independent leaders and generals.

Triumph of the Independents.

The victorious Independents then made their celebrated proposals to the king, as the Presbyterians had done before them; only the conditions which the former imposed were more liberal, and would have granted to the king powers almost as great as are now exercised by the sovereign. But he would not accept them, and continued to play his game of kingcraft.

Shortly after, the king contrived to escape from Windsor to the Isle of Wight, with the connivance of Cromwell. At Carisbrook Castle, where he quartered himself, he was more closely guarded than before. Seeing this, he renewed his negotiations with the Scots, and attempted to escape. But escape was impossible. He was now in the hands of men who aimed at his life. A strong party in the army, called the *Levellers*, openly advocated his execution, and the establishment of a republic; and parliament itself resolved to have no further treaty with him. His only hope was now from the Scots, and they prepared to rescue him.

Although the government of the country was now virtually in the hands of the Independents and of the army, the state of affairs was extremely critical, and none other than Cromwell could have extricated the dominant party from the difficulties. In one quarter was an imprisoned and intriguing king in league with the Scots, while the royalist party was waiting for the first reverse to rise up again with new strength in various parts of the land. Indeed, there were several insurrections, which required all the vigor of Cromwell to suppress. The city of London, which held the purse-strings, was at heart Presbyterian, and was extremely dissatisfied with the course affairs were taking. Then, again, there was a large, headstrong, levelling, mutineer party in the army, which clamored for violent courses, which at that time would have ruined every thing. Finally, the Scotch parliament had voted to raise a force of forty thousand men, to invade England and rescue the king. Cromwell, before he could settle the peace of the country, must overcome all these difficulties. Who, but he, could have triumphed over so many obstacles, and such apparent anarchy?

The first thing Cromwell did was to restore order in England; and therefore he obtained leave to march against the rebels, who had arisen in various parts of the country. Scarcely were these subdued, before he heard of the advance of the Scottish army, under the Duke of Hamilton. A second civil war now commenced, and all parties witnessed the result with fearful anxiety.

The army of Hamilton was not as large as he had hoped. Still he had fifteen thousand men, and crossed the borders, while Cromwell was besieging Pembroke, in a distant part of the kingdom. But Pembroke soon surrendered; and Cromwell advanced, by rapid marches, against the Scottish army, more than twice as large as his own. The hostile forces met in Lancashire. Hamilton was successively defeated at Preston, Wigan, and Warrington. Hamilton was taken prisoner at Uttoxeter, August 25, 1648, and his invading army was completely annihilated.

Cromwell Invades Scotland.

Cromwell then resolved to invade, in his turn, Scotland itself, and, by a series of military actions, to give to the army a still greater ascendency. He was welcomed at Edinburgh by the Duke of Argyle, the head of an opposing faction, and was styled "the Preserver of Scotland." That country was indeed rent with most unhappy divisions, which Lieutenant-General Cromwell remedied in the best way he could; and then he rapidly retraced his steps, to compose greater difficulties at home. In his absence, the Presbyterians had rallied, and were again negotiating with the king on the Isle of Wight, while Cromwell was openly denounced in the House of Lords as ambitious, treacherous, and perfidious. Fairfax, his superior in command, but inferior in influence, was subduing the rebel royalists, who made a firm resistance at Colchester, and all the various parties were sending their remonstrances to parliament.

Among these was a remarkable one from the regiments of Ireton, Ingoldsby, Fleetwood, Whalley, and Overton, which imputed to parliament the neglect of the affairs of the realm, called upon it to proclaim the sovereignty of the people and the election of a supreme magistrate, and threatened to take matters into their own hands. This was in November, 1646; but, long before this, a republican government was contemplated, although the leaders of the army had not joined in with the hue and cry which the fanatical Levellers had made.

Seizure of the King a Second Time.

In the midst of the storm which the petition from the army had raised, the news arrived that the king had been seized a second time, and had been carried a prisoner to Hurst Castle, on the coast opposite the island, where he was closely confined by command of the army. Parliament was justly indignant, and the debate relative to peace was resumed with redoubled earnestness. It is probable that, at this crisis, so irritated was parliament against the army, peace would have been made with the king, and the Independent party suppressed, had not most decisive measures been taken by the army. A rupture between the parliament and the army was inevitable. But Cromwell and the army chiefs had resolved upon their courses. The mighty stream of revolution could no longer be checked. Twenty thousand men had vowed that parliament should be purged. On the morning of December 6, Colonel Pride and Colonel Rich, with troops, surrounded the House of Commons; and, as the members were going into the house, the most obnoxious were seized and sent to prison, among whom were Primrose, who had lost his ears in his contest against the crown, Waller, Harley, Walker, and various other men, who had distinguished themselves as advocates of constitutional liberty. None now remained in the House of Commons but some forty Independents, who were the tools of the army, and who voted to Cromwell their hearty thanks. "The minority had now become a majority," —which is not unusual in revolutionary times, —and proceeded to the work, in good earnest, which he had long contemplated.

Trial of the King.

This was the trial of the king, whose apartments at Whitehall were now occupied by his victorious general, and whose treasures were now lavished on his triumphant soldiers.

On the 17th of December, 1648, in the middle of the night, the drawbridge of the Castle of Hurst was lowered, and a troop of horse entered the yard. Two days after, the king was removed to Windsor. On the 23d, the Commons voted that he should be brought to trial. On the 20th of January, Charles Stuart, King of England, was brought before the Court of High Commission, in Westminster Hall, and placed at the bar, to be tried by this self-constituted body for his life. In the indictment, he was charged with being a tyrant, traitor, and murderer. To such an indictment, and before such a body, the dignified but unfortunate successor of William the Conqueror demurred. He refused to acknowledge the jurisdiction of the court. But the solemn mockery of the trial proceeded nevertheless, and on the 27th, sentence of death was pronounced upon the prisoner—that prisoner the King of England, a few years before the absolute ruler of the state. On January 30, the bloody sentence was executed, and the soul of the murdered king ascended to that God who pardons those who put their trust in him, in spite of all their mistakes, errors, and delusions. The career of Charles I. is the most melancholy in English history. That he was tyrannical, that he disregarded the laws by which he swore to rule, that he was narrow, and bigoted, that he was deceitful in his promises, that he was bent on overturning the liberties of England, and did not comprehend the wants and circumstances of his times, can scarcely be questioned. But that he was sincere in his religion, upright in his private life, of respectable talents, and good intentions, must also be admitted. His execution, or rather his martyrdom, made a deep and melancholy impression in all Christian countries, and was the great blunder which the republicans made—a blunder which Hampden would have avoided. His death, however, removed from England a most dangerous intriguer, and, for a while, cemented the power of Cromwell and his party, who now had undisputed ascendency in the government of the realm. Charles's exactions and tyranny provoked the resistance of parliament, and the indignation of the people, then intensely excited in discussing the abstract principles of civil and religious liberty. The resistance of parliament created the necessity of an army, and the indignation of the people filled it with enthusiasts. The army flushed with success, forgot its relations and duties, and usurped the government it had destroyed, and a military dictatorship, the almost inevitable result of revolution, though under the name of a republic, succeeded to the despotism of the Stuart kings. This republic, therefore, next claims attention.

References.—The standard Histories of England. Guizot's History of the English Revolution. Clarendon's History of the Rebellion. Forster's Life of the Statesmen of the Commonwealth. Neal's History of the Puritans. Macaulay's Essays. Lives of Bacon, Raleigh, Strafford, Laud, Hampden, and Cromwell. These works furnish all the common information. Few American students have the opportunity to investigate Thurlow's State Papers, or Rushworth, Whitelocke, Dugdale, or Mrs. Hutchinson.

CHAPTER XIII
PROTECTORATE OF OLIVER CROMWELL

The Protectorate.

On the day of the king's execution, January 30, 1649, the House of Commons—being but the shadow of a House of Commons, yet ostensibly the supreme authority in England—passed an act prohibiting the proclamation of the Prince of Wales, or any other person, to be king of England. On the 6th of February, the House of Peers was decreed useless and dangerous, and was also dispensed with. On the next day, royalty was formally abolished. The supreme executive power was vested in a council of state of forty members, the president of which was Bradshaw, the relative and friend of Milton, who employed his immortal genius in advocating the new government. The army remained under the command of Fairfax and Cromwell; the navy was controlled by a board of admiralty, headed by Sir Harry Vane. A greater toleration of religion was proclaimed than had ever been known before, much to the annoyance of the Presbyterians, who were additionally vexed that the state was separated entirely from the church.

The Independents pursued their victory with considerable moderation, and only the Duke of Hamilton, and Lords Holland and Capel, were executed for treason, while a few others were shut up in the Tower. Never was so mighty a revolution accomplished with so little bloodshed. But it required all the wisdom and vigor of Fairfax and Cromwell to repress the ultra radical spirit which had crept into several detachments of the army, and to baffle the movements which the Scots were making in favor of Charles Stuart, who had already been proclaimed king by the parliament of Scotland, and in Ireland by the Marquis of Ormond.

Storming of Drogheda and Wexford.

The insurrection in Ireland first required the notice of the new English government. Cromwell accepted the conduct of the war, and the office of lord lieutenant. Dublin and Derry were the only places which held out for the parliament. All other parts of the country were in a state of insurrection. On the 15th of August, Cromwell and his son-in-law, Ireton, landed near Dublin with an army of six thousand foot and three thousand horse only;

but it was an army of Ironsides and Titans. In six months, the complete reconquest of the country was effected. The policy of the conqueror was severe and questionable; but it was successful. In the hope of bringing the war to a speedy termination, Cromwell proceeded in such a way as to bring terror to his name, and curses on his memory. Drogheda and Wexford were not only taken by storm, but nearly the whole garrison, of more than five thousand men, were barbarously put to the sword. The Irish quailed before such a victor, and town after town hastened to make peace. Cromwell's excuse for his undeniable cruelties was, the necessity of the case, of which we may reasonably suppose him to be a judge. Scotland was in array, and English affairs, scarcely settled, demanded his presence in London. An imperfect conquest, on the principles of Rousseau's philanthropy, did not suit the taste or the notions of Cromwell. If he had consumed a few more months than he actually employed, either in treaty-making with a deceitful though oppressed people, or in battles on the principles of the military science then in vogue, the cause of Independency would have been lost; and that cause, associated with that of liberty, in the eyes of Cromwell, was of more value than the whole Irish nation, or any other nation. Cromwell was a devotee to a cause. Principles, with him, were every thing; men were nothing in comparison. To advance the principles for which he fought, he scrupled to use no means or instruments. In this he may have erred. But this policy was the secret of his success. We cannot justify his cruelties in war, because it is hard to justify the war itself. But if we acknowledge its necessity, we should remember that such a master of war as was Cromwell knew his circumstances better than we do or can know. To his immortal glory it can be said that he never inflicted cruelty when he deemed it unnecessary; that he never fought for the love of fighting; and that he stopped fighting when the cause for which he fought was won. And this is more than can be said of most conquerors, even of those imbued with sentimental horror of bloodshed. Our world is full of cant. Cromwell's language sometimes sounds like it, especially when he speaks of the "hand of the Lord" in "these mighty changes," who "breaketh the enemies of his church in pieces."

When the conquest of Ireland was completed, Cromwell hastened to London to receive the thanks of parliament and the acclamations of the people; and then he hurried to Scotland to do battle with the Scots, who had made a treaty with the king, and were resolved to establish Presbyterianism and royalty. Cromwell now superseded Fairfax, and was created captain-general of the forces of the commonwealth. Cromwell passed the borders, reached Edinburgh without molestation, and then advanced on the Scotch army of twenty-seven thousand men, under Lesley, at Dunbar, where was fought a most desperate battle, but which Cromwell gained with marvellous intrepidity and skill. Three thousand men were killed, and ten thousand taken prisoners, and the hopes of the Scots blasted. The lord-general made a halt, and the whole army sang the one hundred and seventeenth psalm, and then advanced upon the capital, which opened its gates. Glasgow followed the example; the whole south of Scotland submitted; while the king fled towards the Highlands, but soon rallied, and even took the bold resolution of marching into England, while Cromwell was besieging Perth. Charles reached Worcester before he was overtaken, established himself with sixteen thousand men, but was attacked by Cromwell, was defeated, and with difficulty fled. He reached France, however, and quietly rested until he was brought back by General Monk.

Battle of Worcester.

With the battle of Worcester, September 3, 1651, which Cromwell called his "crowning mercy," ended his military life. From that day to the time when be became protector, the most noticeable point in his history is his conduct towards the parliament. And this conduct is the most objectionable part of his life and character; for in this he violated the very principles he originally professed, and committed the same usurpations which he condemned in Charles I. Here he was not true to himself or his cause. Here he laid himself open to the censure of all posterity; and although he had great excuses, and his course has many palliations, still it would seem a mockery of all moral distinctions not to condemn in him what we would condemn in another, or what Cromwell himself condemned in the murdered king. It is true he did not, at once, turn usurper, not until circumstances seemed to warrant the usurpation—the utter impossibility of governing England, except by exercising the rights and privileges of an absolute monarch. On the principles of expediency, he has been vindicated, and will be vindicated, so long as his cause is advocated by partisan historians, or expediency itself is advocated as a rule of life.

Policy of Cromwell.

After the battle of Worcester, Cromwell lost, in a measure, his democratic sympathies, and naturally, in view of the great excesses of the party with which he had been identified. That he desired the public good we cannot reasonably doubt; and he adapted himself to those circumstances which seemed to advance it, and which a spirit of wild democratic license assuredly did not. So far as it contributed to overturn the throne of the Stuarts, and the whole system of public abuses, civil and ecclesiastical, Cromwell favored it. But no further. When it seemed subversive of law and order, the grand ends of all civil governments, then he opposed it. And in this he showed that he was much more conservative in his spirit than has often been supposed;

and, in this conservatism he resembled Luther and other great reformers, who were not unreflecting incendiaries, as is sometimes thought—men who destroy, but do not reconstruct. Luther, at heart, was a conservative, and never sought a change to which he was not led by strong inward tempests—forced to make it by the voice of his conscience, which he ever obeyed, and loyalty to which so remarkably characterized the early reformers, and no class of men more than the Puritans. Cromwell abhorred the government of Charles, because it was not a government which respected justice, and which set at defiance the higher laws of God. It was not because Charles violated the constitution, it was because he violated truth and equity, and the nation's good, that he opposed him. Cromwell usurped his prerogatives, and violated the English constitution; but he did not transgress those great primal principles of truth, for which constitutions are made. He looked beyond constitutions to abstract laws of justice; and it never can be laid to his charge that he slighted these, or proved a weak or wicked ruler. He quarrelled with parliament, because the parliament wished to perpetuate its existence unlawfully and meanly, and was moreover unwilling and unable to cope with many difficulties which constantly arose. It may be supposed that Cromwell may thus have thought: "I will not support the parliament, for it will not maintain law; it will not legislate wisely or beneficently; it seeks its own, not the nation's good. And therefore I take away its existence, and rule myself; for I have the fear of God before my eyes, and am determined to rule by his laws, and to advance his glory." Deluded he was; blinded by ambition he may have been but he sought to elevate his country; and his efforts in her behalf are appreciated and praised by the very men who are most severe on his undoubted usurpation.

The Rump Parliament.

Dispersion of the Parliament.

Shortly after the Long Parliament was purged, at the instigation of Cromwell, and had become the Rump Parliament, as it was derisively called, it appointed a committee to take into consideration the time when their powers should cease. But the battle of Worcester was fought before any thing was done, except to determine that future parliaments should consist of four hundred members, and that the existing members should be returned, in the next parliament, for the places they then represented. At length, in December, 1651, it was decided, through the urgent entreaties of Cromwell, but only by a small majority, that the present parliament should cease in November, 1654. Thus it was obvious to Cromwell that the parliament, reduced as it was, and composed of Independents, was jealous of him, and also was aiming to perpetuate its own existence, against all the principles of a representative government. Such are men, so greedy of power themselves, so censorious in regard to the violation of justice by others, so blind to the violation of justice by themselves. Cromwell was not the man to permit the usurpation of power by a body of forty or sixty Independents, however willing he was to assume it himself. Beside, the Rump Parliament was inefficient, and did not consult the interests of the country. There was general complaint. But none complained more bitterly than Cromwell himself. Meeting Whitelock, who then held the great seal, he said that the "army was beginning to have a strange distaste against them; that their pride, and ambition, and self-seeking; their engrossing all places of honor and profit to themselves and their friends; their daily breaking into new and violent parties; their delays of business, and design to perpetuate themselves, and continue the power in their own hands; their meddling in private matters between party and party, their injustice and partiality; the scandalous lives of some of them, do give too much ground for people to open their mouths against them; and unless there be some power to check them, it will be impossible to prevent our ruin." These things Whitelock admitted, but did not see how they could be removed since both he and Cromwell held their commissions from this same parliament, which was the supreme authority. But Cromwell thought there was nothing to hope, and every thing to fear, from such a body of men; that they would destroy what the Lord had done. "We all forget God," said he, "and God will forget us. He will give us up to confusion, and these men will help it on, if left to themselves." Then he asked the great lawyer and chancellor, "What if a man should take upon himself to be king?"—evidently having in view the regal power. But Whitelock presented such powerful reasons against it, that Cromwell gave up the idea, though he was resolved to destroy the parliament. He then held repeated conferences with the officers of the army, who sympathized with him, and who supported him. At last, while parliament was about to pass an obnoxious bill, Cromwell hurried to the House, taking with him a file of musketeers, having resolved what he would do. These he left in the lobby, and, taking his seat, listened a while to the discussion, and then rose, and addressed the House. Waxing warm, he told them, in violent language, "that they were deniers of justice, were oppressive, profane men, were planning to bring in Presbyterians, and would lose no time in destroying the cause they had deserted." Sir Harry Vane and Sir Peter Wentworth rose to remonstrate, but Cromwell, leaving his seat, walked up and down the floor, with his hat on, reproached the different members, who again remonstrated. But Cromwell, raising his voice, exclaimed, "You are no parliament. Get you gone. Give way to honester men." Then, stamping with his feet, the door opened, and the musketeers entered, and the members were dispersed, after giving vent to their feelings in the language of reproach. Most of them wore swords, but none offered resistance to the man they feared, and tamely departed.

Thus was the constitution utterly subverted, and parliament, as well as the throne, destroyed. Cromwell published, the next day, a vindication of his conduct, setting forth the incapacity, selfishness and corruption of the parliament, in which were some of the best men England ever had, including Sir Harry Vane, Algernon Sydney, and Sir Peter Wentworth.

His next step was to order the continuance of all the courts of justice, as before, and summon a new parliament, the members of which were nominated by himself and his council of officers. The army, with Cromwell at the head, was now the supreme authority.

The new parliament, composed of one hundred and twenty persons, assembled on the 4th of July, when Cromwell explained the reason of his conduct, and set forth the mercies of the Lord to England. This parliament was not constitutional, since it was not elected by the people of England, but by Cromwell, and therefore would be likely to be his tool. But had the elections been left free, the Presbyterians would have been returned as the largest party, and they would have ruined the cause which Cromwell and the Independents sought to support. In revolutions, there cannot be pursued half measures. Revolutions are the contest between parties. The strongest party gains the ascendency, and keeps it if it can—never by old, constituted laws. In the English Revolution the Independents gained this ascendency by their valor, enthusiasm, and wisdom. And their great representative ruled in their name.

Cromwell Assumes the Protectorship.

The new members of parliament reappointed the old Council of State, at the head of which was Cromwell, abolished the High Court of Chancery, nominated commissioners to preside in courts of justice, and proceeded to other sweeping changes, which alarmed their great nominator, who induced them to dissolve themselves and surrender their trust into his hands, under the title of Lord Protector of England, Scotland, and Ireland. On the 16th of December, he was installed in his great office, with considerable pomp, in the Court of Chancery, and the new constitution was read, which invested him with all the powers of a king. It, however, ordained that he should rule with the aid of a parliament, which should have all the functions and powers of the old parliaments, should be assembled within five months, should last three years, and should consist of four hundred and sixty members. It provided for the maintenance of the army and navy, of which the protector was the head, and decided that the great officers of state should be chosen by approbation of parliament. Religious toleration was proclaimed, and provision made for the support of the clergy.

The Dutch War.

Thus was the constitution of the nation changed, and a republic substituted for a monarchy, at the head of which was the ablest man of his age. And there was need of all his abilities. England then was engaged in war with the Dutch, and the internal state of the nation demanded the attention of a vigorous mind and a still more vigorous arm.

The Dutch war was prosecuted with great vigor, and was signalized by the naval victories of Blake, Dean, and Monk over the celebrated Van Tromp and De Ruyter, the Dutch admirals. The war was caused by the commercial jealousies of the two nations, and by the unwillingness of the Prince of Orange, who had married a daughter of Charles I., to acknowledge the ambassador of the new English republic. But the superiority which the English sailors evinced, soon taught the Dutch how dangerous it was to provoke a nation which should be its ally on all grounds of national policy, and peace was therefore honorably secured after a most successful war.

The war being ended, the protector had more leisure to attend to business at home. Sir Matthew Hale was made chief justice, and Thurloe, secretary of state; disorganizers were punished; an insurrection in Scotland was quelled by General Monk; and order and law were restored.

Meanwhile, the new parliament, the first which had been freely elected for fourteen years, soon manifested a spirit of opposition to Cromwell, deferred to vote him supplies, and annoyed him all in its power. Still he permitted the members to discuss trifling subjects and waste their time for five months; but, at the earliest time the new constitution would allow, he summoned them to the Painted Chamber, made them a long speech, reminded them of their neglect in attending to the interests of the nation, while disputing about abstract questions, even while it was beset with dangers and difficulties, and then dissolved them, (January 22, 1656.)

Cromwell Rules without a Parliament.

For the next eighteen months, he ruled without a parliament and found no difficulty in raising supplies, and supporting his now unlimited power. During this time, he suppressed a dangerous insurrection in England itself, and carried on a successful and brilliant war against Spain, a power which he hated with all the capacity of hatred of which his nation has shown itself occasionally so capable. In the naval war with Spain, Blake was again the hero. During the contest the rich island of Jamaica was conquered from the Spanish, a possession which England has ever since greatly valued.

Encouraged by his successes, Cromwell now called a third parliament, which he opened the 17th of September, 1656, after ejecting one hundred of the members, on account of their political sentiments. The new House voted for the prosecution of the Spanish war, granted ample supplies, and offered to Cromwell the title of king. But his council violently opposed it, and Cromwell found it expedient to relinquish this object of his heart. But his protectorate was continued to him, and he was empowered to nominate his successor.

In a short time, however, the spirit of the new parliament was manifested, not only by violent opposition to the protector, but in acts which would, if carried out, have subverted the government again, and have plunged England in anarchy. It was plain that the protector could not rule with a real representation of the nation. So he dissolved it; and thus ended the last effort of Cromwell to rule with a parliament; or, as his advocates say, to restore the constitution of his country. It was plain that there was too much party animosity and party ambition to permit the protector, shackled by the law, to carry out his designs of order and good government. Self-preservation compelled him to be suspicious and despotic, and also to prohibit the exercise of the Catholic worship, and to curtail the religious rights of the Quakers, Socinians, and Jews. The continual plottings and political disaffections of these parties forced him to rule on a system to which he was not at first inclined. England was not yet prepared for the civil and religious liberty at which the advocates of revolution had at first aimed.

So Cromwell now resolved to rule alone. And he ruled well. His armies were victorious on the continent, and England was respected abroad, and prospered at home. The most able and upright men were appointed to office. The chairs of the universities were filled with illustrious scholars, and the bench adorned with learned and honest judges. He defended the great interests of Protestantism on the Continent, and formed alliances which contributed to the political and commercial greatness of his country. He generously assisted the persecuted Protestants in the valleys of Piedmont, and refused to make treaties with hostile powers unless the religious liberties of the Protestants were respected. He lived at Hampton Court, the old palace of Cardinal Wolsey, in simple and sober dignity; nor was debauchery or riot seen at his court. He lived simply and unostentatiously, and to the last preserved the form, and perhaps the spirit, of his early piety. He surrounded himself with learned men, and patronized poets and scholars. Milton was his familiar guest, and the youthful Dryden was not excluded from his table. An outward morality, at least, was generally observed, and the strictest discipline was kept at his court.

Had Cromwell's life been prolonged to threescore and ten, the history of England might have been different for the next two hundred years. But such was not his fortune. Providence removed him from the scene of his conflicts and his heroism not long after the dissolution of his last parliament. The death of a favorite daughter preyed upon his mind, and the cares of government undermined his constitution. He died on the 3d of September, 1658, the anniversary of his great battles of Worcester and Dunbar, in the sixtieth year of his age.

Two or three nights before he died, he was heard to ejaculate the following prayer, in the anticipation of his speedy departure; "Lord, though I am a miserable and wretched creature, I am in covenant with thee, through thy grace; and I may, I will come to thee, for thy people. Thou hast made me, though very unworthy, a mean instrument to do them good, and Thee service; and many of them have set too high value upon me, though others wish and would be glad of my death. Lord, however Thou disposest of me, continue and go on to do good to them. Give them consistency of judgment, one heart, and mutual love; and, with the work of reformation, go on to deliver them, and make the name of Christ glorious in the world. Teach those who look too much on thy instrument to depend more upon Thyself. Pardon such as desire to trample upon the dust of a poor worm, for they are Thy people too. And pardon the folly of this short prayer, even for Jesus Christ's sake. And give me a good night, if it be Thy pleasure. Amen."

Thus closed the career of Oliver Cromwell, the most remarkable man in the list of England's heroes. His motives and his honesty have often been impeached, and sometimes by the most excellent and discriminating, but oftener by heated partisans, who had no sympathy with his reforms or opinions. His genius, however, has never been questioned, nor his extraordinary talent, for governing a nation in the most eventful period of its history. And there is a large class, and that class an increasing one, not confined to Independents or republicans, who look upon him as one habitually governed by a stern sense of duty, as a man who feared God and regarded justice, as a man sincerely devoted to the best interests of his country, and deserving of the highest praises of all enlightened critics. No man has ever been more extravagantly eulogized, or been the subject of more unsparing abuse and more cordial detestation. Some are incapable of viewing him in any other light than as a profound hypocrite and ambitious despot, while others see in him nothing but the saint and unspotted ruler. He had his defects; for human nature, in all instances, is weak; but in spite of these, and of many and great inconsistencies, from which no sophistry can clear him, his great and varied excellences will ever entitle him to the rank accorded to him by such writers as Vaughan and Carlyle.

Regal Government Restored.

With the death of Cromwell virtually ended the republic. "Puritanism without its king, is kingless, anarchic, falls into dislocation, staggers, and plunges into even deeper anarchy." His son Richard, according to his will, was proclaimed protector in his stead. But his reign was short. Petitions poured in from every quarter for the restoration of parliament. It was restored, and also with it royalty itself. General Monk advanced with his army from Scotland, and quartered in London. In May, 1660, Charles II. was proclaimed king at the gates of Westminster Hall. The experiment of a republic had been tried, and failed. Puritanism veiled its face. It was no longer the spirit of the nation. A great reaction commenced. Royalty, with new but disguised despotism, resumed its sway.

References.—Carlyle's, Dr. Vaughan's, and D'Aubigné's Life of Cromwell. Neal's History of the Puritans. Macaulay's History of England. Godwin's Commonwealth. The common histories of England. Milton's prose writings may be profitably read in this connection, and the various reviews and essays which have of late been written, on the character of Cromwell.

CHAPTER XIV
THE REIGN OF CHARLES II

The Restoration.

Great Public Rejoicings.

Few events in English history have ever been hailed with greater popular enthusiasm than the restoration of Charles II. On the 25th of May, 1660, he landed near Dover, with his two brothers, the Dukes of York and Gloucester. On the 29th of May, he made his triumphal entry into London. It was his birthday, he was thirty years of age, and in the full maturity of manly beauty, while his gracious manners and captivating speech made him the favorite of the people, as well as of the old nobility. The season was full of charms, and the spirits of all classes were buoyant with hope. Every thing conspired to give a glow to the popular enthusiasm. A long line of illustrious monarchs was restored. The hateful fires of religious fanaticism were apparently extinguished. An accomplished sovereign, disciplined in the school of adversity, of brilliant talents, amiable temper, fascinating manners, and singular experiences, had returned to the throne of his ancestors, and had sworn to rule by the laws, to forget old offences, and promote liberty of conscience. No longer should there be a government of soldiers, nor the rule of a man hostile to those pleasures and opinions which had ever been dear to the English people. With the return of the exiled prince, should also return joy, peace, and prosperity. For seventeen years, there had been violent political and social animosities, war, tyranny, social restraints, and religious fanaticism. But order and law were now to be reëstablished, and the reign of cant and hypocrisy was now to end. Justice and mercy were to meet together in the person of a king who was represented to have all the virtues and none of the vices of his station and his times. So people reasoned and felt, of all classes and conditions. And why should they not rejoice in the restoration of such blessings? The ways were strewn with flowers, the bells sent forth a merry peal, the streets were hung with tapestries; while aldermen with their heavy chains, nobles in their robes of pomp, ladies with their silks and satins, and waving handkerchiefs, filling all the balconies and windows; musicians, dancers, and exulting crowds,—all welcomed the return of Charles. Never was there so great a jubilee in London; and never did monarch receive such addresses of flattery and loyalty. "Dread monarch," said the Earl of Manchester, in the House of Lords, "I offer no flattering titles. You are the desire of three kingdoms, the strength and stay of the tribes of the people." "Most royal sovereign," said one of the deputations, "the hearts of all are filled with veneration for you, confidence in you, longings for you. All degrees, and ages, and sexes, high, low, rich and poor, men, women, and children, join in sending up to Heaven one prayer, 'Long live King Charles II.;' so that the English air is not susceptible of any other sound, bells, bonfires, peals of ordnance, shouts, and acclamations of the people bear no other moral; nor can his majesty conceive with what joy, what cheerfulness, what lettings out of the soul, what expressions of transported minds, a stupendous concourse of people attended the proclamation of their most potent, most mighty, and most undoubted king." Such was the adulatory language addressed by the English people to the son of the king they had murdered, and to a man noted for every frivolity and vice that could degrade a sovereign. What are we to think of that public joy, and public sycophancy, after so many years of hard fighting for civil and religious liberty? For what were the battles of Naseby and Worcester? For what the Solemn League and Covenant? For what the trial and execution of Charles I.? For what the elevation of Cromwell? Alas! for what were all the experiments and sufferings of twenty years, the breaking up of old and mighty customs, and twenty years of blood, usurpation, and change? What were the benefits of the Revolution? Or, had it no benefits? How happened it that a whole nation should simultaneously rise and expel their monarch from a throne which his ancestors had enjoyed for six hundred years, and then, in so short a time, have elevated to this old throne, which was supposed to be subverted forever, the son of their insulted, humiliated, and murdered king? and this without bloodshed, with every demonstration of national rejoicings, and with every external mark of repentance for their past conduct. Charles, too, was restored without any of those limitations by which the nation sought to curtail the power of his father. The nation surrendered to him more absolute power than the most ambitious kings, since the reign of John, had ever claimed,—more than he ever dared to expect. How shall we explain these things? And what is the moral which they teach?

Reaction to Revolutionary Principles.

One fact is obvious,—that a great reaction had taken place in the national mind as to revolutionary principles. It is evident that a great disgust for the government of Cromwell had succeeded the antipathy to the royal government of Charles. All classes as ardently desired the restoration, as they had before favored the rebellion. Even the old parliamentarians hailed the return of Charles, notwithstanding it was admitted that the protectorate was a vigorous administration; that law and order were enforced; that religious liberty was proclaimed; that the rights of conscience were respected; that literature and science were encouraged; that the morals of the people were purified; that the ordinances of religion were observed; that vice and folly were discouraged; that justice was ably administered; that peace and plenty were enjoyed; that prosperity attended the English arms abroad; and that the nation was as much respected abroad as it was prosperous at home. These things were admitted by the very people who rejoiced in the restoration. And yet, in spite of all these substantial blessings, the reign of Cromwell was odious. Why was this?

It can only be explained on the supposition that there were *unendurable evils* connected with the administration of Cromwell, which more than balanced the benefits he conferred; or, that expectations were held out by Charles of national benefits greater than those conferred by the republic; or, that the nation had so retrograded in elevation of sentiment as to be unable to appreciate the excellences of Cromwell's administration.

There is much to support all of these suppositions. In regard to the evils connected with the republic, it is certain that a large standing army was supported, and was necessary to uphold the government of the protector, in order to give to it efficiency and character. This army was expensive, and the people felt the burden. They always complain under taxation, whether necessary or not. Taxes ever make any government unpopular, and made the administration of Cromwell especially so. And the army showed the existence of a military despotism, which, however imperatively called for, or rendered unavoidable by revolution, was still a hateful fact. The English never have liked the principle of a military despotism. And it was a bitter reflection to feel that so much blood and treasure had been expended to get rid of the arbitrary rule of the Stuarts, only to introduce a still more expensive and arbitrary government, under the name of a republic. Moreover, the eyes of the people were opened to the moral corruptions incident to the support of a large army, without which the power of Cromwell would have been unsubstantial. He may originally have desired to establish his power on a civil basis, rather than a military one; but his desires were not realized. The parliaments which he assembled were unpractical and disorderly. He was forced to rule without them. But the nation could not forget this great insult to their liberties, and to those privileges which had ever been dear to them. The preponderance of the civil power has, for several centuries, characterized the government; and no blessings were sufficiently great to balance the evil, in the eye of an Englishman, of the preponderance of a military government, neither the excellence of Cromwell's life, nor the glory and greatness to which he raised the nation.

Excellences in Charles's Government.

Again, much was expected of Charles II., and there was much in his character and early administration to produce content. His manners were agreeable. He had no personal antipathies or jealousies. He selected, at first, the wisest and best of all parties to be his counsellors and ministers. He seemed to forget old offences. He was fond of pleasure; was good-natured and affable. He summoned a free parliament. His interests were made to appear identical with those of the people. He promised to rule by the laws. He did not openly infringe on the constitution. And he restored, what has ever been so dear to the great body of the nation, the Episcopal Church in all its beauty and grandeur, while he did not recommence the persecution of Puritans until some time had elapsed from his restoration. Above all, he disbanded the army, which was always distasteful to the people,—odious, onerous, and oppressive. The civil power again triumphed over that of the military, and circumstances existed which rendered the subversion of liberty very difficult. Many adverse events transpired during his unfortunate and disgraceful reign; but these, in the early part of it, had not, of course, been anticipated.

Failure of the Puritan Experiment.

There is also force in the third supposition, that the nation had retrograded in moral elevation. All writers speak of a strong reaction to the religious fervor of the early revolutionists. The moral influence of the army had proved destructive to the habits and sentiments of the people. A strong love of pleasure and demoralizing amusements existed, when Charles was recalled. A general laxity of morals was lamented by the wisest and best of the nation. The religious convictions of enthusiasts survived their sympathies. Hypocrisy and cant succeeded fervor and honesty. Infidelity lurked in many a bosom in which devotional ardor had once warmly burned. Distrust of all philanthropy and all human virtue was as marked, as faith in the same previously had been. The ordinances of religion became irksome, and it was remembered with bitterness that the Puritans, in the days of their ascendency, had cruelly proscribed the most favorite pleasures and time-honored festivals of old England. But the love of them returned with redoubled vigor. May-poles, wrestling-matches, bear-baitings, puppet-shows, bowls, horse-racing, betting, rope-dancing, romping under the mistletoe on Christmas, eating boars' heads, attending the theatres, health-drinking,—all these old-fashioned ways, in which the English sought merriment, were restored. The evil was chiefly in the excess to which these pleasures were carried; and every thing, which bore any resemblance to the Puritans, was ridiculed and despised. The nation, as a nation, did not love Puritanism, or any thing pertaining to it, after the deep religious excitement had passed away. The people were ashamed of prayer-meetings, of speaking through their noses, of wearing their hair straight, of having their garments cut primly, of calling their children by the name of Moses, Joshua, Jeremiah, Obadiah, &c.; and, in short, of all customs and opinions peculiar to the Extreme Puritans. So general was the disgust of Puritanism, so eager were all to indulge in the pleasures that had been forbidden under the reign of Cromwell, so sick were they of the very name of republicanism, that Puritanism may be said to have proved, in England, a signal failure.

Such were some of the reasons of popular acclamation on the restoration of Charles II., and which we cannot consider entirely without force. A state of mind existed in England as favorable to the encroachments of royalty, as, twenty years before, it had been unfavorable.

Charles was not a high-minded, or honest, or patriotic king; and therefore we might naturally expect the growth of absolutism during his reign. The progress of absolutism is, indeed, one of its features. This, for a time, demands our notice.

On the restoration of Charles II., his subjects made no particular stipulations respecting their liberties, which were incautiously intrusted to his hands. But, at first, he did not seem inclined to grasp at greater powers than what the constitution allowed him. He had the right to appoint the great officers of state, the privilege of veto on legislative enactments, the control of the army and navy, the regulation of all foreign intercourse, and the right of making peace and war. But the constitution did not allow him to rule without a parliament, or to raise taxes without its consent. The parliament might grant or withhold supplies at pleasure, and all money bills originated and were discussed in the House of Commons alone. These were the great principles of the English constitution, which Charles swore to maintain.

Repeal of the Triennial Bill.

The first form in which the encroaching temper of the king was manifested was, in causing the Triennial Bill to be repealed. This was indeed done by the parliament, but through the royal influence. This bill was not that a parliament should be assembled every three years, but that the interval between one session and another should not exceed that period. But this wise law, which had passed by acclamation during the reign of Charles I., and for which even Clarendon had voted, was regarded by

Charles II. as subversive of the liberty of his crown; and a supple, degenerate and sycophantic parliament gratified his wishes.

About the same time was passed the Corporation Act, which enjoined all magistrates, and persons of trust in corporations, to swear that they believed it unlawful, under any pretence whatever to take arms against the king. The Presbyterians refused to take this oath; and they were therefore excluded from offices of dignity and trust. The act bore hard upon all bodies of Dissenters and Roman Catholics, the former of whom were most cruelly persecuted in this reign.

Secret Alliance with Louis XIV.

The next most noticeable effort of Charles to extend his power independently of the law, was his secret alliance with Louis XIV. This was not known to the nation, and even but to few of his ministers, and was the most disgraceful act of his reign. For the miserable stipend of two hundred thousand pounds a year, he was ready to compromise the interests of the kingdom, and make himself the slave of the most ambitious sovereign in Europe. He became a pensioner of France, and yet did not feel his disgrace. Clarendon, attached as he was to monarchy, and to the house of Stuart, could not join him in his base intrigues; and therefore lost, as was to be expected, the royal favor. He had been the companion and counsellor of Charles in the days of his exile; he had attempted to enkindle in his mind the desire of great deeds and virtues; he had faithfully served him as chancellor and prime minister; he was impartial and incorruptible; he was as much attached to Episcopacy, as he was to monarchy; he had even advised Charles to rule without a parliament; and yet he was disgraced because he would not comply with all the wishes of his unscrupulous master. But Clarendon was, nevertheless, unpopular with the nation. He had advised Charles to sell Dunkirk, the proudest trophy of the Revolution, and had built for himself a splendid palace, on the site of the present Clarendon Hotel, in Albemarle Street, which the people called *Dunkirk House*. He was proud, ostentatious, and dictatorial, and was bitterly hostile to all democratic influences. He was too good for one party, and not good enough for the other, and therefore fell to the ground; but he retired, if not with dignity, at least with safety. He retreated to the Continent, and there wrote his celebrated history of the Great Rebellion, a partial and bitter history, yet a valuable record of the great events of the age of revolution which he had witnessed and detested.

Charles received the bribe of two hundred thousand pounds from the French king, with the hope of being made independent of his parliament, and with the condition of assisting Louis XIV. in his aggressive wars on the liberties of Europe, especially those of Holland. He was, at heart an absolutist, and rejoiced in the victories of the "Grand Monarch." But this supply was scarcely sufficient even for his pleasures, much less to support the ordinary pomp of a monarchy, and the civil and military powers of the state. So he had to resort to other means.

Venality and Sycophancy of Parliament.

It happened, fortunately for his encroachments, but unfortunately for the nation, that the English parliament, at that period, was more corrupt, venal, base, and sycophantic than at any period under the Tudor kings, or at any subsequent period under the Hanoverian princes. The House of Commons made no indignant resistance; it sent up but few spirited remonstrances; but tamely acquiesced in the measures of Charles and his ministers. Its members were bought and sold with unblushing facility, and even were corrupted by the agents of the French king. One member received six thousand pounds for his vote. Twenty-nine of the members received from five hundred to twelve hundred pounds a year. Charles I. attempted to rule by opposition to the parliament; Charles II. by corrupting it. Hence it was nearly silent in view of his arbitrary spirit, his repeated encroachments, and his worthless public character.

Among his worst acts was his shutting up the Exchequer, where the bankers and merchants had been in the habit of depositing money on the security of the funds, receiving a large interest of from eight to ten per cent. By closing the Exchequer, the bankers, unable to draw out their money, stopped payment; and a universal panic was the consequence, during which many great failures happened. By this base violation of the public faith, Charles obtained one million three hundred thousand pounds. But it undermined his popularity more than any of his acts, since he touched the pockets of the people. The odium, however, fell chiefly on his ministers, especially those who received the name of the *Cabal*, from the fact that the initials of their names spelt that odious term of reproach, not unmerited in their case.

These five ministers were Clifford, Arlington, Buckingham, Ashley, and Lauderdale, and they were the great instruments of his tyranny. None of them had the talents or audacity of Strafford, or the narrowness and bigotry of Laud; but their counsels were injurious to the nation.

Restrictions on the Press.

Clifford and Arlington were tolerably respectable but indifferent to the glory and shame of their country; while Buckingham, Ashley, and Lauderdale were profligate, unprincipled, and dishonest to a great degree. They aided Charles to corrupt the parliament and deceive the nation. They removed all restraints on his will, and pandered to his depraved tastes.

It was by their suggestion that the king shut up the Exchequer. They also favored restrictions on the press.

These restrictions were another abomination in the reign of Charles, but one ever peculiar to a despotic government. No book could be printed out of London, York, or the Universities. But these were not made wholly with a view of shackling the mind, but to prevent those libels and lampoons which made the government ridiculous in the eyes of the people.

Nothing caused more popular indignation, during this reign, than the Forfeiture of the Corporation of the City of London. The power of the democracy resided, at this time, with the corporations, and as long as they were actuated by the spirit of liberty, there was no prospect of obtaining a parliament entirely subservient to the king. It was determined to take away their charters; and the infamous Judge Jeffreys was found a most subservient tool of royalty in undermining the liberties of the country. The corporation of London, however, received back its charter, after having yielded to the king the right of conferring the appointments of mayor, recorder, and sheriffs.

Among other infringements on the constitution was the fining of jurors when they refused to act according to the direction of the judges. Juries were constantly intimidated, and their privileges were abridged. A new parliament, moreover, was not convoked after three years had elapsed from the dissolution of the old one, which infringement was the more reprehensible, since the king had nothing to fear from the new House of Commons, the members of which vied with each other in a base compliancy with the royal will.

But their sycophancy was nothing compared with what the bishops and clergy of the Established Church generally evinced. Absolute non-resistance was inculcated from the pulpits, and the doctrine ridiculed that power emanated from the people. The divine rights of kings, and the divine ordination of absolute power were the themes of divines, while Oxford proclaimed doctrines worthy of Mariana and the Jesuits.

Thus various influences contributed to make Charles II. absolute in England—the Courts of Justice, the Parliaments, the Universities, and the Church of England. Had he been as ambitious as he was fond of pleasure, as capable of ruling as he was capable of telling stories at the dinner table, he would, like Louis XIV., have reared an absolute throne in England. But he was too easy, too careless, too fond of pleasure to concentrate his thoughts on devising means to enslave his subjects.

Habeas Corpus Act.

It must not, however, be supposed that all his subjects were indifferent to his encroachments, in spite of the great reaction which had succeeded to liberal sentiments. Before he died, the spirit of resistance was beginning to be seen, and some checks to royal power were imposed by parliament itself. The Habeas Corpus Act, the most important since the declaration of Magna Charta, was passed, and through the influence of one of his former ministers, Ashley, now become Earl of Shaftesbury, who took the popular side, after having served all sides, but always with a view of advancing his own interests, a man of great versatility of genius, of great sagacity, and of varied learning. Had Charles continued much longer on the throne, it cannot be doubted that the nation would have been finally aroused to resist his spirit of encroachment, for the principles of liberty had not been proclaimed in vain.

Charles II. was a tyrant, and one of the worst kings that ever sat on the English throne. His leading defect was want of earnestness of character, which made him indifferent to the welfare of his country. England, during his reign, was reduced to comparative insignificance in the eyes of foreigners, and was neither feared nor respected. Her king was neither a powerful friend nor an implacable enemy, and left the Continental Powers to pursue their own ends unmolested and unrebuked. Most of the administrations of the English kings are interlinked with the whole system of European politics. But the reign of Charles is chiefly interesting in relation to the domestic history of England. This history is chiefly the cabals of ministers, the intrigues of the court, the pleasures and follies of the king, the attacks he made on the constitution without any direct warfare with his parliament and the system of religious persecution, which was most intolerant.

The king was at heart a Catholic; and yet the persecution of the Catholics is one of the most signal events of the times. We can scarcely conceive, in this age, of the spirit of distrust and fear which pervaded the national mind in reference to the Catholics. Every calumny was believed. Every trifling offence was exaggerated, and by nearly all classes in the community, by the Episcopalians, as well as by the Presbyterians and the Independents.

Titus Oates.

The most memorable of all the delusions and slanders of the times was produced by the perjuries of an unprincipled wretch called Titus Oates, who took advantage of the general infatuation to advance his individual interests. Like an artful politician, he had only to appeal to a dominant passion or prejudice, and he was sure of making his fortune. Like a cunning, popular orator, he had only to inflame the passions of the people, and he would pass as a genius and a prophet. Few are so abstractedly and coldly intellectual as not to be mainly governed by their tastes or passions. Even men of strong intellect have frequently strong prejudices, and one has only to make himself master of these, in order to lead those who are infinitely their superiors. There is no proof that all who persecuted the Catholics in Charles's time were either weak or ignorant. But there is evidence of unbounded animosity, a traditional hatred, not much diminished since the Gunpowder Plot of Guy Fawkes. The whole nation was ready to believe any thing against the Catholics, and especially against their church, which was supposed to be persecuting and diabolical in all its principles and in all its practice. In this state of the popular mind, Oates made his hideous revelations.

Oates's Revelations.

He was a broken-down clergyman of the Established Church, and had lost caste for disgraceful irregularities. But he professed to hate the Catholics, and such a virtue secured him friends. Among these was the Rev. Dr. Tonge, a man very weak, very credulous, and full of fears respecting the intrigues of the Catholics but honest in his fears. Oates went to this clergyman, and a plan was concerted between them, by which Oates should get a knowledge of the supposed intrigues of the Church of Rome. He professed himself a Catholic, went to the Continent, and entered a Catholic seminary, but was soon discharged for his scandalous irregularities. But he had been a Catholic long enough for his purposes. He returned to London, and revealed his pretended discoveries, among which he declared that the Jesuits had undertaken to restore the Catholic religion in England by force; that they were resolved to take the king's life, and had actually offered a bribe of fifteen thousand pounds to the queen's physician; that they had planned to burn London, and to set fire to all the shipping in the Thames; that they were plotting to make a general massacre of the Protestants; that a French army was about to invade England; and that all the horrors of St. Bartholomew were to be again acted over! Ridiculous as were these assertions, they were believed, and without a particle of evidence; so great was the national infatuation. The king and the Duke of York both pronounced the whole matter a forgery, and laughed at the credulity of the people, but had not sufficient generosity to prevent the triumph of the libellers. But Oates's testimony was not enough to convict any one, the law requiring two witnesses. But, in such a corrupt age, false witnesses could easily be procured. An infamous wretch, by the name of Bedloe, was bribed, a man who had been imprisoned in Newgate for swindling. Others equally unscrupulous were soon added to the list of informers, and no calumnies, however gross and absurd, prevented the people from believing them.

It happened that a man, by the name of Coleman, was suspected of intrigues. His papers were searched, and some passages in them, unfortunately, seemed to confirm the statements of Oates. To impartial eyes, these papers simply indicated a desire and a hope that the Catholic religion would be reëstablished, in view of the predilections of Charles and James, and the general posture of affairs, just as some enthusiastic Jesuit missionary in the valley of the Mississippi may be supposed to write to his superior that America is on the eve of conversion to Catholicism.

Penal Laws against Catholics.

But the general ferment was still more increased by the disappearance of an eminent justice of the peace, who had taken the depositions of Oates against Coleman. Sir Edmondsbury Godfrey was found dead, and with every mark of violence, in a field near London, and was probably murdered by some fanatical persons in the communion of the Church of Rome. But if so, the murder was a great blunder. It was worse than a crime. The whole community were mad with rage and fear. The old penal laws were strictly enforced against the Catholics. The jails were filled with victims. London wore the appearance of a besieged city. The houses of the Catholics were every where searched, and two thousand of them imprisoned. Posts were planted in the street, that chains might be thrown across them on the first alarm. The military, the train bands, and the volunteers were called out. Forty thousand men were kept under guard during the night. Numerous patrols paraded the streets. The gates of the Palace were closed, and the guards of the city were doubled. Oates was pronounced to be the savior of his country, lodged at Whitehall and pensioned with twelve hundred pounds a year.

Then flowed more innocent blood than had been shed for a long period. Catholics who were noble, and Catholics who were obscure, were alike judicially murdered; and the courts of justice, instead of being places of refuge, were disgraced by the foulest abominations. Every day new witnesses were produced of crimes which never happened, and new victims were offered up to appease the wrath of a prejudiced people. Among these victims of popular frenzy was the Earl of Stafford, a venerable and venerated nobleman of sixty-nine years of age, against whom sufficient evidence was not found to convict him; and whose only crime was in being at the head of the Catholic party. Yet he was found guilty by the House of Peers, fifty-five out of eighty-six having voted for his execution. He died on the scaffold, but with the greatest serenity, forgiving his persecutors, and compassionating their delusions. A future generation, during the reign of George IV., however, reversed his attainder, and did justice to his memory, and restored his descendants to their rank and fortune.

Persecution of Dissenters.

If no other illustrious victims suffered, persecution was nevertheless directed into other channels. Parliament passed an act that no person should sit in either House, unless he had previously taken the oath of allegiance and supremacy, and subscribed to the declaration that the worship of the Church of Rome was idolatrous. Catholics were disabled from prosecuting a suit in any court of law, from receiving any legacy, and from acting as executors or administrators of estates. This horrid bill, which outlawed the whole Catholic population, had repeatedly miscarried, but, under influence of the panic which Oates and his confederates created, was now triumphantly passed. Charles himself gave his royal assent because he was afraid to stem the torrent of popular infatuation. And the English nation permitted one hundred and thirty years to elapse before the civil disabilities of the Catholics were removed, and then only by the most strenuous exertions of such a statesman as Sir Robert Peel.

It is some satisfaction to know that justice at last overtook the chief authors of this diabolical infatuation. During the reign of James II., Oates and others were punished as they deserved. Oates's credit gradually passed away. He was fined, imprisoned, and whipped at the pillory until life itself had nearly fled. He died unlamented and detested, leaving behind him, to all posterity an infamous notoriety.

But the sufferings of the Catholics, during this reign, were more than exceeded by the sufferings of Dissenters, who were cruelly persecuted. All the various sects of the Protestants were odious and ridiculous in the eyes of the king. They were regarded as hostile in their sympathies, and treasonable in their designs. They were fined, imprisoned, mutilated, and whipped. An Act of Uniformity was passed, which restored the old penal laws of Elizabeth, and which subjected all to their penalty who did not use the Book of Common Prayer, and adhere strictly to the ritual of the Church of England. The oligarchical power of the bishops was restored, and two thousand ministers were driven from their livings, and compelled to seek a precarious support. Many other acts of flagrant injustice were passed by a subservient parliament, and cruelly carried into execution by unfeeling judges. But the religious persecution of dissenters was not consummated until the reign of James under whose favor or direction the inhuman Jeffreys inflicted the most atrocious crimes which have ever been committed under the sanction of the law. But these will be more appropriately noticed under the reign of James II. Charles was not so cruel in his temper, or bigoted in his sentiments, as his brother James. He was rather a Gallio than a persecutor. He would permit any thing rather than suffer himself to be interrupted in his pleasures. He was governed by his favorites and his women. He had not sufficient moral elevation to be earnest in any thing, even to be a bigot in religion. He vacillated between the infidelity of Hobbes and the superstitions of Rome. He lived a scoffer, and died a Catholic. His temper was easy, but so easy as not to prevent the persecution and ruin of his best supporters, when they had become odious to the nation. If he was incapable of enmity, he was also incapable of friendship. If he hated no one with long-continued malignity, it was only because it was too much trouble to hate perseveringly. But he loved with no more constancy than he hated. He had no patriotism, and no appreciation of moral excellence. He would rather see half of the merchants of London ruined, and half of the Dissenters immured in gloomy prisons, than lose two hours of inglorious dalliance with one of his numerous concubines. A more contemptible prince never sat on the English throne, or one whose whole reign was disgraced by a more constant succession of political blunders and social crimes. And yet he never fully lost his popularity, nor was his reign felt to be as burdensome as was that of the protector, Cromwell, thus showing how little the moral excellence of rulers is ordinarily appreciated or valued by a wilful or blinded generation. We love not the rebukers of our sins, or the opposers of our pleasures. We love those who prophesy smooth things, and "cry peace, when there is no peace." Such is man in his weakness and his degeneracy; and only an omnipotent power can change this ordinary temper of the devotees to pleasure and inglorious gains.

Execution of Russell and Sydney.

Among the saddest events during the reign of Charles, were the executions of Lord Russell and Algernon Sydney. They were concerned, with a few other great men, in a conspiracy, which had for its object the restoration of greater liberty. They contemplated an insurrection, known by the name of the *Rye House Plot*; but it was discovered, and Russell and Sydney became martyrs. The former was the son of the Earl of Bedford, and the latter was the brother of the Earl of Leicester. Russell was a devoted Churchman, of pure morals, and greatly beloved by the people. Sydney was a strenuous republican, and was opposed to any particular form of church government. He thought that religion should be like a divine philosophy in the mind, and had great veneration for the doctrines of Plato. Nothing could save these illustrious men. The Duke of York and Jeffreys declared that, if they were not executed, there would be no safety for themselves. They both suffered with great intrepidity, and the friends of liberty have ever since cherished their memory with peculiar fondness.

Manners and Customs of England.

Milton — Dryden.

Mr. Macaulay, in his recent History, has presented the manners and customs of England during the disgraceful reign of Charles II. It is impossible, in this brief survey, to allude to all those customs; but we direct particularly the attention of readers to them, as described in his third chapter, from which it would appear, that a most manifest and most glorious progress has been made since that period in all the arts of civilization, both useful and ornamental. In those times, travelling was difficult and slow, from the badness of the roads and the imperfections of the carriages. Highwaymen were secreted along the thoroughfares, and, in mounted troops, defied the law, and distressed the whole travelling community. The transmission of letters by post was tardy and unfrequent, and the scandal of coffee-houses supplied the greatest want and the greatest luxury of modern times, the newspaper. There was great scarcity of books in the country places, and the only press in England north of the Trent seems to have been at York. Literature was but feebly cultivated by country squires or country parsons, and female education was disgracefully neglected. Few rich men had libraries as large or valuable as are now common to shopkeepers and mechanics; while the literary stores of a lady of the manor were confined chiefly to the prayer-book and the receipt-book. And those works which were produced or read were disgraced by licentious ribaldry, which had succeeded religious austerity. The drama was the only department of literature which compensated authors, and this was scandalous in the extreme. We cannot turn over the pages of one of the popular dramatists of the age without being shocked by the most culpable indecency. Even Dryden was no exception to the rule; and his poetry, some of which is the most beautiful in the language, can hardly be put into the hands of the young without danger of corrupting them. Poets and all literary men lived by the bounty of the rich and great, and prospered only as they pandered to depraved passions. Many, of great intellectual excellence, died from want and mortification; so that the poverty and distress of literary men became proverbial, and all worldly-wise people shunned contact with them as expensive and degrading. They were hunted from cocklofts to cellars by the minions of the law, and the foulest jails were often their only resting-place. The restoration of Charles proved unfortunate to one great and immortal genius, whom no temptations could assail, and no rewards could bribe. He "possessed his soul in patience," and "soared above the Aonian mount," amid general levity and profligacy. Had he written for a pure, classic, and learned age, he could not have written with greater moral beauty. But he lived when no moral excellence was appreciated, and his claims on the gratitude of the world are beyond all estimation, when we remember that he wrote with the full consciousness, like the great Bacon, that his works would only be valued or read by future generations. Milton was, indeed, unmolested;

but he was sadly neglected in his blindness and in his greatness. But, like all the great teachers of the world, he was sustained by something higher than earthly applause, and labored, like an immortal artist, from the love which his labor excited,—labored to realize the work of art which his imagination had conceived, as well as to propagate ideas and sentiments which should tend to elevate mankind. Dryden was his contemporary, but obtained a greater homage, not because he was more worthy, but because he adapted his genius to the taste of a frivolous and corrupt people. He afterwards wrote more unexceptionably, composed lyrics instead of farces, and satires instead of plays. In his latter days, he could afford to write in a purer style; and, as he became independent, he reared the superstructure of his glorious fame. But Dryden spent the best parts of his life as a panderer to the vices of the town, and was an idol chiefly, in Wills's Coffee House, of lampooners, and idlers, and scandal-mongers. Nor were there many people, in the church or in the state, sufficiently influential and noble to stem the torrent. The city clergy were the most respectable, and the pulpits of London were occupied with twelve men who afterwards became bishops, and who are among the great ornaments of the sacred literature of their country. Sherlock, Tillotson, Wake, Collier, Burnet, Stillingfleet, Patrick, Fowler, Sharp, Tennison, and Beveridge made the Established Church respected in the town; but the country clergy, as a whole, were ignorant and depressed. Not one living in fifty enabled the incumbent to bring up a family comfortably or respectably. The clergyman was disdained even by the county attorney, was hardly tolerated at the table of his patron, and could scarcely marry beyond the rank of a cook or housekeeper. And his poverty and bondage continued so long that, in the times of Swift, the parson was a byword and a jest among the various servants in the households of the great. Still there were eminent clergymen amid the general depression of their order, both in and out of the Established Church. Besides the London preachers were many connected with the Universities and Cathedrals; and there were some distinguished Dissenters, among whom Baxter, Howe, and Alleine if there were no others, would alone have made the name of Puritan respectable.

Condition of the People.

The saddest fact, in connection with the internal history of England, at this time, was the condition of the people. They had small wages, and many privations. They had no social rank, and were disgraced by many vices. They were ignorant and brutal. The wages of laborers only averaged four shillings a week, while those of mechanics were not equal to what some ordinarily earn, in this country and in these times, in a single day. Both peasants, and artisans were not only ill paid, but ill used, and they died, miserably and prematurely, from famine and disease. Nor did sympathy exist for the misfortunes of the poor. There were no institutions of public philanthropy. Jails were unvisited by the ministers of mercy, and the abodes of poverty were left by a careless generation to be dens of infamy and crime. Such was England two hundred years ago; and there is no delusion more unwarranted by sober facts than that which supposes that those former times were better than our own, in any thing which abridges the labors or alleviates the miseries of mankind. "It is now the fashion to place the golden age of England in times when noblemen were destitute of comforts the want of which would be intolerable to a modern footman; when farmers and shopkeepers breakfasted on loaves the very sight of which would raise a riot in a modern workhouse, when men died faster in the purest country air than they now die in the most pestilential lanes of our towns; and when men died faster in the lanes of our towns than they now die on the coast of Guinea. But we too shall, in our turn, be outstripped, and, in our turn, envied. There is constant improvement, as there also is constant discontent; and future generations may talk of the reign of Queen Victoria as a time when England was truly merry England, when all classes were bound together by brotherly sympathy, when the rich did not grind the faces of the poor, and when the poor did not envy the splendor of the rich."

> References. — Of all the works which have yet appeared, respecting this interesting epoch, the new History of Macaulay is the most brilliant and instructive. Indeed, the student scarcely needs any other history, in spite of Macaulay's Whig doctrines. He may sacrifice something to effect; and he may give us pictures, instead of philosophy; but, nevertheless, his book has transcendent merit, and will be read, by all classes, so long as English history is prized. Mackintosh's fragment, on the same period, is more philosophical, and possesses very great merits. Lingard's History is very valuable on this reign, and should be consulted. Hume, also, will never cease to please. Burnet is a prejudiced historian, but his work is an authority. The lives of Milton, Dryden, and Clarendon should also be read in this connection. Hallam has but treated the constitutional history of these times. See also Temple's Works; the Life of William Lord Russell; Rapin's History. Pepys, Dalrymple, Rymeri Fœdera, the Commons' Journal, and the Howell State Trials are not easily accessible, and not necessary, except to the historian.

CHAPTER XV
REIGN OF JAMES II

Accession of James II.

Charles II. died on the 6th of February, 1685, and his brother, the Duke of York, ascended his throne, without opposition, under the title of *James II.* As is usual with princes, on their accession, he made many promises of ruling by the laws, and of defending the liberties of the nation. And he commenced his administration under good auspices. The country was at peace, he was not unpopular, and all classes and parties readily acquiesced in his government.

He retained all the great officers who had served under his brother that he could trust; and Rochester became prime minister, Sunderland kept possession of the Seals, and Godolphin was made lord chamberlain. He did not dismiss Halifax, Ormond, or Guildford, although he disliked and distrusted them, but abridged their powers, and mortified them by neglect.

The Commons voted him one million two hundred thousand pounds, and the Scottish parliament added twenty-five thousand pounds more, and the Customs for life. But this sum he did not deem sufficient for his wants, and therefore, like his brother, applied for aid to Louis XIV., and consented to become his pensioner and vassal, and for the paltry sum of two hundred thousand pounds. James received the money with tears of gratitude, hoping by this infamous pension to rule the nation without a parliament. It was not, of course, known to the nation, or even to his ministers, generally.

He was scarcely crowned before England was invaded by the Duke of Monmouth, natural son of Charles II., and Scotland by the Duke of Argyle, with a view of ejecting James from the throne.

Both these noblemen were exiles in Holland, and both were justly obnoxious to the government for their treasonable intentions and acts. Argyle was loath to engage in an enterprise so desperate as the conquest of England; but he was an enthusiast, was at the head of the most powerful of the Scottish clans, the Campbells, and he hoped for a general rising throughout Scotland, to put down what was regarded as idolatry, and to strike a blow for liberty and the Kirk.

Having concerted his measures with Monmouth, he set sail from Holland, the 2d of May, 1685, in spite of all the efforts of the English minister, and landed at Kirkwall, one of the Orkney Islands. But his objects were well known, and the whole militia of the land were put under arms to resist him. He, however, collected a force of two thousand five hundred Highlanders, and marched towards Glasgow; but he was miserably betrayed and deserted. His forces were dispersed, and he himself was seized while attempting to escape in disguise, brought to Edinburgh, and beheaded. His followers were treated with great harshness, but the rebellion was completely suppressed.

Monmouth Lands in England.

Monmouth had agreed to sail in six days from the departure of Argyle; but he lingered at Brussels, loath to part from a beautiful mistress, the Lady Henrietta Wentworth. It was a month before he set sail from the Texel, with about eighty officers and one hundred and fifty followers—a small force to overturn the throne. But he relied on his popularity with the people, and on a false and exaggerated account of the unpopularity of James. He landed at Lyme, in Dorsetshire, about the middle of June, and forthwith issued a flaming proclamation, inviting all to join his standard, as a deliverer from the cruel despotism of a Catholic prince, whom he accused of every crime—of the burning of London, of the Popish Plot, of the condemnation of Russell and Sydney, of poisoning the late king, and of infringements on the constitution. In this declaration, falsehood was mingled with truth, but well adapted to inflame the passions of the people. He was supported by many who firmly believed that his mother, Lucy Walters, was the lawful wife of Charles II. He, of course, claimed the English throne, but professed to waive his rights until they should be settled by a parliament. The adventurer grossly misunderstood the temper of the people, and the extent to which his claims were recognized. He was unprovided with money, with generals, and with troops. He collected a few regiments from the common people, and advanced to Somersetshire. At Taunton his reception was flattering. All classes welcomed him as a deliverer from Heaven, and the poor rent the air with acclamations and shouts. His path was strewed with flowers, and the windows were crowded with ladies, who waved their handkerchiefs, and even waited upon him with a large deputation. Twenty-six lovely maidens presented the handsome son of Charles II. with standards and a Bible, which he kissed, and promised to defend.

Battle of Sedgemoor.

Death of Monmouth.

But all this enthusiasm was soon to end. The Duke of Albemarle—the son of General Monk, who restored Charles II.—advanced against him with the militia of the country, and Monmouth was supported only by the vulgar, the weak, and the credulous. Not a single nobleman joined his standard, and but few of the gentry. He made innumerable blunders. He lost time by vain attempts to drill the peasants and farmers who followed his fortunes. He slowly advanced to the west of England, where he hoped to be joined by the body of the people. But all men of station and influence stood aloof. Discouraged and dismayed, he reached Wells, and pushed forward to capture Bristol, then the second city in the kingdom. He was again disappointed. He was forced, from unexpected calamities, to abandon the enterprise. He then turned his eye to Wilts; but when he arrived at the borders of the county, he found that none of the bodies on which he had calculated had made their appearance. At Phillips Norton was a slight skirmish, which ended favorably to Monmouth, in which the young Duke of Grafton, natural son of Charles II., distinguished himself against his half brother; but Monmouth was discouraged, and fell back to Bridgewater. Meanwhile the royal army approached, and encamped at Sedgemoor. Here was fought a decisive battle, which was fatal to the rebels, "the last deserving the name of *battle*, that has been fought on English ground." Monmouth, when all was lost, fled from the field, and hastened to the British Channel, hoping to gain the Continent. He was found near the New Forest, hidden in a ditch, exhausted by hunger and fatigue. He was sent, under a strong guard, to Ringwood; and all that was left him was, to prepare to meet the death of a rebel. But he clung to life, so justly forfeited, with singular tenacity. He abjectly and meanly sued for pardon from that inexorable tyrant who never forgot or forgave the slightest resistance from a friend, when even that resistance was lawful, much less rebellion from a man he both hated and despised. He was transferred to London, lodged in the Tower, and executed in a bungling manner by "Jack Ketch" —the name given for several centuries to the public executioner. He was buried under St. Peter's Chapel, in the Tower, where reposed the headless bodies of so many noted saints and political martyrs— the great Somerset, and the still greater Northumberland, the two Earls of Essex, and the fourth Duke of Norfolk, and other great men who figured in the reigns of the Plantagenets and the Tudors.

Monmouth's rebellion was completely suppressed, and a most signal vengeance was inflicted on all who were concerned in it. No mercy was shown, on the part of government, to any party or person.

Of the agents of James in punishing all concerned in the rebellion, there were two, preëminently, whose names are consigned to an infamous immortality. The records of English history contain no two names so loathsome and hateful as Colonel Kirke and Judge Jeffreys.

The former was left, by Feversham, in command of the royal forces at Bridgewater, after the battle of Sedgemoor. He had already gained an unenviable notoriety, as governor of Tangier, where he displayed the worst vices of a tyrant and a sensualist; and his regiment had imitated him in his disgraceful brutality. But this leader and these troops were now let loose on the people of Somersetshire. One hundred captives were put to death during the week which succeeded the battle. His irregular butcheries, however, were not according to the taste of the king. A more systematic slaughter, under the sanctions of the law, was devised, and Jeffreys was sent into the Western Circuit, to try the numerous persons who were immured in the jails of the western counties.

Sir George Jeffreys, Chief Justice of the Court of the King's Bench, was not deficient in talent, but was constitutionally the victim of violent passions. He first attracted notice as an insolent barrister at the Old Bailey Court, who had a rare tact in cross-examining criminals and browbeating witnesses. According to Macaulay, "impudence and ferocity sat upon his brow, while all tenderness for the feelings of others, all self-respect, all sense of the becoming, were obliterated from his mind. He acquired a boundless command of the rhetoric in which the vulgar express hatred and contempt. The profusion of his maledictions could hardly be rivalled in the Fish Market or Bear Garden. His yell of fury sounded, as one who often heard it said, like the thunder of the judgment day. He early became common serjeant, and then recorder of London. As soon as he obtained all the city could give, he made haste to sell his forehead of brass and his tongue of venom to the court." He was just the man whom Charles II. wanted as a tool. He was made chief justice of the highest court of criminal law in the realm, and discharged its duties entirely to the satisfaction of a king resolved on the subjection of the English nation. His violence, at all times, was frightful; but when he was drunk, it was terrific: and he was generally intoxicated. His first exploit was the judicial murder of Algernon Sydney. On the death of Charles, he obtained from James a peerage, and a seat in the Cabinet, a signal mark of royal approbation. In prospect of yet greater honors, he was ready to do whatever James required. James wished the most summary vengeance inflicted on the rebels, and Jeffreys, with his tiger ferocity, was ready to execute his will.

Brutality of Jeffreys.

Nothing is more memorable than those "bloody assizes" which he held in those counties through which Monmouth had passed. Nothing is remembered with more execration. Nothing ever equalled the brutal cruelty of the judge. His fury seemed to be directed with peculiar violence upon the Dissenters. "Show me," said he, "a Presbyterian, and I will show thee a lying knave. Presbyterianism has all manner of villany in it. There is not one of those lying, snivelling, canting Presbyterians, but, one way or another, has had a hand in the rebellion." He sentenced nearly all who were accused, to be hanged or burned; and the excess of his barbarities called forth pity and indignation even from devoted loyalists. He boasted that he had hanged more traitors than all his predecessors together since the Conquest. On a single circuit, he hanged three hundred and fifty; some of these were people of great worth, and many of them were innocent; while many whom he spared from an ignominious death, were sentenced to the most cruel punishments—to the lash of the pillory, to imprisonment in the foulest jails, to mutilation, to banishment, and to heavy fines.

King James watched the conduct of the inhuman Jeffreys with delight, and rewarded him with the Great Seal. The Old Bailey lawyer had now climbed to the greatest height to which a subject could aspire. He was Lord Chancellor of England—the confidential friend and agent of the king, and his unscrupulous instrument in imposing the yoke of bondage on an insulted nation.

Persecution of the Dissenters.

At this period, the condition of the Puritans was deplorable. At no previous time was persecution more inveterate, not even under the administration of Laud and Strafford. The persecution commenced soon after the restoration of Charles II., and increased in malignity until the elevation of Jeffreys to the chancellorship. The sufferings of no class of sectaries bore any proportion to theirs. They found it difficult to meet together for prayer or exhortation even in the smallest assemblies. Their ministers were introduced in disguise. Their houses were searched. They were fined, imprisoned, and banished. Among the ministers who were deprived of their livings, were Gilpin, Bates, Howe, Owen, Baxter, Calamy, Poole, Charnock, and Flavel, who still, after a lapse of one hundred and fifty years, enjoy a wide-spread reputation as standard writers on theological subjects. These great lights of the seventeenth century were doomed to privation and poverty, with thousands of their brethren, most of whom had been educated at the Universities, and were among the best men in the kingdom. All the Stuart kings hated the Dissenters, but none hated them more than Charles II. and James II. Under their sanction, complying parliaments passed repeated acts of injustice and cruelty. The laws which were enacted during Queen Elizabeth's reign were reënacted and enforced. The Act of Uniformity, in one day, ejected two thousand ministers from their parishes, because they refused to conform to the standard of the Established Church. The Conventicle Act ordained that if any person, above sixteen years of age, should be present at any religious meeting, in any other manner than allowed by the Church of England, he should suffer three months' imprisonment, or pay a fine of five pounds, that six months imprisonment and ten pounds fine should be inflicted as a penalty for the second offence, and banishment for the third. Married women taken at "conventicles," were sentenced to twelve months' imprisonment. It is calculated that twenty-five thousand Dissenters were immured in gloomy prisons, and that four thousand of the sect of the Quakers died during their imprisonment in consequence of the filth and malaria of the jails, added to cruel treatment.

Among the illustrious men who suffered most unjustly, was Richard Baxter, the glory of the Presbyterian party. He was minister at Kidderminster, where he was content to labor in an humble sphere, having refused a bishopric. He had written one hundred and forty-five distinct treatises, in two hundred volumes, which were characterized for learning and talent. But neither his age, nor piety, nor commanding virtues could screen him from the cruelties of Jeffreys; and, in fifteen years, he was five times imprisoned. His sufferings drew tears from Sir Matthew Hale, with whose friendship he had been honored. "But he who had enjoyed the confidence of the best of judges, was cruelly insulted by the worst." When he wished to plead his cause, the drunken chief justice replied, "O Richard, Richard, thou art an old fellow and an old knave. Thou hast written books enough to load a cart, every one of which is as full of sedition as an egg is full of meat. I know that thou hast a mighty party, and I see a great many of the brotherhood in corners, and a doctor of divinity at your elbow; but, by the grace of God, I will crush you all."

Entirely a different man was John Bunyan, not so influential or learned, but equally worthy. He belonged to the sect of the Baptists, and stands at the head of all unlettered men of genius—the most successful writer of allegory that any age has seen. The Pilgrim's Progress is the most popular religious work ever published, full of genius and beauty, and a complete exhibition of the Calvinistic theology, and the experiences of the Christian life. This book shows the triumph of genius over learning, and the people's appreciation of exalted merit. Its author, an illiterate tinker, a travelling preacher, who spent the best part of his life between the houses of the poor and the county jails, the object of reproach and ignominy, now, however, takes a proud place, in the world's estimation, with the master minds of all nations—with Dante, Shakspeare, and Milton. He has arisen above the prejudices of the great and fashionable; and the learned and aristocratic Southey has sought to be the biographer of his sorrows and the expounder of his visions. The proud bishops who disdained him, the haughty judges who condemned him, are now chiefly known as his persecutors, while he continues to be more honored and extolled with every succeeding generation.

George Fox.

Another illustrious victim of religious persecution in that age, illustrious in our eyes, but ignoble in the eyes of his contemporaries, was George Fox, the founder of the sect of the Quakers. He, like Bunyan, was of humble birth and imperfect education. Like him, he derived his knowledge from communion with his own soul—from inward experiences—from religious contemplations. He was a man of vigorous intellect, and capable of intense intellectual action. His first studies were the mysteries of theology—the great questions respecting duty and destiny; and these agitated his earnest mind almost to despair. In his anxiety, he sought consolation from the clergy, but they did not remove the burdens of his soul. Like an old Syriac monk, he sought the fields and unfrequented solitudes, where he gave loose to his imagination, and where celestial beings came to comfort him. He despised alike the reasonings of philosophers, the dogmas of divines, and the disputes of wrangling sectarians. He rose above all their prejudices, and sought light and truth from original sources. His peace was based on the conviction that God's Holy Spirit spoke directly to his soul; and this was above reason, above authority, a surer guide than any outward or written revelation. While this divine voice was above the Scriptures, it never conflicted with them, for they were revealed also to inspired men. Hence the Scriptures were not to be disdained, but were to be a guide, and literally to be obeyed. He would not swear, or fight, to save his life, nor to save a world, because he was directly commanded to abstain from swearing and fighting. He abhorred all principles of expediency, and would do right, or what the inspired voice within him assured him to be right, regardless of all consequences and all tribulations. He believed in the power of justice to protect itself, and reposed on the moral dignity of virtue. Love, to his mind, was an omnipotent weapon. He disdained force to accomplish important ends, and sought no control over government, except by intelligence. He believed that ideas and truth alone were at the basis of all great and permanent revolutions; these he was ever ready to declare; these were sure to produce, in the end, all needed reforms; these would be revealed to the earnest inquirer. He disliked all forms and pompous ceremonials in the worship of God, for they seemed useless and idolatrous. God was a Spirit, and to be worshipped in spirit and in truth. And set singing was to be dispensed with, like set forms of prayer, and only edifying as prompted by the Spirit. He even objected to splendid places for the worship of God, and dispensed with steeples, and bells, and organs. The sacraments, too, were needless, being mere symbols, or shadows of better things, not obligatory, but to be put on the same footing as those Jewish ceremonies which the Savior abrogated. The mind of Fox discarded all aids to devotion, all titles of honor, all distinctions which arose in pride and egotism. Hypocrisy he abhorred with his whole soul. It was the vice of the Pharisees, on whom Christ denounced the severest judgments. He, too, would denounce it with the most unsparing severity, whenever he fancied he detected it in rulers, or in venerated dignitaries of the church, or in the customs of conventional life. He sought simplicity and sincerity in all their forms. Truth alone should be his polar star, and this would be revealed by the "inner light," the peculiar genius of his whole system, which, if it led to many new views of duty and holiness, yet was the cause of many delusions, and the parent of conceit and spiritual pride—the grand peculiarity of fanaticism in all ages and countries. What so fruitful a source of error as the notion of special divine illumination?

Persecution of the Quakers.

No wonder that Fox and his followers were persecuted, for they set at nought the wisdom of the world and the customs and laws of ages. They shocked all conservative minds; all rulers and dignitaries; all men attached to systems; all syllogistic reasoners and dialectical theologians; all fashionable and worldly people; all sects and parties attached to creeds and forms. Neither their inoffensive lives, nor their doctrine of non-resistance, nor their elevated spiritualism could screen them from the wrath of judges, bishops, and legislators. They were imprisoned, fined, whipped, and lacerated without mercy. But they endured their afflictions with patience, and never lost their faith in truth, or their trust in God. Generally, they belonged to the humbler classes, although some men illustrious for birth and wealth joined their persecuted ranks, the most influential of whom was William Penn, who lived to be their intercessor and protector, and the glorious founder and legislator of one of the most flourishing and virtuous colonies that, in those days of tribulation, settled in the wilderness of North America; a colony of men who were true to their enlightened principles, and who were saved from the murderous tomahawk of the Indian, when all other settlements were scenes of cruelty and vengeance.

James had now suppressed rebellion; he had filled the Dissenters with fear; and he met with no resistance from his parliaments. The judges and the bishops were ready to coöperate with his ministers in imposing a despotic yoke. All officers of the crown were dismissed the moment they dissented from his policy, or protested against his acts. Even judges were removed to make way for the most unscrupulous of tools.

Despotic Power of James.

His power, to all appearance, was consolidated; and he now began, without disguise, to advance the two great objects which were dearest to his heart—the restoration of the Catholic religion, and the imposition of a despotic yoke. He wished to be, like Louis XIV., a despotic and absolute prince; and, to secure this end, he was ready to violate the constitution of his country. The three inglorious years of his reign were a succession of encroachments and usurpations.

Indeed, among his first acts was the collection of the revenue without an act of parliament. To cover this stretch of arbitrary power, the court procured addresses from public bodies, in which the king was thanked for the royal care he extended to the customs and excise.

In order to protect the Catholics, who had been persecuted under the last reign, he was obliged to show regard to other persecuted bodies. So he issued a warrant, releasing from confinement all who were imprisoned for conscience' sake. Had he simply desired universal toleration, this act would merit our highest praises; but it was soon evident that he wished to elevate the Catholics at the expense of all the rest. James was a sincere but bigoted devotee to the Church of Rome, and all things were deemed lawful, if he could but advance the interests of a party, to which nearly the whole nation was bitterly opposed. Roman Catholics were proscribed by the laws. The Test Act excluded from civil and military office all who dissented from the Established Church. The laws were unjust, but still they were the laws which James had sworn to obey. Had he scrupulously observed them, and kept his faith, there can be no doubt that they would, in good time have been modified.

Favor Extended to Catholics.

But James would not wait for constitutional measures. He resolved to elevate Catholics to the highest offices of both the state and the church, and this in defiance of the laws and of the wishes of a great majority of the nation. He accordingly gave commissions to Catholics to serve as officers in the army; he made Catholics his confidential advisers; he introduced Jesuits into London; he received a Papal nuncio, and he offered the livings of the Church of England to needy Catholic adventurers. He sought, by threats and artifices, to secure the repeal of the Test Act, by which Catholics were excluded from office. Halifax, the ablest of his ministers, remonstrated, and he was turned out of his employments. But he formed the soul and the centre of an opposition, which finally drove the king from his throne. He united with Devonshire and other Whig nobles, and their influence was sufficient to defeat many cherished objects of the king. When opposition appeared, however, in parliament, it was prorogued or dissolved, and the old courses of the Stuart kings were resorted to.

High Commission Court.

Among his various acts of infringement, which gave great scandal, even in those degenerate times, was the abuse of the dispensing power—a prerogative he had inherited, but which had never been strictly defined. By means of this, he intended to admit Catholics to all offices in the realm. He began by granting to the whole Roman Catholic body a dispensation from all the statutes which imposed penalties and tests. A general indulgence was proclaimed, and the courts of law were compelled to acknowledge that the right of dispensing had not been infringed. Four of the judges refused to accede to what was plainly illegal. They were dismissed; for, at that time, even judges held office during the pleasure of the king, and not, as in these times, for life. They had not the independence which has ever been so requisite for the bench. Nor would all his counsellors and ministers accede to his design, and those who were refractory were turned out. As soon as a servile bench of judges recognized this outrage on the constitution, four Catholic noblemen were admitted as privy counsellors, and some clergymen, converted to Romanism, were permitted to hold their livings. James even bestowed the deanery of Christ Church, one of the highest dignities in the University of Oxford, on a notorious Catholic, and threatened to do at Cambridge what had been done at Oxford. The bishopric of Oxford was bestowed upon Parker, who was more Catholic than Protestant, and that of Chester was given to a sycophant of no character. James made no secret of his intentions to restore the Catholic religion, and systematically labored to destroy the Established Church. In order to effect this, he created a tribunal, which not materially differed from the celebrated High Commission Court of Elizabeth, and to break up which was one great object of the revolutionists who brought Charles I. to the block—the most odious court ever established by royal despotism in England. The members of this High Commission Court, which James instituted to try all ecclesiastical cases, were, with one or two exceptions, notoriously the most venal and tyrannical of all his agents—Jeffreys, the Chancellor; Crewe, Bishop of Durham; Sprat, Bishop of Rochester; the Earl of Rochester, Lord Treasurer; Sunderland, the Lord President; and Herbert, Chief Justice of the King's Bench. This court summoned Compton, the Bishop of London, to its tribunal, because he had not suspended Dr. Sharp, one of the clergy of London, when requested to do so by the king—a man who had committed no crime, but simply discharged his duty with fidelity. The bishop was suspended from his spiritual functions, and the charge of his diocese was committed to two of his judges. But this court, not content with depriving numerous clergymen of their spiritual functions, because they would not betray their own church, went so far as to sit in judgment on the two greatest corporations in the land,—the Universities of Oxford and Cambridge,—institutions which had ever befriended the Stuart kings in their crimes and misfortunes. James was infatuated enough to quarrel with these great bodies, because they would not approve of his measures to overturn the church with which they were connected, and which it was their duty and interest to uphold. The king had commanded Cambridge to bestow the degree of master of arts on a Benedictine monk, which was against the laws of the University and of parliament. The University refused to act against the law, and, in consequence, the vice-chancellor and the senate, which consisted of doctors and masters, were summoned to the Court of High Commission. The vice-chancellor, Pechell, was deprived of his office and emoluments, which were of the nature of freehold property. But this was not the worst act of the infatuated monarch. He insisted on imposing a Roman Catholic in the presidential chair of Magdalen College, one of the richest and most venerable of the University of Oxford, against even the friendly remonstrances of his best friends, even of his Catholic counsellors, and not only against the advice of his friends, but against all the laws of the land and of the rights of the University; for the proposed president, Farmer, was a Catholic, and was not a fellow of the college, and therefore especially disqualified. He was also a man of depraved morals. The fellows refused to elect Farmer, and chose John Hough instead. They were accordingly cited to the infamous court of which Jeffreys was the presiding and controlling genius. Their election was set aside, but Farmer was not confirmed, being too vile even for Jeffreys to sustain.

Quarrel with the Universities.

The king was exceedingly enraged at the opposition he received from the University. He resolved to visit it. On his arrival, he summoned the fellows of Magdalen College, and commanded them to obey him in the matter of a president. They still held out in opposition, and the king, mortified and enraged, quitted Oxford to resort to bolder measures. A special commission was instituted. Hough was forcibly ejected, and the Bishop of Oxford installed, against the voice of all the fellows but two. But the blinded king was not yet content. The fellows were expelled from the University by a royal edict, and the high commissioner pronounced the ejected fellows incapable of ever holding any church preferment.

But these severities were blunders, and produced a different effect from what was anticipated. The nation was indignant; the Universities lost all reverence; the clergy, in a body, were alienated; and the whole aristocracy were filled with defiance.

Magdalen College.

But the king, nevertheless, for a time, prevailed against all opposition; and, now that the fellows of Magdalen College were expelled, he turned it into a Popish seminary, admitted in one day twelve Roman Catholics as fellows, and appointed a Roman Catholic bishop to preside over them. This last insult was felt to the extremities of the kingdom; and bitter resentment took the place of former loyalty. James was now regarded, by his old friends even, as a tyrant, and as a man destined to destruction. And, indeed, he seemed like one completely infatuated, bent on the ruin of that church which even James I. and the other Stuart kings regarded as the surest and firmest pillar of the throne.

The bishops of the English Church had in times past, as well as the Universities, inculcated the doctrine of passive obedience; and oppression must be very grievous indeed which would induce them to oppose the royal will. But James had completely alienated them, and they, reluctantly, at last, threw themselves into the ranks of opposition. Had they remained true to him, he might still have held his sceptre; but it was impossible that any body of men could longer bear his injustice and tyranny.

Prosecution of the Seven Bishops.

From motives as impossible to fathom, as it is difficult to account for the actions of a madman, he ordered that the Declaration of Indulgence, an unconstitutional act, should be read publicly from all the pulpits in the kingdom. The London clergy, the most respectable and influential in the realm, made up their minds to disregard the order, and the bishops sustained them in their refusal. The archbishop and six bishops accordingly signed a petition to the king, which embodied the views of the London clergy. It was presented to the tyrant, by the prelates in a body, at his palace. He chose to consider it as a treasonable and libellous act—as nothing short of rebellion. The conduct of the prelates was generally and enthusiastically approved by the nation, and especially by the Dissenters, who now united with the members of the Established Church. James had recently courted the Dissenters, not wishing to oppose too many enemies at a time. He had conferred on them many indulgences, and had elevated some of them to high positions, with the hope that they would unite with him in breaking down the Establishment. But while some of the more fanatical were gained over, the great body were not so easily deceived. They knew well enough that, after crushing the Church of England, he would crush them. And they hated Catholicism and tyranny more than they did Episcopacy, in spite of their many persecutions. Some of the more eminent of the Dissenters took a noble stand, and their conduct was fully appreciated by the Established clergy. For the first time, since the accession of Elizabeth, the Dissenters and the Episcopalians treated each other with that courtesy and forbearance which enlightened charity demands. The fear of a common enemy united them. But time, also, had, at length, removed many of their mutual asperities.

Nothing could exceed the vexation of James when he found that not only the clergy had disobeyed his orders, but that the Seven Bishops were sustained by the nation. When this was discovered, he should have yielded, as Elizabeth would have done. But he was a Stuart. He was a bigoted, and self-willed, and infatuated monarch, marked out most clearly by Providence for destruction. He resolved to prosecute the bishops for a libel, and their trial and acquittal are among the most interesting events of an inglorious reign. They were tried at the Court of the King's Bench. The most eminent lawyers in the realm were employed as their counsel, and all the arts of tyranny were resorted to by the servile judges who tried them. But the jury rendered a verdict of acquittal, and never, within man's memory, were such shouts and tears of joy manifested by the people. Even the soldiers, whom the king had ordered to Hounslow Heath to overawe London, partook of the enthusiasm and triumph of the people. All classes were united in expressions of joy that the tyrant for once was baffled. The king was indeed signally defeated; but his defeat did not teach him wisdom. It only made him the more resolved to crush the liberties of the Church, and the liberties of the nation. But it also arrayed against him all classes and all parties of Protestants, who now began to form alliances, and devise measures to hurl him from his throne. Even the very courts which James had instituted to crush liberty proved refractory. Sprat, the servile Bishop of Rochester, sent him his resignation as one of the Lord Commissioners. The very meanness of his spirit and laxity of his principles made his defection peculiarly alarming, and the unblushing Jeffreys now began to tremble. The Court of High Commission shrunk from a conflict with the Established Church, especially when its odious character was loudly denounced by all classes in the kingdom—even by some of the agents of tyranny itself. The most unscrupulous slaves of power showed signs of uneasiness.

Tyranny and Infatuation of James.

But James resolved to persevere. The sanction of a parliament was necessary to his system, but the sanction of a free parliament it was impossible to obtain. He resolved to bring together, by corruption and intimidation, by violent exertions of prerogative, by fraudulent distortions of law, an assembly which might call itself a parliament, and might be willing to register any edict he proposed. And, accordingly, every placeman, from the highest to the lowest, was made to understand that he must support the throne or lose his office. He set himself vigorously to pack a parliament.

A committee of seven privy counsellors sat at Whitehall for the purpose of regulating the municipal corporations. Father Petre was made a privy councillor. Committees, after the model of the one at Whitehall, were established in all parts of the realm. The lord lieutenants received written orders to go down to their respective counties, and superintend the work of corruption and fraud. But half of them refused to perform the ignominious work, and were immediately dismissed from their posts, which were posts of great honor and consideration. Among these were the great Earls of Oxford, Shrewsbury, Dorset, Pembroke, Rutland, Bridgewater, Thanet, Northampton, Abingdon, and Gainsborough, whose families were of high antiquity, wealth, and political influence. Nor could those nobles, who consented to conform to the wishes and orders of the king, make any progress in their counties, on account of the general opposition of the gentry. The county squires, as a body, stood out in fierce resistance. They refused to send up any men to parliament who would vote away the liberties and interests of the nation. The justices and deputy lieutenants declared that they would sustain, at all hazard, the Protestant religion. And these persons were not odious republicans, but zealous royalists, now firmly united and resolved to oppose unlawful acts, though commanded by the king.

James and his ministers next resolved to take away the power of the municipal corporations. The boroughs were required to surrender their charters. But a great majority firmly refused to part with their privileges. They were prosecuted and intimidated, but still they held out. Oxford, by a vote of eighty to two, voted to defend its franchises. Other towns did the same. Meanwhile, all the public departments were subjected to a strict inquisition, and all, who would not support the policy of the king, were turned out of office, and among them were some who had been heretofore the zealous servants of the crown.

Organized Opposition.

It was now full time for the organization of a powerful confederacy against the king. It was obvious, to men of all parties, and all ranks, that he meditated the complete subversion of English liberties. The fundamental laws of the kingdom had been systematically violated. The power of dispensing with acts of parliament had been strained, so that the king had usurped nearly all legislative authority. The courts of justice had been filled with unscrupulous judges, who were ready to obey all the king's injunctions, whether legal or illegal. Roman Catholics had been elevated to places of dignity in the Established Church. An infamous and tyrannical Court of High Commission had been created; persons, who could not legally set foot in England, had been placed at the head of colleges, and had taken their seat at the royal council-board. Lord lieutenants of counties, and other servants of the crown, had been dismissed for refusing to obey illegal commands; the franchises of almost every borough had been invaded; the courts of justice were venal and corrupt; an army of Irish Catholics, whom the nation abhorred, had been brought over to England; even the sacred right of petition was disregarded, and respectful petitioners were treated as criminals; and a free parliament was prevented from assembling.

Under such circumstances, and in view of these unquestioned facts, a great conspiracy was set on foot to dethrone the king and overturn the hateful dynasty.

Among the conspirators were some of the English nobles, the chief of whom was the Earl of Devonshire, and one of the leaders of the Whig party. Shrewsbury and Danby also joined them, the latter nobleman having been one of the most zealous advocates of the doctrine of passive obedience which many of the High Churchmen and Tories had defended in the reign of Charles II. It was under his administration, as prime minister, that a law had been proposed to parliament to exclude all persons from office who refused to take an oath, declaring that they thought resistance in all cases unlawful. Compton, the Bishop of London, who had been insolently treated by the court, joined the conspirators, whose designs were communicated to the Prince of Orange by Edward Russell and Henry Sydney, brothers of those two great political martyrs who had been executed in the last reign. The Prince of Orange, who had married a daughter of James II., agreed to invade England with a well-appointed army.

William, Prince of Orange.

William of Orange was doubtless the greatest statesman and warrior of his age, and one of the ablest men who ever wore a crown. He was at the head of the great Protestant party in Europe, and was the inveterate foe of Louis XIV. When a youth, his country had been invaded by Louis, and desolated and abandoned to pillage and cruelty. It was amid unexampled calamities, when the population were every where flying before triumphant armies, and the dikes of Holland had been opened for the ravages of the sea in order to avoid the more cruel ravages of war, that William was called to be at the head of affairs. He had scarcely emerged from boyhood; but his boyhood was passed in scenes of danger and trial, and his extraordinary talents were most precociously developed. His tastes were warlike; but he was a warrior who fought, not for the love of fighting, not for military glory, but to rescue his country from a degrading yoke, and to secure the liberties of Europe from the encroachments of a most ambitious monarch. Zeal for those liberties was the animating principle of his existence; and this led him to oppose so perseveringly the policy and enterprises of the French king, even to the disadvantage of his native country and the country which adopted him.

William was ambitious, and did not disdain the overtures which the discontented nobles of England made to him. Besides, his wife, the Princess Mary, was presumptive heir to the crown before the birth of the Prince of Wales. The eyes of the English nation had long been fixed upon him as their deliverer from the tyranny of James. He was a sincere Protestant, a bold and enterprising genius, and a consummate statesman. But he delayed taking any decisive measures until affairs were ripe for his projects—until the misgovernment and encroachments of James drove the nation to the borders of frenzy. He then obtained the consent of the States General for the meditated invasion of England, and made immense preparations, which, however, were carefully concealed from the spies and agents of James. They did not escape, however, the scrutinizing and jealous eye of Louis XIV., who remonstrated with James on his blindness and self-confidence, and offered to lend him assistance. But the infatuated monarch would not believe his danger, and rejected the proffered aid of Louis with a spirit which ill accorded with his former servility and dependence. Nor was he aroused to a sense of his danger until the Declaration of William appeared, setting forth the tyrannical acts of James, and supposed to be written by Bishop Burnet, the intimate friend of the Prince of Orange. Then he made haste to fit out a fleet; and thirty ships of the line were put under the command of Lord Dartmouth. An army of forty thousand men—the largest that any king of England had ever commanded—was also sent to the seaboard; a force more than sufficient to repel a Dutch invasion.

Critical Condition of James.

At the same time, the king made great concessions. He abolished the Court of High Commission. He restored the charter of the city of London. He permitted the Bishop of Winchester, as visitor of Magdalen College, to make any reforms he pleased. He would not, however, part with an iota of his dispensing power, and still hoped to rout William, and change the religion of his country. But all his concessions were too late. Whigs and Tories, Dissenters and Churchmen, were ready to welcome their Dutch deliverer. Nor had James any friends on whom he could rely. His prime minister, Sunderland, was in treaty with the conspirators, and waiting to betray him. Churchill, who held one of the highest commissions in the army, and who was under great obligations to the king, was ready to join the standard of William. Jeffreys, the lord chancellor, was indeed true in his allegiance, but his crimes were past all forgiveness by the nation; and even had he rebelled,—and he was base enough to do so,—his services would have been spurned by William and all his adherents.

Invasion of England by William.

On the 29th of October, 1688, the armament of William put to sea; but the ships had scarcely gained half the distance to England when they were dispersed and driven back to Holland by a violent tempest. The hopes of James revived; but they were soon dissipated. The fleet of William, on the 1st of November, again put to sea. It was composed of more than six hundred vessels, five hundred of which were men of war, and they were favored by auspicious gales. The same winds which favored the Dutch ships retarded the fleet of Dartmouth. On the 5th of November, the troops of William disembarked at Brixham, near Torbay in Devonshire, without opposition. On the 6th, he advanced to Newton Abbot, and, on the 9th, reached Exeter. He was cordially received, and magnificently entertained. He and his lieutenant-general, Marshal Schomberg, one of the greatest commanders in Europe, entered Exeter together in the grand military procession, which was like a Roman triumph. Near him also was Bentinck, his intimate friend and counsellor, the founder of a great ducal family. The procession marched to the splendid Cathedral, the *Te Deum* was sung, and Burnet preached a sermon.

Thus far all things had been favorable, and William was fairly established on English ground. Still his affairs were precarious, and James's condition not utterly hopeless or desperate. In spite of the unpopularity of the king, his numerous encroachments, and his disaffected army, the enterprise of William was hazardous. He was an invader, and the slightest repulse would have been dangerous to his interests. James was yet a king, and had the control of the army, the navy, and the treasury. He was a legitimate king, whose claims were undisputed. And he was the father of a son, and that son, notwithstanding the efforts of the Protestants to represent him as a false heir, was indeed the Prince of Wales. William had no claim to the throne so long as that prince was living. Nor had the nobles and gentry flocked to his standard as he had anticipated. It was nearly a week before a single person of rank or consequence joined him. Devonshire was in Derbyshire, and Churchill had still the confidence of his sovereign. The forces of the king were greatly superior to his own. And James had it in his power to make concessions which would have satisfied a great part of the nation.

But William had not miscalculated. He had profoundly studied the character of James, and the temper of the English. He knew that a fatal blindness and obstinacy had been sent upon him, and that he never would relinquish his darling scheme of changing the religion of the nation; and he knew that the nation would never acquiesce in that change; that Popery was hateful in their sight. He also trusted to his own good sword, and to fortunate circumstances.

Flight of the King.

And he was not long doomed to suspense, which is generally so difficult to bear. In a few days, Lord Cornbury, colonel of a regiment, and son of the Earl of Clarendon, and therefore a relative of James himself, deserted. Soon several disaffected nobles joined him in Exeter. Churchill soon followed, the first general officer that ever in England abandoned his colors. The Earl of Bath, who commanded at Plymouth, placed himself, in a few days, at the prince's disposal, with the fortress which he was intrusted to guard. His army swelled in numbers and importance. Devonshire raised the standard of rebellion at Chatsworth. London was in a ferment. James was with his army at Salisbury, but gave the order to retreat, not daring to face the greatest captain in Europe. Soon after, he sent away the queen and the Prince of Wales to France, and made preparations for his own ignominious flight—the very thing his enemies desired, for his life was in no danger, and his affairs even then might have been compromised, in spite of the rapid defection of his friends, and the advance of William, with daily augmenting forces, upon London. On the 11th of December, the king fled from London, with the intention of embarking at Sheerness, and was detained by the fishermen of the coast; but, by an order from the Lords, was set at liberty, and returned to the capital. William, nearly at the same time, reached London, and took up his quarters at St. James's Palace. It is needless to add, that the population of the city were friendly to his cause, and that he was now virtually the king of England. It is a satisfaction also to add, that the most infamous instrument of royal tyranny was seized in the act of flight, at Wapping, in the mean disguise of a sailor. He was discovered by the horrible fierceness of his countenance. Jeffreys was committed to the Tower; and the Tower screened him from a worse calamity, for the mob would have torn him in pieces. Catholic priests were also arrested, and their chapels and houses destroyed.

Meanwhile parliament assembled and deliberated on the state of affairs. Many propositions were made and rejected. The king fled a second time, and the throne was declared vacant. But the crown was not immediately offered to the Prince of Orange, although addresses were made to him as a national benefactor. Many were in favor of a regency. Another party was for placing the Princess Mary on the throne, and giving to William, during her life, the title of king, and such a share of the administration as she chose to give him.

But William had risked every thing for a throne, and nothing less than the crown of England would now content him. He gave the convention to understand that, much as he esteemed his wife, he would never accept a subordinate and precarious place in her government; "that he would not submit to be tied to the apron-strings of the best of wives;" that, unless he were offered the crown for life, he should return to Holland.

It was accordingly settled by parliament that he should hold the regal dignity conjointly with his wife, but that the whole power of the government should be placed in his hands. And the Princess Mary willingly acceded, being devoted to her husband, and unambitious for herself.

Consummation of the Revolution.

Declaration of Rights.

Thus was consummated the English Revolution of 1688, bloodless, but glorious. A tyrant was ejected from an absolute throne, and a noble and magnanimous prince reigned in his stead, after having taken an oath to observe the laws of the realm—an oath which he never violated. Of all revolutions, this proved the most beneficent. It closed the long struggle of one hundred and fifty years. Royal prerogative bowed before the will of the people, and true religious and civil liberty commenced its reign. The Prince of Orange was called to the throne by the voice of the nation, as set forth in an instrument known as the Declaration of Rights. This celebrated act of settlement recapitulated the crimes and errors of James, and merely asserted the ancient rights and liberties of England—that the dispensing power had no legal existence; that no money could be raised without grant of parliament; and that no army could be kept up in time of peace without its consent; and it also asserted the right of petition, the right of electors to choose their representatives freely, the right of parliament to freedom of debate, and the right of the nation to a pure and merciful administration of justice. No new rights were put forth, but simply the old ones were reëstablished. William accepted the crown on the conditions proposed, and swore to rule by the laws. "Not a single flower of the crown," says Macaulay, "was touched. Not a single new right was given to the people. The Declaration of Rights, although it made nothing law which was not law before, contained the germ of the law which gave religious freedom to the Dissenters; of the law which secured the independence of judges; of the law which limited the duration of parliaments; of the law which placed the liberty of the press under the protection of juries; of the law which abolished the sacramental test; of the law which relieved the Roman Catholics from civil disabilities; of the law which reformed the representative system; of every good law which has been passed during one hundred and sixty years; of every good law which may hereafter, in the course of ages, be found necessary to promote the public weal, and satisfy the demands of public opinion."

References.—Macaulay's, Hume's, Hallam's, and Lingard's Histories of England. Mackintosh's Causes of the Revolution of 1688. Fox's History of the Reign of James—a beautiful fragment. Burnet's History of his Own Times. Neal's History of the Puritans. Life and Times of Richard Baxter. Southey's Life of Bunyan. Memoir of George Fox, by Marsh. Life of William Penn. Chapters on religion, science, and the condition of the people, in the Pictorial History of England. Russell's Modern Europe. Woolrych's Life of Judge Jeffreys.

CHAPTER XVI
LOUIS XIV

Louis XIV.

We turn now from English affairs to contemplate the reign of Louis XIV.—a man who filled a very large space in the history of Europe during the seventeenth century. Indeed, his reign forms an epoch of itself, not so much from any impulse he gave to liberty or civilization, but because, for more than half a century, he was the central mover of European politics. His reign commemorates the triumph in France, of despotic principles, the complete suppression of popular interests, and almost the absorption of national interests in his own personal aggrandizement. It commemorates the ascendency of fashion, and the great refinement of material life. The camp and the court of Louis XIV. ingulphed all that is interesting in the history of France during the greater part of the seventeenth century. He reigned seventy-two years, and, in his various wars, a million of men are supposed to have fallen victims to his vain-glorious ambition. His palaces consumed the treasures which his wars spared. He was viewed as a sun of glory and power, in the light of which all other lights were dim. Philosophers, poets, prelates, generals, and statesmen, during his reign, were regarded only as his satellites. He was the central orb around which every other light revolved, and to contribute to his glory all were supposed to be born. He was, most emphatically, the state. He was France. A man, therefore, who, in the eye of contemporaries, was so grand, so rich, so powerful, and so absolute, claims a special notice. It is the province of history to record great influences, whether they come from the people, from great popular ideas, from literature and science, or from a single man. The lives of individuals are comparatively insignificant in the history of the United States; but the lives of such men as Cæsar, Cromwell, and Napoleon, furnish very great subjects for the pen of the philosophical historian, since great controlling influences emanated from them, rather than from the people whom they ruled.

His Power and Resources.

Louis XIV. was not a great general, like Henry IV., nor a great statesman, like William III., nor a philosopher, like Frederic the Great, nor a universal genius, like Napoleon; but his reign filled the eyes of contemporaries, and circumstances combined to make him the absolute master of a great empire. Moreover, he had sufficient talent and ambition to make use of fortunate opportunities, and of the resources of his kingdom, for his own aggrandizement. But France, nevertheless, was sacrificed. The French Revolution was as much the effect of his vanity and egotism, as his own power was the fruit of the policy of Cardinals Richelieu and Mazarin. By their labors in the cause of absolutism, he came in possession of armies and treasures. But armies and treasures were expended in objects of vain ambition, for the gratification of selfish pleasures, for expensive pageants, and for gorgeous palaces. These finally embarrassed the nation, and ground it down to the earth by the load of taxation, and maddened it by the prospect of ruin, by the poverty and degradation of the people, and, at the same time, by the extravagance and insolence of an overbearing aristocracy. The aristocracy formed the glory and pride of the throne and both nobles and the throne fell, and great was the fall thereof.

Our notice of Louis XIV. begins, not with his birth, but at the time when he resolved to be his own prime minister, on the death of Cardinal Mazarin, (1661.)

Louis XIV. was then twenty-three years of age—frank, beautiful, imperious, and ambitious. His education had been neglected, but his pride and selfishness had been stimulated. During his minority, he had been straitened for money by the avaricious cardinal; but avaricious for his youthful master, since, at his death, besides his private fortune, which amounted to two hundred millions of livres, he left fifteen millions of livres, not specified in his will, which, of course, the king seized, and thus became the richest monarch of Europe. He was married, shortly before the death of Mazarin, to the Infanta Maria Theresa, daughter of Philip IV., King of Spain. But, long before his marriage, he had become attached to Mary de Mancini, niece of Mazarin, who returned his love with passionate ardor. She afterwards married Prince Colonna, a Roman noble, and lived a most abandoned life.

The enormous wealth left by Cardinal Mazarin was, doubtless, one motive which induced Louis XIV., though only a young man of twenty-three, to be his own prime minister. Henceforth, to his death, all his ministers made their regular reports to him, and none were permitted to go beyond the limits which he prescribed to them.

He accepted, at first, the ministers whom the dying cardinal had recommended. The most prominent of these were Le Tellier, De Lionne, and Fouquet. The last was intrusted with the public chest, who found the means to supply the dissipated young monarch with all the money he desired for the indulgence of his expensive tastes and ruinous pleasures.

Habits and Pleasures of Louis.

The thoughts and time of the king, from the death of Mazarin, for six or seven years, were chiefly occupied with his pleasures. It was then that the court of France was so debauched, splendid, and far-famed. It was during this time that the king was ruled by La Vallière, one of the most noted of all his favorites, a woman of considerable beauty and taste, and not so unprincipled as royal favorites generally have been. She was created a duchess, and her children were legitimatized, and also became dukes and princes. Of these the king was very fond, and his love for them survived the love for their unfortunate mother, who, though beautiful and affectionate, was not sufficiently intellectual to retain the affections with which she inspired the most selfish monarch of his age. She was supplanted in the king's affections by Madame de Montespan, an imperious beauty, whose extravagances and follies shocked and astonished even the most licentious court in Europe; and La Vallière, broken-hearted, disconsolate, and mortified, sought the shelter of a Carmelite convent, in which she dragged out thirty-six melancholy and dreary years, amid the most rigorous severities of self-inflicted penance, in the anxious hope of that heavenly mansion where her sins would be no longer remembered, and where the weary would be at rest.

It was during these years of extravagance and pleasure that Versailles attracted the admiring gaze of Christendom, the most gorgeous palace which the world has seen since the fall of Babylon. Amid its gardens and groves, its parks and marble halls, did the modern Nebuchadnezzar revel in a pomp and grandeur unparalleled in the history of Europe, surrounded by eminent prelates, poets, philosophers, and statesmen, and all that rank and beauty had ennobled throughout his vast dominions. Intoxicated by their united flatteries, by all the incense which sycophancy, carried to a science, could burn before him, he almost fancied himself a deity, and gave no bounds to his self-indulgence, his vanity, and his pride. Every thing was subordinate to his pleasure and his egotism—an egotism alike regardless of the tears of discarded favorites, and the groans of his overburdened subjects.

His Military Ambition.

But Louis, at last, palled with pleasure, was aroused from the festivities of Versailles by dreams of military ambition. He knew nothing of war, of its dangers, its reverses, or of its ruinous expenses; but he fancied it would be a beautiful sport for a wealthy and absolute monarch to engage in the costly game. He cast his eyes on Holland, a state extremely weak in land forces, and resolved to add it to the great kingdom over which he ruled.

The only power capable of rendering effectual assistance to Holland, when menaced by Louis XIV., was England; but England was ruled by Charles II., and all he cared for were his pleasures and independence from parliamentary control. The French king easily induced him to break his alliance with the Dutch by a timely bribe, while, at the same time, he insured the neutrality of Spain, by inflaming the hereditary prejudices of the Spanish court against the Low Countries.

War, therefore, without even a decent pretence, and without provocation, was declared against Holland, with a view of annexing the Low Countries to France.

William, Prince of Orange.

Before the Dutch were able to prepare for resistance, Louis XIV. appeared on the banks of the Rhine with an army of one hundred and twenty thousand, marshalled by such able generals as Luxembourg, Condé, and Turenne. The king commanded in person, and with all the pomp of an ancient Persian monarch, surrounded with women and nobles. Without any adequate force to resist him, his march could not but be triumphant. He crossed the Rhine,—an exploit much celebrated, by his flatterers, though nothing at all extraordinary,—and, in the course of a few weeks, nearly all the United Provinces had surrendered to the royal victor. The reduction of Holland and Zealand alone was necessary to crown his enterprise with complete success. But he wasted time in vain parade at Utrecht, where he held his court, and where his splendid army revelled in pleasure and pomp. Amsterdam alone, amid the general despondency and consternation which the French inundation produced, was true to herself, and to the liberties of Holland; and this was chiefly by means of the gallant efforts of the Prince of Orange.

At this time, (1672,) he was twenty-two years of age, and had received an excellent education, and shown considerable military abilities. In consequence of his precocity of talent, his unquestioned patriotism, and the great services which his family had rendered to the state, he was appointed commander-in-chief of the forces of the republic, and was encouraged to aspire to the office of stadtholder, the highest in the commonwealth. And his power was much increased after the massacre of the De Witts—the innocent victims of popular jealousy, who, though patriotic and illustrious, inclined to a different policy than what the Orange party advocated. William advised the States to reject with scorn the humiliating terms of peace which Louis XIV. offered, and to make any sacrifice in defence of their very last ditch. The heroic spirit which animated his bosom he communicated to his countrymen, on the borders of despair, and in the prospect of national ruin; and so great was the popular enthusiasm, that preparations were made for fifty thousand families to fly to the Dutch possessions in the East Indies, and establish there a new empire, in case they were overwhelmed by their triumphant enemy.

Never, in the history of war, were such energies put forth as by the Hollanders in the hour of their extremity. They opened their dikes, and overflowed their villages and their farms. They rallied around the standard of their heroic leader, who, with twenty-two thousand men, kept the vast armies of Condé and Turenne at bay. Providence, too, assisted men who were willing to help themselves. The fleets of their enemies were dispersed by storms, and their armies were driven back by the timely inundation.

The heroism of William called forth universal admiration. Louis attempted to bribe him, and offered him the sovereignty of Holland, which offer he unhesitatingly rejected. He had seen the lowest point in the depression of his country, and was confident of ultimate success.

The resistance of Holland was unexpected, and Louis, wearied with the campaign, retired to Versailles, to be fed with the incense of his flatterers, and to publish the manifestoes of his glory and success.

The states of Europe, jealous of the encroachments of Louis, at last resolved to come to the assistance of the struggling republic of Holland. Charles II. ingloriously sided with the great despot of Europe; but the Emperor of Germany, the Elector of Brandenburg, and the King of Spain declared war against France. Moreover, the Dutch gained some signal naval battles. The celebrated admirals De Ruyter and Van Tromp redeemed the ancient glories of the Dutch flag. The French were nearly driven out of Holland; and Charles II., in spite of his secret treaties with Louis, was compelled to make peace with the little state which had hitherto defied him in the plenitude of his power.

Second Invasion of Holland.

But the ambitious King of France was determined not to be baffled in his scheme, since he had all the mighty resources of his kingdom at his entire disposal, and was burning with the passion of military aggrandizement. So he recommenced preparations for the conquest of Holland on a greater scale than ever, and assembled four immense armies. Condé led one against Flanders, and fought a bloody but indecisive battle with the Prince of Orange, in which twelve thousand men were killed on each side. Turenne commanded another on the side of Germany, and possessed himself of the Palatinate, gained several brilliant successes, but disgraced them by needless cruelties. Manheim, and numerous towns and villages, were burnt, and the country laid waste and desolate. The elector was so overcome with indignation, that he challenged the French general to single combat, which the great marshal declined.

Louis himself headed a third army, and invaded Franche Comté, which he subdued in six weeks. The fourth army was sent to the frontiers of Roussillon, but effected nothing of importance.

Dutch War.

This great war was prosecuted for four years longer, in which the contending parties obtained various success. The only decisive effect of the contest was to reduce the strength of all the contending powers. Some great battles were fought, but Holland still held out with inferior forces. Louis lost the great Turenne, who was killed on the eve of a battle with the celebrated Montecuculi, who commanded the German armies; but, in a succeeding campaign, this loss was compensated by the surrender of Valenciennes, by the victories of Luxembourg over the Prince of Orange, and by another treaty of peace with Charles II.

At last, all the contending parties were exhausted, and Louis was willing to make terms of peace. He had not reduced Holland, but, on account of his vast resources, he had obtained considerable advantages. The treaty of Nimeguen, in 1678, secured to him Franche Comté, which he had twice conquered, and several important cities and fortresses in Flanders. He considerably extended his dominions, in spite of a powerful confederacy, and only retreated from the field of triumph to meditate more gigantic enterprises.

For nine years, Europe enjoyed a respite from the horrors of war, during which Louis XIV. acted like a universal monarch. During these nine years, he indulged in his passion of palace building, and surrounded himself with every pleasure which could intoxicate a mind on which, already, had been exhausted all the arts of flattery, and all the resources of wealth.

The man to whom Louis was most indebted for the means to prosecute his victories and build his palaces, was Colbert, minister of finance, who succeeded Fouquet. France was indebted to this able and patriotic minister for her richest manufactures of silks, laces, tapestries, and carpets, and for various internal improvements. He founded the Gobelin tapestries; erected the Royal Library, the colonnade of the Louvre, the Royal Observatory, the Hotel of the Invalids, and the palaces of the Tuileries, Vincennes, Meudon, and Versailles. He encouraged all forms of industry, and protected the

Huguenots. But his great services were not fully appreciated by the king, and he was obnoxious to the nobility, who envied his eminence, and to the people, because he desired the prosperity of France more than the gratification of their pleasures. He was succeeded by Louvois, who long retained a great ascendency by obsequious attention to all the king's wishes.

Madame Montespan.

At this period, the reigning favorite at court was Madame de Montespan—the most infamous and unprincipled, but most witty and brilliant of all the king's mistresses, and the haughtiest woman of her age. Her tastes were expensive, and her habits extravagant and luxurious. On her the sovereign showered diamonds and rubies. He could refuse her nothing. She received so much from him, that she could afford to endow a convent—the mere building of which cost one million eight hundred thousand livres. Her children were legitimatized, and declared princes of the blood. Through her the royal favors flowed. Ambassadors, ministers, and even prelates, paid their court to her. On her the reproofs of Bossuet fell without effect. Secure in her ascendency over the mind of Louis, she triumphed over his court, and insulted the nation. But, at last, he grew weary of her, although she remained at court eighteen years, and she was dismissed from Versailles, on a pension of a sum equal to six hundred thousand dollars a year. She lived twenty-two years after her exile from court, and in great splendor, sometimes hoping to regain the ascendency she had once enjoyed, and at others in those rigorous penances which her church inflicts as the expiation for sin. To the last, however, she was haughty and imperious, and kept up the vain etiquette of a court. Her husband, whom she had abandoned, and to whom, after her disgrace, she sought to be reconciled, never would hear her name mentioned; and the king, whom, for nearly twenty years, she had enthralled, heard of her death with indifference, as he was starting for a hunting excursion. "Ah, indeed," said Louis XIV., "so the marchioness is dead! I should have thought that she would have lasted longer. Are you ready, M. de la Rochefoucauld? I have no doubt that, after this last shower, the scent will lie well for the dogs. Let us be off at once."

Madame de Maintenon.

As the Marchioness de Montespan lost her power over the royal egotist, Madame de Maintenon gained hers. She was the wife of the poet Scarron, and was first known to the king as the governess of the children of Montespan. She was an estimable woman on the whole, very intellectual, very proper, very artful, and very ambitious. No person ever had so great an influence over Louis XIV. as she; and hers was the ascendency of a strong mind over a weak one. She endeavored to make peace at court, and to dissuade the king from those vices to which he had so long been addicted. And she partially reclaimed him, although, while her counsels were still regarded, Louis was enslaved by Madame de Fontanges—a luxurious beauty, whom he made a duchess, and on whom he squandered the revenues of a province. But her reign was short. Mere physical charms must soon yield to the superior power of intellect and wit, and, after her death, the reign of Madame de Maintenon was complete. As the king could not live without her, and as she refused to follow the footsteps of her predecessors, the king made her his wife. And she was worthy of his choice; and her influence was, on the whole, good, although she befriended the Jesuits, and prompted the king to many acts of religious intolerance. It was chiefly through her influence, added to that of the Jesuits, that the king revoked the edict of Nantes, and its revocation was attended by great sufferings and privations among the persecuted Huguenots. He had, on ascending the throne, in 1643, confirmed the privileges of the Protestants; but, gradually, he worried them by exactions and restraints, and, finally, in 1685, by the revocation of the edict which Henry IV. had passed, he withdrew his protection, and subjected them to a more bitter persecution than at any preceding period. All the Protestant ministers were banished, or sent to the galleys, and the children of Protestants were taken from their parents, and committed to the care of their nearest Catholic relations, or such persons as judges appointed. All the terrors of military execution, all the artifices of priestcraft, were put forth to make converts and such as relapsed were subjected to cruel torments. A twentieth part of them were executed, and the remainder hunted from place to place. By these cruelties, France was deprived of nearly six hundred thousand of the best people in the land—a great misfortune, since they contributed, in their dispersion and exile, to enrich, by their agriculture and manufactures, the countries to which they fled.

From this period of his reign to his death, Louis XIV. was a religious bigot, and the interests of the Roman Church, next to the triumph of absolutism, became the great desire of his life. He was punctual and rigid in the outward ceremonials of his religion, and professed to regret the follies and vices of his early life. Through the influence of his confessor, the Jesuit La Chaise, and his wife, Madame de Maintenon, he sent away Montespan from his court, and discouraged those gayeties for which it had once been distinguished. But he was always fond of ceremony of all kinds, and the etiquette of his court was most irksome and oppressive, and wearied Madame de Maintenon herself, and caused her to exclaim, in a letter to her brother, "Save those who fill the highest stations, I know of none more unfortunate than those who envy them."

The favorite minister of the king at this time was Louvois, a very able but extremely prodigal man, who plunged Louis XIV. into innumerable expenses, and encouraged his taste both for palaces and war. It was probably through his intrigues, in order to make himself necessary to the king, that a general war again broke out in Europe.

League of Augsburg.

In 1687 was formed the famous League of Augsburg, by which the leading princes of Europe united in a great confederacy to suppress the power and encroachments of the French king. Louvois intrigued to secure the election of the Cardinal de Furstemberg to the archbishopric of Cologne, in opposition to the interests of Bavaria, the natural ally of France, conscious that, by so doing, he must provoke hostilities. But this act was only the occasion, not the cause, of war. Louis had enraged the Protestant world by his persecution of the Huguenots. He had insulted even the pope himself by sending an ambassador to Rome, with guards and armed attendants equal to an army, in order to enforce some privileges which it was not for the interest or the dignity of the pope to grant; he had encouraged the invasion of Germany by the Turks; he had seized Strasburg, the capital of Alsace; he bombarded Genoa, because they sold powder to the Algerines, and compelled the doge to visit him as a suppliant; he laid siege to some cities which belonged to Spain; and he prepared to annex the Low Countries to his dominions. Indeed, he treated all other powers as if he were the absolute monarch of Europe, and fear and jealousy united them against them. Germany, Spain, and Holland, and afterwards England, Denmark, Sweden, and Savoy, coöperated together to crush the common enemy of European liberties.

Louis made enormous exertions to resist this powerful confederacy. Four hundred thousand men were sent into the field, divided into four armies. Two of these were sent into Flanders, one into Catalonia, and one into Germany, which laid waste the Palatinate with fire and sword. Louvois gave the order, and Louis sanctioned it, which was executed with such unsparing cruelty that all Europe was filled with indignation and defiance.

Opposing Armies and Generals.

The forces of Louis were immense, but those of the allies were greater. The Spaniards, Dutch, and English, had an army of fifty thousand men in Flanders, eleven thousand of whom were commanded by the Earl of Marlborough. The Germans sent three more armies into the field; one commanded by the Elector of Bavaria, on the Upper Rhine; another by the Duke of Lorraine, on the Middle Rhine; and a third by the Elector of Brandenburg, on the Lower Rhine; and these, in the first campaign, obtained signal successes. The next year, the Duke of Savoy joined the allies, whose army was commanded by Victor Amadeus; but he was beaten by Marshal Catinat, one of the most distinguished of the French generals. Luxembourg also was successful in Flanders, and gained the great battle of Charleroi over the Germans and Dutch: The combined fleet of the English and Dutch was also defeated by the French at the battle of Beachy Head. In the next campaign, Prince Eugene and the Duke of Schomberg distinguished themselves in checking the victorious career of Catinat; but nothing of importance was effected. The following spring, William III. and Louis XIV., the two great heads of the contending parties, took the field themselves; and Louis, with the aid of Luxembourg, took Namur, in spite of the efforts of William to succor it. Some other successes were gained by the French, and Louis retired to Versailles to celebrate the victories of his generals. The next campaign witnessed another splendid victory over William and the allies, by Luxembourg, at Neerwinden, when twelve thousand men were killed; and also another, by Catinat, at Marsaglia, in Italy, over the Duke of Savoy. The military glory of Louis was now at its height; but, in the campaign of 1694-95, he met with great reverses. Luxembourg, the greatest of his generals, died. The allies retook Huy and Namur, and the French king, exhausted by the long war, was forced to make peace. The treaty of Ryswick, in 1697, secured the tranquillity of Europe for four years—long enough only for the contending parties to recover their energies, and prepare for a more desperate contest. Louis XIV., however, now acted on the defensive. The allied powers were resolved on his complete humiliation.

War of the Spanish Succession.

War broke out again in 1701, and in consequence of the accession of Philip V., grandson of Louis XIV., to the throne of Spain. This great war of the Spanish Succession, during which Marlborough so greatly distinguished himself, claims a few explanatory remarks.

Charles II., King of Spain, and the last of the line of the Austrian princes, being without an heir, and about to die, selected as his successor Leopold of Bavaria, a boy five years of age, whose grandmother was Maria Theresa. But there were also two other claimants—the Duke of Anjou, grandson of Louis XIV., whose claim rested in being the grandson of Maria Theresa, daughter of Philip IV., and sister of Charles II., and the Emperor of Germany, whose mother was the daughter of Philip III. The various European states looked with extreme jealousy on the claims of the Emperor of Germany and the Duke of Anjou, because they feared that the balance of power would be seriously disturbed if either an Austrian or a Bourbon prince became King of Spain. They, therefore, generally supported the claims of the Bavarian prince, especially England and Holland.

But the Prince of Bavaria suddenly died, as it was supposed by poison, and Louis XIV. so successfully intrigued, that his grandson was nominated by the Spanish monarch as heir to his throne. This incensed Leopold II. of Germany, and especially William III., who was resolved that the house of Bourbon should be no further aggrandized.

On the accession of the Duke of Anjou to the Spanish throne, in 1701, a grand alliance was formed, headed by the Emperor of Germany and the King of England, to dethrone him. Louis XIV. long hesitated between his ambition and the interests of his kingdom; but ambition triumphed. He well knew that he could only secure a crown to his grandson by a desperate contest with indignant Europe. Austria, Holland, Savoy, and England were arrayed against France. And this war of the Spanish Succession was the longest, the bloodiest, and the most disastrous war in which Louis was ever engaged. It commenced the last year of the reign of William III., and lasted thirteen years.

Duke of Marlborough.

The great hero of this war was doubtless the Duke of Marlborough, although Prince Eugene gained with him as imperishable glories as war can bestow. John Churchill, Duke of Marlborough, cannot be said to be one of those geniuses who have impressed their minds on nations and centuries; but he was a man who gave great lustre to the British name, and who attained to a higher pitch of military fame than any general whom England has produced since Oliver Cromwell, with the exception of Wellington.

He was born in 1650, of respectable parents, and was page of honor to the Duke of York, afterwards James II. While a mere boy, his bent of mind was discernible, and he solicited and obtained from the duke an ensign's commission, and rapidly passed through the military grades of lieutenant, captain, major, and colonel. During the infamous alliance between Louis XIV. and Charles II., he served under Marshal Turenne, and learned from him the art of war. But he also distinguished himself as a diplomatic agent of Charles II., in his intrigues with Holland and France. Before the accession of James II., he was created a Scottish peer, by the title of Baron Churchill. He followed his royal patron in his various peregrinations, and, when he succeeded to the English throne, he was raised to an English peerage. But Marlborough deserted his patron on the landing of William III., and was made a member of his Privy Council, and lord of the bed-chamber. Two days before the coronation of William, he was made Earl of Marlborough; but was not intrusted with as high military command as his genius and services merited, William being apparently jealous of his fame. On the accession of Anne, he was sent to the Continent with the supreme command of the English armies in the war with Louis about the Spanish Succession. His services in the campaign of 1702 secured a dukedom, and deservedly, for he contended against great obstacles—against the obstinacy and stupidity of the Dutch deputies; against the timidity of the English government at home; and against the veteran armies of Louis, led on by the celebrated Villars. But neither the campaigns of 1702 or 1703 were marked by any decisive battles. In 1704 was fought the celebrated battle of Blenheim, by which the French power was crippled, and the hopes of Louis prostrated.

The campaign of 1703 closed disastrously for the allies. Europe was never in greater peril. Bavaria united with France and Spain to crush Austria. The Austrians had only twenty thousand men, while the Bavarians had forty-five thousand men in the centre of Germany, and Marshal Tallard was posted, with forty-five thousand men, on the Upper Rhine. Marshal Villeroy opposed Marlborough in the Netherlands.

Battle of Blenheim.

But Marlborough conceived the bold project of marching his troops to the banks of the Danube, and there uniting with the Imperialists under Prince Eugene, to cut off the forces of the enemy before they could unite. So he left the Dutch to defend themselves against Villeroy, rapidly ascended the Rhine, before any of the enemy dreamed of his designs. From Mentz, he proceeded with forty thousand men to Heidelberg, and from Heidelberg to Donauworth, on the Danube, where his troops, which had effected a junction with the Austrians and Prussians, successfully engaged the Bavarians. But the Bavarians and the French also succeeded in uniting their forces; and both parties prepared for a desperate conflict. There were about eighty thousand men on each side. The French and Bavarians were strongly intrenched at the village of Blenheim; and Marlborough, against the advice of most of his generals, resolved to attack their fortified camp before it was reënforced by a large detachment of troops which Villeroy had sent. "I know the danger," said Marlborough; "but a battle is absolutely necessary." He was victorious. Forty thousand of the enemy were killed or taken prisoners; Tallard himself was taken, and every trophy was secured which marks a decisive victory. By his great victory, the Emperor of Austria was relieved from his fears, the Hungarians were overawed, Bavaria fell under the sway of the emperor, and the armies of Louis were dejected and discouraged. Marlborough marched back again to Holland without interruption, was made a prince of the empire, and received pensions and lands from the English government, which made him one of the richest and greatest of the English nobility. The palace of Blenheim was built, and he received the praises and plaudits of the civilized world.

The French were hardly able to cope with Marlborough during the next campaign, but rallied in 1706, during which year the great battle of Ramillies was fought, and won by Marlborough. The conquest of Brabant, and the greater part of Spanish Flanders, resulted from this victory; and Louis, crippled and humiliated, made overtures of peace. Though equitable, they were rejected; the allies having resolved that no peace should be made with the house of Bourbon while a prince of that house continued to sit upon the throne of Spain. Louis appealed now, in his distress, to the national honor, sent his plate to the mint, and resolved, in his turn, to contend, to the last extremity, with his enemies, whom success had intoxicated.

The English, not content with opposing Louis in the Netherlands and in Germany, sent their armies into Spain, also, who, united with the Austrians, overran the country, and nearly completed its conquest. One of the most gallant and memorable exploits of the war was the siege and capture of Barcelona by the Earl of Peterborough, the city having made one of the noblest and most desperate defences since the siege of Numantia.

Exertions and Necessities of Louis.

The exertions of Louis were equal to his necessities; and, in 1707, he was able to send large armies into the field. None of his generals were able to resist the Duke of Marlborough, who gained new victories, and took important cities; but, in Spain, the English met with reverses. In 1708, Louis again offered terms of peace, which were again rejected. His country was impoverished, his resources were exhausted, and a famine carried away his subjects. He agreed to yield the whole Spanish monarchy to the house of Austria, without any equivalent; to cede to the emperor his conquests on the Rhine, and to the Dutch the great cities which Marlborough had taken; to acknowledge the Elector of Brandenburg as King of Prussia, and Anne as Queen of England; to remove the Pretender from his dominions; to acknowledge the succession of the house of Hanover; to restore every thing required by the Duke of Savoy; and agree to the cessions made to the King of Portugal.

And yet these conditions, so honorable and advantageous to the allies, were rejected, chiefly through the influence of Marlborough, Eugene, and the pensionary Heinsius, who acted from entirely selfish motives. Louis was not permitted to cherish the most remote hope of peace without surrendering the strongest cities of his dominions as pledges for the entire evacuation of the Spanish monarchy by his grandson. This he would not agree to. He threw himself, in his distress, upon the loyalty of his people. Their pride and honor were excited; and, in spite of all their misfortunes, they prepared to make new efforts. Again were the French defeated at the great battle of Malplaquet, when ninety thousand men contended on each side; and again did Louis sue for peace. Again were his overtures rejected, and again did he rally his exhausted nation. Some victories in Spain were obtained over the confederates; but the allies gradually were hemming him around, and the king-hunt was nearly up, when unexpected dissensions among the allies relieved him of his enemies.

Treaty of Utrecht.

These dissensions were the struggles between the Whigs and Tories in England; the former maintaining that no peace should be made; the latter, that the war had been carried far enough, and was prolonged only to gratify the ambition of Marlborough. The great general, in consequence, lost popularity; and the Tories succeeded in securing a peace, just as Louis was on the verge of ruin. Another campaign, had the allies been united, would probably have enabled Marlborough to penetrate to Paris. That was his aim; that was the aim of his party. But the nation was weary of war, and at last made peace with Louis. By the treaty of Utrecht, (1713,) Philip V. resumed the throne of Spain, but was compelled to yield his rights to the crown of France in case of the death of a sickly infant, the great-grandson of Louis XIV., who was heir apparent to the throne; but, in other respects, the terms were not more favorable than what Louis had offered in 1706, and very inadequate to the expenses of the war. The allies should have yielded to the overtures of Louis before, or should have persevered. But party spirit, and division in the English cabinet and parliament, prevented the consummation which the Whigs desired, and Louis was saved from further humiliation and losses.

Last Days of Louis.

But his power was broken. He was no longer the autocrat of Europe, but a miserable old man, who had lived to see irreparable calamities indicted on his nation, and calamities in consequence of his ambition. His latter years were melancholy. He survived his son and his grandson. He saw himself an object of reproach, of ridicule, and of compassion. He sought the religious consolation of his church, but was the victim of miserable superstition, and a tool of the Jesuits. He was ruled by his wife, the widow of the poet Scarron, whom his children refused to honor. His last days were imbittered by disappointments and mortifications, disasters in war, and domestic afflictions. No man ever, for a while, enjoyed a prouder preëminence. No man ever drank deeper of the bitter cup of disappointed ambition and alienated affections. No man ever more fully realized the vanity of this world. None of the courtiers, by whom he was surrounded, he could trust, and all his experiences led to a disbelief in human virtue. He saw, with shame, that his palaces, his wars, and his pleasures, had consumed the resources of the nation, and had sowed the seeds of a fearful revolution. He lost his spirits; his temper became soured; mistrust and suspicion preyed upon his mind. His love of pomp survived all his other weaknesses, and his court, to the last, was most rigid in its wearisome formalities. But the pageantry of Versailles was a poor antidote to the sorrows which bowed his head to the ground, except on those great public occasions when his pride triumphed over his grief. Every day, in his last years, something occurred to wound his vanity, and alienate him from all the world but Madame de Maintenon, the only being whom he fully trusted, and who did not deceive him. Indeed, the humiliated monarch was an object of pity as well as of reproach, and his death was a relief to himself, as well as to his family. He died in 1715, two years after the peace of Utrecht, not much regretted by the nation.

His Character.

Louis XIV. cannot be numbered among the monsters of the human race who have worn the purple of royalty. His chief and worst vice was egotism, which was born with him, which was cultivated by all the influences of his education, and by all the circumstances of his position. This absorbing egotism made him insensible to the miseries he inflicted, and cherished in his soul the notion that France was created for him alone. His mistresses, his friends, his wives, his children, his court, and the whole nation, were viewed only as the instruments of his pride and pleasure. All his crimes and blunders proceeded from his extraordinary selfishness. If we could look on him without this moral taint, which corrupted and disgraced him, we should see an indulgent father and a generous friend. He attended zealously to the duties of his station, and sought not to shake off his responsibilities. He loved pleasure, but, in its pursuit, he did not forget the affairs of the realm. He rewarded literature, and appreciated merit. He honored the institutions of religion, and, in his latter days, was devoted to its duties, so far as he understood them. He has been foolishly panegyrized, and as foolishly censured. Still his reign was baneful, on the whole, especially to the interests of enlightened Christianity and to popular liberty. He was a bigoted Catholic, and sought to erect, on the ruins of states and empires, an absolute and universal throne. He failed; and instead of bequeathing to his successors the power which he enjoyed, he left them vast debts, a distracted empire, and a discontented people. He bequeathed to France the revolution which hurled her monarch from his throne, but which was overruled for her ultimate good.

References.—Louis XIV. et son Siècle. Voltaire's and Miss Pardoe's Histories of the Reign of Louis XIV. James's

Life of Louis XIV. Mémoires du Duc de St. Simon. The Abbé Millot's History. D'Anquetil's Louis XIV., sa Cour, et le Régent. Sismondi's History of France. Crowe's and Rankin's Histories of France. Lord Mahon's War of the Spanish Succession. Temple's Memoirs. Coxe's Life of Marlborough. Memoirs of Madame de Maintenon. Madame de Sévigné's Letters. Russell's Modern Europe. The late history by Miss Pardoe is one of the most interesting ever written. It may have too much gossip for what is called the "dignity of history;" but that fault, if fault it be, has been made by Macaulay also, and has been condemned, not unfrequently, by those most incapable of appreciating philosophical history.

CHAPTER XVII
WILLIAM AND MARY

William and Mary.

From Louis XIV. we turn to consider the reign of his illustrious rival, William III., King of England, who enjoyed the throne conjointly with Mary, daughter of James II.

The early life and struggles of this heroic prince have been already alluded to, in the two previous chapters, and will not be further discussed. On the 12th day of February, 1689, he arrived at Whitehall, the favorite palace of the Stuart kings, and, on the 11th of April, he and Mary were crowned in Westminster Abbey.

Their reign is chiefly memorable for the war with Louis XIV., the rebellion in Ireland, fomented by the intrigues of James II., and for the discussion of several great questions pertaining to the liberties and the prosperity of the English nation, questions in relation to the civil list, the Place Bill, the Triennial Bill, the liberty of the press, a standing army, the responsibility of ministers, the veto of the crown, the administration of Ireland, the East India Company, the Bank of England, and the funded debt. These topics make the domestic history of the country, especially in a constitutional point of view, extremely important.

The great struggle with Louis XIV. has already received all the notice which the limits of this work will allow, in which it was made to appear that, if Louis XIV. was the greater king, William III. was the greater man; and, although his military enterprises were, in one sense, unsuccessful, since he did not triumph in splendid victories, still he opposed successfully what would have been, without his heroism, an overwhelming torrent of invasion and conquest, in consequence of vastly superior forces. The French king was eventually humbled, and the liberties of continental Europe were preserved.

Under the wise, tolerant, and liberal administration of William, the British empire was preserved from disunion, and invaluable liberties and privileges were guaranteed.

Irish Rebellion.

Scarcely was he seated on the throne, which his wife inherited from the proud descendants of the Norman Conqueror, when a rebellion in Ireland broke out, and demanded his presence in that distracted and unfortunate country.

The Irish people, being Roman Catholics, had sympathized with James II. in all his troubles, and were resolved to defend his cause against a Calvinistic king. In a short time after his establishment at St. Germain's, through the bounty of the French king, he began to intrigue with the disaffected Irish chieftains. The most noted of these was Tyrconnel, who contrived to deprive the Protestants of Lord Mountjoy, their most trusted and able leader, by sending him on a mission to James II., by whose influence he was confined, on his arrival at Paris, in the Bastile. Tyrconnel then proceeded to disarm the Protestants, and recruit the Catholic army, which was raised in two months to a force of forty thousand men, burning to revenge their past injuries, and recover their ancient possessions and privileges. James II. was invited by the army to take possession of his throne. He accepted the invitation, and, early in 1689, made his triumphal entry into Dublin, and was received with a pomp and homage equal to his dignity. But James did not go to Ireland merely to enjoy the homage and plaudits of the Irish people, but to defend the last foothold which he retained as King of England, trusting that success in Ireland would eventually restore to him the throne of his ancestors. And he was cordially, but not powerfully, supported by the French king, who was at war with England, and who justly regarded Ireland as the most assailable part of the British empire.

The Irish parliament, in the interest of James, passed an act of attainder against all Protestants who had assisted William, among whom were two archbishops, one duke, seventeen earls, eighteen barons, and eighty-three clergymen. By another act, Ireland was made independent of England. The Protestants were every where despoiled and insulted.

But James was unequal to the task he had assumed, incapable either of preserving Ireland or retaking England. He was irresolute and undecided. He could not manage an Irish House of Commons any better than he could an English one. He debased the coin, and resorted to irritating measures to raise money.

At last he concluded to subdue the Protestants in Ulster, and advanced to lay siege to Londonderry, upon which depended the fate of the north of Ireland. It was bravely defended by the inhabitants, and finally relieved by the troops sent over from England under the command of Kirke—the same who inflicted the cruelties in the west of England under James II. But

William wanted able officers, and he took them indiscriminately from all parties. Nine thousand people miserably perished by famine and disease in the town, before the siege was raised, one of the most memorable in the annals of war.

Ulster was now safe, and the discomfiture of James was rapidly effected. Old Marshal Schomberg was sent into Ireland with sixteen thousand veteran troops, and, shortly after, William himself (June 14, 1690) landed at Carrickfergus, near Belfast, with additional men, who swelled the Protestant army to forty thousand.

King James in Ireland.

The contending forces advanced to the conflict, and on the 1st of July was fought the battle of the Boyne, in which Schomberg was killed, but which resulted in the defeat of the troops of James II. The discomfited king fled to Dublin, but quitted it as soon as he had entered it, and embarked hastily at Waterford for France, leaving the Earl of Tyrconnel to contend with vastly superior forces, and to make the best terms in his power.

The country was speedily subdued, and all the important cities and fortresses, one after the other, surrendered to the king. Limerick held out the longest, and made an obstinate resistance, but finally yielded to the conqueror; and with its surrender terminated the final efforts of the old Irish inhabitants to regain the freedom which they had lost. Four thousand persons were outlawed, and their possessions confiscated. Indeed, at different times, the whole country has been confiscated, with the exception of the possessions of a few families of English blood. In the reign of James I., the whole province of Ulster, containing three millions of acres, was divided among the new inhabitants. At the restoration, eight millions of acres, and, after the surrender of Limerick, one million more of acres, were confiscated. During the reign of William and Mary, the Catholic Irish were treated with extreme rigor, and Ireland became a field for place-hunters. All important or lucrative offices in the church, the state, and the army, were filled with the needy dependants of the great Whig families. Injustice to the nation was constantly exercised, and penal laws were imposed by the English parliament, and in reference to matters which before came under the jurisdiction of the Irish parliament. But, with all these rigorous measures, Ireland was still ruled with more mildness than at any previous period in its history, and no great disturbance again occurred until the reign of George III.

But the reign of William III., however beneficial to the liberties of England and of Europe, was far from peaceful. Apart from his great struggle with the French king, his comfort and his composure of mind were continually disturbed by domestic embarrassments, arising from the jealousies between the Whigs and Tories, the intrigues of statesmen with the exiled family, and discussions in parliament in reference to those great questions which attended the settlement of the constitution. A bill was passed, called the *Place Bill*, excluding all officers of the crown from the House of Commons, which showed the jealousy of the people respecting royal encroachments. A law also was passed, called the *Triennial Bill*, which limited the duration of parliament to three years, but which, in a subsequent reign, was repealed, and one substituted which extended the duration of a parliament to seven years. An important bill was also passed which regulated trials in case of treason, in which the prisoner was furnished with a copy of the indictment, with the names and residences of jurors, with the privilege of peremptory challenge, and with full defence of counsel. This bill guaranteed new privileges and rights to prisoners.

Freedom of the Press.

The great question pertaining to the Liberty of the Press was discussed at this time—one of the most vital questions which affect the stability of government on the one side, and the liberties of the people on the other. So desirable have all governments deemed the control of the press by themselves, that parliament, when it abolished the Star Chamber, in the reign of Charles I., still assumed its powers respecting the licensing of books. Various modifications were, from time to time, made in the laws pertaining to licensing books, until, in the reign of William, the liberty of the press was established nearly upon its present basis.

William, in general, was in favor of those movements which proved beneficial in after times, or which the wisdom of a subsequent age saw fit to adopt. Among these was the union of England and Scotland, which he recommended. Under his auspices, the affairs of the East India Company were considered and new charters granted; the Bank of England was erected; benevolent action for the suppression of vice and for the amelioration of the condition of the poor took place; the coinage was adjusted and financial experiments were made.

The crown, on the whole, lost power during this reign, which was transferred to the House of Commons. The Commons acquired the complete control of the purse, which is considered paramount to all other authority. Prior to the Revolution, the supply for the public service was placed at the disposal of the sovereign, but the definite sum of seven hundred thousand pounds, yearly, was placed at the disposal of William, to defray the expense of the civil list and his other expenses, while the other contingent expenses of government, including those for the support of the army and navy, were annually appropriated by the Commons.

Act of Settlement — Death of William III.

The most important legislative act of this reign was the Act of Settlement, March 12, 1701, which provided that England should be freed from the obligation of engaging in any war for the defence of the foreign dominions of the king; that all succeeding kings must be of the communion of the Church of England; that no succeeding king should go out of the British dominions without consent of parliament; that no person in office, or pensioner, should be a member of the Commons; that the religious liberties of the people should be further secured; that the judges should hold office during good behavior, and have their salaries ascertained; and that the succession to the throne should be confined to Protestant princes.

King William reigned in England thirteen years, with much ability, and sagacity, and prudence, and never attempted to subvert the constitution, for which his memory is dear to the English people. But most of his time, as king, was occupied in directing warlike operations on the Continent, and in which he showed a great jealousy of the genius of Marlborough, whose merits he nevertheless finally admitted. He died March 8, 1702, and was buried in the sepulchre of the kings of England.

Character of William.

Notwithstanding the animosity of different parties against William III., public opinion now generally awards to him, considering the difficulties with which he had to contend, the first place among the English kings. He had many enemies and many defects. The Jacobites hated him because "he upset their theory of the divine rights of kings; the High Churchmen because he was indifferent to the forms of church government; the Tories because he favored the Whigs; and the Republicans because he did not again try the hopeless experiment of a republic." He was not a popular idol, in spite of his great services and great qualities, because he was cold, reserved, and unyielding; because he disdained to flatter, and loved his native better than his adopted country. But his faults were chiefly offences against good manners, and against the prejudices of the nation. He distrusted human nature, and disdained human sympathy. He was ambitious, and his ambition was allied with selfishness. He permitted the slaughter of the De Witts, and never gave Marlborough a command worthy of his talents. He had no taste for literature, wit, or the fine arts. His favorite tastes were hunting, gardening and upholstery. That he was, however, capable of friendship, is attested by his long and devoted attachment to Bentinck, whom he created Earl of Portland, and splendidly rewarded with rich and extensive manors in every part of the land. His reserve and coldness may in part be traced to his profound knowledge of mankind, whom he feared to trust. But if he was not beloved by the nation, he secured their eternal respect by being the first to solve the problem of constitutional monarchy, and by successfully ruling, at a very critical period, the Dutch, the English, the Scotch, and the Irish, who had all separate interests and jealousies; by yielding, when in possession of great power, to restraints he did not like; and by undermining the intrigues and power of so mighty an enemy of European liberties as Louis XIV. His heroism shone brilliantly in defeat and disaster, and his courage and exertion never flagged when all Europe desponded, and when he himself labored under all the pains and lassitude of protracted disease. He died serenely, but hiding from his attendants, as he did all his days, the profoundest impressions which agitated his earnest and heroic soul.

Sir Isaac Newton and John Locke.

Among the great men whom he encouraged and rewarded, may be mentioned the historian Burnet, whom he made Bishop of Salisbury, and Tillotson and Tennison, whom he elevated to archiepiscopal thrones. Dr. South and Dr. Bentley also adorned this age of eminent divines. The great poets of the period were Prior, Dryden, Swift, and Pope, who, however, are numbered more frequently among the wits of the reign of Anne. Robert Boyle distinguished himself for experiments in natural science, and zeal for Christian knowledge; and Christopher Wren for his genius in architectural art. But the two great lights of this reign were, doubtless, Sir Isaac Newton and John Locke, to whom the realm of natural and intellectual philosophy is more indebted than to any other men of genius from the time of Bacon. The discoveries of Newton are scarcely without a parallel, and he is generally regarded as the greatest mathematical intellect that England has produced. To him the world is indebted for the binomial theorem, discovered at the age of twenty-two; for the invention of fluxions; for the demonstration of the law of gravitation; and for the discovery of the different refrangibility of rays of light. His treatise on Optics and his *Principia*, in which he brought to light the new theory of the universe, place him at the head of modern philosophers—on a high vantage ground, to which none have been elevated, of his age, with the exception of Leibnitz and Galileo. But his greatest glory was his modesty, and the splendid tribute he rendered to the truths of Christianity, whose importance and sublime beauty he was ever most proud to acknowledge in an age of levity and indifference.

John Locke is a name which almost exclusively belongs to the reign of William III., and he will also ever be honorably mentioned in the constellation of the very great geniuses and Christians of the world. His treatises on Religious Toleration are the most masterly ever written, while his Essay on the Human Understanding is a great system of truth, as complete, original, and logical, in the department of mental science, as was the system of Calvin in the realm of theology. Locke's Essay has had its enemies and detractors, and, while many eminent men have dissented from it, it nevertheless remains, one of the most enduring and proudest monuments of the immortal and ever-expanding intellect of man.

Anne.

On the death of William III., (1702,) the Princess Anne, daughter of James II., peaceably ascended the throne. She was thirty-seven years of age, a woman of great weaknesses, and possessing but few interesting qualities. Nevertheless, her reign is radiant with the glory of military successes, and adorned with every grace of fancy, wit, and style in literature. The personal talent and exclusive ambition of William suppressed the national genius; but the incapacity of Anne gave scope for the commanding abilities of Marlborough in the field, and Godolphin in the cabinet.

The memorable events connected with her reign of twelve years, were, the war of the Spanish succession, in which Marlborough humbled the pride of Louis XIV.; the struggles of the Whigs and Tories; the union of Scotland with England; the discussion and settlement of great questions pertaining to the constitution, and the security of the Protestant religion; and the impulse which literature received from the constellation of learned men who were patronized by the government, and who filled an unusual place in public estimation.

In a political point of view, this reign is but the continuation of the reign of William, since the same objects were pursued, the same policy was adopted, and the same great characters were intrusted with power. The animating object of William's life was the suppression of the power of Louis XIV.; and this object was never lost sight of by the English government under the reign of Anne.

Hence the great political event of the reign was the war of the Spanish succession, which, however, pertains to the reign of Louis as well as to that of Anne. It was during this war that the great battles of Blenheim, Ramillies, and Malplaquet attested the genius of the greatest military commander that England had ever sent into the field. It was this war which exhausted the energies and resources of all the contending states of Europe, and created a necessity for many years of slumbering repose. It was this war which completed the humiliation of a monarch who aspired to the sovereignty of Europe, which preserved the balance of power, and secured the liberties of Europe. Yet it was a war which laid the foundation of the national debt, inflamed the English mind with a mad passion for military glory, which demoralized the nation, and fostered those international jealousies and enmities which are still a subject of reproach to the two most powerful states of Europe. This war made England a more prominent actor on the arena of European strife, and perhaps contributed to her political aggrandizement. The greatness of the British empire begins to date from this period, although this greatness is more to be traced to colonial possessions, manufactures, and commercial wealth, than to the victories of Marlborough.

It will ever remain an open question whether or not it was wise in the English nation to continue so long the struggle with Louis XIV. In a financial and material point of view, the war proved disastrous. But it is difficult to measure the real greatness of a country, and solid and enduring blessings, by pounds, shillings, and pence. All such calculations, however statistically startling, are erroneous and deceptive. The real strength of nations consists in loyalty, patriotism, and public spirit; and no sacrifices can be too great to secure these unbought blessings—"this cheap defence." If the victories of Marlborough secured these, gave dignity to the British name, and an honorable and lofty self-respect to the English people, they were not dearly purchased. But the settlement of these questions cannot be easily made.

The Duke of Marlborough.

As to the remarkable genius of the great man who infused courage into the English mind, there can be no question. Marlborough, in spite of his many faults, his selfishness and parsimony, his ambition and duplicity, will ever enjoy an enviable fame. He was not so great a moral hero as William, nor did he contend against such superior forces as the royal hero. But he was a great hero, nevertheless. His glory was reached by no sudden indulgence of fortune, by no fortunate movements, by no accidental circumstances. His fame was progressive. He never made a great mistake; he never lost the soundness of his judgment. No success unduly elated him, and no reverses discouraged him. He never forgot the interests of the nation in his own personal annoyances or enmities. He was magnanimously indulgent to those Dutch deputies who thwarted his measures, criticized his plans, and lectured him on the art of war. The glory of his country was the prevailing desire of his soul. He was as great in diplomacy and statesmanship as on the field of Blenheim. He ever sacrificed his feelings as a victorious general to his duty as a subject. His sagacity was only equalled by his prudence and patience, and these contributed, as well as his personal bravery, to his splendid successes, which secured for him magnificent rewards—palaces and parks, peerages, and a nation's gratitude and praise.

But there is a limit to all human glory. Marlborough was undermined by his political enemies, and he himself lost the confidence of the queen whom he had served, partly by his own imperious conduct, and partly from the overbearing insolence of his wife. From the height of popular favor, he descended to the depth of popular hatred. He was held up, by the sarcasm of the writers whom he despised, to derision and obloquy; was accused of insolence, cruelty, ambition, extortion, and avarice, discharged from his high offices, and obliged to seek safety by exile. He never regained the confidence of the nation, although, when he died, parliament decreed him a splendid funeral, and a grave in Westminster Abbey.

Character of Marlborough.

In private life, he was amiable and kind; was patient under contradiction, and placid in manners; had great self-possession, and extraordinary dignity. His person was beautiful, and his address commanding. He was feared as a general, but loved as a man. He never lost his affections for his home, and loved to idolatry his imperious wife, his equal, if not superior, in the knowledge of human nature. These qualities as a man, a general, and a statesman, in spite of his defects, have immortalized his name, and he will, for a long time to come, be called, and called with justice, the *great* Duke of Marlborough.

Scarcely less than he, was Lord Godolphin, the able prime minister of Anne, with whom Marlborough was united by family ties, by friendship, by official relations, and by interest. He was a Tory by profession, but a Whig in his policy. He rose with Marlborough, and fell with him, being an unflinching advocate for the prosecution of the war to the utmost limits, for which his government was distasteful to the Tories. His life was not stainless; but, in an age of corruption, he ably administered the treasury department, and had control of unbounded wealth, without becoming rich—the highest praise which can ever be awarded to a minister of finance. It was only through the coöperation of this sagacious and far-sighted statesman that Marlborough himself was enabled to prosecute his brilliant military career.

Whigs and Tories.

It was during his administration that party animosity was at its height—the great struggle which has been going on, in England, for nearly two hundred years, between the Whigs and Tories. These names originated in the reign of Charles II., and were terms of reproach. The court party reproached their antagonists with their affinity to the fanatical conventiclers in Scotland, who were known by the name of the *Whigs*; and the country party pretended to find a resemblance between the courtiers and the Popish banditti of Ireland, to whom the appellation of *Tory* was affixed. The High Church party and the advocates of absolutism belonged to the Tories; the more liberal party and the advocates of constitutional reform, to the Whigs. The former were conservative, the latter professed a sympathy with improvements. But the leaders of both parties were among the greatest nobles in the realm, and probably cared less for any great innovation than they did for themselves. These two great parties, in the progress of society, have changed their views, and the opinions once held by the Whigs were afterwards adopted by the Tories. On the whole, the Whigs were in advance in liberality of mind, and in enlightened plans of government. But both parties, in England, have ever been aristocratic, and both have felt nearly an equal disgust of popular influences. Charles and James sympathized with the Tories more than with the Whigs; but William III. was supported by the Whigs, who had the ascendency in his reign. Queen Anne was a Tory, as was to be expected from a princess of the house of Stuart; but, in the early part of her reign, was obliged to yield to the supremacy of the Whigs. The advocates for war were Whigs, and those who desired peace were Tories. The Whigs looked to the future glory of the country; the Tories, to the expenses which war created. The Tories at last got the ascendency, and expelled Godolphin, Marlborough, and Sunderland from power.

Of the Tory leaders, Harley, (Earl of Oxford,) St. John, (Lord Bolingbroke,) the Duke of Buckingham, and the Duke of Ormond, the Earl of Rochester, and Lord Dartmouth, were the most prominent, but this Tory party was itself divided, in consequence of jealousies between the chiefs, the intrigues of Harley, and the measureless ambition of Bolingbroke. Under the ascendency of the Tories the treaty of Utrecht was made, now generally condemned by historians of both Whig and Tory politics. It was disproportioned to the success of the war, although it secured the ends of the grand alliance.

Dr. Henry Sacheverell.

One of the causes which led to the overthrow of the Whigs was the impeachment and trial of Dr. Henry Sacheverell, an event which excited intense interest at the time, and, though insignificant in itself, touched some vital principles of the constitution.

This divine was a man of mean capacity, and of little reputation for learning or virtue. He had been, during the reign of William, an outrageous Whig; but, finding his services disregarded, he became a violent Tory. By a sort of plausible effrontery and scurrilous rhetoric, he obtained the applause of the people, and the valuable living of St. Saviour, Southwark. The audacity of his railings against the late king and the revolution at last attracted the notice of government; and for two sermons which he printed, and in which he inculcated, without measure, the doctrine of passive obedience, consigned Dissenters to eternal damnation, and abused the great principle of religious toleration, he was formally impeached. All England was excited by the trial. The queen herself privately attended, to encourage a man who was persecuted for his loyalty, and persecuted for defending his church. The finest orators and lawyers of the day put forth all their energies. Bishop Atterbury wrote for Sacheverell his defence, which was endorsed by a conclave of High Church divines. The result of the trial was the condemnation of the doctor, and with it the fall of his adversaries. He was suspended for three years, but his defeat was a triumph. He was received, in college halls and private mansions, with the pomp of a sovereign and the reverence of a saint. His sentence made his enemies unpopular. The great body of the English nation, wedded to High Church principles, took sides in his favor. But the arguments of his accusers developed some great principles—led to the assertion of the doctrines of toleration; for, if passive obedience to the rulers of the state and church were obligatory, then all Dissenters might be curbed and suppressed. The Whig managers of the trial, by opposing the bigoted Churchmen, aided the cause of dissent, justified the revolution, and upheld the conquest by William III. And their speeches are upon record, that they asserted the great principles of civil and religious liberty, in the face of all the authority, dignity, and wisdom of the realm. It is true they lost as a party, on account of the bigotry of the times; but they furnished another pillar to uphold the constitution, and adduced new and powerful arguments in support of constitutional liberty. The country gained, if they, as a party, lost; and though Sacheverell was lauded by his church, his conviction was a triumph to the friends of freedom. Good resulted in many other ways. Political leaders learned moral wisdom; they saw the folly of persecuting men for libels, when such men had the sympathy of the people; that such persecutions were undignified, and that, while they gained their end, they lost more by victory than by defeat. The trial of Sacheverell, while it brought to view more clearly some great constitutional truths, also more effectually advanced the liberty of the press; for, surely, restriction on the press is a worse evil, than the violence and vituperation of occasional libels.

Union of Scotland and England.

The great domestic event of this reign was doubtless the union of Scotland and England; a consummation of lasting peace between the two countries, which William III. had proposed. Nothing could be more beneficent for both the countries; and the only wonder is, that it was not done before, when James II. ascended the English throne; and nothing then, perhaps, prevented it, but the bitter jealousy which had so long existed between these countries; a jealousy, dislike, and prejudice which have hardly yet passed away.

Scotland, until the reign of James II., was theoretically and practically independent of England, but was not so fortunately placed, as the latter country, for the development of energies. The country was smaller, more barren, and less cultivated. The people were less civilized; and had less influence on the political welfare of the state. The aristocracy were more powerful, and were more jealous of royal authority. There were constant feuds and jealousies between dominant classes, which checked the growth in political importance, wealth, and civilization. But the people were more generally imbued with the ultra principles of the Reformation, were more religious, and cherished a peculiar attachment to the Presbyterian form of church government, and a peculiar hatred of every thing which resembled Roman Catholicism. They were, moreover, distinguished for patriotism, and had great jealousy of English influences.

James II. was the legitimate King of Scotland, as well as of England; but he soon acquired a greater love for England, than he retained for his native country; and England being the greater country, the interests of Scotland were frequently sacrificed to those of England.

Queen Anne, as the daughter of James II., was also the legitimate sovereign of Scotland; and, on her decease, the Scotch were not bound to acknowledge the Elector of Hanover as their legitimate king.

Duke of Hamilton.

Many ardent and patriotic Scotchmen, including the Duke of Hamilton and Fletcher of Saltoun, deemed it a favorable time to assert, on the death of Queen Anne, their national independence, since the English government was neither just nor generous to the lesser country.

Under these circumstances, there were many obstacles to a permanent union, and it was more bitterly opposed in Scotland than in England. The more patriotic desired complete independence. Many were jealous of the superior prosperity of England. The people in the Highlands and the north of Scotland were Jacobinical in their principles, and were attached to the Stuart dynasty. The Presbyterians feared the influence of English Episcopacy, and Scottish peers deprecated a servile dependence on the parliament of England.

But the English government, on the whole, much as it hated Scotch Presbyterianism and Scotch influence, desired a union, in order to secure the peaceful succession of the house of Hanover, for the north of Scotland was favorable to the Stuarts, and without a union, English liberties would be endangered by Jacobinical intrigues. English statesmen felt this, and used every measure to secure this end.

The Scotch were overreached. Force, bribery, and corruption were resorted to. The Duke of Hamilton proved a traitor, and the union was effected—a union exceedingly important to the peace of both countries, but especially desirable to England. Important concessions were made by the English, to which they were driven only by fear. They might have ruled Scotland as they did Ireland, but for the intrepidity and firmness of the Scotch, who while negotiations were pending, passed the famous Act of Security, by which the Scottish parliament decreed the succession in Scotland, on the death of the queen, open and elective; the independence and power of parliaments; freedom in trade and commerce; and the liberty of Scotland to engage or not in the English continental wars. The English parliament retaliated, indeed, by an act restricting the trade of Scotland, and declaring Scotchmen aliens throughout the English dominions. But the conflicts between the Whigs and Tories induced government to repeal the act; and the commissioners for the union secured their end.

It was agreed, in the famous treaty they at last effected, that the two kingdoms of England and Scotland be united into one, by the name of *Great Britain*.

That the succession to the United Kingdom shall remain to the Princess Sophia, Duchess Dowager of Hanover, and the heirs of her body, being Protestants; and that all Papists, and persons marrying Papists, shall be excluded from, and be forever incapable of inheriting, the crown of Great Britain;

That the whole people of Great Britain shall be represented by one parliament, in which sixteen peers and forty-five commoners, chosen for Scotland, should sit and vote;

That the subjects of the United Kingdom shall enjoy an entire freedom and intercourse of trade and navigation, and reciprocal communication of all other rights, privileges, and advantages belonging to the subjects of either kingdom;

That the laws, in regard to public rights and civil government, shall be the same in both countries, but that no alteration shall be made in the laws respecting private rights, unless for the evident utility of the subjects residing in Scotland;

That the Court of Session, and all other courts of judicature in Scotland, remain as before the union, subject, however, to such regulations as may be made by the parliament of Great Britain.

Beside these permanent regulations, a sum of three hundred and ninety-eight thousand pounds was granted to Scotland, as an equivalent to the augmentation of the customs and excise.

By this treaty, the Scotch became identified with the English in interest. They lost their independence; but they gained security and peace; and rose in wealth and consequence. The nation moreover, was burdened by the growth of the national debt. The advantage was mutual, but England gained the greater advantage by shifting a portion of her burdens on Scotland, by securing the hardy people of that noble country to fight her battles, and by converting a nation of enemies into a nation of friends.

We come now to glance at those illustrious men who adorned the literature of England in this brilliant age, celebrated for political as well as literary writings.

Of these, Addison, Swift, Bolingbroke, Bentley, Warburton, Arbuthnot, Gay, Pope, Tickell, Halifax, Parnell, Rowe, Prior, Congreve, Steele, and Berkeley, were the most distinguished. Dryden belonged to the preceding age; to the period of license and gayety—the greatest but most immoral of all the great poets of England, from the time of Milton to that of Pope.

Wits of Queen Anne's Reign.

The wits of Queen Anne's reign were political writers as well as poets, and their services were sought for and paid by the great statesmen of the times, chiefly of the Tory party. Marlborough neglected the poets, and they contributed to undermine his power.

Of these wits the most distinguished and respectable was Addison, born 1672. He was well educated, and distinguished himself at Oxford, and was a fellow of Magdalen College. His early verses, which would now be pronounced very inferior, however attracted the notice of Dryden, then the great autocrat of letters, and the oracle of the literary clubs. At the age of twenty-seven, Addison was provided with a pension from the Whig government, and set out on his travels. He was afterwards made secretary to Lord Halifax, and elected a member of the House of Commons, but was never able to make a speech. He, however, made up for his failure as an orator by his power as a writer, being a perfect master of elegant satire. He was also charming in private conversation, and his society was much sought by eminent statesmen, scholars, and noblemen. In 1708, he became secretary for Ireland, and, while he resided at Dublin, wrote those delightful papers on which his fame chiefly rests. Not as the author of Rosamond, nor of Latin verses, nor of the treatise on Medals, nor of Letters from Italy, nor of the tragedy of Cato, would he now be known to us. His glory is derived from the Tatler and Spectator—an entirely new species of writing in his age, original, simple, and beautiful, but chiefly marked for polished and elegant satire against the follies and bad taste of his age. Moreover, his numbers of the Spectator are distinguished for elevation of sentiment, and moral purity, without harshness, and without misanthropy. He wrote three sevenths of that immortal production, and on every variety of subject, without any attempt to be eloquent or *intense,* without pedantry and without affectation. The success of the work was immense, and every one who could afford it, had it served on the breakfast table with the tea and toast. It was the general subject of conversation in all polite circles, and did much to improve the taste and reform the morals of the age. There was nothing which he so severely ridiculed as the show of learning without the reality, coxcombry in conversation, extravagance in dress, female flirts and butterflies, gay and fashionable women, and all false modesty and affectation. But he blamed without bitterness, and reformed without exhortation, while he exalted what was simple, and painted in most beautiful colors the virtues of contentment, simplicity, sincerity, and cheerfulness.

His latter days were imbittered by party animosity, and the malignant stings of literary rivals. Nor was he happy in his domestic life, having married a proud countess, who did not appreciate his genius. He also became addicted to intemperate habits. Still he was ever honored and respected, and, when he died, was buried in Westminster Abbey.

Swift.

Next to Addison in fame, and superior in genius, was Swift, born in Ireland, in 1677, educated at Dublin, and patronized by Sir William Temple. He was rewarded, finally, with the deanery of St. Patrick's. He was very useful to his party by his political writings; but his fame rests chiefly on his poetry, and his Gulliver's Travels, marked and disgraced by his savage sarcasm on woman, and his vilification of human nature. He was a great master of venomous satire. He spared neither friends nor enemies. He was ambitious, misanthropic and selfish. His treatment of woman was disgraceful and heartless in the extreme. But he was witty, learned, and natural. He was never known to laugh, while he convulsed the circles into which he was thrown. He was rough to his servants, insolent to inferiors, and sycophantic to men of rank. His distinguishing power was his unsparing and unscrupulous sarcasm and his invective was as dreadful as the personal ridicule of Voltaire. As a poet he was respectable, and as a writer he was original. He was indifferent to literary fame, and never attempted any higher style of composition than that in which he could excel. His last days were miserable, and he lingered a long while in hopeless and melancholy idiocy.

Pope — Bolingbroke — Gay — Prior.

Pope properly belongs to a succeeding age, though his first writings attracted considerable attention during the life of Addison, who first raised him from obscurity. He is the greatest, after Dryden, of all the second class poets of his country. His Rape of the Lock, the most original of his poems, established his fame. But his greatest works were the translations of the Iliad and Odyssey, the Dunciad, and his Essay on Man. He was well paid for his labors, and lived in a beautiful villa at Twickenham, the friend of Bolingbroke, and the greatest literary star of his age. But he was bitter and satirical, irritable, parsimonious, and vain. As a versifier, he has never been equalled. He died in 1744, in the Romish faith, beloved but by few, and disliked by the world generally.

Writers of the Age of Queen Anne.

Bolingbroke was not a poet, but a man of vast genius, a great statesman, and a great writer on history and political philosophy, a man of most fascinating manners and conversation, brilliant, witty, and learned, but unprincipled and intriguing, the great leader of the Tory party. Gay, as a poet, was respectable, but poor, unfortunate, a hanger on of great people, and miserably paid for his sycophancy. His fame rests on his Fables and his Beggar's Opera. Prior first made himself distinguished by his satire called A City Mouse and a Country Mouse, aimed against Dryden. He was well rewarded by government, and was sent as minister to Paris. Like most of the wits of his time, he was convivial, and not always particular in the choice of his associates. Humor was the natural turn of his mind. Steele was editor of the Spectator and wrote some excellent papers, although vastly inferior to Addison's. He is the father of the periodical essay, was a man of fashion and pleasure, and had great experience in the follies and vanities of the world. It is doubtful whether the writings of the great men who adorned the age of Anne will ever regain the ascendency they once enjoyed, since they have all been surpassed in succeeding times. They had not the fire, enthusiasm, or genius which satisfies the wants of the present generation. As poets, they had no greatness of fancy; and as philosophers, they were cold and superficial. Nor did they write for the people, but for the great, with whom they sought to associate, by whose praises they were consoled, and by whose bread they were sustained. They wrote for a class, and that class alone, that chiefly seeks to avoid ridicule and abstain from absurdity, that never attempts the sublime, and never sinks to the ridiculous; a class keen of observation, fond of the satirical, and indifferent to all institutions and enterprises which have for their object the elevation of the masses, or the triumph of the abstract principles of truth and justice.

References.—Lord Mahon's History of England, which commences with the peace of Utrecht, is one of the most useful and interesting works which have lately appeared. Smollett's continuation of Hume should be consulted, although the author was greater as a novelist than as an historian. Burnet's history on this period is a standard. Hallam should be read in reference to all constitutional questions. Coxe's Life of Marlborough throws great light on the period, and is very valuable. Macaulay's work will, of course, be read. See, also, Bolingbroke's Letters, and the Duke of Berwick's Memoirs. A chapter in the Pictorial History is very good as to literary history and the progress of the arts and sciences. See, also, Johnson's Lives of the Poets; Nichols's Life of Addison; Scott's Life of Swift; Macaulay's Essay on Addison; and the Spectator and Tatler.

CHAPTER XVIII
PETER THE GREAT, AND RUSSIA

While Louis XIV. was prosecuting his schemes of aggrandizement, and William III. was opposing those schemes; while Villeroy, Villars, Marlborough, and Eugene were contending, at the head of great armies, for their respective masters; a new power was arising at the north, destined soon to become prominent among the great empires of the world. The political importance of Russia was not appreciated at the close of the seventeenth century, until the great resources of the country were brought to the view of Europe by the extraordinary genius of Peter the Great.

Early History of Russia.

The history of Russia, before the reign of this great prince, has not excited much interest, and is not particularly eventful or important. The Russians are descended from the ancient Sclavonic race, supposed to be much inferior to the Germanic or Teutonic tribes, to whom most of the civilized nations of Europe trace their origin.

The first great event in Russian history is the nominal conversion of a powerful king to Christianity, in the tenth century, named Vladimir, whose reign was a mixture of cruelty, licentiousness, and heroism. Seeing the necessity of some generally recognized religion, he sent ten of his most distinguished men into all the various countries then known, to examine their religious systems. Being semi-barbarians, they were disposed to recommend that form which had the most imposing ceremonial, and appealed most forcibly to the senses. The commissioners came to Mecca, but soon left with contempt, since Mohammedanism then made too great demands upon the powers of self-control, and prohibited the use of many things to which the barbarians were attached. They were no better pleased with the Manichean philosophy, which then extensively prevailed in the East; for this involved the settlement of abstract ideas, for which barbarians had no relish. They disliked Roman Catholicism, on account of the arrogant claims of the pope. Judaism was spurned, because it had no country, and its professors were scattered over the face of the earth. But the lofty minarets of St. Sophia, and the extravagant magnificence of the Greek worship, filled the commissioners with admiration; and they easily induced Vladimir to adopt the forms of the Greek Church; which has ever since been the established religion of Russia. But Christianity, in its corrupted form, failed to destroy, and scarcely alleviated, the traits of barbarous life. Old superstitions and vices prevailed; nor were the Russian territories on an equality with the Gothic kingdoms of Europe, in manners, arts learning, laws, or piety.

The Tartar Conquest.

When Genghis Khan, with his Tartar hordes, overran the world Russia was subdued, and Tartar princes took possession of the throne of the ancient czars. But the Russian princes, in the thirteenth century, recovered their ancient power. Alexander Nevsky performed exploits of great brilliancy; gained important victories over Danes, Swedes, Lithuanians, and Teutonic knights; and greatly enlarged the boundaries of his kingdom. In the fourteenth century, Moscow became a powerful city, to which was transferred the seat of government, which before was Novgorod. Under the successor of Ivan Kalita, the manners, laws, and institutions of the Russians became fixed, and the absolute power of the czars was established. Under Ivan III., who ascended the Muscovite throne in 1462, the Tartar rule was exterminated, and the various provinces and principalities, of which Russia was composed, were brought under a central government. The Kremlin, with its mighty towers and imposing minarets, arose in all the grandeur of Eastern art and barbaric strength. The mines of the country were worked, the roads cleared of banditti, and a code of laws established. The veil which concealed Russia from the rest of Europe was rent. An army of three hundred thousand men was enlisted, Siberia was discovered, the printing press introduced, and civilization commenced. But the czar was, nevertheless, a brutal tyrant and an abandoned libertine, who massacred his son, executed his nobles, and destroyed his cities.

His successors were disgraced by every crime which degrades humanity; and the whole population remained in rudeness and barbarism, superstition and ignorance. The clergy wielded enormous power; which, however, was rendered subservient to the interests of absolutism.

Accession of Peter the Great.

Such was Russia, when Peter, the son of Alexis Michaelovitz, ascended the throne, in 1682—a boy, ten years of age. He early exhibited great sagacity and talent, but was addicted to gross pleasures. These, strangely, did not enervate him, or prevent him from making considerable attainments. But he was most distinguished for a military spirit, which was treated with contempt by the Regent Sophia, daughter of Alexis by a first marriage. As soon, however, as her eyes were open to his varied studies and his ambitious spirit, she became jealous, and attempted to secure his assassination. In this she failed, and the youthful sovereign reigned supreme in Moscow, at the age of seventeen.

No sooner did he assume the reins of empire, than his genius blazed forth with singular brilliancy, and the rapid development of his powers was a subject of universal wonder. Full of courage and energy, he found nothing too arduous for him to undertake; and he soon conceived the vast project of changing the whole system of his government, and reforming the manners of his subjects.

He first directed his attention to the art of war, and resolved to increase the military strength of his empire. With the aid of Le Fort, a Swiss adventurer, and Gordon, a Scotch officer, he instituted, gradually, a standing army of twenty thousand men, officered, armed, and disciplined after the European model; cut off the long beards of the soldiers, took away their robes, and changed their Asiatic dress.

He then conceived the idea of a navy, which may be traced to his love of sailing in a boat, which he had learned to navigate himself. He studied assiduously the art of ship-building, and soon laid the foundation of a navy.

His enterprising and innovating spirit created, as it was to be expected, considerable disaffection among the partisans of the old *régime*—the old officers of the army, and the nobles, stripped of many of their privileges. A rebellion was the consequence; which, however, was soon suppressed, and the conspirators were executed with unsparing cruelty.

He then came to the singular resolution of visiting foreign countries, in order to acquire useful information, both in respect to the arts of government and the arts of civilization. Many amusing incidents are recorded of him in his travels. He journeyed incognito; clambered up the sides of ships, ascended the rigging, and descended into the hold; he hired himself out as a workman in Holland, lived on the wretched stipend which he earned as a ship-carpenter, and mastered all the details of ship-building. From Holland he went to England, where he was received with great honor by William III.; studied the state of manufactures and trades, and sought to gain knowledge on all common subjects. From England he went to Austria, intending to go afterwards to Italy; but he was compelled to return home, on account of a rebellion of the old military guard, called the *Strelitz*, who were peculiarly disaffected. But he easily suppressed the discontents, and punished the old soldiers with unsparing rigor. He even executed thirty with his own hands.

Peter's Reforms.

He then turned himself, in good earnest, to the work of reform. His passions were military, and he longed to conquer kingdoms and cities. But he saw no probability of success, unless he could first civilize his subjects, and teach the soldiers the great improvements in the art of war. In order to conquer, he resolved first to reform his nation. His desires were selfish, but happened to be directed into channels which benefited his country. Like Napoleon, his ruling passion was that of the aggrandizement of himself and nation. But Providence designed that his passions should be made subservient to the welfare of his race. It is to his glory that he had enlargement of mind sufficient to perceive the true sources of national prosperity. To secure this, therefore, became the aim of his life. He became a reformer; but a reformer, like Hildebrand, of the despotic school.

The first object of all despots is the improvement of the military force. To effect this, he abolished the old privileges of the soldiers, disbanded them, and drafted them into the new regiments, which he had organized on the European plan.

He found more difficulty in changing the dress of the people, who, generally, wore the long Asiatic robe, and the Tartar beard; and such was the opposition made by the people, that he was obliged to compromise the matter, and compelled all who would wear beards and robes to pay a heavy tax, except priests and peasants: having granted the indulgence to priests on account of the ceremonial of their worship, and to peasants in order to render their costume ignominious.

His next important measure was the toleration of all religions, and all sects, with the exception of the Jesuits, whom he hated and feared. He caused the Bible to be translated into the Sclavonic language; founded a school for the marine, and also institutions for the encouragement of literature and art. He abolished the old and odious laws of marriage, by which women had no liberty in the choice of husbands. He suppressed all useless monasteries; taxed the clergy as well as the laity; humiliated the patriarch, and assumed many of his powers. He improved the administration of justice, mitigated laws in relation to woman, and raised her social rank. He established post-offices, boards of trade, a vigorous police, hospitals and almshouses. He humbled the nobility, and abolished many of their privileges; for which the people honored him, and looked upon him as their benefactor.

Having organized his army, and effected social reforms, he turned his attention to war and national aggrandizement.

His War with Charles XII.

Charles XII.

His first war was with Sweden, then the most powerful of the northern states, and ruled by Charles XII., who, at the age of eighteen, had just ascended the throne. The *cause* of the war was the desire of aggrandizement on the part of the czar; the *pretence* was, the restitution of some lands which Sweden had obtained from Denmark and Poland. Taking advantage of the defenceless state of Sweden,—attacked, at that time, by Denmark on the one side, and by Poland on the other,—Peter invaded the territories of Charles with an army of sixty thousand men, and laid siege to Narva. The Swedish forces were only twenty thousand; but they were veterans, and they were headed by a hero. Notwithstanding the great disproportion between the contending parties, the Russians were defeated, although attacked in their intrenchments, and all the artillery fell into the hands of the Swedes. The victory at Narva settled the fame of Charles, but intoxicated his mind, and led to a presumptuous self-confidence; while the defeat of Peter did not discourage him, but braced him to make still greater exertions—one of the numerous instances, so often seen in human life, where defeat is better than victory. But the czar was conscious of his strength, and also of his weakness. He knew he had unlimited resources, but that his troops were inexperienced; and he made up his mind for disasters at the beginning, in the hope of victory in the end. "I know very well," said he, "that the Swedes will have the advantage over us for a considerable time; but they will teach us, at length, to beat them." The Swede, on the other hand, was intoxicated with victory, and acquired that fatal presumption which finally proved disastrous to himself and to his country. He despised his adversary; while Peter, without overrating his victorious enemy, was led to put forth new energies, and develop the great resources of his nation. He was sure of final success; and he who can be sustained by the consciousness of ultimate triumph, can ever afford to wait. It is the spirit which sustains the martyr. It constitutes the distinguishing element of enthusiasm and exalted heroism.

But Peter not only made new military preparations, but prosecuted his schemes of internal improvement, and projected, after his unfortunate defeat at Narva, the union, by a canal, of the Baltic and Caspian Seas. About this time, he introduced into Russia flocks of Saxony sheep, erected linen and paper manufactories, built hospitals, and invited skilful mechanics, of all trades, to settle in his kingdom. But Charles thought only of war and glory, and did not reconstruct or reproduce. He pursued his military career by invading Poland, then ruled by the Elector of Saxony; while Peter turned his attention to the organization of new armies, melting bells into cannon, constructing fleets, and attending to all the complicated cares of a mighty nation with the most minute assiduity. He drew plans of fortresses, projected military reforms, and inspired his soldiers with his own enthusiasm. And his energy and perseverance were soon rewarded. He captured Marianburgh, a strong city on the confines of Livonia and Ingria, and among the captives was a young peasant girl, who eventually became the Empress Catharine, and to whose counsels Peter was much indebted for his great success.

She was the daughter of a poor woman of Livonia; lost her mother at the age of three years; and, at that early age, attracted the notice of the parish clerk, a Lutheran clergyman: was brought up with his own daughters, and married a young sergeant of the army, who was killed in the capture of the city. She interested the Russian general, by her intense grief and great beauty; was taken into his family, and, soon after, won the favor of Prince Menzikoff, the prime minister of the czar; became mistress of his palace; there beheld Peter himself, captivated him, and was married to him,—at first privately, and afterwards publicly. Her rise, from so obscure a position, in a distant country town, to be the wife of the absolute monarch of an empire of thirty-three millions of people, is the most extraordinary in the history of the world. When she enslaved the czar by the power of her charms, she was only seventeen years of age; two years after the foundations of St. Petersburg were laid.

Building of St. Petersburg.

The building of this great northern capital was as extraordinary as the other great acts of this monarch. Amid the marshes, at the mouth of the Neva, a rival city to the ancient metropolis of the empire arose in five months. But one hundred thousand people perished during the first year, in consequence of the severity of their labors, and the pestilential air of the place. The new city was an object of as great disgust to the nobles of Russia and the inhabitants of the older cities, as it was the delight and pride of the czar, who made it the capital of his vast dominions. And the city was scarcely built, before its great commercial advantages were appreciated; and vessels from all parts of the world, freighted with the various treasures of its different kingdoms and countries, appeared in the harbor of Cronstadt.

Charles XII. looked with contempt on the Herculean labors of his rival to civilize and enrich his country, and remarked "that the czar might amuse himself as he saw fit in building a city, but that he should soon take it from him, and set fire to his wooden house;" a bombastic boast, which, like most boasting, came most signally to nought.

New War with Sweden.

Indeed, success now turned in favor of Peter, whose forces had been constantly increasing, while those of Charles had been decreasing. City after city fell into the hands of Peter, and whole provinces were conquered from Sweden. Soon all Ingria was added to the empire of the czar, the government of which was intrusted to Menzikoff, a man of extraordinary abilities raised from obscurity, as a seller of pies in the streets of Moscow to be a prince of the empire. His elevation was a great mortification to the old and proud nobility. But Peter not only endeavored to reward and appropriate merit, but to humble the old aristocracy, who were averse to his improvements. And Peter was as cold and haughty to them, as he was free and companionable with his meanest soldiers. All great despots are indifferent to grades of rank, when their own elevation is above envy or the reach of ambition. The reward of merit by the czar, if it alienated the affections of his nobles, increased the veneration and enthusiasm of the people, who are, after all, the great permanent foundation on which absolute power rests; illustrated by the empire of the popes, as well as the despotism of Napoleon.

While Peter contended, with various success, with the armies of Sweden, he succeeded in embroiling Sweden in a war with Poland, and in diverting Charles from the invasion of Russia. Had Charles, at first, and perseveringly, concentrated all his strength in an invasion of Russia, he might have changed the politics of Europe. But he was induced to invade Poland, and soon drove the luxurious and cowardly monarch from his capital and throne, and then turned towards Russia, to play the part of Alexander. But he did not find a Darius in the czar, who was ready to meet him, at the head of immense armies.

The Russian forces amounted to one hundred thousand men; the Swedish to eighty thousand, and they were veterans. Peter did not venture to risk the fate of his empire, by a pitched battle, with such an army of victorious troops. So he attempted a stratagem, and succeeded. He decoyed the Swedes into a barren and wasted territory; and Charles, instead of marching to Moscow, as he ought to have done, followed his expected prey where he could get no provisions for his men, or forage for his horses. Exhausted by fatigue and famine, his troops drooped in the pursuit, and even suffered themselves to be diverted into still more barren sections. Under these circumstances, they were defeated in a disastrous battle. Charles, struck with madness, refused to retreat. Disasters multiplied. The victorious Russians hung upon his rear. The Cossacks cut off his stragglers. The army of eighty thousand melted away to twenty-five thousand. Still the infatuated Swede dreamed of victory, and expected to see the troops of his enemy desert. The winter set in with its northern severity, and reduced still further his famished troops. He lost time by marches and counter-marches, without guides, and in the midst of a hostile population. At last he reached Pultowa, a village on the banks of the Vorskla. Peter hastened to meet him, with an army of sixty thousand, and one of the bloodiest battles in the history of war was fought. The Swedes performed miracles of valor. But valor could do nothing against overwhelming strength. A disastrous defeat was the result, and Charles, with a few regiments, escaped to Turkey.

Had the battle of Pultowa been decided differently; had Charles conquered instead of Peter, or had Peter lost his life, the empire of Russia would probably have been replunged into its original barbarism, and the balance of power, in Europe, been changed.

War with the Turks.

But Providence, which ordained the civilization of Russia, also ordained that the triumphant czar should not be unduly aggrandized, and should himself learn lessons of humility. The Turks, in consequence of the intrigues of Charles, and their hereditary jealousy, made war upon Peter, and advanced against him with an army of two hundred and fifty thousand men. His own army was composed of only forty thousand. He was also indiscreet, and soon found himself in the condition of Charles at Pultowa. On the banks of the Pruth, in Moldavia, he was surrounded by the whole Turkish force, and famine or surrender seemed inevitable. It was in this desperate and deplorable condition that he was rescued by the Czarina Catharine, by whose address a treaty was made with his victorious enemy, and Peter was allowed to retire with his army. Charles XII. was indignant beyond measure with the Turkish general, for granting such easy conditions, when he had the czar in his power; and to his reproaches the vizier of the sultan replied, "I have a right to make peace or war; and our law commands us to grant peace to our enemies, when they implore our clemency." Charles replied with an insult; and, though a fugitive in the Turkish camp, he threw himself on a sofa, contemptuously cast his eye on all present, stretched out his leg, and entangled his spur in the vizier's robe; which insult the magnanimous Turk affected to consider an accident.

After the defeat of Peter on the banks of the Pruth, he devoted himself with renewed energy to the improvement of his country. He embellished St. Petersburg, his new capital, with palaces, churches, and arsenals. He increased his army and navy, strengthened himself by new victories, and became gradually master of both sides of the Gulf of Finland, by which his vast empire was protected from invasion.

Peter Makes a Second Tour.

He now reached the exalted height to which he had long aspired. He assumed the title of *emperor*, and his title was universally acknowledged. He then meditated a second tour of Europe, with a view to study the political constitutions of the various states. Thirteen years had elapsed, since, as a young enthusiast, he had visited Amsterdam and London. He now travelled, a second time, with the additional glory of a great name, and in the full maturity of his mind. He visited Hamburg, Stockholm, Lubec, Amsterdam, and Paris. At this latter place he was much noticed. Wherever he went, his course was a triumphal procession. But he disdained flattery, and was wearied with pompous ceremonies. He could not be flattered out of his simplicity, or the zeal of acquiring useful knowledge. He visited all the works of art, and was particularly struck with the Gobelin tapestries and the tomb of Richelieu. "Great man," said he, apostrophizing his image, "I would give half of my kingdom to learn of thee how to govern the other half." His residence in Paris inspired all classes with profound respect; and from Paris he went to Berlin. There he found sympathy with Frederic William, whose tastes and character somewhat resembled his own; and from him he learned many useful notions in the art of government. But he was suddenly recalled from Berlin by the bad conduct of his son Alexis, who was the heir to his throne. He was tried, condemned, disgraced, humiliated, and disinherited. He probably would have been executed by his hard and rigorous father, had he not died in prison. He was hostile to his father's plans of reform, and indecently expressed a wish for his death. The conduct of Peter towards him is generally considered harsh and unfeeling; but it has many palliations, if the good of his subjects and the peace of the realm are more to be desired than the life of an ignominious prince.

Peter prosecuted his wars and his reforms. The treaty of Neustadt secured to Russia, after twenty years of unbroken war, a vast increase of territory, and placed her at the head of the northern powers. The emperor also enriched his country by opening new branches of trade, constructing canals, rewarding industry, suppressing gambling and mendicity, introducing iron and steel manufacture, building cities, and establishing a vigorous police.

Elevation of Catharine.

After having settled the finances and trade of his empire, subdued his enemies at home and abroad, and compelled all the nobles and clergy to swear fealty to the person whom he should select as his successor, he appointed his wife, Catharine; and she was solemnly crowned empress in 1724, he himself, at her inauguration, walking on foot, as captain of her guard. He could not have made a better choice, as she was, in all substantial respects, worthy of the exalted position to which she was raised.

In about a year after, he died, leaving behind him his principles and a mighty name. Other kings have been greater generals; but few have derived from war greater success. Some have commanded larger armies; but he created those which he commanded. Many have destroyed; but he reconstructed. He was a despot, but ruled for the benefit of his country. He was disgraced by violent passions, his cruelty was sanguinary, and his tastes were brutal; but his passions did not destroy his judgment, nor his appetites make him luxurious. He was incessantly active and vigilant, his prejudices were few, and his views tolerant and enlightened. He was only cruel when his authority was impeached. His best portraiture is in his acts. He found a country semi-barbarous, convulsed by disorders, a prey to petty tyrannies, weak from disunion, and trembling before powerful neighbors. He left it a first-class power, freed in a measure from its barbarous customs, improved in social life, in arts, in science, and, perhaps, in morals. He left a large and disciplined army, a considerable navy, and numerous institutions for the civilization of the people. He left more—the moral effect of a great example, of a man in the possession of unbounded riches and power, making great personal sacrifices to improve himself in the art of governing for the welfare of the millions over whom he was called to rule. These virtues and these acts have justly won for him the title of Peter the *Great*—a title which the world has bestowed upon but few of the great heroes of ancient or modern times.

The reign of Charles XII. is intimately connected with that of Peter the Great; these monarchs being contemporaries and rivals, both reigning in northern countries of great extent and comparative barbarism. The reign of Peter was not so exclusively military as that of Charles, with whom war was a passion and a profession. The interest attached to Charles arises more from his eccentricities and brilliant military qualities, than from any extraordinary greatness of mind or heart. He was barbarous in his manners, and savage in his resentments; a stranger to the pleasures of society, obstinate, revengeful, unsympathetic, and indifferent to friendship and hatred. But he was brave, temperate, generous, intrepid in danger, and firm in misfortune.

Early History of Sweden.

Before his singular career can be presented, attention must be directed to the country over which he reigned, and which will be noticed in connection with Denmark; these two countries forming a greater part of the ancient Scandinavia, from which our Teutonic ancestors migrated, the land of Odin, and Frea, and Thor, those half-fabulous deities, concerning whom there are still divided opinions; some supposing that they were heroes, and others, impersonations of virtues, or elements and wonders of nature. The mythology of Greece does not more fully abound with gods and goddesses, than that of the old Scandinavia with rude deities,—dwarfs, and elfs, and mountain spirits. It was in these northern regions that the Normans acquired their wild enthusiasm, their supernatural daring, and their magnificent superstitions. It was from these regions that the Saxons brought their love of liberty, their spirit of enterprise, and their restless passion for the sea. The ancient Scandinavians were heroic, adventurous, and chivalrous robbers, holding their women in great respect, and profoundly reverential in their notions of a supreme power. They were poor in silver, in gold, in the fruits of the earth, in luxuries, and in palaces, but rich in poetic sentiments and in religious ideas. Their chief vices were those of gluttony and intemperance, and their great pleasures were those of hunting and gambling.

Fabulous as are most of their legends as to descent, still Scandinavia was probably peopled with hardy races before authentic history commences. Under different names, and at different times, they invaded the Roman empire. In the fifth century, they had settled in its desolated provinces—the Saxons in England, the Goths in Spain and Italy, the Vandals in Africa, the Burgundians in France, and the Lombards in Italy.

Among the most celebrated of these northern Teutonic nations were the pirates who invaded England and France, under the name of *Northmen*. They came from Denmark, and some of their chieftains won a great name in their generation, such as Harold, Canute, Sweyn, and Rollo.

Introduction of Christianity.

Christianity was probably planted in Sweden about the middle of the ninth century. St. Anscar, a Westphalian monk, was the first successful missionary, and he was made Archbishop of Hamburg, and primate of the north.

The early history of the Swedes and Danes resembles that of England under the Saxon princes, and they were disgraced by the same great national vices. During the Middle Ages, no great character appeared worthy of especial notice. Some of the more powerful kings, such as Valdemar I. and II., and Canute VI., had quarrels with the Emperors of Germany, and invaded some provinces of their empire. Some of these princes were warriors, some cruel tyrants, none very powerful, and all characterized by the vices of their age—treachery, hypocrisy, murder, drunkenness, and brutal revenge.

The most powerful of these kings was Christian I., who founded the dynasty of Oldenburgh, and who united under his sway the kingdoms of Denmark, Sweden, and Norway. He reigned from 1448 to 1481; and in his family the crown of Sweden remained until the revolution effected by Gustavus Vasa, in 1525, and by which revolution Sweden was made independent of Denmark.

Gustavus Vasa.

Gustavus Vasa was a nobleman descended from the ancient kings of Sweden, and who, from the oppression to which his country was subjected by Christian and the Archbishop of Upsal, was forced to seek refuge amid the forests of Dalecarlia. When Stockholm was pillaged and her noblest citizens massacred by the cruel tyrant of the country, Gustavus headed an insurrection, defeated the king's forces, and was made king himself by the Diet. He, perceiving that the Catholic clergy were opposed to the liberties and the great interests of his country, seized their fortresses and lands, became a convert to the doctrine of the reformers, and introduced Lutheranism into the kingdom, which has ever since been the established religion of Sweden. He was despotic in his government, but ruled for the good of his subjects, and was distinguished for many noble qualities.

The celebrated Gustavus Adolphus was his descendant, and was more absolute and powerful than even Gustavus Vasa. But he is chiefly memorable as the great hero of the Thirty Years' War, and as the greatest general of his age. Under his sway, Sweden was the most powerful of the northern kingdoms.

He was succeeded by his daughter Christina, a woman of most extraordinary qualities; a woman of genius, of taste, and of culture; a woman who, at twenty-seven, became wearied of the world, and of the enjoyment of unlimited power, and who changed her religion, retired from her country, and abdicated her throne, that she might, unmolested, enjoy the elegant pleasures of Rome, and be solaced by the literature, religion, and art of that splendid capital. It was in the society of men of genius that she spent most of her time, and was the life of the most intellectual circle which then existed in Europe.

She was succeeded by her cousin, who was elected King of Sweden, by the title of *Charles Gustavus X.*, and he was succeeded by Charles XI., the father of Charles XII.

Charles XII. was fifteen years of age when he came to the throne, in the year 1697, and found his country strong in resources, and his army the best disciplined in Europe. His territories were one third larger than those of France when ruled by Louis XIV., though not so thickly populated.

Early Days of Charles XII.

The young monarch, at first, gave but few indications of the remarkable qualities which afterwards distinguished him. He was idle, dissipated, haughty, and luxurious. When he came to the council chamber, he was absent and indifferent, and generally sat with both legs thrown across the table.

But his lethargy and indifference did not last long. Three great monarchs had conspired to ruin him, and dismember his kingdom. These were the Czar Peter, Frederic IV. of Denmark, and Frederic Augustus, King of Poland, and also Elector of Saxony; and their hostile armies were on the point of invading his country.

The greatness of the danger brought to light his great qualities. He vigorously prepared for war. His whole character changed. Quintus Curtius became his text-book, and Alexander his model. He spent no time in sports or magnificence. He clothed himself like a common soldier, whose hardships he resolved henceforth to share. He forswore the society and the influence of woman. He relinquished wine and all the pleasures of the table. Love of glory became his passion, and continued through life; and this ever afterwards made him insensible to reproach, danger, toil, fear, hunger, and pain. Never was a more complete change effected in a man's moral character; and never was an improved moral character consecrated to a worse end. He was not devoted to the true interests of his country, but to a selfish, base, and vain passion for military fame.

But his conduct, at first, called forth universal admiration. His glorious and successful defence against enemies apparently overwhelming gave him a great military reputation, and secured for him the sympathies of Christendom. Had he died when he had repelled the Russian, the Danish, and the Polish armies, he would have secured as honorable an immortality as that of Gustavus Adolphus. But he was not permitted to die prematurely, as was his great ancestor. He lived long enough to become intoxicated with success, to make great political blunders, and to suffer the most fatal and mortifying misfortunes.

The commencement of his military career was beautifully heroic. "Gentlemen," said the young monarch of eighteen to his counsellors, when he meditated desperate resistance, "I am resolved never to begin an unjust war, and never to finish a just one but with the destruction of my enemies."

In six weeks he finished, after he had begun, the Danish war having completely humbled his enemy, and succored his brother-in-law, the Duke of Holstein.

Charles's Heroism.

His conflict with Peter has been presented, when with twenty thousand men he attacked and defeated sixty thousand Russians in their intrenchments, took one hundred and fifty pieces of cannon, and killed eighteen thousand men. The victory of Narva astonished all Europe, and was the most brilliant which had then been gained in the annals of modern warfare.

Charles was equally successful against Frederic Augustus. He routed his Saxon troops, and then resolved to dethrone him, as King of Poland. And he succeeded so far as to induce the Polish Diet to proclaim the throne vacant. Augustus was obliged to fly, and Stanislaus Leczinski was chosen king in his stead, at the nomination of the Swedish conqueror. The country was subjugated, and Frederic Augustus became a fugitive.

But Charles was not satisfied with expelling him from Poland. He resolved to attack him also in Saxony itself. Saxony was then, next to Austria, the most powerful of the German states. Nevertheless, Saxony could not arrest the victorious career of Charles. The Saxons fled as he approached. He penetrated to the heart of the electorate, and the unfortunate Frederic Augustus was obliged to sue for peace, which was only granted on the most humiliating terms; which were, that the elector should acknowledge Stanislaus as king of Poland; that he should break all his treaties with Russia, and should deliver to the King of Sweden all the men who had deserted from his army. The humbled elector sought a personal interview with Charles, after he had signed the conditions of peace, with the hope of securing better terms. He found Charles in his jack boots, with a piece of black taffeta round his neck for a cravat, and clothed in a coarse blue coat with brass buttons. His conversation turned wholly on his jack boots; and this trifling subject was the only one on which he would deign to converse with one of the most accomplished monarchs of his age.

Charles had now humbled and defeated all his enemies. He should now have returned to Sweden, and have cultivated the arts of peace. But peace and civilization were far from his thoughts. The subjugation of all the northern powers became the dream of his life. He invaded Russia, resolved on driving Peter from his throne.

His Misfortunes.

He was eminently successful in defensive war, and eminently unsuccessful in aggressive war. Providence benevolently but singularly comes to the aid of all his children in distress and despair. Men are gloriously strong in defending their rights; but weak, in all their strength, when they assail the rights of others. So signal is this fact, that it blazes upon all the pages of history, and is illustrated in common life as well as in the affairs of nations.

When Charles turned as an assailant of the rights of his enemies, his unfortunate reverses commenced. At the head of forty-three thousand veterans, loaded with the spoils of Poland and Saxony, he commenced his march towards Russia. He had another army in Poland of twenty thousand, and another in Finland of fifteen thousand. With these he expected to dethrone the czar.

His mistakes and infatuation have been noticed, and his final defeat at Pultowa, a village at the eastern extremity of the Ukraine. This battle was more decisive than that of Narva; for in the latter the career of Peter was only arrested, but in the former the strength of Charles was annihilated. And so would have been his hopes, had he been an ordinary man. But he was a madman, and still dreamed of victory, with only eighteen hundred men to follow his fortunes into Turkey, which country he succeeded in reaching.

His conduct in Turkey was infamous and extraordinary. No reasonings can explain it. It was both ridiculous and provoking. At first, he employed himself in fomenting quarrels, and devising schemes to embark the sultan in his cause. Vizier after vizier was flattered and assailed. He rejected every overture for his peaceable return. He lingered five years in endless intrigues and negotiations, in order to realize the great dream of his life—the dethronement of the czar. He lived recklessly on the bounty of the sultan, taking no hints that even imperial hospitality might be abused and exhausted. At last, his inflexible obstinacy and dangerous intrigues so disgusted his generous host, that he was urged to return, with the offer of a suitable escort, and a large sum of money. He accepted and spent the twelve hundred purses, and still refused to return. The displeasure of the Sultan Achmet was now fairly excited. It was resolved upon by the Porte that he should be removed by force, since he would not be persuaded. But Charles resisted the troops of the sultan who were ordered to remove him. With sixty servants he desperately defended himself against an army of janizaries, and killed twenty of them with his own hand; and it was not until completely overwhelmed and prostrated that he hurled his sword into the air. He was now a prisoner of war, and not a guest; but still he was treated with the courtesy and dignity due to a king, and conducted in a chariot covered with gold and scarlet to Adrianople. From thence he was removed to Demotica, where he renewed his intrigues, and zealously kept his bed, under pretence of sickness, for ten months.

While he remained in captivity, Frederic Augustus recovered the crown of Poland, King Stanislaus was taken by the Turks, and Peter continued his conquest of Ingria, Livonia, and Finland, provinces belonging to Sweden. The King of Prussia also invaded Pomerania, and Frederic IV. of Denmark claimed Bremen, Holstein, and Scania. The Swedes were divested of all their conquests, and one hundred and fifty thousand of them became prisoners in foreign lands.

Such were the reverses of a man who had resolved to play the part of Alexander, but who, so long as he contented himself with defending his country against superior forces, was successful, and won a fame so great, that his misfortunes could never reduce him to contempt.

Charles's Return to Sweden.

When all was lost, he signified to the Turkish vizier his desire to return to Sweden. The vizier neglected no means to rid his master of so troublesome a person. Charles returned to his country impoverished, but not discouraged. The charm of his name was broken. His soldiers were as brave and devoted as ever, but his resources were exhausted. He succeeded, however, in raising thirty-five thousand men, in order to continue his desperate game of conquest, not of defence. Europe beheld the extraordinary spectacle of this infatuated hero passing, in the depth of a northern winter, over the frozen hills and ice-bound rocks of Norway, with his devoted army, in order to conquer that hyperborean region. So inured was he to cold and fatigue, that he slept in the open air on a bed of straw, covered only with his cloak, while his soldiers dropped down dead at their posts from cold. In the month of December, 1718, he commenced the siege of Fredericshall, a place of great strength and importance, but, having exposed himself unnecessarily, was killed by a ball from the fortress. Many, however, suppose that he was assassinated by his own officers who were wearied with endless war, from which they saw nothing but disaster to their exhausted country.

His Death.

His death was considered as a signal for the general cessation of arms; but Sweden never recovered from the mad enterprises of Charles XII. It has never since been a first class power. The national finances were disordered, the population decimated, and the provinces dismembered. Peter the Great gained what his rival lost. We cannot but compassionate a nation that has the misfortune to be ruled by such an absolute and infatuated monarch as was Charles XII. He did nothing for the civilization of his subjects, or to ameliorate the evils he caused. He was, like Alaric or Attila, a scourge of the Almighty, sent on earth for some mysterious purpose, to desolate and to destroy. But he died unlamented and unhonored. No great warrior in modern times has received so little sympathy from historians, since he was not exalted by any great moral qualities of affection or generosity, and unscrupulously sacrificed both friends and enemies to gratify a selfish and a depraved passion.

References.—Voltaire's History of Russia, a very attractive book, on account of its lively style. Voltaire's Life of Charles XII., also, is equally fascinating. There are tolerable histories of both Russia and Sweden in Lardner's Cabinet Cyclopedia; also in the Family Library. See, also, a History of Russia and Sweden in the Universal History. Russell's Modern Europe.

CHAPTER XIX
GEORGE I., AND THE ADMINISTRATION
OF SIR ROBERT WALPOLE

Accession of George I.

Queen Anne died in 1714, soon after the famous treaty of Utrecht was made, and by which the war of the Spanish Succession was closed. She was succeeded by George I., Elector of Hanover. He was grandson of Elizabeth, only daughter of James I., who had married Frederic, the King of Bohemia. He was fifty-four years of age when he ascended the English throne, and imperfectly understood the language of the nation whom he was called upon to govern.

George I. was not a sovereign who materially affected the interests or destiny of England; nor was he one of those interesting characters that historians love to delineate. It is generally admitted that he was respectable, prudent, judicious, and moral; amiable in his temper, sincere in his intercourse, and simple in his habits,—qualities which command respect, but not those which dazzle the people. It is supposed that he tolerably understood the English Constitution, and was willing to be fettered by the restraints which the parliaments imposed. He supported the Whigs,—the dominant party of the time,—and sympathized with liberal principles, so far as a monarch can be supposed to advance the interests of the people, and the power of a class ever hostile to the prerogatives of royalty. He acquiesced in the rule of his ministers—just what was expected of him, and just what was wanted of him; and became—what every King of England, when popular, has since been—the gilded puppet of a powerful aristocracy. His social and constitutional influence was not, indeed, annihilated; he had the choice of ministers, and collected around his throne the great and proud, who looked to him as the fountain of all honor and dignity. But, still, from the accession of the house of Hanover the political history of England is a history of the acts of parliaments, and of those ministers who represented the dominant parties of the nation. Few nobles were as great as some under the Tudor and Stuart princes; but the power of the aristocracy, as a class, was increased. From the time of George I. to Queen Victoria, the ascendency of the parliaments has been most marked composed chiefly of nobles, great landed proprietors, and gigantic commercial monopolists. The people have not been, indeed, unheard or unrepresented; but, literally speaking, have had but a feeble influence, compared with the aristocracy. Parliaments and ministers, therefore, may be not unjustly said to be the representatives of the aristocracy—of the wise, the mighty, and the noble.

When power passes from kings to nobles, then the acts of nobles constitute the genius of political history, as fully as the acts of kings constitute history when kings are absolute, and the acts of the people constitute history where the people are all-powerful.

Sir Robert Walpole.

A notice, therefore, of that great minister who headed the Whig party of aristocrats, and who, as their organ, swayed the councils of England for nearly forty years, demands our attention. His political career commenced during the reign of Anne, and continued during the reign of George I., and part of the reign of George II. George I., as a man or as a king, dwindled into insignificance, when compared with his prime minister, Sir Robert Walpole. And he is great, chiefly, as the representative of the Whigs; that is, of the dominant party of rich and great men who sat in parliament; a party of politicians who professed more liberal principles than the Tories, but who were equally aristocratic in the social sympathies, and powerful from aristocratic connections. What did the great Dukes of Devonshire or Bedford care for the poor people, who, politically, composed no part of the nation? But they were Whigs, and King George himself was a Whig.

Sir Robert belonged to an ancient, wealthy, and honorable family; was born 1676, and received his first degree at King's College, Cambridge, in 1700. He entered parliament almost immediately after, became an active member, sat on several committees, and soon distinguished himself for his industry and ability. He was not eloquent, but acquired considerable skill as a debater. In 1705, Lord Godolphin, the prime minister of Anne, made him one of the council to Prince George of Denmark; in 1706, Marlborough selected him as secretary of war; in 1709, he was made treasurer of the navy; and in 1710, he was the acknowledged leader of the House of Commons. He lost office, however, when the Whigs lost power, in 1710; was subjected to cruel political persecution, and even impeached, and imprisoned in the Tower. This period is memorable for the intense bitterness and severe conflicts between the Whigs and Tories; not so much on account of difference of opinion on great political principles, as the struggle for the possession of place and power.

On the accession of George I., Walpole became paymaster of the forces, one of the most lucrative offices in the kingdom. Townshend was made secretary of state. The other great official dignitaries were the Lords Cowper, Marlborough, Wharton, Sunderland, Devonshire, Oxford, and Somerset; but Townshend and Walpole were the most influential. They impeached their great political enemies, Ormond and Bolingbroke, the most distinguished leaders of the Tory party. Bolingbroke, in genius and learning, had no equal in parliament, and was a rival of Walpole at Eton.

The Pretender.

The first event of importance, under the new ministry, was the invasion of Great Britain by the Pretender—the Prince James Frederic Edward Stuart, only son of James II. His early days were spent at St. Germain's, the palace which the dethroned monarch enjoyed by the hospitality of Louis XIV. He was educated under influences entirely unfavorable to the recovery of his natural inheritance, and was a devotee to the pope and the interests of absolutism. But he had his adherents, who were called *Jacobites*, and who were chiefly to be found in the Highlands of Scotland. In 1705, an unsuccessful effort had been made to regain the throne of his father, but the disasters attending it prevented him from milking any renewed effort until the death of Anne.

When she died, many discontented Tories fanned the spirit of rebellion; and Bishop Atterbury, a distinguished divine, advocated the claims of the Pretender. Scotland was ripe for revolt. Alarming riots took place in England. William III. was burned in effigy at Smithfield. The Oxford students pulled down a Presbyterian meeting-house, and the sprig of oak was publicly displayed on the 29th of May. The Earl of Mar hurried into Scotland to fan the spirit of insurrection; while the gifted, brilliant, and banished Bolingbroke joined the standard of the chevalier. The venerable and popular Duke of Ormond also assisted him with his counsels.

Invasion of Scotland.

Advised by these great nobles, assisted by the King of France, and flattered by the Jacobite faction, the Pretender made preparations to recover his rights. His prospects were apparently better than were those of William, when he landed in England. The Earl of Mar was at the head of ten thousand men; but the chevalier was no general, and was unequal to his circumstances. When he landed in Scotland, he surrendered himself to melancholy and inaction. His sadness and pusillanimity dispirited his devoted band of followers. He retreated before inferior forces, and finally fled from the country which he had invaded. The French king was obliged to desert his cause, and the Pretender retreated to Italy, and died at the advanced age of seventy-nine, after witnessing the defeat of his son, Charles Edward, whose romantic career and misfortunes cannot now be mentioned. By the flight of the Pretender from Scotland, in 1715, the insurrection was easily suppressed, and the country was not molested by the intrigues of the Stuart princes for thirty years.

The year which followed the invasion of Scotland was signalized by the passage of a great bill in parliament, which is one of the most important events in parliamentary history. In 1716, the famous Septennial Act, which prolonged parliament from three to seven years, was passed. So many evils, practically, resulted from frequent elections, that the Whigs resolved to make a change; and the change contributed greatly to the tranquillity of the country, and the establishment of the House of Brunswick. The duration of the English parliament has ever since, constitutionally, been extended to seven years, but the average duration of parliaments has been six years— the term of office of the senators of the United States.

After the passage of the Septennial Act, the efforts of Walpole were directed to a reduction of the national debt. He was then secretary of the treasury. But before he could complete his financial reforms, he was driven from office by the cabals of his colleagues, and the influence of the king's German favorites and mistresses. The Earl of Sunderland, who had married a daughter of the Duke of Marlborough, was at the head of the cabal party, and was much endeared to the Whigs by his steady attachment to their principles. He had expected, and probably deserved, to be placed at the head of the administration. When disappointed, he bent all his energies to undermine Townsend and Walpole, and succeeded for a while. But Walpole's opposition to the new administration was so powerful, that it did not last long. Sunderland had persuaded the king to renounce his constitutional prerogative of creating peers; and a bill, called the *Peerage Bill*, was proposed, which limited the House of Lords to its actual existing number, the tendency of which was to increase the power and rank of the existing peers, and to raise an eternal bar to the aspirations of all commoners to the peerage, and thus widen the gulf between the aristocracy and the people. Walpole presented these consequences so forcibly, and showed so clearly that the proposed bill would diminish the consequence of the landed gentry, and prove a grave to honorable merit, that the Commons were alarmed, and rejected the bill by a large and triumphant majority of two hundred and sixty-nine to one hundred and seventy-seven.

The defeat of this bill, and the great financial embarrassments of the country, led to the restoration of Walpole to office. His genius was eminently financial, and his talents were precisely those which have ever since been required of a minister—those which characterized Sir Robert Peel and

William Pitt. The great problem of any government is, how to raise money for its great necessities; and the more complicated the relations of society are, the more difficult becomes the problem.

The South Sea Bubble.

At that period, the English nation were intoxicated and led astray by one of those great commercial delusions which so often take place in all civilized countries. No mania ever was more marked, more universal, and more fatal than that of the South Sea Company. The bubble had turned the heads of politicians, merchants, and farmers; all classes, who had money to invest, took stock in the South Sea Company. The delusion, however, passed away; England was left on the brink of bankruptcy, and a master financier was demanded by the nation, to extricate it from the effects of folly and madness. All eyes looked to Sir Robert Walpole, and he did all that financial skill could do, to repair the evils which speculation and gambling had caused.

The desire for sudden wealth is one of the most common passions of our nature, and has given rise to more delusions than religious fanaticism, or passion for military glory. The South Sea bubble was kindred to that of John Law, who was the author of the Mississippi Scheme, which nearly ruined France in the reign of Louis XV., and which was encouraged by the Duke of Orleans, as a means of paying off the national debt.

The South Sea Company.

The wars of England had created a national debt, under the administration of Godolphin and Marlborough; but which was not so large but that hopes were entertained of redeeming it. Walpole proposed to pay it off by a sinking fund; but this idea, not very popular, was abandoned. It was then the custom for government to borrow of corporations, rather than of bankers, because the science of brokerage was not then understood, and because no individuals were sufficiently rich to aid materially an embarrassed administration. As a remuneration, companies were indulged with certain commercial advantages. As these advantages enabled companies to become rich, the nation always found it easy to borrow. During the war of the Spanish Succession, the prime minister, Harley, afterwards Earl of Oxford, in order to raise money, projected the South Sea Company. This was in 1710, and the public debt was ten million pounds sterling, thought at that time to be insupportable. The interest on that debt was six per cent. In order to liquidate the debt, Oxford made the duties on wines, tobacco, India goods, silks, and a few other articles, permanent. And, to allure the public creditor, great advantages were given to the new company, and money was borrowed of it at five per cent. This gain of one per cent., by money borrowed from the company, was to constitute a sinking fund to pay the debt.

But the necessities of the nation increased so rapidly, that a leading politician of the day, Sir John Blount, proposed that the South Sea Company should become the sole national creditor, and should loan to the government new sums, at an interest of four per cent. New monopolies were to be given to the company; and it, on the other hand, offered to give a bonus of three million pounds to the government. The Bank of England, jealous of the proposal, offered five millions. The directors of the company then bid seven millions for a charter, nearly enough to pay off the whole redeemable debt of the nation; which, however, could not be redeemed, so long as there were, in addition, irredeemable annuities to the amount of eight hundred thousand pounds yearly. It became, therefore, an object of the government to get rid, in the first place, of these irredeemable annuities; and this could be effected, if the national creditor could be induced to accept of shares in the South Sea Company, instead of his irredeemable annuities, or, as they are now variously called, consols, stocks, and national funds. The capital was not desired; only the interest on capital. So many monopolies and advantages were granted to the company, that the stock rose, and the national creditor was willing to part with his annuities for stock in the company. The offer was, therefore, accepted, and the government got rid of irredeemable annuities, and obtained seven millions besides, but became debtor to the company. A company which could apparently afford to pay so large a bonus to government for its charter, and loan such large sums as the nation needed, in addition, at four per cent., was supposed to be making most enormous profits. Its stock rose rapidly in value. The national creditor hastened to get rid of irredeemable annuities—a national stock which paid five per cent.—in order to buy shares which might pay ten per cent.

Opposition of Walpole.

Walpole, then paymaster of the forces, opposed the scheme of Blount with all his might, showed that the acceptance of the company's proposal would countenance stockjobbing, would divert industry from its customary channels, and would hold out a dangerous lure to the unsuspecting to part with real for imaginary property. He showed the misery and confusion which existed in France from the adoption of similar measures, and proved that the whole success of the scheme must depend on the rise of the company's stock; that, if there were no rise, the company could not afford the bonus, and would fail, and the obligation of the nation remain as before. But his reasonings were of no avail. All classes were infatuated. All people speculated in the South Sea stock. And, for a while, all people rejoiced; for, as long as the stock continued to rise, all people were gainers.

And the stock rose rapidly. It soon reached three hundred per cent, above the original par value, and this in consequence of the promise of great dividends. All hastened to buy such lucrative property. The public creditor willingly gave up three hundred pounds of irredeemable stock for one hundred pounds of the company's stock.

Mania for Speculation.

And this would have been well, had there been a moral certainty of the stockholder receiving a dividend of twenty per cent. But there was not this certainty, nor even a chance of it. Still, in consequence of the great dividends promised, even as high as fifty per cent., the stock gradually rose to one thousand per cent. Such was the general mania. And such was the extent of it, that thirty-seven millions of pounds sterling were subscribed on the company's books.

And the rage for speculation extended to all other kinds of property; and all sorts of companies were formed, some of the shares of which were at a premium of two thousand per cent. There were companies formed for fisheries, companies for making salt, for making oil, for smelting metals, for improving the breed of horses, for the planting of madder, for building ships against pirates, for the importation of jackasses, for fattening hogs, for wheels of perpetual motion, for insuring masters against losses from servants. There was one company for carrying on an undertaking of great advantage, but no one knew for what. The subscriber, by paying two guineas as a deposit, was to have one hundred pounds per annum for every hundred subscribed. It was declared, that, in a month, the particulars were to be laid open, and the remainder of the subscription money was then to be paid. Notwithstanding this barefaced, swindling scheme, two thousand pounds were received one morning as a deposit. The next day, the proprietor was not to be found.

Now, in order to stop these absurd speculations, and yet to monopolize all the gambling in the kingdom, the directors of the South Sea Company obtained an act from parliament, empowering them to prosecute all the various bubble companies that were projected. In a few days, all these bubbles burst. None were found to be buyers. Stock fell to nothing.

Bursting of the South Sea Bubble.

But the South Sea Company made a blunder. The moral effect of the bursting of so many bubbles was to open the eyes of the nation to the greatest bubble of all. The credit of the South Sea Company declined. Stocks fell from one thousand per cent to two hundred in a few days. All wanted to sell, nobody to buy. Bankers and merchants failed, and nobles and country gentlemen became impoverished.

In this general distress, Walpole was summoned to power, in older to extricate the nation, on the eve of bankruptcy. He proposed a plan, which was adopted, and which saved the credit of the nation. He ingrafted nine millions of the South Sea stock into the Bank of England, and nine millions more into the East India Company; and government gave up the seven millions of bonus which the company had promised.

By this assistance, the company was able to fulfil its engagements, although all who purchased stock when it had arisen beyond one hundred per cent. of its original value, lost money. It is strange that the stock, after all, remained at a premium of one hundred per cent.; of course, the original proprietors gained one hundred per cent., and those who paid one hundred per cent. premium lost nothing. But these constituted a small fraction of the people who had speculated, and who paid from one hundred to nine hundred per cent. premium. Government, too, gained by reducing interest on irredeemable bonds from five to four per cent., although it lost the promised bonus of seven millions.

The South Sea bubble did not destroy the rage for speculation, although it taught many useful truths—that national prosperity is not advanced by stockjobbing; that financiers, however great their genius, generally overreach themselves; that great dividends are connected with great risk; that circumstances beyond human control will defeat the best-laid plan; that it is better to repose upon the operation of the ordinary laws of trade; and that nothing but strict integrity and industry will succeed in the end. From the time of Sir Robert Walpole, money has seldom been worth, in England, over five per cent., and larger dividends on vested property have generally been succeeded by heavy losses, however plausible the promises and clear the statements of stockjobbers and speculators.

Enlightened Policy of Walpole.

After the explosion of the South Sea Company, Walpole became possessed of almost unlimited power. And one of the first objects to which he directed attention, after settling the finances, was the removal of petty restrictions on commerce. He abolished the export duties on one hundred and six articles of British manufacture, and allowed thirty-eight articles of raw material to be imported duty free. This regulation was made to facilitate trade with the colonies, and prevent them from manufacturing; and this regulation accomplished the end desired. Both England and the colonies were enriched. It was doubtless the true policy of British statesmen then, as now, to advance the commercial, manufacturing, and agricultural interests of Great Britain, rather than meddle with foreign wars, or seek glory on the field of battle. The principles of Sir Robert Walpole were essentially pacific;

and under his administration, England made a great advance in substantial prosperity. In this policy he surpassed all the statesmen who preceded or succeeded him, and this constituted his glory and originality.

But liberal and enlightened as was the general course of Walpole, he still made blunders, and showed occasional illiberality. He caused a fine of one hundred thousand pounds to be inflicted on the Catholics, on the plea that they were a disaffected body. He persecuted Bishop Atterbury, and permitted Bolingbroke, with his restless spirit of intrigue, to return to his country, and to be reinstated in his property and titles. He flattered the Duchess of Kendall, the mistress of the king, and stooped to all the arts of corruption and bribery. There never was a period of greater political corruption than during the administration of this minister. Sycophancy, meanness, and hypocrisy were resorted to by the statesmen of the age, who generally sought their own interests rather than the welfare of the nation. There were, however, exceptions. Townsend, the great rival and coadjutor of Walpole, retired from office with an unsullied fame for integrity and disinterestedness; and Walpole, while he bribed others, did not enrich himself.

King George I. died on the 11th of June, 1727, suddenly, by apoplexy, and was succeeded by his son George II., a man who resembled his father in disposition and character, and was superior to him in knowledge of the English constitution, though both were inclined to steer the British bark by the Hanoverian rudder. Like his father, he was reserved, phlegmatic, cautious, sincere, fond of business, economical, and attached to Whig principles. He was fortunate in his wife, Queen Caroline, one of the most excellent women of the age, learned, religious, charitable, and sensible; the patroness of divines and scholars; fond of discussion on metaphysical subjects, and a correspondent of the distinguished Leibnitz.

The new king disliked Walpole, but could not do without him, and therefore continued him in office. Indeed, the king had the sense to perceive that England was to be governed only by the man in whom the nation had confidence.

East India Company.

In 1730, Walpole rechartered the East India Company, the most gigantic monopoly in the history of nations. As early as 1599, an association had been formed in England for trade to the East Indies. This association was made in consequence of the Dutch and Portuguese settlements and enterprises, which aroused the commercial jealousy of England. The capital was sixty-eight thousand pounds. In 1600, Queen Elizabeth gave the company a royal charter. By this charter, the company obtained the right of purchasing land, without limit, in India, and the monopoly of the trade for fifteen years. But the company contended with many obstacles. The first voyage was made by four ships and one pinnace, having on board twenty-eight thousand pounds in bullion, and seven thousand pounds in merchandise, such as tin, cutlery, and glass.

During the civil wars, the company's affairs were embarrassed, owing to the unsettled state of England. On the accession of Charles II., the company obtained a new charter, which not only confirmed the old privileges, but gave it the power of making peace and war with the native princes of India. The capital stock was increased to one million five hundred thousand pounds.

Much opposition was made by Bolingbroke and the Tories to the recharter of this institution; but the ministry carried their point, and a new charter was granted on the condition of the company paying to government two hundred thousand pounds, and reducing the interest of the government debts one per cent. per annum. By this time, the company, although it had not greatly enlarged its jurisdiction in India, had accumulated great wealth. Its powers and possessions will be more fully treated when the victories of Clive shall be presented.

About this time, the Duke of Newcastle came into the cabinet whose future administration will form the subject of a separate chapter.

Resignation of Townsend.

In 1730 also occurred the disagreement between Walpole and Lord Townsend, which ended in the resignation of the latter, a man whose impetuous and frank temper ill fitted him to work with so cautious and non-committal a statesman as his powerful rival. He passed the evening of his days in rural pursuits and agricultural experiments, keeping open house, devoting himself to his family and friends, never hankering after the power he had lost, never even revisiting London, and finding his richest solace in literature and simple agricultural pleasures—the pattern of a lofty and cultivated nobleman.

The resignation of Townsend enabled Walpole to take more part in foreign negotiations; and he exerted his talents, like Fleury in France, to preserve the peace of Europe. The peace policy of Walpole entitles him to the gratitude of his country. More than any other man of his age, he apprehended the true glory and interests of nations. Had Walpole paid as much attention to the intellectual improvement of his countrymen, as he did to the refinements of material life and to physical progress, he would have merited still higher praises. But he despised learning, and neglected literary men. And they turned against him and his administration, and, by their sarcasm and invective, did much to undermine his power. Pope, Swift, and Gay might have lent him powerful aid by their satirical pen; but he passed them by with contemptuous indifference, and they gave to Bolingbroke what they withheld from Walpole.

Next to the pacific policy of the minister, the most noticeable peculiarity of his administration was his zeal to improve the finances. He opposed speculations, and sought a permanent revenue from fixed principles. He regarded the national debt as a great burden, and strove to abolish it; and, when that was found to be impracticable, sought to prevent its further accumulation. He was not, indeed, always true to his policy; but he pursued it on the whole, consistently. He favored the agricultural interests, and was inclined to raise the necessary revenue by a tax on articles used, rather than by direct taxation on property or income, or articles imported. Hence he is the father of the excise scheme—a scheme still adopted in England, but which would be intolerable in this country. In this scheme, his grand object was to ease the landed proprietor, and to prevent smuggling, by making smuggling no object. But the opposition to the Excise Bill was so great that Sir Robert abandoned it; and this relinquishment of his favorite scheme is one of the most striking peculiarities of his administration. He never pushed matters to extremity. He ever yielded to popular clamor. He perceived that an armed force would be necessary in order to collect the excise, and preferred to yield his cherished measures to run the danger of incurring greater evils than financial embarrassments. His spirit of conciliation, often exercised in the plenitude of power, prolonged his reign. This policy was the result of immense experience and practical knowledge of human nature, of which he was a great master.

Unpopularity of Walpole.

But Sir Robert was not allowed to pursue to the end his pacific, any more than his financial policy. The clamors of interested merchants, the violence of party spirit, and the dreams of heroic grandeur on the part of politicians, overcame the repugnance of the minister, and plunged England in a disastrous Spanish war; and a war soon succeeded by that of the Austrian Succession, in which Maria Theresa was the injured, and Frederic the Great the offending party. But this war, which was carried on chiefly during the subsequent administration, will be hereafter alluded to.

Although Walpole was opposed by some of the ablest men in England— by Pulteney, Sir William Windham, and the Lords Chesterfield, Carteret, and Bolingbroke, his power was almost absolute from 1730 to 1740. His most powerful assistance was derived from Mr. Yorke, afterwards the

Lord Chancellor Hardwicke, one of the greatest lawyers that England has produced.

Decline of his Power.

In 1740, his power began to decline, and rapidly waned. He lost a powerful friend and protector by the death of Queen Caroline, whose intercessions with the king were ever listened to with respectful consideration. But he had almost insurmountable obstacles to contend with — the distrust of the king, the bitter hatred of the Prince of Wales, the violent opposition of the leading statesmen in parliament, and universal envy. Moreover, he had grown careless and secure. He fancied that no one could rule England but himself. But hatred, opposition, envy, and unsuccessful military operations, forced him from his place. No shipwrecked pilot ever clung to the rudder of a sinking ship with more desperate tenacity than did this once powerful minister to the helm of state. And he did not relinquish it until he was driven from it by the desertion of all his friends, and the general clamor of the people. The king, however, appreciated the value of his services, and created him Earl of Orford, a dignity which had been offered him before, but which, with self-controlling policy, he had unhesitatingly declined. Like Sir Robert Peel in later times, he did not wish to be buried in the House of Lords.

His retirement (1742) amid the beeches and oaks of his country seat was irksome and insipid. He had no taste for history, or science, or elegant literature, or quiet pleasures. His tumultuous public life had engendered other tastes. "I wish," said he to a friend, "I took as much delight in reading as you do. It would alleviate my tedious hours." But the fallen minister, though uneasy and restless, was not bitter or severe. He retained his good humor to the last, and to the last discharged all the rites of an elegant hospitality. Said his enemy, Pope, —

> "Seen him I have, but in his happier hour
> Of social pleasure — ill exchanged for power;
> Seen him, uncumbered by the venal tribe,
> Smile without art, and win without a bribe."

He had the habit of "laughing the heart's laugh," which it is only in the power of noble natures to exercise. His manners were winning, his conversation frank, and his ordinary intercourse divested of vanity and pomp. He had many warm personal friends, and did not enrich himself, as Marlborough did, while he enriched those who served him. He kept a public table at Houghton, to which all gentlemen in the country had free access. He was fond of hunting and country sports, and had more taste for pictures than for books. He was not what would be called a man of genius or erudition, but had a sound judgment, great sagacity, wonderful self-command, and undoubted patriotism. As a wise and successful ruler, he will long be held in respect, though he will never secure veneration.

It was during the latter years of the administration of Walpole that England was electrified by the preaching of Whitefield and Wesley, and the sect of the Methodists arose, which has exercised a powerful influence on the morals, religion, and social life of England.

John Wesley.

John Wesley, who may rank with Augustine, Pelagius, Calvin, Arminius, or Jansen, as the founder of a sect, was demanded by the age in which he lived. Never, since the Reformation, was the state of religion so cold in England. The Established Church had triumphed over all her enemies. Puritanism had ceased to become offensive, and had even become respectable. The age of fox-hunting parsons had commenced, and the clergy were the dependants of great families, easy in their manners, and fond of the pleasures of the table. They were not expected to be very great scholars, or very grave companions. If they read the service with propriety, did not scandalize their cause by gross indulgences, and did not meddle with the two exciting subjects of all ages,—politics and religion,—they were sure of peace and plenty. But their churches were comparatively deserted, and infidel opinions had been long undermining respect for the institutions and ministers of religion. Swearing and drunkenness were fashionable vices among the higher classes, while low pleasures and lamentable ignorance characterized the people. The dissenting sects were more religious, but were formal and cold. Their ministers preached, too often, a mere technical divinity, or a lax system of ethics. The Independents were inclined to a frigid Arminianism, and the Presbyterians were passing through the change from ultra Calvinism to Arianism and Socinianism.

The reformation was not destined to come from Dissenters, but from the bosom of the Established Church, a reformation which bore the same relation to Protestantism as that effected by St. Francis bore to Roman Catholicism in the thirteenth century; a reformation among the poorer classes, who did not wish to be separated from the Church Establishment.

Early Life of Wesley.

John Wesley belonged to a good family, his father being a respectable clergyman in a market town. He was born in 1703, was educated at Oxford, and for the church. At the age of twenty, he received orders from the Bishop of Oxford, and was, shortly after, chosen fellow of Lincoln College, and then Greek lecturer.

While at Oxford, he and his brother Charles, who was also a fellow and a fine scholar, excited the ridicule of the University for the strictness of their lives, and their methodical way of living, which caused their companions to give them the name of *Methodists*. Two other young men joined them— James Hervey, author of the Meditations, and George Whitefield. The fraternity at length numbered fifteen young men, the members of which met frequently for religious purposes, visited prisons and the sick, fasted zealously on Wednesdays and Fridays, and bound themselves by rules, which, in many respects, resembled those which Ignatius Loyola imposed on his followers. The Imitation of Christ, by A Kempis, and Taylor's Holy Living, were their grand text-books, both of which were studied for their devotional spirit. But the Holy Living was the favorite book of Wesley, who did not fully approve of the rigid asceticism of the venerable mystic of the Middle Ages. The writings of William Law, also, had great influence on the mind of Wesley; but his religious views were not matured until after his return from Georgia, where he had labored as a missionary, under the auspices of Oglethorpe. The Moravians, whom he met with both in America and Germany, completed the work which Taylor had begun; and from their beautiful establishments he also learned many principles of that wonderful system of government which he so successfully introduced among his followers.

Wesley continued his labors with earnestness; but these were also attended with some extravagances, which Dr. Potter, the worthy Bishop of London, and other Churchmen, could not understand. And though he preached with great popular acceptance, and gained wonderful eclat, though he was much noticed in society and even dined with the king at Hampton Court, and with the Prince of Wales at St. James's, still the churches were gradually shut against him. When Whitefield returned from Georgia, having succeeded Wesley as a missionary in that colony, and finding so much opposition from the dignitaries of the Church, although neither he nor Wesley had seceded from the Church; and, above all, excited by the popular favor he received,—for the churches would not hold half who flocked to hear him preach,—he resolved to address the people in the open air. The excitement he produced was unparalleled. Near Bristol, he sometimes assembled as many as twenty thousand. But they were chiefly the colliers, drawn forth from their subterranean working places. But his eloquence had equal fascination for the people of London and the vicinity. In Moorfields, on Kennington Common, and on Blackheath, he sometimes drew a crowd of forty thousand people, all of whom could hear his voice. He could draw tears from Hume, and money from Dr. Franklin. He could convulse a congregation with terror, and then inspire them with the brightest hopes.

He was a greater artist than Bossuet or Bourdaloue. He never lost his self-possession, or hesitated for appropriate language. But his great power was in his thorough earnestness, and almost inspired enthusiasm. No one doubted his sincerity, and all were impressed with the spirituality and reality of the great truths which he presented. And wonderful results followed from his preaching, and from that of his brethren. A great religious revival spread over England, especially among the middle and lower classes, the effects of which last to this day.

Whitefield.

Whitefield was not so learned, or intellectual as Wesley. He was not so great a genius. But he had more eloquence, and more warmth of disposition. Wesley was a system maker, a metaphysician, a logician. He was also profoundly versed in the knowledge of human nature, and curiously adapted his system to the wants and circumstances of that class of people over whom he had the greatest power. Both Wesley and Whitefield were demanded by their times, and only such men as they were could have succeeded. They were reproached for their extravagances, and for a zeal which was confounded with fanaticism; but, had they been more proper, more prudent, more yielding to the prejudices of the great, they would not have effected so much good for their country. So with Luther. Had he possessed a severer taste, had he been more of a gentleman, or more of a philosopher, or even more humble, he would not so signally have succeeded. Germany, and the circumstances of the age, required a rough, practical, bold, impetuous reformer to lead a movement against dignitaries and venerable corruptions. England, in the eighteenth century, needed a man to arouse the common people to a sense of their spiritual condition; a man who would not be trammelled by his church; who would not be governed by the principles of expediency; who would trust in God, and labor under peculiar discouragement and self-denial.

Wesley was like Luther in another respect. He quarrelled with those who would not conform to all his views, whether they had been friends or foes. He had been attracted by the Moravians. Their simplicity, fervor, and sedateness had won his regard. But when the Moravians maintained that there was delusion in those ravings which Wesley considered as the work of grace, when they asserted that sin would remain with even regenerated man until death, and that it was in vain to expect the purification of the soul by works of self-denial, Wesley opposed them, and slandered them. He also entered the lists against his friend and fellow-laborer, Whitefield. The latter did not agree with him respecting perfection, nor election, nor predestination; and, when this disagreement had become fixed, an alienation took place, succeeded by actual bitterness and hostility. Wesley, however, in his latter days, manifested greater charity and liberality, and was a model of patience and gentleness. He became finally reconciled to Whitefield, and the union continued until the death of the latter, at Newburyport, in 1770.

The greatness of Wesley consisted in devising that wonderful church polity which still governs the powerful and numerous sect which he founded. It is from the system of the Methodists, rather than from their theological opinions, that their society spread so rapidly over Great Britain and America, and which numbered at his death, seventy-one thousand persons in England, and forty-eight thousand in this country.

Institution of Wesley.

And yet his institution was not wholly a matter of calculation, but was gradually developed as circumstances arose. When contributions were made towards building a meeting-house in Bristol, it was observed that most of the brethren were poor, and could afford but little. Then said one of the number, "Put eleven of the poorest with me, and if they give any thing, it is well. I will call on each of them weekly, and if they give nothing, I will give for them as well as for myself." This suggested the idea of a system of supervision. In the course of the weekly calls, the persons who had undertaken for a class discovered some irregularities among those for whose contributions they were responsible, and reported them to Wesley. He saw, at once, the advantage to be derived from such an arrangement. It was what he had long desired. He called together the leaders, and desired that each should make a particular inquiry into the behavior of all under their respective supervision. They did so. The custom was embraced by the whole body, and became fundamental. But it was soon found to be inconvenient to visit each person separately in his own house weekly, and then it was determined that all the members of the class should assemble together weekly, when quarrels could be made up, and where they might be mutually profited by each other's prayers and exhortations. Thus the system of classes and class-leaders arose, which bears the same relation to the society at large that town meetings do to the state or general government in the American democracy—which, as it is known, constitute the genius of our political institutions.

Itinerancy.

Itinerancy also forms another great feature of Methodism; and this resulted from accident. But it is the prerogative and peculiarity of genius to take advantage of accidents and circumstances. It cannot create them. Wesley had no church; but, being an ordained clergyman of the Establishment, and a fellow of a college beside, he had the right to preach in any pulpit, and in any diocese. But the pulpits were closed against him, in consequence of his peculiarities; so he preached wherever he could collect a congregation. Itinerancy and popularity gave him notoriety, and flattered ambition, of which he was not wholly divested. He and his brethren wandered into every section of England, from the Northumbrian moorlands to the innermost depths of the Cornish mines, in the most tumultuous cities and in the most unfrequented hamlets.

Great Influence and Power of Wesley.

As he was the father of the sect, all appointments were made by him, and, as he deserved respect and influence, the same became unbounded. When power was vested to an unlimited extent in his hands, and when the society had become numerous and scattered over a great extent of territory, he divided England into circuits, and each circuit had a certain number of ministers appointed to it. But he held out no worldly rewards as lures. The conditions which he imposed were hard. The clergy were to labor with patience and assiduity on a mean pittance, with no hope of wealth or ease. Rewards were to be given them by no earthly judge. The only recompense for toil and hunger was that of the original apostles—the approval of their consciences and the favor of Heaven.

To prevent the overbearing intolerance and despotism of the people, the chapels were not owned by the congregation nor even vested in trustees, but placed at the absolute disposal of Mr. Wesley and the conference.

If the rule of Wesley was not in accordance with democratic principles, still its perpetuation in the most zealous of democratic communities, and its escape, thus far, from the ordinary fate of all human institutions,—that of corruption and decay,—shows its remarkable wisdom, and also the great virtue of those who have administered the affairs of the society. It effected, especially in England,—what the Established Church and the various form of Dissenters could not do,—the religious renovation of the lower classes; it met their wants; it stimulated their enthusiasm. And while Methodism promoted union and piety among the people, especially those who were ignorant and poor, it did not undermine their loyalty or attachment to the political institutions of the country. Other Dissenters were often hostile to the government, and have been impatient under the evils which have afflicted England; but the Methodists, taught subordination to superiors and rulers, and have ever been patient, peaceful, and quiet.

References.—Lord Mahon's History should be particularly read; also Coxe's Memoirs of Walpole. Consult Smollett's and Tindall's History of England, and Belsham's History of George II. Smyth's Lectures are very valuable on this period of English history. See, also, Bolingbroke's State of Parties; Burke's Appeal from the Old to the New Whigs; Lord Chesterfield's Characters; and Cobbett's Parliamentary Debates. Reminiscences by Horace Walpole. For additional information respecting the South Sea scheme, see Anderson's and Macpherson's Histories of Commerce, and Smyth's Lectures. The lives of the Pretenders have been well written by Ray and Jesse. Tytler's History of Scotland should be consulted; and Waverley may be read with profit. The rise of the Methodists, the great event of the reign of George I., has been generally neglected. Lord Mahon has, however, written a valuable chapter. See also Wesley's Letters and Diary, and Lives, by Southey and Moore.

CHAPTER XX
THE COLONIZATION OF AMERICA
AND THE EAST INDIES

Commercial Enterprise.

During the administration of Sir Robert Walpole, the English colonies in America, and the East India Company's settlements began to attract the attention of ministers, and became of considerable political importance. It is, therefore, time to consider the history of colonization, both in the East and West, and not only by the English, but by the Spaniards, the Portuguese, the Dutch, and the French.

The first settlements in the new world by Europeans, and their conquests in the unknown regions of the old, were made chiefly in view of commercial advantages. The love of money, that root of all evil, was overruled by Providence in the discovery of new worlds, and the diffusion of European civilization in countries inhabited by savages, or worn-out Oriental races. But the mere ignoble love of gain was not the only motive which incited the Europeans to navigate unknown oceans and colonize new continents. There was also another, and this was the spirit of enterprise, which magically aroused the European mind in the fifteenth and sixteenth centuries. Marco Polo, when he visited the East; the Portuguese, when they doubled the Cape of Good Hope; Columbus, when he discovered America; and Magellan, when he entered the South Sea, were moved by curiosity and love of science, more than by love of gold. But the vast wealth, which the newly-discovered countries revealed, stimulated, in the breasts of the excited Europeans, the powerful passions of ambition and avarice; and the needy and grasping governments of Spain, Portugal, Holland, France, and England patronized adventurers to the new El Dorado, and furnished them with ships and stores, in the hope of receiving a share of the profits of their expedition. And they were not disappointed. Although many disasters happened to the early navigators, still country after country was added to the possessions of European kings, and vast sums of gold and silver were melted into European coin. No conquests were ever more sudden, and brilliant than those of Cortez and Pizarro, nor did wealth ever before so suddenly enrich the civilized world. But sudden and unlawful gains produced their natural fruit. All the worst evils which flow from extravagance, extortion, and pride prevailed in the old world and the new; and those advantages and possessions, which had been gained by enterprise, were turned into a curse, for no wealth can balance the vices of avarice, injustice, and cruelty.

Spanish Conquests and Settlements.

The most important of all the early settlements of America were made by the Spaniards. Their conquests were the most brilliant, and proved the most worthless. The spirit which led to their conquests and colonization was essentially that of avarice and ambition. It must, however, be admitted that religious zeal, in some instances, was the animating principle of the adventurers and of those that patronized them.

The first colony was established in Hispaniola, or, as it was afterwards called, St. Domingo, a short time after the discovery of America by Columbus. The mines of the island were, at that period, very productive, and the aggressive Spaniards soon compelled the unhappy natives to labor in them, under their governor, Juan Ponce de Leon. But Hispaniola was not sufficiently large or productive to satisfy the cupidity of the governor, and Porto Rico was conquered and enslaved. Cuba also, in a few years, was added to the dominions of Spain.

At length, the Spaniards, who had explored the coasts of the Main land, prepared to invade and conquer the populous territories of Montezuma, Emperor of Mexico. The people whom he governed had attained a considerable degree of civilization, having a regular government, a system of laws, and an established priesthood. They were not ignorant of the means of recording great events, and possessed considerable skill in many useful and ornamental arts. They were rich in gold and silver, and their cities were ornamented with palaces and gardens. But their riches were irresistible objects of desire to the European adventurers, and, therefore, proved their misfortune. The story of their conquest by Fernando Cortez need not here be told; familiarized as are all readers and students with the exquisite and artistic narrative of the great American historian, whose work and whose fame can only perish with the language itself.

About ten years after the conquest of Mexico, Pizarro landed in Peru, which country was soon added to the dominions of Philip II. And the government of that country was even more oppressive and unjust than that of Mexico. All Indians between the ages of fifteen and fifty were compelled to work in the mines; and so dreadful was the forced labor, that four out of five of those who worked in them were supposed to perish annually. There was no limit to Spanish rapacity and cruelty, and it was exercised over all the other countries which were subdued — Chili, Florida, and the West India Islands.

Enormous and unparalleled quantities of the precious metals were sent to Spain from the countries of the new world. But, from the first discovery of Peru and Mexico, the mother country declined in wealth and political importance. With the increase of gold, the price of labor and of provision, and of all articles of manufacturing industry, also increased, and nearly in the same ratio. The Spaniards were insensible to this truth, and, instead of cultivating the soil or engaging in manufactures, were contented with the gold which came from the colonies. This, for a while, enriched them; but it was soon scattered over all Christendom, and was exchanged for the necessities of life. Industry and art declined, and those countries alone were the gainers which produced those articles which Spain was obliged to purchase.

Portuguese Discoveries.

Portugal soon rivalled Spain in the extent and richness of colonial possessions. Brazil was discovered in 1501, and, in about half a century after, was colonized. The native Brazilians, inferior in civilization to the Mexicans and Peruvians, were still less able than they to resist the arms of the Europeans. They were gradually subdued, and their beautiful and fertile country came into possession of the victors. But the Portuguese also extended their empire in the East, as well as in the West. After the discovery of a passage round the Cape of Good Hope by Vasco de Gama, the early navigators sought simply to be enriched by commerce with the Indies. They found powerful rivals in the Arabs, who had heretofore monopolized the trade. In order to secure their commerce, and also to protect themselves against their rivals and enemies, the Portuguese, under the guidance of Albuquerque, procured a grant of land in India, from one of the native princes. Soon after, Goa was reduced, and became the seat of government; and territorial acquisition commenced, which, having been continued nearly three centuries by the various European powers, is still progressive. In about sixty years, the Portuguese had established a great empire in the East, which included the coasts and islands of the Persian Gulf, the whole Malabar and Coromandel coasts, the city of Malacca, and numerous islands of the Indian Ocean. They had effected a settlement in China, obtained a free trade with the empire of Japan, and received tribute from the rich Islands of Ceylon, Java, and Sumatra.

Portuguese Settlements.

The same moral effects happened to Portugal, from the possession of the Indies, that the conquests of Cortez and Pizarro produced on Spain.

Goa was the most depraved spot in the world: and the vices which wealth engendered, wherever the Europeans formed a settlement, can now scarcely be believed. When Portugal fell under the dominion of Philip II., the ruin of her settlements commenced. They were supplanted by the Dutch, who were more moral, more united and enterprising, though they provoked, by their arrogance and injustice, the hostility of the Eastern princes.

The conquests and settlements of the Dutch rapidly succeeded those of the Portuguese. In 1595, Cornelius Houtman sailed, with a well-provided fleet, for the land of gems and spices. A company was soon incorporated, in Holland, for managing the Indian trade. Settlements were first made in the Moluccas Islands, which soon extended to the possession of the Island of Java, and to the complete monopoly of the spice trade. The Dutch then gained possession of the Island of Ceylon, which they retained until it was wrested from them by the English. But their empire was only maintained at a vast expense of blood and treasure; nor were they any exception to the other European colonists and adventurers, in the indulgence of all those vices which degrade our nature.

Neither the French nor the English made any important conquests in the East, when compared with those of the Portuguese and Dutch. Nor did their acquisitions in America equal those of the Spaniards. But they were more important in their ultimate results.

Early English Enterprise.

English enterprise was manifested shortly after the first voyage of Columbus. Henry VII. was sufficiently enlightened, envious, and avaricious, to listen to the proposals of a Venetian, resident in Bristol, by the name of Cabot; and, in 1495, he commissioned him to sail under the banner of England, to take possession of any new countries he might discover. Accordingly, in about two years after, Cabot, with his second son, Sebastian, embarked at Bristol, in one of the king's ships, attended by four smaller vessels, equipped by the merchants of that enterprising city.

Impressed with the idea of Columbus, and other early navigators, that the West India Islands were not far from the Indian continent, he concluded that, if he steered in a more northerly direction, he should reach India by a shorter course than that pursued by the great discoverer. Accordingly, sailing in that course, he discovered Newfoundland and Prince Edwards', and, soon after, the coast of North America, along which he sailed, from Labrador to Virginia. But, disappointed in not finding a westerly passage to India, he returned to England, without attempting, either by settlement or conquest, to gain a footing on the great continent which the English were the second to visit, of all the European nations.

England was prevented, by various circumstances, from deriving immediate advantage from the discovery. The unsettled state of the country; the distractions arising from the civil wars, and afterwards from the Reformation; the poverty of the people, and the sordid nature of the king,— were unfavorable to settlements which promised no immediate advantage; and it was not until the reign of Elizabeth that any deliberate plans were made for the colonization of North America. The voyages of Frobisher and Drake had aroused a spirit of adventure, if they had not gratified the thirst for gold.

Among those who felt an intense interest in the new world, was Sir Humphrey Gilbert, a man of enlarged views and intrepid boldness. He secured from Elizabeth (1578) a liberal patent, and sailed, with a considerable body of adventurers, for the new world. But he took a too northerly direction, and his largest vessel was shipwrecked on the coast of Cape Breton. The enterprise from various causes, completely failed, and the intrepid navigator lost his life.

Sir Walter Raleigh.

The spirit of the times raised up, however, a greater genius, and a more accomplished adventurer, and no less a personage than Sir Walter Raleigh,—the favorite of the queen; one of the greatest scholars and the most elegant courtier of the age; a soldier, a philosopher, and a statesman. He obtained a patent, substantially the same as that which had been bestowed on Gilbert. In 1584, Raleigh despatched two small exploring vessels, under the command of Amidas and Barlow, which seasonably arrived off the coast of North Carolina. From the favorable report of the country and the people, a larger fleet, of seven ships, was despatched to America, commanded by Sir Richard Grenville. But he was diverted from his course by the prevailing passion for predatory enterprise, and hence only landed one hundred and eight men at Roanoke, (1585.) The government of this feeble band was intrusted to Captain Lane. But the passion for gold led to a misunderstanding with the natives. The colony became enfeebled and reduced, and the adventurers returned to England, (1586,) bringing with them some knowledge of the country, and also that singular weed, which rapidly enslaved the courtiers of Queen Elizabeth, and which soon became one of the great staple commodities in the trade of the civilized world. Modern science has proved it to be a poison, and modern philanthropy has lifted up its warning voice against the use of it. But when have men, in their degeneracy, been governed by their reason? What logic can break the power of habit, or counteract the seductive influences of those excitements which fill the mind with visionary hopes, and lull a tumultuous spirit into the repose of pleasant dreams and oblivious joys? Sir Walter Raleigh, to his shame or his misfortune, was among the first to patronize a custom which has proved more injurious to civilized nations than even the use of opium itself, because it is more universal and more insidious.

But smoking was simply an amusement with him. He soon turned his thoughts to the reëstablishment of his colony. Even before the return of the company under Lane, Sir Richard Grenville had visited the Roanoke, with the necessary stores. But he arrived too late; the colony was abandoned.

But nothing could abate the zeal of the most enterprising genius of the age. In 1587, he despatched three more ships, under the command of Captain White, who founded the city of Raleigh. But no better success attended the new band of colonists. White sailed for England, to secure new supplies; and, when he returned, he found no traces of the colony he had planted; and no subsequent ingenuity or labor has been able to discover the slightest vestige.

The patience of Raleigh was not wasted; but new objects occupied his mind, and he parted with his patent, which made him the proprietary of a great part of the Southern States. Nor were there any new attempts at colonization until 1606, in the reign of James.

London Company Incorporated.

Through the influence of Sir Ferdinand Gorges, a man of great wealth; Sir John Popham, lord chief justice of England; Richard Hakluyt, the historian; Bartholomew Gosnold, the navigator, and John Smith, the enthusiastic adventurer,—King James I. granted a royal charter to two rival companies, for the colonization of America. The first was composed of noblemen, gentlemen, and merchants, in and about London, who had an exclusive right to occupy regions from thirty-four to thirty-eight degrees of north latitude. The other company, composed of gentlemen and merchants in the west of England, had assigned to them the territory between forty-one and forty-five degrees. But only the first company succeeded.

The territory, appropriated to the London or southern colony, preserved the name which had been bestowed upon it during the reign of Elizabeth,— Virginia. The colonists were authorized to transport, free of the custom-house, for the term of seven years, what arms and provisions they required; and their children were permitted to enjoy the same privileges and liberties, in the American settlements, that Englishmen had at home. They had the right to search for mines, to coin money, and, for twenty-one years, to impose duties, on vessels trading to their harbors, for the benefit of the colony. But, after this period, the duty was to be taken for the king, who also preserved a control over both the councils established for the government of the colony,—the one in England itself, and the other in Virginia; a control inconsistent with those liberties which the colonists subsequently asserted and secured.

Hardships of the Virginia Colony.

The London Company promptly applied themselves to the settlement of their territories; and, on the 19th of December, 1606, a squadron of three small vessels set sail for the new world; and, on May 13, 1607, a company of one hundred and five men, without families, disembarked at Jamestown. This was the first permanent settlement in America by the English. But great misfortunes afflicted them. Before September, one half of the colonists had perished, and the other half were suffering from famine, dissension, and fear. The president, Wingfield, attempted to embezzle the public stores, and escape to the West Indies. He was supplanted in his command by Ratcliffe, a man without capacity. But a deliverer was raised up in the person of Captain John Smith, who extricated the suffering and discontented band from the evils which impended. He had been a traveller and a warrior; had visited France, Italy, and Egypt; fought in Holland and Hungary; was taken a prisoner of war in Wallachia, and sent as a slave to Constantinople. Removed to a fortress in the Crimea, and subjected to the hardest tasks, he yet contrived to escape, and, after many perils, reached his native country. But greater hardships and dangers awaited him in the new world, to which he was impelled by his adventurous curiosity. He was surprised and taken by a party of hostile Indians, when on a tour of exploration, and would have been murdered, had it not been for his remarkable presence of mind and singular sagacity, united with the intercession of the famous Pocahontas, daughter of a great Indian chief, from whom some of the best families in Virginia are descended. It would be pleasant to detail the romantic incidents of this brief captivity; but our limits forbid. Smith, when he returned to Jamestown, found his company reduced to forty men, and they were discouraged and disheartened. Moreover, they were a different class of men from those who colonized New England. They were gentlemen adventurers connected with aristocratic families, were greedy for gold, and had neither the fortitude nor the habits requisite for success. They were not accustomed to labor, at least with the axe and plough. Smith earnestly wrote to the council of the company in England, to send carpenters, husbandmen, gardeners, fishermen, and blacksmiths, instead of "vagabond gentlemen and goldsmiths." But he had to organize a colony with such materials as avarice or adventurous curiosity had sent to America. And, in spite of dissensions and natural indolence, he succeeded in placing it on a firm foundation; surveyed the Chesapeake Bay to the Susquehannah, and explored the inlets of the majestic Potomac. But he was not permitted to complete the work which he had so beneficently begun. His administration was unacceptable to the company in England, who cared very little for the welfare of the infant colony, and only sought a profitable investment of their capital. They were disappointed that mines of gold and silver had not been discovered, and that they themselves had not become enriched. Even the substantial welfare of the colony displeased them; for this diverted attention from the pursuit of mineral wealth.

New Charter of the London Company.

The original patentees, therefore, sought to strengthen themselves by new associates and a new charter. And a new charter was accordingly granted to twenty-one peers, ninety-eight knights, and a great number of doctors, esquires, gentlemen, and merchants. The bounds of the colony were enlarged, the council and offices in Virginia abolished, and the company in England empowered to nominate all officers in the colony. Lord Delaware was appointed governor and captain-general of the company, and a squadron of nine ships, with five hundred emigrants were sent to Virginia. But these emigrants consisted, for the most part, of profligate young men, whom their aristocratic friends sent away to screen themselves from shame; broken down gentlemen, too lazy to work; and infamous dependants on powerful families. They threw the whole colony into confusion, and provoked, by their aggression and folly, the animosities of the Indians, whom Smith had appeased. The settlement at Jamestown was abandoned to famine and confusion, and would have been deserted had it not been for the timely arrival of Lord Delaware, with ample supplies and new recruits. His administration was wise and efficient, and he succeeded in restoring order, if he did not secure the wealth which was anticipated.

In 1612, the company obtained a third patent, by which all the islands within three hundred leagues of the Virginia shore were granted to the patentees, and by which a portion of the power heretofore vested in the council was transferred to the whole company. The political rights of the colonists remained the same but they acquired gradually peace and tranquillity. Tobacco was extensively cultivated, and proved a more fruitful source of wealth than mines of silver or gold.

The jealousy of arbitrary power, and impatience of liberty among the new settlers, induced the Governor of Virginia, in 1619, to reinstate them in the full possession of the rights of Englishmen; and he accordingly convoked a Provincial Assembly, the first ever held in America, which consisted of the governor, the council, and a number of burgesses, elected by the eleven existing boroughs of the colony. The deliberation and laws of this infant legislature were transmitted to England for approval; and so wise and judicious were these, that the company, soon after, approved and ratified the platform of what gradually ripened into the American representative system.

Rapid Colonization.

The guarantee of political rights led to a rapid colonization. "Men were now willing to regard Virginia as their home. They fell to building houses and planting corn." Women were induced to leave the parent country to become the wives of adventurous planters; and, during the space of three years, thirty-five hundred persons, of both sexes, found their way to Virginia. In the year 1620, a Dutch ship, from the coast of Guinea, arrived in James River, and landed twenty negroes for sale; and, as they were found more capable of enduring fatigue, in a southern climate, than the Europeans, they were continually imported, until a large proportion of the inhabitants of Virginia was composed of slaves. Thus was introduced, at this early period, that lasting system of injustice and cruelty which has proved already an immeasurable misfortune to the country, as well as a disgrace to the institutions of republican liberty, but which is lamented, in many instances, by no class with more sincerity than by those who live by the produce of slave labor itself.

Indian Warfare.

The succeeding year, which witnessed the importation of negroes, beheld the cultivation of tobacco, which before the introduction of cotton, was the great staple of southern produce.

In 1622, the long-suppressed enmity of the Indians broke out in a savage attempt to murder the whole colony. A plot had been formed by which all the English settlements were to be attacked on the same day, and at the same hour. The conspiracy was betrayed by a friendly Indian, but not in time to prevent a fearful massacre of three hundred and forty-seven persons, among whom were some of the wealthiest and most respectable inhabitants. Then followed all the evils of an Indian war, and the settlements were reduced from eighty to eight plantations; and it was not until after a protracted struggle that the colonists regained their prosperity.

Scarcely had hostilities with the Indians commenced, before dissensions among the company in England led to a quarrel with the king, and a final abrogation of their charter. The company was too large and too democratic. The members were dissatisfied that so little gain had been derived from the colony; and moreover they made their courts or convocations, when they assembled to discuss colonial matters, the scene of angry political debate. There was a court party and a country party, each inflamed with violent political animosities. The country party was the stronger, and soon excited the jealousy of the arbitrary monarch, who looked upon their meetings "as but a seminary to a seditious parliament." A royal board of commissioners were appointed to examine the affairs of the company, who reported unfavorably; and the king therefore ordered the company to surrender its charter. The company refused to obey an arbitrary mandate; but upon its refusal, the king ordered a writ of *quo warranto* to be issued, and the Court of the King's Bench decided, of course, in favor of the crown. The company was accordingly dissolved. But the dissolution, though arbitrary, operated beneficially on the colony. Of all cramping institutions, a sovereign company of merchants is the most so, since they seek simply commercial gain, without any reference to the political, moral, or social improvement of the people whom they seek to control.

Governor Harvey.

Before King James had completed his scheme for the government of the colony, he died; and Charles I. pursued the same arbitrary policy which his father contemplated. He instituted a government which combined the unlimited prerogative of an absolute prince with the narrow and selfish maxims of a mercantile corporation. He monopolized the profits of its trade, and empowered the new governor, whom he appointed, to exercise his authority with the most undisguised usurpation of those rights which the colonists had heretofore enjoyed. Harvey's disposition was congenial with the rapacious and cruel system which he pursued, and he acted more like the satrap of an Eastern prince than the representative of a constitutional monarch. The colonists remonstrated and complained; but their appeals to the mercy and justice of the king were disregarded, and Harvey continued his course of insolence and tyranny until that famous parliament was assembled which rebelled against the folly and government of Charles. In 1641, a new and upright governor, Sir William Berkeley, was sent to Virginia, and the old provincial liberties were restored. In the contest between the king and parliament Virginia espoused the royal cause. When the parliament had triumphed over the king, Virginia was made to feel the force of republican displeasure, and oppressive restrictions were placed upon the trade of the colony, which were the more provoking in view of the indulgence which the New England colonies received from the protector. A revolt ensued, and Sir William Berkeley was forced from his retirement, and made to assume the government of the rebellious province. Cromwell, fortunately for Virginia, but unfortunately for the world, died before the rebellion, could be suppressed; and when Charles II. was restored, Virginia joyfully returned to her allegiance. The supremacy of the Church of England was established by law, stipends were allowed to her ministers, and no clergymen were permitted to exercise their functions but such as held to the supremacy of the Church of England.

Arbitrary Policy of Charles II.

But Charles II. was as incapable as his father of pursuing a generous and just policy to the colonies; and parliament itself looked upon the colonies as a source of profit to the nation, rather than as a part of the nation. No sooner was Charles seated on the throne, than parliament imposed a duty of five per cent. on all merchandise exported from, or imported into, any of the dominions belonging to the crown; and the famous Navigation Act was passed, which ordained that no commodities should be imported into any of the British settlements but in vessels built in England or in her colonies; and that no sugar, tobacco, cotton, wool, indigo and some other articles produced in the colonies, should be shipped from them to any other country but England. As a compensation, the colonies were permitted the exclusive cultivation of tobacco. The parliament, soon after, in 1663, passed additional restrictions; and, advancing, step by step, gradually subjected the colonies to a most oppressive dependence on the mother country, and even went so far as to regulate the trade of the several colonies with each other. This system of monopoly and exclusion, of course, produced indignation and disgust, and sowed the seeds of ultimate rebellion. Indian hostilities were added to provincial discontent, and even the horrors of civil war disturbed the prosperity of the colony. An ambitious and unprincipled adventurer, by the name of Bacon, succeeded in fomenting dissension, and in successfully resisting the power of the governor. Providence arrested the career of the rebel in the moment of his triumph; and his sickness and death fortunately dissipated the tempest which threatened to be fatal to the peace and welfare of Virginia. Berkeley, on the suppression of the rebellion, punished the offenders with a severity which ill accorded with his lenient and pacific character. His course did not please the government in England, and he was superseded by Colonel Jeffries. But he died before his successor arrived. A succession of governors administered the colony as their disposition prompted, some of whom were wise and able, and others tyrannical and rapacious.

The English revolution of 1688 produced also a change in the administration of the colony. Its dependence on the personal character of the sovereign was abolished, and its chartered liberties were protected. The king continued to appoint the royal governor, and the parliament continued to oppress the trade of the colonists; but they, on the whole, enjoyed the rights of freemen, and rapidly advanced in wealth and prosperity. On the accession of William and Mary, the colony contained fifty thousand inhabitants and forty-eight parishes; and, in 1676, the customs on tobacco alone were collected in England to the amount of one hundred and thirty-five thousand pounds. The people generally belonged to the Episcopal Church, and the clergy each received, in every parish, a house and glebe, together with sixteen thousand pounds of tobacco. The people were characterized for hospitality and urbanity, but were reproached for the indolence which a residence in scattered villages, a hot climate, and negro slavery must almost inevitably lead to. Literature, that solace of the refined and luxurious in the European world, was but imperfectly cultivated; nor was religion, in its stern and lofty developments, the animating principle of life, as in the New England settlements. But the people of Virginia were richer, more cultivated, and more aristocratic than the Puritans, more refined in manners, and more pleasing as companions.

Settlement of New England.

The settlements in New England were made by a very different class of men from those who colonized Virginia. They were not adventurers in quest of gain; they were not broken-down gentlemen of aristocratic connections; they were not the profligate and dissolute members of powerful families. They were Puritans, they belonged to the middle ranks of society; they were men of stern and lofty virtue, of invincible energy, and hard and iron wills; they detested both the civil and religious despotism of their times, and desired, above all worldly consideration, the liberty of worshipping God according to the dictates of their consciences. They were chiefly Independents and Calvinists, among whom religion was a life, and not a dogma. They sought savage wilds, not for gain, not for ease, not for aggrandizement, but for liberty of conscience; and, for the sake of that inestimable privilege, they were ready to forego all the comforts and elegances of civilized life, and cheerfully meet all the dangers and make all the sacrifices which a residence among savage Indians, and in a cold and inhospitable climate, necessarily incurred.

The efforts at colonization attempted by the company in the west of England, to which allusion has been made, signally failed. God did not design that New England should be settled by a band of commercial adventurers. A colony was permanently planted at Plymouth, within the limits of the corporation, of forty persons, to whom James had granted enormous powers, and a belt of country from the fortieth to the forty-eighth degree of north latitude in width, and from the Atlantic to the Pacific in length.

Arrival of the Mayflower.

On the 5th of August, 1620, the Mayflower and the Speedwell, freighted with the first Puritan colony, set sail from Southampton. It composed a band of religious and devoted men, with their wives and children, who had previously sought shelter in Holland for the enjoyment of their religious opinions. The smaller vessel, after a trial on the Atlantic, was found incompetent to the voyage, and was abandoned. The more timid were allowed to disembark at old Plymouth. One hundred and one resolute souls again set sail in the Mayflower, for the unknown wilderness, with all its countless dangers and miseries. No common worldly interest could have sustained their souls. The first adventurers embarked for Virginia, without women or children; but the Puritans made preparation for a permanent residence. Providence, against their design, guided their little vessel to the desolate shores of the most barren part of Massachusetts. On the 9th of November, it was safely moored in the harbor of Cape Cod. On the 11th, the colonists solemnly bound themselves into a body politic, and chose John Carver for their governor. On the 11th of December, (O. S.,) after protracted perils and sufferings, this little company landed on Plymouth Rock. Before the opening spring, more than half the colony had perished from privation, fatigue, and suffering, among whom was the governor himself. In the autumn, their numbers were recruited; but all the miseries of famine remained. They lived together as a community; but, for three or four months together, they had no corn whatever. In the spring of 1623, each family planted for itself, and land was assigned to each person in perpetual fee. The needy and defenceless colonists were fortunately preserved from the hostility of the natives, since a famine had swept away the more dangerous of their savage neighbors; nor did hostilities commence for several years. God protected the Pilgrims, in their weakness, from the murderous tomahawk, and from the perils of the wilderness. They suffered, but they existed. Their numbers slowly increased, but they were all Puritans, — were just the men to colonize the land, and lay the foundation of a great empire. From the beginning, a strict democracy existed, and all enjoyed ample exemption from the trammels of arbitrary power. No king took cognizance of their existence, or imposed upon them a despotic governor. They appointed their own rulers, and those rulers governed in the fear of God. Township independence existed from the first; and this is the nursery and the genius of American institutions. The Plymouth colony was a self-constituted democracy; but it was composed of Englishmen, who loved their native land, and, while they sought unrestrained freedom, did not disdain dependence on the mother country, and a proper connection with the English government. They could not obtain a royal charter from the king; but the Grand Council of Plymouth—a new company, to which James had given the privileges of the old one—granted all the privileges which the colonists desired. They were too insignificant to attract much attention from the government, or excite the jealousy of a great corporation.

Unobtrusive and unfettered, the colony slowly spread. But wherever it spread, it took root. It was a tree which Providence planted for all generations. It was established upon a rock. It was a branch of the true church, which was destined to defy storms and changes, because its strength was in the Lord.

Settlement of New Hampshire.

But all parts of New England were not, at first, settled by Puritan Pilgrims, or from motives of religion merely. The council of Plymouth issued grants of domains to various adventurers, who were animated by the spirit of gain. John Mason received a patent for what is now the state of New Hampshire. Portsmouth and Dover had an existence as early as 1623. Gorges obtained a grant of the whole district between the Piscataqua and the Kennebec. Saco, in 1636, contained one hundred and fifty people. But the settlements in New Hampshire and Maine, having disappointed the expectations of the patentees in regard to emolument and profit, were not very flourishing.

In the mean time, a new company of Puritans was formed for the settlement of the country around Boston. The company obtained a royal charter, (1629,) which constituted them a body politic, by the name of the *Governor and Company of the Massachusetts Bay*. It conferred on the colonists the rights of English subjects, although it did not technically concede freedom of religious worship, or the privilege of self-government. The main body of the colonists settled in Salem. They were a band of devout and lofty characters; Calvinists in their religious creed, and republicans in their political opinions. Strict independency was the basis and the genius of their church. It was self-constituted, and all its officers were elected by the members.

The charter of the company had been granted to a corporation consisting chiefly of merchants resident in London, and was more liberal than could have been expected from so bigoted and zealous a king as Charles I. If it did not directly concede the rights of conscience, it seemed to be silent respecting them; and the colonists were left to the unrestricted enjoyment of their religious and civil liberties. The intolerance and rigor of Archbishop Laud caused this new colony to be rapidly settled; and, as many distinguished men desired to emigrate, they sought and secured, from the company in England, a transfer of all the powers of government to the actual settlers in America. By this singular transaction, the municipal rights and privileges of the colonists were established on a firm foundation.

Constitution of the Colony.

In 1630, not far from fifteen hundred persons, with Winthrop as their leader and governor, emigrated to the new world, and settled first in Charlestown, and afterwards in Boston. In accordance with the charter which gave them such unexpected privileges, a General Court was assembled, to settle the government. But the privilege of the elective franchise was given only to the members of the church, and each church was formed after the model of the one in Salem. It cannot be said that a strict democracy was established, since church membership was the condition of the full enjoyment of political rights. But if the constitution was somewhat aristocratic and exclusive, aristocracy was not based on wealth or intellect. The Calvinists of Massachusetts recognized a government of the elect,—a sort of theocracy, in which only the religious, or those who professed to be so, and were admitted to be so, had a right to rule. This was the notion of Cromwell himself, the great idol and representative of the Independents, who fancied that the government of England should be intrusted only to those who were capable of saving England, and were worthy to rule England. As his party constituted, in his eyes, this elect body, and was, in reality, the best party,—composed of men who feared God, and were willing to be ruled by his laws,—therefore his party, as he supposed, had a right to overturn thrones, and establish a new theocracy on earth.

Doctrines of the Puritans.

This notion was a delusion in England, and proved fatal to all those who were blinded by it. Not so in America. Amid the unbroken forests of New England, a colony of men was planted who generally recognized the principles of Cromwell; and one of the best governments the world has seen controlled the turbulent, rewarded the upright, and protected the rights and property of all classes with almost paternal fidelity and justice. The colony, however,—such is the weakness of man, such the degeneracy of his nature,—was doomed to dissension. Bigotry, from which no communities or individuals are fully free, drove some of the best men from the limits of the colony. Roger Williams, a minister in Salem, and one of the most worthy and enlightened men of his age, sought shelter from the persecution of his brethren amid the wilds on Narragansett Bay. In June, 1636, the lawgiver of Rhode Island, with five companions, embarked in an Indian canoe, and, sailing down the river, landed near a spring, on a sheltered spot, which he called *Providence*. He was gradually joined by others, who sympathized with his tolerant spirit and enlightened views, and the colony of Rhode Island became an asylum for the persecuted for many years. And there were many such. The Puritans were too earnest to live in harmony with those who differed from them on great religious questions; and a difference of views must have been expected among men so intellectual, so acute, and so fearless in speculation. How could dissenters from prevailing opinions fail to arise?—mystics, fanatics, and heretics? The idea of special divine illumination—ever the prevailing source of fanaticism, in all ages and countries—led astray some; and the desire for greater spiritual liberty animated others. Anne Hutchinson adopted substantially the doctrine of George Fox, that the spirit of God illuminates believers, independently of his written word; and she communicated her views to many others, who became, like her, arrogant and conceited, in spite of their many excellent qualities. Harry Vane, the governor, was among the number. But there was no reasoning with fanatics, who fancied themselves especially inspired; and, as they disturbed the peace of the colony, the leaders were expelled. Vane himself returned to England, to mingle in scenes more congenial with his excellent but excitable temper. In England, this illustrious friend of Milton greatly distinguished himself for his efforts in the cause of liberty, and ever remained its consistent advocate; opposing equally the tyranny of the king, and the encroachments of those who overturned his throne.

Pequod War.

Connecticut, though assigned to a company in England, was early colonized by a detachment of Pilgrims from Massachusetts. In 1635, settlements were made at Hartford, Windsor, and Wethersfield. The following year, the excellent and illustrious Hooker led a company of one hundred persons through the forests to the delightful banks of the Connecticut, whose rich alluvial soil promised an easier support than the hard and stony land in the vicinity of Boston. They were scarcely settled before the Pequod war commenced, which involved all the colonies in a desperate and bloody contest with the Indians. But the Pequods were no match for Europeans, especially without firearms; and, in 1637, the tribe was nearly annihilated. The energy and severity exercised by the colonists, fighting for their homes, struck awe in the minds of the savages; and it was long before they had the courage to rally a second time. The Puritans had the spirit of Cromwell, and never hesitated to act with intrepid boldness and courage, when the necessity was laid upon them. They were no advocates of half measures. Their subsequent security and growth are, in no slight degree, to be traced to these rigorous measures,—measures which, in these times, are sometimes denounced as too severe, but the wisdom of which can scarcely be questioned when the results are considered. All the great masters of war, and of war with barbarians, have pursued a policy of unmitigated severity; and when a temporizing or timid course has been adopted with men incapable of being governed by reason, and animated by savage passions, that course has failed.

Union of the New England Colonies.

After the various colonies were well established in New England, and more than twenty thousand had emigrated from the mother country, they were no longer regarded with benevolent interest by the king or his ministers. The Grand Council of Plymouth surrendered its charter to the king, and a writ of *quo warranto* was issued against the Massachusetts colony. But the Puritans refused to surrender their charter, and prepared for resistance against the malignant scheme of Strafford and Laud. Before they could be carried into execution, the struggle between the king and the Long Parliament had commenced. The less resistance was forgotten in the greater. The colonies escaped the vengeance of a bigoted government. When the parliament triumphed, they were especially favored, and gradually acquired wealth and power. The different colonies formed a confederation to protect themselves against the Dutch and French on the one side, and the Indians on the other. And this happily continued for half a century, and was productive of very important results. But the several colonies continued to make laws for their own people, to repress anarchy, and favor the cause of religion and unity. They did not always exhibit a liberal and enlightened policy. They destroyed witches; persecuted the Baptists and Quakers, and excluded them from their settlements. But, with the exception of religious persecution, their legislation was wise, and their general conduct was virtuous. They encouraged schools, and founded the University of Cambridge. They preserved the various peculiarities of Puritanism in regard to amusements, to the observance of the Sabbath, and to antipathy to any thing which reminded them of Rome, or even of the Church of England. But Puritanism was not an odious crust, a form, a dogma. It was a life, a reality; and was not unfavorable to the development of the most beautiful virtues of charity and benevolence, in a certain sphere. It was not a mere traditional Puritanism, which clings with disgusting tenacity to a form, when the spirit of love has departed; but it was a harmonious development of living virtues, which sympathized with education, with freedom, and with progress; which united men together by the bond of Christian love, and incited them to deeds of active benevolence and intrepid moral heroism. Nor did the Puritan Pilgrims persecute those who did not harmonize with them in order to punish them, but simply to protect themselves, and to preserve in their midst, and in their original purity, those institutions and those rights, for the possession of which they left their beloved native land for a savage wilderness, with its countless perils and miseries. But their hardships and afflictions were not of long continuance. With energy, industry, frugality, and love, they soon obtained security, comfort, and health. And it is no vain and idle imagination which assigns to those years, which succeeded the successful planting of the colony, the period of the greatest happiness and virtue which New England has ever enjoyed.

Equally fortunate with the Puritans were those interesting people who settled Pennsylvania. If the Quakers were persecuted in the mother country and in New England, they found a shelter on the banks of the Delaware. There they obtained and enjoyed that freedom of religious worship which had been denied to the great founder of the sect, and which had even been withheld from them by men who had struggled with them for the attainment of this exalted privilege.

William Penn.

In 1677, the Quakers obtained a charter which recognized the principle of democratic equality in the settlements in West Jersey; and in 1680, William Penn received from the king, who was indebted to his father, a grant of an extensive territory, which was called *Pennsylvania*, of which he was constituted absolute proprietary. He also received a liberal charter, and gave his people privileges and a code of laws which exceeded in liberality any that had as yet been bestowed on any community. In 1682 he landed at Newcastle, and, soon after, at his new city on the banks of the Delaware, under the shelter of a large, spreading elm, made his immortal treaty with the Indians. He proclaimed to the Indian, heretofore deemed a foe never to be appeased, the principles of love which animated Fox, and which "Mary Fisher had borne to the Grand Turk." "We meet," said the lawgiver, "on the broad pathway of good faith and good will. No advantage shall be taken on either side, but all shall be openness and love. I will not call you children, for parents sometimes chide their children too severely; nor brothers only, for brothers differ. The friendship between me and you I will not compare to a chain, for that the rains might rust, or the felling tree might break. We are the same as if one man's body were to be divided into two parts; we are all one flesh and blood."

Such were the sublime doctrines which the illustrious founder of Pennsylvania declared to the Indians, and which he made the basis of his government, and the rule of his intercourse with his own people and with savage tribes. These doctrines were already instilled into the minds of the settlers, and they also found a response in the souls of the Indians. The sons of the wilderness long cherished the recollection of the covenant, and never forgot its principles. While all the other settlements of the Europeans were suffering from the hostility of the red man, Pennsylvania alone enjoyed repose. "Not a drop of Quaker blood was ever shed by an Indian."

William Penn, although the absolute proprietor of a tract of country which was nearly equal in extent to England, sought no revenue and no arbitrary power. He gave to the settlers the right to choose their own magistrates, from the highest to the lowest, and only reserved to himself the power to veto the bills of the council—the privilege which our democracies still allow to their governors.

Such a colony as he instituted could not but prosper. Its rising glories were proclaimed in every country of Europe, and the needy and distressed of all countries sought this realized Utopia. In two years after Philadelphia was settled, it contained six hundred houses. Peace was uninterrupted, and the settlement spread more rapidly than in any other part of North America.

New Jersey, Maryland, North and South Carolina, and Georgia, were all colonized by the English, shortly after the settlement of Virginia and New England, either by emigration from England, or from the other colonies. But there was nothing in their early history sufficiently marked to warrant a more extended sketch. In general, the Southern States were colonized by men who had not the religious elevation of the Puritans, nor the living charity of the Quakers. But their characters improved by encountering the evils to which they were subjected, and they became gradually imbued with those principles which in after times secured independence and union.

Settlement of New York.

The settlement of New York, however, merits a passing notice, since it was colonized by emigrants from Holland, which was by far the most flourishing commercial state of Europe in the seventeenth century. The Hudson River had been discovered (1609) by an Englishman, whose name it bears, but who was in the service of the Dutch East India Company. The right of possession of the country around it was therefore claimed by the United Provinces, and an association of Dutch merchants fitted out a ship to trade with the Indians. In 1614, a rude fort was erected on Manhattan Island, and, the next year, the settlement at Albany commenced, chiefly with a view of trading with the Indians. In 1623, New Amsterdam, now New York, was built for the purpose of colonization, and extensive territories were appropriated by the Dutch for the rising colony. This appropriation involved them in constant contention with the English, as well as with the Indians; nor was there the enjoyment of political privileges by the people, as in the New England colonies. The settlements resembled lordships in the Netherlands, and every one who planted a colony of fifty souls, possessed the absolute property of the lands he colonized, and became *Patroon*, or Lord of the Manor. Very little attention was given to education, and the colonists were not permitted to make cotton, woollen, or linen cloth, for fear of injury to the monopolists of the Dutch manufactures. The province had no popular freedom, and no public spirit. The poor were numerous, and the people were disinclined to make proper provision for their own protection.

Conquest of New Netherlands.

But the colony of the New Netherlands was not destined to remain under the government of the Dutch West India Company. It was conquered by the English in 1664, and the conquerors promised security to the customs, the religion, the institutions, and the possessions of the Dutch; and this promise was observed. In 1673, the colony was reconquered, but finally, in 1674, was ceded to the English, and the brother of Charles II. resumed his possession and government of New York, and delegated his power to Colonel Nichols, who ruled with wisdom and humanity. But the old Dutch Governor Stuyvesant remained in the city over which he had so honorably presided, and prolonged the empire of Dutch manners, if not of Dutch arms. The banks of the Hudson continued also to be peopled by the countrymen of the original colonists, who long preserved the language, customs, and religion of Holland. New York, nevertheless, was a royal province, and the administration was frequently intrusted to rapacious, unprincipled, and arbitrary governors.

Thus were the various states which border on the Atlantic Ocean colonized, in which English laws, institutions, and language were destined to be perpetuated. In 1688, the various colonies, of which there were twelve, contained about two hundred thousand inhabitants; and all of these were Protestants; all cherished the principles of civil and religious liberty, and sought, by industry, frugality and patience, to secure independence and prosperity. From that period to this, no nation has grown more rapidly; no one has ever developed more surprising energies; no one has ever enjoyed greater social, political, and religious privileges.

But the shores of North America were not colonized merely by the English. On the banks of the St. Lawrence and Mississippi another body of colonists arrived, and introduced customs and institutions equally foreign to those of the English and Spaniards. The French settlements in Canada and Louisiana are now to be considered.

Discovery of the St. Lawrence.

Within seven years from the discovery of the continent, the fisheries of Newfoundland were known to French adventurers. The St. Lawrence was explored in 1506, and plans of colonization were formed in 1518. In 1534, James Cartier, a native of St. Malo, sailed up the River St. Lawrence; but the severity of the climate in winter prevented an immediate settlement. It was not until 1603 that any permanent colonization was commenced. Quebec was then selected by Samuel Champlain, the father of the French settlements in Canada, as the site for a fort. In 1604, a charter was given, by Henry IV., to an eminent Calvinist, De Monts, which gave him the sovereignty of Acadia, a tract embraced between the fortieth and forty-sixth degrees of north latitude. The Huguenot emigrants were to enjoy their religion, the monopoly of the fur trade, and the exclusive control of the soil. They arrived at Nova Scotia the same year, and settled in Port Royal.

In 1608, Quebec was settled by Champlain, who aimed at the glory of founding a state; and in 1627 he succeeded in establishing the authority of the French on the banks of the St. Lawrence. But Champlain was also a zealous Catholic, and esteemed the salvation of a soul more than the conquest of a kingdom. He therefore selected Franciscan monks to effect the conversion of the Indians. But they were soon supplanted by the Jesuits, who, patronized by the government in France, soon made the new world the scene of their strange activity.

Jesuit Missionaries.

At no period and in no country were Jesuit missionaries more untiring laborers than amid the forests of North America. With the crucifix in their hands, they wandered about with savage tribes, and by unparalleled labors of charity and benevolence, sought to convert them to the Christianity of Rome. As early as 1635, a college and a hospital were founded, by munificent patrons in France, for the benefit of all the tribes of red men from the waters of Lake Superior to the shores of the Kennebec. In 1641 Montreal, intended as a general rendezvous for converted Indians was occupied, and soon became the most important station in Canada, next to the fortress of Quebec. Before Eliot had preached to the Indians around Boston, the intrepid missionaries of the Jesuits had explored the shores of Lake Superior, had penetrated to the Falls of St. Mary's, and had visited the Chippeways, the Hurons, the Iroquois, and the Mohawks. Soon after, they approached the Dutch settlements on the Hudson, explored the sources of the Mississippi, examined its various tributary streams, and floated down its mighty waters to its mouth. The missionaries claimed the territories on the Gulf of Mexico for the king of France, and in 1684, Louisiana was colonized by Frenchmen. The indefatigable La Salle, after having explored the Mississippi, from the Falls of St. Anthony to the sea, was assassinated by one of his envious followers, but not until he had earned the immortal fame of being the father of western colonization.

Thus were the North American settlements effected. In 1688, England possessed those colonies which border on the Atlantic Ocean, from Maine to Georgia. The French possessed Nova Scotia, Canada, Louisiana, and claimed the countries bordering on the Mississippi and its branches, from the Gulf of Mexico to Lake Superior, and also the territories around the great lakes.

A mutual jealousy, as was to be expected, sprung up between France and England respecting their colonial possessions. Both kingdoms aimed at the sovereignty of North America. The French were entitled, perhaps, by right of discovery, to the greater extent of territory; but their colonies were very unequal to those of the English in respect to numbers, and still more so in moral elevation and intellectual culture.

But Louis XIV., then in the height of his power, meditated the complete subjection of the English settlements. The French allied themselves with the Indians, and savage wars were the result. The Mohawks and other tribes, encouraged by the French, committed fearful massacres at Deerfield and Haverhill, and the English settlers were kept in a state of constant alarm and fear. By the treaty of Utrecht, in 1713, the colonists obtained peace and considerable accession of territory. In 1720, John Law proposed his celebrated financial scheme to the prince regent of France, and the Mississippi Company was chartered, and Louisiana colonized. Much profit was expected to be derived from this company. It will be seen, in another chapter, how miserably it failed. It was based on wrong foundations, and the project of deriving wealth from the colonies came to nought; nor did it result in a rapid colonization.

Prosperity of the English Colonies.

Meanwhile the English colonies advanced in wealth, numbers, and political importance, and attracted the notice of the English government. Sir Robert Walpole, in 1711, was solicited to tax the colonies; but he nobly rejected the proposal. He encouraged trade to the utmost latitude, and tribute was only levied by means of consumption of British manufactures. But restrictions were subsequently imposed on colonial enterprise, which led to collisions between the colonies and the mother country. The Southern colonies were more favored than the Northern, but all of them were regarded with the view of promoting the peculiar interests of Great Britain. Other subjects of dispute also arose; but, nevertheless, the colonies, especially those of New England, made rapid strides. There was a general diffusion of knowledge, the laws were well observed, and the ministers of religion were an honor to their sacred calling. The earth was subdued, and replenished with a hardy and religious set of men. Sentiments of patriotism and independence were ardently cherished. The people were trained to protect themselves; and, in their town meetings, learned to discuss political questions, and to understand political rights. Some ecclesiastical controversies disturbed the peace of parishes and communities, but did not retard the general prosperity. Some great lights also appeared. David Brainerd performed labors of disinterestedness and enlightened piety, which have never been surpassed, and never equalled, even in zeal and activity, except by those of the earlier Jesuits. Jonathan Edwards stamped his genius on the whole character of New England theology, and won the highest honor as a metaphysician, even from European admirers. His treatise on the Freedom of the Will has secured the praises of philosophers and divines of all sects and parties from Hume to Chalmers, and can "never be attentively perused without a sentiment of admiration at the strength and stretch of the human understanding." Benjamin Franklin also had arisen: he had not, at this early epoch, distinguished himself for philosophical discoveries; but he had attracted attention as the editor of a newspaper, in which he fearlessly defended freedom of speech and the great rights of the people. But greater than Franklin, greater than any hero which modern history has commemorated, was that young Virginia planter, who was then watching, with great solicitude, the interests and glory of his country, and preparing himself for the great conflicts which have given him immortality.

The growth of the colonies, and their great importance in the eyes of the Europeans, had now provoked the jealousy of the two leading powers of Europe, and the colonial struggle between England and France began.

French Encroachments.

The French claimed the right of erecting a chain of fortresses along the Ohio and the Mississippi, with a view to connect Canada with Louisiana, and thus obtain a monopoly of the fur trade with the Indians, and secure the possession of the finest part of the American continent. But these designs were displeasing to the English colonists, who had already extended their settlements far into the interior. The English ministry was also indignant in view of these movements, by which the colonies were completely surrounded by military posts. England protested; but the French artfully protracted negotiations until the fortifications were completed.

It was to protest against the erection of these fortresses that George Washington, then twenty-three years of age, was sent by the colony of Virginia to the banks of the Ohio. That journey through the trackless wilderness, attended but by one person, in no slight degree marked him out, and prepared him for his subsequently great career.

While the disputes about the forts were carried on between the cabinets of France and England, the French prosecuted their encroachments in America with great boldness, which doubtless hastened the rupture between the two countries. Orders were sent to the colonies to drive the French from their usurpations in Nova Scotia, and from their fortified posts upon the Ohio. Then commenced that great war, which resulted in the loss of the French possessions in America. But this war was also allied with the contests which grew out of the Austrian Succession, and therefore will be presented in a separate chapter on the Pelham administration, during which the Seven Years' War, in the latter years of the reign of George II., commenced.

European Settlements in the East.

But the colonial jealousy between England and France existed not merely in view of the North American colonies, but also those in the East Indies; and these must be alluded to in order to form a general idea of European colonization, and of the causes which led to the mercantile importance of Great Britain, as well as to the great wars which desolated the various European nations.

From the difficulties in the American colonies, we turn to those, therefore, which existed in the opposite quarter of the globe. Even to those old countries had European armies penetrated; even there European cupidity and enterprise were exercised.

As late as 1742, the territories of the English in India scarcely extended beyond the precincts of the towns in which were located the East India Company's servants. The first English settlement of importance was on the Island of Java; but, in 1658, a grant of land was obtained on the Coromandel coast, near Madras, where was erected the strong fortress of St. George. In 1668, the Island of Bombay was ceded by the crown of Portugal to Charles II., and appointed the capital of the British settlements in India. In 1698, the English had a settlement on the Hooghly, which afterwards became the metropolis of British power.

French Settlements in India.

But the Dutch, and Portuguese, and French had also colonies in India for purposes of trade. Louis XIV. established a company, in imitation of the English, which sought a settlement on the Hooghly. The French company also had built a fort on the coast of the Carnatic, about eighty miles south of Madras, called Pondicherry, and had colonized two fertile islands in the Indian Ocean, which they called the Isle of France and the Isle of Bourbon. The possessions of the French were controlled by two presidencies, one on the Isle of France, and the other at Pondicherry.

La Bourdonnais and Dupleix.

When the war broke out between England and France, in 1744, these two French presidencies were ruled by two men of superior genius,—La Bourdonnais and Dupleix,—both of them men of great experience in Indian affairs, and both devoted to the interests of the company, so far as their own personal ambition would permit. When Commodore Burnet, with an English squadron, was sent into the Indian seas, La Bourdonnais succeeded in fitting out an expedition to oppose it, and even contemplated the capture of Madras. No decisive action was fought at sea; but the French governor succeeded in taking Madras. This success displeased the Nabob of the Carnatic, and he sent a letter to Dupleix, and complained of the aggression of his countrymen in attacking a place under his protection. Dupleix, envious of the fame of La Bourdonnais, and not pleased with the terms of capitulation, as being too favorable to the English, claimed the right of annulling the conquest, since Madras, when taken, would fall under his own presidency.

The contentions between these two Frenchmen prevented La Bourdonnais from following up the advantage of his victory, and he failed in his attempts to engage the English fleet, and, in consequence, returned to France, and died from the effects of an unjust imprisonment in the Bastile.

Dupleix, after the departure of La Bourdonnais, brought the principal inhabitants of Madras to Pondicherry. But some of them contrived to escape. Among them was the celebrated Clive, then a clerk in a mercantile house. He entered as an ensign into the company's service, and soon found occasion to distinguish himself.

But Dupleix, master of Madras, now formed the scheme of founding an Indian empire, and of expelling the English from the Carnatic. And India was in a state to favor his enterprises. The empire of the Great Mogul, whose capital was Delhi, was tottering from decay. It had been, in the sixteenth century, the most powerful empire in the world. The magnificence of his palaces astonished even Europeans accustomed to the splendor of Paris and Versailles. His viceroys ruled over provinces larger and richer than either France or England. And even the lieutenants of these viceroys frequently aspired to independence.

The Nabob of Arcot was one of these latter princes. He hated the French, and befriended the English. On the death of the Viceroy of the Deccan, to whom he was subject, in 1748, Dupleix conceived his gigantic scheme of conquest. To the throne of this viceroy there were several claimants, two of whom applied to the French for assistance. This was what the Frenchman desired, and he allied himself with the pretenders. With the assistance of the French, Mirzappa Juy obtained the viceroyalty. Dupleix was splendidly rewarded, and was intrusted with the command of seven thousand Indian cavalry, and received a present of two hundred thousand pounds.

The only place on the Carnatic which remained in possession of the rightful viceroy was Trichinopoly, and this was soon invested by the French and Indian forces.

To raise this siege, and turn the tide of French conquest, became the object of Clive, then twenty-five years of age. He represented to his superior the importance of this post, and also of striking a decisive blow. He suggested the plan of an attack on Arcot itself, the residence of the nabob. His project was approved, and he was placed at the head of a force of three hundred sepoys and two hundred Englishmen. The city was taken by surprise, and its capture induced the nabob to relinquish the siege of Trichinopoly in order to retake his capital. But Clive so intrenched his followers, that they successfully defended the place after exhibiting prodigies of valor. The fortune of war turned to the side of the gallant Englishman, and Dupleix, who was no general, retreated before the victors. Clive obtained the command of Fort St. David, an important fortress near Madras, and soon controlled the Carnatic.

About this time, the settlements on the Hooghly were plundered by Suraj-w Dowlah, Viceroy of Bengal. Bengal was the most fertile and populous province of the empire of the Great Mogul. It was watered by the Ganges, the sacred river of India, and its cities were surprisingly rich. Its capital was Moorshedabad, a city nearly as large as London; and here the young viceroy lived in luxury and effeminacy, and indulged in every species of cruelty and folly. He hated the English of Calcutta, and longed to plunder them. He accordingly seized the infant city, and shut up one hundred and forty of the colonists in a dungeon of the fort, a room twenty feet by fourteen, with only two small windows; and in a few hours, one hundred and seventeen of the English died. The horrors of that night have been splendidly painted by Macaulay in his essay on Clive, and the place of torment, called the *Black Hole of Calcutta*, is synonymous with suffering and misery. Clive resolved to avenge this insult to his countrymen. An expedition was fitted out at Madras to punish the inhuman nabob, consisting of nine hundred Europeans and fifteen hundred sepoys. It was a small force, but proved sufficient. Calcutta was recovered and the army of the nabob was routed. Clive intrigued with the enemies of the despot in his own city; and, by means of unparalleled treachery, dissimulation, art, and violence, Suraj-w Dowlah was deposed, and Meer Jaffier, one of the conspirators, was made nabob in his place. In return for the services of Clive, the new viceroy splendidly rewarded him. A hundred boats conveyed the treasures of Bengal down the river to

Calcutta. Clive himself, who had walked between heaps of gold and silver, crowned with diamonds and rubies, condescended to receive a present of three hundred thousand pounds. His moderation has been commended by his biographers in not asking for a million.

The elevation of Meer Jaffier was, of course, displeasing to the imbecile Emperor of India, and a large army was sent to dethrone him. The nabob appealed, in his necessity, to his allies, the English, and, with the powerful assistance of the Europeans, the forces of the successor of the great Aurungzebe were signally routed. But the great sums he was obliged to bestow on his allies, and the encroaching spirit which they manifested, changed his friendship into enmity. He plotted with the Dutch and the French to overturn the power of the English. Clive divined his object, and Meer Jaffier was deposed in his turn. The Viceroy of Bengal was but the tool of his English protectors, and British power was firmly planted in the centre of India. Calcutta became the capital of a great empire, and the East India Company, a mere assemblage of merchants and stockjobbers, by their system of perfidy, craft and violence, became the rulers and disposers of provinces which Alexander had coveted in vain. The servants of this company made their fortunes, and untold wealth was transported to England. Clive obtained a fortune of forty thousand pounds a year, an Irish peerage, and a seat in the House of Commons. He became an object of popular idolatry, courted by ministers, and extolled by Pitt. He was several times appointed governor-general of the country he had conquered, and to him England is indebted for the foundation of her power in India. But his fame and fortune finally excited the jealousy of his countrymen, and he was made to bear the sins of the company which he had enriched. The malignity with which he was pursued, and the disease which he acquired in India, operated unfortunately on a temper naturally irritable; his reason became overpowered, and he died, in 1774, by his own hand.

Conquest of India.

The subsequent career of Hastings, and final conquest of India, form part of the political history of England itself, during those administrations which yet remain to be described. The colonization of America and the East Indies now became involved with the politics of rival statesmen; and its history can only be appreciated by considering those acts and principles which marked the career of the Newcastles and the Pitts. The administration of the Pelhams, therefore, next claims attention.

References.—The best histories pertaining to the conquests of the Spaniards are undoubtedly those of Mr. Prescott. Irving's Columbus should also be consulted. For the early history of the North American colonies, the attention of students is directed to Grahame's and Bancroft's Histories of the United States. In regard to India, see Elphinstone's, Gleig's, Ormes's, and Mills's Histories of India; Malcolm's Life of Clive; and Macaulay's Essay on Clive. For the contemporaneous history of Great Britain, the best works are those of Tyndal, Smollett, Lord Mahon, and Belsham; Russell's Modern Europe; the Pictorial History of England; and the continuation of Mackintosh, in Lardner's Cabinet Cyclopedia.

CHAPTER XXI
THE REIGN OF GEORGE II

The English nation acquiesced in the government of Sir Robert Walpole for nearly thirty years—the longest administration in the annals of the country. And he was equal to the task, ruling, on the whole, beneficently, promoting peace, regulating the finances, and encouraging those great branches of industry which lie at the foundation of English wealth and power. But the intrigues of rival politicians, and the natural desire of change, which all parties feel after a long repose, plunged the nation into war, and forced the able minister to retire. The opposition, headed by the Prince of Wales, supported by such able statesmen as Bolingbroke, Carteret, Chesterfield, Pulteney, Windham, and Pitt, and sustained by the writings of those great literary geniuses whom Walpole disdained and neglected, compelled George II., at last, to part with a man who had conquered his narrow prejudices.

But the Tories did not come into power on the retirement of Walpole. His old confederates remained at the head of affairs, and Carteret, afterwards Lord Granville, the most brilliant man of his age, became the leading minister. But even he, so great in debate, and so distinguished for varied attainments, did not long retain his place. None of the abuses which existed under the former administration were removed; and moreover the war which the nation had clamored for, had proved disastrous. He also had to bear the consequences of Walpole's temporizing policy which could no longer be averted.

The Pelhams.

The new ministry was headed by Henry Pelham, as first lord of the treasury and chancellor of the exchequer, and by the Duke of Newcastle, as principal secretary of state. These two men formed, also, a coalition with the leading members of both houses of parliament, Tories as well as Whigs; and, for the first time since the accession of the Stuarts, there was no opposition. This great coalition was called the "Broad Bottom," and comprehended the Duke of Bedford, the Earls of Chesterfield and Harrington, Lords Lyttleton and Hardwicke, Sir Henry Cotton, Mr Doddington, Mr. Pitt, Mr. Fox, and Mr. Murray. The three latter statesmen were not then formidable.

The Pelhams were descended from one of the oldest, proudest and richest families in England, and had an immense parliamentary influence from their aristocratic connections, their wealth, and their experience. They were not remarkable for genius so much as for sagacity, tact, and intrigue. They were extremely ambitious, and fond of place and power. They ruled England as the representatives of the aristocracy—the last administration which was able to defy the national will. After their fall, the people had a greater voice in the appointment of ministers. Pitt and Fox were commoners in a different sense from what Walpole was, and represented that class which has ever since ruled England,—not nobles, not the democracy, but a class between them, composed of the gentry, landed proprietors, lawyers, merchants, manufacturers, men of leisure, and their dependants.

The administration of the Pelhams is chiefly memorable for the Scotch rebellion of 1745, and for the great European war which grew out of colonial and commercial ambition, and the encroachments of Frederic the Great.

The Pretender Charles Edward Stuart.

The Scotch rebellion was produced by the attempts of the young Pretender, Charles Edward Louis Philip Casimir Stuart, to regain the throne of his ancestors. His adventures have the interest of romance, and have generally excited popular sympathy. He was born at Rome in 1720; served, at the age of fifteen, under the Duke of Berwick, in Spain, and, at the age of twenty, received overtures from some discontented people of Scotland to head an insurrection. There was, at this time, great public distress, and George II. was exceedingly unpopular. The Jacobites were powerful, and thousands wished for a change, including many persons of rank and influence.

With only seven followers, in a small vessel, he landed on one of the Western Islands, 18th of July, 1745. Even had the promises which had been made to him by France, or by people in Scotland, been fulfilled, his enterprise would have been most hazardous. But, without money, men, or arms, his hopes were desperate. Still he cherished that presumptuous self-confidence which so often passes for bravery, and succeeded better than could have been anticipated. Several chieftains of the Highland clans joined his standard, and he had the faculty of gaining the hearts of his followers. At Borrodaile occurred his first interview with the chivalrous Donald Cameron of Lochiel, who was perfectly persuaded of the desperate character of his enterprise, but nevertheless aided it with generous self-devotion.

The standard of Charles Edward was raised at Glenfinnan, on the 19th of August, and a little band of seven hundred adventurers and enthusiastic Highlanders resolved on the conquest of England! Never was devotion to an unfortunate cause more romantic and sincere. Never were energies more generously made, or more miserably directed. But the first gush of enthusiasm and bravery was attended with success, and the Pretender soon found himself at the head of fifteen hundred men, and on his way to Edinburgh, marching among people friendly to his cause, whom he endeared by every attention and gentlemanly artifice. The simple people of the north of Scotland were won by his smiles and courtesy, and were astonished at the exertions which the young prince made, and the fatigues he was able to endure.

On the 15th of September, Charles had reached Linlithgow, only sixteen miles from Edinburgh, where he was magnificently entertained in the ancient and favorite palace of the kings of Scotland. Two days after, he made his triumphal entry into the capital of his ancestors, the place being unprepared for resistance. Colonel Gardiner, with his regiment of dragoons, was faithful to his trust, and the magistrates of Edinburgh did all in their power to prevent the surrender of the city. But the great body of the citizens preferred to trust to the clemency of Charles, than run the risk of defence.

Surrender of Edinburgh.

Thus, without military stores, or pecuniary resources, or powerful friends, simply by the power of persuasion, the Pretender, in the short space of two months from his landing in Scotland, quietly took possession of the most powerful city of the north. The Jacobites put no restraint to their idolatrous homage, and the ladies welcomed the young and handsome chevalier with extravagant adulation. Even the Whigs pitied him, and permitted him to enjoy his brief hour of victory.

At Edinburgh, Charles received considerable reënforcement, and took from the city one thousand stand of arms. He gave his followers but little time for repose, and soon advanced against the royal army commanded by Sir John Cope. The two armies met at Preston Pans, and were of nearly equal force. The attack was made by the invader, and was impetuous and unlooked for. Nothing could stand before the enthusiasm and valor of the Highlanders, and in five minutes the rout commenced, and a great slaughter of the regular army occurred. Among those who fell was the distinguished Colonel Gardiner, an old veteran, who refused to fly.

Success of the Pretender.

Charles followed up his victory with moderation, and soon was master of all Scotland. He indulged his taste for festivities, at Holyrood, for a while, and neglected no means to conciliate the Scotch. He flattered their prejudices, gave balls and banquets, made love to their most beautiful women, and denied no one access to his presence. Poets sang his praises, and women extolled his heroism and beauty. The light, the gay, the romantic, and the adventurous were on his side; but the substantial and wealthy classes were against him, for they knew he must be conquered in the end.

Still his success had been remarkable, and for it he was indebted to the Highlanders, who did not wish to make him king of England, but only king of Scotland. But Charles deceived them. He wanted the sceptre of George II.; and when he commenced his march into England, their spirits flagged, and his cause became hopeless. There was one class of men who were inflexibly hostile to him—the Presbyterian ministers. They looked upon him, from the first, with coldness and harshness, and distrusted both his religion and sincerity. On them all his arts, and flattery, and graces were lost; and they represented the substantial part of the Scottish nation. It is extremely doubtful whether Charles could ever have held Edinburgh, even if English armies had not been sent against him.

But Charles had played a desperate game from the beginning, for the small chance of winning a splendid prize. He, therefore, after resting his troops, and collecting all the force he could, turned his face to England at the head of five thousand men, well armed and well clothed, but discontented and dispirited. They had never contemplated the invasion of England, but only the recovery of the ancient independence of Scotland.

On the 8th of November, the Pretender set foot upon English soil, and entered Carlisle in triumph. But his forces, instead of increasing, diminished, and no popular enthusiasm supported the courage of his troops. But he advanced towards the south, and reached Derby unmolested on the 4th of December. There he learned that the royal army, headed by the Duke of Cumberland, with twelve thousand veterans, was advancing rapidly against him.

His followers clamored to return, and refused to advance another step. They now fully perceived that success was not only hopeless, but that victory would be of no advantage to them; that they would be sacrificed by a man who only aimed at the conquest of England.

The Retreat of the Pretender.

Charles was well aware of the desperate nature of the contest, but had no desire to retreat. His situation was not worse than what it had been when he landed on the Hebrides. Having penetrated to within one hundred and twenty miles of London, against the expectations of every one, why should he not persevere? Some unlooked-for success, some lucky incidents, might restore him to the throne of his grandfather. Besides, a French army of ten thousand was about to land in England. The Duke of Norfolk, the first nobleman in the country, was ready to declare in his favor. London was in commotion. A chance remained.

But his followers thought only of their homes, and Charles was obliged to yield to an irresistible necessity. Like Richard Cœur de Lion after the surrender of Acre, he was compelled to return, without realizing the fruit of bravery and success. Like the lion-hearted king, pensive and sad, sullen and miserable, he gave the order to retreat. His spirits, hitherto buoyant and gladsome, now fell, and despondency and despair succeeded vivacity and hope. He abandoned himself to grief and vexation, lingered behind his retreating army, and was reckless of his men and of their welfare. And well he may have been depressed. The motto of Hampden, "*Vestigia nulla retrorsum*," had also governed him. But others would not be animated by it, and he was ruined.

Battle of Culloden.

But his miserable and dejected army succeeded in reaching their native soil, although pursued by the cavalry of two powerful armies, in the midst of a hostile population, and amid great sufferings from hunger and fatigue. On the 26th of December, he entered Glasgow, levied a contribution on the people, and prepared himself for his final battle. He retreated to the Highlands, and spent the winter in recruiting his troops, and in taking fortresses. On the 15th of April, 1746, he drew up his army on the moor of Culloden, near Inverness, with the desperate resolution of attacking, with vastly inferior forces, the Duke of Cumberland, intrenched nine miles distant. The design was foolish and unfortunate. It was early discovered; and the fresh troops of the royal duke attacked the dispirited, scattered, and wearied followers of Charles Edward before they could form themselves in battle array. They defended themselves with valor. But what is valor against overwhelming force? The army of Charles was totally routed, and his hopes were blasted forever.

The most horrid barbarities and cruelties were inflicted by the victors. The wounded were left to die. The castles of rebel chieftains were razed to the ground. Herds and flocks were driven away, and the people left to perish with hunger. Some of the captives were sent to Barbadoes, others were imprisoned, and many were shot. A reward of thirty thousand pounds was placed on the head of the Pretender; but he nevertheless escaped. After wandering a while as a fugitive, disguised, wearied, and miserable, hunted from fortress to fortress, and from island to island, he succeeded, by means of the unparalleled loyalty and fidelity of his few Highland followers, in securing a vessel, and in escaping to France. His adventures among the Western Islands, especially those which happened while wandering, in the disguise of a female servant, with Flora Macdonald, are highly romantic and wonderful. Equally wonderful is the fact that, of the many to whom his secret was intrusted, not one was disposed to betray him, even in view of so splendid a bribe as thirty thousand pounds. But this fact, though surprising, is not inconceivable. Had Washington been unfortunate in his contest with the mother country, and had he wandered as a fugitive amid the mountains of Vermont, would not many Americans have shielded him, even in view of a reward of one hundred thousand pounds?

Latter Days of the Pretender.

The latter days of the Pretender were spent in Rome and Florence. He married a Polish princess, and assumed the title of *Duke of Albany*. He never relinquished the hope of securing the English crown, and always retained his politeness and grace of manner. But he became an object of pity, not merely from his poverty and misfortunes, but also from the vice of intemperance, which he acquired in Scotland. He died of apoplexy, in 1788, and left no legitimate issue. The last male heir of the house of Stuart was the Cardinal of York, who died in 1807, and who was buried in St. Peter's Cathedral; over whose mortal remains was erected a marble monument, by Canova, through the munificence of George IV., to whom the cardinal had left the crown jewels which James II. had carried with him to France. This monument bears the names of James III., Charles III., and Henry IX., kings of England; titles never admitted by the English. With the battle of Culloden expired the hopes of the Catholics and Jacobites to restore Catholicism and the Stuarts.

The great European war, which was begun by Sir Robert Walpole, not long before his retirement, was another great event which happened during the administration of the Pelhams, and with which their administration was connected. The Spanish war was followed by the war of the Austrian Succession.

Maria Theresa.

Maria Theresa, Queen of Hungary, ascended the oldest and proudest throne of Europe,—that of Germany,—amid a host of claimants. The Elector of Bavaria laid claim to her hereditary dominions in Bohemia; the King of Sardinia made pretension to the duchy of Milan; while the Kings of Poland, Spain, France, and Prussia disputed with her her rights to the whole Austrian succession. Never were acts of gross injustice meditated with greater audacity. Just as the young and beautiful princess ascended the throne of Charlemagne, amid embarrassments and perplexities,—such as an exhausted treasury, a small army, a general scarcity, threatened hostilities with the Turks, and absolute war with France, — the new king of Prussia, Frederic, surnamed the Great, availing himself of her distresses, seized one of the finest provinces of her empire. The first notice which the queen had of the seizure of Silesia, was an insulting speech from the Prussian ambassador. "I come," said he, "with safety for the house of Austria on the one hand, and the imperial crown for your royal highness on the other. The troops of my master are at the service of the queen, and cannot fail of being acceptable, at a time when she is in want of both. And as the king, my master, from the situation of his dominions, will be exposed to great danger from this alliance with the Queen of Hungary, it is hoped that, as an indemnification, the queen will not offer him less than the whole duchy of Silesia."

The queen, of course, was indignant in view of this cool piece of villany, and prepared to resist. War with all the continental powers was the result. France joined the coalition to deprive the queen of her empire. Two French armies invaded Germany. The Elector of Bavaria marched, with a hostile army, to within eight miles of Vienna. The King of Prussia made himself master of Silesia. Abandoned by all her allies, — without an army, or ministers, or money, — the queen fled to Hungary, her hereditary dominions, and threw herself on the generosity of her subjects. She invoked the states of the Diet, and, clad in deep mourning, with the crown of St. Stephen on her head, and a cimeter at her side, she traversed the hall in which her nobles were assembled, and addressed them, in the immortal language of Rome, respecting her wrongs and her distresses. Her faithful subjects responded to her call; and youth, beauty, and rank, in distress, obtained their natural triumph. "A thousand swords leaped from their scabbards," and the old hall rung with the cry, "We will die for our queen, Maria Theresa." Tears started from the eyes of the queen, whom misfortunes and insult could not bend, and called forth, even more than her words, the enthusiasm of her subjects.

It was in defence of this injured and noble queen that the English parliament voted supplies and raised armies. This was the war which characterized the Pelham administration, and to which Walpole was opposed. But it will be further presented, when allusion is made to Frederic the Great.

France no sooner formed an alliance with Prussia, against Austria, than the "balance of power" seemed to be disturbed. To restore this balance, and preserve Austria, was the aim of England. To the desire to preserve this power may be traced most of the wars of the eighteenth century. The idea of a balance of power was the leading principle which animated all the diplomatic transactions of Europe for more than a century.

By the treaty of Breslau, (1742,) Maria Theresa yielded up to Frederic the province of Silesia, and Europe might have remained at peace. But as England and France were both involved in the contest, their old spirit of rivalry returned; and, from auxiliaries, they became principals in the war, and soon renewed it. The theatre of strife was changed from Germany to Holland, and the arms of France were triumphant. The Duke of Cumberland was routed by Marshal Saxe at the great battle of Fontenoy; and this battle restored peace, for a while, to Germany. The Grand Duke of Tuscany, husband of Maria Theresa, was elected Emperor of Germany, and assumed the title of Francis I.

But it was easier to restore tranquillity to Germany, than peace between England and France; both powers panting for military glory, and burning with mutual jealousy. The peace of Aix la Chapelle, in 1748, was a truce rather than a treaty; and France and England soon found occasion to plunge into new hostilities.

Capture of Louisburg.

During the war of the Austrian Succession, hostilities had not been confined to the continent of Europe. As colonial jealousy was one of the animating principles of two of the leading powers in the contest, the warfare extended to the colonies themselves. A body of French, from Cape Breton, surprised the little English garrison of Canseau, destroyed the fort and fishery, and removed eighty men, as prisoners of war, to Louisburg— the strongest fortress, next to Quebec, in French America. These men were afterwards sent to Boston, on parole, and, while there, communicated to Governor Shirley the state of the fortress in which they had been confined. Shirley resolved to capture it, and the legislature of Massachusetts voted supplies for the expedition. All the New England colonies sent volunteers; and the united forces, of about four thousand men were put under the command of William Pepperell, a merchant at Kittery Point, near Portsmouth. The principal part of the forces was composed of fishermen; but they were Yankees. Amid the fogs of April, this little army, rich in expedients, set sail to take a fortress which five hundred men could defend against five thousand. But they were successful, aided by an English fleet; and, after a siege of three months, Louisburg surrendered, (1745)—justly deemed the greatest achievement of the whole war.

Great Colonial Contest.

But the French did not relinquish their hopes of gaining an ascendency on the American continent, and prosecuted their labors of erecting on the Ohio their chain of fortifications, to connect Canada with Louisiana. The erection of these forts was no small cause of the breaking out of fresh hostilities. When the contest was renewed between Maria Theresa and Frederic the Great, and the famous Seven Years' War began, the English resolved to conquer all the French possessions in America.

Without waiting, however, for directions from England, Governor Dinwiddie, of Virginia, raised a regiment of troops, of which George Washington was made lieutenant-colonel, and with which he marched across the wilderness to attack Fort Du Quesne, now Pittsburg, at the junction of the Alleghany and Monongahela Rivers.

That unsuccessful expedition was the commencement of the great colonial contest in which Canada was conquered. Early in 1755, General Braddock was sent to America to commence offensive operations. The colonies coöperated, and three expeditions were planned; one to attack Fort Du Quesne, a second to attack Fort Niagara, and a third to attack Crown Point. The first was to be composed of British troops, under Braddock, the second of American, under Governor Shirley, and the third of militia of the northern colonies.

The expedition against Fort Du Quesne was a memorable failure. Braddock was a brave man, but unfitted for his work, Hyde Park having hitherto been the only field of his military operations. Moreover, with that presumption and audacity which then characterized his countrymen, he affected sovereign contempt for his American associates, and would listen to no advice. Unacquainted with Indian warfare, and ignorant of the country, he yet pressed towards the interior, until, within ten miles of Fort Du Quesne, he was surprised by a body of French and Indians, and taken in an ambuscade. Instant retreat might still have saved him; but he was too proud not to fight according to rule; and he fell mortally wounded. Washington was the only mounted officer that escaped being killed or wounded. By his prudent and skilful management, he saved half of his men, who formed after the battle, and effected a retreat.

The other two expeditions also failed, chiefly through want of union between the provincial governor and the provincial assemblies, and also from the moral effects of the defeat of Braddock. Moreover, the colonies perfectly understood that they were fighting, not for liberty, but for the glory and ambition of the mother country, and therefore did not exhibit the ardor they evinced in the revolutionary struggle.

But the failure of these expeditions contributed to make the ministry of the Duke of Newcastle unpopular. Other mistakes were also made in the old world. The conduct of Admiral Byng in the Mediterranean excited popular clamor. The repeated disappointments and miscarriages, the delay of armaments, the neglect of opportunities, the absurd disposition of fleets, were numbered among the misfortunes which resulted from a weak and incapable ministry. Stronger men were demanded by the indignant voice of the nation, and the Duke of Newcastle, first lord of the treasury, since the death of his brother, was obliged to call Mr. Pitt and Mr. Legge—the two most popular commoners of England—into the cabinet. But the new administration did not work harmoniously. It was an emblem of that image which Nebuchadnezzar beheld in a vision, with a head of gold, and legs of iron, and feet of clay. Pitt and Legge were obliged by their colleague to resign. But their removal incensed the whole nation, and so great was the clamor, that the king was compelled to reinstate the popular idols—the only men capable of managing affairs at that crisis. Pitt became secretary of state, and Legge chancellor of the exchequer. The Duke of Newcastle, after being at the head of administration ten years, was, reluctantly, compelled to resign. The Duke of Devonshire became nominally the premier, but Pitt was the ruling spirit in the cabinet.

Character of the Duke of Newcastle.

The character of the Duke of Newcastle is thus sketched by Horace Walpole; "He had no pride, but infinite self-love. Jealousy was the great source of all his faults. There was no expense to which he was addicted but generosity. His houses, gardens, table, and equipage, swallowed immense sums, and the sums he owed were only exceeded by those he wasted. He loved business immoderately, but was always doing it; he never did it. His speeches were copious in words, but empty and unmeaning, his professions extravagant, and his curiosity insatiable. He was a secretary of state without intelligence, a duke without money, a man of infinite intrigue without secrecy, and a minister hated by all parties, without being turned out by either." "All able men," adds Macaulay, "ridiculed him as a dunce, a driveller, a child who never knew his own mind an hour together; and yet he overreached them all."

Unpopularity of the Pelhams.

The Pelham administration cannot, on the whole, be called fortunate, nor, on the other hand, a disgraceful one. The Pelhams "showed themselves," says Smyth, "friendly to the principles of mild government." With all their faults, they were tolerant, peaceful, prudent; they had the merit of respecting public opinion; and though they were not fitted to advance the prosperity of their country by any exertions of political genius, they were not blind to such opportunities as fairly presented themselves. But they were not fitted for the stormy times in which they lived, and quietly yielded to the genius of a man whom they did not like, and whom the king absolutely hated.

George II., against his will, was obliged to intrust the helm of state to the only man in the nation capable of holding it.

The administration of William Pitt is emphatically the history of the civilized world, during a period of almost universal war. It was for his talents as a war minister that he was placed at the head of the government, and his policy, like that of his greater son, in a still more stormy epoch, was essentially warlike. In the eyes of his contemporaries, his administration was brilliant and successful, and he undoubtedly raised England to a high pitch of military glory; but glory, alas! most dearly purchased, since it led to the imposition of taxes beyond a parallel, and the vast increase of the national debt.

Rise of William Pitt.

He was born in 1708, of good family, his grandfather having been governor of Madras, and the purchaser of the celebrated diamond which bears his name, and which was sold to the regent of France for one hundred and thirty-five thousand pounds. William Pitt was sent to Oxford at the age of seventeen, and at twenty-seven, became a member of parliament. From the first, he was heard with attention, and, when years and experience had given him wisdom and power, his eloquence was overwhelming. No one ever equalled him in brilliant invective and scorching sarcasm. He had not the skill of Fox in debate, nor was he a great reasoner, like Murray; he did not talk philosophy, like Burke, nor was he master of details, like his son; but he had an air of sincerity, a vehemence of feeling, an intense enthusiasm, and a moral elevation of sentiment, which bore every thing away before him.

When Walpole was driven from power, Pitt exerted his eloquence in behalf of the Pelham government. Being personally obnoxious to the king, he obtained no office. But he was not a man to be amused by promises long, and, as he would not render his indispensable services without a reward, he was made paymaster of the forces—a lucrative office, but one which did not give him a seat in the cabinet. This office he retained for eight years, which were years of peace. But when the horizon was overclouded by the death of Henry Pelham, in 1754, and difficulties arose between France and England respecting North America and the East Indies; when disasters in war tarnished the glory of the British arms, and the Duke of Newcastle showed his incapacity to meet the national crisis, Pitt commenced a furious opposition. Of course he was dismissed from office. But the Duke of Newcastle could not do without him, and the king was obliged to call him into the cabinet as secretary of state, in 1756. But the administration did not work. The king opposed the views of Pitt, and he was compelled to resign. Then followed disasters and mistakes. The resignation of the Duke of Newcastle became an imperative necessity. Despondency and gloom hung over the nation, and he was left without efficient aid in the House of Commons. Nothing was left to the king but to call in the aid of the man he hated; and Pitt, as well as Legge, were again reinstated, the Duke of Devonshire remaining nominally at the head of the administration.

But this administration only lasted five months, during which Admiral Byng was executed, and the Seven Years' War, of which Frederic of Prussia was the hero, fairly commenced. In 1757, Pitt and his colleague were again dismissed. But never was popular resentment more fierce and terrible. Again was the king obliged to bend to the "great commoner." An arrangement was made, and a coalition formed. Pitt became secretary of state, and virtual premier, but the Duke of Newcastle came in as first lord of the treasury. But Pitt selected the cabinet. His brother-in-law, Lord Temple, was made keeper of the privy seal, and Lord Grenville was made treasurer of the navy; Fox became paymaster of the forces; the Duke of Bedford received the lord lieutenancy of Ireland; Hardwicke, the greatest lawyer of his age became lord chancellor; Legge, the ablest financier, was made chancellor of the exchequer. Murray, a little while before, had been elevated to the bench, as Lord Mansfield. There was scarcely an eminent man in the House of Commons who was not made a member of the administration. All the talent of the nation was laid at the feet of Pitt, and he had the supreme direction of the army and of foreign affairs.

Then truly commenced the brilliant career of Pitt. He immediately prosecuted hostilities with great boldness, and on a gigantic scale. Immense armies were raised and sent to all parts of the world.

Brilliant Military Successes.

But nothing raised the reputation of Pitt so highly as military operations in America. He planned, immediately on his assumption of supreme power as virtual dictator of England, three great expeditions—one against Louisburg, a second against Ticonderoga, and a third against Fort Du Quesne. Two of these were attended with triumphant success, (1758.)

Louisburg, which had been surrendered to France by the treaty of Aix la Chapelle, was reduced by General Amherst, though only with a force of fourteen thousand men.

General Forbes marched, with eight thousand men, against Fort Du Quesne; but it was abandoned by the enemy before he reached it.

Ticonderoga was not, however, taken, although the expedition was conducted by General Abercrombie, with a force of sixteen thousand men.

Thus nearly the largest military force ever known at one time in America was employed nearly a century ago, by William Pitt, composed of fifty thousand men, of whom twenty-two thousand were regular troops.

Military Successes in America.

The campaign of 1759 was attended with greater results than even that of the preceding year. General Amherst succeeded Abercrombie, and the plan for the reduction of Canada was intrusted to him for execution. Three great expeditions were projected: one was to be commanded by General Wolfe, who had distinguished himself at the siege of Louisburg, and who had orders from the war secretary to ascend the St. Lawrence, escorted by the fleet, and lay siege to Quebec. The second army, of twelve thousand men, under General Amherst, was ordered to reduce Ticonderoga and Crown Point, cross Lake Champlain, and proceed along the River Richelieu to the banks of the St. Lawrence, join General Wolfe, and assist in the reduction of Quebec. The third army was sent to Fort Niagara, the most important post in French America, since it commanded the lakes, and overawed the whole country of the Six Nations. After the reduction of this fort, the army was ordered down the St. Lawrence to besiege Montreal.

That this project was magnificent, and showed the comprehensive military genius of Pitt, cannot be doubted. But that it was easy of execution may well be questioned, when it is remembered that the navigation of the St. Lawrence was difficult and dangerous; that the fortifications and strength of Quebec were unrivalled in the new world; that the French troops between Montreal and Quebec numbered nine thousand men, besides Indians, commanded, too, by so great a general as Montcalm. Still all of these expeditions were successful. Quebec and Niagara were taken, and Crown Point and Ticonderoga were abandoned.

The most difficult part of the enterprise was the capture of Quebec, which was one of the most brilliant military exploits ever performed, and which raised the English general to the very summit of military fame. He was disappointed in the expected coöperation of General Amherst, and he had to take one of the strongest fortresses in the world, defended by troops superior in number to his own. He succeeded in climbing the almost perpendicular rock on which the fortress was built, and in overcoming a superior force. Wolfe died in the attack, but lived long enough to hear of the flight of the enemy. Nothing could exceed the tumultuous joy in England with which the news of the fall of Quebec was received; nothing could surpass the interest with which the distant expedition was viewed; and the depression of the French was equal to the enthusiasm of the English. Wolfe gained an immortal name, and a monument was erected to him in Westminster Abbey. But Pitt reaped the solid and substantial advantages which resulted from the conquest of Canada, which soon followed the reduction of Quebec. He became the nation's idol, and was left to prosecute the various wars in which England was engaged, in his own way.

Victories of Clive in India.

While the English armies, under the direction of Pitt, were wresting from the French nearly all their possessions in America, Clive was adding a new empire to the vast dominions of Great Britain. India was conquered, and the British power firmly planted in the East. Moreover, the English allies on the continent—the Prussians—obtained great victories, which will be alluded to in the chapter on Frederic the Great. On all sides the English were triumphant, and were intoxicated with joy. The stocks rose, and the bells rang almost an incessant peal for victories.

In the midst of these public rejoicings, King George II. died. He was a sovereign who never secured the affections of the nation, whose interests he sacrificed to those of his German electorate, "He had neither the qualities which make libertinism attractive nor the qualities which make dulness respectable. He had been a bad son, and he made a worse father. Not one magnanimous action is recorded of him, but many meannesses. But his judgment was sound, his habits economical, and his spirit bold. These qualities prevented him from being despised, if they did not make him honored."

His grandson, George III., entered upon his long reign, October, 1760, in the twenty-third year of his age, and was universally admitted to be the most powerful monarch in Christendom—or, rather, the monarch of the most powerful kingdom. He, or, rather, his ministers, resolved to prosecute the war with vigor, and parliament voted liberal supplies. The object of Pitt was the humiliation of both France and Austria, and also the protection of Prussia, struggling against almost overwhelming forces. He secured his object by administering to the nation those draughts of flattery and military glory which intoxicated the people.

Resignation of Pitt.

However sincere the motives and brilliant the genius of the minister, it was impossible that a practical nation should not awake from the delusion, which he so powerfully contributed to produce. People at last inquired "why England was to become a party in a dispute between two German powers, and why were the best English regiments fighting on the Maine?" What was it to the busy shopkeeper of London that the Tower guns were discharged, and the streets illuminated, if he were to be additionally taxed? Statesmen began to calculate the enormous sums which had been wasted in an expensive war, where nothing had been gained but glory. Besides, jealousies and enmities sprung up against Pitt. Some were offended by his haughtiness, and others were estranged by his withering invective. And his enemies were numerous and powerful. Even the cabinet ministers, who were his friends, turned against him. He wished to declare war against Spain, while the nation was bleeding at every pore. But the cabinet could not be persuaded of the necessity of the war, and Pitt, of course, resigned. But it was inevitable, and took place under his successor. Pitt left the helm of state with honor. He received a pension of three thousand pounds a year, and his wife was made a baroness.

The Earl of Bute succeeded him as premier, and was the first Tory minister since the accession of the house of Hanover. His watchword was *prerogative*. The sovereign should no longer be a gilded puppet, but a real king—an impossible thing in England. But his schemes pleased the king, and Oxford University, and Dr. Johnson; while his administration was assailed with a host of libels from Wilkes, Churchill, and other kindred firebrands.

His main act was the peace he secured to Europe. The Whigs railed at it then, and rail at it now; and Macaulay falls in with the lamentation of his party, and regrets that no better terms should have been made. But what can satisfy the ambition of England? The peace of Paris, in 1763, stipulated that Canada, with the Island of St. John, and Cape Breton, and all that part of Louisiana which lies east of the Mississippi, except New Orleans, should be ceded to Great Britain, and that the fortifications of Dunkirk should be destroyed; that Spain should relinquish her claim to fish on the Banks of Newfoundland, should permit the English to cut mahogany on the shores of Honduras Bay, and cede Florida and Minorca to Great Britain. In return for these things, the French were permitted to fish on the Banks of Newfoundland, and the Islands of Martinique, Guadaloupe, Belleisle, and St. Lucia were restored to them, and Cuba was restored to Spain.

Peace of Paris.

The peace of Paris, in 1763, constitutes an epoch; and we hence turn to survey the condition of France since the death of Louis XIV., and also other continental powers.

References. — Archdeacon Coxe's History of the Pelham Administration. Thackeray's Life of Lord Chatham. Macaulay's Essay on Chatham. Horace Walpole's Reminiscences. Smyth's Lectures on Modern History. Jesse's Memoirs of the Pretenders. Graham's History of the United States, an exceedingly valuable work, but not sufficiently known. Lord Mahon's, Smollett's, Tyndal's, and Belsham's, are the standard histories of England, at this period; also, the continuation of Mackintosh, and the Pictorial History, are valuable. See also the Marchmont Papers, Ray's History of the Rebellion, Horace Walpole's Memoirs of George II., Lord Waldegrave's Memoirs, and Doddington's Diary.

CHAPTER XXII
LOUIS XV

The reign of Louis XV. was one of the longest on record extending from 1715 to 1774—the greater part of the eighteenth century. But he was a child, only five years of age, on the death of his great grandfather, Louis XIV.; and, even after he came to his majority, he was ruled by his ministers and his mistresses. He was not, like Louis XIV., the life and the centre of all great movements in his country. He was an automaton, a pageant; not because the constitution imposed checks on his power, but because he was weak and vacillating. He, therefore, performing no great part in history, is only to be alluded to, and attention should be mainly directed to his ministers.

Regency of the Duke of Orleans.

During the minority of the king, the reins of government were held by the Duke of Orleans, as regent, and who, in case of the king's death, would be the next king, being grand-nephew of Louis XIV. The administration of the Duke of Orleans is nearly contemporaneous with that of Sir Robert Walpole. The most pressing subject which demanded the attention of the regent, was that of the finances. The late king had left a debt of one thousand millions of livres—an enormous sum in that age. To get rid of this burden, the Duke of St. Simon proposed a bankruptcy. "This," said he, "would fall chiefly on the commercial and moneyed classes, who were not to be feared or pitied; and would, moreover, be not only a relief to the state, but a salutary warning to the ignoble classes not to lend their money." This speech illustrates the feelings and opinions of the aristocratic class in France, at that time. But the minister of finance would not run the risk of incurring the popular odium which such a measure would have produced, and he proposed calling together the States General. The regent duke, however, would not hear of that measure, and yet did not feel inclined to follow fully the advice of St. Simon. He therefore compromised the matter, and resolved to rob the national creditor. He established a commission to verify the bills of the public creditors, and, if their accounts did not prove satisfactory, to cancel them entirely. Three hundred and fifty millions of livres—equal, probably, to three hundred millions of dollars in this age—were thus swept away. But it was resolved not only to refuse to pay just debts, but to make people repay the gains which they had made. Those who had loaned money to the state, or had farmed the revenues, were flung into prison, and threatened with confiscation of their goods, and even death,—treated as Jews were treated in the Dark Ages,—unless they redeemed themselves by purchasing a pardon. Never before did men suffer such a penalty for having befriended an embarrassed state. To this injustice and cruelty the magistracy winked. But, in addition to this, the coin was debased to such an extent, that seventy-two millions of livres were thus added to the treasury. Yet even these gains were not enough to satisfy a profligate government. There still continued a constant pressure. The national debt had increased even to fifteen hundred millions of livres, or almost seventy millions sterling—equivalent to what would now be equal to at least one thousand millions of dollars.

John Law.

To get rid of this debt, the regent listened to the schemes of the celebrated John Law, a Scotch adventurer and financier, who had established a bank, had grown rich, and was reputed to be a wonderful political economist.

Law proposed, in substance, to increase the paper currency of the country, and thus supersede the necessity for the use of the precious metals.

The regent, moreover, having great faith in Law's abilities, and in his wealth, converted his private bank into a royal one—made it, in short, the Bank of France. This bank was then allied with the two great commercial companies of the time—the East India and the Mississippi. Great privileges were bestowed on each. The latter had the exclusive monopoly of the trade with Louisiana, and all the countries on the Mississippi River, and also of the fur trade in Canada. Louisiana was then supposed to be rich in gold mines, and great delusions arose from the popular notion.

Mississippi Company.

The capital of this gigantic corporation was fixed at one hundred millions and Law, who was made director-general, aimed to make the notes of the company preferable to specie, which, however could lawfully be demanded for the notes. So it was settled that the shares of the company could only be purchased by the paper of the bank. As extravagant hopes of gain were cherished respecting the company, its shares were in great demand. And, as only Law's bank bills could purchase the shares, the gold and silver of the realm flowed into Law's bank. Law and the regent had, therefore, the fabrication of both shares and bank bills to an indefinite amount.

The national creditor was also paid in the notes of the bank, and, as unbounded confidence existed, both in the genius of Law and in the profits of the Mississippi Company,—as the shares were constantly in demand,

and were rising in value,—the creditor was satisfied. In a short time, one half of the national debt was transferred. Government owed the bank, and not the individuals and corporations from whom loans had been originally obtained. These individuals, instead of government scrip, had shares in the Mississippi Company.

And all would have been well, had the company's shares been valuable, or had they retained their credit, or even had but a small part of the national debt been transferred. But the people did not know the real issues of the bank, and so long as new shares could be created and sold to pay the interest, the company's credit was good. For a while the delusion lasted. Law was regarded as a great national benefactor. His house was thronged with dukes and princes. He became controller-general of the finances—virtually prime minister. His fame extended far and wide. Honors were showered upon him from every quarter. He was elected a member of the French Academy. His schemes seemed to rain upon Paris a golden shower. He had freed the state from embarrassments, and he had, apparently, made every body rich, and no one poor. He was a deity, as beneficent as he was powerful. He became himself the richest man in Europe. Every body was intoxicated. The golden age had come. Paris was crowded with strangers from all parts of the world. Five hundred thousand strangers expended their fortunes, in hope of making greater ones. Twelve hundred new coaches were set up in the city. Lodgings could scarcely be had for money. The highest price was paid for provisions. Widow ladies, clergymen, and noblemen deserted London to speculate in stocks at Paris. Nothing was seen but new equipages, new houses, new apparel, new furniture. Nothing was felt but universal exhilaration. Every man seemed to have made his fortune. The stocks rose every day. The higher they rose, the more new stock was created. At last, the shares of the company rose from one hundred to twelve hundred per cent., and three hundred millions were created, which were nominally worth, in 1719, three thousand six hundred millions of livres—one hundred and eighty times the amount of all the gold and silver in Europe at that time.

Popular Delusion.

In this public delusion, the directors were wise enough to convert *their* shares into silver and gold. A great part of the current coin in the kingdom was locked up in the houses or banks of a few stockjobbers and speculators.

But the scarcity of gold and silver was felt, people's eyes were opened, and the bubble burst, but not until half of the national debt had been paid off by this swindling transaction.

The nation was furious. A panic spread among all classes; the bank had no money with which to redeem its notes; the shares fell almost to nothing; and universal bankruptcy took place. Those who, a few days before, fancied themselves rich, now found themselves poor. Property of all kinds fell to less than its original value. Houses, horses, carriages, upholstery, every thing, declined in price. All were sellers, and few were purchasers.

But popular execration and vengeance pursued the financier who had deceived the nation. He was forced to fly from Paris. His whole property was confiscated, and he was reduced to indigence and contempt. When his scheme was first suggested to the regent, he was worth three millions of livres. He had better remained a private banker.

The bursting of the Mississippi bubble, of course, inflamed the nation against the government, and the Duke of Orleans was execrated, for his agency in the business had all the appearance of a fraud. But he was probably deluded with others, and hoped to free the country from its burdens. The great blunder was in the over-issue of notes when there was no money to redeem them.

Nor could any management have prevented the catastrophe.

Fatal Effects of the Delusion.

It was not possible that the shares of the company should advance so greatly, and the public not perceive that they had advanced beyond their value; it was not possible, that, while paper money so vastly increased in quantity, the numerical prices of all other things should not increase also, and that foreigners who sold their manufactures to the French should not turn their paper into gold, and carry it out of the kingdom; it was not possible that the disappearance of the coin should not create alarm, notwithstanding the edicts of the regent, and the reasonings of Law; it was not possible that annuitants should not discover that their old incomes were now insufficient and less valuable, as the medium in which they were paid was less valuable; it was not possible that the small part of society which may be called the sober and reasoning part, should not be so struck with the sudden fortunes and extravagant enthusiasm which prevailed, as not to doubt of the solidity of a system, unphilosophical in itself, and which, after all, had to depend on the profits of a commercial company, the good faith of the regent, and the skill of Law; it was impossible, on these and other accounts, but that gold and silver should be at last preferred to paper notes, of whatever description or promise. These were inevitable consequences. Hence the failure of the scheme of Law, and the ruin of all who embarked in it, owing to a change in public opinion as to the probable success of the scheme, and, secondly, the over-issue of money.

By this great folly, four hundred thousand families were ruined, or greatly reduced; but the government got rid of about eight hundred millions of debts. The sufferings of the people, with such a government, did not, however, create great solicitude; the same old course of folly and extravagance was pursued by the court.

Nor was there a change for the better when Louis XV. attained his majority. His vices and follies exceeded all that had ever been displayed before. The support of his mistresses alone was enough to embarrass the nation. Their waste and extravagance almost exceeded belief. Who has not heard of the disgraceful and disgusting iniquities of Pompadour and Du Barry?

The regency of the Duke of Orleans occupied the first eight years of the reign of Louis XV. The prime minister of the regent was Dubois, at first his tutor, and afterwards Archbishop of Cambray. He was rewarded with a cardinal's hat for the service he rendered to the Jesuits in their quarrel with the Jansenists, but was a man of unprincipled character; a fit minister to a prince who pretended to be too intellectual to worship God, and who copied Henry IV. only in his licentiousness.

The first minister of Louis XV., after he assumed himself the reins of government, was the Duke of Bourbon, lineal heir of the house of Condé, and first prince of the blood. But he was a man of no character, and his short administration was signalized by no important event.

Administration of Cardinal Fleury.

Cardinal Fleury succeeded the Duke of Bourbon as prime minister. He had been preceptor of the king, and was superior to all the intrigues of the court; a man of great timidity, but also a man of great probity, gentleness, and benignity. Fortunately, he was intrusted with power at a period of great domestic tranquillity, and his administration was, like that of Walpole, pacific. He projected, however, no schemes of useful reform, and made no improvements in laws or finance. But he ruled despotically, and with good intentions, from 1726 to 1743.

The most considerable subject of interest connected with his peaceful administration, was the quarrel between the Jesuits and the Jansenists. Fleury took the side of the former, although he was never an active partisan; and he was induced to support the Jesuits for the sake of securing the cardinal's hat—the highest honor, next to that of the tiara, which could be conferred on an ecclesiastic. The Jesuits upheld the crumbling power of the popes, and the popes rewarded the advocates of that body of men, who were their ablest supporters.

The Jansenist controversy is too important to be passed over with a mere allusion. It was the great event in the history of Catholic Europe during the seventeenth century. It involved principles of great theological, and even political interest.

Cornelius Jansen.

The Jansenist controversy grew out of the long-disputed questions pertaining to grace and free will—questions which were agitated with great spirit and acrimony in the seventeenth century as they had previously been centuries before by Augustine and Pelagius. The Jesuits had never agreed with the great oracle of the Western church in his views on certain points, and it was their aim to show the absolute freedom of the human will—that it had a self-determining power, a perfect liberty to act or not to act. Molina, a Spanish Jesuit, had been a great defender of this ancient Pelagianism, and his views were opposed by the Dominicans, and the controversy was carried into all the universities of Europe. The Council of Trent was too wise to meddle with this difficult question; but angry theologians would not let it rest, and it was discussed with peculiar fervor in the Catholic University of Louvaine. Among the doctors who there distinguished themselves in reviving the great contest of the fifth and sixth centuries, were Cornelius Jansen of Holland, and Jean de Verger of Gascony. Both these doctors hated the Jesuits, and lamented the dangerous doctrines which they defended, and advocated the views of Augustine and the Calvinists. Jansen became professor of divinity in the university, and then Bishop of Ypres. After an uninterrupted study of twenty years, he produced his celebrated book called *Augustinus*, in which he set forth the servitude of the will, and the necessity of divine grace to break the bondage, which, however, he maintained, like Calvin, is imparted only to a few, and in pursuance of a decree existing in the divine mind before the creation of our species. But Jansen died before the book was finished, and two years elapsed before it was published, but, when published, it was the signal for a contest which distracted Europe for seventy years.

St. Cyran — Arnauld — Le Maitre.

While Jansen was preparing this work, his early companion and friend, De Verger, a man of family and rank, had become abbot of the monastery of St. Cyran in Paris, and had formed, in the centre of that gay city, a learned and ascetic hermitage. This was during the reign of Louis XIII. His reputation, as a scholar and a saint, attracted the attention of Richelieu, and his services were solicited by that able minister. But neither rewards, nor flatteries, nor applause had power over the mind of St. Cyran, as he was now called. The cardinal hated and feared a man whom he could not bribe or win, and soon found means to quarrel with him, and sent him to the gloomy fortress of Vincennes. But there, in his prison, he devoted himself, with renewed ardor, to his studies and duties, subduing his appetites and passions by an asceticism which even his church did not require, and devoting all his thoughts and words to the service of God. Like Calvin and Augustine, he had so profound a conception of the necessity of an inward change, that he made grace precede repentance. A man so serene in trial, so humble in spirit, so natural and childlike in ordinary life, and yet so distinguished for talents and erudition, could not help exciting admiration, and making illustrious proselytes. Among them was Arnauld D'Antilly, the intimate friend of Richelieu and Anne of Austria; Le Maitre, the most eloquent lawyer and advocate in France; and Angelique Arnauld, the abbess of Port Royal. This last was one of the most distinguished ladies of her age, noble by birth, and still more noble by her beautiful qualities of mind and heart. She had been made abbess of her Cistercian convent at the age of eleven years, and at that time was gay, social, and light-hearted. The preaching of a Capuchin friar had turned her thoughts to the future world, and she closed the gates of her beautiful abbey, in the vale of Chevreuse, against all strangers, and devoted herself to the ascetic duties which her church and age accounted most meritorious. She soon after made the acquaintance of St. Cyran, and he imbued her mind with the principles of the Augustinian theology. When imprisoned at Vincennes, he was still the spiritual father of Port Royal. Amid this famous retreat were collected the greatest scholars and the greatest saints of the seventeenth century—Antoine Le Maitre, De Lericourt, Le Maitre de Saci, Antoine Arnauld, and Pascal himself. Le Maitre de Saci gave to the world the best translation of the Bible in French; Arnauld wrote one hundred volumes of controversy, and, among them, a noted satire on the Jesuits, which did them infinite harm; while Pascal, besides his wonderful mathematical attainments, and his various meditative works, is immortalized for his Provincial Letters, written in the purest French, and with matchless power and beauty. This work, directed against the Jesuits, is an inimitable model of elegant irony, and the most effective sarcasm probably ever elaborated by man. In the vale of Port Royal also dwelt Tillemont, the great ecclesiastical historian; Fontaine and Racine, who were controlled by the spirit of Arnauld, as well as the Prince of Conti, and the Duke of Liancourt. There resided, under the name of *Le Merrier*, and in the humble occupation of a gardener, one of the proudest nobles of the French court; and there, too, dwelt the celebrated Duchess of Longueville, sister of the Prince of Condé, the life of the Fronde, the idol of the Parisian mob, and the once gay patroness of the proudest festivities.

The Labors of the Port Royalists.

But it is the labors of these saints, scholars, and nobles to repress the dangerous influence of the Jesuits for which they were most distinguished. The Jansenists of Port Royal did not deny the authority of the pope, nor the great institutions of the papacy. They sought chiefly, in their controversy with the Jesuits, to enforce the doctrines of Augustine respecting justification. But their efforts were not agreeable to the popes, nor to the doctors of the Sorbonne, who had no sympathy with their religious life, and detested their bold spirit of inquiry. The doctors of the Sorbonne, accordingly, extracted from the book of Jansen five propositions which they deemed heretical, and urged the pope to condemn them. The Port Royalists admitted that these five propositions were indefensible if they were declared heretical by the sovereign pontiff, but denied that they were actually to be found in the book of Jansen. They did not quarrel with the pope on grounds of faith. They recognized his infallibility in matters of religion, but not in matters of fact. The pope, not wishing to push things to extremity, which never was the policy of Rome, pretended to be satisfied. But the Jesuits would not let him rest, and insisted on the condemnation of the Jansenist opinions. The case was brought before a great council of French bishops and doctors, and Arnauld, the great champion of the Jansenists, was voted guilty of heresy for denying that the five propositions which the pope condemned were actually in the book of Jansen. The pope, moreover, was induced to issue a formula of an oath, to which all who wished to enjoy any office in the church were obliged to subscribe, and which affirmed that the five condemned propositions were actually to be found in Jansen's book. This act of the pope was justly regarded by the Jansenists as intolerably despotic, and many of the most respectable of the French clergy sided with them in opinion. All France now became interested in the controversy, and it soon led to great commotions. The Jansenists then contended that the pope might err in questions of fact, and that, therefore, they were not under an obligation to subscribe to the required oath. The Jesuits, on the other hand, maintained the pope's infallibility in matters of fact, as well as in doctrine; and, as they had the most powerful adherents, the Jansenists were bitterly persecuted. But, as twenty-two bishops were found to take their side, the matter was hushed up for a while. For ten years more, the Port Royalists had peace and protection, chiefly through the great influence of the Duchess of Longueville; but, on her death, persecution returned. Arnauld was obliged to fly to the Netherlands, and the beautiful abbey of Port Royal was despoiled of its lands and privileges. Louis XIV. had ever hated its inmates, being ruled by Madame de Maintenon, who, in turn, was a tool of the Jesuits.

But the demolition of the abbey, the spoliation of its lands, and the dispersion of those who sought its retreat, did not stop the controversy.

Pascal continued it, and wrote his Provincial Letters, which had a wonderful effect in making the Jesuits both ridiculous and hateful. That book was the severest blow this body of ambitious and artful casuists ever received.

Principles of Jansenism.

Nor was the Jansenist controversy merely a discussion of grace and free will. The principles of Jansenism, when carried out, tended to secure independence to the national church, and to free the consciences of men from the horrible power of their spiritual confessors. Jansenism was a timid protest against spiritual tyranny, a mild kind of Puritanism, which found sympathy with many people in France. The Parliament of Paris caught the spirit of freedom, and protected the Jansenists and those who sympathized with them. It so happened that a certain bishop published a charge to his clergy which was strongly imbued with the independent doctrines of the Jansenists. He was tried and condemned by a provincial council, and banished by the government. The Parliament of Paris, as the guardian of the law, took up the quarrel, and Cardinal Fleury was obliged to resort to a *Bed of Justice* in order to secure the registry of a decree. A Bed of Justice was the personal appearance of the sovereign in the supreme judicial tribunal of the nation, and his command to the members of it to obey his injunctions was the last resort of absolute power. The parliament, of course, obeyed, but protested the next day, and drew up resolutions which declared the temporal power to be independent of the spiritual. It then proceeded to Meudon, one of the royal palaces, to lay its remonstrance before the king; and Louis XV., indignant and astonished, refused to see the members. The original controversy was forgotten, and the cause of the parliament, which was the cause of liberty, became the cause of the nation. The resistance of the parliament was technically unsuccessful, yet, nevertheless, sowed the seeds of popular discontent, and contributed to that great insurrection which finally overturned the throne.

Functions of the Parliament.

The Bull Unigenitus.

It may be asked how the Parliament of Paris became a judicial tribunal, rather than a legislative assembly, as in England. When the Justinian code was introduced into French jurisprudence, in the latter part of the Middle Ages, the old feudal and clerical judges—the barons and bishops—were incapable of expounding it, and a new class of men arose—the lawyers, whose exclusive business it was to study the laws. Being best acquainted with them, they entered upon the functions of judges, and the secular and clerical lords yielded to their opinions. The great barons, however, still continued to sit in the judicial tribunals, although ignorant of the new jurisprudence; and their decisions were directed by the opinions of the lawyers who had obtained a seat in their body, as is the case at present in the English House of Lords when it sits as a judicial body. The necessity of providing some permanent repository for the royal edicts, induced the kings of France to enroll them in the journals of the courts of parliament, being the highest judicial tribunal; and the members of these courts gradually availed themselves of this custom to dispute the legality of any edict which had not been thus registered. As the influence of the States General declined, the power of the parliament increased. The encroachments of the papacy first engaged its attention, and then the management of the finances by the ministers of Francis I. called forth remonstrances. During the war of the Fronde, the parliament absolutely refused to register the royal decrees. But Louis XIV. was sufficiently powerful to suppress the spirit of independence, and accordingly entered the court, during the first years of his reign, with a whip in his hand, and compelled it to register his edicts. Nor did any murmur afterwards escape the body, until, at the close of his reign the members opposed the bull *Unigenitus*—that which condemned the Jansenists—as an infringement of the liberties of the Gallican Church. And no sooner had the great monarch died, than, contrary to his will, they vested the regency in the hands of the Duke of Orleans. Then freedom of expostulation respecting the ruinous schemes of Law induced him to banish them, and they only obtained their recall by degrading concessions. Their next opposition was during the administration of Fleury. The minister of finance made an attempt to inquire into the wealth of the clergy, which raised the jealousy of the order; and the clergy, in order to divert the attention of the court, revived the opposition of the parliament to the bull *Unigenitus*. It was resolved by the clergy to demand confessional notes from dying persons, and that these notes should be signed by priests adhering to the bull, before extreme unction should be given. The Archbishop of Paris, at the head of the French clergy, was opposed by the parliament, and this high judicial court imprisoned such of the clergy as refused to administer the sacraments. The king, under the guidance of Fleury, forbade the parliament to take cognizance of ecclesiastical proceedings, and to suspend its prosecutions. Instead of acquiescing, the parliament presented new remonstrances, and the members refused to attend to any other functions, and resolved that they could not obey this injunction without violating their consciences. They cited the Bishop of

Orleans before their tribunal, and ordered all his writings, which denied the jurisdiction of the court, to be publicly burnt by the executioner. By aid of the military, the parliament enforced the administration of the sacraments, and became so interested in the controversy as to neglect other official duties. The king, indignant, again banished the members, with the exception of four, whom he imprisoned. And, in order not to impede the administration of justice, the king established another tribunal for the prosecution of civil suits. But the lawyers, sympathizing with the parliament, refused to plead before the new court. This resolute conduct, and other evils happening at the time, induced the king to yield, in order to conciliate the people, and the parliament was recalled. This was a popular triumph, and the archbishop was banished in his turn. Shortly after, Cardinal Fleury died, and a new policy was adopted. The quarrel of the parliament and the clergy was forgotten in a still greater quarrel between the king and the Jesuits.

The policy of Fleury, like that of Walpole, was pacific; and yet, like him, he was forced into a war against his own convictions. And success attended the arms of France, in the colonial struggle with England, until Pitt took the helm of state.

Until the death of Fleury, in 1743, who administered affairs with wisdom, moderation, and incorruptible integrity, he was beloved, if he was not venerated. But after this event, a great change took place in his character and measures, and the reign of mistresses commenced, and to an extent unparalleled in the history of Europe. Louis XIV. bestowed the revenue of the state on unworthy favorites, yet never allowed them to govern the nation; but Louis XV. intrusted the most important state matters to their direction, and the profoundest state secrets to their keeping.

Madame de Pompadour.

Among these mistresses, Madame de Pompadour was the most noted; a woman of talent, but abominably unprincipled. Ambition was her master-passion, and her *boudoir* was the council chamber of the royal ministers. Most of the great men of France paid court to her, and to neglect her was social ruin. Even Voltaire praised her beauty, and Montesquieu flattered her intellect. And her extravagance was equal to her audacity. She insisted on drawing bills on the treasury without specifying the service. The comptroller-general was in despair, and the state was involved in inextricable embarrassments.

It was through her influence that the Duke de Choiseul was made the successor of Fleury. He was not deficient in talent, but his administration proved unfortunate. Under his rule, Louis lost the Canadas, and France plunged into a contest with Frederic the Great. The Seven Years' War, which occurred during his administration, had made the age an epoch; but as this is to be considered in the chapter on Frederic III., no notice of it will be taken in this connection.

The most memorable event which arose out of the policy and conduct of Choiseul was the fall of the Jesuits.

The Jesuits.

Their arts and influence had obtained from the pope the bull *Unigenitus*, designed to suppress their enemies, the Jansenists; and the king, governed by Fleury, had taken their side.

But they were so unwise as to quarrel with the powerful mistress of Louis XV. They despised her, and defied her hatred. Indeed, the Jesuits had climbed to so great a height that they were scornful of popular clamor, and even of regal distrust. But there is no man, and no body of men, who can venture to provoke enmity with impunity; and destruction often comes from a source the least suspected, and apparently the least to be feared. Who could have supposed that the ruin of this powerful body, which had reigned so proudly in Christendom for a century; which had imposed its Briareus's arms on the necks of princes; which had its confessors in the courts of the most absolute monarchs; which, with its hundred eyes, had penetrated the secrets of all the cabinets of Europe; and which had succeeded in suppressing in so many places every insurrection of human intelligence, in spite of the fears of kings, the jealousy of the other monastic orders, and the inveterate animosity of philosophers and statesmen,—would receive a fatal wound from the hands of a woman, who scandalized by her vices even the depraved court of an enervated prince? But so it was. Madame de Pompadour hated the Jesuits because they attempted to undermine her influence with the king. And she incited the prime minister, whom she had raised by her arts to power, to unite with Pombal in Portugal, in order to effect their ruin.

Exposure of the Jesuits.

In no country was the power of the Jesuits more irresistible than in Portugal. There their ascendency was complete. But the prime minister of Joseph I., the Marquis of Pombal, a man of great energy, had been insulted by a lady of the highest rank, and he swore revenge. An opportunity was soon afforded. The king happened to be fired at and wounded in his palace by some unknown enemy. The blow was aimed at the objects of the minister's vengeance—the Marchioness of Tavora, her husband, her family, and her friends the Jesuits. And royal vengeance followed, not merely on an illustrious family, but on those persons whom this family befriended. The Jesuits were expelled in the most summary manner from the kingdom. The Duke de Choiseul and Madame Pompadour hailed their misfortunes with delight, and watched their opportunity for revenge. This was afforded by the failure of La Valette, the head of the Jesuits at Martinique. It must be borne in mind that the Jesuits had embarked in commercial enterprises, while they were officiating as missionaries. La Valette aimed to monopolize, for his order, the trade with the West Indies, which commercial ambition excited the jealousy of mercantile classes in France, and they threw difficulties in his way. And it so happened that some of his most valuable ships were taken and plundered by the English cruisers, which calamity, happening at a time of embarrassment, caused his bills to be protested, and his bankers to stop payment. They, indignant, accused the Jesuits, as a body, of peculation and fraud, and demanded repayment from the order. Had the Jesuits been wise, they would have satisfied the ruined bankers. But who is wise on the brink of destruction? *"Quem deus vult perdere, prius dementat."* The Jesuits refused to sacrifice La Valette to the interests of their order, which course would have been in accordance with their general policy. The matter was carried before the Parliament of Paris, and the whole nation was interested in its result. It was decided by this supreme judicial tribunal, that the Jesuits were responsible for the debts of La Valette. But the commercial injury was weak in comparison with the moral. In the course of legal proceedings, the books and rule of the Jesuits were demanded—that mysterious rule which had never been exposed to the public eye, and which had been so carefully guarded. When this rule was produced, all minor questions vanished; mistresses, bankruptcies, politics, finances, wars,—all became insignificant, compared with those questions which affected the position and welfare of the society. Pascal became a popular idol, and "Tartuffe grew pale before Escobar." The reports of the trial lay on every toilet table, and persons of both sexes, and of all ages and conditions, read with avidity the writings of the casuists. Nothing was talked about but "probability," "surrender of conscience," and "mental reservations." Philosophers grew jealous of the absorbing interest with which every thing pertaining to the *régime* of the Jesuits was read, and of the growing popularity of the Jansenists, who had exposed it. "What," said Voltaire, "will it profit us to be delivered from the foxes, if we are to be given up to the wolves?" But the philosopher had been among the first to raise the cry of alarm against the Jesuits, and it was no easy thing to allay the storm.

Their Expulsion from France.

The Jesuits, in their distress, had only one friend sufficiently powerful to protect them, and he was the king. He had been their best friend, and he still wished to come to their rescue. He had been taught to honor them, and he had learned to fear them. He stood in fear of assassination, and dreaded a rupture with so powerful and unscrupulous a body. And his resistance to the prosecution would have been insurmountable, had it not been for the capriciousness of his temper, which more than balanced his superstitious fears. His minister and his mistress circumvented him. They represented that, as the parliament and the nation were both aroused against the Jesuits, his resistance would necessarily provoke a new Fronde. Nothing he dreaded so much as civil war. The wavering monarch, placed in the painful necessity of choosing, as he supposed, between a war and the ruin of his best friends, yielded to the solicitations of his artful advisers. But he yielded with a moderation which did him honor. He would not consent to the expulsion of the Jesuits until efforts had been made to secure their reform. He accordingly caused letters to be written to Rome, demanding an immediate attention to the subject. Choiseul himself prepared the scheme of reformation. But the Jesuits would not hear of any retrenchment of their power or privileges. "Let us remain as we are, or let us exist no longer," was their reply. The parliament, the people, the minister, and the mistress renewed their clamors. The parliament decreed that the constitution of the society was an encroachment on the royal authority, and the king was obliged to yield. The members of the society were forbidden to wear the habit of the society, or to enjoy any clerical office or dignity. Their colleges were closed, their order was dissolved, and they were expelled from the kingdom with rigor and severity, in spite of the wishes of the king and many entreaties and tears from the zealous advocates of Catholicism, and even of religious education.

Suppression in Spain.

But the Jesuits were too powerful, even in their misfortunes, to be persecuted without the effort to annihilate them. Having secured their expulsion from France and Portugal, Choiseul and Pombal turned their attention to Spain, and so successfully intrigued, so artfully wrought on the jealousy and fears of Charles III., that this weak prince followed the example of Joseph I. and Louis XV. But the king and his minister D'Aranda, however, prosecuted their investigations with the utmost secrecy—did not even tell their allies of their movements. Of course, the Jesuits feared nothing from the king of Spain. But when his measures were completed, an edict was suddenly declared, decreeing the suppression of the order in the land of Inquisitions. The decree came like a thunderbolt, but was instantly executed. "On the same day, 2d April, 1767, and at the same hour, in Spain, in Africa, in Asia, in America, and in all the islands belonging to the Spanish monarchy, the alcaldes of the towns opened their despatches from Madrid, by which they were ordered, on pain of the severest penalties, immediately to enter the establishments of the Jesuits, to seize their persons, expel them from their convents, and transport them, within twenty-four hours, to such places as were designated. Nor were the Jesuits permitted to carry away their money or their papers. Only a purse, a breviary, and some apparel were given them."

The government feared a popular insurrection from an excitement so sudden, and a persecution so dreadful, and therefore issued express prohibition to all the ecclesiastical authorities to prevent any allusion to the event from the pulpit. All classes were required to maintain absolute silence, and any controversy, or criticism, or remark was regarded as high treason. Such is despotism. Such is religious persecution, when fear, as well as hatred, prompts to injustice and cruelty.

The Jesuits, in their misfortunes, managed with consummate craft. Their policy was to appear in the light of victims of persecution. There was to them no medium between reigning as despots or dying as martyrs. Mediocrity would have degraded them. Ricci, the general of the order, would not permit them to land in Italy, to which country they were sent by the king of Spain. Six thousand priests, in misery and poverty, were sent adrift upon the Mediterranean, and after six months of vicissitude, suffering, and despair, they found a miserable refuge on the Island of Corsica.

Pope Clement XIV.

Soon after, the pope, their most powerful protector, died. A successor was to be appointed. But France, Spain, and Portugal, bent on the complete suppression of the Jesuits, resolved that no pope should be elected who would not favor their end. A cardinal was found,—Ganganelli,—who promised the ambassadors that, if elected pope, he would abolish the order. They, accordingly, intrigued to secure his election. The Jesuits, also, strained every nerve, and put forth marvellous talent and art, to secure a pope who would *protect them*. But the ambassadors of the allied powers overreached even the Jesuits. Ganganelli was the plainest, and, apparently, the most unambitious of men. His father had been a peasant; but, by the force of talent and learning, he had arisen, from the condition of his father, to be a Roman cardinal. Under the garb of a saint, he aspired to the tiara. There was only one condition of success; and that was, to destroy the best supporters of that fearful absolutism which had so long enslaved the world. The sacrifice was tremendous; but it was made, and he became a pope. Then commenced in his soul the awful struggle. Should he fulfil his pledge, and jeopardize his cause and throne, and be branded, by the zealots of his church, with eternal infamy? or should he break his word, and array against himself, with awful enmity, the great monarchs of Europe, and perhaps lose the allegiance of their subjects to him as the supreme head of the Catholic Church? The decision was the hardest which mortal man had ever been required to make. Whatever course he pursued was full of danger and disgrace. Poor Ganganelli! he had better remained a cowherd, a simple priest, a bishop, a cardinal,—any thing,—rather than to have been made a pope! But such was his ambition, and he was obliged to reap its penalty. Long did the afflicted pontiff delay to fulfil his pledge; long did he practise all the arts of dissimulation, of which he was such a master. He delayed, he flattered, he entreated, he coaxed. But the monarchs called peremptorily for the fulfilment of his pledge, and all Europe now understood the nature of the contest. It was between the Jesuits and the monarchs of Europe. Ganganelli was compelled to give his decision. His health declined, his spirits forsook him, his natural gayety fled. He courted solitude, he wept, he prayed. But he must, nevertheless, decide. The Jesuits threatened assassination, and exposed, with bitter eloquence, the ruin of his church, if he yielded her privileges to kings. And kings threatened secession from Rome, deposition—ten thousand calamities. His agony became insupportable; but delay was no longer possible. He decided to suppress the order of the Jesuits; and sixty-nine colleges were closed, their missions were broken up, their churches were given to their rivals, and twenty-two thousand priests were left without organization, wealth, or power.

Death of Ganganelli.

Their revenge was not an idle threat. One day, the pope, on arising from table, felt an internal shock, followed by great cold. Gradually he lost his voice and strength. His blood became corrupted; and his moral system gave way with the physical. He knew that he was doomed—that he was poisoned—that he must die. The fear of hell was now added to his other torments. "*Compulsus, feci, compulsus, feci!*" — "O, mercy, mercy, I have been compelled!" he cried, and died — died by that slow but sure poison, such as old Alexander VI. knew so well how to administer to his victims when he sought their wealth. Pope Clement XIV. inflicted, it was supposed, a mortal wound upon his church and upon her best friends. He, indeed, reaped the penalty of ambition; but the cause which he represented did not perish, nor will it lose vitality so long as the principle of evil on earth is destined to contend with the principle of good. On the restoration of the Bourbons, the order of the Jesuits was restored; and their flaming sword, with its double edge, was again felt in every corner of the world.

Death of Louis XV.

The Jesuits, on their expulsion, found shelter in Prussia, and protection from the royal infidel who had been the friend of Voltaire. A schism between the crowned heads of Europe and infidel philosophers had taken place. Frederic, who had sympathized with their bitter mockery, at last perceived the tendency of their writings; that men who assailed obedience to divine laws would not long respect the institutions and governments which mankind had recognized. He perceived, too, the natural union of absolutism in the church with absolutism in the state, and came to the rescue of the great, unchanged, unchangeable, and ever-consistent advocates of despotism. The frivolous Choiseul, the extravagant Pompadour, and the debauched Sardanapalus of his age, did not perceive the truth which the King of Prussia recognized in his latter days. Nor would it have availed any thing, if they had been gifted with the clear insight of Frederic the Great. The stream, on whose curious banks the great and the noble of France had been amusing themselves, soon swelled into an overwhelming torrent. That devastating torrent was the French Revolution, whose awful swell was first perceived during the latter years of Louis XV. He himself caught glimpses of the future; but, with the egotism of a Bourbon, he remarked "that the throne would last during his time." Soon after this heartless speech was made, he was stricken with the small-pox, and died 1774, after a long and inglorious reign. He was deserted in his last hours, and his disgusting and loathsome remains were huddled into their last abode by the workmen of his palace.

Before the reign of Louis XVI. can be described, it is necessary to glance at the career of Frederic the Great, and the condition of the various European states, at a period contemporary with the Seven Years' War — the great war of the eighteenth century, before the breaking out of the French Revolution.

References.—For a general view of the reign of Louis XV., see the histories of Lacretelle, Voltaire, and Crowe. The scheme of Law is best explained in Smyth's Lectures, and Anderson's History of Commerce. The struggles between the king and the Parliament of Paris are tolerably described in the History of Adolphus. For a view of the Jansenist Controversy, see Du Pin's Ecclesiastical History, Ranke's History of the Popes, Pascal's Provincial Letters, and Stephens's article in the Edinburgh Review, on the Port Royalists. The fall of the Jesuits has been admirably treated by Quinet. James has written a good sketch of the lives of Fleury and Choiseul. For the manners of the court of Louis XV., the numerous memoirs and letters, which were written during the period, must be consulted; the most amusing of which, and, in a certain sense, instructive, are too infamous to be named.

CHAPTER XXIII
FREDERIC THE GREAT

Frederic William.

Frederic II. of Prussia has won a name which will be immortal on Moloch's catalogue of military heroes. His singular character extorts our admiration, while it calls forth our aversion, admiration for his great abilities, sagacity, and self-reliance, and disgust for his cruelties, his malice, his suspicions, and his tricks. He had no faith in virtue or disinterestedness, and trusted only to mechanical agencies—to the power of armies—to the principle of fear. He was not indifferent to literature, or the improvement of his nation; but war was alike his absorbing passion and his highest glory. Peter the Great was half a barbarian, and Charles XII. half a madman; but Frederic was neither barbarous in his tastes, nor wild in his schemes. Louis XIV. plunged his nation in war from puerile egotism, and William III. fought for the great cause of religious and civil liberty; but Frederic, from the excitement which war produced, and the restless ambition of plundering what was not his own.

He was born in the royal palace of Berlin, in 1712—ten years after Prussia had become a kingdom, and in the lifetime of his grandfather, Frederic I. The fortunes of his family were made by his great-grandfather, called the *Great Elector*, of the house of Hohenzollern. He could not make Brandenburg a fertile province; so he turned it into a military state. He was wise, benignant, and universally beloved. But few of his amiable qualities were inherited by his great-grandson. Frederic II. resembled more his whimsical and tyrannical father, Frederic William, who beat his children without a cause, and sent his subjects to prison from mere caprice. When his ambassador, in London, was allowed only one thousand pounds a year, he gave a bounty of thirteen hundred pounds to a tall Irishman, to join his famous body-guard, a regiment of men who were each over six feet high. He would kick women in the streets, abuse clergymen for looking on the soldiers, and insult his son's tutor for teaching him Latin. But, abating his coarseness, his brutality, and his cruelty, he was a Christian, after a certain model. He had respect for the institutions of religion, denounced all amusements as sinful, and read a sermon aloud, every afternoon, to his family. His son perceived his inconsistencies, and grew up an infidel. There was no sympathy between father and son, and the father even hated the heir of his house and throne. The young prince was kept on bread and water; his most moderate wishes were disregarded; he was surrounded with spies; he was cruelly beaten and imprisoned, and abused as a monster and a heathen. The cruel treatment which the prince received induced him to fly; his flight was discovered; he was brought back to Berlin, condemned to death as a deserter and only saved from the fate of a malefactor by the intercession of half of the crowned heads of Europe. A hollow reconciliation was effected; and the prince was permitted, at last, to retire to one of the royal palaces, where he amused himself with books, billiards, balls, and banquets. He opened a correspondence with Voltaire, and became an ardent admirer of his opinions.

Accession of Frederic the Great.

In 1740, the old king died, and Frederic II. mounted an absolute throne. He found a well filled treasury, and a splendidly disciplined army. His customary pleasures were abandoned, and dreams of glory filled his ambitious soul.

Scarcely was he seated on his throne before military aggrandizement became the animating principle of his life.

His first war was the conquest of Silesia, one of the richest provinces of the Austrian empire. It belonged to Maria Theresa, Queen of Hungary and Bohemia, daughter of the late emperor of Germany, whose succession was guaranteed by virtue of the Pragmatic Sanction—a law which the Emperor Charles passed respecting his daughter's claim, and which claim was recognized by the old king of Prussia, and ratified by all the leading powers of Europe. Without a declaration of war, without complaints, without a cause, scarcely without a pretext, from the mere lust of dominion, Frederic commenced hostilities, in the depth of winter, when invasion was unexpected, and when the garrisons were defenceless. Without a battle, one of the oldest provinces of Austria was seized, and the royal robber returned in triumph to his capital.

Such an outrage and crime astonished and alarmed the whole civilized world, and Europe armed itself to revenge and assist the unfortunate queen, whose empire was threatened with complete dismemberment. Frederic was alarmed, and a hollow peace was made. But, in two years, the war again broke out. To recover Silesia and to humble Frederic was the aim of Maria Theresa. She succeeded in securing the coöperation of Russia, France, Sweden, and Saxony. No one doubted of the ruin of the house of Brandenburg. Six hundred thousand men were arrayed to crush an upstart monarchy, and an unprincipled king, who had trampled on all the laws of nations and all the principles of justice.

The Seven Years' War.

The resistance of Frederic to these immense forces constitutes the celebrated *Seven Years' War*—the most gigantic war which Europe had seen, from the Reformation to the French Revolution. This contest began during the latter years of George II., and was connected with the colonial wars of Great Britain and France, during which Wolfe was killed and the Canadas were gained. This war called out all the energies of the elder Pitt, and placed Great Britain on the exalted height which it has since retained.

Frederic was not so blinded as not to perceive the extent of his dangers; and his successful resistance to the armies which his own offensive war had raised up against him, has given him his claims to the epithet of *Great*. Although he provoked the war, his successful defence of his country placed him on the very highest pinnacle of military fame. He would gladly have been relieved from the contest, but it was inevitable; and when the tempest burst upon his head, he showed all the qualities of exalted heroism.

Great and overwhelming odds were arrayed against him. But he himself had some great advantages. He was absolute master of his army, of his treasury, and of his territories. The lives and property of his subjects were at his disposal; his subjects were brave and loyal; he was popular with the people, and was sustained by the enthusiasm of the nation; his army was well disciplined; he had no sea-coast to defend, and he could concentrate all his forces upon any point he pleased, in a short time.

His only hope was in energetic measures. He therefore invaded Saxony, at once, with sixty thousand men. His aim was to seize the state papers at Dresden, which contained the proofs of the confederation. These were found and published, which showed that now, at least, he acted on the defensive.

The campaign of 1756 commenced, and the first great battle was won by the Prussians. By the victory of Lowositz, Frederic was in a better condition to contend with Austria. By this he got possession of Saxony.

The campaign of 1757 was commenced under great solicitude. Five hundred thousand men were arrayed against two hundred thousand. Near Prague, Frederic obtained a victory, but lost twelve thousand men. He then invested Prague. General Daun, with a superior army, advanced to its relief. Another bloody battle was fought, and lost by the Prussian king. This seemed to be a fatal stroke. At the outset, as it were, of the war, he had received a check. The soldiers' confidence was weakened. Malevolent sarcasm pointed out mistakes. The siege of Prague was raised, and Bohemia was abandoned. A French army, at the same time, invaded Germany; and Frederic heard also of the death of his mother—the only person whom he loved. His spirits fell, and he became haggard and miserable.

The only thing for him to do now was, to protect Saxony, and secure that conquest—no very easy task. His dominions were now assailed by a French, a Swedish, and a Russian army. His capital was in the hands of the Croatians, and he was opposed by superior Austrian forces. No wonder that he was oppressed with melancholy, and saw only the ruin of his house. On one thing, however, he was resolved—never to be taken alive. So he provided himself with poison, which he ever carried about his person.

The heroic career of Frederic dates from this hour of misfortune and trial. Indeed, the heroism of all great men commences in perplexity, difficulty, and danger. Success is glorious; but success is obtained only through struggle. Frederic's career is a splendid example of that heroism which rises above danger, and extricates a man from difficulties when his cause is desperate.

Battle of Rossbach.

The King of Prussia first marched against the French. The two armies met at Rossbach. The number of the French was double that of the Prussians; but the Prussians were better disciplined, and were commanded by an abler general. The French, however felt secure of victory; but they were defeated: seven thousand men were taken prisoners, together with their guns, ammunition, parrots, hair powder, and pomatum. The victory of Rossbach won for Frederic a great name, and diffused universal joy among the English and Prussians.

Battle of Leuthen.

After a brief rest, he turned his face towards Silesia, which had again fallen into the hands of the Austrians. It was for this province that he provoked the hostilities of Europe; and pride, as well as interest, induced him to bend all his energies to regain it. Prince Charles of Lorraine commanded the forces of Maria Theresa, which numbered eighty thousand men. Frederic could only array against him an army of thirty thousand. And yet, in spite of the disparity of forces, and his desperate condition, he resolved to attack the enemy. His generals remonstrated; but the hero gave full permission to all to retire, if they pleased. None were found to shun the danger. Frederic, like Napoleon, had the talent of exciting the enthusiasm of his troops. He both encouraged and threatened them. He declared that any cavalry regiment which did not, on being ordered, burst impetuously on the foe, should after the battle, be dismounted, and converted into a garrison regiment. But he had no reason to complain. On the 5th of December, the day of the ever-memorable battle of Leuthen, he selected an officer with fifty men as his body-guard. "I shall," said he, "expose myself much to-day; you are not to leave me for an instant: if I fall, cover me quickly with a mantle, place me in a wagon and tell the fact to no one. The battle cannot be avoided, and must be won." And he obtained a glorious victory. The Austrian general abandoned a strong position, because he deemed it beneath his dignity to contend with an inferior force in a fortified camp. His imprudence lost him the battle. According to Napoleon, it was a masterpiece on the part of the victor, and placed him in the first rank of generals. Twenty thousand Austrians were either killed or taken. Breslau opened its gates to the Prussians, and Silesia was reconquered. The king's fame filled the world. Pictures of him were hung in almost every house. The enthusiasm of Germany was not surpassed by that of England. London was illuminated; the gay scions of aristocracy proposed to the Prussian king to leave their country and join his army; an annual subsidy of seven hundred thousand pounds was granted by government. The battle of Leuthen was the most brilliant in Prussian annals; out the battle of Rossbach, over the French, was attended by greater moral results. It showed, for the first time for several centuries, that the Germans were really a great people, and were a match for the French, hitherto deemed invincible.

Early in the spring of 1758, Frederic was ready for a new campaign, which was soon signalized by a great victory over the Russians, at Zorndorff. It was as brilliant and decisive as the battles of Rossbach and Leuthen. A force of thirty-two thousand men defeated an army of fifty-two thousand. Twenty-two thousand Russians lay dead on the field. This victory placed Frederic at the zenith of military fame. In less than a year, he had defeated three great armies; in less than a year, and when nearly driven to despair, — when his cause seemed hopeless, and his enemies were rejoicing in their strength,—he successively triumphed over the French, the Austrians, and the Russians; the three most powerful nations on the continent of Europe. And his moderation after victory was as marked as his self-reliance after defeat. At this period, he stood out, to the wondering and admiring eyes of the world, as the greatest hero and general of modern times. But, after this, his career was more checkered, and he was still in danger of being overwhelmed by his powerful enemies.

Fall of Dresden.

The remainder of the campaign of 1758 was spent in driving the Austrians from Silesia, and in capturing Dresden. No capital in Europe has suffered more in war than this elegant and polished city. It has been often besieged and taken, but the victors have always spared its famous picture gallery—the finest collection of the works of the old masters, probably, in existence.

But Frederic was now assailed by a new enemy, Pope Benedict XIV. He sent a consecrated sword, a hat of crimson velvet, and a dove of pearls,— "the mystic symbol of the divine Comforter,"—to Marshal Daun, the ablest of the Austrian generals, and the conqueror at Kolin and Hochkirchen. It was the rarest of the papal gifts, and had been only bestowed, in the course of six centuries, on Godfrey of Bouillon, by Urban II., when he took Jerusalem; on Alva, after his massacres in Holland; and on Sobieski, after his deliverance of Vienna, when besieged by the Turks. It had never been conferred, except for the defence of the "Holy Catholic Church." But this greatest of papal gifts made no impression on the age which read Montesquieu and Voltaire. A flood of satirical pamphlets inundated Christendom, and the world laughed at the impotent weapons which had once been thunderbolts in the hands of Hildebrand or Innocent III.

Reverses of Frederic.

The fourth year of the war proved disastrous to Frederic. He did not lose military reputation, but he lost his cities and armies. The forces of his enemies were nearly overwhelming. The Austrians invaded Saxony, and menaced Silesia, while the Russians gained a victory over the Prussians at Kunersdorf, and killed eighteen thousand men. The Russians did not improve this great victory over Frederic, which nearly drove him to despair. But he rallied, and was again defeated in three disastrous battles. In his distress, he fed his troops on potatoes and rye bread, took from the peasant his last horse, debased his coin, and left his civil functionaries unpaid.

The campaign of 1760 was, at first, unfavorable to the Prussians. Frederic had only ninety thousand men, and his enemies had two hundred thousand, in the field. He was therefore obliged to maintain the defensive. But still disasters thickened. General Loudon obtained a great victory over his general, Fouqué, in Silesia. Instead of being discouraged by this new defeat, he formed the extraordinary resolution of wresting Dresden from the hands of the Austrians. But he pretended to retreat from Saxony, and advance to Silesia. General Daun was deceived, and decoyed from Saxony in pursuit of him. As soon as Frederic had retired a considerable distance from Dresden, he returned, and bombarded it. But he did not succeed in taking it, and was forced to retreat to Silesia. It was there his good fortune to gain a victory over the Austrians, and prevent their junction with the Russians. At Torgau, he again defeated an army of sixty-four thousand of the enemy, with a force of only forty-four thousand. This closed the campaign, and the position of the parties was nearly the same as at the commencement of it. The heart of

Frederic was now ulcerated with bitterness in view of the perseverance of his enemies, who were resolved to crush him. He should, however, have remembered that he had provoked their implacable resentment, by the commission of a great crime.

Although Frederic, by rare heroism, had maintained his ground, still his resources were now nearly exhausted, and he began to look around, in vain, for a new supply of men, horses, and provisions. The circle which his enemies had drawn around him was obviously becoming smaller. In a little while, to all appearance, he would be crushed by overwhelming forces.

Continued Disasters.

Under these circumstances, the campaign in 1761 was opened; but no event of importance occurred until nearly the close of the year. On the whole, it was disastrous to Prussia. Half of Silesia was taken by the Austrians, and the Russian generals were successful in Pomerania. And a still greater misfortune happened to Frederic in consequence of the resignation of Pitt, who had ever been his firmest ally, and had granted him large subsidies, when he was most in need of them. On the retirement of the English minister, these subsidies were withdrawn, and the party which had thwarted William III., which had persecuted Marlborough, and had given up the Catalans, came into power—the Tories. "It was indifferent to them whether the house of Hohenstaufen or Hohenzollern should be dominant in Germany." But Pitt and the Whigs argued that no sacrifice would be too great to preserve the balance of power. The defection of England, however, filled the mind of Frederic with implacable hatred, and he never could bear to hear even the name of England mentioned. The defection of this great ally made his affairs desperate; and no one, taking a dispassionate view of the contending parties, could doubt but that the ruin of the Prussian king was inevitable. Maria Theresa was so confident of success, that she disbanded twenty thousand of her troops.

But Providence had ordered otherwise. A great and unexpected change came over the fortunes of Frederic. His heroism was now to be rewarded—not the vulgar heroism which makes a sudden effort, and gains a single battle, but that well-sustained heroism which strives in the midst of defeat, and continues to hope when even noble hearts are sinking in despair. On the 5th of January, 1762, Elizabeth, the empress of Russia, died; and her successor, Peter III., who was an admirer of Frederic, and even a personal friend, returned the Prussian prisoners, withdrew his troops from the Prussian territories, dressed himself in a Prussian uniform, and wore the black eagle of Prussia on his breast. He even sent fifteen thousand troops to reënforce the army of Frederic.

England and France had long been wearied of this war, and formed a separate treaty for themselves. Prussia and Austria were therefore left to combat each other. If Austria, assisted by France and Russia, could not regain Silesia and ruin Prussia, it certainly was not strong enough to conquer Frederic single-handed. The proud Maria Theresa was compelled to make peace with that heroic but unprincipled robber, who had seized one of the finest provinces of the Austrian empire. In February, the treaty of Hubertsburg was signed, by which Frederic retained his spoil. He, in comparison with the other belligerent parties was the gainer. But no acquisition of territory could compensate for those seven years of toil, expense, and death. After six years, he entered his capital in triumph; but he beheld every where the melancholy marks of devastation and suffering. The fields were untilled, houses had been sacked, population had declined, and famine and disease had spread a funereal shade over the dwellings of the poor. He had escaped death, but one sixth of the whole male population of Prussia had been killed, and untold millions of property had been destroyed. In some districts, no laborers but women were seen in the fields, and fifteen thousand houses had been burnt in his own capital.

It is very remarkable that no national debt was incurred by the king of Prussia, in spite of all his necessities. He always, in the worst of times, had a year's revenue in advance; and, at the close of the war, to show the world that he was not then impoverished, he built a splendid palace at Potsdam, which nearly equalled the magnificence of Versailles.

Exhaustion of Prussia by the War.

But he also did all in his power to alleviate the distress which his wars had caused. Silesia received three millions of thalers, and Pomerania two millions. Fourteen thousand houses were rebuilt; treasury notes, which had depreciated, were redeemed; officers who had distinguished themselves were rewarded; and the widows and children of those who had fallen were pensioned.

The possession of Silesia did not, indeed, compensate for the Seven Years' War; but the struggles which the brave Prussians made for their national independence, when assailed on all sides by powerful enemies, were not made in vain. Had they not been made, worse evils would have happened. Prussia would not have held her place in the scale of nations, and the people would have fallen in self-respect. It was wrong in Frederic to seize the possession of another. In so doing, he was in no respect better than a robber: and he paid a penalty for his crime. But he also fought in self-defence. This defence was honorable and glorious, and this entitles him to the name of *Great*.

After the peace of Hubertsburg, in 1763, Prussia, for a time, enjoyed repose, and the king devoted himself to the improvement of his country. But the army received his greatest consideration, and a peace establishment of one hundred and sixty thousand men was maintained; an immense force for so small a kingdom, but deemed necessary in such unsettled times. Frederic amused himself in building palaces, in writing books, and corresponding with literary friends. But schemes of ambition were, after all, paramount in his mind.

The Seven Years' War had scarcely closed before the partition of Poland was effected, the greatest political crime of that age, for which the king of Prussia was chiefly responsible.

The Bavarian war was the next great political event of importance which occurred during the reign of Frederic. The emperor of Germany formed a project for the dismemberment of the electorate of Bavaria. The liberties of the Germanic body were in danger, and Frederic came to the rescue. On this occasion, he was the opposer of lawless ambition. In 1778, he took the field with a powerful army; but no action ensued. The Austrian court found it expedient to abandon the design, and the peace of Teschen prevented another fearful contest. The two last public acts of Frederic were the establishment, in 1785, of the Germanic Union for preserving the constitution of the empire, and a treaty of amity and commerce, in 1786, with the United States of America, which was a model of liberal policy respecting the rights of independent nations, both in peace and war.

Death of Frederic.

He died on the 17th of August, 1786, in the seventy-fifth year of his age, and the forty-seventh of his reign. On the whole, he was one of the most remarkable men of his age, and had a great influence on the condition of his country.

His distinguishing peculiarity was his admiration of, and devotion to, the military profession, which he unduly exalted. An ensign in his army ranked higher than a counsellor of legation or a professor of philosophy. His ordinary mode of life was simple and unostentatious, and his favorite residence was the palace of Sans Souci, at Potsdam. He was very fond of music, and of the society of literary men; but he mortified them by his patronizing arrogance, and worried them by his practical jokes. His favorite literary companions were infidel philosophers, and Voltaire received from him marks of the highest distinction. But the king of letters could not live with the despot who solicited his society, and an implacable hatred succeeded familiarity and friendship. The king had considerable literary reputation, and was the author of several works. He was much admired by his soldiers, and permitted in them uncommon familiarity. He was ever free from repulsive formality and bolstered dignity. He was industrious, frugal, and vigilant. Nothing escaped his eye, and he attended to the details of his administration. He was probably the most indefatigable sovereign that ever existed, but displayed more personal ability than enlarged wisdom.

Character of Frederic.

But able and successful as he was as a ruler, he was one of those men for whom it is impossible to entertain a profound respect. He was cruel, selfish, and parsimonious. He was prodigal of the blood of his subjects, and ungenerous in his treatment of those who had sacrificed every thing for his sake. He ruled by fear rather than by love. He introduced into every department the precision of a rigid military discipline, and had no faith in any power but that of mechanical agencies. He quarrelled with his best friends, and seemed to enjoy the miseries he inflicted. He was contemptuous of woman, and disdainful of Christianity. His egotism was not redeemed by politeness or affability, and he made no efforts to disguise his unmitigated selfishness and heartless injustice. He had no loftiness of character, and no appreciation of elevation of sentiment in others. He worshipped only himself and rewarded those only who advanced his ambitious designs.

References. — The Posthumous Works of
Frederic II. Gillies's View of the Reign of
Frederic II. Thiebault's Mémoires de Frédéric le Grand.
Voltaire's Idée du Roi de Prusse. Life of Baron Trenck.
Macaulay's Essay on the Life and Times of Frederic the
Great. Coxe's House of Austria. Tower's, Johnson's, and
Campbell's Life of Frederic the Great.

CHAPTER XXIV
MARIA THERESA AND CATHARINE II

Contemporaneous with Frederic the Great were Maria Theresa and Catharine II.—two sovereigns who claim an especial notice, as representing two mighty empires. The part which Maria Theresa took in the Seven Years' War has been often alluded to and it is not necessary to recapitulate the causes or events of that war. She and Catharine II. were also implicated with Frederic in the partition of Poland. The misfortunes of that unhappy country will be separately considered. In alluding to Maria Theresa, we cannot but review the history of that great empire over which she ruled, the most powerful of the German states. The power of Austria, at different times since the death of the Emperor Charles V., threatened the liberties of Europe; and, to prevent her ascendency, the kings of France, England, and Prussia have expended the treasure and wasted the blood of their subjects.

The Germanic Constitution.

By the peace of Westphalia, in 1648, at the close of the Thirty Years' War, the constitution of Germany was established upon a firm basis. The religious differences between the Catholics and the Protestants were settled, and religious toleration secured in all the states of the empire. It was settled that no decree of the Diet was to pass without a majority of suffrages, and that the Imperial Chamber and the Aulic Council should be composed of a due proportion of Catholics and Protestants. The former was instituted by the Emperor Maximilian I., in 1495, at the Diet of Worms, and was a judicial tribunal, and the highest court of appeal. It consisted of seventeen judges nominated by the emperor, and took cognizance of Austrian affairs chiefly. The Aulic Council was also judicial, and was composed of eighteen persons and attended chiefly to business connected with the empire. The members of these two great judicial tribunals were Catholics; and there were also frequent disputes between them as to their respective jurisdictions. It was ordained by the treaty of Westphalia that a perfect equality should be observed in the appointment of the members of these two important courts; but, in fact, twenty-four Protestants and twenty-six Catholics were appointed to the Imperial Chamber. The various states had the right of presenting members, according to political importance. The Aulic Council was composed of six Protestants and twelve Catholics, and was a tribunal to settle difficulties between the various states of which Germany was composed.

These states were nearly independent of each other, but united under one common head. Each state had its own peculiar government, which was generally monarchical, and regulated its own coinage, police, and administration of justice. Each kingdom, electorate, principality, and imperial city, which were included in the states of Germany, had the right to make war, form alliances, conclude peace, and send ambassadors to foreign courts.

The Diet of the empire consisted of representatives of each of the states, appointed by the princes themselves, and took cognizance of matters of common interest, such as regulations respecting commerce, the license of books, and the military force which each state was required to furnish.

The emperor had power, in some respects, over all these states; but it was chiefly confined to his hereditary dominions. He could not exercise any despotic control over the various princes of the empire; but, as hereditary sovereign of Austria, Styria, Moravia, Bohemia, Hungary, and the Tyrol, he was the most powerful prince in Europe until the aggrandisement of Louis XIV.

Ferdinand III. was emperor of Germany at the peace of Westphalia; but he did not long survive it. He died in 1657, and his son Leopold succeeded him as sovereign of all the Austrian dominions. He had not completed his eighteenth year, but nevertheless was, five months after, elected Emperor of Germany by the Electoral Diet.

Great events occurred during the reign of Leopold I. — the Turkish war, the invasion of the Netherlands by Louis XIV., the heroic struggles of the Prince of Orange, the French invasion of the Palatinate, the accession of a Bourbon prince to the throne of Spain, the discontents of Hungary, and the victories of Marlborough and Eugene. Most of these have been already alluded to, especially in the chapter on Louis XIV., and, therefore, will not be further discussed.

The Hungarian War.

The most important event connected with Austrian affairs, as distinct from those of France, England, and Holland, was the Hungarian war. Hungary was not a province of Austria, but was a distinct state. In 1526, the crowns of the two kingdoms were united, like those of England and Hanover under George I. But the Hungarians were always impatient of the rule of the Emperor of Germany, and, in the space of a century, arose five times in defence of their liberties.

In 1667, one of these insurrections took place, occasioned by the aggressive policy and government of Leopold. The Hungarians conspired to secure their liberties, but in vain. So soon as the emperor was aware of the conspiracy of his Hungarian subjects, he adopted vigorous measures, quartered thirty thousand additional troops in Hungary, loaded the people with taxes, occupied the principal fortresses, banished the chiefs, and changed the constitution of the country. He also attempted to suppress Protestantism, and committed all the excesses of a military despotism. These accumulated oppressions drove a brave but turbulent people to despair, and both Catholics and Protestants united for their common safety. The insurgents were assisted by the Prince of Transylvania, and were supplied with money and provisions by the French. They also found a noble defender in Emeric Tekeli, a young Hungarian noble, who hated Austria as intensely as Hannibal hated Rome, and who, at the head of twenty thousand men, defended his country against the emperor. Moreover, he successfully intrigued with the Turks, who invaded Hungary with two hundred thousand men, and advanced to lay siege to Vienna. This immense army was defeated by John Sobieski, to whom Leopold appealed in his necessities, and the Turks were driven out of Hungary. Tekeli was gradually insulated from those who had formed the great support of his cause, and, in consequence of jealousies which Leopold had fomented between him and the Turks, was arrested and sent in chains to Constantinople. New victories followed the imperial army, and Leopold succeeded in making the crown of Hungary, hitherto elective, hereditary in his family. He instituted in the conquered country a horrible inquisitorial tribunal, and perpetrated cruelties which scarcely find a parallel in the proscriptions of Marius and Sylla. His son Joseph, at the age of ten, was crowned king of Hungary with great magnificence, and with the usual solemnities.

When the Hungarian difficulties were settled, Leopold had more leisure to prosecute his war with the Turks, in which he gained signal successes. The Ottoman Porte was humbled and crippled, and a great source of discontent to the Christian powers of Europe was removed. By the peace of Carlovitz, (1697,) Leopold secured Hungary and Sclavonia, which had been so long occupied by the Turks, and consolidated his empire by the acquisition of Transylvania.

Leopold I. lived only to witness the splendid victories of Marlborough and Eugene, by which the power of his great rival, Louis, was effectually reduced. He died in 1705, having reigned forty-six years; the longest reign in the Austrian annals, except that of Frederic III.

He was a man of great private virtues; pure in his morals, faithful to his wife, a good father, and a kind master. He was minute in his devotions, unbounded in his charities, and cultivated in his taste. But he was reserved, cold, and phlegmatic. His jealousy of Sobieski was unworthy of his station, and his severities in Hungary made him the object of execration. He was narrow, bigoted, and selfish. But he lived in an age of great activity, and his reign forms an era in the military and civil institutions of his country. The artillery had been gradually lightened, and received most of the improvements which at present are continued. Bayonets had been added to muskets, and the use of pikes abandoned. Armies were increased from twenty or thirty thousand men to one hundred thousand, more systematically formed. A police was established in the cities, and these were lighted and paved. Jurisprudence was improved, and numerous grievances were redressed.

The Emperor Joseph.

Leopold was succeeded by his eldest son, Joseph, who had an energetic and aspiring mind. His reign is memorable for the continuation of the great War of the Spanish Succession, signalized by the victories of Marlborough and Eugene, the humiliation of the French, and the career of Charles XII. of Sweden. He also restored Bohemia to its electoral rights, rewarded the elector palatine with the honors and territories wrested from his family by the Thirty Years' War, and confirmed the house of Hanover in the possession of the ninth electorate. He had nearly restored tranquillity to his country, when he died (1711) of the small-pox—a victim to the ignorance of his physicians. He was a lover and patron of the arts, and spoke several languages with elegance and fluency. But he had the usual faults of absolute princes; was prodigal in his expenditures, irascible in his temper, fond of pageants and pleasure, and enslaved by women.

Accession of Maria Theresa.

He was succeeded by his brother, the Archduke Charles, under the title of Charles VI. Soon after his accession, the tranquillity of Europe was established by the peace of Utrecht, and Austria once more became the preponderating power in Europe. But Charles VI. was not capable of appreciating the greatness of his position, or the true sources of national power. He, however, devoted himself zealously to the affairs of his empire, and effected some useful reforms. As he had no male issue, he had drawn up a solemn law, called the *Pragmatic Sanction*, according to which he transferred to his daughter, Maria Theresa, his vast hereditary possessions. He found great difficulty in securing the assent of the European powers to this law; but, after a while, he effected his object. On his death, (1740,) Maria Theresa succeeded to all the dominions of the house of Austria.

No princess ever ascended a throne under circumstances of greater peril, or in a situation which demanded greater energy and fortitude. Her army had dwindled to thirty thousand; her treasury contained only one hundred thousand florins; a general scarcity of provisions distressed the people, and the vintage was cut off by the frost.

Under all these embarrassing circumstances, the Elector of Bavaria laid claim to her territory, and Frederic II. marched into Silesia. It has been already stated that England sympathized with her troubles, and lent a generous aid. Her appeal to her Hungarian subjects, and the enthusiasm they manifested in her cause, have also been described. The boldness of Frederic and the distress of Maria Theresa drew upon them the eyes of all Europe. Hostilities were prosecuted four years, which resulted in the acquisition of Silesia by the King of Prussia. The peace of Dresden (1745) gave a respite to Germany, and Frederic and Maria Theresa prepared for new conflicts.

The Seven Years' War has been briefly described, in connection with the reign of Frederic, and need not be further discussed. The war was only closed by the exhaustion of all the parties engaged in it.

In 1736, Maria Theresa was married to Francis Stephen, Grand Duke of Tuscany, and he was elected (1745) Emperor of Germany, under the title of *Francis I*. He died soon after the peace of Hubertsburg was signed, and his son Joseph succeeded to the throne of the empire, and was co-regent, as his father had been, with Maria Theresa. But the empress queen continued to be the real, as she was the legitimate, sovereign of Austria, and took an active part in all the affairs of Europe.

Maria Theresa Institutes Reforms.

When the tranquillity of her kingdom was restored, she founded various colleges, reformed the public schools, promoted agriculture and instituted many beneficial regulations for the prosperity of her subjects. She reformed the church, diminished the number of superfluous clergy, suppressed the Inquisition and the Jesuits, and formed a system of military economy which surpassed the boasted arrangements of Frederic II. "She combined private economy with public liberality, dignity with condescension, elevation of soul with humility of spirit, and the virtues of domestic life with the splendid qualities which grace a throne." Her death, in 1780, was felt as a general loss to the people, who adored her; and her reign is considered as one of the most illustrious in Austrian annals.

Her reign was, however, sullied by the partition of Poland, in which she was concerned with Frederic the Great and Catharine II. Before this is treated, we will consider the reign of the Russian empress.

The reign of Catharine II., like that of Maria Theresa, is interlinked with that of Frederic. But some remarks concerning her predecessors, after the death of Peter the Great, are first necessary.

Successors of Peter the Great.

Catharine, the wife of Peter, was crowned empress before his death. The first years of her reign were agreeable to the people, because she diminished the taxes, and introduced a mild policy in the government of her subjects. She intrusted to Prince Menzikoff an important share in the government of the realm.

But Catharine, who, during the reign of Peter I., had displayed so much enterprise and intrepidity, very soon disdained business, and abandoned herself to luxury and pleasure. She died in 1727, and Peter II. ascended her throne, chiefly in consequence of the intrigues of Menzikoff, who, like Richelieu, wished to make the emperor his puppet.

Peter II. was only thirteen years of age when he became emperor. He was the son of Alexis, and, consequently, grandson of Peter I. His youth did not permit him to assume the reins of government, and every thing was committed to the care of Menzikoff, who reigned, for a time, with absolute power. But he, at last, incurred the displeasure of his youthful master, and was exiled to Siberia. But Peter II. did not long survive the disgrace of his minister. He died of the small-pox, in 1730.

He was succeeded by Anne, Duchess of Holstein, and eldest daughter of Catharine I. But she lived but a few months after her accession to the throne, and the Princess Elizabeth succeeded her.

The Empress Elizabeth resembled her mother, the beautiful Catharine, but was voluptuous and weak. She abandoned herself to puerile amusements and degrading follies. And she was as superstitious as she was debauched. She would continue whole hours on her knees before an image, to which she spoke, and which she ever consulted; and then would turn from bigotry to infamous sensuality. She hated Frederic II., and assisted Maria Theresa in her struggles. Russia gained no advantage from the Seven Years' War, except that of accustoming the Russians to the tactics of modern warfare. She died in 1762, and was succeeded by the Grand Duke Peter Fedorowitz, son of the Duke of Holstein and Anne, daughter of Peter I. He assumed the title of Peter III.

Murder of Peter III.

Peter III. was a weak prince, but disposed to be beneficent. One of his first acts was to recall the numerous exiles whom the jealousy of Elizabeth had consigned to the deserts of Siberia. Among them was Biren, the haughty lover and barbarous minister of the Empress Anne and Marshal Munich, a veteran of eighty-two years of age. Peter also abolished the Inquisition, established by Alexis Michaelowitz, and promoted commerce, the arts, and sciences. He attempted to imitate the king of Prussia, for whom he had an extravagant admiration. He set at liberty the Prussian prisoners, and made peace with Frederic II. He had a great respect for Germany, but despised the country over which he was called to reign. But his partiality for the Germans, and his numerous reforms, alienated the affections of his subjects, and he was not sufficiently able to curb the spirit of discontent. He imitated his immediate predecessors in the vices of drunkenness and sensuality, and was guilty of great imprudences. He reigned but a few months, being dethroned and murdered. His wife, the Empress Catharine, was the chief of the conspirators; and she was urged to the bloody act by her own desperate circumstances. She was obnoxious to her husband, who probably would have destroyed her, had his life been prolonged. She, in view of his hostility, and prompted by an infernal ambition, sought to dethrone her husband. She was assisted by some of the most powerful nobles, and gained over most of the regiments of the imperial guard. The Archbishop of Novgorod and the clergy were friendly to her, because they detested the reforms which Peter had attempted to make. Catharine became mistress of St. Petersburg, and caused herself to be crowned Empress of Russia, in one of the principal churches. Peter had timely notice of the revolt, but not the energy to suppress it. He listened to the entreaties of women, rather than to the counsels of those veteran generals who still supported his throne. He was timid, irresolute, and vacillating. He was doomed. He was a weak and infatuated prince, and nothing could save him. He surrendered himself into the hands of Catharine, abdicated his empire, and, shortly after, died of poison. His wife seated herself, without further opposition, on his throne; and the principal nobles of the empire, the army, and the clergy, took the oath of allegiance, and the monarchs of Europe acknowledged her as the absolute sovereign of Russia. In 1763, she was firmly established in the power which had been before wielded by Catharine I. She had dethroned an imbecile prince, whom she abhorred; but the revolution was accomplished without bloodshed, and resulted in the prosperity of Russia.

Catharine was a woman of great moral defects; but she had many excellences to counterbalance them; and her rule was, on the whole, able and beneficent. She was no sooner established in the power which she had usurped, than she directed attention to the affairs of her empire, and sought to remedy the great evils which existed. She devoted herself to business, advanced commerce and the arts, regulated the finances, improved the jurisprudence of the realm, patronized all works of internal improvement, rewarded eminent merit, encouraged education, and exercised a liberal and enlightened policy in her intercourse with foreign powers. After engaging in business with her ministers, she would converse with scholars and philosophers. With some she studied politics, and with others literature. She tolerated all religions, abolished odious courts, and enacted mild laws. She held out great inducements for foreigners to settle in Russia, and founded colleges and hospitals in all parts of her empire.

Assassination of Ivan.

Beneficent as her reforms were, she nevertheless committed some great political crimes. One of these was the assassination of the dethroned Ivan, the great-grandson of the Czar Ivan Alexejewitsch, who was brother of Peter the Great. On the death of the Empress Anne, in 1731, he had been proclaimed emperor: but when Elizabeth was placed upon the throne, the infant was confined in the fortress of Schlussenburg. Here he was so closely guarded and confined, that he was never allowed access to the open air or the light of day. On the accession of Catharine, he was twenty-three years of age, and was extremely ignorant and weak. But a conspiracy was formed to liberate him, and place him on the throne. The attempt proved abortive, and the prince perished by the sword of his jailers, who were splendidly rewarded for their infamous services.

Her scheme of foreign aggrandizement, and especially her interference in the affairs of Poland, caused the Ottoman Porte to declare war against her, which war proved disastrous to Turkey, and contributed to aggrandize the empire of Russia. The Turks lost several battles on the Pruth, Dniester, and Danube; the provinces of Wallachia, and Moldavia, and Bessarabia submitted to the Russian arms; while a great naval victory, in the Mediterranean, was gained by Alexis Orloff, whose share in the late revolution had raised him from the rank of a simple soldier to that of a general of the empire, and a favorite of the empress. The naval defeat of the Turks at Tschesmé, by Orloff and Elphinstone, was one of the most signal of that age, and greatly weakened the power of Turkey. The war was not terminated until 1774, when the Turks were compelled to make peace, by the conditions of which, Russia obtained a large accession of territory, a great sum of money, the free navigation of the Black Sea, and a passage through the Dardanelles.

In 1772 occurred the partition of Poland between Austria, Prussia, and Russia. Catharine and Frederic II. were the chief authors of this great political crime, which will be treated in the notice on Poland.

The reign of Catharine was not signalized by any other great political events which affected materially the interests of Europe, except the continuation of the war with the Turks, which broke out again in 1778, and which was concluded in 1792, by the treaty of Jassy. In this war, Prince Potemkin, the favorite and prime minister of Catharine, greatly distinguished himself; also General Suwarrow, afterwards noted for his Polish campaigns. In this war Russia lost two hundred thousand men, and the Turks three hundred and thirty thousand, besides expending two hundred and fifty millions of piasters. The most important political consequence was the aggrandizement of Russia, whose dominion was established on the Black Sea.

Death of Catharine.

Catharine, having acquired, either by arms or intrigues, almost half of Poland, the Crimea, and a part of the frontiers of Turkey, then turned her arms against Persia. But she died before she could realize her dreams of conquest. At her death, she was the most powerful sovereign that ever reigned in Russia. She was succeeded by her son, Paul I., (1796,) and her remains were deposited by the side of her murdered husband, while his chief murderers, Alexis Orloff and Prince Baratinski, were ordered to stand at her funeral, on each side of his coffin as chief mourners.

Catharine, though a woman of great energy and talent, was ruled by favorites; the most distinguished of whom were Gregory Orloff and Prince Potemkin. The former was a man of brutal manners and surprising audacity; the latter was more civilized, but was a man disgraced, like Orloff, by every vice. His memory, however, is still cherished in Russia on account of his military successes. He received more honors and rewards from his sovereign than is recorded of any favorite and minister of modern times. His power was equal to what Richelieu enjoyed, and his fortune was nearly as great as Mazarin's. He was knight of the principal orders of Prussia, Sweden, Poland, and Russia, field-marshal, commander-in-chief of the Russian armies, high admiral of the fleets, great hetman of the Cossacks, and chamberlain of the empress. He received from her a fortune of fifty millions of roubles; equal to nearly twenty-five millions of dollars. The Orloffs received also about seventeen millions in lands, and palaces, and money, with forty-five thousand peasants.

Her Character.

Catharine had two passions which never left her but with her last breath—the love of the other sex, which degenerated into the most unbounded licentiousness, and the love of glory, which sunk into vanity. She expended ninety millions of roubles on her favorites, the number of which is almost incredible; and she was induced to engage in wars, which increased the burdens of her subjects.

With the exception of these two passions, her character is interesting and commanding. Her reign was splendid, and her court magnificent. Her institutions and monuments were to Russia what the magnificence of Louis XIV. was to France. She was active and regular in her habits; was never hurried away by anger, and was never a prey to dejection; caprice and ill humor were never perceived in her conduct; she was humorous, gay, and affable; she appreciated literature, and encouraged good institutions; and, with all her faults, obtained the love and reverence of her subjects. She had not the virtues of Maria Theresa, but had, perhaps, greater energy of character. Her foulest act was her part in the dismemberment of Poland, which now claims a notice.

References.—For the reign of Maria Theresa, see
Archdeacon Coxe's Memoirs of the House of Austria,
which is the most interesting and complete. See also
Putter's Constitution of the Germanic Empire; Kolhrausch's
History of Germany; Heeren's Modern History; Smyth's
Lectures; also a history of Germany, in Dr. Lardner's
Cyclopædia. For a life of Catharine, see Castina's Life,
translated by Hunter; Tooke's Life of Catharine II.; Ségur's
Vie de Catharine II.; Coxe's Travels; Heeren's and Russell's
Modern History.

CHAPTER XXV
CALAMITIES OF POLAND

Calamities of Poland.

No kingdom in Europe has been subjected to so many misfortunes and changes, considering its former greatness, as the Polish monarchy. Most of the European states have retained their ancient limits, for several centuries, without material changes, but Poland has been conquered, dismembered, and plundered. Its ancient constitution has been completely subverted, and its extensive provinces are now annexed to the territories of Russia, Austria, and Prussia. The greatness of the national calamities has excited the sympathy of Christian nations, and its unfortunate fate is generally lamented.

In the sixteenth century, Poland was a greater state than Russia, and was the most powerful of the northern kingdoms of Europe. The Poles, as a nation, are not, however, of very ancient date. Prior to the ninth century, they were split up into numerous tribes, independent of each other, and governed by their respective chieftains. Christianity was introduced in the tenth century, and the earliest records of the people were preserved by the monks. We know but little, with certainty, until the time of Piast, who united the various states, and whose descendants reigned until 1386, when the dynasty of the Jagellons commenced, and continued till 1572. Under the princes of this line, the government was arbitrary and oppressive. War was the great business and amusement of the princes, and success in it brought the highest honors. The kings were, however, weak, cruel, and capricious, ignorant, fierce, and indolent. The records of their reigns are the records of drunkenness, extortion, cruelty, lust, and violence—the common history of all barbarous kings. There were some of the Polish princes who were benignant and merciful, but the great majority of them, like the Merovingian and Carlovingian princes of the Dark Ages, were unfit to reign, were the slaves of superstition, and the tools of designing priests. There is a melancholy gloom hanging over the annals of the Middle Ages, especially in reference to kings. And yet their reigns, though stained by revolting crimes, generally were to be preferred to the anarchy of an interregnum, or the overgrown power of nobles.

The brightest period in the history of Poland was during the reigns of the Jagellon princes, especially when Casimir I. held the sceptre of empire. During his reign, Lithuania, which then comprised Hungary, Bohemia, and Silesia, was added to his kingdom. The university of Cracow was founded, and Poland was the great resort of the Jews, to whom were committed the trade and commerce of the land. But the rigors of the feudal system, and the vast preponderance of the aristocracy, proved unfortunate for the prosperity of the kingdom. What in England was the foundation of constitutional liberty, proved in Poland to be subversive of all order and good government. In England, the representative of the nation was made an instrument in the hands of the king of humbling the great nobility. Absolutism was established upon the ruins of feudalism. But, in Poland, the Diet of the nation controlled the king, and, as the representatives of the nobility alone, perpetuated the worst evils of the feudal system.

The Crown of Poland Made Elective.

When Sigismund II., the last male heir of the house of Jagellon, died, in 1572, the nobles were sufficiently powerful to make the crown elective. From this period we date the decline of Poland. The Reformation, so beneficent in its effects, did not spread to this Sclavonic country; and the barbarism of the Middle Ages received no check. On the death of Sigismund, the nobles would not permit the new sovereign to be elected by the Diet, but only by the whole body of the nobility. The plain of Praga was the place selected for the election; and, at the time appointed, such a vast number of nobles arrived, that the plain, of twelve miles in circumference, was scarcely large enough to contain them and their retinues. There never was such a sight seen since the crusaders were marshalled on the field of Chalcedon, for all the nobles were gorgeously apparelled, and decked with ermine, gold, and jewels. The Polish horseman frequently invests half his fortune in his horse and dress. In the centre of the field was the tent of the late king, capable of accommodating eight thousand men. The candidates for the crown were Ernest Archduke of Austria; the Czar of Russia; a Swedish prince, and Henry of Valois, Duke of Anjou, and brother of Charles IX., king of France.

Election of Henry, Duke of Anjou.

The first candidate was rejected because the house of Austria was odious to the Polish nobles; the second, on account of his arrogance; and the third, because he was not powerful enough to bring advantage to the republic. The choice fell on the Duke of Anjou; and he, for the title of a king, agreed to the ignominious conditions which the Poles proposed, viz., that he should not attempt to influence the election of his successors, or assume the title of heir of the monarchy, or declare war without the consent of the Diet, or impose taxes of any description, or have power to appoint his ambassadors, or any foreigner to a benefice in the church; that he should convoke the Diet every two years; and that he should not marry without its permission. He also was required to furnish four thousand French troops, in case of war; to apply annually, for the sole benefit of the Polish state, a considerable part of his hereditary revenues; to pay the debts of the crown; and to educate, at his own expense, at Paris or Cracow, one hundred Polish nobles. He had scarcely been crowned when his brother died, and he was called to the throne of France. But he found it difficult to escape from his kingdom, the government of which he found to be burdensome and vexatious. No criminal ever longed to escape from a prison, more than this prince to break the fetters which bound him to his imperious subjects. He resolved to run away; concealed his intentions with great address; gave a great ball at his palace; and in the midst of the festivities, set out with full speed towards Silesia. He was pursued, but reached the territories of the emperor of Germany before he was overtaken. He reached Paris in safety, and was soon after crowned as king of France.

Sobieski Assists the Emperor Leopold.

He was succeeded by Stephen, Duke of Transylvania; and he, again, by Sigismund, Prince of Sweden. The two sons of Sigismund, successively, were elected kings of Poland, the last of whom, John II., was embroiled in constant war. It was during his disastrous reign that John Sobieski, with ten thousand Poles, defeated eighty thousand Cossacks, the hereditary enemies of Poland. On the death of Michael, who had succeeded John II., Sobieski was elected king, and he assumed the title of *John III.* He was a native noble, and was chosen for his military talents and successes. Indeed, Poland needed a strong arm to defend her. Her decline had already commenced, and Sobieski himself could not avert the ruin which impended. For some time, Poland enjoyed cessation from war, and the energies of the monarch were directed to repair the evils which had disgraced his country. But before he could prosecute successfully any useful reforms, the war between the Turks and the eastern powers of Europe broke out, and Vienna was besieged by an overwhelming army of two hundred thousand Mohammedans. The city was bravely defended, but its capture seemed inevitable. The emperor of Germany, Leopold, in his despair, implored the aid of Sobieski. He was invested with the command of the allied armies of Austrians, Bavarians, Saxons, and Poles, amounting to seventy thousand men. With this force he advanced to relieve Vienna. He did not hesitate to attack the vast forces encamped beneath the walls of the Austrian capital, and obtained one of the most signal victories in the history of war. Immense treasures fell into his hands, and Vienna and Christendom were saved.

But the mean-spirited emperor treated his deliverer with arrogance and chilling coldness. No gratitude was exhibited or felt. But the pope sent him the rarest of his gifts—"the dove of pearls." Sobieski, in spite of the ingratitude of Leopold, pursued his victories over the Turks; and, like Charles Martel, ten centuries before, freed Europe from the danger of a Mohammedan yoke. But he saved a serpent, when about to be crushed, which turned and stung him for his kindness. The dismemberment of his country soon followed the deliverance of Vienna.

He was succeeded, in 1696, by Frederic Augustus, Elector of Saxony, whose reign was a constant succession of disasters. During his reign, Poland was invaded and conquered by Charles XII. of Sweden. He was succeeded by his son, Frederic Augustus II., the most beautiful, extravagant, luxurious, and licentious monarch of his age. But he was a man of elegant tastes, and he filled Dresden with pictures and works of art, which are still the admiration of travellers. His reign, as king of Poland, was exceedingly disastrous. Muscovite and Prussian armies traversed the plains of Poland at pleasure, and extorted whatever they pleased. Faction was opposed by faction in the field and in the Diet. The national assembly was dissolved by the *veto*, the laws were disregarded, and brute force prevailed on every side. The miserable peasants in vain besought the protection of their brutal yet powerless lords. Bands of robbers infested the roads, and hunger invaded the cottages. The country rapidly declined in wealth, population, and public spirit.

Under the reign of Stanislaus II., who succeeded Frederic Augustus II., in 1764, the ambassadors of Prussia, Austria, and Russia, informed the miserable king that, in order to prevent further bloodshed, and restore peace to Poland, the three powers had determined to insist upon their claims to some of the provinces of the kingdom. This barefaced and iniquitous scheme for the dismemberment of Poland originated with Frederic the Great. So soon as the close of the Seven Years' War allowed him repose, he turned his eyes to Poland, with a view of seizing one of her richest provinces. Territories inhabited by four million eight hundred thousand people, were divided between Frederic, Maria Theresa, and Catharine II. There were no scruples of conscience in the breast of Frederic, or of Catharine, a woman of masculine energy, but disgraceful morals. The conscience of Maria Theresa, however, long resisted. "The fear of hell," said she, "restrains me from seizing another's possessions;" but sophistry was brought to bear upon her mind, and the lust of dominion asserted its powerful sway. This crime was regarded with detestation by the other powers of Europe; but they were too much occupied with their own troubles to interfere, except by expostulation. England was disturbed by difficulties in the colonies, and France was distracted by revolutionary tumults.

The Liberum Veto.

Stanislaus, robbed of one third of his dominions, now directed his attention to those reforms which had been so long imperatively needed. He intrusted to the celebrated Zamoyski the task of revising the constitution. The patriotic chancellor recommended the abolition of the "liberum veto," a fatal privilege, by which any one of the armed equestrians, who assembled on the plain of Praga to elect a king, or deliberate on state affairs, had power to nullify the most important acts, and even to dissolve the assembly. A single word, pronounced in the vehemence of domestic strife, or by the influence of external corruption, could plunge the nation into a lethargic sleep. And faction went so far as often to lead to the dissolution of the assembly. The treasury, the army, the civil authority then fell into a state of anarchy. Zamoyski also recommended the emancipation of serfs, the encouragement of commerce, the elevation of the trading classes, and the abolition of the fatal custom of electing a king. But the Polish nobles, infatuated and doomed, opposed these wholesome reforms. They even had the madness to invoke the aid of the Empress Catharine to protect them in their ancient privileges. She sent an army into Poland, and great disturbances resulted.

The Fall of Poland.

Too late, at last, the nobles perceived their folly, and adopted some of the proposed reforms. But these reforms gave a new pretence to the allied powers for a second dismemberment. An army of one hundred thousand men invaded Poland, to effect a new partition. The unhappy country, without fortified towns or mountains, abandoned by all the world, distracted by divisions, and destitute of fortresses and military stores, was crushed by the power of gigantic enemies. There were patriotism and bravery left, but no union or organized strength. The patriots made a desperate struggle under Kosciusko, a Lithuanian noble, but were forced to yield to inevitable necessity. Warsaw for a time held out against fifty thousand men; but the Polish hero was defeated in a decisive engagement, and unfortunately taken prisoner. His countrymen still rallied, and another bloody battle was fought at Praga, opposite Warsaw, on the other side of the Vistula, and ten thousand were slain; Praga was reduced to a heap of ruins; and twelve thousand citizens were slaughtered in cold blood. Warsaw soon after surrendered, Stanislaus was sent as a captive to Russia, and the final partition of the kingdom was made.

"Sarmatia fell," but not "unwept," or "without a crime." "She fell," says Alison, "a victim of her own dissensions, of the chimera of equality falsely pursued, and the rigor of aristocracy unceasingly maintained. The eldest born of the European family was the first to perish, because she had thwarted all the ends of the social union; because she united the turbulence of democratic to the exclusion of aristocratic societies; because she had the vacillation of a republic without its energy, and the oppression of a monarchy without its stability. The Poles obstinately refused to march with other nations in the only road to civilization; they had valor, but it could not enforce obedience to the laws; it could not preserve domestic tranquillity; it could not restrain the violence of petty feuds and intestine commotions; it could not preserve the proud nobles from unbounded dissipation and corruption; it could not prevent foreign powers from interfering in the affairs of the kingdom; it could not dissolve the union of these powers with discontented parties at home; it could not inspire the slowly-moving machine of government with vigor, when the humblest partisan, corrupted with foreign money, could arrest it with a word; it could not avert the entrance of foreign armies to support the factious and rebellious; it could not uphold, in a divided country, the national independence against the combined effects of foreign and domestic treason; finally, it could not effect impossibilities, nor turn aside the destroying sword which had so long impended over it."

But this great crime was attended with retribution. Prussia, in her efforts to destroy Poland, paralyzed her armies on the Rhine. Suwarrow entered Warsaw when its spires were reddened by the fires of Praga; but the sack of the fallen capital was forgotten in the conflagration of Moscow. The remains of the soldiers of Kosciusko sought a refuge in republican France, and served with distinction, in the armies of Napoleon, against the powers that had dismembered their country.

The ruin of Poland, as an independent state, was not fully accomplished until the year 1832, when it was incorporated into the great empire of Russia. But the history of the late revolution, with all its melancholy results, cannot be well presented in this connection.

References.—Fletcher's History of Poland. Rulhière's Histoire de l'Anarchie de Pologne. Coyer's Vie de Sobieski. Parthenay's History of Augustus II. Hordynski's History of the late Polish Revolution. Also see Lives of Frederic II., Maria Theresa, and Catharine II.; contemporaneous histories of Prussia, Russia, and Austria; Alison's History of Europe; Smyth's Lectures; Russell's Modern Europe; Heeren's Modern History.

CHAPTER XXVI
THE DECLINE OF THE OTTOMAN EMPIRE

Saracenic Empire.

While the great monarchies of Western Europe were struggling for preëminence, and were developing resources greater than had ever before been exhibited since the fall of the Roman empire, that great power which had alarmed and astonished Christendom in the sixteenth and seventeenth centuries, began to show the signs of weakness and decay. Nothing, in the history of society, is more marvellous than the rise of Mohammedan kingdoms. The victories of the Saracens and Turks were rapid and complete; and in the tenth century, they were the most successful warriors on the globe, and threatened to subvert the world. They had planted the standard of the Prophet on the walls of Eastern capitals, and had extended their conquests to India on the east, and to Spain on the west. Powerful Mohammedan states had arisen in Asia, Africa, and Europe, and the Crusaders alone arrested the progress of these triumphant armies. The enthusiasm which the doctrines of Mohammed had kindled, cannot easily be explained; but it was fresh, impetuous, and self-sacrificing. Successive armies of Mohammedan invaders overwhelmed the ancient realms of civilization, and reduced the people whom they conquered and converted to a despotic yoke. But success enervated the victorious conquerors of the East, the empire of the Caliphs was broken up, and great changes took place even in those lands where the doctrines of the Koran prevailed. Mohammed perpetuated a religion, but not an empire. Different Saracenic chieftains revolted from the "Father of the Faithful," and established separate kingdoms, or viceroyalties, nearly independent of the acknowledged successors of Mohammed. The Saracenic empire was early dismembered, and the sultans of Egypt, Spain, and Syria contested for preëminence.

Rise of the Turks.

But a new power arose on the ruins of the Saracen empire, and became the enthusiastic defenders of the religion of Islam. The Turks were an obscure tribe of barbarians when Bagdad was the seat of a powerful monarchy. Their origin has been traced to the wilds of Scythia; but they early deserted their native forests in search of more fruitful regions. When Apulia and Sicily were subdued by the Norman pirates, a swarm of these Scythian shepherds settled in Armenia, probably in the ninth century, and, by their valor and simplicity, soon became a powerful tribe. Not long after they were settled in their new abode, the Sultan of Persia invoked their aid to assist him in his wars against the Caliph of Bagdad, his great rival. The Turks complied with his request, and their arms were successful. The sultan then refused to part with such useful auxiliaries, and moreover, fearing their strength, designed to employ them in his wars against the Hindoos, and to shut them up in the centre of his dominions. The Turkmans rebelled, withdrew into a mountainous part of the country, became robbers, and devastated the adjacent countries. The band of robbers gradually swelled into a powerful army, gained a great victory over the troops of the Sultan Mohammed, and placed their chieftain upon the Persian throne, (1038.) According to Gibbon, the new monarch was chosen by lot, and Seljuk had the fortune to win the prize of conquest, and became the founder of the dynasty of the Shepherd kings. During the reign of his grandson Togrul, the ancient Persian princes were expelled, and the Turks embraced the religion of the conquered. In 1055, the Turkish sultan delivered the Caliph of Bagdad from the arms of the Caliph of Egypt, who disputed with him the title of *Commander of the Faithful.* For this service he was magnificently rewarded by the grateful successor of the Prophet, who, at that time, banqueted in his palace at Bagdad—a venerable phantom of power. The victorious sultan was publicly commissioned as lieutenant of the caliph, and he was virtually seated on the throne of the Abbassides. Shortly after, the Turkish conqueror invaded the falling empire of the Greeks, and its Asiatic provinces were irretrievably lost. In the latter part of the eleventh century, the Turkish power was established in Asia Minor, and Jerusalem itself had fallen into the hands of the sultan. He exacted two pieces of gold from the Christian pilgrim, and treated him, moreover, with greater cruelty than the Saracens had ever exercised. The extortion and oppression of the Turkish masters of the Sacred City led to the Crusades and the final possession of Western Asia by the followers of the Prophet. The Turkish power constantly increased with the decline of the Saracenic and Greek empires, but the Seljukian dynasty, like that of Abbassides at Bagdad, at last run out, and Othman, a soldier of fortune, became sultan of the Turks. He is regarded as the founder of the Ottoman empire, and under his reign, from 1299 to 1326, the Moslems made rapid strides in the progress of aggrandizement.

Turkish Conquerors.

Orkham, his son, instituted the force of the Janizaries, completed the conquest of Bithynia, and laid the foundation of Turkish power in

Europe. Under his successor, Amurath I., Adrianople became the capital of the Ottoman empire, and the rival of Constantinople. Bajazet succeeded Amurath, and his conquests extended from the Euphrates to the Danube. In 1396, he defeated, at Nicopolis, a confederate army of one hundred thousand Christians; and, in the intoxication of victory, declared that he would feed his horse with a bushel of oats on the altar of St. Peter, at Rome. Had it not been for the victories of Tamerlane, Constantinople, which contained within its walls the feeble fragments of a great empire, would also have fallen into his hands. He was unsuccessful in his war with the great conqueror of Asia, and was defeated at the battle of Angora, (1402,) and taken captive, and carried to Samarcand, by Tamerlane, in an iron cage.

The great Bajazet died in captivity, and Mohammed I. succeeded to his throne. He restored, on a firmer basis, the fabric of the Ottoman monarchy, and devoted himself to the arts of peace. His successor, Amurath II., continued hostilities with the Greeks, and laid siege to Constantinople. But this magnificent city, the last monument of Roman greatness, resisted the Turkish arms only for a while. In 1453, it fell before an irresistible force of three hundred thousand men, supported by a fleet of three hundred sail. The Emperor Constantine succeeded in maintaining a siege of fifty-three days; and the religion and empire of the Christians were trodden to the dust by the Moslem conquerors. The city was sacked, the people were enslaved, and the Church of St. Sophia was despoiled of the oblations of ages, and converted into a Mohammedan mosque. One hundred and twenty thousand manuscripts perished in the sack of Constantinople, and the palaces and treasure of the Greeks were transferred to semi-barbarians.

Progress of the Turks.

From that time, the Byzantine capital became the seat of the Ottoman empire; and, for more than two centuries, Turkish armies excited the fears and disturbed the peace of the world. They gradually subdued and annexed Macedonia, the Peloponnesus, Epirus, Bulgaria, Servia, Bosnia, Armenia, Cyprus, Syria, Egypt, India, Tunis, Algiers, Media, Mesopotamia, and a part of Hungary, to the dominions of the sultan. In the sixteenth century, the Ottoman empire was the most powerful in the world. Nor should we be surprised, in view of the great success of the Turks, when we remember their singular bravery, their absorbing ambition, their almost incredible obedience to the commands of the sultan, and the unity which pervaded the national councils. They also fought to extend their religion, to which they were blind devotees. After the capture of Constantinople, a succession of great princes sat on the most absolute throne known in modern times; men disgraced by many crimes, but still singularly adapted to extend their dominion.

The progress of the Turks justly alarmed the Emperor Charles V., and he exerted all his energies to unite the German princes against them, but unsuccessfully. The Sultan Solyman, called the *Magnificent*, maintained his supremacy over Transylvania, Wallachia, and Moldavia, ravaged Hungary, wrested Rhodes from the Knights of St. John, conquered the whole of Arabia, and attacked the Portuguese dominion in India. He raised the Turkish empire to the highest pitch of its greatness, and died while besieging Sigeth, as he was completing the conquest of Hungary. His empire was one vast camp, and his decrees were dated from the imperial stirrup. The iron sceptre which he and his successors wielded was imbrued in blood; and discipline alone was the politics of his soldiers, and rapine their resources.

Selim II. succeeded Solyman, and set the ruinous example of not going himself to the wars, and of carrying them on by his lieutenants. His son, Murad III., penetrated into Russia and Poland, and made war on the Emperor of Germany. Mohammed III., who died in 1604, murdered all his brothers, nineteen in number, and executed his own son. It was usual, when an emperor mounted the throne, for him to put to death his brothers and nephews. Indeed, the characters of the sultans were marked by unusual ferocity and jealousy, and they were unscrupulous in the means they took to advance their power. The world has never seen more suspicious tyrants; and it ever must excite our wonder that they were so unhesitatingly obeyed. But they were, however, sometimes dethroned by the Janizaries, who constituted a sort of imperial guard. Osman II., fearing their power, and disgusted with their degeneracy, resolved to destroy them, as dangerous to the state. But his design was discovered, and he himself lost his life, (1622.) Several monsters of tyranny and iniquity succeeded him, whose reigns were disgraced by every excess of debauchery and cruelty. Their subjects, however, had not, as yet, lost vigor, temperance, and ambition, and still continued to furnish troops unexampled for discipline and bravery, and bent on conquest and dominion.

The Turkish power received no great checks until the reign of Mohammed IV., during which Sobieski defeated an immense army, which had laid siege to Vienna. By the peace of Carlovitz, in 1699, Transylvania was ceded to the Emperor of Germany, and a barrier was raised against Mohammedan invasion.

The Russians, from the time of Peter the Great, looked with great jealousy on the power of the sultan, and several wars were the result. No Russian sovereign desired the humiliation of the Porte more than Catharine II. A bloody contest ensued, signalized by the victories of Galitzin, Suwarrow, Romanzoff, and Orloff, by which Turkey became a second class power, no longer feared by the European states.

Decline of Turkish Power.

From the peace of Carlovitz, the decline of the Ottoman empire has been gradual, but marked, owing to the indifference of the Turks to all modern improvements, and a sluggish, conservative policy, hostile to progress, and sceptical of civilization. The Turks have ever been bigoted Mohammedans, and hostile to European influences. The Oriental dress has been preserved in Constantinople, and all the manners and customs of the people are similar to what they were in Asia several centuries ago.

Turkish Institutions.

One of the peculiarities of the Turkish government, in the most flourishing period of its history, was the institution of the Janizaries—a guard of soldiers, to whom was intrusted the guardianship of the sultan, and the protection of his capital. When warlike and able princes were seated on the throne, this institution proved a great support to the government; but when the reins were held by effeminate princes, the Janizaries, like the Prætorian Guards of Rome, acquired an undue ascendency, and even deposed the monarchs whom they were bound to obey. They were insolent, extortionate, and extravagant, and became a great burden to the state. At first they were brave and resolute; but they gradually lost their skill and their courage, were uniformly beaten in the later wars with the Russians, and retained nothing of the soldier but the name. Mahmoud II., in our own time, succeeded in dissolving this dangerous body, and in introducing European tactics into his army.

Turkish Character.

The Turkish institutions have reference chiefly to the military character of the nation. All Mussulmans, in the eye of the law, are soldiers, to whom the extension of the empire and the propagation of their faith were the avowed objects of warfare. They may be regarded, wherever they have conquered, as military colonists, exercising great tyranny, and treating all vanquished subjects with contempt. The government has ever been a pure despotism, and both the executive and legislative authorities have been vested in the sultan. He is the sole fountain of honor; for, in Turkey, birth confers no privilege. His actions are regarded as prescribed by an inevitable fate, and his subjects suffer with resignation. The evils of despotism are aggravated by the ignorance and effeminacy of those to whom power is intrusted, although the grand vizier, who is the prime minister of the empire, is generally a man of great experience and talent. All the laws of the country are founded upon the precepts of the Koran, the example of Mohammed, the precepts of the four first caliphs, and the decision of learned doctors upon disputed cases. Justice is administered promptly, but without much regard to equity or mercy; and the course of the grand vizier is generally marked with blood. The character of the people partakes of the nature of their government, religion, and climate. They are arrogant, ignorant, and austere; passing from devotion to obscenity; fastidiously abstemious in some things, and grossly sensual in others. They have cherished the virtues of hospitality, and are fond of conversation but their domestic life is spent in voluptuous idleness, and is dull and insipid compared with that of Europeans. But the Turks have degenerated. In the fifteenth and sixteenth centuries, they were simple, brave, and religious. They founded an immense empire on the ruins of Asiatic monarchies, and filled the world with the terror of their arms. For two hundred years their power has been retrograding, and there is much reason now to believe that a total eclipse of their glory is soon to take place.

References.—See Knolle's History of Turkey. Eton's Survey of the Turkish Empire. Upham's History of the Ottoman Empire. Encyclopædia Britannica. Heeren's Modern History. Madden's Travels in Turkey. Russell's Modern Europe. Life of Catharine II.

CHAPTER XXVII
REIGN OF GEORGE III. TO THE
ADMINISTRATION OF WILLIAM PITT

Great subjects were discussed in England, and great events happened in America, during the latter years of the reigns of Frederic II., Catharine II., and Maria Theresa. These now demand attention.

Military Successes in America.

George III. ascended the throne of Great Britain at a period of unparalleled prosperity, when the English arms were victorious in all parts of the world, and when commerce and the arts had greatly enriched his country and strengthened its political importance. By the peace of Paris, (1763,) the dominions of George III. were enlarged, and the country over which he reigned was the most powerful in Europe.

Mr. George Grenville succeeded the Earl of Bute as the prime minister of the king, and he was chiefly assisted by the Earls of Egremont and Halifax. His administration was signalized by the prosecution of Wilkes, and by schemes for the taxation of the American colonies.

Mr. Wilkes was a member of parliament, but a man of ruined fortunes and profligate morals. As his circumstances were desperate, he applied to the ministry for some post of emolument; but his application was rejected. Failure enraged him, and he swore revenge, and resolved to libel the ministers, under the pretext of exercising the liberty of the press. He was editor of the North Briton, a periodical publication of some talent, but more bitterness. In the forty-fifth number, he assailed the king, charging him with a direct falsehood. The charge should have been dismissed with contempt; for it was against the dignity of the government to refute an infamous slander. But, in an evil hour, it was thought expedient to vindicate the honor of the sovereign; and a warrant was therefore issued against the editor, puɔlisher, and printer of the publication. The officers of the law entered Wilkes's house late one evening, seized his papers, and committed him to the Tower. He sued out a writ of habeas corpus, in consequence of which he was brought up to Westminster Hall. Being a member of parliament, and a man of considerable abilities and influence, his case attracted attention. The judges decided that his arrest was illegal, since a member of parliament could not be imprisoned except for treason, felony, or breach of the peace. He had not committed any of these crimes, for a libel had only a *tendency* to disturb the peace. Still, had he been a private person, his imprisonment would have been legal; but being unconstitutional, he was discharged. Lord Chief Justice Pratt gained great popularity by his charge in favor of the liberation of Wilkes, and ever nobly defended constitutional liberty. He is better known as Lord Camden, the able lord chancellor and statesman during a succeeding administration, and one of the greatest lawyers England has produced, ranking with Lord Hardwicke, Lord Ellenborough, and Lord Eldon.

Prosecution of Wilkes.

After the discharge of Wilkes, the attorney-general was then ordered to commence a state prosecution, and he was arraigned at the bar of the House of Commons. It was voted, by a great majority, that the forty-fifth number of the North Briton was a scandalous and seditious libel, and tending to excite traitorous insurrections. It was further voted that the paper should be burned by the common hangman. Wilkes then complained to the House of a breach of privilege, which complaint, being regular, was considered. But the Commons decided that the privilege of parliament does not extend to a libel, which resolution was against the decision of the Court of Common Pleas, and the precedents upon record in their own journals. However scandalous and vulgar the vituperation of Wilkes, and especially disgraceful in a member of parliament, still his prosecution was an attack on the constitution. Wilkes was arrested on what is called a *general warrant*, which, if often resorted to, would be fatal to the liberties of the people. Many, who strongly disliked the libeller, still defended him in this instance, among whom were Pitt, Beckford, Legge, Yorke, and Sir George Saville. But party spirit and detestation of Wilkes triumphed over the constitution, and the liberties of members of parliament were abridged even by themselves. But Wilkes was not discouraged, and immediately brought an action, in Westminster Hall, against the Earl of Halifax, the secretary of state, for seizing his papers, and, after a hearing of fifteen hours, before Lord Chief Justice Pratt and a special jury, obtained a verdict in his favor of one thousand pounds damages and costs.

While the Commons were prosecuting Wilkes for a libel, the Lords also continued the prosecution. Wilkes, in conjunction with Potter, a dissipated son of Archbishop Potter, during some of their bacchanalian revels, had written a blasphemous and obscene poem, after the model of Pope's Essay on Man, called *An Essay on Woman*. The satire was not published, but a few copies of it were printed privately for the authors. Lord Sandwich had contrived to secure a copy of it, and read it before the House; and the Lords, indignant and disgusted, voted an address to the king to institute a prosecution against the author. The Lords, by so doing, departed from the dignity of their order, and their ordinary functions, and their persecution served to strengthen, instead of weaken, the cause of Wilkes.

Churchill.

Associated with him, in his writings and his revels, was the poet Churchill, a clergyman of the Establishment, but as open a contemner of decency as Wilkes himself. For some years, his poetry had proved as bad as his sermons, his time being spent in low dissipation. An ill-natured criticism on his writings called forth his energies, and he started, all at once, a giant in numbers, with all the fire of Dryden and all the harmony of Pope. Imagination, wit, strength, and sense, were crowded into his compositions; but he was careless of both matter and manner, and wrote just what came in his way. "This bacchanalian priest," says Horace Walpole, "now mouthing patriotism, and now venting libertinism, the scourge of bad men, and scarce better than the worst, debauching wives, and protecting his gown by the weight of his fist, engaged with Wilkes in his war on the Scots, and set himself up as the Hercules that was to cleanse the state and punish its oppressors. And true it is, the storm that saved us was raised in taverns and night-cellars; so much more effectual were the orgies of Churchill and Wilkes than the dagger of Cato and Brutus. Earl Temple joined them in mischief and dissipation, and whispered where they might find torches, though he took care never to be seen to light one himself. This triumvirate has even made me reflect that nations are most commonly saved by the worst men in them. The virtuous are too scrupulous to go the lengths which are necessary to rouse the people against their tyrants."

Grafton's Administration.

The ferment created by the prosecution of Wilkes led to the resignation of Mr. Grenville, in 1765, and the Marquis of Rockingham succeeded him as head of the administration. He continued, however, the prosecution. He retained his place but a few months, and was succeeded by the Duke of Grafton, the object of such virulent invective in the Letters of Junius, a work without elevation of sentiment, without any appeal to generous principle, without recognition of the eternal laws of justice, and without truthfulness, and yet a work which produced a great sensation, and is to this day regarded as a masterpiece of savage and unscrupulous sarcasm. The Duke of Grafton had the same views as his predecessor respecting Wilkes, who had the audacity, notwithstanding the sentence of outlawry which had been passed against him, to return from Paris, to which he had, for a time, retired, and to appear publicly at Guildhall, and offer himself as a candidate for the city of London. He was contemptuously rejected, but succeeded in being elected as member for Middlesex county.

Mr. Wilkes, however, recognizing the outlawry that had been passed against him, surrendered himself to the jurisdiction of the Court of the King's Bench, which was then presided over by Lord Mansfield. This great lawyer and jurist confirmed the verdicts against him, and sentenced him to pay a fine of one thousand pounds, to suffer two years' imprisonment, and to find security for good behavior for seven years. This sentence was odious and severe, and the more unjustifiable in view of the arbitrary and unprecedented alteration of the records on the very night preceding the trial.

Popularity of Wilkes.

The multitude, enraged, rescued their idol from the officers of the law, as they were conducting him to prison, and carried him with triumph through the city; but, through his entreaties, they were prevailed upon to abstain from further acts of outrage. Mr. Wilkes again surrendered himself, and was confined in prison. When the Commons met, Wilkes was again expelled, in order to satisfy the vengeance of the court. But the electors of Middlesex again returned him to parliament, and the Commons voted that, being once expelled, he was incapable of sitting, even if elected, in the same parliament. The electors of Middlesex, equally determined with the Commons, chose him, for a third time, their representative; and the election, for the third time, was declared void by the commons. In order to terminate the contest, Colonel Lutterell, a member of the House, vacated his seat, and offered himself a candidate for Middlesex. He received two hundred and ninety-six votes, and Wilkes twelve hundred and forty-three, but Lutterell was declared duly elected by the Commons, and took his seat for Middlesex.

This decision threw the whole nation into a ferment, and was plainly an outrage on the freedom of elections; and it was so considered by some of the most eminent men in England, even by those who despised the character of Wilkes. Lord Chatham, from his seat, declared "that the laws were despised, trampled upon, destroyed; those laws which had been made by the stern virtues of our ancestors, those iron barons of old, to whose spirit in the hour of contest, and to whose fortitude in the triumph of victory, the silken barons of this day owe all their honors and security."

Mr. Wilkes subsequently triumphed; the Commons grew weary of a contest which brought no advantage and much ignominy, and the prosecution was dropped; but not until the subject of it had been made Lord

Mayor of London. From 1768 to 1772, he was the sole unrivalled political idol of the people, who lavished on him all in their power to bestow. They subscribed twenty thousand pounds for the payment of his debts, besides gifts of plate, wine, and household goods. Every wall bore his name and every window his picture. In china, bronze, or marble, he stood upon the chimney-pieces of half the houses in London, and he swung from the sign-board of every village, and every great road in the environs of the metropolis. In 1770 he was discharged from his imprisonment, in 1771 was permitted to take his seat, and elected mayor. From 1776, his popularity declined, and he became involved in pecuniary difficulties. He, however, emerged from them, and enjoyed a quiet office until his death (1797.) He was a patriot from accident, and not from principle, and corrupt in his morals; but he was a gentleman of elegant manners and cultivated taste. He was the most popular political character ever known in England; and his name, at one time, was sufficient to blow up the flames of sedition, and excite the lower orders to acts of violence bordering on madness.

Taxation of the Colonies.

During his prosecution, important events occurred, of greater moment to the world. The disputes about the taxation of America led to the establishment of a new republic, whose extent and grandeur have never been equalled, and whose future greatness cannot well be exaggerated.

These disputes commenced during the administration of George Grenville. The proposal to tax the American colonies had been before proposed to Sir Robert Walpole, but this prudent and sagacious minister dared not run the risk. Mr. Grenville was not, however, daunted by the difficulties and dangers which the more able Walpole regarded. In order to lighten the burden which resulted from the ruinous wars of Pitt, the minister proposed to raise a revenue from the colonies. The project pleased the house, and the Stamp Duties were imposed. It is true that the tax was a light one, and was so regarded by Mr. Grenville; but he intended it as a precedent; he was resolved to raise a revenue from the colonies sufficiently great to lighten the public burden. He regarded the colonists as subjects of the King of Great Britain, in every sense of the word; and, since they received protection from the government, they were bound to contribute to its support.

Indignation of the Colonies.

But the colonists, now scattered along the coast from Maine to Georgia, took other views. They maintained that, though subject in some degree to English legislation, they could not be taxed, any more than other subjects of Great Britain, without their consent. They were willing to be ruled in accordance with those royal charters which had, at different times, been given them. They were even willing to assist the mother country, which they loved and revered, and with which were connected their brightest and most cherished associations, in expelling its enemies from adjoining territories, and to fight battles in its defence. They were willing to receive the literature, the religion, the fashions, and the opinions of their brethren in England. But they looked upon the soil which they cultivated in the wilderness with so many difficulties, hardships, and dangers, as their own, and believed that they were bound to raise taxes only to defend the soil, and promote good government, religion, and morality in their midst. But they could not understand why they were bound to pay taxes to support English wars on the continent of Europe. It was for their children, and for the sacred privilege of religious liberty, that they had originally left the mother country. It was only for themselves and their children that they felt bound to labor. They sought no political influence in England. They did not wish to control elections, or regulate the finances, or interfere with the projects of military aggrandizement. They were not represented in the English parliament, and they composed, politically speaking, no part of the English nation. Great, therefore, was their indignation, when they learned that the English government was interfering with their chartered rights, and designed to raise a revenue from them to lighten taxes at home, merely to support the government in foolish wars. If they could be taxed, without their consent, in any thing, they could be taxed without limit; and they would be in danger of becoming mere slaves of the mother country, and be bound to labor for English aggrandizement. On one point they insisted with peculiar earnestness—that taxation, in a free country, without a representation of interests in parliament, was an outrage. It was on account of this arbitrary taxation that Charles I. lost his crown, and the second revolution was effected, which placed the house of Hanover on the throne. The colonies felt that, if the subjects of the king at home were justified in resisting unlawful taxes, they surely, on another continent, and without a representation, had a right to do so also; that, if they were to be taxed without their consent, they would be in a worse condition than even the people of Ireland; would be in the condition of a conquered people, without the protection which even a conquered country enjoyed. Hence they remonstrated, and prepared themselves for resistance.

The Stamp Act.

The English government was so blinded as not to perceive or feel the force of the reasoning of the colonists, and obstinately resolved to resort to measures which, with a free and spirited people, must necessarily lead to violence and strife. The House of Commons would not even hear the reports of the colonial agents, but proceeded, with strange infatuation and obstinate bigotry, to impose the Stamp Act, (1765.) There were some, however, who perceived its folly and injustice. General Conway protested against the assumed right of the government, and Colonel Barré, a speaker of great eminence, exclaimed, in reply to the speech of Charles Townshend, who styled the colonies "children planted by our care, and nourished by our indulgence," — "They planted by your care! — No! your oppressions planted them in America; they fled from your tyranny to a then uncultivated wilderness, exposed to all the hardships to which human nature is liable! They nourished by your indulgence!—No! they grew by your neglect; your *care* of them was displayed in sending persons to govern them who were the deputies of deputies of ministers—men whose behavior, on many occasions, has caused the blood of those sons of liberty to recoil within them; men who have been promoted to the highest seats of justice in a foreign country, in order to escape being brought to the bar of a court of justice in their own." Mr. Pitt opposed the fatal policy of Grenville with singular eloquence; by arguments which went beyond acts of parliament; by an appeal to the natural reason; and by recognition of the great, inalienable principles of liberty. He maintained that the House had *no right* to lay an internal tax upon America, *that country not being represented.* Burke, too, then a new speaker, raised his voice against the folly and injustice of taxing the colonies; but it was in vain. The commons were bent on imposing the Stamp Act.

But the passage of this act created great disturbances in America, and was every where regarded as the beginning of great calamities. Throughout the colonies there was a general combination to resist the stamp duty; and it was resolved to purchase no English manufactures, and to prevent the adoption of stamped paper.

Such violent and unexpected opposition embarrassed the English ministry; which, in addition to the difficulties attending the prosecution of Wilkes, led to the retirement of Grenville, who was succeeded by the Marquis of Rockingham. During his short administration, the Stamp Act was repealed, although the Commons still insisted on their right to tax America. The joy which this repeal created in the colonies was unbounded; and the speech of Pitt, who proposed the repeal, and defended it with unprecedented eloquence, was every where read with enthusiasm, and served to strengthen the conviction, among the leading men in the colonies, that their cause was right. Lord Rockingham did not long remain at the head of the government, and was succeeded by the Duke of Grafton; although Mr. Pitt, recently created Earl of Chatham, was virtually the prime minister. Lord Rockingham retired from office with a high character for pure and disinterested patriotism, and without securing place, pension, or reversion, to himself or to any of his adherents.

Lord Chatham.

The elevation of Lord Chatham to the peerage destroyed his popularity and weakened his power. No man ever made a greater mistake than he did in consenting to an apparent elevation. He had long been known and designated as the *Great Commoner*. The people were proud of him and, as a commoner, he could have ruled the nation, in spite of all opposition. No other man could have averted the national calamities. But, as a peer, he no longer belonged to the people, and the people lost confidence in him, and abandoned him. What he gained in dignity he lost in power and popularity. The people now compared him with Lord Bath, and he became the object of universal calumny.

And Chatham felt the change which had taken place in the nation. He had ever loved and courted popularity, and that was the source of his power. He now lost his spirits, and interested himself but little in public affairs. He relapsed into a state of indolence and apathy. He remained only the shadow of a mighty name; and, sequestered in the groves of his family residence, ceased to be mentioned by the public. He became melancholy, nervous, and unfit for business. Nor could he be induced to attend a cabinet council, even on the most pressing occasions. He pretended to be ill, and would not hold conference with his colleagues. Nor did he have the influence with the king which he had a right to expect. Being no longer beloved by the people, he was no longer feared by the king. He was like Samson when deprived of his locks—without strength; for his strength lay in the confidence and affections of the nation. He opposed his colleagues in their resolution to impose new taxes on America, but his counsels were disregarded.

These taxes were in the shape of duties on glass, paper, lead, and painters' colors, from which no considerable revenue could be gained, and much discontent would inevitably result. When the news of this new taxation reached the colonies, it destroyed all the cheerfulness which the repeal of the Stamp Act had caused. Sullenness and gloom returned. Trust in parliament was diminished. New combinations of opposition were organized, and the newspapers teemed with invective.

In the midst of these disturbances, Lord Chatham resigned the Privy Seal, the office he had selected, and retired from the administration, (1768.)

Administration of Lord North.

In 1770, the Duke of Grafton also resigned his office as first lord of the treasury, chiefly in consequence of the increasing difficulties with America;

and Lord North, who had been two years chancellor of the exchequer, took his place. He was an amiable and accomplished nobleman, and had many personal friends, and few personal enemies; but he was unfit to manage the helm of state in the approaching storm.

It was his misfortune to be minister in the most unsettled and revolutionary times, and to misunderstand not merely the spirit of the age, but the character and circumstances of the American colonies. George III., with singular obstinacy and blindness, sustained the minister against all opposition; and under his administration the American war was carried on, which ended so disastrously to the mother country.

As this great and eventful war will be the subject of the next chapter, the remaining events of interest, connected with the domestic history of England, will be first presented.

The most important of these were the discontents of the Irish.

As early as 1762, associations of the peasantry were formed with a view to political reforms and changes, and these popular demonstrations of the discontented have ever since marked the history of the Irish nation—ever poor, ever oppressed, ever on the eve of rebellion.

Functions of the Parliament.

The first circumstance, however, after the accession of George III., which claims particular notice, was the passing of the Octennial Bill, in 1788. The Irish parliament, unlike the English, continued in existence during the life of the sovereign. In 1761, an attempt had been made by the patriotic party to limit its duration, and to place it upon the same footing as the parliament of England; but this did not succeed. Lord Townshend, at this period, was lord lieutenant, and it was the great object of his government to break the power of the Irish aristocracy, and to take out of their hands the distribution of pensions and places, which hitherto had, from motives of policy, been allowed them. He succeeded in his object, though by unjustifiable means, and the British government became the source of all honor and emolument. During his administration, some disturbances broke out in Ulster, in consequence of the system which then prevailed of letting land on fines. As a great majority of the peasantry and small farmers were unable to pay these fines, and were consequently deprived of their farms, they became desperate, and committed violent outrages on those who had taken their lands. Government was obliged to resort to military force, and many distressed people were driven to America for subsistence. To Ireland there appeared no chance of breaking the thraldom which England in other respects also exercised, when the American war broke out. This immediately changed the language and current of the British government in reference to Ireland; proposals were made favorable to Irish commerce; and some penal statutes against Catholics were annulled. Still the patriots of Ireland aimed at much greater privileges than had as yet been granted, and the means to secure these were apparent. England had drawn from Ireland nearly all the regular forces, in order to send them to America, and the sea-coast of Ireland was exposed to invasion. In consequence of the defenceless state of the country, the inhabitants of the town of Belfast, in 1779, entered into armed associations to defend themselves in case of necessity. This gave rise to a system of volunteers, which soon was extended over the island. The Irish now began to feel their strength; and even Lord North admitted, in the House of Commons, the necessity of granting to them still greater privileges, and carried a bill through parliament, which removed some grievous commercial restrictions. But the Irish looked to greater objects, and especially since Lord North, in order to carry his bill, represented it as a boon resumable at pleasure, rather than as a right to which the Irish were properly entitled. This bill, therefore, instead of quieting the patriots, led to a desire for an independent parliament of their own. A union was formed of volunteers to secure this end, not composed of the ignorant peasantry, but of all classes, at the head of which was the Duke of Leinster himself. In 1781, this association of volunteers had a force of fifty thousand disciplined men; and it moreover formed committees of correspondence, which naturally alarmed the British government.

These and other disturbances, added to the disasters in America, induced the House of Commons to pass censure on Lord North and his colleague, as incapable of managing the helm of state. The king, therefore, was compelled to dismiss his ministers, whose administration had proved the most disastrous in British annals. Lord North, however, had uncommon difficulties to contend with, and might have governed the nation with honor in ordinary times. He resigned in 1782, four years after the death of Chatham, and the Marquis of Buckingham, a second time, was placed at the head of the government. Mr. Fox and Mr. Burke also obtained places, and the Whigs were once more triumphant.

Irish Discontents.

The attention of the new ministry was imperatively demanded by the discontents in Ireland, and important concessions were made. Mr. Grattan moved an address to the king, which was unanimously carried in both Houses, in which it was declared that "the crown of Ireland was inseparably annexed to the crown of Great Britain; but that the kingdom of Ireland was a distinct kingdom, with a parliament of her own, the sole legislature thereof; that in this right they conceived the very essence of their liberty to exist; that in behalf of all the people of Ireland, they claimed this as their birthright, and could not relinquish it but with their lives; that they had a high veneration for the British character; and that, in sharing the freedom of England, it was their determination to share also her fate, and to stand and fall with the British nation." The new lord lieutenant, the Duke of Portland, assured the Irish parliament that the British legislature had resolved to remove the cause of discontent, and a law was actually passed which placed the Irish parliament on the same footing as that of England. Acts were also passed for the right of habeas corpus, and for the independence of the judges.

The volunteers, having accomplished the objects which they originally contemplated, did not, however, disband, but now directed their efforts to a reform in parliament. But the House of Commons rejected the proposition offered by Mr. Flood, and the convention, appointed by the volunteers, indefinitely adjourned without persevering, as it should have done. The volunteer system soon after declined.

The cause of parliamentary reform, though no longer supported by the volunteers in their associate character, was not deserted by the people, or by their advocates in parliament. Among these advocates was William Pitt himself. But in 1783, he became prime minister, and changed his opinions.

Protestant Association.

But before the administration of Pitt can be presented, an event in the domestic history of England must be alluded to, which took place during the administration of Lord North. This was the Protestant Association, headed by Lord George Gordon, and the riots to which it led.

Lord George Gordon's Riots.

In 1780, parliament had passed an act relieving Roman Catholics from some of the heavy penalties inflicted on them in the preceding century. It relieved bishops, priests, and schoolmasters from prosecution and imprisonment, gave security to the rights of inheritance, and permission to purchase lands on fee simple. This act of toleration was generally opposed in England; but the fanatical spirit of Presbyterianism in Scotland was excited in view of this reasonable indulgence, to a large body of men, of the rights of conscience and civil liberty. On the bare rumor of the intended indulgence, great tumults took place in Edinburgh and Glasgow; the Roman Catholic chapel was destroyed, and the houses of the principal Catholics were attacked and plundered. Nor did the magistracy check or punish these disorders with any spirit, but secretly favored the rioters. Encouraged by the indifference of the magistrates, the fanatics formed themselves into a society called the *Protestant Association*, to oppose any remission of the present unjust laws; and of this association Lord George Gordon was chosen president. He was the son of the Duke of Gordon, belonging to one of the most ancient of the Scottish nobility, but a man in the highest degree wild and fanatical. He was also a member of parliament, and opposed the views of the most enlightened statesmen of his time, and with an extravagance which led to the belief that he was insane. He calumniated the king, defied the parliament, and boasted of the number of his adherents. He pretended that he had, in Scotland, one hundred and sixty thousand men at his command, who would cut off the king's head, if he did not keep his coronation oath. The enthusiasm of the Scotch soon spread to the English; and, throughout the country, associations were affiliated with the parent societies in London and Edinburgh, of both of which Lord Gordon was president. At Coachmakers' Hall he assembled his adherents; and, in an incendiary harangue, inflamed the minds of an immense audience in regard to the Church of Rome, with the usual invectives respecting its idolatry and corruption. He urged them to violent courses, as the only way to stop the torrent of Catholicism which was desolating the land. Soon after, this association assembled at St. George's Fields, to the astonishing number of fifty thousand people, marshalled in separate bands, with blue cockades; and this immense rabble proceeded through the city of London to the House of Parliament, preceded by a man carrying a petition signed by twelve hundred thousand names. The rabble took possession of the lobby of the house, making the old palace ring with their passionate cries of "No popery! no popery!" This mob was harangued by Lord Gordon himself, in the lobby of the house, while the matter was discussed among the members. The military were drawn out, and the mob was dispersed for a time, but soon assembled again, and became still more alarming. Houses were plundered, churches were entered, and the city set on fire in thirty-six different places. The people were obliged to chalk on their houses "No popery," and pay contributions to prevent their being sacked. The prisons were emptied of both felons and debtors. Lord Mansfield's splendid residence was destroyed, together with his pictures, furniture, and invaluable law library. Martial law was finally proclaimed — the last resort in cases of rebellion, and never resorted to but in extreme cases; and the military did what magistrates could not do—restored order and law. Had not the city been decreed to be in a state of rebellion, the rioters would have taken the bank, which they had already attacked. Five hundred persons were killed in the riot, and Lord George Gordon was committed to the Tower. He, however, escaped conviction, through the extraordinary talents of his counsel, Mr. Erskine and Mr. Kenyon; but one hundred others were capitally convicted. This disgraceful riot opened the eyes of the people to the horrors of popular insurrection, and perhaps prevented a revolution in England, when other questions, of more practical importance, agitated the nation.

But no reform of importance took place until the administration of William Pitt. Mr. Burke attempted to secure some economical retrenchments, which were strongly opposed. But what was a retrenchment of two hundred thousand pounds a year, when compared with the vast expenditures of the British armies in America and in India? But though the reforms which Burke projected were not radical or important, they contributed to raise his popularity with the people, who were more annoyed by the useless offices connected with the king's household, than by the expenditure of millions in war. At first, his scheme received considerable attention, and the members listened to his propositions so long as they were abstract and general. But when he proceeded to specific reforms, they no longer regarded his voice, and he was obliged to abandon his task as hopeless. William Pitt made his first speech in the debate which Burke had excited, and argued in favor of retrenchment with the eloquence of his father, but with more method and clearness. The bill was lost, but Burke finally succeeded in carrying his measures; and the offices of the master of the harriers, the master of the staghounds, the clerk of the green cloth, and some other unimportant sinecures, were abolished.

Parliamentary Reforms.

Reform Questions.

The first attempt at that great representative reform which afterwards convulsed the nation, was made by William Pitt. He brought forward two resolutions, to prevent bribery at elections, and secure a more equitable representation. But he did not succeed; and Pitt himself, when his cause was advocated by men of a different spirit,—men inflamed by revolutionary principles,—changed his course, and opposed parliamentary reform with more ardor than he had at first advocated it. But parliamentary reform did not become an object of absorbing interest until the times of Henry Brougham and Lord John Russell.

No other great events were sufficiently prominent to be here alluded to, until the ministry of William Pitt. The American Revolution first demands attention.

References.—Belsham's History of the Reign of George III. Walpole's Memoir of the same reign. Holt's Private and Domestic Life of George III. Lord Brougham's Statesmen of the Reign of George III. Smyth's Lectures. Thackeray's Life of the Earl of Chatham. Correspondence of the Earl of Chatham. Annual Register, from 1765 to 1775. Debret's Parliamentary Debates. Stephens' Life of Horne Tooke. Campbell's Lives of the Lord Chancellors. Macaulay's Essay on Chatham. Burke's Thoughts on the Present Discontents.

CHAPTER XXVIII
THE AMERICAN REVOLUTION

The American Revolution.

The American Revolution, if contemplated in view of its ultimate as well as immediate consequences, is doubtless the greatest event of modern times. Its importance was not fully appreciated when it took place, but still excited a great interest throughout the civilized world. It was the main subject which engrossed the attention and called out the energies of British statesmen, during the administration of Lord North. In America, of course, all other subjects were trivial in comparison with it. The contest is memorable for the struggles of heroes, for the development of unknown energies, for the establishment of a new western empire, for the triumph of the cause of liberty, and for the moral effects which resulted, even in other countries, from the examples of patriots who preferred the glory and honor of their country to their own aggrandizement.

The causes of the struggle have been already alluded to in the selfishness and folly of British statesmen, who sought to relieve the burdens of the English people by taxing the colonies. The colonies were doubtless regarded by the British parliament without proper affection or consideration; somewhat in the light of a conquered nation, from which England might derive mercantile advantage. The colonies were not ruled in a spirit of conciliation, nor were the American people fully appreciated. Some, perhaps, like Chatham and Burke, may have known the virtues and the power of the colonial population, and may have had some glimpse of the glory and greatness to which America was destined. But they composed but a small minority of the nation, and their advice and remonstrances were generally disregarded.

Causes of the Revolution.

Serious disturbances did not take place until Lord North commenced his unfortunate administration, (1770.) Although the colonies were then resolved not to submit to unlawful taxation, and to an oppressive government, independence was not contemplated. Conciliatory measures, if they had been at that time adopted, probably would have deferred the

Revolution. But the contest must have occurred, at a later date; for nothing, in the ordinary course of events, could have prevented the ultimate independence of the colonies. Their rapid growth, the extent of the country in which settlements were made, its distance from England, the spirit of liberty which animated the people, their general impatience under foreign restraint, and the splendid prospects of future greatness which were open to their eyes, must have led to a rupture with the mother country at no distant time.

The colonies, at the commencement of their difficulties, may have exaggerated their means of resistance, but not their future greatness. All of them, from New Hampshire to Georgia, were animated by a spirit of liberty which no misfortunes could crush. A large majority of the people were willing to incur the dangers incident to revolution, not for themselves merely, but for the sake of their posterity, and for the sacred cause of liberty. They felt that their cause was just, and that Providence would protect and aid them in their defence.

A minute detail of the events of the American Revolution, of course, cannot be expected in a history like this. Only the more prominent events can be alluded to. The student is supposed to be familiar with the details of the conflict, which are to be read in the works of numerous American authors.

Lord North, at the commencement of his administration, repealed the obnoxious duties which had been imposed in 1767, but still retained the duty on tea, with a view chiefly to assert the supremacy of Great Britain, and her right to tax the colonies. This course of the minister cannot be regarded in any other light than that of the blindest infatuation.

The imposition of the port duties, by Grenville, had fomented innumerable disturbances, and had led to universal discussion as to the nature and extent of parliamentary power. A distinction, at first, had been admitted between internal and external taxes; but it was soon asserted that Great Britain had no right to tax the colonies, either internally or externally. It was stated that the colonies had received charters, under the great seal, which had given them all the rights and privileges of Englishmen at home and therefore that they could not be taxed, except by their own consent; that this consent had never been asked or granted; that they were unrepresented in the imperial parliament; and that the taxes which had been imposed by their own respective legislatures were, in many instances, greater than what were paid by the people of England—taxes too, incurred, to a great degree, to preserve the jurisdiction of Great Britain on the American continent. The colonies were every where exceedingly indignant with the course the mother country had pursued with reference to them. Patrick Henry, a Virginian, supported the cause of liberty with unrivalled eloquence and power, as did John Adams, Josiah Quincy, Jr., James Otis, and other patriots in Massachusetts. Riots took place in Boston, Newport, and New York, and assemblies of citizens in various parts expressed an indignant and revolutionary spirit.

Riots and Disturbances.

The residence of the military at Boston was, moreover, the occasion of perpetual tumult. The people abused the soldiers, vilified them in newspapers, and insulted them in the street. Mutual animosity was the result. Rancor and insults produced riot, and the troops fired upon the people. So great was the disturbances, that the governor was reluctantly obliged to remove the military from the town. The General Court was then removed to Cambridge, but refused to enter upon business unless it were convened in Boston. Fresh disturbances followed. The governor quarrelled with the legislature, and a complete anarchy began to prevail. The public mind was inflamed by effigies, paintings, and incendiary articles in the newspapers. The parliament was represented as corrupt, the ministry as venal, the king as a tyrant, and England itself as a rotten, old, aristocratic structure, crumbling to pieces. The tide was so overwhelming in favor of resistance, that even moderate men were borne along in the current; and those who kept aloof from the excitement were stigmatized as timid and selfish, and the enemies of their country. The courts of justice were virtually silenced, since juries disregarded the charges of the judges. Libels were unnoticed, and the rioters were unpunished. Smuggling was carried on to a great extent, and revenue officers were insulted in the discharge of their duties. Obnoxious persons were tarred and feathered, and exposed to public derision and scorn. In Providence, they burnt the revenue cutter, and committees were formed in the principal towns who fanned the flame of sedition. The committee in Boston, in 1773, framed a celebrated document, called the *Bill of Rights*, in which the authority of parliament to legislate for the colonies, in any respect, was denied, and in which the salaries decreed by the crown to the governor and judges were considered as a systematic attempt to enslave the land.

The public discontents were further inflamed by the information which Dr. Franklin, then in London, afforded the colonies, and the advice he gave them to persevere, assuring them that, if they were firm, they had nothing to apprehend. Moreover, he got into his possession a copy of the letters of Governor Hutchinson to the ministry, which he transmitted to the colonies, and which by them were made public. These letters were considered by the legislature of Massachusetts as unjust and libellous, and his recall was demanded. Resolutions, of an offensive character to the English, were every where passed, and all things indicated an approaching storm. The crisis was at hand. The outrage, in Boston harbor, of throwing overboard three hundred and forty-two chests of tea, which the East India Company had sent to America, consummated the difficulties, and induced the government to resort to more coercive measures.

Duty on Tea.

It was in the power of Lord North to terminate the difficulties with the colonies when the East India Company urged him to repeal the duty of threepence per pound on tea, and offered to pay sixpence per pound in lieu of it, as export duty, if permitted to import it into the colonies duty free. The company was induced to make this proposition in view of the great accumulation of tea in England; but the government, more solicitous about the right than the revenue, would not consent. The colonists were equally determined to resist taxation, not on account of immediate burdens, but upon principle, and therefore resolved to prevent the landing of the tea. A multitude rushed to the wharf, and twenty persons, disguised as Indians, went on board the ships laden with it, staved the chests, and threw their contents into the sea. In New York and Philadelphia, as no persons could be found who would venture to receive the tea sent to those ports, the ships laden with it returned to England.

The ministers of the crown were especially indignant with the province of Massachusetts, which had always been foremost in resistance, and the scene of the greatest disorders, and therefore resolved to block up the port of Boston. Accordingly, in 1774 they introduced a bill to discontinue the lading and shipping of goods, wares, and merchandise at Boston, and to remove the custom-house to Salem. The bill received the general approbation of the House, and passed by a great majority.

No measure could possibly have been more impolitic. A large force should have been immediately sent to the colonies, to coerce them, before they had time to organize sufficient force to resist the mother country, or conciliatory measures should have been adopted. But the House was angry and infatuated, and the voice of wisdom was disregarded.

Soon after, Lord North introduced another bill for the better government of the provinces, which went to subvert the charter of the colony, and to violate all the principles of liberty and justice. By this bill, the nomination of counsellors, judges, sheriffs, and magistrates of all kinds, was vested in the crown; and these were also removable at pleasure. The ministers, in advocating the bill, urged the ground of necessity, the universal spirit of disaffection, which bordered on actual rebellion. The bill was carried, by a majority of two hundred and thirty-nine against sixty-four voices, May 2, 1774.

The next step of the minister was to bring in a bill which provided that, in case any person was indicted in Massachusetts for a capital offence, and that, if it should appear that a fair trial could not be had in the province, the prisoner might be sent to any other colony, or even to Great Britain itself, to be tried. This was insult added to injury, and met with vigorous resistance even in parliament itself. But it nevertheless passed through both Houses.

Port of Boston Closed.

When intelligence arrived concerning it, and of the other bills, a fire was kindled in the colonies not easily to be extinguished. There was scarcely a place which did not convene its assembly. Popular orators, in the public halls and in the churches, every where inflamed the people by incendiary discourses; organizations were made to abstain from all commerce with the mother country; and measures were adopted to assemble a General Congress, to take into consideration the state of the country. People began to talk of defending their rights by the sword. Every where was heard the sound of the drum and the fife. All were fired by the spirit of liberty. Associations were formed for the purchase of arms and ammunition. Addresses were printed and circulated calling on the people to arm themselves, and resist unlawful encroachment. All proceedings in the courts of justice were suspended. Jurors refused to take their oaths; the reign of law ceased, and that of violence commenced. Governor Gage, who had succeeded Hutchinson, fortified Boston Neck, and cut off the communication of the town with the country.

Meeting of Congress.

In the mean time, the Continental Congress met at Philadelphia, in which all the colonies were represented but Georgia. Congress passed resolutions approving the course of Massachusetts, and also a bill called a *Declaration of Rights*. It sent an address to the king, framed with great ability, in which it discussed the rights of the colonies, complained of the mismanagement of ministers, and besought a redress of the public evils.

Speech of Burke.

But this congress was considered by the government of Great Britain as an illegal body, and its petition was disregarded. But the ministers no longer regarded the difficulties as trifling, and sought to remedy them, though not in the right way. The more profound of the English statesmen fully perceived the danger and importance of the crisis, and many of them took the side of liberty. Dean Tucker, who foresaw a long war, with all its expenses, urged, in a masterly treatise, the necessity of giving the Americans, at once, the liberty they sought. Others, who overrated the importance of the colonies in a mercantile view, wished to retain them, but to adopt conciliatory measures. Lord Chatham put forth all the eloquence of which he was such a master, to arouse the ministers. He besought them to withdraw the troops from Boston. He showed the folly of metaphysical refinements about the right of taxation when a continent was in arms. He spoke of the means of enforcing thraldom as inefficient and ridiculous. Lord Camden sustained Chatham in the House of Lords, and declared, not as a philosopher, but as a constitutional lawyer, that England had no right to tax America. Mr. Burke moved a conciliatory measure in the House of Commons, fraught with wisdom and knowledge. "My hold of the colonies," said this great oracle of moral wisdom, "is the close affection which grows from the common names, from the kindred blood, from similar privileges, and from equal protection. These are the ties which, though light as air, are as strong as links of iron. Let the colonies always keep the idea of their civil rights associated with your government; they will cling and grapple with you, and no power under heaven will be able to tear them from their allegiance. But let it once be understood that your government may be one thing, and their privileges another, then the cement is gone, and every thing hastens to dissolution. It is the love of the people, it is their attachment to your government from the sense in the deep stake they have in such glorious institutions, which gives you your army and navy, and infuses into both that liberal obedience without which your army would be but a base rabble, and your navy nothing but rotten timber." But this elevated and sublime wisdom was regarded as a philosophical abstraction, as a vain and impractical view of political affairs, well enough for a writer on the "sublime and beautiful," but absurd in a British statesman. Colonel Barré and Fox supported Burke; but their eloquence had not much effect on the Commons, and the ministry was supported in their measures. The colonies were declared to be in a state of rebellion, and measures were adopted to crush them.

To declare the colonies in a state of rebellion was, in fact, to declare war. And this was perfectly understood by the popular leaders who fanned the spirit of resistance. All ideas of reconciliation now became chimerical. Necessity stimulated the timid, and vengeance excited the bold. It was felt that the people were now to choose between liberty and slavery, and slavery was, of course, regarded as worse than death. "We must look back," said the popular orators, "no more! We must conquer or die! We are placed between altars smoking with the most grateful incense of glory and gratitude on the one part, and blocks and dungeons on the other. Let each, then, rise and gird himself for the conflict. The dearest interests of the world command it; our most holy religion requires it. Let us banish fear, and remember that fortune smiles only on the brave."

Such was the general state of feeling; and there only needed a spark to kindle a conflagration. That spark was kindled at Lexington. General Gage, the governor, having learned that military stores and arms were deposited at Concord, resolved to seize them. His design was suspected, and the people prepared to resist his orders. The alarm bells were rung, and the cannons were fired. The provincial militia assembled, and the English retreated to Lexington. That village witnessed the commencement of a long and sanguinary war. The tide of revolution could no longer be repressed. The colonies were now resolved to achieve their independence.

The Continental Congress met on the 10th of May, 1775, shortly after the first blood had been shed at Lexington, and immediately proceeded to raise an army, establish a paper currency, and to dissolve the compact between Great Britain and the Massachusetts colony. John Hancock was chosen president of the assembly, and George Washington commander-in-chief of the continental army. He accepted the appointment with a modesty only equalled by his merit, and soon after departed for the seat of war. For his associates, Congress appointed Artemas Ward, Charles Lee, Philip Schuyler, and Israel Putnam as major-generals, and Seth Pomeroy, Richard Montgomery, David Wooster, William Heath, Joseph Spencer, John Thomas, John Sullivan, and Nathanael Greene as brigadiers. Horatio Gates received the appointment of adjutant-general, with the rank of brigadier.

Battle of Bunker Hill.

On the 17th of June was fought the battle of Bunker Hill, which proved the bravery of the Americans, and which was followed by great moral results. But the Americans unfortunately lost, in this battle, Dr. Warren, who had espoused the cause of revolution with the same spirit that Hampden did in England, and whom he resembled in genius, patriotism, and character. He had been chosen major-general four days before his death, but fought at Bunker Hill as a simple volunteer. On the 2d of July, Washington took command of the army, and established his head-quarters at Cambridge. The American army amounted to seventeen thousand men, of whom twenty-five hundred were unfit for duty. They were assembled on the spur of the occasion, and had but few tents and stores, no clothing, no military chest and no general organization. They were collected from the various provinces and were governed by their own militia laws. Of this material he constructed the first continental army, and under innumerable vexations and difficulties. No man was ever placed in a more embarrassing situation. His troops were raw and undisciplined; and the members of the Continental Congress, from whom he received his commission, were not united among themselves. He had all the responsibility of the war, and yet had not sufficient means to prosecute it with the vigor which the colonies probably anticipated. His success, in the end, *was* glorious and unequivocal; but none other than he could have secured it, and not he, even, unless he had been sustained by a loftiness of character almost preternatural.

The English forces, at this time, were centred in Boston under the command of General Gage, and were greatly inferior in point of numbers to the American troops who surrounded them. But the troops of Gage were regulars and veterans, and were among the best in the English army. He was recalled in order to give information to the government in reference to the battle of Bunker Hill, and was succeeded in October by General Howe.

Death of Montgomery.

The first campaign of the war was signalized by the invasion of Canada by the American troops, with the hope of wresting that province from the English, which was not only disaffected, but which was defended by an inconsiderable force. General Montgomery, with an army of three thousand, advanced to Montreal, which surrendered. The fortresses of Crown Point and Ticonderoga had already been taken by Colonel Ethan Allen. But the person who most distinguished himself in this unfortunate expedition was Colonel Benedict Arnold, who, with a detachment of one thousand men, penetrated through the forests, swamps, and mountains of Maine, beyond the sources of the Kennebec and, in six weeks from his departure at Boston, arrived on the plains of Canada, opposite Quebec. He there effected a junction with the troops of Montgomery, and made an assault on the strongest fortress in America, defended by sixteen hundred men. The attack was unsuccessful, and Montgomery was killed. Arnold did not retire from the province, but remained encamped upon the Heights of Abraham. This enterprise, though a failure, was not without great moral results, since it showed to the English government the singular bravery and intrepidity of the nation it had undertaken to coerce.

The ministry then resolved upon vigorous measures, and, finding a difficulty in raising men, applied to the Landgrave of Hesse for seventeen thousand mercenaries. These, added to twenty-five thousand men enlisted in England, and the troops already sent to America, constituted a force of fifty-five thousand men—deemed amply sufficient to reduce the rebellious colonies. But these were not sent to America until the next year.

In the mean time, General Howe was encamped in Boston with a force, including seamen, of eleven thousand men, and General Washington, with an army of twenty-eight thousand, including militia, was determined to attack him. In February, 1776, he took possession of Dorchester Heights, which command the harbor. General Howe found it expedient to evacuate Boston, and sailed for Halifax with his army, and Washington repaired to Philadelphia to deliberate with Congress.

But Howe retired from Boston only to occupy New York; and when his arrangements were completed, he landed at Staten Island, waiting for the arrival of his brother, Lord Howe, with the expected reinforcements. By the middle of August they had all arrived, and his united forces amounted to twenty-four thousand men. Washington's army, though it nominally numbered twenty thousand five hundred, still was composed of only about eleven thousand effective men, and these imperfectly provided with arms and ammunition. Nevertheless, Washington gave battle to the English; but the result was disastrous to the Americans, owing to the disproportion of the forces engaged. General Howe took possession of Long Island, the Americans evacuated New York, and, shortly after, the city fell into the hands of the English. Washington, with his diminished army, posted himself at Haerlem Heights.

Declaration of American Independence.

But before the victory of Howe on Long Island was obtained, Congress had declared the Independence of the American States, (4th July, 1776.) This Declaration of Independence took the English nation by surprise, and firmly united it against the colonies. It was received by the Americans, in every section of the country, with unbounded enthusiasm. Reconciliation was now impossible, and both countries were arrayed against each other in fierce antagonism.

The remainder of the campaign of 1776 was occupied by the belligerents in skirmishing, engagements, marchings and countermarchings, in the states of New York and New Jersey. The latter state was overrun by the English army, and success, on either side, was indecisive. Forts Washington and Lee were captured. General Lee was taken prisoner. The capture of Lee, however, was not so great a calamity as it, at first, seemed; for, though a man of genius and military experience, his ambition, vanity, and love of glory would probably have led to an opposition to his superior officer, and to Congress itself. To compensate for the disasters in New Jersey, Washington, invested with new and extraordinary power by Congress, gained the battles of Princeton and Trenton, which were not only brilliant victories, but were attended by great moral effects, and showed the difficulty of subduing a people determined to be free. "Every one applauded the firmness, the prudence, and the bravery of Washington. All declared him to be the savior of his country; all proclaimed him equal to the most renowned commanders of antiquity, and especially distinguished him by the name of the *American Fabius.*"

The greatness of Washington was seen, not so much by his victories at Princeton and Trenton, or by his masterly retreat before superior forces, as by his admirable prudence and patience during the succeeding winter. He had, for several months, a force which scarcely exceeded fifteen hundred men, and these suffered all manner of hardships and privations. After the first gush of enthusiasm had passed, it was found exceedingly difficult to enlist men, and still more difficult to pay those who had enlisted. Congress, composed of great men, and of undoubted patriotism, on the whole, harmonized with the commander-in-chief, whom, for six months, it invested with almost dictatorial power; still there were some of its members who did not fully appreciate the character or condition of Washington, and threw great difficulties in his way.

Commissioners Sent to France.

Congress about this time sent commissioners to France to solicit money and arms. These commissioners were Dr. Franklin, Silas Deane, and Arthur Lee. They were not immediately successful; for the French king, doubtful of the result of the struggle, did not wish to incur prematurely the hostility of Great Britain; but they induced many to join the American cause, and among others, the young Marquis de La Fayette, who arrived in America in the spring of 1777, and proved a most efficient general, and secured the confidence and love of the nation he assisted.

Capture of Burgoyne.

The campaign of 1777 was marked by the evacuation of the Jerseys by the English, by the battles of Bennington and Brandywine, by the capture of Philadelphia, and the surrender of Burgoyne. Success, on the whole, was in favor of the Americans. They suffered a check at Brandywine, and lost the most considerable city in the Union at that time. But these disasters were more than compensated by the victory at Bennington and the capture of Burgoyne.

Moral Effects of Burgoyne's Capture.

This indeed was the great event of the campaign. Burgoyne was a member of parliament, and superseded General Carleton in the command of the northern army—an injudicious appointment, but made by the minister in order to carry his measures more easily through the House of Commons. The troops under his command amounted to over seven thousand veterans, besides a corps of artillery. He set out from St. John's, the 16th of June, and advanced to Ticonderoga, which he invested. The American forces, under General Schuyler, destined to oppose this royal army, and to defend Ticonderoga, were altogether insufficient, being not over five thousand men. The fortress was therefore abandoned, and the British general advanced to the Hudson, hoping to open a communication between it and Lake Champlain, and thus completely surround New England, and isolate it from the rest of the country. But the delays attending the march of the English army through the forests enabled the Americans to rally. The defeat of Colonel Baum at Bennington, by Colonel Stark, added to the embarrassments of Burgoyne, who now was straitened for provisions; nevertheless, he continued his march, hoping to reach Albany unmolested. But the Americans, commanded by General Gates, who had superseded Schuyler, were strongly intrenched at the principal passes on his route, and had fortified the high grounds. The army of Burgoyne was moreover attacked by the Americans at Stillwater, and he was forced to retreat to Saratoga. His army was now reduced to five thousand men; he had only three days' provisions; all the passes were filled by the enemy, and he was completely surrounded by fifteen thousand men. Under these circumstances, he was forced to surrender. His troops laid down their arms, but were allowed to embark at Boston for Europe. The Americans, by this victory, acquired forty-two pieces of brass artillery, four thousand six hundred muskets, and an immense quantity of military stores. This surrender of Burgoyne was the greatest disaster which the British troops had thus far experienced, and raised the spirits of the Americans to the highest pitch. Indeed, this surrender decided the fate of the war, for it proved the impossibility of conquering the Americans. It showed that they fought under infinitely greater advantages, since it was in their power always to decline a battle, and to choose their ground. It showed that the country presented difficulties which were insurmountable. It mattered but little that cities were taken, when the great body of the people resided in the country, and were willing to make sacrifices, and were commanded by such generals as Washington, Gates, Greene, Putnam, and Lee. The English ministry ought to have seen the nature of the contest; but a strange infatuation blinded the nation. There were some, however, whom no national pride could blind. Lord Chatham was one of these men. "No man," said this veteran statesman, "thinks more highly of the virtues and valor of British troops than I do. I know that they can achieve any thing except impossibilities. But the conquest of America is an impossibility."

There was one nation in Europe who viewed the contest with different eyes. This nation was France, then on the eve of revolution itself, and burning with enthusiastic love of the principles on which American independence was declared. The French government may not have admired the American cause, but it hated England so intensely, that it was resolved to acknowledge the independence of America, and aid the country with its forces.

Arrival of La Fayette.

In the early part of the war, the American Congress had sent commissioners to France, in order to obtain assistance. In consequence of their representations, La Fayette, then a young man of nineteen years of age, freighted a ship at his own expense, and joined the American standard. Congress, in consideration of his illustrious rank and singular enthusiasm, gave him a commission of major-general. And gloriously did he fulfil the great expectations which were formed of him; richly did he deserve the gratitude and praise of all the friends of liberty.

La Fayette embarked in the American cause as a volunteer. The court of France, in the early period of the contest, did not think it expedient openly to countenance the revolution. But, after the surrender of Burgoyne, and it was evident that the United States would succeed in securing their independence, then it was acknowledged, and substantial aid was rendered.

The winter which succeeded the surrender of Burgoyne is memorable for the sufferings of the American army encamped at Valley Forge, about twenty miles from Philadelphia. The army was miserably supplied with provisions and clothing, and strong discontent appeared in various quarters. Out of eleven thousand eight hundred men, nearly three thousand were barefooted and otherwise naked. But the sufferings of the army were not the only causes of solicitude to the commander-in-chief, on whom chiefly rested the responsibility of the war. The officers were discontented, and were not prepared, any more than the privates, to make permanent sacrifices. They were obliged to break in upon their private property, and were without any prospect of future relief. Washington was willing to make any sacrifices himself, and refused any payment for his own expenses; but, while he exhibited the rarest magnanimity, he did not expect it from others, and urged Congress to provide for the future pay of the officers, when the war should close. He looked upon human nature as it was, not as he wished it to be, and recognized the principles of self-interest as well as those of patriotism. It was his firm conviction that a long and lasting war could not, even in those times, be sustained by the principle of patriotism alone, but required, in addition, the prospect of interest, or some reward. The members of Congress did not all agree with him in his views, and expected that officers would make greater sacrifices than private citizens, but, after a while, the plan of half-pay for life, as Washington proposed, was adopted by a small majority, though afterwards changed to half-pay for seven years. There was also a prejudice in many minds against a standing army, besides the jealousies and antipathies which existed between different sections of the Union. But Washington, with his rare practical good sense, combated these, as well as the fears of the timid and the schemes of the selfish. The history of the Revolution impresses us with the greatness and bravery of the American nation; and every American should feel proud of his ancestors for the efforts they made, under so many discouragements, to secure their liberties; but it would be a mistake to suppose that nothing but exalted heroism was exhibited. Human nature showed its degeneracy in the camp and on the field of battle, among heroes and among patriots. The perfection of character, so far as man is ever perfect, was exhibited indeed, by Washington, but by Washington alone.

The army remained at Valley Forge till June, 1778. In the mean time, Lord North made another ineffectual effort to procure reconciliation. But he was too late. His offers might have been accepted at the commencement of the contest; but nothing short of complete independence would now satisfy the Americans, and this North was not willing to concede. Accordingly, new measures of coercion were resorted to by the minister, although the British forces in America were upwards of thirty-three thousand.

Evacuation of Philadelphia.

On the 18th of June, Sir Henry Clinton, who had succeeded Sir William Howe in command of the British forces, evacuated Philadelphia, the possession of which had proved of no service to the English, except as winter quarters for the troops. It was his object to proceed to New York, for which place he marched with his army, having sent his heavy baggage by water. The Americans, with superior forces, hung upon his rear, and sought an engagement. An indecisive one occurred at Monmouth, during which General Lee disregarded the orders of his superior in command, and was suspended for twelve months. There never was perfect harmony between Washington and Lee; and the aid of the latter, though a brave and experienced officer, was easily dispensed with.

No action of importance occurred during this campaign, and it was chiefly signalized by the arrival of the Count d'Estaing, with twelve ships of the line and four frigates, to assist the Americans. But, in consequence of disagreements and mistakes, this large armament failed to engage the English naval forces.

The campaign of 1779 was not more decisive than that of the preceding year. Military operations were chiefly confined to the southern sections of the country, in which the English generally gained the advantage, having superior forces. They overran the country, inflamed the hostility of the

Indians, and destroyed considerable property. But they gained no important victory, and it was obvious to all parties that conquest was impossible.

The Treason of Arnold.

The campaign of 1780 is memorable for the desertion of General Arnold. Though not attended by important political results, it produced an intense excitement. He was intrusted with the care of the fortress of West Point, which commanded the Hudson River; but, dissatisfied, extravagant, and unprincipled, he thought to mend his broken fortunes by surrendering it to the British, who occupied New York. His treason was discovered when his schemes were on the point of being accomplished; but he contrived to escape, and was made a brigadier-general in the service of the enemy. Public execration loaded his name with ignominy, and posterity has not reversed the verdict of his indignant countrymen. His disgrace and ruin were primarily caused by his extravagance and his mortified pride. Washington fully understood his want of moral principle, but continued to intrust him with power, in view of the great services he had rendered his country, and his unquestioned bravery and military talents. After his defection, the American commander-in-chief was never known to intrust an important office to a man in whose virtue he had not implicit faith. The fate of Major André, who negotiated the treason with Arnold, and who was taken as a spy, was much lamented by the English Neither his family, nor rank, nor accomplishments, nor virtues nor the intercession of Sir Henry Clinton, could save him from military execution, according to the established laws of war. Washington has been blamed for not exercising more forbearance in the case of so illustrious a prisoner; but the American general never departed from the rigid justice which he deemed it his duty to pursue.

During this year, the American currency had singularly depreciated, so that forty dollars were worth only one in specie—a fact which shows the embarrassments of the country, and the difficulty of supporting the army. But the prospects of ultimate success enabled Congress, at length, to negotiate loans, and the army was kept together.

Surrender of Lord Cornwallis.

The great event in the campaign of 1781 was the surrender of Lord Cornwallis, at Yorktown, which decided the fate of the war. Lord Cornwallis, who was an able commander, had been successful at the south, although vigorously and skilfully opposed by General La Fayette. But he had at last to contend with the main body of the American army, and French forces in addition, so that the combined armies amounted to over twelve thousand men. He was compelled to surrender to superior forces; and seven thousand prisoners, with all their baggage and stores, fell into the hands of the victors, 19th of October, 1781. This great event diffused universal joy throughout America, and a corresponding depression among the English people.

After this capitulation, the conviction was general that the war would soon be terminated. General La Fayette obtained leave to return to France, and the recruiting service languished. The war nevertheless, was continued until 1783; without, however, being signalized by any great events. On the 30th of November, 1782, preliminary articles of peace were signed at Paris, by which Great Britain acknowledged the independence of the United States, and by which the whole country south of the lakes and east of the Mississippi was ceded to them, and the right of fishing on the Banks of Newfoundland.

On the 25th of November, 1783, the British troops evacuated New York; and, shortly after, the American army was disbanded. The 4th of December, Washington made his farewell address to his officers; and, on the 23d of December, he resigned his commission into the hands of the body from which he received it, and retired to private life; having discharged the great trust reposed in him in a manner which secured the gratitude of his country and which will probably win the plaudits of all future generations.

Resignation of Lord North.

The results of the Revolutionary War can only be described by enumerating the progressive steps of American aggrandizement from that time to this, and by speculating on the future destinies of the Anglo-Saxon race on the American continent. The success which attended this long war is in part to be traced to the talents and matchless wisdom and integrity of the commander-in-chief; to the intrepid courage and virtues of the armies he directed; to the self-confidence and inexperience of the English generals; to the difficulties necessarily attending the conquest of forests, and swamps, and scattered towns; to the assistance of the French nation; and, above all, to the superintending providence of God, who designed to rescue the sons of the Pilgrims from foreign oppression, and, in spite of their many faults, to make them a great and glorious nation, in which religious and civil liberty should be perpetuated, and all men left free to pursue their own means of happiness, and develop the inexhaustible resources of a great and boundless empire.

The English nation acquiesced in an event which all felt to be inevitable; but Lord North was compelled to resign, and a change of measures was pursued. It is now time to contemplate English affairs, until the French Revolution.

References.—The books written on the American Revolution are very numerous, an index to which may be seen in Botta's History, as well as in the writings of those who have treated of this great event. Sparks's Life and Correspondence of Washington is doubtless the most valuable work which has yet appeared since Marshall wrote the Life of Washington. Guizot's Essay on Washington is exceedingly able; nor do I know any author who has so profoundly analyzed the character and greatness of the American hero. Botta's History of the Revolution is a popular but superficial and overlauded book. Mr. Hale's History of the United States is admirably adapted to the purpose for which it is designed, and is the best compendium of American history. Stedman is the standard authority in England. Belsham, in his History of George III., has written candidly and with spirit. Smyth, in his lectures on Modern History, has discussed the Revolution with great ability. See also the works of Ramsay, Winterbotham, Allen, and Gordon. The lives of the prominent American generals, statesmen, and orators, should also be read in connection; especially of Lee, Greene, Franklin, Adams, and Henry, which are best described in Sparks's American Biography.

CHAPTER XXIX
ADMINISTRATION OF WILLIAM PITT

William Pitt.

We come now to consider the most eventful administration, in many important respects, in British annals. The greatness of military operations, the magnitude of reforms, and the great number of illustrious statesmen and men of genius, make the period, when Pitt managed the helm of state, full of interest and grandeur.

Early Life of Pitt.

William Pitt, second son of the first Earl of Chatham, entered public life at a very early age, and was prime minister of George III. at a period of life when most men are just completing a professional education. He was a person of extraordinary precocity. He entered Cambridge University at the age of fourteen, and at that period was a finished Greek and Latin scholar. He spent no idle hours, and evinced but little pleasure in the sports common to boys of his age. He was as successful in mastering mathematics as the languages, and was an admirer of the profoundest treatises of intellectual philosophy. He excelled in every branch of knowledge to which he directed his attention. In 1780, at the age of twenty-one, he became a resident in Lincoln's Inn, entered parliament the succeeding spring, and immediately assumed an active part. His first speech astonished all who heard him, notwithstanding that great expectations were formed concerning his power. He was made chancellor of the exchequer at the age of twenty-three, and at a time when it required a finance minister of the greatest experience. Nor would the Commons have acquiesced in his appointment to so important a post, in so critical a state of the nation, had not great confidence existed as to his abilities. From his first appearance, Pitt took a commanding position as a parliamentary orator; nor, as such, has he ever, on the whole, been surpassed. His peculiar talents fitted him for the highest post in the gift of his sovereign, and the circumstances of the times, in addition, were such as were calculated to develop all the energies and talents he possessed. He was not the most commanding intellect of his age, but he was, unquestionably, the greatest orator that England has produced, and exercised, to the close of his career, in spite of the opposition of such men as Burke, Fox, and Sheridan, an overwhelming parliamentary influence. He was a prodigy; as great in debate, and in executive power, as Napoleon was in the field, Bacon in philosophy, or Shakspeare in poetry. It is difficult for us to conceive how a young man, just emerging from college halls, should be able to answer the difficult questions of veteran statesmen who had been all their lives opposing the principles he advanced, and to assume at once the powers with which his father was intrusted only at a mature period of life. Pitt was almost beyond envy, and the proud nobles and princely capitalists of the richest, proudest, and most conservative country in the world, surrendered to him the guardianship of their liberties with no more fear or distrust than the hereditary bondmen of Turkey or Russia would have shown in hailing the accession of a new emperor. He was born to command, one of nature's despots, and he assumed the reins of government with a perfect consciousness of his abilities to rule.

He was only twenty-four years of age when he began to reign; for, as prime minister of George III., he was, during his continuance in office, the absolute ruler of the British empire. He had, virtually, the nomination of his colleagues, and, through them, the direction of all executive affairs. He was controlled by the legislature only, and parliament was subservient to his will. What a proud position for a young man to occupy! A commoner, with a limited fortune, to give laws to a vast empire, and to have a proud nobility obedient to his will; and all this by the force of talents alone— talents which extorted admiration and respect. He selected Lord Thurlow as chancellor, Lord Gower as president of the council, the Duke of Richmond as lord privy seal, Lords Carmarthen and Sydney as secretaries of state, and Lord Howe as first lord of the admiralty. These were his chief associates in resisting a powerful opposition, and in regulating the affairs of a vast empire—the concerns of India, the national debt, the necessary taxation, domestic tranquillity, and intercourse with foreign powers. But he deserved the confidence of his sovereign and of the nation, and they sustained him in his extraordinary embarrassments and difficulties.

Policy of Pitt.

The policy of the administration is not here to be discussed; but it was the one pursued, in the main, by his father, and one which gratified the national pride. The time has not yet come for us to decide, with certainty, on the wisdom of his course. He was the advocate of measures which had for their object national aggrandizement. He was the strenuous defender of war, and he would oppose Napoleon and all the world to secure preëminence to Great Britain. He believed that glory was better than money; he thought that an overwhelming debt was a less evil than national disgrace; he exaggerated the resources and strength of his country, and believed that it was destined to give laws to the world; he underrated the abilities of other nations to make great advances in mechanical skill and manufacturing enterprise; he supposed that English manufactures would be purchased forever by the rest of the world, and therefore that England, in spite of the debt, would make all nations contribute to her glory and wealth. It was to him a matter of indifference how heavily the people were taxed to pay the interest on a fictitious debt, provided that, by their commerce and manufactures, they could find abundant means to pay this interest. And so long as England could find a market for her wares, the nation would not suffer from taxation. His error was in supposing that England, forever, would manufacture for the world; that English skill was superior to the skill of all other nations; that there was a superiority in the very nature of an Englishman which would enable him, in any country, or under any circumstances, to overcome all competitors and rivals. Such views were grateful to his nation; and he, by continually flattering the national vanity, and ringing the changes on glory and patriotism, induced it to follow courses which may one day result in overwhelming calamities. Self-exaggeration is as fatal to a nation as it is to an individual, and constitutes that pride which precedes destruction. But the mere debt of England, being owed to herself, and not to another nation, is not so alarming as it is sometimes supposed. The worst consequence, in a commercial point of view, is national bankruptcy; but if England becomes bankrupt, her factories, her palaces, her warehouses, and her ships remain. These are not destroyed. Substantial wealth does not fly from the island, but merely passes from the hands of capitalists to the people. The policy of Pitt has merely enriched the few at the expense of the many—has confirmed the power of the aristocracy. When manufacturers can no longer compete with those of other countries, upon such unequal terms as are rendered necessary in consequence of unparalleled taxation to support the public creditors, then the public creditors must suffer rather than the manufacturer himself. The manufacturer must live. This class composes a great part of the nation. The people must be fed, and they will be fed; and they can be fed as cheaply as in any country, were it not for taxes. The policy of Pitt, during the period of commercial prosperity, tended, indeed, to strengthen the power of the aristocracy—that class to which he belonged, and to which the House of Commons, who sustained him, belonged. But it was suicidal, as is the policy of all selfish men; and ultimately must tend to revolutionary measures, even though those measures may not be carried by massacres and blazing thrones.

But we must hasten to consider the leading events which characterized the administration of William Pitt. These were the troubles in Ireland, parliamentary reforms, the aggrandizement of the East India Company, the trial of Hastings, debates on the slave trade, and the war with France in consequence of the French Revolution.

Difficulties with Ireland.

The United Irishmen.

The difficulties with Ireland did not become alarming until the French Revolution had created a spirit of discontent and agitation in all parts of Great Britain. Soon after his accession to power, Mr. Flood, a distinguished member of the Irish House of Commons, brought in a bill of parliamentary reform, which, after a long debate, was negatived. Though his measure was defeated in the House, its advocates out of doors were not cast down, but took measures to form a national congress, for the amelioration of the evils which existed. A large delegation of the people actually met at Dublin, and petitioned parliament for the redress of grievances. Mr. Pitt considered the matter with proper attention, and labored to free the commerce of Ireland from the restraints under which it labored. But, in so doing, he excited the jealousy of British merchants and manufacturers, and they induced him to remodel his propositions for the relief of Ireland, which were then adopted. Tranquillity was restored until the year 1791, when there appeared at Belfast the plan of an association, under the name of the *United Irishmen*, whose object was a radical reform of all the evils which had existed in Ireland since its connection with England. This association soon extended throughout the island, and numbered an immense body of both Protestants and Catholics who were disaffected with the government. In consequence of the disaffections, especially among the Catholics, the English ministry made many concessions, and the legislature allowed Catholics to practice law, to intermarry with Protestants, and to obtain an unrestrained education. But parliament also took measures to prevent the assembling of any convention of the people, and augmented the militia in case of disturbance. But disturbances took place, and the United Irishmen began to contemplate an entire separation from England, and other treasonable designs. In consequence of these commotions, the Habeas Corpus Act was suspended, and a military government was enforced with all its rigor. The United Irish pretended to submit, but laid still deeper schemes, and extended their affiliations. In May, 1797, the number of men enrolled by the union in Ulster alone was one hundred thousand, and their organization was perfect. The French government was aware of the union, which gradually numbered five hundred thousand men, and promised it assistance. The Irish, however, relied chiefly upon themselves, and prepared to resist the English government, which was resolved on pursuing the most vigorous measures. A large military force was sent to Ireland, and several ringleaders of the contemplated insurrection were arrested.

But the timely discovery of the conspiracy prevented one of the most bloody contests which ever happened in Ireland. Nevertheless, the insurrection broke out in some places, and in the county of Wexford was really formidable. The rebels numbered twenty thousand men. They got possession of Wexford, and committed great barbarities; but they were finally subdued by Lord Cornwallis. Had the French coöperated, as they had promised, with a force of fifteen thousand, it is not improbable that Ireland would have been wrested from England. But the French had as much as they could do, at this time, to take care of themselves; and Ireland was again subjected to greater oppressions than before.

The Irish parliament had hitherto been a mere body of perpetual dictators. By the Octennial Bill, this oligarchy was disbanded, and the House of Commons wore something of the appearance of a constitutional assembly, and there were found in it some men of integrity and sagacity. Ireland also had her advocates in the British senate; but whenever the people or the parliament gained a victory over the viceroy, some accident or blunder deprived the nation of reaping the fruits. The Commons became again corrupted, and the independence which Ireland obtained ceased to have a value. The corrupted Commons basely surrendered all that had been obtained. In vain the eloquence of Curran and Grattan. The Irish nation, without public virtue, a prey to faction, and a scene of corruption, became at last powerless and politically helpless. The rebellion of 1798 was a mere peasants' war, without intelligence to guide, or experience to counsel. It therefore miserably failed, but did not fail until fifty thousand rebels and twenty thousand royalists had perished.

Union of England and Ireland.

In June, 1800, the union of Ireland and England was effected, on the same basis as that between England and Scotland in the time of Anne. It was warmly opposed by some of the more patriotic of the Irish statesmen, and only carried by corruption and bribery. By this union, foreign legislation took the place of the guidance of those best qualified to know the national grievances; the Irish members became, in the British senate, merely the tools of the administration. Absenteeism was nearly doubled, and the national importance nearly annihilated in a political point of view. But, on the other hand, an oligarchal tyranny was broken, and the bond of union which bound the countries was strengthened, and the nation subsided into a greater state of tranquillity. Twenty-eight peers and one hundred commoners were admitted into the English parliament.

Notwithstanding the suppression of the rebellion of 1798, only five years elapsed before another one was contemplated—the result of republican principles, and of national grievances. The leaders were Robert Emmet and Thomas Russell. But their treasonable designs were miserably supported by their countrymen, and they were able to make but a feeble effort, which immediately failed. These men were arrested, tried, and executed. The speech of Emmet, before his execution, has been much admired for its spirit of patriotism and pensive eloquence. His grand mistake consisted in overrating the strength of democratic influences, and in supposing that, by violent measures, he could overturn a strong military government. The Irish were not prepared for freedom, still less republican freedom. There was not sufficient concert, or patriotism, or intelligence, to secure popular liberty, and the antipathy between the Catholic and Protestant population was too deeply seated and too malignant to hope, reasonably, for a lasting union.

Condition of Ireland.

All the measures which have been adopted for the independence and elevation of Ireland have failed, and the country is still in as lamentable a state as ever. It presents a grand enigma and mystery to the politician. All the skill of statesmen is baffled in devising means for the tranquillity and improvement of that unhappy and unfortunate country. The more privileges the people gain, and the greater assistance they receive, the more unreasonable appear to be their demands, and the more extravagant their expectations. Still, there are great and shameful evils, which ought to be remedied. There are nearly five millions of acres of waste land in the country, capable of the highest cultivation. The soil is inexhaustibly rich, the climate is most delightful, and the natural advantages for agriculture and commerce unprecedented. Still the Irish remain oppressed and poor; enslaved by their priests, and ground down to the earth by exacting landlords and a hostile government. There is no real union between England and Ireland, no sympathy between the different classes, and an implacable animosity between the Protestant and Catholic population. The northern and Protestant part of the island is the most flourishing; but Ireland, in any light it may be viewed, is the most miserable country, with all the gifts of nature, the worst governed, and the most afflicted, in Christendom; and no human sagacity or wisdom has yet been able to devise a remedy for the innumerable evils which prevail. The permanent causes of the degradation of the Irish peasantry, in their own country, have been variously attributed to the Roman Catholic priesthood, to the tyranny of the government, to the system by which the lands are leased and cultivated, and to the natural elements of the Irish character. These, united, may have produced the effects which all philanthropists deplore; but no one cause, in particular, can account for so fine a nation sinking into such poverty and wretchedness, especially when it is considered that the same idle and miserable peasantry, when transplanted to America, exhibit very different dispositions and tastes, and develop traits of character which command respect and secure prosperity.

Parliamentary Reform.

The first plan for parliamentary reform was brought forward by Pitt in 1782, before he was prime minister, in consequence of a large number of the House representing no important interests, and dependent on the minister. But his motion was successfully opposed. In May, 1783, he brought in another bill to add one hundred members to the House of Commons, and to abolish a proportionate number of the small and obnoxious boroughs. This plan, though supported by Fox, was negatived by a great majority. In 1785, he made a third attempt to secure a reform of parliament, and again failed; and with this last attempt ended all his efforts for this object. So persuaded was he of the impracticability of the measure, that he even uniformly opposed the object when attempted by others. Moreover, he changed his opinions when he perceived the full connection and bearing of the subject with other agitating questions. He was desirous of a reform, if it could be obtained without mischief; but when it became a democratic measure, he opposed it with all his might. Indeed, he avowed that he preferred to have parliament remain as it was, forever, rather than risk any prospects of reform when the country was so deeply agitated by revolutionary discussions. Mr. Pitt perfectly understood that those persons who were most eager for parliamentary reform, desired the overthrow of the existing institutions of the land, or, at least, such as were inconsistent with the hereditary succession to the throne, hereditary titles, and the whole system of entailed estates. Mr. Pitt, as he grew older, more powerful, and more experienced, became more aristocratic and conservative; feared to touch any of the old supports of the constitution for fear of producing a revolution—an evil which, of all evils, he most abhorred. Mr. Burke, though opposed to the minister, here defended him, and made an eloquent speech against revolutionary measures. Nor can we wonder at the change of opinion, which Mr. Pitt and others admitted, when it is considered that the advocates of parliamentary reform also were associated with men of infidel and dangerous principles. Thomas Paine was one of the apostles of liberty in that age, and his writings had a very great and very pernicious influence on the people at large. It is very singular, but nevertheless true, that some of the most useful reforms have been projected by men of infidel principles, and infidelity and revolutionary excess have generally been closely connected.

But the reform question did not deeply agitate the people of England until a much later period. One of the most exciting events, in the domestic history of England during the administration of Pitt, was the trial of Hastings and the difficulties which grew out of the aggrandizement of the East India Company.

Warren Hastings.

In the chapter on colonization, allusion was made to Indian affairs until the close of the administration of Lord Clive. Warren Hastings continued the encroachments and conquests which Clive had so successfully begun. He went to India in 1750, at the age of seventeen, as a clerk in the service of the company. It was then merely a commercial corporation. His talents and sagacity insured his prosperity. He gradually was promoted, and, in 1772, was appointed head of the government in Bengal. But the governor was not then, as he now is, nearly absolute, and he had only one vote in the council which represented the company at Calcutta. He was therefore frequently overruled, and his power was crippled. But he contrived to make important changes, and abolished the office of the minister to whom was delegated the collection of the revenue and the general regulation of internal affairs—an office which had been always held by a native. Hastings transferred the internal administration to the servants of the company, and in various other ways improved the finances of the company, the members of which were indifferent, comparatively, to the condition of the people of India, provided that they themselves were enriched. To enrich the company and extend its possessions, even at the expense of justice and humanity, became the object of the governor-general. He succeeded; but success brought upon him the imprecations of the natives and the indignant rebukes of his own countrymen. In less than two years after he had assumed the government, he added four hundred thousand pounds to the annual income of the company, besides nearly a million in ready money. But the administration of Hastings cannot be detailed. We can only notice that part of it which led to his trial in England.

War with Hyder Ali.

The great event which marked his government was the war with Hyder Ali, the Mohammedan sovereign of Mysore. The province of Bengal and the Carnatic had been, for some time, under the protection of the English. Adjoining the Carnatic, in the centre of the peninsula, were the dominions of Hyder Ali. Had Hastings been governor of Madras, he would have conciliated him, or vigorously encountered him as an enemy. But the authorities at Madras had done neither. They provoked him to hostilities, and, with an army of ninety thousand men, he invaded the Carnatic. British

India was on the verge of ruin. Hyder Ali was every where triumphant, and only a few fortified places remained to the English.

Hastings, when he heard of the calamity, instantly adopted the most vigorous measures. He settled his difficulties with the Mahrattas; he suspended the incapable governor of Fort George, and sent Sir Eyre Coote to oppose the great Mohammedan prince who threatened to subvert the English power in India.

But Hastings had not the money which was necessary to carry on an expensive war with the most formidable enemy the English ever encountered in the East. He therefore resolved to plunder the richest and most sacred city of India—Benares. It was the seat of Indian learning and devotion, and contained five hundred thousand people. Its temple, as seen from the Ganges, was the most imposing in the Eastern world, while its bazaars were filled with the most valuable and rare of Indian commodities; with the muslins of Bengal, the shawls of Cashmere, the sabres of Oude, and the silks of its own looms.

This rich capital was governed by a prince nominally subject to the Great Mogul, but who was dependent on the Nabob of Oude, a large province north of the Ganges, near the Himmaleh Mountains. Benares and its territories, being oppressed by the Nabob of Oude, sought the protection of the British. Their protection was, of course, readily extended; but it was fatal to the independence of Benares. The alliance with the English was like the protection Rome extended to Greece when threatened by Asia, and which ended in the subjection of both Greece and Asia. The Rajah of Benares became the vassal of the company, and therefore was obliged to furnish money for the protection he enjoyed.

But the tribute which the Rajah of Benares paid did not satisfy Hastings. He exacted still greater sums, which led to an insurrection and ultimate conquest. The fair domains of Cheyte Sing, the lord of Benares, were added to the dominions of the company together with an increased revenue of two hundred thousand pounds a year. The treasure of the rajah amounted to two hundred and fifty thousand pounds, and this was divided as prize money among the English.

Robbery of the Princesses of Oude.

The rapacious governor-general did not obtain the treasure which he expected to find at Benares, and then resolved to rob the Princesses of Oude, who had been left with immense treasures on the death of Suraj-w Dowlah, the nabob vizier of the Grand Mogul. The only pretext which Hastings could find was, that the insurrection at Benares had produced disturbances at Oude, and which disturbances were imputed to the princesses. Great barbarities were inflicted in order to secure these treasures; but the robbers were successful, and immense sums flowed into the treasury of the company. By these iniquities, the governor found means to conduct the war in the Carnatic successfully, and a treaty was concluded with Tippoo, the son of Hyder Ali, by which the company reigned without a rival on the great Indian peninsula.

When peace was restored to India, and the company's servants had accumulated immense fortunes, Hastings returned to England. But the iniquities he had practised excited great indignation among those statesmen who regarded justice and humanity as better supports to a government than violence and rapine.

Foremost among these patriots was Edmund Burke. He had long been a member of the select committee to investigate Indian affairs, and he had bestowed great attention to them, and fully understood the course which Hastings had pursued.

Through his influence, an inquiry into the conduct of the late governor-general was instituted, and he was accordingly impeached at the bar of the House of Lords. Mr. Pitt permitted matters to take their natural course; but the king, the Lord Chancellor Thurlow, the ministers generally, and the directors of the East India Company espoused his cause. They regarded him as a very great man, whose rule had been glorious to the nation, in spite of the mistakes and cruelties which marked his government. He had added an empire to the British crown, educed order out of anarchy, and organized a system of administration which, in its essential features, has remained to this time. He enriched the company, while he did not enrich himself; for he easily might have accumulated a fortune of three millions of pounds. And he moreover contrived, in spite of his extortions and conquests, to secure the respect of the native population, whose national and religious prejudices he endeavored not to shock. "These things inspired good will. At the same time, his constant success, and the manner in which he extricated himself from every difficulty, made him an object of superstitious admiration; and the more than regal splendor which he sometimes displayed, dazzled a people who have much in common with children. Even now, after the lapse of more than fifty years, the natives of India still talk of him as the greatest of the English, and nurses sing children to sleep with a gingling ballad about the fleet horses and richly-caparisoned elephants of Sahib Warren Hostein."

Prosecution of Hastings.

But neither the admiration of the people of the East for the splendid abilities of Hastings, nor the gratitude of a company of merchants, nor the powerful friends he had in the English parliament, could screen him from the malignant hatred of Francis, or the purer indignation of Burke. The zeal which the latter evinced in his prosecution has never been equalled, and all his energies, for years, were devoted to the exposure of a person whom he regarded as "a delinquent of the first magnitude." "He had just as lively an idea of the insurrection at Benares as of Lord George Gordon's riots, and of the execution of Nuncomar as of the execution of Dr. Dodd." Burke was assisted in his vehement prosecution by Charles James Fox, the greatest debater ever known in the House of Commons, but a man vastly inferior to himself in moral elevation, in general knowledge, in power of fancy, and in profound wisdom.

The trial was at Westminster Hall, the hall which had witnessed the inauguration of thirty kings, and the trials of accused nobles since the time of William Rufus. And he was a culprit not unworthy of that great tribunal before which he was summoned—"a tribunal which had pronounced sentence on Strafford, and pardon on Somers"—the tribunal before which royalty itself had been called to account. Hastings had ruled, with absolute sway, a country which was more populous and more extensive than any of the kingdoms of Europe, and had gained a fame which was bounded only by the unknown countries of the globe. He was defended by three men who subsequently became the three highest judges of the land, and he was encouraged by the appearance and sympathetic smiles of the highest nobles of the realm.

Edmund Burke.

But greater than all were the mighty statesmen who conducted the prosecution. First among them in character and genius was Edmund Burke, who, from the time that he first spoke in the House of Commons, in 1766, had been a prominent member, and had, at length, secured greater fame than any of his contemporaries, Pitt alone excepted, not merely as an orator, but as an enlightened statesman, a philosopher, and a philanthropist. He excelled all the great men with whom he was associated, in the variety of his powers; he was a poet even while a boy; a penetrating philosopher, critic, and historian before the age of thirty; a statesman of unrivalled moral wisdom; an orator whose speeches have been read with increasing admiration in every succeeding age; a judge of the fine arts to whose opinions Reynolds submitted; and a writer on various subjects, in which he displayed not only vast knowledge, but which he treated in a style of matchless beauty and force. All the great men of his age—Johnson, Reynolds, Goldsmith, Garrick, Pitt, Fox, Sheridan, Windham, North, Thurlow, Parr—scholars, critics, divines, and statesmen—bore testimony to his commanding genius and his singular moral worth, to his hatred of vice, and his passionate love of virtue. But these great and varied excellences, which secured him the veneration of the finest minds in Europe, were not fully appreciated by his own nation, which was astonished rather than governed by his prophetic wisdom. But Burke was remarkable, not merely for his knowledge, eloquence, and genius but also for an unblemished private life, for the habitual exercise of all those virtues, and the free expression of all those noble sentiments which only have marked exalted Christian characters. In his political principles, he was a conservative, and preferred to base his views on history and experience, rather than to try experiments, especially when these were advocated by men whose moral character or infidel sentiments excited his distrust or aversion. He did not shut his eyes to abuse, but aimed to mend deliberately and cautiously. His admonition to his country respecting America corresponded with his general sentiments. "Talk not of your abstract rights of government; I hate the very sound of them; follow experience and common sense." He believed that love was better than force, and that the strength of any government consisted in the affections of the people. And these he ever strove to retain, and for these he was willing to relinquish momentary gain and selfish aggrandizement. He advocated concession to the Irish legislature; justice and security to the people of India; liberty of conscience to Dissenters; relief to small debtors; the suppression of general warrants; the extension of the power of juries; freedom of the press; retrenchment in the public expenditures; the removal of commercial restrictions; and the abolition of the slave trade. He had a great contempt for "mechanical politicians," and "pedler principles." And he lived long enough to see the fulfilment of his political prophecies, and the horrors of that dreadful revolution which he had predicted and disliked, not because the principles which the French apostles of liberty advocated, were not abstractedly true, but because they were connected with excesses, and an infidel recklessness in the violation of established social rights, which alarmed and disgusted him. He died in 1797, in the sixty-eighth year of his age, beloved and honored by the good and great in all Christian countries.

Charles James Fox.

Next to Burke, among the prosecutors of Hastings, for greatness and popularity, was Charles James Fox; inferior to Burke in knowledge, imagination, and moral power, but superior in all the arts of debate, the most logical and accomplished forensic orator which that age of orators produced. His father, Lord Holland, had been the rival of the great Chatham, and he himself was opposed, nearly the whole of his public life, to the younger Pitt. His political principles were like those of Burke until the French Revolution, whose principles he at first admired. He was emphatically the man of the people, easy of access, social in his habits, free in his intercourse, without reserve or haughtiness, generous, magnanimous, and conciliatory. He was unsurpassed for logical acuteness, and for bursts of overpowering passion. He reached high political station, although his habits were such as destroyed, in many respects, the respect of those great men with whom he was associated.

Richard Brinsley Sheridan.

Richard Brinsley Sheridan, another of the public accusers of Hastings, was a different man from either Burke or Fox. He was born in Ireland, but was educated at Harrow, and first distinguished himself by writing plays. In 1776, on the retirement of Garrick, he became manager of Drury Lane Theatre; and shortly after appeared the School for Scandal, which placed him on the summit of dramatic fame. In 1780, he entered parliament, and, when Hastings was impeached, was in the height of his reputation, both as a writer and orator. His power consisted in brilliant declamation and sparkling wit, and his speech in relation to the Princesses of Oude produced an impression almost without a parallel in ancient or modern times. Mr. Burke's admiration was sincere and unbounded, but Fox thought it too florid and rhetorical. His fame now rests on his dramas. But his life was the shipwreck of genius, in consequence of his extravagance, his recklessness in incurring debts, and his dissipated habits, which disorganized his moral character and undermined the friendships which his brilliant talents at first secured to him.

But in spite of the indignation which these illustrious orators excited against Hastings, he was nevertheless acquitted, after a trial which lasted eight years, in consequence of the change of public opinion; and, above all, in view of the great services which he had really rendered to his country. The expenses of the trial nearly ruined him; but the East India Company granted him an annual income of four thousand pounds, which he spent in ornamenting and enriching Daylesford, the seat which had once belonged to his family, and which he purchased after his return from India.

Bill for the Regulation of India.

Although Warren Hastings was eventually acquitted by the House of Lords, still his long and protracted trial brought to light many evils connected with the government of India; and, in 1784, acts were passed which gave the nation a more direct control over the East India Company—the most gigantic monopoly the world has ever seen. That a company of merchants in Leadenhall Street should exercise an unlimited power over an empire larger than the whole of Europe with the exception of Russia, and sacrifice the interests of humanity to base pecuniary considerations, at length aroused the English nation. Accordingly, Mr. Pitt brought in a bill, which passed both Houses, which provided that the affairs of the company should be partly managed by a Board of Control, partly by the Court of Directors, and partly by a general meeting of the stockholders of the company. The Board of Control was intrusted to five privy counsellors, one of whom was secretary of state. It was afterwards composed of a president, such members of the privy council as the king should select, and a secretary. This board superintends and regulates all civil, military, and revenue officers, and political negotiations, and all general despatches. The Board of Directors, composed of twenty-four men, six of whom are annually elected, has the nomination of the governor-general, and the appointment of all civil and military officers. These two boards operate as a check against each other.

The first governor-general, by the new constitution, was Lord Cornwallis, a nobleman of great military experience and elevated moral worth; a man who was intrusted with great power, even after his misfortunes in America, and a man who richly deserved the confidence reposed in him. Still, he was seldom fortunate. He made blunders in India as well as in America. He did not fully understand the institutions of India, or the genius of the people. He was soon called to embark in the contests which divided the different native princes, and with the usual result. The simple principle of English territorial acquisition is, in defending the cause of the feebler party. The stronger party was then conquered, and became a province of the East India Company, while the weaker remained under English protection, until, by oppression, injustice, and rapacity on the part of the protectors, it was driven to rebellion, and then subdued.

When Lord Cornwallis was sent to India, in 1786, the East India Company had obtained possession of Bengal, a part of Bahar, the Benares district of Allahabad, part of Orissa, the Circars, Bombay, and the Jaghire of the Carnatic—a district of one hundred miles along the coast. The other great Indian powers, unconquered by the English, were the Mahrattas, who occupied the centre of India, from Delhi to the Krishna, and from the Bay of Bengal to the Arabian Sea; also, Golconda, the western parts of the Carnatic, Mysore, Oude, and the country of the Sikhs. Of the potentates who ruled over these extensive provinces, the Sultan of Mysore, Tippoo Saib, was the most powerful, although the Mahrattas country was the largest.

War with Tippoo Saib.

The hostility of Tippoo, who inherited his father's prejudices against the English, excited the suspicions of Lord Cornwallis, and a desperate war was the result, in which the sultan showed the most daring courage. In 1792, the English general invested the formidable fortress of Seringapatam, with sixteen thousand Europeans and thirty thousand sepoys, and with the usual success. Tippoo, after the loss of this strong fort, and of twenty-three thousand of his troops, made peace with Lord Cornwallis, by the payment of four millions of pounds, and the surrender of half his dominions. Lord Cornwallis, after the close of this war, returned home, and was succeeded by Sir John Shore; and he by Marquis Wellesley, (1798,) under whose administration the war with Tippoo was renewed, in consequence of the intrigues of the sultan with the French at Pondicherry, to regain his dominions. The Sultan of Mysore, was again defeated, and slain; the dynasty of Hyder Ali ceased to reign, and the East India Company took possession of the whole southern peninsula. A subsequent war with the Mahratta powers completely established the British supremacy in India. Delhi, the capital of the Great Mogul, fell into the hands of the English, and the emperor himself became a stipendiary of a company of merchants. The conquest of the country of the Mahrattas was indeed successful, but was attended by vast expenses, which entailed a debt on the company of about nineteen millions of pounds. The brilliant successes of Wellesley, however, were not appreciated by the Board of Directors, who wanted dividends rather than glory, and he was recalled.

Conquest of India.

There were no new conquests until 1817, under the government of the Earl of Moira, afterwards Marquis of Hastings. He made war on the Pindarries, who were bands of freebooters in Central India. They were assisted by several native powers, which induced the governor-general to demand considerable cessions of territory. In 1819, the British effected a settlement at Singapore by which a lucrative commerce was secured to Great Britain.

Lord Hastings was succeeded by the Earl of Amherst, under whose administration the Burmese war commenced, and by which large territories, between Bengal and China, were added to the British empire, (1826.)

On the overthrow of the Mogul empire, the kingdom of the Sikhs, in the northern part of India, and that of the Affghans, lying west of the Indus, arose in importance—kingdoms formerly subject to Persia. The former, with all its dependent provinces, has recently been conquered, and annexed to the overgrown dominions of the Company.

In 1833, the charter of the East India Company expired, and a total change of system was the result. The company was deprived of its exclusive right of trade, the commerce with India and China was freely opened to all the world, and the possessions and rights of the company were ceded to the nation for an annual annuity of six hundred and thirty thousand pounds. The political government of India, however, was continued to the company until 1853.

Consequences of the Conquest.

Thus has England come in possession of one of the oldest and most powerful of the Oriental empires, containing a population of one hundred and thirty millions of people, speaking various languages, and wedded irrecoverably to different social and religious institutions. The conquest of India is complete, and there is not a valuable office in the whole country which is not held by an Englishman. The native and hereditary princes of provinces, separately larger and more populous than Great Britain itself, are divested of all but the shadow of power, and receive stipends from the East India Company. The Emperor of Delhi, the Nabobs of Bengal and the Carnatic, the Rajahs of Tanjore and Benares, and the Princes of the house of Tippoo, and other princes, receive, indeed, an annual support of over a million sterling; but their power has passed away. An empire two thousand miles from east to west, and eighteen hundred from north to south, and containing more square miles than a territory larger than all the States between the Mississippi and the Atlantic Ocean, has fallen into the hands of the Anglo-Saxon race. It is true that a considerable part of Hindostan is nominally held by subsidiary allies, under the protection of the British government; but the moment that these dependent princes cease to be useful, this protection will be withdrawn. There can be no reasonable doubt that the English rule is beneficent in many important respects. Order and law are better observed than formerly under the Mohammedan dynasty; but no compensation is sufficient, in the eyes of the venerable Brahmin, for interference in the laws and religion of the country. India has been robbed by the armies of European merchants, and is only held in bondage by an overwhelming military force, which must be felt as burdensome and expensive when the plundered country shall no longer satisfy the avarice of commercial corporations. But that day may be remote. Calcutta now rivals in splendor and importance the old capital of the Great Mogul. The palace of the governor-general is larger than Windsor Castle or Buckingham Palace; the stupendous fortifications of Fort William rival the fortress of Gibraltar; the Anglo-Indian army amounts to two hundred thousand men; while the provinces of India are taxed, directly or indirectly, to an amount exceeding eighteen millions of pounds per annum. It is idle to speculate on the destinies of India, or the duration of the English power. The future is ever full of gloom, when scarcely any thing is noticeable but injustice and oppression on the part of rulers, and poverty and degradation among the governed. It is too much to suppose that one hundred and eighty millions of the human race can be permanently governed by a power on the opposite side of the globe, and where there never can exist any union or sympathy between the nation that rules and the nations that are ruled, in any religious, social, or political institution; and when all that is dear to the heart of man, and all that is consecrated by the traditions of ages, are made to subserve the interests of a mercantile state.

But it is time to hasten to the consideration of the remaining subjects connected with the administration of William Pitt.

The agitations of moral reformers are among the most prominent and interesting. The efforts of benevolent statesmen and philanthropists to abolish the slave trade produced a great excitement throughout Christendom, and were followed by great results.

In 1787, William Wilberforce, who represented the great county of York, brought forward, in the House of Commons, a motion for the abolition of the slave trade. The first public movements to put a stop to this infamous traffic were made by the Quakers in the Southern States of America, who presented petitions for that purpose to their respective legislatures. Their brethren in England followed their example, and presented similar petitions to the House of Commons. A society was formed, and a considerable sum was raised to collect information relative to the traffic, and to support the expense of application to parliament. A great resistance was expected and made, chiefly by merchants and planters. Mr. Wilberforce interested himself greatly in this investigation, and in May brought the matter before parliament, and supported his motion with overwhelming arguments and eloquence. Mr. Fox, Mr. Burke, Mr. William Smith, and Mr. Whitbread supported Mr. Wilberforce. Mr. Pitt defended the cause of abolition with great eloquence and power; but the House was not then in favor of immediate abolition, nor was it carried until Mr. Fox and his friends came into power.

War with France.

The war with France, in consequence of the progress of the revolution, is too great a subject to be treated except in a chapter by itself. Mr. Pitt abstained from all warlike demonstrations until the internal tranquillity of

England itself was affected by the propagation of revolutionary principles. But when, added to these, it was feared that the French were resolved to extend their empire, and overturn the balance of power, and encroach on the liberties of England, then Pitt, sustained by an overwhelming majority in parliament, declared war upon France, (1793.) The advocates of the French Revolution, however, take different views, and attribute the rise and career of Napoleon to the jealousy and encroachments of England herself, as well as of Austria and Prussia. Whether the general European war might not have been averted, is a point which merits inquiry, and on which British statesmen are not yet agreed. But the connection of England with this great war will be presented in the following chapter.

Mr. Pitt continued to manage the helm of state until 1806; but all his energies were directed to the prosecution of the war, and no other events of importance took place during his administration.

Policy of Pitt.

His genius most signally was displayed in his financial skill in extricating his nation from the great embarrassments which resulted from the American war, and in providing the means to prosecute still more expensive campaigns against Napoleon and his generals. He also had unrivalled talent in managing the House of Commons against one of the most powerful oppositions ever known, and in a period of great public excitements. He was always ready in debate, and always retained the confidence of the nation. He is probably the greatest of the English statesmen, so far as talents are concerned, and so far as he represented the ideas and sentiments of his age. But it is a question which will long perplex philosophers whether he was the wisest of that great constellation of geniuses who enlightened his brilliant age. To him may be ascribed the great increase of the national debt. If taxes are the greatest calamity which can afflict a nation, then Pitt has entailed a burden of misery which will call forth eternal curses on his name, in spite of all the brilliancy of his splendid administration. But if the glory and welfare of nations consist in other things—in independence, patriotism, and rational liberty; if it was desirable, above all material considerations, to check the current of revolutionary excess, and oppose the career of a man who aimed to bring all the kings and nations of Europe under the yoke of an absolute military despotism, and rear a universal empire on the ruins of ancient monarchies and states,—then Pitt and his government should be contemplated in a different light.

That mighty contest which developed the energies of this great statesman, as well as the genius of a still more remarkable man, therefore claims our attention.

References.—Tomline's Life of Pitt. Belsham's History of George III. Prior's and Bissett's Lives of Burke. Moore's Life of Sheridan. Walpole's Life of Fox. Life of Wilberforce, by his sons. Annual Register, from 1783 to 1806. Macaulay's Essay on Warren Hastings. Elphinstone's and Martin's Histories of India. Mill's British India. Russell's Modern Europe. Correspondence of Rt. Hon. Edmund Burke. Campbell's Lives of the Lord Chancellors. Boswell's Life of Johnson. Burke's Works. Schlosser's Modern History.

CHAPTER XXX
THE FRENCH REVOLUTION

If the American war was the greatest event in modern times, in view of ultimate results, the French Revolution may be considered the most exciting and interesting to the eye of contemporaries. The wars which grew out of the Revolution in France were conducted on a scale of much greater magnitude, and embroiled all the nations of Europe. A greater expenditure of energies took place than from any contest in the annals of civilized nations. Nor has any contest ever before developed so great military genius. Napoleon stands at the head of his profession, by general consent; and it is probable that his fame will increase, rather than diminish, with advancing generations.

It is impossible to describe, in a few pages, the great and varied events connected with the French Revolution, or even allude to all the prominent ones. The causes of this great movement are even more interesting than the developments.

Causes of the French Revolution.

The question is often asked, could Louis XVI. have prevented the catastrophe which overturned his throne? He might, perhaps, have delayed it; but it was an inevitable event, and would have happened, sooner or later. There were evils in the government of France, and in the condition of the people, so overwhelming and melancholy, that they would have produced an outbreak. Had Richelieu never been minister; had the Fronde never taken place; had Louis XIV. and XV. never reigned; had there been no such women as disgraced the court of France in the eighteenth century; had there been no tyrannical kings, no oppressive nobles, no grievous taxes, no national embarrassments, no luxurious courts, no infidel writings, and no discontented people,—then Louis XVI. might have reigned at Versailles, as Louis XV. had done before him. But the accumulated grievances of two centuries called imperatively for redress, and nothing short of a revolution could have removed them.

Now, what were those evils and those circumstances which, of necessity, produced the most violent revolutionary storm in the annals of the world? The causes of the French revolution may be generalized under five heads:

First, the influence of the writings of infidel philosophers; second, the diffusion of the ideas of popular rights; third, the burdens of the people, which made these abstract ideas of right a mockery; fourth, the absurd infatuation of the court and nobles; fifth, the derangement of the finances, which clogged the wheels of government, and led to the assembling of the States General. There were also other causes: but the above mentioned are the most prominent.

Helvetius — Voltaire.

Of those philosophers whose writings contributed to produce this revolution, there were four who exerted a remarkable influence. These were Helvetius, Voltaire, Rousseau, and Diderot.

Helvetius was a man of station and wealth, and published, in 1758, a book, in which he carried out the principles of Condillac and of other philosophers of the sensational, or, as it is sometimes called, the sensuous school. He boldly advocated a system of undisguised selfishness. He maintained that man owed his superiority over the lower animals to the superior organization of the body. Proceeding from this point, he asserted, further, that every faculty and emotion are derived from sensation; that all minds are originally equal; that pleasure is the only good, and self-interest the only ground of morality. The materialism of Helvetius was the mere revival of pagan Epicurianism; but it was popular, and his work, called *De l'Esprit*, made a great sensation. It was congenial with the taste of a court and a generation that tolerated Madame de Pompadour. But the Parliament of Paris condemned it, and pronounced it derogatory to human nature, inasmuch as it confined our faculties to animal sensibility, and destroyed the distinctions between virtue and vice.

His fame was eclipsed by the brilliant career of Voltaire, who exercised a greater influence on his age than any other man. He is the great apostle of French infidelity, and the great oracle of the superficial thinkers of his nation and age. He was born in 1694, and early appeared upon the stage. He was a favorite at Versailles, and a companion of Frederic the Great—as great an egotist as he, though his egotism was displayed in a different way. He was an aristocrat, made for courts, and not for the people, with whom he had no sympathy, although the tendency of his writings was democratic. In all his satirical sallies, he professed to respect authority. But he was never in earnest, was sceptical, insincere, and superficial. It would not be rendering him justice to deny that he had great genius. But his genius was to please, to amuse a vain-glorious people, to turn every thing into ridicule, to pull down, and substitute nothing instead. He was a modern Lucian, and his satirical mockery destroyed reverence for God and truth. He despised and defied the future, and the future has rendered a verdict which can never be reversed—that he was vain, selfish, shallow, and cold, without faith in any spiritual influence to change the world. But he had a keen perception of what was false, with all his superficial criticism, a perception of what is now called *humbug*; and it cannot be denied that, in a certain sense, he had a love of truth, but not of truth in its highest development, not of the positive, the affirmative, the real. Negation and denial suited him better, and suited the age in which he lived better; hence he was a "representative man," was an exponent of his age, and led the age. He hated the Jesuits, but chiefly because they advocated a blind authority; and he strove to crush Christianity, because its professors so often were a disgrace to it, while its best members were martyrs and victims. Voltaire did not, like Helvetius, propose any new system of philosophy, but strove to make all systems absurd. He set the ball of Atheism in motion, and others followed in a bolder track: pushed out, not his principles, for he had none, but his spirit, into the extreme of mockery and negation. And such a course unsettled the popular faith, both in religion and laws, and made men indifferent to the future, and to their moral obligations.

Rousseau.

Quite a different man was Rousseau. He was not a mocker, or a leveller, or a satirist, or an atheist. He resembled Voltaire only in one respect—in egotism. He was not so learned as Voltaire, did not write so much, was not so highly honored or esteemed. But he had more genius, and exercised a greater influence on posterity. His influence was more subtle and more dangerous, for he led astray people of generous impulses and enthusiastic dispositions, with but little intelligence or experience. He abounded in extravagant admiration of unsophisticated nature, professed to love the simple and earnest, affected extraordinary friendship and sympathy, and was most enthusiastic in his rhapsodies of sentimental love. Voltaire had no cant, but Rousseau was full of it. Voltaire was the father of Danton, but Rousseau of Robespierre, that sentimental murderer who as a judge, was too conscientious to hang a criminal, but sufficiently unscrupulous to destroy a king. The absurdities of Rousseau can be detected in the ravings of the ultra Transcendentalists, in the extravagance of Fourierism, in the mock philanthropy of such apostles of light as Eugene Sue and Louis Blanc. The whole mental and physical constitution of Rousseau was diseased, and his actions were strangely inconsistent with his sentiments. He gave the kiss of friendship, and it proved the token of treachery; he expatiated on simplicity and earnestness in most bewitching language, but was a hypocrite, seducer, and liar. He was always breathing the raptures of affection, yet never succeeded in keeping a friend; he was always denouncing the selfishness and vanity of the world, and yet was miserable without its rewards and praises; no man was more dependent on society, yet no man ever professed to hold it in deeper contempt; no man ever had a prouder spirit, yet no man ever affected a more abject humility. He dilated, with apparent rapture, on disinterested love, and yet left his own children to cold neglect and poverty. He poisoned the weak and the susceptible by pouring out streams of passion in eloquent and exciting language, under the pretence of unburdening his own soul and revealing his own sorrows. He was always talking about philanthropy and generosity, and yet seldom bestowed a charity. No man was ever more eloquent in paradox, or sublime in absurdity. He spent his life in gilding what is corrupt, and glossing over what is impure. The great moral effect of his writings was to make men commit crimes under the name of patriotism, and permit them to indulge in selfish passion under the name of love.

Diderot.

But more powerful than either of these false prophets and guides, in immediate influence, was Diderot; and with him the whole school of bold and avowed infidels, who united open atheism with a fierce democracy. The Encyclopedists professed to know every thing, to explain every thing, and to teach every thing, they discovered that there was no God, and taught that truth was a delusion, and virtue but a name. They were learned in mathematical, statistical, and physical science, but threw contempt on elevated moral wisdom, on the lessons of experience, and the eternal truths of divine revelation. They advocated changes, experiments, fomentations, and impracticable reforms. They preached a gospel of social rights, inflamed the people with disgust of their condition, and with the belief that wisdom and virtue resided, in the greatest perfection, with congregated masses.

General Influence of the Philosophers.

They incessantly boasted of the greatness of philosophy, and the obsolete character of Christianity. They believed that successive developments of human nature, without the aid of influences foreign to itself, would gradually raise society to a state of perfection. What they could not explain by their logical formularies, they utterly discarded. They denied the reality of a God in heaven, and talked about the divinity of man on earth, especially when associated masses of the ignorant and brutal asserted what they conceived to be their rights. They made truth to reside, in its greatest lustre, with passionate majorities; and virtue, in its purest radiance, with felons and vagabonds, if affiliated into a great association. They flattered the people that they were wiser and better than any classes above them, that rulers were tyrants, the clergy were hypocrites, the oracles of former days mere fools and liars. To sum up, in few words, the French Encyclopedists, "they made Nature, in her outward manifestations, to be the foundation of all great researches, man to be but a mass of organization, mind the development of our sensations, morality to consist in self-interest, and God to be but the diseased fiction of an unenlightened age. The whole intellect, being concentrated on the outward and material, gave rise, perhaps, to some improvements in physical science; but religion was disowned, morality degraded, and man made to be but the feeble link in the great chain of events by which Nature is inevitably accomplishing her blind designs." From such influences, what could we expect but infidelity, madness, anarchy, and crimes?

The second cause of the French revolution was the diffusion of the ideas of democratic liberty. Rousseau was a republican in his politics, as he was a sentimentalist in religion. Thomas Paine's Age of Reason had a great influence on the French mind, as it also had on the English and American. Moreover, the apostles of liberty in France were much excited in view of the success of the American Revolution, and fancied that the words "popular liberty," "sovereignty of the people," the "rights of man," "liberty and equality," meant the same in America as they did when pronounced by a Parisian mob. The French people were unduly flattered, and made to believe, by the demagogues, that they were philosophers, and that they were as fit for liberty as the American nation itself. Moreover, it must be confessed that the people had really made considerable advances, and discovered that there was no right or justice in the oppressions under which they groaned. The exhortations of popular leaders and the example of American patriots prepared the people to make a desperate effort to shake off their fetters. What were rights, in the abstract, if they were to be ground down to the dust? What a mockery was the watchword of liberty and equality, if they were obliged to submit to a despotism which they knew to be, in the highest degree, oppressive and tyrannical?

Sufferings of the People.

Hence the real and physical evils which the people of France endured, had no small effect in producing the revolution. Abstract ideas prepared the way, and sustained the souls of the oppressed; but the absolute burdens which they bore aroused them to resistance.

Degradation of the People.

These evils were so great, that general discontent prevailed among the middle and lower classes through the kingdom. The agricultural population was fettered by game laws and odious privileges to the aristocracy. "Game of the most destructive kind, such as wild boars and herds of deer, were permitted to go at large through spacious districts, in order that the nobles might hunt as in a savage wilderness." Numerous edicts prohibited weeding, lest young partridges should be disturbed, and mowing of hay even, lest their eggs should be destroyed. Complaints for the infraction of these edicts were carried before courts where every species of oppression and fraud prevailed. Fines were imposed at every change of property and at every sale. The people were compelled to grind their corn at their landlord's mill, to press their grapes in his press, and bake their bread in his oven. In consequence of these feudal laws and customs, the people were very poor, their houses dark and comfortless, their dress ragged and miserable, their food coarse and scanty. Not half of the enormous taxes which they paid reached the royal treasury, or even the pockets of the great proprietors. Officers were indefinitely multiplied. The governing classes looked upon the people only to be robbed. Their cry was unheard in the courts of justice, while the tear of sorrow was unnoticed amid the pageantry of the great, whose extravagance, insolence, and pride were only surpassed by the misery and degradation of those unfortunate beings on whose toils they lived. Justice was bought and sold like any other commodity, and the decisions of judges were influenced by the magnitude of the bribes which were offered them. Besides feudal taxes, the clergy imposed additional burdens, and swarmed wherever there was plunder to be obtained. The people were so extravagantly taxed that it was no object to be frugal or industrious. Every thing beyond the merest necessaries of life was seized by various tax-gatherers. In England, severe as is taxation, three fourths of the produce of the land go to the farmer, while in France only one twelfth went to the poor peasant. Two thirds of his earnings went to the king. Nor was there any appeal from this excessive taxation, which ground down the middle and lower classes, while the clergy and the nobles were entirely exempted themselves. Nor did the rich proprietor live upon his estates. He was a non-resident, and squandered in the cities the money which was extorted from his dependents. He took no interest in the condition of the peasantry, with whom he was not united by any common ties. Added to this oppression, the landlord was cruel, haughty, and selfish; and he irritated by his insolence as well as oppressed by his injustice. All situations in the army, the navy, the church, the court, the bench, and in diplomacy were exclusively filled by the aristocracy, of whom there were one hundred and fifty thousand people—a class insolent, haughty, effeminate, untaxed; who disdained useful employments, who sought to live by the labor of others, and who regarded those by whose toils they were enabled to lead lives of dissipation and pleasure, as ignoble minions, who were unworthy of a better destiny, and unfit to enjoy those rights which God designed should be possessed by the whole human race.

The privileges and pursuits of the aristocratic class, from the king to a lieutenant in his army, were another cause of revolution. Louis XV. squandered twenty million pounds sterling in pleasures too ignominious to be even named in the public accounts, and enjoyed almost absolute power. He could send any one in his dominions to rot in an ignominious prison, without a hearing or a trial. The odious *lettre de cachet* could consign the most powerful noble to a dungeon, and all were sent to prison who were offensive to government. The king's mistresses sometimes had the power of sending their enemies to prison without consulting the king. The lives and property of the people were at his absolute disposal, and he did not scruple to exercise his power with thoughtless, and sometimes inhuman cruelty.

Derangement of Finances.

But these evils would have ended only in disaffection, and hatred, and unsuccessful resistance, had not the royal finances been deranged. So long as the king and his ministers could obtain money, there was no immediate danger of revolution. So long as he could pay the army, it would, if decently treated, support an absolute throne.

But the king at last found it difficult to raise a sufficient revenue for his pleasures and his wars. The annual deficit was one hundred and ninety million of francs a year. The greater the deficit, the greater was the taxation, which, of course, increased the popular discontent.

Such was the state of things when Louis XVI. ascended the throne of Hugh Capet, (1774,) in his twentieth year, having married, four years before, Marie Antoinette, daughter of Maria Theresa, empress of Austria. He was grandson of Louis XV., who bequeathed to him a debt of four thousand millions of livres.

The new king was amiable and moral, and would have ruled France in peaceful times, but was unequal to a revolutionary crisis. "Of all the monarchs," says Alison, "of the Capetian line, he was the least able to stem, and yet the least likely to provoke, a revolution. The people were tired of the arbitrary powers of their monarch, and he was disposed to abandon them; they were provoked at the expensive corruptions of the court, and he was both innocent in his manners, and unexpensive in his habits; they demanded reformation in the administration of affairs, and he placed his chief glory in yielding to the public voice. His reign, from his accession to the throne to the meeting of the States General, was nothing but a series of ameliorations, without calming the public effervescence. He had the misfortune to wish sincerely for the public good, without possessing the firmness necessary to secure it; and with truth it may be said that reforms were more fatal to him than the continuance of abuses would have been to another sovereign."

Maurepas — Turgot — Malesherbes.

He made choice of Maurepas as his prime minister, an old courtier without talent, and who was far from comprehending the spirit of the nation or the genius of the times. He accustomed the king to half measures, and pursued a temporizing policy, ill adapted to revolutionary times. The discontents of the people induced the king to dismiss him, and Turgot, for whom the people clamored, became prime minister. He was an honest man, and contemplated important reforms, even to the abolition of feudal privileges and the odious *lettres de cachet*, which were of course opposed by the old nobility, and were not particularly agreeable to the sovereign himself.

Necker — Calonne.

Malesherbes, a lawyer who adopted the views of Turgot, succeeded him, and, had he been permitted, would have restored the rights of the people, and suppressed the *lettres de cachet*, reënacted the Edict of Nantes, and secured the liberty of the press. But he was not equal to the crisis, with all his integrity and just views, and Necker became financial minister.

He was a native of Geneva, a successful banker, and a man who had won the confidence of the nation. He found means to restore the finances, and to defray the expenses of the American war. But he was equally opposed by the nobles, who wanted no radical reform, and he was not a man of sufficient talent to stem the current of revolution. Financial skill was certainly desirable, but no financiering could save the French nation on the eve of bankruptcy with such vast expenditures as then were deemed necessary. The nobles indeed admitted the extent of the evils which existed, and descanted, on their hunting parties, in a strain of mock philanthropy, but would submit to no sacrifices themselves, and Necker was compelled to resign.

M. de Calonne took his place; a man of ready invention, unscrupulous, witty, and brilliant. Self-confident and full of promises, he succeeded in imparting a gleam of sunshine, and pursued a plan directly the opposite to that adopted by Necker. He encouraged the extravagance of the court, derided the future, and warded off pressing debts by contracting new ones. He pleased all classes by his captivating manners, brilliant conversation, and elegant dress. The king, furnished with what money he wanted, forgot the burdens of the people, and the minister went on recklessly contracting new loans, and studiously concealing from the public the extent of the annual deficit.

But such a policy could not long be adopted successfully, and the people were overwhelmed with amazement when it finally appeared that, since the retirement of Necker in 1781, Calonne had added sixteen hundred and forty-six millions of francs to the public debt. National bankruptcy stared every body in the face. It was necessary that an extraordinary movement should be made; and Calonne recommended the assembling of the Notables, a body composed chiefly of the nobility, clergy, and magistracy, with the hope that these aristocrats would consent to their own taxation.

He was miserably mistaken. The Notables met, (1787,) the first time since the reign of Henry IV., and demanded the dismissal of the minister, who was succeeded by Brienne, Archbishop of Toulouse.

He was a weak man, and owed his elevation to his influence with women. He won the queen by his pleasing conversation, but had no solid acquirements. Occupying one of the highest positions in his church, he yet threw himself into the arms of atheistical philosophers. A man so inconsistent and so light was not fit for his place.

However, the Notables agreed to what they had refused to Calonne. They consented to a land tax, to the stamp duty, to provincial assemblies, and to the suppression of the gratuitous service of vassals. These were popular measures, but were insufficient. Brienne was under the necessity of proposing the imposition of new taxes. But the Parliament of Paris refused to register the edict. A struggle between the king and the parliament resulted; and the king, in order to secure the registration of new taxes, resorted to the *bed of justice*—the last stretch of his royal power.

States General.

During one of the meetings of the parliament, when the abuses and prodigality of the court were denounced, a member, punning upon the word *états*, (statements,) exclaimed, "It is not statements but States General that we want."

From that moment, nothing was thought of or talked about but the assembling of the States General; to which the minister, from his increasing embarrassments, consented. Moreover, the court hoped, in view of the continued opposition of the parliament, that the Tiers État would defend the throne against the legal aristocracy.

All classes formed great and extravagant expectations from the assembling of the States General, and all were doomed to disappointment, but none more than those who had most vehemently and enthusiastically called for its convocation.

The Archbishop of Toulouse soon after retired, unable to stem the revolutionary current. But he contrived to make his own fortune, by securing benefices to the amount of eight hundred thousand francs, the archbishopric of Sens, and a cardinal's hat. At his recommendation Necker was recalled.

On Necker's return, he found only two hundred and fifty thousand francs in the royal treasury; but the funds immediately rose, thirty per cent., and he was able to secure the loans necessary to carry on the government, rich capitalists fearing that absolute ruin would result unless they came to his assistance.

Then followed discussions in reference to the Tiers État, as to what the third estate really represented, and as to the number of deputies who should be called to the assembly of the States General. "The Tiers État," said the Abbé Sièyes, in an able pamphlet, "is the French nation, *minus* the noblesse and the clergy."

It was at last decided that the assembly should be at least one thousand, and that the number of deputies should equal the representatives of the nobles and clergy. The elections, were carelessly conducted, and all persons, decently dressed, were allowed to vote. Upwards of three millions of electors determined the choice of deputies. Necker conceded too much, and opened the flood-gates of revolution. He had no conception of the storm, which was to overwhelm the throne.

On the 4th of May, 1789, that famous Assembly, which it was hoped would restore prosperity to France, met with great pomp in the cathedral church of Notre Dame, and the Bishop of Nancy delivered the sermon, and, the next day, the assembly was opened in the hall prepared for the occasion. The king was seated on a magnificent throne, the nobles and the clergy on both sides of the hall, and the third estate at the farther end. Louis XVI. pronounced a speech full of disinterested sentiments, and Necker read a report in reference to the state of the finances.

The Tiers État.

The next day, the deputies of the Tiers État were directed to the place allotted to them, which was the common hall. The nobles and clergy repaired to a separate hall. It was their intention, especially in view of the great number of the deputies, to deliberate in distinct halls. But the deputies insisted upon the three orders deliberating together in the same room. Angry discussions and conferences took place. But there was not sufficient union between the nobles and the clergy, or sufficient energy on the part of the court. There happened also to be some bold and revolutionary spirits among the deputies, and they finally resolved, by a majority of four hundred and ninety-one to ninety, to assume the title of *National Assembly,* and invited the members of the other chamber to join them. They erected themselves into a sovereign power, like the Long Parliament of Charles I., disregarding both the throne and the nobility.

Some of the most resolute of the nobles urged the king to adopt vigorous measures against the usurpation of the third estate; but he was timid and irresolute.

The man who had, at that time, the greatest influence in the National Assembly was Mirabeau, a man of noble birth, but who had warmly espoused the popular side. He was disagreeable in his features, licentious in his habits, and a bankrupt in reputation, but a man of commanding air, of great abilities, and unrivalled eloquence. His picture has been best painted by Carlyle, both in his essays and his history of the revolution.

The National Assembly contained many great men, who would never have been heard of in quiet times; some of great virtues and abilities, and others of the most violent revolutionary principles. There were also some of the nobility, who joined them, not anticipating the evils which were to come. Among them were the Dukes of Orleans, Rochefoucault, and Liancourt, Count Lally Tollendal, the two brothers Lameth, Clermont Tonnerre, and the Marquis de La Fayette, all of whom were guillotined or exiled during the revolution.

Commotions.

The discussions in the Assembly did not equal the tumults of the people. All classes were intoxicated with excitement, and believed that a new era was to take place on earth; that all the evils which afflicted society were to be removed, and a state of unbounded liberty, plenty, and prosperity, was about to take place.

In the midst of the popular ferments, the regiment of guards, comprising three thousand six hundred men, revolted: immense bodies of workmen assembled together, and gave vent to the most inflammatory language; the Hotel of the Invalids was captured; fifty thousand pikes were forged and distributed among the people; the Bastile was stormed; and military massacres commenced. Soon after, the tricolored cockade was adopted, the French guards were suppressed by the Assembly, the king and his family were brought to Paris by a mob, and the Club of the Jacobins was established. Before the year 1789 was ended, the National Assembly was the supreme power in France, and the king had become a shadow and a mockery; or, rather, it should be said that there was no authority in France but what emanated from the people, and no power remained to suppress popular excesses and insurrections. The Assembly published proclamations against acts of violence; but it was committed in a contest with the crown and aristocracy, and espoused the popular side. A famine, added to other horrors, set in at Paris; and the farmers, fearing that their grain would be seized, no longer brought it to market. Manufactures of all kinds were suspended, and the public property was confiscated to supply the immediate wants of a starving and infuriated people. A state was rapidly hastening to universal violence, crime, misery, and despair.

Rule of the People.

The year 1790 opened gloomily, and no one could tell when the agitating spirit would cease, or how far it would be carried, for the mob of Paris was rapidly engrossing the power of the state. One of the first measures of the Assembly was to divest the provinces of France of their ancient privileges, since they were jealous of the sovereignty exercised by the Assembly, and to divide the kingdom into eighty-four new departments, nearly equal in extent and population. A criminal tribunal was established for each department and a civil court for each of the districts into which the department was divided. The various officers and magistrates were elected by the people, and the qualification for voting was a contribution to the amount of three days' labor. By this great stop, the whole civil force in the kingdom was placed at the disposal of the lower classes. They had the nomination of the municipality, and the control of the military, and the appointment of judges, deputies, and officers of the National Guard. Forty-eight thousand communes, or municipalities, exercised all the rights of sovereignty, and hardly any appointment was left to the crown. A complete democratic constitution was made, which subverted the ancient divisions of the kingdom, and all those prejudices and interests which had been nursed for centuries. The great extension of the electoral franchise introduced into the Assembly a class of men who were prepared to make the most impracticable changes, and commit the most violent excesses.

The next great object of the Assembly was the regulation of the finances. Further taxation was impossible, and the public necessities were great. The revenue had almost failed, and the national debt had alarmingly increased,—twelve hundred millions in less than three years. The capitalists would advance nothing, and voluntary contributions had produced but a momentary relief. Under these circumstances, the spoliation of the church was resolved, and Talleyrand, Bishop of Autun, was the first to propose the confiscation of the property of his order. The temptation was irresistible to an infidel and revolutionary assembly; for the church owned nearly one half of the whole landed property of the kingdom. Several thousand millions of francs were confiscated, and the revenues of the clergy reduced to one fifth of their former amount.

This violent measure led to another. There was no money to pay for the great estates which the Assembly wished to sell. The municipalities of the large cities became the purchasers, and gave promissory notes to the public creditors until payment should be made; supposing that individuals would buy in small portions. Sales not being effected by the municipalities, as was expected and payment becoming due, recourse was had to government bills. Thus arose the system of *Assignats*, which were issued to a great amount on the security of the church lands, and which resulted in a paper circulation, and the establishment of a vast body of small landholders, whose property sprung out of the revolution, and whose interests were identified with it. The relief, however great, was momentary. New issues were made at every crisis, until the over issue alarmed the reflecting portion of the community, and assignats depreciated to a mere nominal value. At the close of the year, the credit of the nation was destroyed, and the precious metals were withdrawn, in a great measure, from circulation.

Soon after, the assembly abolished all titles of nobility, changed the whole judicial system, declared its right to make peace and war, and established the National Guard, by which three hundred thousand men were enrolled in support of revolutionary measures.

National Federation.

On the 14th of July, the anniversary of the capture of the Bastile, was the celebrated National Federation, when four hundred thousand persons repaired to the Champ de Mars, to witness the king, his ministers, the assembly, and the public functionaries, take the oath to the new constitution; the greatest mockery of the whole revolution, although a scene of unparalleled splendor.

Towards the close of the year, an extensive emigration of the nobles took place; a great blunder on their part, since their estates were immediately confiscated, and since the forces left to support the throne were much diminished. The departure of so many distinguished persons, however, displeased the Assembly, and proposals were made to prevent it. But Mirabeau, who, until this time, had supported the popular side, now joined the throne, and endeavored to save it. His popularity was on the decline, when a natural death relieved him from a probable execution. He had contributed to raise the storm, but he had not the power to allay it. He exerted his splendid abilities to arrest the revolution, whose consequences, at last, he plainly perceived. But in vain. His death, however, was felt as a public calamity, and all Paris assembled to see his remains deposited, with extraordinary pomp, in the Pantheon, by the side of Des Cartes. Had he lived, he might possibly have saved the lives of the king and queen, but he could not have prevented the revolution.

Flight of the King.

Soon after, the royal family, perceiving, too late, that they were mere prisoners in the Tuileries, undertook to escape, and fly to Coblentz, where the great body of emigrants resided. The unfortunate king contrived to reach Varennes, was recognized, and brought back to Paris. But the National Assembly made a blunder in not permitting him to escape; for it had only to declare the throne vacant by his desertion, and proceed to institute a republican government. The crime of regicide might have been avoided, and further revolutionary excesses prevented. But his return increased the popular ferments, and the clubs demanded his head. He was suspended from his functions, and a guard placed over his person.

On the 29th of September, 1791, the Constituent Assembly dissolved itself; having, during the three years of its existence enacted thirteen hundred and nine laws and decrees relative to the general administration of the state. It is impossible, even now, to settle the question whether it did good or ill, on the whole; but it certainly removed many great and glaring evils, and enacted many wise laws. It abolished torture, the *lettres de cachet*, the most oppressive duties, the privileges of the nobility, and feudal burdens. It established a uniform system of jurisprudence, the National Guards, and an equal system of finance. "It opened the army to men of merit, and divided the landed property of the aristocracy among the laboring classes; which, though a violation of the rights of property, enabled the nation to bear the burdens which were subsequently imposed, and to prosper under the evils connected with national bankruptcy, depreciated assignats, the Reign of Terror, the conscription of Napoleon, and the subjugation of Europe."

The Legislative Assembly, composed of inexperienced men,—country attorneys and clerks for the most part, among whom there were not fifty persons possessed of one hundred pounds a year,—took the place of the Constituent Assembly, and opened its sittings on the 1st of October.

In the first assembly there was a large party attached to royal and aristocratical interests, and many men of great experience and talents. But in the second nearly all were in favor of revolutionary principles. They only differed in regard to the extent to which revolution should be carried.

The members of the right were called the *Feuillants*, from the club which formed the centre of their power, and were friends of the constitution, or the limited monarchy which the Constituent Assembly had established. The national guard, the magistrates, and all the constituted authorities, were the supporters of this party.

The Girondists and the Jacobins.

The *Girondists,* comprehending the more respectable of the republicans, and wishing to found the state on the model of antiquity, formed a second party, among whom were numbered the ablest men in the assembly. Brissot, Vergniaud, Condorcet, Guadet, and Isnard, were among the leading members.

There was also a third party, headed by Chabot, Bazin, and Merlin, which was supported by the clubs of the *Jacobins* and the *Cordeliers.* The great oracles of the Jacobins were Robespierre, Varennes, and Collot d'Herbois; while the leaders of the Cordeliers were Danton and Desmoulins. Robespierre was excluded, as were others of the last assembly, from the new one, by a sort of self-denying ordinance which he himself had proposed. His influence, at that time, was immense, from the extravagance of his opinions, the vehemence of his language, and the reputation he had acquired for integrity.

Between these three parties there were violent contentions, and the struggle for ascendency soon commenced, to end in the complete triumph of the Jacobinical revolutionists.

In the mean time, the restrictions imposed on the king, who still enjoyed the shadow of authority, the extent of popular excesses, and the diffusion of revolutionary principles, induced the leading monarchs of Europe to confederate together, in order to suppress disturbances in France. In July, the Emperor Leopold appealed to the sovereigns of Europe to unite for the deliverance of Louis XVI. Austria collected her troops, the emigrants at Coblentz made warlike demonstrations, and preparations were made for a contest, which, before it was finished, proved the most bloody and extensive which has desolated the world since the fall of the Roman empire.

The Constituent Assembly rejected with disdain the dictation of the various European powers; and the new ministry, of which Dumourier and Roland were the most prominent members, prepared for war. All classes in France were anxious for it, and war was soon declared. On the 25th of July, the Duke of Brunswick, with an army of one hundred and forty-eight thousand Prussians, Austrians, and Hessians, entered the French territory. The spirit of resistance animated all classes, and the ardor of the multitude was without a parallel. The manifesto of the allied powers indicated the dispositions of the court and emigrants. Revolt against the throne now seemed necessary, in order to secure the liberty of the people, who now had no choice between victory and death. On the 25th of July, the Marseillais arrived in Paris, and augmented the strength and confidence of the insurgents. Popular commotions increased, and the clubs became unmanageable. On the 10th of August, the tocsin sounded, the *générale* beat in every quarter of Paris, and that famous insurrection took place which overturned the throne. The Hotel de Ville was seized by the insurgents, the Tuileries was stormed, and the Swiss guards were massacred. The last chance for the king to regain his power was lost, and Paris was in the hands of an infuriated mob.

The confinement of the king in the Temple, the departure of the foreign ambassadors, the flight of emigrants, the confiscation of their estates, the massacres in the prisons, the sack of palaces, the fall and flight of La Fayette, and the dissolution of the Legislative Assembly, rapidly succeeded.

The National Convention.

On the 21st of September, the National Convention was opened, and was composed of the most violent advocates of revolution. It was ruled by those popular orators who had the greatest influence in the clubs. The most influential of these leaders were Danton, Marat, and Robespierre. Danton was the hero of the late insurrection; was a lawyer, a man of brutal courage, the slave of sensual passions, and the idol of the Parisian mob. He was made minister of justice, and was the author of the subsequent massacres in the prisons. But, with all his ferocity, he was lenient to individuals, and recommended humanity after the period of danger had passed.

Marat — Danton — Robespierre.

Marat was a journalist, president of the Jacobin Club, a member of the convention, and a violent advocate of revolutionary excesses. His bloody career was prematurely cut off by the hand of a heroine, Charlotte Corday, who offered up her own life to rid the country of the greatest monster which the annals of crime have consigned to an infamous immortality.

Robespierre was a sentimentalist, and concealed, under the mask of patriotism and philanthropy, an insatiable ambition, inordinate vanity, and implacable revenge. He was above the passion of money, and, when he had at his disposal the lives and fortunes of his countrymen, lived upon a few francs a day. It is the fashion to deny to him any extraordinary talent; but that he was a man of domineering will, of invincible courage, and austere enthusiasm appears from nearly all the actions of his hateful career.

It was in the midst of the awful massacre in the prisons, where more than five thousand perished to appease the infatuated vengeance of the Parisian mob, that the National Convention commenced its sittings.

Its first measure was, to abolish the monarchy, and proclaim a republic; the next, to issue new assignats. The two preceding assemblies had authorized the fabrication of twenty-seven hundred millions of francs, and the Convention added millions more on the security of the national domains. On the 7th of November, the trial of the king was decreed; and, on the 11th of December, his examination commenced. On his appearance at the bar of the Convention, the president, Barrere, said, "Louis, the French nation accuses you; you are about to hear the charges that are to be preferred. Louis, be seated."

The charges consisted of the whole crimes of the revolution, to which he replied with dignity, simplicity, and directness. He was defended, in the mock trial, by Desèze, Tronchet, and Malesherbes; but his blood was demanded, and the assembly unanimously pronounced the condemnation of their king. That seven hundred men, with all the natural differences of opinion, could be found to do this, shows the excess of revolutionary madness. On the 20th of January, Santerre appeared in the royal prison, and read the sentence of death; and only three days were allowed the king to prepare for the last hour of anguish. On the 24th of January, he mounted the scaffold erected between the garden of the Tuileries and the Champs Élysées, and the fatal axe separated his head from his body. His remains were buried in the ancient cemetery of the Madeleine, over which Napoleon commenced, after the battle of Jena, a splendid temple of glory, but which was not finished until the restoration of the Bourbons, who converted it into the beautiful church which bears the name of the ancient cemetery. The spot where Louis XVI. offered up his life, in expiation of the crimes of his ancestors, is now marked by the colossal obelisk of red granite, which the French government, in 1831, brought from Egypt, a monument which has witnessed the march of Cambyses, and may survive the glory of the French nation itself.

General War.

The martyrdom of Louis XVI. was the signal for a general war. All the powers of Europe united to suppress the power and the principles of the French revolutionists. The Convention, after declaring war against England, Holland, Spain, Austria, Prussia, Portugal, the Two Sicilies, the Roman States, Sardinia, and Piedmont,—all of which had combined together,—ordered a levy of three hundred thousand men, instituted a military tribunal, and imposed a forced loan on the rich of one thousand millions, and prepared to defend the principles of liberty and the soil of France. The enthusiasm of the French was unparalleled, and the energies put forth were most remarkable. Patriotism and military ardor were combined, and measures such as only extraordinary necessities require were unhesitatingly adopted.

A Committee of Public Safety was appointed, and the dictatorship of Danton, Marat, and Robespierre commenced, marked by great horrors and barbarities, but signalized by wonderful successes in war, and by exertions which, under common circumstances, would be scarcely credited.

This committee was composed of twenty-five persons at first, and twelve afterwards; but Robespierre and Marat were the leading members. The committee assigned to ruling Jacobins the different departments of the government. St. Just was intrusted with the duty of denouncing its enemies; Couthon for bringing forward its general measures; Billaud Varennes and Collot d'Herbois with the management of departments; Carnot was made minister of war; and Robespierre general dictator. This committee, though required to report to the Convention, as the supreme authority, had really all the power of government. "It named and dismissed generals, judges, and juries; brought forward all public measures in the Convention; ruled provinces and armies; controlled the Revolutionary Tribunal; and made requisitions of men and money; and appointed revolutionary committees, which sprung up in every part of the kingdom to the frightful number of fifty thousand. It was the object of the Committee of Public Safety to destroy all who opposed the spirit of the most violent revolutionary measures. Marat declared that two hundred and sixty thousand heads must fall before freedom was secure; the revolutionary committees discovered that seven hundred thousand persons must be sacrificed."

Reign of Terror.

Then commenced the Reign of Terror, when all the prisons of France were filled with victims, who were generally the most worthy people in the community, and whose only crime was in being obnoxious to the reigning powers. Those who were suspected fled, if possible, but were generally unable to carry away their property. Millions of property was confiscated; the prisons were crowded with the rich, the elegant, and the cultivated classes; thousands were guillotined; and universal anarchy and fear reigned without a parallel. Deputies, even those who had been most instrumental in bringing on the Revolution, were sacrificed by the triumphant Jacobins. Women and retired citizens were not permitted to escape their fear and vengeance. Marie Antoinette, and the Princess Elizabeth, and Madame Roland, were among the first victims. Then followed the executions of Bailly, Mayor of Paris; Barnave, one of the most eloquent and upright members of the Constituent Assembly; Dupont Dutertre, one of the ministers of Louis XVI.; Lavoisier, the chemist; Condorcet, the philosopher; General Custine; and General Houchard; all of whom had been the allies of the present dominant party. The Duke of Orleans, called *Égalité*, who had supported the revolt of the 10th of August, and had voted for the execution of the king, shared the fate of Louis XVI. He was the father of Louis Philippe, and, of all the victims of the revolution, died the least lamented.

The "Decemvirs" had now destroyed the most illustrious advocates of constitutional monarchy and of republican liberty. The slaughter of their old friends now followed. The first victim was Danton himself, who had used his influence to put a stop to the bloody executions which then disgraced the country, and had recognized the existence of a God and the rights of humanity. For such sentiments he was denounced and executed, together with Camille Desmoulins, and Lacroix, who perished because they were less wicked than their associates. Finally, the anarchists themselves fell before the storm which they had raised, and Hebert, Gobet, Clootz, and Vincent died amid the shouts of general execration. The Committee of Public Safety had now all things in their own way, and, in their iron hands, order resumed its sway from the influence of terror. "The history of the world has no parallel to the horrors of that long night of suffering, because it has no parallel to the guilt which preceded it; tyranny never assumed so hideous a form, because licentiousness never required so severe a punishment."

The Committee of Public Safety, now confident of its strength, decreed the disbanding of the revolutionary army, raised to overawe the capital, and the dissolution of all the popular societies which did not depend on the Jacobin Club, and devoted all their energies to establish their power. But death was the means which they took to secure it, and two hundred thousand victims filled the prisons of France.

Death of Robespierre.

At last, fear united the members of the Convention, and they resolved to free the country of the great tyrant who aimed at the suppression of all power but his own. "Do not flatter yourselves," said Tallien to the Girondists, "that he will spare you, for you have committed an unpardonable offence in being freemen." "Do you still live?" said he to the Jacobins; "in a few days, he will have your heads if you do not take his." All parties in the assembly resolved to overthrow their common enemy. Robespierre, the chief actor of the bloody tragedy, Dumas, the president of the Revolutionary Tribunal, Henriot, the commander of the National Guard, Couthon and St. Just, the tools of the tyrant, were denounced, condemned, and executed. The last hours of Robespierre were horrible beyond description. When he was led to execution, the blood flowed from his broken jaw, his face was deadly pale, and he uttered yells of agony, which filled all hearts with terror. But one woman, nevertheless, penetrated the crowd which surrounded him, exclaiming, "Murderer of my kindred! your agony fills me with joy; descend to hell, covered with the curses of every mother in France."

Thus terminated the Reign of Terror, during which, nearly nineteen thousand persons were guillotined; and among these were over two thousand nobles and one thousand priests, besides immense numbers of other persons, by war or the axe, in other parts of France.

But vigorous measures had been adopted to carry on the war against united Christendom. No less than two hundred and eighty thousand men were in the field, on the part of the allies, from Basle to Dunkirk. Toulon and Lyons had raised the standard of revolt, Mayence gave the invaders a passage into the heart of the kingdom, while sixty thousand insurgents in La Vendée threatened to encamp under the walls of Paris. But under the exertions of the Committee, and especially of Carnot, the minister of war, still greater numbers were placed under arms, France was turned into an immense workshop of military preparations, and the whole property of the state, by means of confiscations and assignats, put at the disposal of the government. The immense debts of the government were paid in paper money, while conscription filled the ranks with all the youth of the state. Added to all this force which the government had at its disposal, it must be remembered that the army was burning with enthusiastic dreams of liberty, and of patriotism, and of glory. No wonder that such a nation of soldiers and enthusiasts should have been able to resist the armies of united Christendom.

New Constitution.

On the death of Robespierre, (July, 1794,) a great reaction succeeded the Reign of Terror. His old associates and tools were executed or transported, the club of the Jacobins was closed, the Revolutionary Tribunals were suppressed, the rebellious faubourgs were subdued, the National Guard was reorganized, and a new constitution was formed.

The Directory.

The constitution of 1798, framed under different influences, established the legislative power among two councils,—that of the *Five Hundred*, and that of the *Ancients*. The former was intrusted with the power of originating laws; the latter had the power to reject or pass them. The executive power was intrusted to five persons, called *Directors*, who were nominated by the Council of Five Hundred, and approved by that of the Ancients. Each individual was to be president by rotation during three months, and a new director was to be chosen every year. The Directory had the entire disposal of the army, the finances, the appointment of public functionaries, and the management of public negotiations.

But there were found powerful enemies to the new constitution. Paris was again agitated. The National Guard took part with the disaffected, and the Convention, threatened and perplexed, summoned to its aid a body of five thousand regular troops. The National Guard mustered in great strength, to the number of thirty thousand men, and resolved to overawe the Convention, which was likened to the Long Parliament in the times of Cromwell. The Convention intrusted Barras with its defence, and he demanded, as his second in command, a young officer of artillery who had distinguished himself at the siege of Toulon. By his advice, a powerful train of artillery was brought to Paris by a lieutenant called *Murat*. On the 4th of October, 1795, the whole neighborhood of the Tuileries resembled an intrenched camp. The commander of the Convention then waited the attack of the insurgents, and the action soon commenced. Thirty thousand men surrounded the little army of six thousand, who defended the Convention and the cause of order and law. Victory inclined to the regular troops, who had the assistance of artillery, and, above all, who were animated by the spirit of their intrepid leader—*Napoleon Bonaparte*. The insurgents were not a rabble, but the flower of French citizens; but they were forced to yield to superior military skill, and the reign of the military commenced.

Thus closed what is technically called the French Revolution; the most awful political hurricane in the annals of modern civilized nations. It closed, nominally, with the accession of the Directory to power, but really with the accession of Napoleon; for, shortly after, his victories filled the eyes of the French nation, and astonished the whole world.

Reflections.

It is impossible to pronounce on the effects of this great Revolution, since a sufficient time has not yet elapsed for us to form healthy judgments. We are accustomed to associate with some of the actors every thing that is vile and monstrous in human nature. But unmitigated monsters rarely appear on earth. The same men who excite our detestation, had they lived in quiet times might have been respected. Even Robespierre might have retained an honorable name to his death, as an upright judge. But the French mind was deranged. New ideas had turned the brains of enthusiasts. The triumph of the abstract principles of justice seemed more desirable than the preservation of human life. The sense of injury and wrong was too vivid to allow heated partisans to make allowances for the common infirmities of man. The enthusiasts in liberty could not see in Louis XVI. any thing but the emblem of tyranny in the worst form. They fancied that they could regenerate society by their gospel of social rights, and they overvalued the virtues of the people. But, above all, they over-estimated themselves, and placed too light a value on the imperishable principles of revealed religion; a religion which enjoins patience and humility, as well as encourages the spirit of liberty and progress. But whatever may have been their blunders and crimes, and however marked the providence of God in overruling them for the ultimate good of Europe, still, all contemplative men behold in the

Revolution the retributive justice of the Almighty, in humiliating a proud family of princes, and punishing a vain and oppressive nobility for the evils they had inflicted on society.

> References.—Alison's History of the French Revolution, marked by his English prejudices, heavy in style, and inaccurate in many of his facts, yet lofty, temperate, and profound. Thiers's History is more lively, and takes different views. Carlyle's work is extremely able, but the most difficult to read of all his works, in consequence of his affected and abominable style. Lamartine's History of the Girondists is sentimental, but pleasing and instructive. Mignet's History is also a standard. Lacretelle's Histoire de France, and the Memoirs of Mirabeau, Necker, and Robespierre should be read. Carlyle's Essays on Mirabeau and Danton are extremely able. Burke's Reflections should be read by all who wish to have the most vivid conception of the horrors of the awful event which he deprecated. The Annual Register should be consulted. For a general list of authors who have written on this period, see Alison's index of writers, prefixed to his great work, but which are too numerous to be mentioned here.

CHAPTER XXXI
NAPOLEON BONAPARTE

Napoleon Bonaparte.

Mr. Alison has found it necessary to devote ten large octavo volumes to the life and times of Napoleon Bonaparte; nor can the varied events connected with his brilliant career be satisfactorily described in fewer volumes. The limits of this work will not, however, permit a notice extending beyond a few pages. Who, then, even among those for whom this History is especially designed, will be satisfied with our brief review? But only a brief allusion to very great events can be made; for it is preposterous to attempt to condense the life of the greatest actor on the stage of real tragedy in a single chapter. And yet there is a uniformity in nearly all of the scenes in which he appears. The history of war is ever the same—the exhibition of excited passions, of restless ambition, of dazzling spectacles of strife, pomp, and glory. Pillage, oppression, misery, crime, despair, ruin, and death— such are the evils necessarily attendant on all war, even glorious war, when men fight for their homes, for their altars, or for great ideas. The details of war are exciting, but painful. We are most powerfully reminded of our degeneracy, of our misfortunes, of the Great Destroyer. The "Angel Death" appears before us, in grim terrors, punishing men for crimes. But while war is so awful, and attended with all the evils of which we can conceive, or which it is the doom of man to suffer, yet warriors are not necessarily the enemies of mankind. They are the instruments of the Almighty to scourge a wicked world, or to bring, out of disaster and suffering, great and permanent blessings to the human race.

Character of Napoleon.

Napoleon is contemplated by historians in both those lights. The English look upon him, generally, as an ambitious usurper, who aimed to erect a universal empire upon universal ruin; as an Alexander, a Cæsar, an Attila, a Charles XII. The French nation regard him almost as a deity, as a messenger of good, as a great conqueror, who fought for light and freedom. But he was not the worst or the best of warriors. His extraordinary and astonishing energies were called into exercise by the circumstances of the times; and he, taking advantage of both ideas and circumstances, attempted to rear a majestic throne, and advance the glory of the country, of which he made himself the absolute ruler. His nature was not sanguinary, or cruel, or revengeful; but few conquerors have ever committed crimes on a greater scale, or were more unscrupulous in using any means, lawful or unlawful, to accomplish a great end. Napoleon had enlightened views, and wished to advance the real interests of the French nation, but not until he had climbed to the summit of power, and realized all those dreams which a most inordinate ambition had excited. He doubtless rescued his country from the dangers which menaced it from foreign invasion; but his conquests and his designs led to still greater combinations, and these, demanding for their support the united energies of Christendom, deluged the world with blood. Napoleon, to an extraordinary degree, realized the objects to which he had aspired; but these were not long enjoyed, and he was hurled from his throne of grandeur and of victory, to impress the world, which he mocked and despised, of the vanity of military glory and the dear-earned trophies of the battle field. No man was ever permitted by Providence to accomplish so much mischief, and yet never mortal had more admirers than he, and never were the opinions of the wise more divided in regard to the effects of his wars. A painful and sad recital may be made of the desolations he caused, so that Alaric, in comparison, would seem but a common robber, while, at the same time, a glorious eulogium might be justly made of the many benefits he conferred upon mankind. The good and the evil are ever combined in all great characters; but the evil and the good are combined in him in such vast proportions, that he seems either a monster of iniquity, or an object of endless admiration. There are some characters which the eye of the mind can survey at once, as the natural eye can take in the proportions of a small but singular edifice; but Napoleon was a genius and an actor of such wonderful greatness and majesty, both from his natural talents and the great events which he controlled, that he rises before us, when we contemplate him, like some vast pyramid or some majestic cathedral, which the eye can survey only in details. Our age is not sufficiently removed from the times in which he lived, we are too near the object of vision, to pronounce upon the general effect of his character, and only prejudiced or vain persons would attempt to do so. He must remain for generations simply an object of awe, of wonder, of dread, of admiration, of hatred, or of love.

Nor can we condense the events of his life any more than we can analyze his character and motives. We do not yet know their relative importance. In the progress of ages, some of them will stand out more beautiful and more remarkable, and some will be entirely lost sight of. Thousands of books will waste away as completely as if they were burned, like the Alexandrian library; and a future age may know no more of the details of Napoleon's battles than we now know of Alexander's marches. But the main facts can never be lost; something will remain, enough to "point a moral or adorn a tale." The object of all historical knowledge is moral wisdom, and this we may learn from narratives as brief as the stories of Joseph and Daniel, or the accounts which Tacitus has left us of the lives of the Roman tyrants.

Early Days of Napoleon.

Napoleon Bonaparte was born in Corsica, the 15th of August, 1769, of respectable parents, and was early sent to a royal military school at Brienne. He was not distinguished for any attainments, except in mathematics; he was studious, reserved, and cold; he also exhibited an inflexible will, the great distinguishing quality of his mind. At the age of fourteen, in view of superior attainments, he was removed to the military school at Paris, and, at the age of seventeen, received his commission as second lieutenant in a regiment of artillery.

Early Services to the Republic.

When the Revolution broke out, Toulon, one of the arsenals of France, took a more decided part in favor of the king and the constitution than either Marseilles or Lyons, and invited the support of the English and Spanish squadrons. The Committee of Public Safety resolved to subdue the city; and Bonaparte, even at that time a brigadier-general, with the command of the artillery at the siege, recommended a course which led to the capture of that important place.

For his distinguished services and talents, he was appointed second in command, by the National Convention, when that body was threatened and overawed by the rebellious National Guard. He saved the state and defended the constitutional authorities, for which service he was appointed second in command of the great army of the interior, and then general-in-chief in the place of Barras, who found his new office as director incompatible with the duties of a general.

The other directors who now enjoyed the supreme command were Reubel, Laréveillère-Lépeaux, Le Tourneur, and Carnot. Sièyes, a man of great genius, had been elected, but had declined. Among these five men, Carnot was the only man of genius, and it was through his exertions that France, under the Committee of Public Safety, had been saved from the torrent of invasion. But Barras, though inferior to Carnot in genius, had even greater influence, and it was through his favor that Bonaparte received his appointments. That a young man of twenty-five should have the command of the army of the interior, is as remarkable as the victories which subsequently showed that his elevation was not the work of chance, but of a providential hand.

The acknowledged favorite of Barras was a young widow, by birth a Creole of the West Indies, whose husband, a general in the army of the Rhine, had been guillotined during the Reign of Terror. Her name was Josephine Beauharnois; and, as a woman of sense, of warm affections, and of rare accomplishments, she won the heart of Bonaparte, and was married to him, March 9, 1796. Her dowry was the command of the army of Italy, which, through her influence, the young general received.

Then commenced his brilliant military career. United with Josephine, whom he loved, he rose in rank and power.

The army which Bonaparte commanded was composed of forty-two thousand men, while the forces of the Italian states numbered one hundred and sixty thousand, and could with ease be increased to three hundred thousand. But Italian soldiers had never been able to contend with either Austrian or French, and Bonaparte felt sure of victory. His soldiers were young men, inured to danger and toil; and among his officers were Berthier, Massena, Marmont, Augereau, Serrurier, Joubert, Lannes, and Murat. They were not then all generals, but they became afterwards marshals of France.

The Italian Campaign.

The campaign of 1796, in Italy, was successful beyond precedent in the history of war; and the battles of Montenotte, Millesimo, and Dego, the passage of the bridge of Lodi, the siege of Mantua, and the victories at Castiglione, Caldiero, Arcola, Rivoli, and Mantua, extended the fame of Bonaparte throughout the world. The Austrian armies were every where defeated, and Italy was subjected to the rule of the French. "With the French invasion commenced tyranny under the name of liberty, rapine under the name of generosity, the stripping of churches, the robbing of hospitals, the levelling of the palaces of the great, and the destruction of the cottages of the poor; all that military license has of most terrible, all that despotic authority has of most oppressive."

While Bonaparte was subduing Italy, the French under Moreau were contending, on the Rhine, with the Austrians under the Archduke Charles. Several great battles were fought, and masterly retreats were made, but without decisive results.

It is surprising that England, France, and the other contending powers, were able at this time to commence the contest, much more so to continue it for more than twenty years. The French Directory, on its accession to power, found the finances in a state of inextricable confusion. Assignats had fallen to almost nothing, and taxes were collected with such difficulty, that there were arrears to the amount of fifteen hundred millions of francs. The armies were destitute and ill paid, the artillery without horses, and the infantry depressed by suffering and defeat. In England, the government of Pitt was violently assailed for carrying on a war against a country which sought simply to revolutionize her own institutions, and which all the armies of Europe had thus far failed to subdue. Mr. Fox, and others in the opposition, urged the folly of continuing a contest which had already added one hundred millions of pounds to the national debt, and at a time when French armies were preparing to invade Italy; but Pitt argued that the French must be nearly exhausted by their great exertions, and would soon be unable to continue the warfare. The nation, generally, took this latter view of the case, and parliament voted immense supplies.

The year 1797 opened gloomily for England. The French had gained immense successes. Bonaparte had subdued Italy, Hoche had suppressed the rebellion in La Vendée, Austria was preparing to defend her last barriers in the passes of the Alps, Holland was virtually incorporated with Republican France, Spain had also joined its forces, and the whole continent was arrayed against Great Britain. England had interfered in a contest in which she was not concerned, and was forced to reap the penalty. The funds fell from ninety-eight to fifty-one, and petitions for a change of ministers were sent to the king from almost every city of note in the kingdom. The Bank of England stopped payment in specie, and the country was overburdened by taxation. Nevertheless, parliament voted new supplies, and made immense preparations, especially for the increase of the navy. One hundred and twenty-four ships of the line, one hundred and eighty frigates, and one hundred and eighty-four sloops, were put in commission, and sent to the various quarters of the globe.

Battle of St. Vincent.

Soon after occurred the memorable mutiny in the English fleet, which produced the utmost alarm; but it was finally suppressed by the vigorous measures which the government adopted, and the happy union of firmness and humanity, justice and concession which Mr. Pitt exercised. The mutiny was entirely disconnected with France, and resulted from the real grievances which existed in the navy; grievances which, to the glory of Pitt, were candidly considered and promptly redressed. The temporary disgrace which resulted to the navy by this mutiny was soon, however, wiped away by the battle of Cape St. Vincent, in which Admiral Jervis, seconded by Nelson and Collingwood, with fifteen ships of the line and six frigates, defeated a Spanish fleet of twenty-seven ships of the line and twelve frigates. This important naval victory delivered England from all fears of invasion, and inspired courage into the hearts of the nation, groaning under the heavy taxes which the war increased. Before the season closed, the Dutch fleet, of fifteen ships of the line and eleven frigates, was defeated by an English one, under Admiral Duncan, consisting of sixteen ships of the line and three frigates. The battles of Camperdown and Cape St. Vincent, in which the genius of Duncan and Nelson were signally exhibited, were among the most important fought at sea during the war, and diffused unexampled joy throughout Great Britain. The victors were all rewarded. Jervis became Earl St. Vincent, Admiral Duncan became a viscount, and Commodore Nelson became a baronet. Soon after the bonfires and illuminations for these victories were ended, Mr. Burke died urging, as his end approached, the ministry to persevere in the great struggle to which the nation was committed.

Conquest of Venice by Napoleon.

While the English were victorious on the water, the French obtained new triumphs on the land. In twenty days after the opening of the campaign of 1797, Bonaparte had driven the Archduke Charles, with an army equal to his own, over the Julian Alps, and occupied Carniola, Carinthia, Trieste, Fiume, and the Italian Tyrol, while a force of forty-five thousand men, flushed with victory, was on the northern declivity of the Alps, within fifty leagues of Vienna. In the midst of these successes, an insurrection broke out in the Venetian territories; and, as Bonaparte was not supported, as he expected, by the Armies of the Rhine, and partly in consequence of the jealousy of the Directory, he resolved to forego all thoughts of dictating peace under the walls of Vienna, and contented himself with making as advantageous terms as possible with the Austrian government. Bonaparte accomplished his object, and directed his attention to the subjugation of Venice, no longer the "Queen of the Adriatic, throned on her hundred isles," but degenerate, weakened, and divided. Bonaparte acted, in his treaty with Austria, with great injustice to Venice, and also encouraged the insurrection of the people in her territories. And when the Venetian government attempted to suppress rebellion in its own provinces, Bonaparte affected great indignation, and soon found means to break off all negotiations. The Venetian senate made every effort to avert the storm, but in vain. Bonaparte declared war against Venice, and her fall soon after resulted. The French seized all the treasure they could find, and obliged the ruined capital to furnish heavy contributions, and surrender its choicest works of art. Soon after, the youthful conqueror established himself in the beautiful chateau of Montebello near Milan, and there dictated peace to the assembled ambassadors of Germany, Rome, Genoa, Venice, Naples, Piedmont, and the Swiss republic. The treaty of Campo Formio exhibited both the strength and the perfidy of Bonaparte, especially in reference to Venice, which was disgracefully despoiled to pay the expenses of the Italian wars. Among other things, the splendid bronze horses, which, for six hundred years, had stood over the portico of the church of St. Mark, to commemorate the capture of Constantinople by the Venetian crusaders, and which had originally been brought from Corinth to Rome by ancient conquerors, were removed to Paris to decorate the Tuileries.

Bonaparte's journey from Italy to Paris, after Venice, with its beautiful provinces, was surrendered to Austria, was a triumphal procession. The enthusiasm of the Parisians was boundless; the public curiosity to see him indescribable. But he lived in a quiet manner, and assumed the dress of a member of the Institute, being lately elected. Great *fêtes* were given to his honor, and his victories were magnified.

Invasion of Egypt.

But he was not content with repose or adulation. His ambitious soul panted for new conquests, and he conceived the scheme of his Egyptian invasion, veiled indeed from the eyes of the world by a pretended attack on England herself. He was invested, with great pomp, by the Directory, with the command of the army of England, but easily induced the government to sanction the invasion of Egypt. It is not probable that Bonaparte seriously contemplated the conquest of England, knowing the difficulty of supporting and recruiting his army, even if he succeeded in landing his forces. He probably designed to divert the attention of the English from his projected enterprise.

When all was ready, Bonaparte (9th May) embarked at Toulon in a fleet of thirteen ships of the line, fourteen frigates, seventy-two brigs, and four hundred transports, containing thirty-six thousand soldiers and ten thousand sailors. He was joined by reinforcements at Genoa, Ajaccio, Civita Castellana, and on the 10th of June arrived at Malta, which capitulated without firing a shot; proceeded on his voyage, succeeded in escaping the squadron of Nelson, and on the 1st of July reached Alexandria. He was vigorously opposed by the Mamelukes, who were the actual rulers of the country, but advanced in spite of them to Cairo, and marched along the banks of the Nile. Near the Pyramids, a great battle took place, and the Mamelukes were signally defeated, and the fate of Egypt was sealed.

Siege of Acre.

But Nelson got intelligence of Bonaparte's movements, and resolved to "gain a peerage, or a grave in Westminster Abbey." Then succeeded the battle of the Nile, and the victory of Nelson, one of the most brilliant but bloody actions in the history of naval warfare. Nelson was wounded, but gained a peerage and magnificent presents. The battle was a mortal stroke to the French army, and made the conquest of Egypt useless. Bonaparte found his army exiled, and himself destined to hopeless struggles with Oriental powers. But he made gigantic efforts, in order to secure the means of support, to prosecute scientific researches, and to complete the conquest of the country. He crossed the desert which separates Africa from Asia, with his army, which did not exceed sixteen thousand men, invaded Syria, stormed Jaffa, massacred its garrison, since he could not afford to support the prisoners,—a most barbarous measure, and not to be excused even in view of the policy of the act,—and then advanced to Acre. Its memorable siege in the time of the Crusades should have deterred Bonaparte from the attempt to subdue it with his little army in the midst of a hostile population. But he made the attack. The fortress, succored by Sir Sidney Smith, successfully resisted the impetuosity of his troops, and they were compelled to retire with the loss of three thousand men. His discomfited army retreated to Egypt, and suffered all the accumulated miseries which fatigue, heat, thirst, plague, and famine could inflict. He, however, amidst all these calamities, added to discontents among the troops, won the great battle of Aboukir, and immediately after, leaving the army under the command of Kleber, returned to Alexandria, and secretly set sail for France, accompanied by Berthier, Lannes, Murat, Marmont, and other generals. He succeeded in escaping the English cruisers, and, on the 8th of October, 1799, landed in France.

Bonaparte, had he not been arrested at Acre by Sir Sidney Smith, probably would have conquered Asia Minor, and established an Oriental empire; but such a conquest would not have been permanent. More brilliant victories were in reserve for him than conquering troops of half-civilized Turks and Arabs.

During the absence of Bonaparte in Egypt, the French Directory became unpopular, and the national finances more embarrassed than ever. But Switzerland was invaded and conquered—an outrage which showed the ambitious designs of the government more than any previous attack which it had made on the liberties of Europe. The Papal States were next seized, the venerable pontiff was subjected to cruel indignities, and the treasures and monuments of Rome were again despoiled. "The Vatican was stripped to its naked walls, and the immortal frescoes of Raphael and Michael Angelo alone remained in solitary beauty amidst the general desolation." The King of Sardinia was driven from his dominions, and Naples yielded to the tricolored flag. Immense military contributions were levied in all these unfortunate states, and all that was beautiful in art was transported to Paris.

Reverses of the French.

In the mean time, the spirits of the English were revived by the victories of Nelson, and greater preparations than ever were made to resist the general, who now plainly aimed at the conquest of Europe. England, Austria, and Russia combined against France and her armies met with reverses in Italy and on the Rhine. Suwarrow, with a large army of Russians united with Austrians gained considerable success, and General Moreau was obliged to retreat before him. Serrurier surrendered with seven thousand men, and Suwarrow entered Milan in triumph, with sixty thousand troops. Turin shared the fate of Milan, and Piedmont and Lombardy were overrun by the allies. The republicans were expelled from Naples. Mantua fell, and Suwarrow marched with his conquering legions into Switzerland.

Napoleon First Consul.

These disasters happened while Bonaparte was in Egypt; and his return to France was hailed with universal joy. His victories in Egypt had prepared the way for a most enthusiastic reception, and for his assumption of the sovereign power. All the generals then in Paris paid their court to him, and his saloon, in his humble dwelling in the Rue Chantereine, resembled the court of a monarch. Lannes, Murat, Berthier, Jourdan, Augereau, Macdonald, Bournonville, Leclerc, Lefebvre, and Marmont, afterwards so illustrious as the marshals of the emperor, offered him the military dictatorship, while Sièyes, Talleyrand, and Régnier, the great civil leaders, concurred to place him at the head of affairs. He himself withdrew from the gaze of the people, affected great simplicity, and associated chiefly with men distinguished for literary and scientific attainments. But he secretly intrigued with Sièyes and with his generals. Three of the Directory sent in their resignations, and Napoleon assumed the reins of government under the title of *First Consul*, and was associated with Sièyes and Roger Ducos. The legislative branches of the government resisted, but the Council of Five Hundred was powerless before the bayonets of the military. A new revolution was effected, and despotic power in the hands of a military chieftain commenced. He, however, signalized himself by the clemency he showed in the moment of victory, and the principles of humanity, even in the government of a military despot, triumphed over the principles of cruelty. Bonaparte chose able men to assist him in the government. Talleyrand was made minister of foreign affairs. Fouché retained his portfolio of police, and the celebrated La Place was made minister of the interior. On the 24th of December, 1799, the new constitution was proclaimed; and, shortly after, Sièyes and Roger Ducos withdrew from the consulate, and gave place to Cambacères and Lebrun, who were in the interests of Napoleon.

The first step of the first consul was to offer peace to Great Britain; and he wrote a letter to the king, couched in his peculiar style of mock philanthropy and benevolence, in which he spoke of peace as the first necessity and truest glory of nations! Lord Grenville, minister of foreign affairs, replied in a long letter, in which he laid upon France the blame of the war, in consequence of her revolutionary principles and aggressive spirit, and refused to make peace while the causes of difficulty remained; in other words, until the Bourbon dynasty was restored. The Commons supported the government by a large majority, and all parties prepared for a still more desperate conflict. Napoleon was obliged to fight, and probably desired to fight, feeling that his power and the greatness of his country would depend upon the victories he might gain; that so long as the *éclat* of his government continued, his government would be strong. Mr. Pitt was probably right in his opinion that no peace could be lasting with a revolutionary power, and that every successive peace would only pave the way for fresh aggressions. Bonaparte could only fulfil what he called his destiny, by continual agitation; and this was well understood by himself and by his enemies. The contest had become one of life and death; and both parties resolved that no peace should be made until one or the other was effectually conquered The land forces of Great Britain, at the commencement of the year 1800, amounted to one hundred and sixty-eight thousand men, exclusive of eighty thousand militia, while one hundred and twenty thousand seamen and marines were voted. The ships in commission were no less than five hundred, including one hundred and twenty-four of the line. The charter of the Bank of England was renewed, and the union with Ireland effected. The various German states made still greater exertions, and agreed to raise a contingent force of three hundred thousand men. They were greatly assisted in this measure by subsidies from Great Britain. Austria, alone, had in the field at this time a force of two hundred thousand men, half of whom belonged to the army of Italy under Melas.

Immense Military Preparations.

To make head against the united forces of England and Austria, with a defeated army, an exhausted treasury, and a disunited people, was the difficult task of Bonaparte. His first object was to improve the finances; his second, to tranquillize La Vendée; his third, to detach Russia from the allies; his fourth, to raise armies equal to the crisis; and all these measures he rapidly accomplished. One hundred and twenty thousand men were raised by conscription, without any exemption from either rank or fortune, and two hundred and fifty thousand men were ready to commence hostilities. The first consul suppressed the liberty of the press, fixed his residence in the Tuileries, and established the usages and ceremonial of a court. He revoked the sentence of banishment on illustrious individuals, established a secret police, and constructed the gallery of the Louvre.

Hostilities commenced in Germany, and General Moreau was successful over General Kray at the battles of Engen, Moeskirch, and Biberach. General Massena fought with great courage in the Maritime Alps, but was obliged to retreat before superior forces, and shut himself up in Genoa, which endured a dreadful siege, but was finally compelled to surrender. The victor, Melas, then set out to meet Bonaparte himself, who was invading Italy, and had just effected his wonderful passage over the Alps by the Great St. Bernard, one of the most wonderful feats in the annals of war; for his artillery and baggage had to be transported over one of the highest and most difficult passes of the Alps. The passes of the St. Gothard and Mount Cenis were also effected by the wings of the army. The first action was at Montebello, which ended in favor of the French; and this was soon followed by a decisive and brilliant victory at Marengo, (June 14,) one of the most obstinately contested during the war, and which was attended with greater results than perhaps any battle that had yet occurred in modern warfare. Moreau also gained a great victory over the Austrians at Hohenlinden, and Macdonald performed great exploits amid the mountains of the Italian Tyrol. The treaty of Lunéville, (February 9, 1801,) in consequence of the victorious career of Bonaparte, ceded to France the possession of Belgium, and the whole left bank of the Rhine. Lombardy was erected into an independent state, Venice was restored to Austria, and the independence of the Batavian, Helvetic, Cisalpine, and Ligurian republics was guaranteed. This peace excited unbounded joy at Paris, and was the first considerable pause in the continental strife.

The Reforms of Napoleon.

Napoleon returned to his capital to reconstruct society, which was entirely disorganized. It was his object to restore the institutions of religion, law, commerce, and education. He did not attempt to give constitutional freedom. This was impracticable; but he did desire to bring order out of confusion. One night, going to the theatre, he narrowly escaped death by the explosion of an "infernal machine." He attributed the design of assassination to the Jacobins, and forthwith transported one hundred and thirty of them, more as a statesman than as a judge. He was determined to break up that obnoxious party, and the design against his life furnished the pretence. Shortly after, he instituted the Legion of Honor, an order of merit which was designed to restore gradually the gradation in the ranks of society. He was violently opposed, but he carried his measures through the Council of State; and this institution, which at length numbered two thousand persons, civil and military, became both popular and useful. He then restored the external institution of religion, and ten archbishops and fifty bishops administered the affairs of the Gallican Church. The restoration of the Sunday, with its customary observances, was hailed by the peasantry with undisguised delight, and was a pleasing sight to the nations of Europe. He then contemplated the complete restoration of all the unalienated national property to the original proprietors, but was forced to abandon the design. A general amnesty, was also proclaimed to emigrants, by which one hundred thousand people returned, not to enjoy their possessions, but to recover a part of them, and breathe the air of their native land. At last, he resolved to make himself first consul for life, and seat his family on a monarchical throne. He was opposed by the Council of State; but he appealed to the people, and three million three hundred and sixty-eight thousand two hundred and nine, out of three million five hundred and fifty-seven thousand eight hundred and eighty-five electors, voted for his elevation.

The Code Napoléon.

The "Code Napoléon" then occupied his attention, indisputably the greatest monument of his reign, and the most beneficial event of his age. All classes and parties have praised the wisdom of this great compilation, which produced more salutary changes than had been effected by all the early revolutionists. Amid these great undertakings of the consul, the internal prosperity of France was constantly increasing, and education, art, and science received an immense impulse. Every thing seemed to smile upon Bonaparte, and all appeared reconciled to the great power which he exercised.

But there were some of his generals who were attached to republican principles, and viewed with ill-suppressed jealousy the rapid strides he was making to imperial power. Moreau, the victor at Hohenlinden, was at the head of these, and, in conjunction with Fouché, who had been turned out of his office on account of the immense power which it gave him, formed a conspiracy of republicans and royalists to overturn the consular throne. But Fouché revealed the plot to Bonaparte, who restored him to power, and Generals Moreau and Pichegru, the Duke d'Enghien, and other illustrious persons were arrested. The duke himself was innocent of the conspiracy, but was sacrificed to the jealousy of Bonaparte, who wished to remove from the eyes of the people this illustrious scion of the Bourbon family, the only member of it he feared. This act was one of the most cruel and unjustifiable, and therefore, impolitic, which Bonaparte ever committed. "It was worse than a crime," said Talleyrand; "it was a blunder." His murder again lighted the flames of continental war, and from it may be dated the commencement of that train of events which ultimately hurled Napoleon from the imperial throne.

That possession was what his heart now coveted, and he therefore seized what he desired, and what he had power to retain. On the 18th of May, 1804, Napoleon was declared Emperor of the French, and an overwhelming majority of the electoral votes of France confirmed him in his usurpation of the throne of Hugh Capet.

His first step, as emperor, was the creation of eighteen marshals, all memorable in the annals of military glory—Berthier, Murat, Moncey, Jourdan, Massena, Augereau, Bernadotte, Soult, Brune, Lannes, Mortier, Ney, Davoust, Bessières, Kellermann, Lefebvre, Pérignon, and Serrurier. The individual lives of these military heroes cannot here be alluded to.

Early in the year 1805, the great powers of England, Austria, and Russia entered into a coalition to reduce France to its ancient limits, and humble the despot who had usurped the throne. Enormous preparations were made by all the belligerent states, and four hundred thousand men were furnished by the allies for active service; a force not, however, much larger than Napoleon raised to prosecute his scheme of universal dominion.

Meditated Invasion of England.

Among other designs, he meditated the invasion of England itself, and assembled for that purpose one of the most splendid armies which had been collected since the days of the Roman legions. It amounted to one hundred and fourteen thousand men, four hundred and thirty-two pieces of cannon, and fourteen thousand six hundred and fifty-four horses. Ample transports were provided to convey this immense army to the shores of England. But the English government took corresponding means of defence, having fathomed the designs of the enemy, who had succeeded in securing the coöperation of Spain. This great design of Napoleon was defeated by the vigilance of the English, and the number of British ships which defended the coasts—the "wooden walls" which preserved England from a most imminent and dreaded danger.

Battle of Austerlitz.

Frustrated in the attempt to invade Great Britain, Napoleon instantly conceived the plan of the campaign of Austerlitz, and without delay gave orders for the march of his different armies to the banks of the Danube. The army of England on the shores of the Channel, the forces in Holland, and the troops in Hanover were formed into seven corps, under the command of as many marshals, comprising altogether one hundred and ninety thousand men, while the troops of his allies in Italy and Germany amounted to nearly seventy thousand more. Eighty thousand new conscripts were also raised, and all of these were designed for the approaching conflict with the Austrians.

But before the different armies could meet together in Germany, Nelson had gained the great and ever-memorable victory of Trafalgar, (October 23,) on the coast of Spain, by which the naval power of France and Spain was so crippled and weakened, that England remained, during the continuance of the war, sovereign mistress of the ocean. Nothing could exceed the transports of exultation which pervaded the British empire on the news of this great naval victory—perhaps the greatest in the annals of war. And all that national gratitude could prompt was done in honor of Nelson. The remains of the fallen victor were buried in St. Paul's Cathedral, over which a magnificent monument was erected. His brother, who inherited his title, was made an earl, with a grant of six thousand pounds a year, and an estate worth one hundred thousand pounds. Admiral Collingwood, the second in command, was raised to the peerage, with a grant of two thousand pounds yearly. But the thoughts of the nation were directed to the departed hero, and countless and weeping multitudes followed him to the grave; and his memory has ever since been consecrated in the hearts of his countrymen, who regard him, and with justice, as the greatest naval commander whom any nation or age has produced.

Early in October, the forces of Napoleon were marshalled on the plains of Germany, and the Austrians, under the Archduke Charles, acted on the defensive. Napoleon advanced rapidly on Vienna, seized the bridge which led from it to the northern provinces of the empire, passed through the city, and established his head-quarters at Schoenbrunn. On the 1st of December was fought the celebrated battle of Austerlitz, the most glorious of all Napoleon's battles, and in which his military genius shone with the greatest lustre, and which decided the campaign. Negotiations with Austria, dictated by the irresistible power of the French emperor, were soon concluded at Presburg, (27th December,) by which that ancient state was completely humbled. The dethronement of the King of Naples followed, and the power of Napoleon was consolidated on the continent of Europe.

The defeat of Austerlitz was a great blow to the allied powers, and the health and spirits of Pitt sunk under the disastrous intelligence. A devouring fever seized his brain, and delirium quenched the fire of his genius. He died on the 23d of January, 1806, at the age of forty-seven, with the exclamation, "Alas, my country!" after having nobly guided the British bark in the most stormy times his nation had witnessed since the age of Cromwell. He was buried with great pomp in Westminster Abbey, and died in debt, after having the control, for so many years, of the treasury of England. Mr. Fox did not long survive his more illustrious rival, but departed from the scene of conflict and of glory the 13th of September.

Battle of Jena.

The humiliation of Prussia succeeded that of Austria. The battle of Jena, the 14th of October, prostrated, in a single day, the strength of the Prussian monarchy, and did what the united armies of Austria, Russia, and France could not accomplish by the Seven Years' War. Napoleon followed up his victories by bold and decisive measures, invested Magdeburg, which was soon abandoned, entered Berlin in triumph, and levied enormous contributions on the kingdom, to the amount of one hundred and fifty-nine millions of francs. In less than seven weeks, three hundred and fifty standards, four thousand pieces of cannon, and eighty thousand prisoners were taken; while only fifteen thousand, out of one hundred and twenty thousand men, were able to follow the standards of the conquered king to the banks of the Vistula. Alarm, as well as despondency, now seized all the nations of Europe. All the coalitions which had been made to suppress a revolutionary state had failed, and the proudest monarchs of Christendom were suppliant at the feet of Napoleon.

The unfortunate Frederic William sued for peace; but such hard conditions were imposed by the haughty conqueror at Berlin, that the King of Prussia prepared for further resistance, especially in view of the fact that the Russians were coming to his assistance At Berlin, Napoleon issued his celebrated decrees against British commerce, which, however, flourished in spite of them.

Napoleon Aggrandizes France.

Napoleon then advanced into Poland to meet the Russian armies, and at Eylau, on the 8th of February, 1807, was fought a bloody battle, in which fifty thousand men perished. It was indecisive, but had the effect of checking the progress of the French armies. But Napoleon ordered new conscriptions, and made unusual exertions, so that he soon had two hundred and eighty thousand men between the Vistula and Memel. New successes attended the French armies, which resulted in a peace with Russia, at Tilsit, on the river Niemen, at which place Napoleon had a personal interview with the Emperor Alexander and the King of Prussia. By this treaty, (7th July,) Poland was erected into a separate principality, and the general changes which Napoleon had made in Europe were ratified by the two monarchs. Soon after, Napoleon, having subdued resistance on the continent of Europe, returned to his capital. He was now at the height of his fame and power, but on an elevation so high that his head became giddy. Moreover, his elevation, at the expense of Italy, Belgium, Switzerland, Austria, Prussia, Saxony, and Russia, to say nothing of inferior powers, excited the envy and the hatred of all over whom he had triumphed, and prepared the way for new intrigues and coalitions.

Napoleon after the peace of Tilsit, devoted all his energies to the preservation of his power and to the improvement of his country, and expected of his numerous subjects the most implicit obedience to his will. He looked upon himself as having received a commission from Heaven to rule and to reign as absolute monarch of a vast empire, as a being upon whom the fate of France depended. The watchwords "liberty," "equality," "fraternity," "the public welfare," were heard no more, and gave place to others which equally flattered the feelings of the French people—"the interests of the empire," "the splendor of the imperial throne." From him emanated all glory and power, and the whole structure of the state, executive, judicial, and legislative, depended upon his will. Freedom, in the eyes of the people, was succeeded by glory, and the *éclat* of victory was more highly prized than any fictitious liberty. The *Code Napoléon* rapidly progressed; schools of science were improved; arts, manufactures, and agriculture revived. Great monuments were reared to gratify the national pride and perpetuate the glory of conquests. The dignity of the imperial throne was splendidly maintained, and the utmost duties of etiquette were observed. He encouraged amusements, festivities, and *fêtes*; and Talma, the actor, as well as artists and scholars, received his personal regard. But his reforms and his policy had reference chiefly to the conversion of France into a nation of soldiers; and his system of conscription secured him vast and disciplined armies, not animated, as were the soldiers of the revolution, by the spirit of liberty, but transformed into mechanical forces. The time was to come, in spite of the military enthusiasm of his veteran soldiers, when it was to be proved that the throne of absolutism is better sustained by love than by mechanism.

Aggrandizement of Napoleon's Family.

Napoleon had already elevated his two brothers, Louis and Joseph, to the thrones of Holland and Naples. He now sought to make his brother Joseph the King of Spain. He availed himself of a quarrel between King Charles and his son; acted as mediator, in the same sense that Hastings and Clive acted as mediators in the quarrels of Indian princes; and prepared to seize, not to humble, one of the oldest and proudest monarchies of Europe.

The details of that long war on the Spanish peninsula, which resulted from the appointment of Joseph Bonaparte to the throne of Spain, have been most admirably traced by Napier, in the best military history that has been written in modern times. The great hero of that war was Wellington; and, though he fought under the greatest disadvantages and against superior forces,—though unparalleled sufferings and miseries ensued among all the belligerent forces,—still he succeeded in turning the tide of French conquest.

Spain did not fall without a struggle. The Spanish Juntas adopted all the means of defence in their power; and the immortal defence of Saragossa, the capital of Arragon, should have taught the imperial robber that the Spanish spirit, though degenerate, was not yet extinguished.

It became almost the universal wish of the English to afford the Spaniards every possible assistance in their honorable struggle, and Sir Arthur Wellesley, the conqueror of the Mahrattas, landed in Portugal in August, 1808. He was immediately opposed by Marshal Junot. Napoleon could not be spared to defend in person the throne of his brother, but his most illustrious marshals were sent into the field; and, shortly after, the battle of Corunna was fought, at which Sir John Moore, one of the bravest of generals, was killed in the moment of victory.

The Peninsular War.

Long and disastrous was that Peninsular war. Before it could be closed, Napoleon was called to make new exertions. Austria had again declared war, and the forces which she raised were gigantic. Five hundred and fifty thousand men, in different armies, were put under the command of the Archduke Charles. Napoleon advanced against him, and was again successful, at Abensberg and at Eckmuhl. Again he occupied Vienna; but its fall did not discourage the Austrians, who, soon after, were marshalled against the French at Wagram, which dreadful battle made Napoleon once more the conqueror of Austria. On the 14th of November, 1809, he returned to Paris, and soon after made the grand mistake of his life.

He resolved to divorce Josephine, whom he loved and respected; a woman fully worthy of his love, and of the exalted position to which she was raised. But she had no children, and Napoleon wanted an heir to the universal empire which he sought to erect on the ruins of the ancient monarchies of Europe. The dream of Charlemagne and of Charles V. was his, also—the revival of the great Western Empire. Moreover, Napoleon sought a domestic alliance with the proud family of the German emperor. He sought, by this, to gratify his pride and strengthen his throne. He perhaps also contemplated, with the Emperor of Austria for his father and ally, the easy conquest of Russia. Alexander so supposed. "His next task," said he, "will be to drive me back to my forests."

The Empress Josephine heard of the intentions of Napoleon with indescribable anguish, but submitted to his will; thus sacrificing her happiness to what she was made to believe would advance the welfare of her country and the interests of that heartless conqueror whom she nevertheless loved with unparalleled devotion. On the 11th of March, 1810, the espousals of Napoleon and Maria Louisa were celebrated at Vienna, the person of the former being represented by his favorite Berthier. A few days afterwards she set out for France; and her marriage, in a domestic point of view, was happy. Josephine had the advantage over her in art and grace, but she was superior in the charms of simplicity and modesty. "It is singular," says Sir Walter Scott, "that the artificial character should have belonged to the daughter of a West India planter; that, marked by nature and simplicity, to a princess of the proudest court in Europe."

War in Spain.

Meanwhile, the war in Spain was prosecuted, and Napoleon was master of its richest and most powerful provinces. Seventy-five thousand men in Andalusia, under Soult; fifty thousand under Marmont, in Leon; sixty thousand under Bessières, at Valladolid and Biscay; forty-five thousand under Macdonald, at Gerona, to guard Catalonia; thirty thousand under Suchet, twenty thousand under Joseph and Jourdan, fifteen thousand under Régnier, besides many more thousand troops in the various garrisons, — in all over three hundred thousand men, — held Spain in military subjection. Against these immense forces, marshalled under the greatest generals of France, Spain and her allies could oppose only about ninety thousand men, for the most part ill disciplined and equipped.

The vital point of resistance was to be found shut up within the walls of Cadiz, which made a successful defence. But Tortosa, Tarragona, Saguntum, and Valentia, after making most desperate resistance, fell. But Wellington gained, on the other hand, the great battle of Albuera, one of the bloodiest ever fought, and which had a great effect in raising the spirits of his army and of the Spaniards. The tide of French conquest was arrested, and the English learned from their enemies those arts of war which had hitherto made Napoleon triumphant.

In the next campaign of 1812, new successes were obtained by Wellington, and against almost overwhelming difficulties. He renewed the siege of Badajoz, and carried this frontier fortress, which enabled him now to act on the offensive, and to enter the Spanish territories. The fall of Ciudad Rodrigo was attended with the same important consequences. Wellington now aimed to reduce the French force on the Peninsula, although vastly superior to his own. He had only sixty thousand men; but, with this force, he invaded Spain, defended by three hundred thousand. Salamanca was the first place of consequence which fell: Marmont was totally defeated. Wellington advanced to Madrid, which he entered the 12th of August, amid the enthusiastic shouts of the Spanish population. Soult was obliged to raise the siege of Cadiz, abandon Andalusia, and hasten to meet the great English general, who had turned the tide of French aggression. Wellington was compelled, of course, to retire before the immense forces which were marching against him, and fell back to Salamanca, and afterwards to Ciudad Rodrigo. The campaign, on the part of the English, is memorable in the annals of successful war, and the French power was effectually weakened, if it was not destroyed.

Invasion of Russia.

In the midst of these successes, Napoleon prepared for his disastrous invasion of Russia; the most gigantic and most unfortunate expedition in the whole history of war.

Napoleon was probably induced to invade Russia in order to keep up the succession of victories. He felt that, to be secure, he must advance; that, the moment he sought repose, his throne would begin to totter; that nothing would sustain the enthusiasm of his countrymen but new triumphs, commensurate with his greatness and fame. Some, however, dissuaded him from the undertaking, not only because it was plainly aggressive and unnecessary, but because it was impolitic. Three hundred thousand men were fighting in Spain to establish his family on the throne of the Bourbons, and the rest of Europe was watching his course, with the intention of assailing him so soon as he should meet with misfortunes.

But neither danger nor difficulty deterred Napoleon from the commission of a gigantic crime, for which no reasonable apology could be given, and which admits of no palliation. He made, however, a fearful mistake, and his rapid downfall was the result. Providence permitted him to humble the powers of Europe, but did not design that he should be permanently aggrandized by their misfortunes.

The forces of all the countries he had subdued were marshalled with the French in this dreadful expedition, and nothing but enthusiasm was excited in all the dominions of the empire. The army of invasion amounted to above five hundred thousand men, only two hundred thousand of whom were native French. To oppose this enormous force, the Russians collected about three hundred thousand men; but Napoleon felt secure of victory.

On the banks of the Niemen he reviewed the principal corps of his army, collected from so many countries, and for the support of which they were obliged to contribute. On the 24th of June, he and his hosts crossed the river; and never, probably, in the history of man, was exhibited a more splendid and imposing scene.

The Russians retreated as the allied armies advanced; and, on the 28th of June, Napoleon was at Wilna, where he foolishly remained seventeen days—the greatest military blunder of his life. The Emperor Alexander hastened to Moscow, collected his armaments, and issued proclamations to his subjects, which excited them to the highest degree of enthusiasm to defend their altars and their firesides.

Battle of Smolensko.

Both armies approached Smolensko about the 16th of July, and there was fought the first great battle of the campaign. The town was taken, and the Russians retreated towards Moscow. But before this first conflict began, a considerable part of the army had perished from sickness and fatigue. At Borodino, another bloody battle was fought, in which more men were killed and wounded than in any battle which history records. Napoleon, in this battle, did not exhibit his usual sagacity or energy, being, perhaps, overwhelmed with anxiety and fatigue. His dispirited and broken army continued the march to Moscow, which was reached the 14th of September. The Sacred City of the Russians was abandoned by the army, and three hundred thousand of the inhabitants took to flight. Napoleon had scarcely entered the deserted capital, and taken quarters in the ancient palace of the czars, before the city was discovered to be on fire in several places; and even the Kremlin itself was soon enveloped in flames. Who could have believed that the Russians would have burnt their capital? Such an event surely never entered into a Frenchman's head. The consternation and horrors of that awful conflagration can never be described, or even conceived. Pillage and murder could scarcely add to the universal wretchedness. Execration, indignation, and vengeance filled the breasts of both the conquerors and the conquered. But who were the conquerors? Alas! those only, who witnessed the complicated miseries and awful destruction of the retreating army, have answered.

Retreat of the French.

The retreat was the saddest tragedy ever acted by man, but rendered inevitable after the burning of Moscow, for Napoleon could not have advanced to St. Petersburg. For some time, he lingered in the vicinity of Moscow, hoping for the submission of Russia. Alexander was too wise to treat for peace, and Napoleon and his diminished army, loaded, however, with the spoil of Moscow, commenced his retreat, in a hostile and desolate country, harassed by the increasing troops of the enemy. Soon, however, heavy frosts commenced, unusual even in Russia, and the roads were strewed by thousands who perished from fatigue and cold. The retreat became a rout; for order, amid general destruction and despair, could no longer be preserved. The Cossacks, too, hung upon the rear of the retreating army, and cut off thousands whom the elements had spared. In less than a week, thirty thousand horses died, and the famished troops preyed upon their remains. The efforts of Napoleon proved in vain to procure provisions for the men, or forage for the horses. Disasters thickened, and all abandoned themselves to despair. Of all the awful scenes which appalled the heart, the passage of the Beresina was the most dreadful. When the ice was dissolved in the following spring, twelve thousand dead bodies were found upon the shore. The shattered remnants of the Grand Army, after unparalleled suffering, at length reached the bank of the Niemen. Not more than twenty thousand of the vast host with which Napoleon passed Smolensko left the Russian territory. Their course might be traced by the bones which afterwards whitened the soil. But before the Polish territories were reached, Napoleon had deserted his army, and bore to Paris himself the first intelligence of his great disaster. One hundred and twenty-five thousand of his troops had died in battle, one hundred and ninety thousand had been taken prisoners, and one hundred and thirty-two thousand had died of cold, fatigue and famine. Only eighty thousand had escaped, of whom twenty-five thousand were Austrians and eighteen thousand were Prussians. The annals of the world furnish no example of so complete an overthrow of so vast an armament, or so terrible a retribution to a vain-glorious nation.

This calamity proved the chief cause of Napoleon's overthrow. Had he retained his forces to fight on the defensive, he would have been too strong for his enemies; but, by his Russian campaign, he lost a great part of his veteran troops, and the veneration of his countrymen.

His failure was immediately followed by the resurrection of Germany. Both Austria and Prussia threw off the ignominious yoke he had imposed, and united with Russia to secure their ancient liberties. The enthusiasm of the Prussians was unbounded, and immense preparations were made by all the allied powers for a new campaign. Napoleon exerted all the energies, which had ever distinguished him, to rally his exhausted countrymen, and a large numerical force was again raised. But the troops were chiefly conscripts, young men, unable to endure the fatigue which his former soldiers sustained, and no longer inspired with their sentiments and ideas.

Battles of Lutzen and Bautzen.

The campaign of 1813 was opened in Germany, signalized by the battles of Lutzen and Bautzen, in which the French had the advantage. Saxony still remained true to Napoleon, and he established his head-quarters in Dresden. The allies retreated, but only to prepare for more vigorous operations. England nobly assisted, and immense supplies were sent to the mouth of the Elbe, and distributed immediately through Germany. While these preparations were going on, the battle of Vittoria, in Spain, was fought, which gave a death blow to French power in the Peninsula, and placed Wellington in the front rank of generals. Napoleon was now more than ever compelled to act on the defensive, which does not suit the genius of the French character, and he resolved to make the Elbe the base of his defensive operations. His armies, along this line, amounted to the prodigious number of four hundred thousand men; and Dresden, the head-quarters of Napoleon, presented a scene of unparalleled gayety and splendor, of licentiousness, extravagance, and folly. But Napoleon was opposed by equally powerful forces, under Marshal Blucher, the Prussian general, a veteran seventy years of age, and Prince Schwartzenberg, who commanded the Austrians. But these immense armies composed not one half of the forces arrayed in desperate antagonism. Nine hundred thousand men in arms encircled the French empire, which was defended by seven hundred thousand.

Battle of Leipsic.

The allied forces marched upon Dresden, and a dreadful battle was fought, on the 27th of August, beneath its walls, which resulted in the retreat of the allies, and in the death of General Moreau, who fought against his old commander. But Napoleon was unable to remain long in that elegant capital, having exhausted his provisions and forage, and was obliged to retreat. On the 15th of October was fought the celebrated battle of Leipsic, in which a greater number of men were engaged than in any previous battle during the war, or probably in the history of Europe—two hundred and thirty thousand against one hundred and sixty thousand. The triumph of the allies was complete. Napoleon was overpowered by the overwhelming coalition of his enemies. He had nothing to do, after his great discomfiture, but to retreat to France, and place the kingdom in the best defence in his power. Misfortunes thickened in every quarter; and, at the close of the campaign, France retained but a few fortresses beyond the Rhine. The contest in Germany was over, and French domination in that country was at an end. Out of four hundred thousand men, only eighty thousand recrossed the Rhine. So great were the consequences of the battle of Leipsic, in which the genius of Napoleon was exhibited as in former times, but which availed nothing against vastly superior forces. A grand alliance of all the powers of Europe was now arrayed against Napoleon—from the rock of Gibraltar to the shores of Archangel; from the banks of the Scheldt to the margin of the Bosphorus; the mightiest confederation ever known, but indispensably necessary. The greatness of Napoleon is seen in his indomitable will in resisting this confederation, when his allies had deserted him, and when his own subjects were no longer inclined to rally around his standard. He still held out, even when over a million of men, from the different states that he had humbled, were rapidly hemming him round and advancing to his capital. Only three hundred and fifty thousand men nominally remained to defend his frontiers, while his real effective army amounted to little over one hundred thousand men. A million of his soldiers in eighteen months had perished, and where was he to look for recruits?

The Allied Powers Invade France.

On the 31st of December, 1814, fourteen hundred and seven years after the Suevi, Vandals, and Burgundians crossed the Rhine and entered without opposition the defenceless provinces of Gaul, the united Prussians, Austrians, and Russians crossed the same river, and invaded the territories of the modern Cæsar. They rapidly advanced towards Paris, and Napoleon went forth from his capital to meet them. His cause, however, was now desperate: but he made great exertions, and displayed consummate abilities, so that the forces of his enemies were for a time kept at bay. Battles were fought and won by both sides, without decisive results. Slowly, but surely, the allied armies advanced, and gradually surrounded him. By the 30th of March, they were encamped on the heights of Montmartre; and Paris, defenceless and miserable, surrendered to the conquerors. They now refused to treat with Napoleon, who, a month before, at the conference of Chatillon, might have retained his throne, if he had consented to reign over the territories of France as they were before the Revolution. Napoleon retired to Fontainebleau; and, on the 4th of April, he consented to abdicate the throne he no longer could defend. His wife returned to her father's protection, and nearly every person of note or consideration abandoned him. On the 11th, he formally abdicated, and the house of Bourbon was restored. He himself retired to the Island of Elba, but was allowed two million five hundred thousand francs a year, the title of emperor, and four hundred soldiers as his body guard. His farewell address to the soldiers of his old guard, at Fontainebleau, was pathetic and eloquent. They retained their attachment amid general desertion and baseness.

Josephine did not long survive the fall of the hero she had loved, and with whose fortunes her own were mysteriously united. She died on the 28th, and her last hours were soothed by the presence of the Emperor Alexander, who promised to take her children under his protection. Of all the great monarchs of his age, he was the most extensively beloved and the most profoundly respected.

Peace of Paris.

The allies showed great magnanimity and moderation after their victory. The monarchy of France was established nearly as it was before the Revolution, and the capital was not rifled of any of its monuments, curiosities, or treasures—not even of those which Napoleon had brought from Italy. Nor was there a military contribution imposed upon the people. The allies did not make war to destroy the kingdom of France, but to dethrone a monarch who had proved himself to be the enemy of mankind. The peace of Paris was signed by the plenipotentiaries of France, Great Britain, Russia, Prussia, and Austria, on the 30th of April; and Christendom, at last, indulged the hope that the awful conflict had ended. The Revolution and its offspring Napoleon were apparently suppressed, after more than three millions of men had perished in the struggle on the part of France and of her allies alone.

Great changes had taken place in the sentiments of all classes, since the commencement of the contest, twenty years before, and its close excited universal joy. In England, the enthusiasm was unparalleled, and not easy to be conceived. The nation, in its gratitude to Wellington, voted him four hundred thousand pounds, and the highest military triumphs. It also conferred rewards and honors on his principal generals; for his successful operations in Spain were no slight cause of the overthrow of Napoleon.

But scarcely were these rejoicings terminated, before Napoleon escaped from Elba, and again overturned the throne of the Bourbons. The impolitic generosity and almost inconceivable rashness of the allies had enabled Napoleon to carry on extensive intrigues in Paris, and to collect a respectable force on the island of which he was constituted the sovereign; while the unpopularity and impolitic measures of the restored dynasty singularly favored any scheme which Napoleon might have formed. The disbanding of an immense military force, the humiliation of those veterans who still associated with the eagles of Napoleon the glory of France, the derangement of the finances, and the discontents of so many people thrown out of employment, naturally prepared the way for the return of the hero of Marengo and Austerlitz.

Napoleon's Return to France.

On the 26th of February, he gave a brilliant ball to the principal people of the island, and embarked the same evening, with eleven hundred troops, to regain the sceptre which had been wrested from him only by the united powers of Europe. On the 1st of March, his vessels cast anchor in the Gulf of St. Juan, on the coast of Provence; and Napoleon immediately commenced his march, having unfurled the tricolored flag. As he anticipated he was welcomed by the people, and the old cry of "*Vive l'Empereur*" saluted his ears.

The court of the Bourbons made vigorous preparations of resistance, and the armies of France were intrusted to those marshals who owed their elevation to Napoleon. Soult, Ney, Augereau, Massena, Oudinot, all protested devotion to Louis XVIII.; and Ney promised the king speedily to return to Paris with Napoleon in an iron cage. But Ney was among the first to desert the cause of law and legitimacy, and threw himself into the arms of the emperor. He could not withstand the arts and the eloquence of that great hero for whose cause he had so long fought. The defection of the whole army rapidly followed. The king was obliged to fly, and Napoleon took possession of his throne, amid the universal transports of the imperial party in France.

The intelligence of his restoration filled Europe with consternation, rage, and disappointment, and greater preparations were made than ever to subdue a man who respected neither treaties nor the interests of his country. The unparalleled sum of one hundred and ten millions of pounds sterling was decreed by the British senate for various purposes, and all the continental powers made proportionate exertions. The genius of Napoleon never blazed so brightly as in preparing for his last desperate conflict with united Christendom; and, considering the exhaustion of his country, the forces which he collected were astonishing. Before the beginning of June, two hundred and twenty thousand veteran soldiers were completely armed and equipped; a great proof of the enthusiastic ardor which the people felt for Napoleon to the last.

The Duke of Wellington had eighty thousand effective men under his command, and Marshal Blucher one hundred and ten thousand. These forces were to unite, and march to Paris through Flanders. It was arranged that the Austrians and Russians should invade France first, by Befort and Huningen, in order to attract the enemy's principal forces to that quarter.

Napoleon's plan was to collect all his forces into one mass, and boldly to place them between the English and Prussians, and attack them separately. He had under his command one hundred and twenty thousand veteran troops, and therefore, not unreasonably, expected to combat successfully the one hundred and ninety thousand of the enemy. He forgot, however, that he had to oppose Wellington and Blucher.

Battle of Waterloo.

On the 18th of June was performed the last sad act of the great tragedy which had for twenty years convulsed Europe with blood and tears. All the combatants on that eventful day understood the nature of the contest, and the importance of the battle. At Waterloo, Napoleon staked his last throw in the desperate game he had hazarded, and lost it; and was ruined, irrevocably and forever.

Little signified his rapid flight, his attempt to defend Paris, or his readiness to abdicate in favor of his son. The allied powers again, on the 7th of July, entered Paris, and the Bourbon dynasty was restored.

Napoleon retired to Rochefort, hoping to escape his enemies and reach America. It was impossible. He then resolved to throw himself upon the generosity of the English. He was removed to St. Helena, where he no longer stood a chance to become the scourge of the nations. And there, on that lonely island, in the middle of the ocean, guarded most effectually by his enemies, his schemes of conquest ended. He supported his hopeless captivity with tolerable equanimity, showing no signs of remorse for the injuries he had inflicted, but meditating profoundly on the mistakes he had committed, and conjecturing vainly on the course he might have adopted for the preservation of his power.

How idle were all his conjectures and meditations! His fall was decreed in the councils of Heaven, and no mortal strength could have prevented his overthrow. His mission of blood was ended; and his nation, after its bitter humiliation, was again to enjoy repose. But he did not live in vain. He lived as a messenger of divine vengeance to chastise the objects of divine indignation. He lived to show to the world what a splendid prize human energy could win; and yet to show how vain, after all, was military glory, and how worthless is the enjoyment of any victory purchased by the sufferings of mankind. He lived to point the melancholy moral, that war, for its own sake, is a delusion, a mockery, and a snare, and that the greater the elevation to which unlawful ambition can raise a man, the greater will be his subsequent humiliation; that "pride goeth before destruction, and a haughty spirit before a fall."

Reflections on Napoleon's Fall.

The allied sovereigns of Europe insisted on the restoration of the works of art which Napoleon had pillaged. "The bronzed horses, brought from Corinth to Rome, again resumed their old station in the front of the Church of St. Mark; the Transfiguration was restored to the Vatican; the Apollo and the Laocoon again adorned St. Peter's; the Venus was enshrined with new beauty at Florence; and the Descent from the Cross was replaced in the Cathedral of Antwerp." By the treaty which restored peace to Europe for a generation, the old dominions of Austria, Prussia, Russia, Spain, Holland, and Italy were restored, and the Bourbons again reigned over the ancient provinces of France. Popular liberty on the continent of Europe was entombed, and the dreams of revolutionists were unrealized; but suffering proved a beneficial ordeal, and prepared the nations of Europe to appreciate, more than ever, the benefits and blessings of peace.

References.—The most complete work, on the whole, though full of faults, and very heavy and prosaic, is Alison's History of the French Revolution. Scott's Life of Napoleon was too hastily written, and has many mistakes. No English author has done full justice to Napoleon. Thiers's Histories are invaluable. Napier's History of the Peninsula War is masterly. Wellington's Despatches are indispensable only to a student. Botta's History of Italy under Napoleon. Dodsley's Annual Register. Labaume's Russian Campaign. Southey's Peninsular War. Liborne's Waterloo Campaign. Southey's Life of Nelson. Sherer's Life of the Duke of Wellington. Gifford's Life of Pitt. Moore's Life of Sir John Moore. James's Naval History. Memoirs of the Duchess d'Abrantes. Berthier's Histoire de l'Expédition d'Égypte. Schlosser's Modern History. The above works are the most accessible, but form but a small part of those which have appeared concerning the French Revolution and the career of Napoleon. For a complete list of original authorities, see the preface of Alison, and the references of Thiers.

CHAPTER XXXII
EUROPE ON THE FALL OF NAPOLEON

Complexity of Modern History.

It would be interesting to trace the history of the civilized world since the fall of Napoleon; but any attempt to bring within the limits of a history like this a notice of the great events which have happened for thirty-five years, would be impossible. And even a notice as extended as that which has been presented of the events of three hundred years would be unsatisfactory to all minds. The common reader is familiar with the transactions of the present generation, and reflections on them would be sure to excite the prejudices of various parties and sects. A chronological table of the events which have transpired since the downfall of Napoleon is all that can be attempted. The author contemplates a continuation of this History, which will present more details, collected from original authorities. The history of the different American States, since the Revolution; the administration of the various presidents; the late war with Great Britain; the Seminole and Mexican wars; the important questions discussed by Congress; the contemporary history of Great Britain under George IV., William IV., and Victoria; the conquests in India and China; the agitations of Ireland; the great questions of Reform, Catholic Emancipation, Education, and Free Trade; the French wars in Africa; the Turkish war; the independence of the Viceroy of Egypt; the progress of Russian territorial aggrandizement; the fall of Poland; the Spanish rebellion; the independence of the South American states; the Dutch and Belgic war; the two last French revolutions; the great progress made in arts and sciences, and the various attempts in different nations to secure liberty;—these, and other great subjects, can only be properly discussed in a separate work, and even then cannot be handled by any one, however extraordinary his talents or attainments, without incurring the imputation of great audacity, which only the wants of the public can excuse.

In concluding the present History, a very brief notice of the state of the civilized world at the fall of Napoleon may be, perhaps, required.

Remarkable Men of Genius.

England suffered less than any other of the great powers from the French Revolution. A great burden was, indeed, entailed on future generations; but the increase of the national debt was not felt so long as English manufactures were purchased, to a great extent, by the Continental States. Six hundred million pounds were added to the national debt; but England, internally, was never more flourishing than during this long war of a quarter of a century. And not only was glory shed around the British throne by the victories of Nelson and Wellington, and the effectual assistance which England rendered to the continental powers, and without which the liberties of Europe would have been subverted, but, during the reign of George III., a splendid constellation of men of genius, in literature and science, illuminated the world. Dr. Johnson made moral reflections on human life which will ever instruct mankind; Burke uttered prophetic oracles which even his age was not prepared to appreciate; and his rivals thundered in the senate with an eloquence and power not surpassed by the orators of antiquity; Gibbon wrote a history which such men as Guizot and Milman pronounced wonderful both for art and learning; Hume, Reid, and Stewart, carried metaphysical inquiry to its utmost depth; Gray, Burns, Goldsmith, Coleridge, Southey, and Wordsworth, were not unworthy successors of Dryden and Pope; Adam Smith called into existence the science of political economy, and nearly brought it to perfection in a single lifetime; Reynolds and West adorned the galleries with pictures which would not have disgraced the land of artists; while scholars, too numerous to mention, astonished the world by the extent of their erudition; and divines, in language which rivalled the eloquence of Chrysostom or Bossuet, declared to an awakened generation the duties and destinies of man.

France, the rival of England, was not probably permanently injured by the Revolution; for, if millions of lives were sacrificed, and millions of property were swept away, still important civil and social privileges were given to the great mass of the people, and odious feudal laws and customs were broken forever. All the glory which war can give, was obtained; and France, for twenty years, was feared and respected. Popular liberty was not secured; but advances were made towards it, and great moral truths were impressed upon the nation,—to be again disregarded, but not to be forgotten. The territorial limits of France were not permanently enlarged, and the conquests of Napoleon were restored to the original rulers. The restoration of the former political system was insisted upon by the Holy Alliance, and the Bourbon kings, in regaining their throne, again possessed all that their ancestors had enjoyed but the possession of the hearts of the people. The allied powers may have restored despotism and legitimacy for a while; they could not eradicate the great ideas of the Revolution, and these were destined once more to overturn their thrones. The reigns of Louis XVIII., Charles X., and Louis Philippe were but different acts of the long tragedy which was opened by the convocation of the States General, and which is not probably closed by the election of Prince Louis Napoleon to the presidency of the French republic. The *ideas* which animated La Fayette and Moreau, and which Robespierre and Napoleon at one time professed, still live, in spite of all the horrors of the Reign of Terror, and all the streams of blood which flowed at Leipsic and Waterloo. Notwithstanding the suicidal doctrines of Socialists and of the various schools of infidel philosophers, and in view of all the evils which papal despotism, and democratic license, and military passions have inflicted, and will continue to inflict, still the immortal principles of liberty are safe under the protection of that Providence which has hitherto advanced the nations of Europe from the barbarism and paganism of ancient Teutonic tribes.

Condition of Germany.

Germany suffered the most, and apparently reaped the least, from the storms which revolutionary discussion had raised. Austria and Prussia were invaded, pillaged, and humiliated. Their cities were sacked, their fields were devastated, and the blood of their sons was poured out like water. But sacrifice and suffering developed extraordinary virtues and energies, united the various states, and gave nationality to a great confederation. The struggles of the Germans were honorable and gigantic, and proved to the world the impossibility of the conquest of states, however afflicted, when they are resolved to defend their rights. The career of Napoleon demonstrated the impossibility of a universal empire in Europe, and least of all, an empire erected over the prostrated thrones and discomfited armies of Germany. The Germans learned the necessity and the duty of union, and proved the strength of their sincere love for their native soil and their venerable institutions. The Germans, though poor in gold and silver, showed that they were rich in patriotic ardor, and in all those glorious sentiments which ennoble a great and progressive nation. After twenty years' contention, and infinite sacrifices and humiliations, the different princes of Germany recovered their ancient territorial possessions, and were seated, more firmly than before on the thrones which legitimacy had consecrated.

Condition of Other Powers.

Condition of Other Powers.

Absolute monarchy was restored also to Spain; but the imbecile Bourbons, the tools of priests and courtiers, revived the ancient principles of absolutism and bigotry, without any of those virtues which make absolutism respectable or bigotry endurable. But in the breasts of Spanish peasants the fires of liberty burned, which all the terrors of priestly rule, and all the evils of priestly corruption, could not quench. They, thus far, have been unfortunate, but no person who has studied the elements of the Spanish character, or has faith in the providence of God, can doubt that the day of deliverance will, sooner or later, come, unless he has the misfortune to despair of any permanent triumph of liberty in our degenerate world.

In the northern kingdoms of Europe, no radical change took place; and Italy, the land of artists, so rich in splendid recollections, so poor in all those blessings which we are taught to value, returned to the dominion of Austria, and to the rule of despotic priests. Italy, disunited, abandoned, and enslaved, has made generous efforts to secure what is enjoyed in more favored nations, but hitherto in vain. So slow is the progress of society! so hard are the struggles to which man is doomed! so long continued are the efforts of any people to secure important privileges!

Greece made, however, a more successful effort, and the fetters of the Turkish sultan were shaken off. The Ottoman Porte looked, with its accustomed indifference, on the struggles of the Christians, and took no active part in the war until absolutely forced. But it looked with the indifference of decrepit age, rather than with the philosophical calmness of mature strength, and exerted all the remaining energies it possessed to prevent the absorption of the state in the vast and increasing empire of the czars. Russia, of all the great powers which embarked in the contest to which we have alluded, arose the strongest from defeat and disaster. The rapid aggrandizement of Russia immediately succeeded the fall of Napoleon.

The spiritual empire of the Popes was again restored, and the Jesuits, with new powers and privileges, were sent into all the nations of the earth to uphold the absolutism of their great head. Again they have triumphed when their cause seemed hopeless; nor is it easy to predict the fall of their empire. So long as the principle of Evil shall contend with the principle of Good, the popes will probably rejoice and weep at alternate victories and defeats.

The United States of America. The United States of America were too far removed from the scene of conflict to be much affected by the fall of thrones. Moreover, it was against the wise policy of the government to interfere with foreign quarrels. But the American nation beheld the conflict with any feelings but those of indifference, and, while its enlightened people speculated on the chances of war, they still devoted themselves with ardor to the improvement of their institutions, to agriculture, and manufacturing interests. Merchants, for a while, made their fortunes by being the masters of the carrying trade of the world, and the nation was quietly enriched. The wise administrations of Washington, Adams, Jefferson, and Madison, much as they conflicted, in some respects, with each other, resulted in the growth of commerce, manufactures, agriculture, and the arts; while institutions of literature and religion took a deep hold of the affections of the people. The country increased and spread with unparalleled rapidity on all sides, and the prosperity of America was the envy and the admiration of the European world. The encroachments of Great Britain, and difficulties which had never been settled, led to a war between the two countries, which, though lamented at the time, is now viewed, by all parties, as resulting in the ultimate advancement of the United States in power and wealth, as well as in the respect of foreign nations. Great questions connected with the rapid growth of the country, unfortunately at different times, have produced acrimonious feelings between different partisans; but the agitation of these has not checked the growth of American institutions, or weakened those sentiments of patriotism and mutual love, which, in all countries and ages, have constituted the glory and defence of nations. The greatness of American destinies is now a favorite theme with popular orators. Nor is it a vain subject of speculation. Our banner of Liberty will doubtless, at no distant day, wave over all the fortresses which may be erected on the central mountains of North America, or on the shores of its far distant oceans; but all national aggrandizement will be in vain without regard to those sacred principles of law, religion, and morality, for which, in disaster and sorrow, both Puritan Settler and Revolutionary Hero contended. The believer in Progress, as affected by influences independent of man, as coming from the benevolent Providence which thus far has shielded us, cannot otherwise than hope for a still loftier national elevation than has been yet attained, with all the aid of circumstances, and all the energies of heroes.

APPENDIX

CHRONOLOGICAL TABLE
FROM THE FALL OF NAPOLEON.

1815.—Battle of Waterloo, (June 18.) Napoleon embarks for St. Helena, (August 7.) Final Treaty at Paris between the Allied Powers, (November 20.) Inauguration of the King of Holland. First Steam Vessels on the Thames.

1816.—Great Agricultural distress in Great Britain. Brazil declared a Kingdom. Consolidation of the Exchequers of England and Ireland. Marriage of the Princess Charlotte with Prince Leopold.

1817.—Disorders in Spain. Renewal of the Bill for the suspension of the Habeas Corpus Act. Inauguration of President Monroe. Death of the Princess Charlotte. Death of Curran.

1818.—Entire Withdrawal of Foreign Forces from France. Seminole War. Great Discussions in Parliament on the Slave Trade. Death of Warren Hastings, of Lord Ellenborough, and of Sir Philip Francis.

1819.—Great depression of Trade and Manufactures in Great Britain. Great Reform meetings in Manchester, Leeds, and other large Towns, Lord John Russell's Motion for a Reform in Parliament. Organized bands of robbers in Spain. Settlement of the Pindarrie War in India. Assassination of Kotzebue.

1820.—Death of George III., (January 23.) Lord Brougham's Plan of Popular Education. Proceedings against Queen Caroline. Rebellion in Spain. Trial of Sir Francis Burdett. Election of Sir Humphrey Davy as President of the Royal Society. Ministry in France of the Duc de Richelieu. Death of Grattan; of the Duke of Kent.

1821.—Second Inauguration of President Monroe. Revolution in Naples and Piedmont. Insurrections in Spain. Independence of Colombia, and fall of Spanish Power in Mexico and Peru. Disturbances in Ireland. War in the Morea. Formal occupation of the Floridas by the United States. Extinction of the Mamelukes. Revolt in Wallachia and Moldavia. Death of Queen Caroline; of Napoleon.

1822.—Mr. Canning's Bill for the admission of Catholic Peers to the House of Lords. Disturbances in Ireland. Sir James Mackintosh's Motion for a reform of Criminal Law. Mr. Canning succeeds the Marquis of Londonderry (Lord Castlereagh) as Secretary of State for Foreign Affairs. Lord Amherst appointed Governor-General of India. Fall of the administration of the Duc de Richelieu. Congress of Vienna. War in Greece. Insurrection of the Janizaries. The Persian War. Settlement of the Canadian Boundary. Suicide of the Marquis of Londonderry.

1823.—Great Agricultural Distress in Great Britain. Debates on Catholic Emancipation, and on the Slave Trade. French Invasion of Spain. Captain Franklin's Voyage to the Polar Seas. Death of Pius VII.

1824.—General Prosperity in England. Capture of Ipsara by the Turks. Visit of La Fayette to the United States. Leaders of the Carbonari suppressed in Italy by the Austrian Government. Repeal of duties between Great Britain and Ireland. Burmese War, and Capture of Rangoon. Censorship of the Press in France. Death of Louis XVIII., (September 16.)

1825.—Inauguration of President Adams. Independence of Brazil acknowledged by Portugal. Coronation of Charles X. Siege of Missolonghi. Inundations in the Netherlands. Death of the Emperor Alexander, (December 1.)

1826.—Bolivar chosen President of Peru for Life. Independence of Hayti acknowledged by France. Riots in Lancashire. Surrender of the fortress of St. Juan d'Ulloa to the Mexicans. Great Debates in Parliament on the Slave Trade. Death of Ex-President Adams; of Jefferson. Coronation of the Emperor Nicholas.

1827.—Death of the Earl of Liverpool, and dissolution of the Ministry. Mr. Canning appointed First Lord of the Treasury; dies four months after; succeeded by Lord Goderich. National Guard disbanded in France. Defeat of the Greek army before Athens. Battle of Navarino. Foundation of the University of London. Death of the Duke of York; of La Place; of Mitford, the Historian; of Eichhorn; of Pestalozzi; of Beethoven; of King Frederic Augustus of Saxony.

1828.—Dissolution of Lord Goderich's Ministry, and new one formed under the Duke of Wellington, Mr. Peel and the Earl of Aberdeen. Repeal of the Test and Corporation Acts. New Corn Law. Riots in Ireland. Mr. O'Connell represents the County of Clare. New and Liberal ministry in France. Final departure of the French Armies from Spain. War between Naples and Tripoli. War between Russia and Turkey. Independence of Greece. Death of Ypsilanti.

1829.—Inauguration of President Jackson. Passage of the Catholic Emancipation Bill. New and Ultra-Royalist ministry in France, under Polignac. Victories of Count Diebitsch against the Turks. Surrender of Adrianople. Civil War in Mexico. Don Miguel acknowledged as King of Portugal by Spain. Burning of York Cathedral. Treaty between the United States and Brazil. Civil War in Chili. Death of Judge Washington.

1830.—Great discussions in Congress on the Tariff. Reform Agitations in England. Death of George IV., (June 26.) New Whig Ministry under Earl Grey and Lord John Russell. Opening of the Liverpool Railroad. Revolution in France, and the Duke of Orleans declared King. Capture of Algiers by the French. Belgium erected into an independent Kingdom. Riots and Insurrections in Germany. Plots of the Carlists in Spain. Murder of Joseph White. Death of Pope Leo XII.; of the King of Naples; of Sir Thomas Lawrence; of the Grand Duke of Baden.

1831.—Dissolution of the Cabinet at Washington. Great discussions on the Reform Bill. Agitations in Ireland. Leopold made King of Belgium. Insurrection in Switzerland. Revolution in Poland. Treaty between the United States and Turkey. Coronation of William IV. Appearance of the Cholera in England. Its great ravages on the Continent. Death of Bolivar; of Robert Hall; of Mrs. Siddons; of William Roscoe; of James Monroe.

1832.—Veto of President Jackson of the Bill to recharter the United States Bank. Discontents in South Carolina, in consequence of the Tariff. War with the Indians. Bristol and Birmingham Riots. Final passage of the Reform Bill. Abolition of the Slave Trade in Brazil. Death of Casimir Périer, Prime Minister of France, who is succeeded by Marshal Soult. Death of Sir Walter Scott; of Sir James Mackintosh; of Spurzheim; of Cuvier; of Goethe; of Champollion; of Adam Clarke; of Andrew Bell; of Anna Maria Porter; of Charles Carroll of Carrollton.

1833.—Second Inauguration of Andrew Jackson. Mr. Clay's Tariff Bill. President Jackson's war with the United States Bank. Recharter of the Bank of England and of the East India Company. Fortifications of Paris commenced. Santa Anna inaugurated President of Mexico. Bill passed to abolish slavery in the British Colonies. Trial of Avery. Death of the King of Spain; of Mr. Wilberforce; of Hannah More; of Caspar Hauser; of Lord Grenville; of Dr. Schleiermacher.

1834.—Discussions on the Corn Laws. Destruction of the two Houses of Parliament. Change of Ministry in France. Congress of Vienna. Donna Maria acknowledged Queen of Portugal. Opening of the Boston and Worcester Railroad. Resignation of Earl Grey, succeeded by Lord Melbourne, who is again shortly succeeded by Sir Robert Peel. Irish Coercion Bill. Death of La

Fayette; of William Wirt; of Dr. Porter; of General Huntingdon; of Coleridge; of Rev. Edward Irving.

1835.—New Ministry of Viscount Melbourne. French expedition to Algiers. Otho made King of Greece. Suppression of the Jesuits in Spain. Remarkable eruption of Vesuvius. Revolt in Spain. Great fire in New York. Death of the Emperor of Austria; of Chief Justice Marshall; of Nathan Dane; of McCrie; of William Cobbett.

1836.—Settlement of the disputes between France and the United States. Resignation of M. Thiers, who is succeeded, as Prime Minister of France, by Count Molé. Military operations against Abd-el-Kader. Massacre of the Carlist Prisoners at Barcelona. Isturitz made Prime Minister of Spain. Prince Louis Napoleon attempts an insurrection at Strasburg. Commutation of Tithes in England. Bill for the Registration of Births and Marriages. Passage of the Irish Municipal Corporation Bill. Agitations in Canada. War between Texas and Mexico. Burning of the Patent Office at Washington. Death of Aaron Burr; of the Abbé Sièyes; of Lord Stowell; of Godwin.

1837.—Inauguration of President Van Buren. Death of William IV., (June 20.) Insurrection in Canada. Suspension of cash payments by the Bank of the United States in Philadelphia, and by the banks in New York. Acknowledgment of the Independence of Texas. Treaty with the Indians. Great failures in New York. Great Protestant Meeting in Dublin. Change of Ministry in Spain. Death of Gustavus Adolphus IV. of Sweden; of M. de Pradt; of Abiel Holmes; of Dr. Griffin; of Charles Botta; of Lovejoy.

1838.—War with the Seminoles. General Scott takes command of the New York Militia on the Frontiers. Affair of the Caroline. Lord Durham Governor-General of Canada. Coronation of Queen Victoria; of the Emperor Ferdinand. Violence of Civil War in Spain. Circassian War. Revolution in Peru and Bolivia. Peace between Russia and Turkey. Great Chartist meetings in England. Emancipation of the West India Negro Apprentices. Death of Lord Eldon; of Talleyrand; of Noah Worcester; of Dr. Bowditch; of Zachary Macaulay.

1839.—Disputes between Maine and New Brunswick. Resignation of the Melbourne Ministry, and the failure of Sir Robert Peel to construct a new one. Birmingham Riots. Chartist Convention. Resignation of Count Molé, who is succeeded, as Prime Minister, by Marshal Soult, and Guizot. Capture of the fortress of St. Juan d'Ulloa by the French. Treaty of Peace between France and Mexico. Affghan War. War between Turkey and Mohammed Ali. Invasion of Syria. Death of Lady Hester Stanhope; of Governor Hayne; of Dr. Bancroft; of Stephen Van Rensselaer; of Zerah Colburn; of Samuel Ward.

1840.—Marriage of Queen Victoria. Penny Postage in England. Affghan War. Difficulties in China respecting the Opium Trade. Blockade of Canton. Ministry of M. Thiers. Arrival of Napoleon's Remains from St. Helena. Abdication of the King of Holland. Continued Civil War in Spain. Burning of the Lexington. Ministry of Espartero. Death of Frederic William III. of Prussia; of Lord Camden; of Dr. Olinthus Gregory; of Blumenbach; of Dr. Follen; of Dr. Kirkland; of John Lowell; of Judge Mellen; of Dr. Emmons; of Prof. Davis.

1841.—Inauguration of President Harrison; his Death; succeeded by John Tyler. Trial of McLeod. Repeal of the Sub-Treasury. Veto, by the President, of the Bill to establish a Bank. Resignation of the Melbourne Ministry, succeeded by that of Sir Robert Peel. War in Scinde. Espartero sole Regent of Spain. Revolution in Mexico. Treaty between Turkey and Egypt. Treaty between the United States and Portugal. Death of Chantrey; of Dr. Marsh; of Dr. Oliver; of Dr. Ripley; of Blanco White; of William Ladd.

1842.—Great Debates in Parliament on the Corn Laws. New Tariff of Sir Robert Peel. Affghan War. Treaty of Peace between England and China. Treaty between England and the United States respecting the North-eastern Boundary Question. Chartist Petitions. Income Tax. Accident on the Paris and Versailles Railroad. Death of the Duke of Orleans; of Lord Hill; of Dr. Charming; of Dr. Arnold; of Jeremiah Smith.

1843.—Activity of the Anti Corn Law League. Repeal Agitation in Ireland. Monster Meetings. Establishment of the Free Presbyterian Church in Scotland. War in Scinde. Sir James Graham's Factory Bill. Repudiation of State Debts. Death of Southey; of Dr. Ware; of Allston; of Legare; of Dr. Richards; of Noah Webster.

1844.—Corn Law Agitations in Great Britain. Passage of the Sugar Duties Bill; of the Dissenters' Chapel Bill. State Trials in Ireland. Opening of the Royal Exchange. Sir Charles Napier's victories in India. Louis Philippe's visit to England. War between France and Morocco. Disturbances on the Livingston and Rensselaer Manors. Insurrection in Mexico. Death of Secretary Upshur.

1845.—Installation of President Polk. Treaty between the United States and China. Great Fire in New York. Municipal disabilities removed from the Jews by Parliament. War in Algeria. Abdication of Don Carlos. Termination of the War in Scinde. Revolution in Mexico. War in the Punjaub.

1846—War between the United States and Mexico. Battle of Monterey. New Tariff Bill. Passage of the Corn Bill in England, and Repeal of Duties. Free Trade policy of Sir Robert Peel. Settlement of the Oregon Question. Distress in Ireland by the failure of the Potato Crop. Resignation of Sir Robert

Peel; succeeded by Lord John Russell. Marriage of the Queen of Spain; and of her sister, the Infanta, to the Due de Montpensier. Escape of Prince Louis Napoleon from Ham. Death of Pope Gregory XVI., and elevation of Pius IX. Death of Louis Napoleon, Ex-King of Holland.

1847.—Splendid military successes of Generals Scott and Taylor in Mexico. Fall of Mexico. Ravages of the Potato Disease. Awful Distress in Ireland. Guizot succeeds Soult as President of the Council. Frequent changes of Ministry in Spain. Civil War in Switzerland. Grant of a Constitution to Prussia. Liberal Measures of Pius IX. Death of the King of Denmark; of Dr. Chalmers; of Silas Wright.

1848.—French Revolution, and Fall of Louis Philippe. Abdication of the King of Bavaria. Tumults in Vienna and Berlin. Riots in Rome. Chartist demonstrations in London. Election of the National Assembly in France. General fermentation throughout Europe. Distress of Ireland. Oregon Territorial Bill. Free Soil Convention in Buffalo. Death of John Quincy Adams. Election of General Taylor for President of the United States.

Footnote 1: Macaulay.